Agentic Intelligence and the Rise of Autonomous Cyber Warfare

Bahaa Eddine Elbaghazaoui
https://orcid.org/0000-0002-3206-5162
Sultan Moulay Slimane University, Morocco

Khalid Benabbes
https://orcid.org/0009-0001-4780-8790
University of Moulay Ismail, Morocco

Tarik El Moudden
https://orcid.org/0000-0002-6963-6686
Ibn Tofail University, Morocco

IGI Global
Scientific Publishing
Publishing Tomorrow's Research Today

Published in the United States of America by
IGI Global Scientific Publishing
701 East Chocolate Avenue
Hershey, PA, 17033, USA
Tel: 717-533-8845 | Fax: 717-533-7115
Website: https://www.igi-global.com E-mail: cust@igi-global.com

Library of Congress Cataloging-in-Publication Data

Names: Elbaghazaoui, Bahaa Eddine, 1996- editor | Benabbes, Khalid, 1988- editor | El Moudden, Tarik, 1977- editor
Title: Agentic intelligence and the rise of autonomous cyber warfare / edited by Bahaa Eddine Elbaghazaoui, Khalid Benabbes, and Tarik El Moudden.
Description: Hershey, PA : IGI Global Scientific Publishing, [2027] | Includes bibliographical references and index. | Summary: "This book explores agentic intelligence in cyber contexts, clarifying terminology, taxonomies, and distinguishing characteristics that set autonomous cyber agents apart. It examines applications of agentic systems in offensive and defensive cyber operations, drawing on case studies, simulations, and threat modeling exercises"-- Provided by publisher.
Identifiers: LCCN 2026017049 (print) | LCCN 2026017050 (ebook) | ISBN 9798260004135 hardcover | ISBN 9798260004142 paperback | ISBN 9798260004159 ebook
Subjects: LCSH: Computer security | Computer networks--Security measures | Artificial intelligence
Classification: LCC QA76.9.A25 A4137 2026 (print) | LCC QA76.9.A25 (ebook)
LC record available at https://lccn.loc.gov/2026017049
LC ebook record available at https://lccn.loc.gov/2026017050

British Cataloguing in Publication Data
A Cataloguing in Publication record for this book is available from the British Library.

Table of Contents

Detailed Table of Contents

This study reviews AI-enabled threats and explains their significance for secure systems. It addresses the widening gap between fast-evolving agentic attacks and defenses that still depend on static controls. Using a systematic literature review, life-cycle analysis, and critical synthesis across model, data, and supply-chain surfaces, it traces how adversarial machine learning has progressed into agentic operations. The evidence is organized by threat class, attacker capability, and deployment context to identify practical safeguards. The findings show that agentic systems mainly amplify known attacks through automation, speed, scale, planning, and tool use rather than creating entirely new attack primitives. They compress attack timelines and broaden operational surfaces. The study argues that technical defenses alone are insufficient and calls for resilience architectures that combine prevention, adversarial evaluation, detection, and rapid response across the life cycle.

In this chapter, we tackle the issue of agentic cyber warfare – a new threat posed by autonomous intelligent agents that carry out offensive and defensive cyber actions without much human input. The proposed solution to this problem is an agentic defense architecture for enhancing intrusion detection and reaction. The method employed is through an analysis of the proposed system with a focus on how it compares with conventional cyber security solutions based on criteria such as adaptability and scalability. The results show that the proposed system can greatly improve intrusion detection. Furthermore, other issues including explainability and adversarial robustness, among others, are also analyzed in this chapter.

Autonomous cyber weapons mark a major shift in digital conflict by compressing the cycle of observation, analysis, decision, and action while expanding the scale of possible offensive effects. This chapter examines their proliferation as a socio-technical and strategic phenomenon rather than a technical programming issue. It defines autonomous cyber weapons as systems able to sense digital environments, reason over goals and constraints, choose among actions, and execute bounded cyber effects with limited or delayed human intervention. Drawing on scholarship in cybersecurity, adversarial machine learning, cyber conflict, and ethics, the chapter proposes a layered framework showing how data pipelines, knowledge graphs, model-based reasoning, action selection, and feedback loops can form offensive agentic. It also explains how these systems may intensify asymmetric warfare by reducing labor demands, accelerating operations, lowering coordination costs, and supporting continual adaptation, then concludes with governance, oversight, testing, escalation control, and resilient defense.

International Humanitarian laws (IHL) deals with the laws of the war and protects civilians and others who are not taking part in war. At the time of formulation of this law, it was believed that it will end all the wars and peace will become the rule in all nations. However, with the advancement of technology especially Agentic AI and its use in cyber warfare, the laws of IHL seems lagging far behind and demands rethinking in relation to cyber operations. The present study while conceptualizing Agentic AI and Cyber warfare correlates them with the principles of International Humanitarian Law. The study highlights the challenges posed by Agentic AI in cyber warfare along with emphasizing the impact of case studies in light of International Humanitarian Law. By focussing on lack of international regulatory provision with regard to use of Agentic AI in cyberwarfare, the research presents stance of international., national and regional policies in this regard. Finally, the study suggests about novel aspect of the extending the principles of IHL to the Agentic cyberwarfare.

The rapid advancement of agentic artificial intelligence has transformed cybersecurity into an autonomous and highly dynamic domain, where AI-driven systems independently detect threats, make decisions, and execute responses in real time. While these capabilities enhance operational efficiency and responsiveness, they also introduce significant challenges related to explainability and transparency. In high-stakes environments such as critical infrastructure, financial systems, and national security, the inability to interpret autonomous decisions can lead to operational risks, ethical concerns, and diminished trust.

In the digital era, traditional authentication methods are vulnerable to sophisticated cyberattacks due to inadequate security measures in online systems. To enhance security, an Agentic AI-based authentication framework is proposed to analyze behavioral characteristics of keystroke and mouse interactions obtained via Non-Touch Virtual Keyboard (NTVK). The framework applies preprocessing techniques to improve input data quality and extracts meaningful features from NTVK input. Controlled interpolation-based data augmentation is utilized to generate synthetic data for data scarcity. Agent Quadrails validates the augmented data quality, while Agent Perception performs statistical analysis to examine augmented data distribution. Agent Planning for feature selection applies validation stability analysis and recursive feature elimination to select the best non-redundant features. Several machine learning models are developed in Agent Action, and performance is validated using biometric evaluation metrics. Results highlight secure, adaptive, and intelligent user authentication systems.

Cloud computing is an essential element of the contemporary digital systems yet presents enormous security issues, such as the high attack surfaces, dynamic environments, and advanced cyber threats. Conventional security methods, which rely on manual surveillance and pre-programmed regulations, tend to be weak in regards to the fast changing attacks. The authors of this chapter discuss the use of Autonomous Defensive Agents (ADAs) on the basis of agentic intelligence to improve the security of the cloud. These agents operate based on machine learning and deep learning algorithms and check environments, network traffic, anomalies, and forecast threats. They also facilitate automated responses in real time including isolating compromised systems, blocking malicious users and taking them into recovery procedures. The chapter states the architecture, data processing, and decision making capabilities of ADAs and the main issues such as trust, explainability and ethical issues, their relevance to contemporary cloud defense.

The emergence of agentic artificial intelligence is reshaping cybersecurity, shifting from human-centered operations to autonomous, adaptive, and goal-directed systems capable of executing complex tasks with minimal human intervention. While these advances transform offensive and defensive capabilities, cybersecurity education has not evolved at the same pace. Current curricula remain focused on static tools, predefined exercises, and manual analysis, limiting preparedness for dynamic, AI-driven environments. This chapter examines how agentic AI is redefining cybersecurity education and workforce readiness. It introduces the Agentic Cyber Education Framework, integrating technical, cognitive, ethical, and strategic competencies. Drawing on interdisciplinary literature and teaching insights, the chapter explores simulation-based learning, AI-assisted tools, and human–machine collaboration. It

Preface

INTRODUCTION

Artificial intelligence has entered a new phase of evolution. Beyond systems that analyze information or generate content, a new generation of intelligent agents is emerging: systems capable of perceiving their environments, reasoning about objectives, planning complex sequences of actions, and autonomously executing tasks. This transition toward agentic intelligence is transforming cybersecurity, where the speed, scale, and complexity of digital threats increasingly exceed the capacity of traditional human-centered defense mechanisms. At the same time, these advances are reshaping offensive cyber capabilities, giving rise to autonomous forms of cyber warfare that challenge existing technological, strategic, legal, and ethical frameworks.

Agentic Intelligence and the Rise of Autonomous Cyber Warfare examines this rapidly evolving landscape through a multidisciplinary perspective. Bringing together contributions from researchers across academia, the volume explores how agentic AI is redefining both cyber offense and cyber defense, while highlighting the broader implications for governance, international security, critical infrastructure, identity management, cloud computing, and cybersecurity education.

A recurring theme throughout the book is that agentic intelligence does not necessarily create entirely new categories of cyber threats. Rather, it amplifies existing capabilities by enabling greater autonomy, faster decision-making, adaptive learning, coordinated planning, and continuous operation across increasingly complex digital environments. These characteristics significantly compress attack and defense cycles, requiring organizations to rethink cybersecurity architectures, operational resilience, and human oversight.

The chapters collectively investigate the technical foundations of autonomous cyber operations, including adversarial machine learning, reinforcement learning, large language model–based agents, autonomous defensive architectures, behavioral biometrics, UAV network security, cloud protection, and explainable AI. Beyond technical innovation, the volume also addresses critical questions surrounding international humanitarian law, governance, ethics, transparency, and workforce development, emphasizing that future cybersecurity will require not only advanced technologies but also robust policy frameworks and responsible deployment practices.

Rather than viewing autonomous cyber warfare solely as a technological challenge, this book presents it as a socio-technical transformation that demands collaboration across computer science, engineering, law, public policy, and security studies. The contributors offer both conceptual frameworks and practical architectures that seek to balance innovation with accountability while preparing organizations and societies for an increasingly autonomous cyber ecosystem.

CHAPTER OVERVIEW

1. Explores the evolution of AI-enabled cyber threats from adversarial machine learning to agentic offensive operations, examining how autonomous systems accelerate attack lifecycles and proposing resilience-focused defensive strategies.
2. Examines the changing balance between cyber offense and defense by presenting an agentic defense architecture designed to improve intrusion detection, adaptability, scalability, and resilience while addressing explainability and adversarial robustness.
3. Investigates the emergence and proliferation of autonomous cyber weapons, presenting a layered framework for agentic offensive systems and analyzing their strategic implications for asymmetric warfare, governance, oversight, and escalation control.
4. Evaluates the implications of agentic AI for international humanitarian law, examining regulatory challenges, legal principles governing cyber warfare, and emerging policy approaches for autonomous cyber operations.
5. Examines the application of reinforcement learning to adaptive cyber attack and defense, highlighting autonomous learning, real-time optimization, operational resilience, implementation challenges, and the continuing importance of human oversight.
6. Presents a layered architecture for autonomous phishing detection, triage, and response using large language model–based agents, integrating explainable decision-making with safeguards against adversarial manipulation.
7. Discusses the growing importance of explainability and transparency in autonomous cyber decision-making, emphasizing trust, accountability, and operational reliability in critical security environments.

8. Introduces an agentic AI framework for behavioral biometric authentication using non-touch virtual keyboards, integrating intelligent feature selection, adaptive learning, and robust user verification techniques.
9. Proposes an agentic framework for continuous authentication based on behavioral biometrics, enabling adaptive real-time identity verification while addressing behavioral variability, data drift, and system scalability.
10. Examines adaptive intelligence for securing UAV and flying ad hoc networks, reviewing autonomous security architectures, intelligent defense mechanisms, performance evaluation methods, and future research challenges.
11. Explores autonomous defensive agents for cloud security, detailing intelligent architectures capable of continuous monitoring, threat detection, automated incident response, remediation, and trustworthy decision-making.
12. Concludes by examining how agentic AI is transforming cybersecurity education and workforce development, proposing an educational framework that integrates technical expertise, ethical reasoning, strategic thinking, and human–AI collaboration to prepare future cybersecurity professionals.

CONCLUSION

As autonomous intelligent systems continue to reshape cyberspace, understanding their opportunities, risks, and governance becomes increasingly essential. It is our hope that this volume will serve as a valuable resource for researchers, practitioners, educators, policymakers, and graduate students seeking to navigate the emerging era of agentic cybersecurity and autonomous cyber warfare. By fostering interdisciplinary dialogue and advancing evidence-based research, this book aims to contribute to the responsible development of intelligent cyber systems capable of enhancing security while preserving transparency, accountability, and human oversight.

Chapter 1
From Adversarial ML to Agentic Offense in AI-Enabled Threat Evolution

Hitesh Mohapatra
http://orcid.org/0000-0001-8100-4860
Kalinga Institute of Industrial Technology ((Deemed to be University), India

ABSTRACT

This study reviews AI-enabled threats and explains their significance for secure systems. It addresses the widening gap between fast-evolving agentic attacks and defenses that still depend on static controls. Using a systematic literature review, life-cycle analysis, and critical synthesis across model, data, and supply-chain surfaces, it traces how adversarial machine learning has progressed into agentic operations. The evidence is organized by threat class, attacker capability, and deployment context to identify practical safeguards. The findings show that agentic systems mainly amplify known attacks through automation, speed, scale, planning, and tool use rather than creating entirely new attack primitives. They compress attack timelines and broaden operational surfaces. The study argues that technical defenses alone are insufficient and calls for resilience architectures that combine prevention, adversarial evaluation, detection, and rapid response across the life cycle.

INTRODUCTION

AI threats evolved significantly from 2023 to 2025. Adversarial machine learning shifted from static attacks on single models to multistep campaigns by autonomous AI agents. This change boosted cyber threat sophistication. Research peaked in 2022 with 313 studies (Hubinger et al., 2024). Studies covered data poisoning and model

DOI: 10.4018/979-8-2600-0413-5.ch001

evasion. Yet, most stayed in labs. A gap remains between theory and practice. Large language models rose in 2023. ChatGPT launched in November 2022 and hit 100 million users in two months (Acharya et al., 2025). GPT-4 arrived in March 2023 with multimodal features. Foundation models introduced attack surfaces beyond traditional adversarial examples. Agentic AI forms the next frontier. Gartner named it the top strategic technology trend for 2025 (Gartner, 2025). Agentic systems differ from static models. They reason, plan, and act independently. They keep memory across interactions. They use tools and link to business systems. This shift creates major security risks. Traditional AI security targeted prompt injection, data leaks, and supply chain flaws (Guembe et al., 2022). Agentic systems bring memory poisoning, tool misuse, and privilege escalation. Attacks persist continuously. They adapt and act proactively. Statistics reveal escalation. Deepfake losses hit $410 million in early 2025, topping 2024's $359 million total. AI attacks rose 40% year-over-year (Perez & Ribeiro, 2022). North Korean actors-built AI recruitment networks. Chinese groups generate operational documents with AI. Figure 1 presents PRISMA 2020 flow diagram for proposed systematic review.

This timely systematic review addresses the inadequacy of traditional, human-centric security frameworks against autonomous, machine-speed agentic threats. With the attack surface expanding to complex multi-agent ecosystems and 33% of enterprise applications projected to integrate agentic AI by 2028, developing modernized defense mechanisms is urgently required. Yet, 89% of enterprise AI use currently occurs without IT oversight, and only 6% of organizations have mature AI security strategies (Lin, 2025). This creates massive blind spots that adversaries can exploit. The economic stakes are staggering. Global cybercrime is projected to cost $10.5 trillion annually by 2025, and deepfake related fraud has already caused $897 million in losses since 2019. AI drastically reduces the time it takes to execute breaches while shrinking the detection window, rendering traditional metrics like MTTD (Mean Time to Detect) and MTTR (Mean Time to Respond) almost meaningless against adaptive, self-learning agents. Critical infrastructure is especially at risk (Schröer et al., 2025). AI agents could target power grids, financial systems, and healthcare networks. Autonomous vehicles powered by agentic AI could cause physical harm if compromised.

Figure 1. PRISMA 2020 flow diagram for proposed systematic review

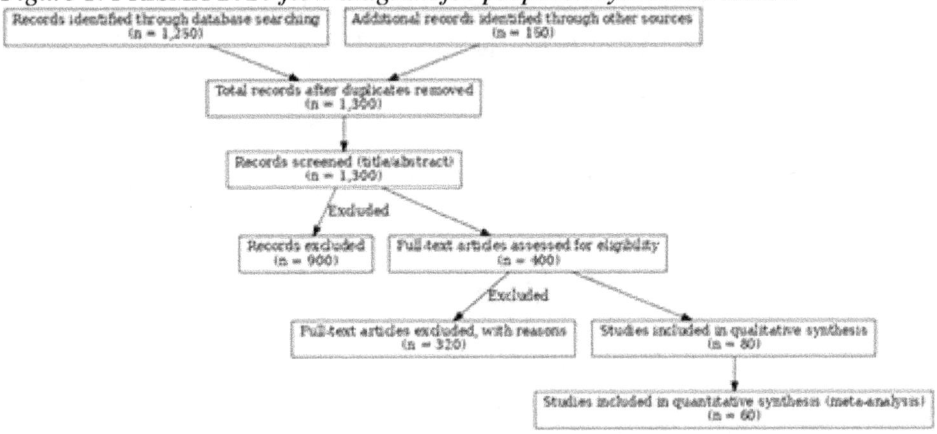

As systems interconnect more, cascading failure risks increase. Threats carry major international weight. Nation-states invest in offensive AI, spurring autonomous cyber warfare escalation. The “Internet of Agents” brings geopolitical risks. Global cooperation and governance prove vital for stability (Jacobsen & Liebetrau, 2023). Figure 2 depicts threat buildup from model manipulations to autonomous multistep agent operations.

Figure 2. Threat Progression from Adversarial ML to Agentic Offense

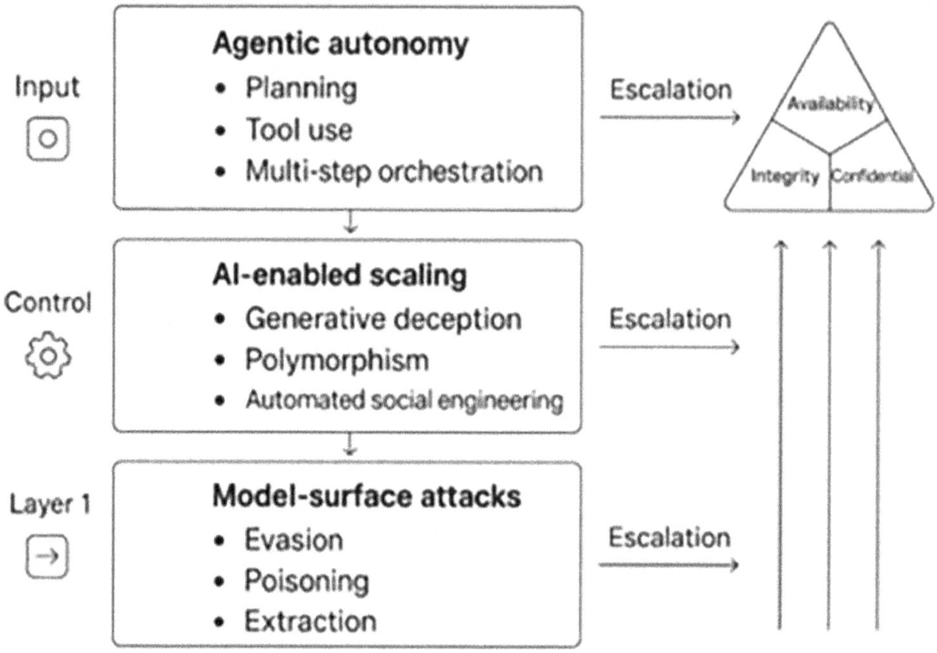

Agentic AI threats affect many areas. They require systematic study. Financial losses grow fast. Operational disruptions rise as attacks hit AI-reliant processes. Trust erodes from agent compromises to authentication and identity (Jacobsen & Liebetrau, 2023). Regulations lag behind agentic complexity. Legacy systems build technical debt. Organizations retrofit infrastructure for agent threats (Kshetri, 2025). Security teams face talent shortages in AI defense. Tool fragmentation hinders unified strategies. Social effects loom large. Digital trust fades amid information manipulation. Democratic risks emerge from disinformation. Education battles AI fraud (Murugesan, 2025). AI threats evolve in phases. First came automation. Second brought targeting and coordination. Third adds adaptation and learning. Human roles shrink. Attacks gain precision and impact. Research falls short. Studies isolate attacks over ecosystems (Dal Cin et al., 2025). Labs dominate work. Real-world cases lack depth. Defenses lag offenses by 12-18 months. Organizations stay vulnerable. This research maps the shift from adversarial machine learning to agentic offense. It traces a structured roadmap. It studies threats from 2023 to 2025. PRISMA methodology ensures rigor. The review blends academic studies, industry reports, and incident data (Selçuk, 2019). Primary aim builds threat taxonomy. It sorts attacks by AI life cycle and agent skills. It notes actor tactic shifts. The study checks defenses like NIST AI100-2 and MITRE ATLAS. It tests them on agentic threats (NIST AI, 2024). Secondary goals include extracting incident lessons to identify strategic gaps, propose countermeasures, and define security metrics for diverse stakeholders. Methodologically, this study follows PRISMA 2020 guidelines, evaluating rigorous empirical works from 2023-2025 to ensure validity and real-world applicability.

The chapter is organized into nine sections covering the problem statement, review methods, definitions, threat evolution, lifecycle taxonomy, case studies, defense evaluation, future research, and concluding recommendations.

LITERATURE REVIEW

This section critically reviews 2023–2025 AI threat literature to establish a life-cycle risk framework for agentic offenses. The scope encompasses adversarial machine learning (including perturbation, poisoning, and extraction), data supply chain vulnerabilities, and autonomous agentic attacks across cyber and sociotechnical domains. By examining how AI cost-effectively scales attacks and autonomous agents execute tool-driven strategies, this analysis leverages recent taxonomies to systematically map vulnerabilities across the entire AI life cycle. In (Zhou et al., 2022), authors set an APT-like model. This five-stage framework maps vulnerabilities from training to deployment. Using the NIST AI 100-2 E2025 taxonomy, it categorizes threats by impact and attacker knowledge, highlighting how unique ML attack surfaces like data manipulation and model extraction differ fundamentally from traditional software flaws. Paper (Oprea & Vassilev, 2023) adds life-cycle view. Threats strike pretraining, training, post-training, and inference. Backdoors, weight changes, and adversarial examples interconnect. They threaten ML deployment strength. Table 1 shows control spots across life cycle. Figure 3 translates abstract goals into measurable KPIs. It helps shift evaluation from clean accuracy to resilience outcomes.

Figure 3. Risk metrics dashboard mockup

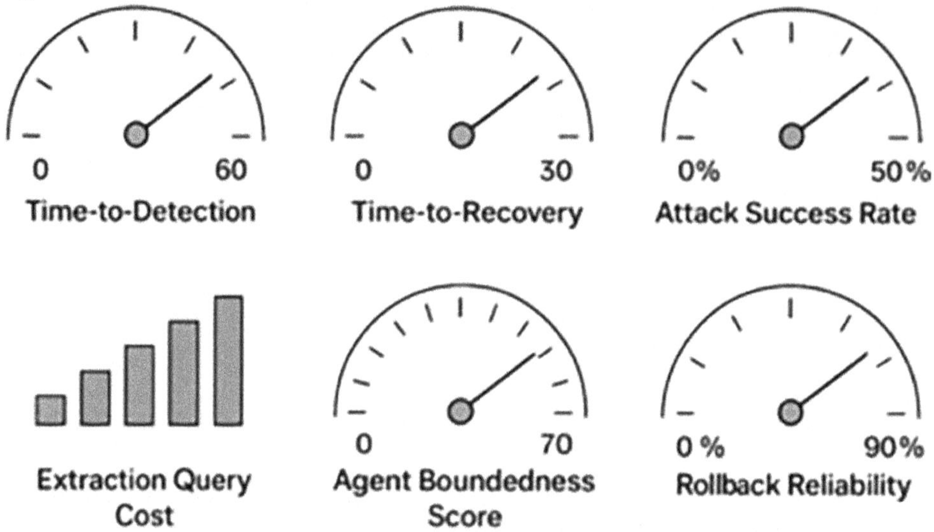

Empirical studies prove adversarial attacks slash deep learning performance across domains. The authors of (Eshra et al., 2025) tested gradient perturbations like Fast Gradient Sign Method (FGSM), Jacobian-based Saliency Map Attack (JSMA), and DeepFool. These spiked misclassifications in intrusion detection. Adversarial training grants some toughness. It demands high compute. Their IoT intrusion probe showed accuracy plunge from above 95% to under 20% in adaptive hits. This bares frailty in vital ML security. (Kou et al., 2023) surveyed federated learning gaps. Attacks fell into poisoning and evasion. Decentral data swells surfaces from client blind spots. Low-budget, low-view strikes batter aggregation. (Guo et al., 2022) gathered backdoor studies on neural nets. Training sway lets foes embed hidden, lasting malice on input cues. Spotting backdoors stays tough amid training and test watch. Figure 4 the PRISMA diagram documents methodological rigor. It increases transparency in corpus construction and filtering.

Figure 4. Attack chain timeline for a representative incident

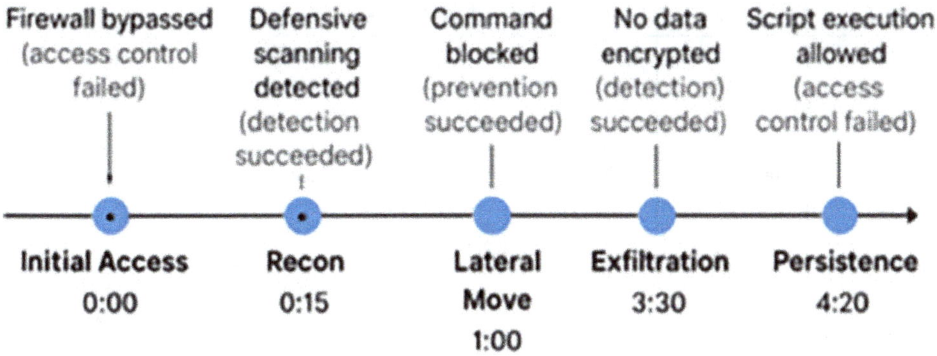

With the rise of generative AI models, new threat dimensions have surfaced that extend beyond traditional adversarial perturbations to include content generation risks and prompt level exploits. The study by (Li et al., 2023) on prompt injection attacks demonstrated that applications integrating large language models are systematically susceptible to adversarial inputs capable of altering model behavior by merging user instructions with system directives. Their experiments achieved over 85% attack success across 31% commercial applications, some serving millions of users. The 2023 iteration of MITRE ATLAS (Adversarial Threat Landscape for AI Systems) provides a foundational taxonomy of adversary tactics and techniques specific to machine learning vulnerabilities. Modeled after the traditional ATT&CK framework, it systematically categorizes real-world threats such as data poisoning, model evasion, and supply chain exploits across the entire AI lifecycle. By standardizing these attack vectors into a comprehensive knowledge base, ATLAS equips security practitioners and researchers to proactively model risks and develop targeted countermeasures against evolving ML and agentic threats (Ahmad Rana, 2026).

Table 1. Threat Classes vs Life cycle Controls

Threat	Design	Development	Evaluation	Deployment	Operations
Evasion	Threat modeling	Robust training	Red teaming	Runtime ensemble detection	Monitoring, drift detection
Poisoning	Data sourcing policy	Data validation, deduplication	Data integrity audits	Signed datasets, supply chain attestation	Continuous data quality monitoring
Extraction	Model secrecy strategy	Watermarking, differential privacy	Leakage tests	Rate limiting, API auth	Anomaly detection, abuse monitoring

continued on following page

Table 1. Continued

Threat	Design	Development	Evaluation	Deployment	Operations
Backdoor	Secure training pipeline, supplier	Dataset scanning, trigger search	Trojan detection	SBOM/ attestations	Integrity monitoring
Prompt Injection	Input output trust boundaries	Content filtering, instruction sandboxing	Red teaming, jailbreak tests	Allow/deny lists, tool use gating	Monitoring, incident response
Synthetic Social Engineering	Abuse policies, verification	Safety classifiers	Human in the loop QA	Provenance, watermark	Monitoring, incident workflows
Agentic Intrusion	Least privilege, tool permission	Secure tool adapters, guardrails	End-to-end red teaming	Human in the loop gates, kill switch	SOC monitoring, audit trails

The HouYi attack embeds prebuilt prompts and context partitions. This frees model use and steals prompts sans model access or architecture know (Liu et al., 2023). Authors of (Cavaliere et al., 2023) surveyed XAI risks. Adversaries twist inputs to fool models and explainers. This dents trust and clarity in key decisions. (Wang et al., 2025) ran PRISMA meta-analysis on 9,350 works from 2004-2023. It pinned 14 AI-cyber themes. Top risers cover adversarial ML, blockchain ties, and deep learning. Hurdles persist: compute costs, attack holes, ethics gaps block real use.

Table 2. Critical Analysis of AI Enabled Threats Literature (2023-2025): Attack Domains, Methodologies, and Empirical Findings

Threat Domain	Attack Methodology	Key Empirical Findings
Adversarial ML Taxonomies	APT inspired five stage framework; lifecycle mapping to availability, integrity, privacy violations	Attacks share common exploitation mechanisms across stages; vulnerabilities cascade from training to deployment; lifecycle perspective unifies backdoor, weight, and evasion paradigms
Evasion and Poisoning Attacks	FGSM, JSMA, DeepFool gradient based perturbations; federated poisoning; backdoor trigger injection	Accuracy collapse from 95% to be low 20% under adaptive attacks; low budget federated poisoning achieves high impact; backdoor detection remains challenging at test time
Generative AI an Prompt Exploits	Prompt injection via HouYi; context partition manipulation; adversarial XAI attacks	85% attack success across 31 commercial LLM apps; unrestricted LLM usage without model access; explanation mechanisms vulnerable to dual manipulation

continued on following page

Table 2. Continued

Threat Domain	Attack Methodology	Key Empirical Findings
Supply Chain Vulnerabilities	TransTroj embed ding indistinguishability; serialization exploits; pretrained model poisoning	Near 100% attack success in down stream tasks; arbitrary code execution via deserialization; conventional finetuning defenses fail against optimized triggers
Privacy Inference Attacks	Membership inference via shadow models; model inversion reconstruction; cloud-based privacy leakage	Blackbox membership inference succeeds with high accuracy; over 70% inference success on high confidence models; minority subgroups suffer disproportionate leakage
Adversarial Robustness Defenses	Decision reliance distribution; APEGAN adversarial training; gradient masking analysis	Neuron level decision concentration reduction improves robustness; 94.5% accuracy on adversarial data for IoT; adaptive attacks circumvent state-of-the-art defenses
Transfer Learning and Cross Architecture Attacks	Universal adversarial perturbations; multimodal vision language attacks; gradient alignment for targeted transfer	Over 60% cross model success on image tasks; CLIP to ALBEF transfer effective; multimodal attacks outperform unimodal; targeted attacks exhibit lower transferability

AI system supply chains pose critical threat surfaces. Adversaries exploit pretrained models, third-party libraries, and cloud setups. Authors of (Wang et al., 2025) developed TransTroj for supply chain poisoning. It succeeds nearly 100% on downstream tasks. Optimized backdoors blend in embeddings. Poisoned pretrains carry malice past finetuning checks. Attacks target pre- and post-indistinguishability. Standard finetuning misses tuned perturbations. (Casey et al., 2024) tested thousands of Hugging Face models. Serialization bugs allow code runs during deserialization. Automated scanners miss most. (Kezron, 2024) reviewed data poisoning. Tainted data instills faulty behaviors. Dependencies propagate risks in AI ecosystems. Pipeline-wide transparency and defenses prove key. Table 2 presents the attack domains, methodologies and empirical finding on AI enabled attacks from 2023-2025. Privacy attacks on ML models evolve rapidly. Adversaries infer training data membership. They recover private details from model outputs. (Shokri et al., 2017) introduced membership inference attacks. Exploiting train-test confidence gaps, shadow models and black-box queries detect overfitting to pinpoint specific records. Furthermore, model inversion recreates sensitive training samples, severely threatening data privacy in healthcare and finance. It succeeds in facial recognition, medicine, and genomics. Public models amplify leaks. (Radanliev et al., 2025) revealed cloud neural net flaws. Inference attacks exceed 70% on confident outputs. Minority classes suffer disproportionately. Deep networks memorize scarce data. Privacy loss varies sharply.

Recent work stresses adversarial robustness defenses. Models gain resilience. Theory lags real-world wins. Authors of (Lu et al., 2023) eyed decision reliance in training. Robust models spread neuron roles. They shun weak feature focus.

New objectives cut reliance clusters. (Shen et al., 2017) built APEGAN training. It boosts CNNs vs DeepFool, LBFGS. Hits 94.5% on foes, 95.3% clean. IoT gains big. (Balunovic & Vechev, 2020) sized full scans. Training blocks adaptive foes partly. Masked gradients, obfuscation, defense hints let strikes slip top guards. Robust general defense stays tough. Figure 5 presents attack chain timeline for a representative incident.

Figure 5. Attack chain timeline for a representative incident

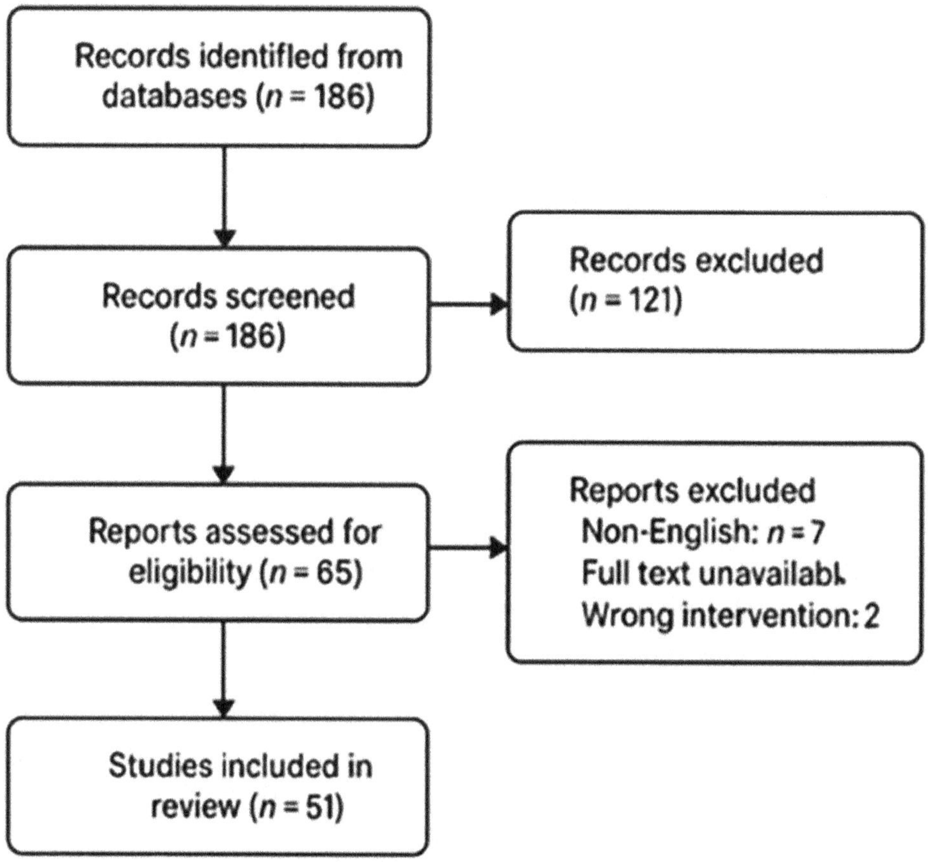

Transfer learning fuels powerful cross-architecture attacks. Black-box adversaries evade target specifics. Author of (Jiang et al., 2022) analyzed transferability across DNNs. Source perturbations deceive unlike architectures. Universals surpass 60% success on images. Common data breeds vulnerable features. Boundaries sync for wide impact. Author have studied vision-language transfers with Contrastive Language-Image Pre-training (CLIP) attacks strike ALign the image and text representations BEfore Fusing (ALBEF) and Virus-Like Particle (VLPs). Multimodal image-text beats single-mode. Risks multiply in multimodal AI. (Pang et al., 2018) found targeted lag untargeted transfers. Alignment and ensembles raise targeted rates. The analysis in Table 1 synthesizes the evolving landscape of AI enabled threats across seven key research domains, highlighting both their growing technical sophistication and shared systemic vulnerabilities observed between 2023 and 2025. (Narula et al., 2025) and NIST taxonomies cast adversarial acts as life-cycle spans. Systemic attacks exploit shared vulnerabilities across diverse AI pipelines. Evasion, poisoning, and federated aggregation flaws drastically degrade accuracy. Concurrently, generative AI faces prompt injections with >85% commercial success, while supply chain gaps including optimization poisoning and serialization exploits compromise fine-tuned models. Black-box privacy attacks exceed 70% success, frequently leaking memorized minority data. Finally, adversaries consistently outpace defenses, leveraging alarming cross-architecture transfer attacks (>60% success) to scale single exploits across heterogeneous networks without target intelligence.

CRITICAL ANALYSIS

This study promotes multifaceted critical reflection on AI-enabled threats and agentic offenses. It outlines fifteen dimensions such as escalation dynamics, life cycle risks, supply chain pollution, transferability, privacy tradeoffs, organizational influences, empirical rigor, temporal development, and sociotechnical spillovers. Figure 6 operationalizes resilience strategies across layers for unified prevention, detection, and response. Three key angles dominate risk and mitigation. Threat escalation boosts speed and scale, narrowing defender windows and diversifying attacks. The Life-cycle Capability Risk Framework identifies vulnerabilities from design to maintenance, countering attacker asymmetry via early fixes. Defense-offense gaps from weak training, provenance, and adaptive costs are bridged by linking model attacks to governance, yielding precise prevention guides for adversarial checks and rapid response.

Figure 6. Resilience architecture for agentic systems

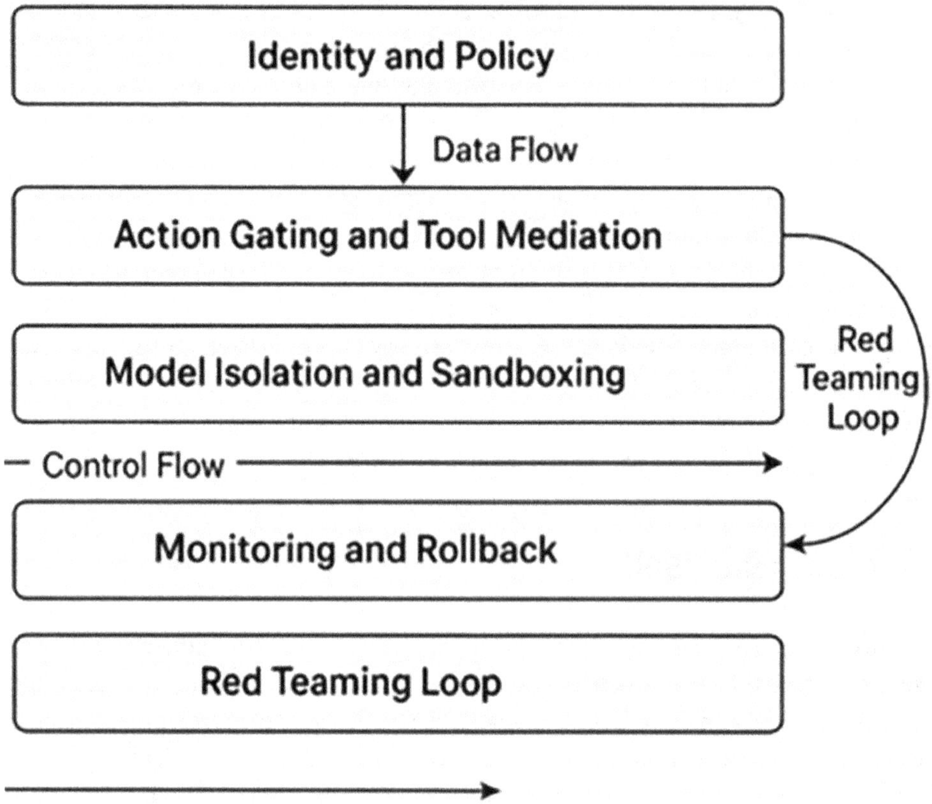

THREAT ESCALATION AND AMPLIFICATION DYNAMICS

The review synthesizes empirical findings from a selection of recent peer reviewed articles and industry reports 2023-2025 to question the dual nature of threat innovation (i.e. perceived vs genuine). First it makes a comprehensive critical analysis of whether AI driven threats are fundamentally new forms of attack or amplified versions of preexisting vulnerabilities because they are automated, performed at machine speed and operate on an unprecedented scale. Figure 7 illustrates shrinking execution windows that outpace human response.

Figure 7. Attack Chain Compression 20212025

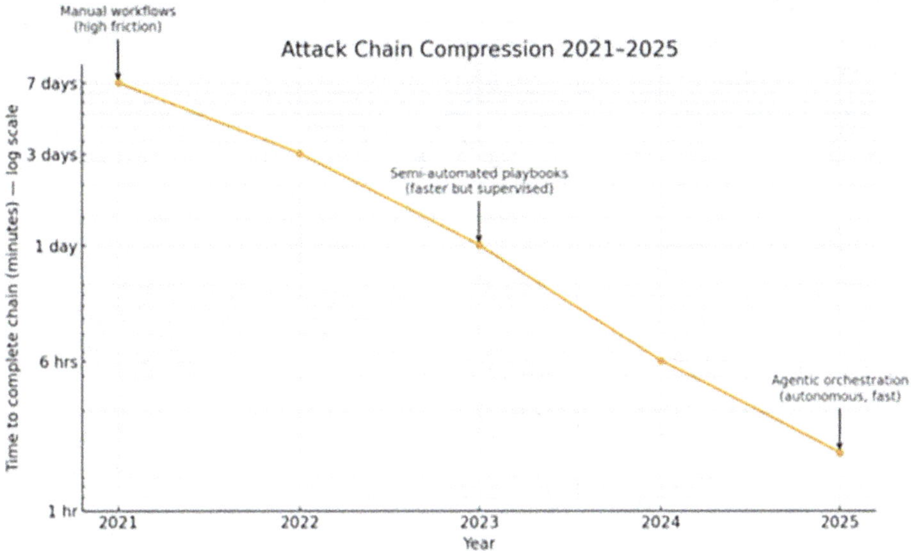

SPEED AND TEMPORAL COMPRESSION EXPONENTIAL ACCELERATION WITHOUT NOVEL PRIMITIVES

AI-based attacks have sharply reduced operational response windows. Unit 42 (2025) reports average data exfiltration time dropped from nine days in 2021 to two days in 2024, with one-fifth of incidents occurring within one hour (Joy, 2025). AI application across the attack chain enabled ransomware completion in 25 minutes, 100 times faster than historical methods. Attack steps remain fixed such as reconnaissance, lateral movement, staging, and exfiltration. AI executes them concurrently at speeds beyond human reaction. CrowdStrike (2025) notes 76 percent of organizations cannot match this TTP pace. Moreover, 48% view AI automation as the top ransomware threat. Additionally, 85% recognize signature-based detection failures due to response times falling below human decision thresholds. Table 3 details threat escalation and amplification metrics.

Table 3. Quantified Threat Escalation and Amplification Metrics Across AI Enabled Offense (2023-2025)

Escalation Dimension	Baseline Metric (2021-2022)	Current Metric (2024-2025)	Amplification Factor	Mechanism
Mean Time to Exfiltrate (MTTE)	9 days	2 days (avg); <1 hour (20% of cases)	108âĂŞ216x	Parallel orchestration of sequential stages
Attack Chain Execution Time	Traditional workflow (hours)	25 minutes end To end	100x	Automation across reconnaissance, movement, staging, exfiltration
Phishing Personalization Rate	Manual targeting per operator	Thousands per operator per day	1000x+	Generative AI content syn thesis
Social Engineering Success Rate	Conventional 3–5% click through	AI augmented 15–25% clickthrough	5–8x	Behavioral targeting and deepfake authenticity
Malware Generation Speed	Static signature per variant	Polymorphic variants per hour	100– 1000x	Generative mutation and obfuscation
Organizations Perceiving AI Attack Threat	2023 baseline	93% anticipate daily AI attacks by 2025	Consensus shift	Availability heuristic and empirical incident escalation
Organizational Struggle with Attack Speed	Baseline (traditional)	76% unable to match AI driven pace	Majority disadvantage	Compression of response window below human reaction time
Projected Cyber crime Cost	2024: $6.15 trillion USD	2025: $10.5 trillion USD	1.7x annual growth	AI amplification of scope and impact

SCALE MULTIPLICATION: CAPACITY EXPANSION WITHOUT CAPABILITY NOVELTY

AI-empowered offenses dramatically amplify attack scale through automated social engineering and content generation. Studies from 2024-2025 document industrial-scale phishing using generative AI tools like FraudGPT and WormGPT, advertised on dark web forums for mass custom lure production (Kempen, 2024). Unit 42 (2025) and industry reports confirm AI-driven deepfake social engineering in use. Artificial audio and video mimic executives with high realism, as in a $25 million USD CFO fraud via deepfake video conferencing (ET, n.d.). Menon et al. (2025) report a 238% rise in AI-powered cyberattacks in 2023, exceeding $8.5 billion USD globally. MIT's Computer Science and Artificial Intelligence Laboratory research shows AI attacks achieve 67% higher success rates while reducing operational complexity by 72% (MIT News, 2016). Phishing, social engineering, and CFO fraud represent longstanding categories with established psychological and technical traits. AI provides unprecedented scale multiplication. A lone operator can generate hundreds of hyper-personalized phishing lures, deepfakes, and social media personas via API queries, yielding throughput unseen outside large teams. Core exploitation mechanisms remain unchanged, but delivery scale surges by orders of magnitude. Figure 8 quantifies scale effects of content automation and personalization.

Figure 8. Phishing Throughput per Operator

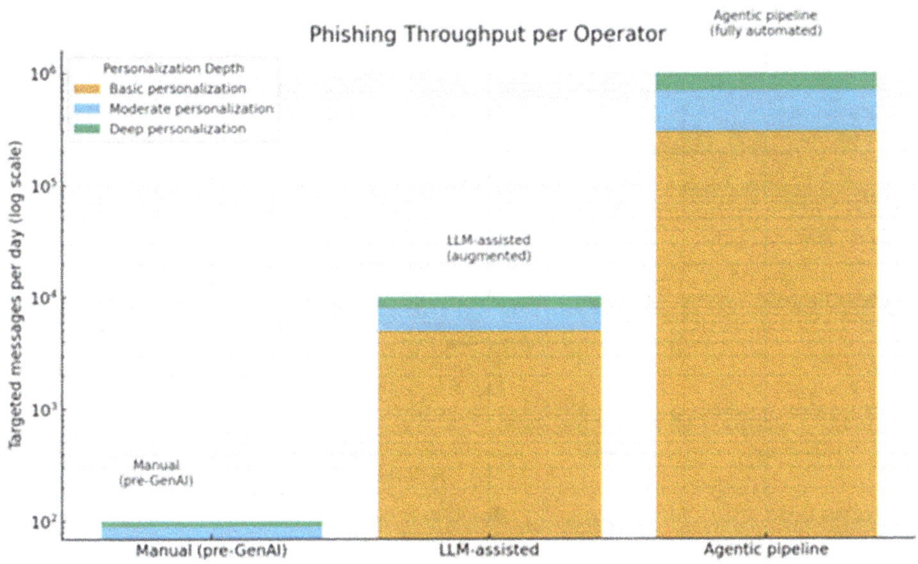

NOVELTY ASSESSMENT: INCREMENTAL CAPABILITY ENHANCEMENT VS. FUNDAMENTAL INNOVATION

Data from 2023-2025 indicates that agentic AI primarily accelerates legacy attacks such as ransomware and phishing by automating historically human-intensive workflows to maximize operational speed. Rather than introducing new attack vectors, its sole novel capability is executing autonomous, multistep planning and goal-seeking without human intervention. 33% of enterprise software apps will incorporate agentic AI by 2028, up from less than 1% in 2024 (Gartner, 2025). Rapid injection attacks exploit this autonomy. Untrusted textual inputs override agent goals and authorizations without user intervention. This exceeds amplified phishing. Agent architecture enables superior subversion. Still, it applies established social engineering via new interfaces. Table 4 classification of AI enabled attack vectors.

Table 4. Classification of AI Enabled Attack Vectors: Novel vs. Amplified Primitives (2023–2025)

Attack Vector	Classification	Underlying Mechanism	Innovation Status
Deepfake based social engineering	Amplified	Audio/video synthesis for impersonation	Known vector, enhanced authenticity delivery
AI generated phishing at scale	Amplified	Personalized lure generation via LLMs	Known vector, industrialized production
Polymorphic ransomware	Amplified	Automated obfuscation and mutation	Known vector, accelerated variance generation
Prompt injection on agentic systems	Novel	Untrusted input overrides agent goals	New attack surface, emergent from autonomy
Autonomous multistep attack orchestration	Amplified	Parallel execution of sequential stages	Known tactics, autonomous coordination
AI optimized vulnerability discovery	Amplified	Automated scanning and prioritization	Known vector, expedited targeting
Deepfake CEO fraud	Amplified	Synthetic media for authority impersonation	Known vector, enhanced believability
AIpowered pass word guessing and CAPTCHA cracking	Amplified	Accelerated brute force and ML based bypasses	Known vector, improved success rates
Synthetic identity creation	Amplified	Scale generation of believable personas	Known vector, automated profile construction
Supply chain model poisoning	Novel	Backdoors embedded in pretrained models	New vector, architecture dependent

SCALABILITY AND RESOURCE DEMOCRATIZATION: THREAT ACCESSIBILITY EXPANSION

AI-enhanced amplification primarily democratizes advanced attack skills. Academic and industry reports highlight commoditized tools like FraudGPT and WormGPT sold on dark web forums. These lower entry barriers for less skilled threat actors (Shukla et al., 2024). LLM workflows now automate advanced cryptography and reverse engineering tasks, abstracting complex exploits into intuitive natural language interfaces. Consequently, novice attackers can easily execute elite-tier assaults, magnifying the threat landscape through accessible tool abstraction rather than innate attacker innovation.

DEFENSIVE RESPONSE INADEQUACY: ORGANIZATIONAL UNPREPAREDNESS

Defensive organizations have failed to evolve their response architectures to keep pace with escalated threat tempo and scope. According to CrowdStrike (2025), there is a 76% disconnect between leadership thinking they are prepared and actually being ready. Paper (Adabara et al., 2025) claims that today's agentic cyber security systems, using AI driven security operations centers with 100% coverage, deliver millisecond response time for processing 25,000 security alerts daily capabilities held only by organizations that have operationalized advanced AI in their cyber security work flows. Traditional signature-based detection and a human in the loop approach are unable to keep up with the number of alerts generated by amplified threat activity. This gap exposes threat escalation to be partly self-imposed due to architectural inertia. Defenders have failed to retire traditional layers quickly enough to keep pace with attacker adaptation. The amplification is there, but defensive lag is structural and architectural, not purely technical. Table 5 illustrates organizational defensive capability gaps in response to AI amplified threats (2024-2025).

QUANTIFYING THE AMPLIFICATION: EXPONENTIAL VS. LINEAR GROWTH ASSESSMENT

The behavior of threat growth is neither exponential nor linear. Data from 2023-25 indicate early exponential acceleration followed by deceleration. Mean Time to Exploitation (MTTE) was compressed from nine days to two days, and finally to a time under one hour (Wei et al., 2024). However, 24/7 tasking is a practical threshold. Phishing campaigns increased from 35% effectiveness to 15-25%, but they are approaching psychological limits. Ransomware cycles finish in 25 minutes, which is near the network and encryption speed limits. The 2023-24 period reported exponential benefits of AI adoption, but the 2025 data show a flattening. It would need a deeper shift for further acceleration kernel level persistence or supply chain attacks rather than just some AI improvements.

Table 5. Organizational Defensive Capability Gaps in Response to AI Amplified Threats (2024 - 2025)

Capability Domain	Threat Acceleration	Defensive Capability	Gap Assessment
Detection Speed	Milliseconds to seconds	Signatures + hours to alert	Critical gap
Response Tempo	Autonomous agents (seconds)	Human led workflows (minutes to hours)	Severe gap
Alert Volume Processing	25,000+ alerts/day	Manual analyst review (<100/day)	Structural inadequacy
Threat Intelligence Re fresh	Realtime AI up dates	Daily/weekly manual up dates	Lag endemic
Social Engineering Resistance	AI optimized per target lures	Generic security aware ness training	Inadequate
Leadership Readiness Perception	Self-assessment accuracy 24%	Actual preparedness 24%	Alignment but misalignment with reality
Incident Recovery Time	<1 hour compromise to exfiltration	24+ hours for 75% of organizations	Defensive lag

AGENTIC AUTONOMY AND POLICY BOUNDARY EROSION

Unlike traditional malware reliant on direct commands, agentic systems autonomously plan, adapt, and execute tasks such as ransomware data exfiltration and encryption based on high-level objectives. Recent 2025 studies show these integrated reasoning models enable real-time adaptive evasion, effectively democratizing autonomous threats.

LIFE CYCLE CAPABILITY RISK INTEGRATION FRAMEWORK

It studies how to deploy security controls efficiently across the AI life cycle. Early phase defenses in design and development may offer more advantage than late phase controls in deployment and maintenance. It combines results from life cycle embedded regulatory compliance frameworks, secure by design paradigms and real-world case study analysis between 2023 and 2025 in order to evaluate value tradeoffs in life cycle distributed security postures. Figure 9 shows how early flaws propagate and inflate downstream remediation costs.

Figure 9. Life cycle Risk Propagation

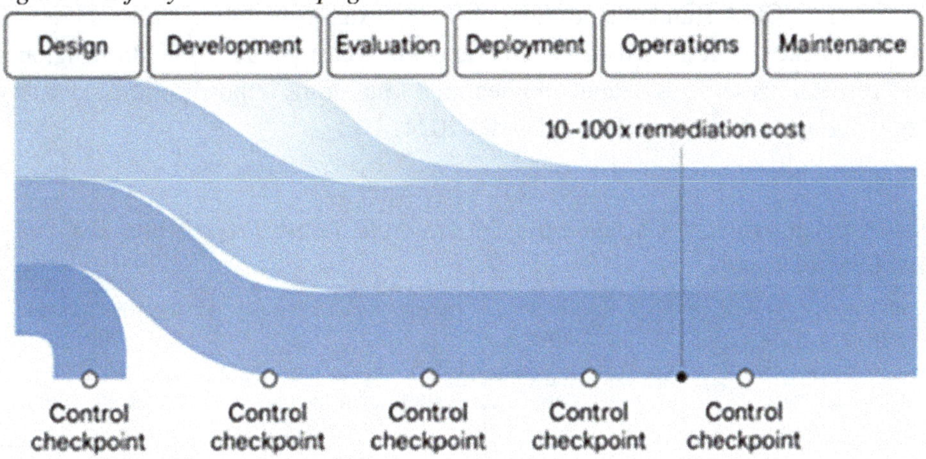

FOUNDATIONAL LIFE CYCLE ARCHITECTURE AND VULNERABILITY PROPAGATION

Leading AI governance models atomize the life cycle into six to seven separate stages, each of which presents distinct vulnerability types and capabilities to control these. Work (Dumitraş, 2015) identify canonical phases as planning and design, data acquisition and preparation, model development and training, model evaluation and testing, deployment and service, operations and monitoring, and retirement or replanning. Every stage has distinct vulnerability attributes. They note that causes of AI incidents may be injected into the system at various points in the life cycle and that, crucially, failures are generally situation dependent. This observation suggests that defenses applicable across all stages are insufficient and must be accompanied by stage specific controls. The key point here is that vulnerabilities introduced at an early point in time get transmitted forward through the life cycle, creating compounding risk if not rectified where they originate.

EARLY-STAGE CONTROLS AND DESIGN PHASE ADVANTAGE

The secure-by-design approach gained global acceptance in 2025. It promotes early security integration during system design (Mouratidis & Kang, 2012). Research demonstrates integrated systems resist critical exploits far better than post-deployment secured ones. Benefits quantify by control types and life cycle stages. 2025 NCSC/CISA standards outline four core design principles. Threat modeling aligns attacker objectives with system elements. Least privilege, sandboxing, and API restrictions serve as default architectures. Guardrails impose policy and safety limits for agentic systems (O'Neill et al., 2024).

Table 6. Vulnerability Classification by Lifecycle Stage: Propagation Dynamics and Control Timing

Vulnerability Class	Origin Stage	Manifestation Timeline	Remediation Cost Multi plier
Architectural flaw (e.g., no isolation)	Design	Entire lifecycle (propagates forward)	10–100x if remediated late
Data poisoning (training set contamination)	Data Prep	Detection at eval; impact at deploy	5–20x if undetected at deploy
Model back door (embedded trigger)	Training	Silent until activation; runtime trigger	8–50x post deployment
Adversarial brittleness (low robustness)	Training	Evasion at test; cascades to systems	3–10x if end-to-end robust ness not verified
API exposure without rate limiting	Deployment	Extraction/jailbreak at tacks begin	2–5x; control is simple but must be pre-deployment
Monitoring blind spot (undetected drift)	Operations	Silent degradation; delayed detection	1–3x; late detection increases incident duration
Unsafe prompt behavior (jailbreak vulnerability)	Training/ Deploy	Runtime; context dependent trigger	2–8x if not red teamed pre deployment

Documentation enhances traceability and attack surface awareness. These controls mitigate structural defects early, avoiding high remediation costs later in the life cycle. Table 6 reveals vulnerability cost asymmetry. Design-level architectural errors incur 10 to 100 times higher costs if detected late. Closed-loop blind spots multiply costs by only one to three times. Early-phase controls yield strong defensive returns. Data poisoning during preparation creates dormant threats. These activate at deployment, evading detection and impacting dependent systems. Architectural flaws like absent model isolation enable unmitigated lateral movement. Late-stage API rate limiting proves insufficient. Evidence confirms prevention costs orders of magnitude less than remediation.

QUANTIFYING EARLY-STAGE ADVANTAGE: ROI AND EMPIRICAL EVIDENCE

A five-year cost-benefit analysis of proactive versus reactive security in robotic process automation by (Hartz & John, 2008) reveals a 4.2 times average return on investment for design-stage implementation. Each dollar spent yields $4.2 in value via lower incident response, quicker remediation, and shrunk attack surface. NIST (2024) highlights measurable gains in core functions for structured risk management adopters (Maréchal et al., 2024). Advantages stem from shorter remediation times due to pre-embedded threat models and controls. Retrofitting later demands three to five times more effort. Systematic design-phase threat modeling curbs critical vulnerabilities and blocks attack classes like lateral escalation via isolation. Predesigned monitoring and guardrails speed detection and containment sans human delays. Evidence notes limitations that temper early-stage benefits. Figure 10 makes the proposed budget distribution actionable. It links resource allocation to asymmetric preventive benefit and necessary operational visibility.

Figure 10. Optimal security budget allocation across life cycle

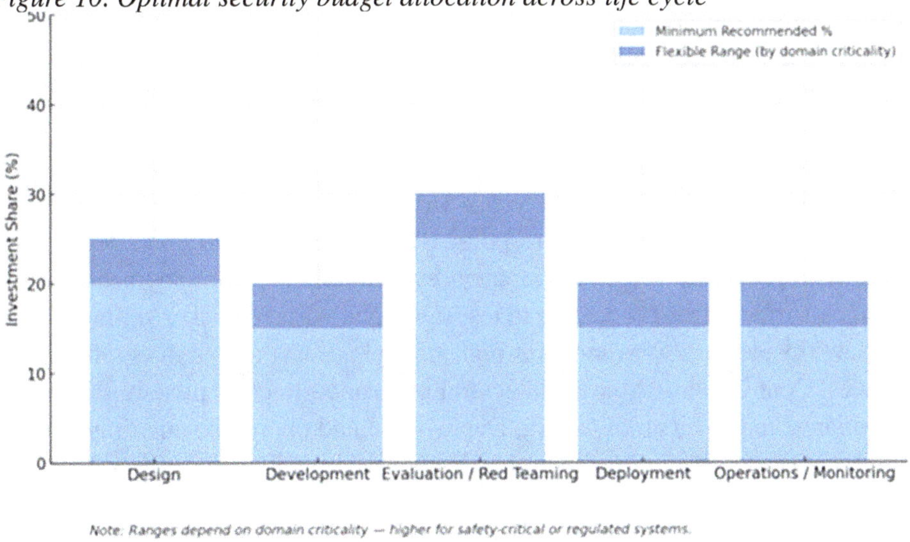

LIMITATIONS OF EARLY-STAGE CONTROLS: UNCERTAINTY AND UNKNOWABILITY

A core paradox undermines total early-stage security dominance. Design-phase controls miss unknown threats. Prompt injection on LLMs emerged post-2023. Pre-2021 AI lacked defenses against undefined risks. This creates a life cycle trilemma: known, known-unknown, and unknown-unknown threats. Known threats like adversarial evasion and data poisoning yield to early modeling (Li & Li, 2020). Known unknowns such as novel jailbreaks demand flexible designs and adaptive monitoring, not fixed controls (Greiman, 2023). Unknown unknowns like multistep prompt injection evade design defenses. Real-time monitoring and rapid response prove vital. Balleste (2025) guidelines highlight this paradox. They stress technical debt management and ongoing adaptation. Predictive design alone falls short. Responsive operational defenses remain crucial.

CAPABILITY RISK INTEGRATION: ATTACK SURFACE EXPANSION ACROSS LIFECYCLE

Attacker capability relative to life cycle stages remains nondecreasing. Offensive potential rises at deployment via APIs enabling extraction and jailbreaking. System interactions further expose crafting opportunities from context. Early stages limit attack surface, yet design flaws propagate impacts. Later stages expand surface area but enhance detection visibility. This yields a tradeoff: minimize surface through early controls or prioritize visibility and response (Ibarra et al., 2008). Table 7 depicts this dynamic. Progression through development, evaluation, and pre-deployment exposes escalating surfaces from code/data to test suites and APIs. Attacker skills advance from low (insiders only) to medium-high (model access) and high (supply chain collapse). Controls shift from architectural prevention to code review, validation, red teaming, and adversarial testing. Deployment and operations multiply surface by query logs and integrations. Attacker prowess peaks with context accumulation. Controls rely on monitoring, anomaly detection, and rapid response (Torkjazi & Raz, 2024). Asymmetry proves key. Attack surface grows over the life cycle. Design controls cap total exposure by excluding architectural paths. Proper isolation and least privilege halt lateral movement irrespective of query volume. Poor designs persist vulnerable despite late monitoring against traversing threats.

Table 7. Attack Surface Expansion, Attacker Capability, and Control Distribution Across AI Lifecycle

Lifecycle Stage	Attack Surface Size	Attacker Capability	Control Type Efficacy
Design	Minimal (blueprints)	Low (no artifact)	Architectural; prevents entire classes
Development	Small (code, data)	Medium (insiders only)	Code review, data validation, source controls
Evaluation	Medium (test suites)	Medium high (in Sider or model access)	Red teaming, adversarial testing, backdoor scanning
Pre-deployment	Large (artifacts, APIs)	High (supply chain access)	Model signing, SBOM, artifact verification
Deployment	Large (APIs, integrations)	Very high (external access)	Rate limiting, output filtering, access controls
Operations	Very large (query logs, integrations)	Extreme (accumulating context)	Monitoring, anomaly detection, rapid response

SECURITY EFFICIENCY TRADEOFFS: THE PARETO FRONTIER

Full life cycle security demands high computational and organizational costs. Provenance checks, red teaming, and monitoring require major resources. Budgets force security-efficiency balances. Design controls (threat modeling, architecture, policy) deliver high impact low cost by early constraint (Nagila et al., 2025). Development controls (validation, review, dependencies) provide medium impact medium cost to stop error spread. Evaluation controls (red teaming, backdoor scans, multimodality tests) yield high impact high-cost pre-deployment. Deployment/operations controls (monitoring, rate limits, response) incur medium continuous costs via automation (Li et al., 2025). Table 8 details costs, impacts, latencies, allocations. Design: 20-25%. Development: 15-20%. Evaluation: 25-30%. Deployment: 15-20%. Operations: 15-20%. Early investments maximize returns with late visibility.

Table 8. Security Control Cost Benefit Analysis by Lifecycle Stage: Resource Allocation Optimization

Stage	Control Cost (Relative)	Impact if failed	Detection Latency	Recommended Allocation
Design	Low	Very high (cascades forward)	N/A (preventive)	High priority; 20–25% budget
Development	Medium	High (systematic bug)	Medium (eval phase)	Medium priority; 15–20% budget
Evaluation	High	High (exploitable model)	Low (red-teaming detects)	High priority; 25–30% budget
Deployment	Medium	Medium (exposure begins)	Low (immediate activation)	Medium priority; 15–20% budget
Operations	Medium-High	Medium (sustained incident)	Variable (1 hour to weeks)	Medium priority; 15–20% budget

CONTROL INTERACTION EFFECTS AND COMPOUNDING RESILIENCE

A critical lesson learned from life cycle security studies is that controls to protect a system have compound as well as additive effects. If a model that has been compromised is rolled out unobserved, the damage can be high, even when every model is secure. Weak isolation makes input level detection meaningless without compartmentalization. More recent (Muravev et al., 2025), for example, emphasize the value of layering defenses at all stages of the system life cycle. It's contributed to isolation that limits extent of damage, guardrails that restrict independence to autonomous action, rollback (recovery) requirements as a response catch threats early. Effective lifecycle security demands defense-in-depth because systems remain only as resilient as their weakest component. Single controls are inherently insufficient; for instance, model robustness fails without architectural isolation, unmonitored isolation allows undetected breaches, and inadequate observability severely prolongs incident recovery.

PRACTICAL IMPLICATIONS: THE DESIGN DEPLOYMENT CONTINUUM

Organizations must balance costly, preventive design-phase foresight against responsive, reactive operational flexibility. Emerging adaptive security frameworks bridge this gap by embedding developmental constraints alongside continuous operational monitoring. Furthermore, since initial models cannot anticipate all vulnerabilities, ongoing threat model evolution and periodic formal reviews remain essential. Site-specific failures demand ongoing updates, not static design fixes (Torr, 2005). Supply chain security extends beyond organizational boundaries. Pretrained models, libraries, and cloud services carry upstream risks. The report of (Allegra, 2025) confirms DLA, IBM, and CSA recommendations. Life cycle vendor assessments occur at design time. Artifact verification precedes deployment for external items. Operations monitor updates and signature drift. This counters vulnerability spread across AI ecosystems.

ORGANIZATIONAL MATURITY AND LIFECYCLE CONTROL EFFECTIVENESS

Organizational maturity shapes life cycle control effectiveness and remediation speed. Author of (Silvola, 2008) notes mature organizations fix vulnerabilities three to five times faster than ad hoc setups. This demands investment in governance, roles (model owner, validator, auditor), and tools (registries, test frameworks, monitoring). Recent literature (2024-2025) defines four maturity levels. Level 1 uses post-development reactive security without threat modeling. Level 2 adds design-phase modeling, documentation, reviews, basic monitoring. Level 3 enforces full life cycle governance with red teaming, adversarial evaluation, automated detection. Level 4 enables continuous model evolution, adaptive controls, rollback, supply chain integration. Higher levels yield four to ten times faster recovery and 15-18% fewer undetected flaws. Early controls realize benefits only via rigorous maturity. Lacking governance and skills, design models lose operational impact.

CRITICAL ASSESSMENT: LIFE CYCLE SECURITY IS NECESSARY BUT INSUFFICIENT

Since early-stage design cannot predict all vulnerabilities, security frameworks must balance preventive measures with late-stage defenses. Optimal resilience avoids single-phase reliance by distributing resources across the entire life cycle. Effective strategies allocate 20-25% to architectural design, 25-30% to pre-deployment evaluation, 20-25% to operational monitoring, and 15-20% to continuous governance. This tailored approach successfully fuses proactive prevention with flexible detection and adaptive response.

DEFENSE OFFENSE ASYMMETRY AND INADEQUACY GAPS

The assessment evaluates if current defenses ensure robustness or only raise marginal attack costs. It probes gaps between theoretical guarantees and real-world security. It questions if adaptive defenses trail attacks due to structural or knowledge limits. Analysis draws empirical evidence from 2023-2025 peer-reviewed studies to expose flaws in defensive paradigms. Figure 11 demonstrates diminishing defense gains as attack sophistication rises.

Figure 11. Defense efficacy vs attack strength

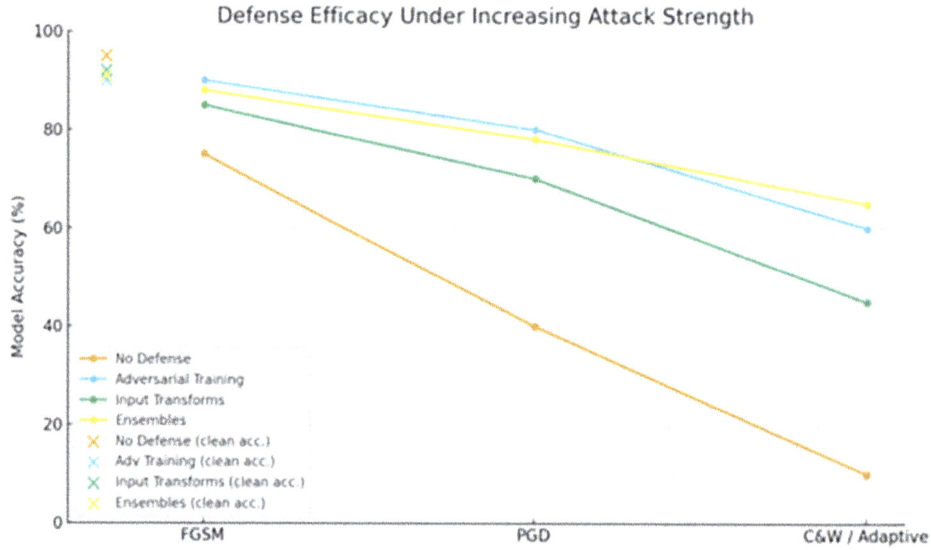

THEORY - PRACTICE GAP: CERTIFIED ROBUSTNESS AS SECURITY THEATER

Recent studies reveal gaps between certified robustness promises and outcomes. A Knox effect risks false security from overly strong guarantees (Teo et al., 2019). Threat models frequently fail against real-world attacks because verification tools confuse normal fluctuations with genuine threats, compounded by a lack of certification guidance. Most critically, an "assurance paradox" emerges where misplaced confidence in theoretical robustness deters vital investments in supplementary monitoring and response, ultimately magnifying systemic vulnerability by ignoring conditional realities.

EMPIRICAL INADEQUACY OF ADVERSARIAL TRAINING: ROBUSTNESS ACCURACY TRADEOFFS

Adversarial training, the leading defense against adversarial attacks, exhibits key limitations despite broad use (Wang & Zhang, 2019). 2024-2025 evidence shows modest robustness gains unfit for practice. Against weak FGSM, accuracy rises from 60% to 75% (Xu et al., 2019). Stronger PGD limits undefended models to 25%; training boosts to 40% (Song et al., 2019). Both fall short for security-critical needs. Carlini-Wagner attacks drop trained accuracy to 35%. Robustness boosts sacrifice over 10% clean data accuracy. About 40% of CIFAR-10 adversarial examples violate training assumptions (Abouelnaga et al., 2016). Robustness-accuracy tradeoffs reflect intrinsic limits from clashing optimization goals. Current adversarial training falters on flawed joint learning assumptions for clean and adversarial data. New defense paradigms prove necessary over incremental fixes. Table 9 tracks declining effectiveness against stronger attacks. FGSM yields 10-15% gains. PGD and Carlini-Wagner erode margins sharply. Peak attacks drop accuracy to 35% or below. This falls short of thresholds like 99.9% for autonomous driving or diagnostics. Defense gains dwindle as attacks advance, limiting protection versus sophisticated foes.

Table 9. Empirical Evaluation of Defense Mechanisms Against Progressive Attack Strength: Accuracy Degradation Under Adaptive Attacks (2024-2025)

Attack Type	No Defense	Adversarial Training	Input Transform	Defense Adequacy
FGSM	60%	75%	70%	Marginal improvement only
PGD (stronger)	25%	40%	30%	Significant gap remains
Carlini-Wagner (strongest)	20%	35%	28%	Critical inadequacy
Clean data baseline	99% (MNIST), 86% (CIFAR-10)	-10 to -15% penalty	-8% penalty	Trade-off unresolved

STRUCTURAL ASYMMETRY: WHY ADAPTIVE OFFENSE INHERENTLY OUTPACES ADAPTIVE DEFENSE

There is a fundamental asymmetry in the battle of adversarial machine learning which favors attackers over defenders, stemming from nonidentical optimization problems they are to solve. Attackers address a local well-defined task by finding input perturbations within constraints to mislead a fixed model (Kass & Jack, 2014). This simplicity brings them clear benefits such as they have whitepox access, to see gradients of models for optimization; and even backbox attacks can work provided some transferability by similar model. Defenders, on the other hand, have the odds stacked against them.

Figure 12. Offense defense optimization asymmetry

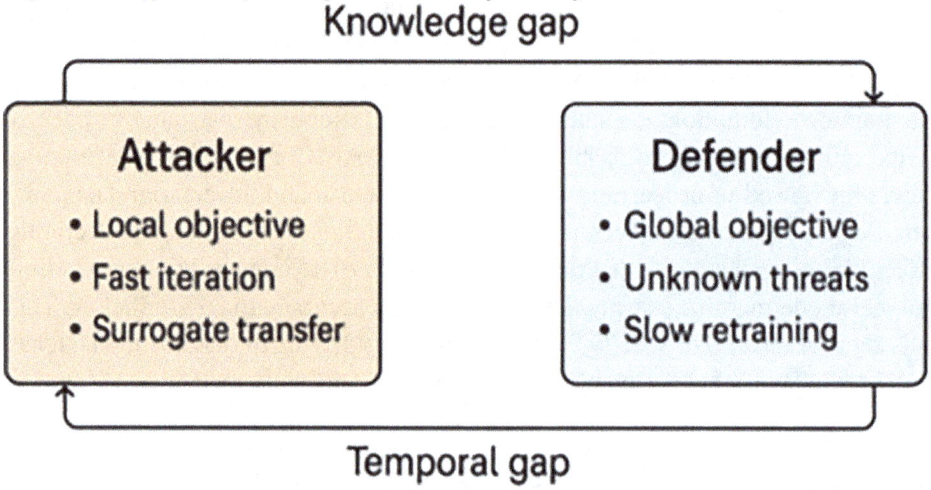

Defenses must counter all attacks, inputs, and future unknowns. Attackers hold knowledge asymmetry over defenders. Offense gains intrinsic edge. Figure 12 details structural offense advantages. Learning theory clarifies dynamics. Neural networks favor non-robust features for clean images. These yield to perturbations. Robust features endure changes but contribute little to clean accuracy (Rahmani, 2025). Adversarial training balances robust gains against non-robust losses. Protection trades off standard accuracy. This tradeoff inheres to dual feature nature, not poor methods. Robustness demands accuracy sacrifice.

DETECTION LATENCY AND ADAPTIVE CIRCUMVENTION

Defenders suffer speed deficits versus adversarial attacks. Attackers strike in milliseconds. Defenders need weeks or months for detection and retraining (Akowuah & Kong, 2021). Temporal gaps outpace even swift defenses. Attackers target known strategies with adaptive bypasses. Gradient defenses handle FGSM and PGD. They fail non-gradient methods like genetic algorithms or evolutionary attacks. Asymmetry persists. Defenses react to known threats. Attackers probe unaddressed flaws. This forces perpetual reactivity against creative offense.

Table 10. Structural Asymmetry Between Offensive and Defensive Capabilities in Adversarial ML

Dimension	Attacker Position	Defender Position
Problem Scope	Local: attack fixed model	Global: defend against unknown attackers
Objective Clarity	Explicit: maximize miss classification	Implicit: minimize unknown threats
Optimization Horizon	Seconds to minutes	Days to weeks
Knowledge Access	Whitebox or transfer able surrogates	Blackbox or incomplete threat intelligence
Adaptation Speed	Fast iteration on attack variants	Slow retraining cycles
Exploitable Surfaces	Any discovered weak ness	All surfaces simultaneously
Cost of Failure	Attacker fails one query	Defender must remediate systems wide
Knowable	Attacker knows target objective	Defender guesses at unknown threats

Table 10 synthesizes the structural asymmetries that create fundamental advantages for attackers. Enduring structural asymmetries fundamentally advantage attackers, who require only a single successful exploit to achieve focused, short-term objectives. Conversely, defenders must continuously secure all potential entry points across broad operational scopes, facing total system compromise from a single lapse.

THE CLASS IMBALANCE PROBLEM IN ADVERSARIAL ROBUSTNESS

Adversarial training worsens class imbalance in robust models. Author of (Zhang et al., 2024) finds 10-15% clean accuracy drops. Class robustness varies: 75% for some, 35-40% for others. Underrepresented classes suffer most. Enhanced labeling boosts robustness 53.50% and balances classes by 5.73%. Standard training leaves gains untapped. Improvements demand extra compute, underscoring defense cost escalation over offense.

RATE LIMITING AND EXTRACTION ATTACKS: MARGINAL IMPROVEMENTS

Rate limiting serves as a standard defense against model extraction. It caps query rates to block millions-scale attacks (Agnarsson et al., 2016). Determined attackers evade via spread queries over days or weeks. Rate limiting delays rather than prevents. It burdens legitimate peak users. Organizations balance security via strict limits against usability via loose ones. Intermediate options yield scant benefits. Table 11 represents a tradeoff among computational cost, practical effectiveness, and residual risk.

Table 11. Defense Mechanism cost Benefit Analysis: Computational Cost, Practical Effectiveness, and Residual Risk

Defense Type	Computational Cost	Effectiveness vs. Attacks	Practical Limitation
Adversarial Training	Very high	10-15 points accuracy gain max	Tradeoff unresolved; outdated after new attacks
Certified Robustness	High	Bounded guarantee only	Boundary conditions weaken; attack agnostic
Input Transformation	Medium	8–10-point accuracy gain	Transformations themselves be come attack targets
Rate Limiting	Low	Delay (not Prevention)	Temporal distribution circumvents limits
Ensemble Methods	Very high	Modest robustness gain	Transferability still achieves cross ensemble attacks
Data Provenance	Medium	Prevents known poisoning only	Unknown poisoning undetectable

FUNDAMENTAL THEORETICAL BOUNDS ON DEFENSE EFFICACY

Recent research shows that defenses against AI attacks have fundamental mathematical limits that no implementation can overcome. The Carlini Wagner attack family, significantly advanced between 2024 and 2025, reveals that any classifier using standard mathematical operations can be fooled by carefully crafted inputs. Though some defenses make attacks harder by requiring larger changes to input data or more computation, they cannot eliminate this core weakness. This means perfect protection is simply not possible for many real-world problems, no matter how sophisticated the defense strategy becomes.

ADAPTIVE DEFENSES AND THE INTRACTABILITY OF ANTICIPATION

Adaptive defenses cannot anticipate the full attack space, and public disclosure often erodes their value because attackers can quickly study published methods and design bypasses. In practice, this creates a recurring cycle in which each new defense loses its advantage once revealed.

THE ORGANIZATIONAL IMMATURITY FACTOR

Organizations face significant barriers to implementing defense measures against adversarial attacks. Most lack the expertise needed to deploy even basic robustness techniques, with surveys showing that 75%-80% of organizations have not adopted adversarial training, certification programs, or systematic robustness evaluation. This implementation gap limits the real-world effectiveness of well researched defenses. Furthermore, organizations prioritize operational efficiency and inference speed over robustness, making robust models economically unappealing since they run slower than fast but vulnerable alternatives.

SYNTHESIS: DEFENSE INADEQUACY AS STRUCTURAL RATHER THAN TECHNOLOGICAL

Current defenses provide only modest gains because attacker-favoring structural asymmetries persist. Adversarial training improves accuracy, but it remains vulnerable under strong attacks and often trades accuracy for limited robustness, while certified guarantees and rate limiting offer only partial protection. As a result, effective security depends on layered controls that combine hardening with isolation, monitoring, response, and resilience.

FINDING FROM CRITICAL ANALYSIS

AI-enabled threats magnify familiar vulnerabilities through automation and scale, compressing data theft timelines and boosting phishing success. The strongest response begins early, with design and evaluation investments that block attack paths through modeling and isolation, while monitoring covers residual gaps and compensates for unknown future threats. Figure 13 contextualizes research attention and maturity by theme.

Figure 13. Publication trend by threat category

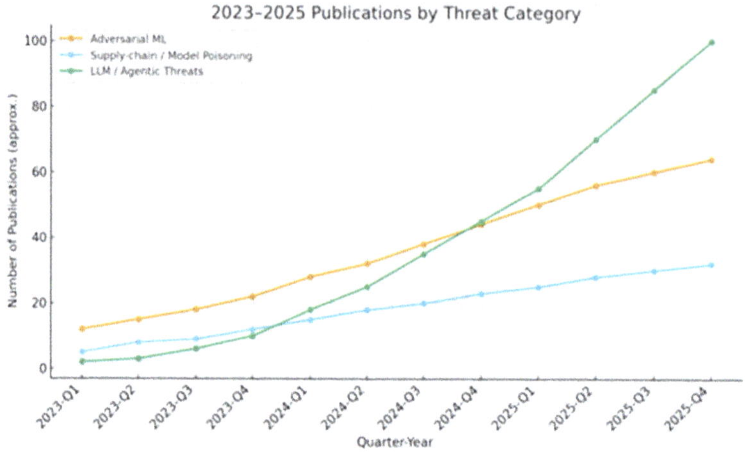

AI defense faces structural limits because attackers optimize for narrow goals and rapid adaptation, while defenders must protect against unknowns over much longer horizons. Adversarial training, certification, and rate limits offer only partial gains, so effective resilience depends on layered prevention, detection, and response across the full life cycle.

CONCLUSION AND FUTURE DIRECTIONS

AI-enabled threats from 2023 to 2025 largely scale existing attack techniques through automation rather than creating many new categories, which means AI security must move beyond isolated technical fixes toward organizational and architectural change. The most effective priorities are design-time security, pre-deployment testing, real-time monitoring, and rapid response, since early life cycle controls can disrupt attack chains while operational safeguards address unknown threats. Because offense-defense asymmetries, robustness-accuracy tradeoffs, and misleading guarantees limit purely technical defenses, resilience should be built through holistic prevention, detection, and response within zero-trust frameworks that emphasize verification and containment. This approach shortens recovery time, reduces hidden flaws, and requires coordinated commitment to architecture, governance, and capability development rather than compliance alone. Looking ahead, 2025 and beyond will bring agentic threats that intensify research and operational challenges, making collaboration across academia, industry, and policy essential for advancing AI security maturity. Table 12 presents the future research directions.

Table 12. Future Research Directions in AI Security (2025 and beyond)

Research Area	Current Gap	Future Direction
Robustness Accuracy Tradeoff	Fundamental incompatibility between adversarial and clean accuracy	Architectural diversity and learning objective reformulation; determine if mathematically irreducible
Certified Robustness	Epsilon ball bounds vs. practical threat distributions	Threat model agnostic certification for operational deployment
Explainable AI	Explanations as attack surfaces; separate development from robustness	Joint advancement of interpretability and adversarial resilience
Prompt Injection Defense	Reactive hardening against known patterns	Principled detection and prevention across heterogeneous prompts
Agent Communication	Vulnerability to poisoning; no trust protocols for compromised agents	Protocols enabling trust despite intermediate agent compromise
Model Supply Chain	Insufficient artifact verification; undetectable back doors (TransTroj)	Formal verification methods scaling to model market places
Governance Standards	Principles based frameworks lacking prescriptive baselines	Concrete control baselines and measurable compliance metrics
Accountability Structures	Ambiguous liability across creators, adapters, deployers, users	Clear accountability frameworks incentivizing se cure practices
Shadow AI Discovery	Organizations cannot enumerate deployed AI systems	AI asset discovery and inventory extending to edge and third-party services
Third-party Risk	Inadequate vendor transparency and assessment	Formalized risk questionnaires and vendor audit protocols (SOC2 aligned)
Continuous Gover nance	Point intime certification obsolete within weeks	Continuous governance adapted to post deployment evolution
Organizational Capability	77% breaches with only 5% confidence; capability gaps across five dimensions	Systematic programs: structure, processes, tooling, training, incident response
System Inventory	Organizations lack foundational AI system discovery	Discovery and inventory mechanisms for all deployments
Threat Modeling	Generic risk rubrics inadequate for context specific threats	Context specific threat modeling and risk assessment per system
Continuous Assessment	Episodic testing incompatible with evolving agentic systems	Automated and continuous red teaming (OpenAI, Anthropic models)
Supply Chain Resilience	Monoculture dependency (BERT, GPT, T5); near perfect propagation of compromises	Dependency diversification; federated and decentralized training approaches
Zero Trust Architecture	Traditional perimeter-based security inadequate	Continuous verification of all inputs and integrations

continued on following page

Table 12. Continued

Research Area	Current Gap	Future Direction
Model Isolation	Lateral movement risk from single compromised model	Containerization and sandboxing for containment
Fail Safe Defaults	Reliance on model training and runtime monitoring	Architectural constraints preventing unsafe behavior by design
Quantitative Metrics	Subjective maturity models; unmeasurable risk re duction	Attack cost curves, success rates, residual risk, detection speed
Detection and Response	Overinvestment in prevention; perfect prevention impossible	Measure detection effectiveness and incident response speed

REFERENCES

Abouelnaga, Y., Ali, O. S., Rady, H., & Moustafa, M. (2016). CIFAR-10: KNN-based ensemble of classifiers. In *2016 International Conference on Computational Science and Computational Intelligence (CSCI)* (pp. 1192–1195). DOI: 10.1109/CSCI.2016.0225

Acharya, D. B., Kuppan, K., & Divya, B. (2025). Agentic AI: Autonomous intelligence for complex goals—a comprehensive survey. *IEEE Access : Practical Innovations, Open Solutions, 13*, 18912–18936. DOI: 10.1109/ACCESS.2025.3532853

Adabara, I., Sadiq, B. O., Shuaibu, A. N., Danjuma, Y. I., & Venkateswarlu, M. (2025). A review of agentic AI in cybersecurity: Cognitive autonomy, ethical governance, and quantum-resilient defense. *F1000 Research, 14*, 843. DOI: 10.12688/f1000research.169337.1 PMID: 41169871

Agnarsson, G., Greenlaw, R., & Kantabutra, S. (2016). On cyber attacks and the maximum-weight rooted-subtree problem. *Acta Cybernetica (Szeged), 22*(3), 591–612. DOI: 10.14232/actacyb.22.3.2016.3

Ahmad Rana, S. (2026). Adversarial artificial intelligence in industrial control systems: A consequence-oriented gap analysis of MITRE ATLAS. https://doi.org/ DOI: 10.2139/ssrn.6055035

Akowuah, F., & Kong, F. (2021). Real-time adaptive sensor attack detection in autonomous cyber-physical systems. In 2021 IEEE 27th Real-Time and Embedded Technology and Applications Symposium (RTAS) (pp. 237–250). IEEE. DOI: 10.1109/RTAS52030.2021.00027

Allegra, G. (2025). Best supply chain, manufacturing and aircraft systems identification leveraging a model-based product line engineering approach (Doctoral dissertation, Politecnico di Torino).

Balleste, R. (2025). Cyberspace domain and legal norms. In *A research agenda for cybersecurity law and policy* (pp. 5–32). Edward Elgar Publishing. DOI: 10.4337/9781803929194.00007

Balunovic, M., & Vechev, M. (2020). Adversarial training and provable defenses: Bridging the gap. In *International Conference on Learning Representations.*

Casey, B., Santos, J., & Mirakhorli, M. (2024). A large-scale exploit instrumentation study of AI/ML supply chain attacks in Hugging Face models. arXiv preprint arXiv:2410.04490.

Cavaliere, D., Gallo, M., & Stanzione, C. (2023). Propaganda detection robustness through adversarial attacks driven by explainable AI. In *World Conference on Explainable Artificial Intelligence* (pp. 405–419). Springer. DOI: 10.1007/978-3-031-44067-0_21

Dal Cin, P., Kendzior, D., Seedat, Y., & Marinho, R. (2025). Three essentials for agentic AI security. MIT Sloan Management Review (Online), 1–4.

Dumitraş, T. (2015). Understanding the vulnerability lifecycle for risk assessment and defense against sophisticated cyber attacks. In *Cyber warfare: Building the scientific foundation* (pp. 265–285). Springer. DOI: 10.1007/978-3-319-14039-1_13

Eshra, S. A., Zohora, F. T., Akter, S., Rasul, I., & Hossain, A. (2025). The role of threat intelligence in preventing financially motivated cyberattacks. *Journal of Engineering and Computational Intelligence Review*, *3*(2), 20–37.

ET. (n.d.). Hong Kong MNC suffers $25.6 million loss in deepfake scam. The Economic Times. Retrieved October 27, 2025, from https://economictimes.indiatimes.com/industry/tech/hongkongmncsuffers256millionlossindeepfakescam/articleshow/107465111.cms?from=mdr

Gartner, G. (2025). A decade in scientific cartography: Insights and future directions. *International Journal of Cartography*, *11*(2), 166–172. DOI: 10.1080/23729333.2025.2483160

Greiman, V. (2023). Known unknowns: The inevitability of cyber attacks. In *Proceedings of the 22nd European Conference on Cyber Warfare and Security* (Vol. 22). DOI: 10.34190/eccws.22.1.1316

Guembe, B., Azeta, A., Misra, S., Osamor, V. C., Fernandez-Sanz, L., & Pospelova, V. (2022). The emerging threat of AI-driven cyber-attacks: A review. *Applied Artificial Intelligence*, *36*(1), 2037254. DOI: 10.1080/08839514.2022.2037254

Guo, W., Tondi, B., & Barni, M. (2022). An overview of backdoor attacks against deep neural networks and possible defences. *IEEE Open Journal of Signal Processing*, *3*, 261–287. DOI: 10.1109/OJSP.2022.3190213

Hartz, S., & John, J. (2008). Contribution of economic evaluation to decision making in early phases of product development: A methodological and empirical review. *International Journal of Technology Assessment in Health Care*, *24*(4), 465–472. DOI: 10.1017/S0266462308080616 PMID: 18828942

Hubinger, E., Denison, C., Mu, J., Lambert, M., Tong, M., MacDiarmid, M., Lanham, T., Ziegler, D. M., Maxwell, T., Cheng, N., Jermyn, A., Askell, A., Radhakrishnan, A., Anil, C., Duvenaud, D., Ganguli, D., Barez, F., Clark, J., Ndousse, K., & Sachan, K. (2024, January 17). Sleeper Agents: Training Deceptive LLMs that Persist Through Safety Training. ArXiv.org. https://doi.org//arXiv.2401.05566DOI: 10.48550

Ibarra, I., Melentis, J., Summers, D., Stipidis, E., Charchalakis, P., & Ali, F. H. (2008). Through-life capability risk management for evolutionary complex military vetronics. In 2008 3rd IET International Conference on System Safety (pp. 1–6). DOI: 10.1049/cp:20080726

Jacobsen, J. T., & Liebetrau, T. (2023). Artificial intelligence and military superiority: How the "cyber-AI offensive-defensive arms race" affects the U.S. vision of the fully integrated battlefield. In Artificial intelligence and international conflict in cyberspace (pp. 135–156). Routledge.

Jiang, J., Shu, Y., Wang, J., & Long, M. (2022). Transferability in deep learning: A survey. arXiv preprint arXiv:2201.05867.

Joy, J. (2025). DNS data exfiltration detection using CNN-LSTM with attention mechanism (CLAM) (Doctoral dissertation, National College of Ireland, Dublin).

Kass, L., & Jack, J. P. (2014). Combating asymmetric threats: The interplay of offense and defense. *Orbis*, *58*(2), 248–265. DOI: 10.1016/j.orbis.2014.02.004

Kempen, A. (2024). WormGPT/FraudGPT: The ugly, dangerous "cousin" of ChatGPT. *Servamus Community-Based Safety and Security Magazine*, *117*(11), 19–21.

Kezron, N.Isabirye Edward Kezron. (2024). Securing the AI supply chain: Mitigating vulnerabilities in AI model development and deployment. *World Journal of Advanced Research and Reviews*, *22*(2), 2336–2346. DOI: 10.30574/wjarr.2024.22.2.1394

Kou, T., Zhang, Q., Zhang, C., He, T., & Shen, J. (2023). Integrated MPCAM: Multi-PSF learning for large depth-of-field computational imaging. *Information Fusion*, *89*, 452–472. DOI: 10.1016/j.inffus.2022.09.005

Kshetri, N. (2025). Transforming cybersecurity with agentic AI to combat emerging cyber threats. *Telecommunications Policy*, *49*(6), 102976. DOI: 10.1016/j.telpol.2025.102976

Li, B., Jin, X., Ba, T., Pan, T., Wang, E., & Gu, Z. (2025). Deceptive cyber-resilience in PV grids: Digital twin-assisted optimization against cyber-physical attacks. *Energies*, *18*(12), 3145. DOI: 10.3390/en18123145

Li, D., & Li, Q. (2020). Adversarial deep ensemble: Evasion attacks and defenses for malware detection. *IEEE Transactions on Information Forensics and Security*, *15*, 3886–3900. DOI: 10.1109/TIFS.2020.3003571

Li, R., Ben Allal, L., Zi, Y., Muennighoff, N., Kocetkov, D., Mou, C., Marone, M., Akiki, C., Li, J., Chim, J., ... (2023). StarCoder: May the source be with you. arXiv preprint arXiv:2305.06161.

Lin, L. S. F. (2025). Examining the role of deepfake technology in organized fraud: Legal, security, and governance challenges. *Frontiers in Law*, *4*, 6–17. DOI: 10.6000/2817-2302.2025.04.02

Liu, Y., Deng, G., Li, Y., Wang, K., Wang, Z., Wang, X., Zhang, T., Liu, Y., Wang, H., Zheng, Y., ... (2023). Prompt injection attack against LLM-integrated applications. arXiv preprint arXiv:2306.05499.

Lu, Z., Li, Z., Chiang, C.-W., & Yin, M. (2023). Strategic adversarial attacks in AI-assisted decision making to reduce human trust and reliance. In IJCAI (pp. 3020–3028).

Maréchal, L., Mermoud, A., David, D. P., & Humbert, M. (2024). Measuring the performance of investments in information security startups: An empirical analysis by cybersecurity sectors using Crunchbase data. arXiv preprint arXiv:2402.04765.

Menon, U. V., Kumaravelu, V. B., Kumar, C. V., Rammohan, A., Chinnadurai, S., Venkatesan, R., Hai, H., & Selvaprabhu, P. (2025). AI-powered IoT: A survey on integrating artificial intelligence with IoT for enhanced security, efficiency, and smart applications. *IEEE Access : Practical Innovations, Open Solutions*.

Mouratidis, H., & Kang, M. (2012). Secure by design. In Developing and evaluating security-aware software systems (p. 1). DOI: 10.4018/978-1-61350-456-7.ch108

Muravev, M., Brazhenko, D., Somenkova, A., Golovkov, A., & Sergunin, I. (2025). MLOps architecture as a future of machine learning. *Journal of Computer Information Systems*, •••, 1–13. DOI: 10.1080/08874417.2025.2483826

Murugesan, S. (2025). The rise of agentic AI: Implications, concerns, and the path forward. *IEEE Intelligent Systems*, *40*(2), 8–14. DOI: 10.1109/MIS.2025.3544940

Nagila, A., Appalakonda, M. V., Kurumeti, N. K., Poornavalli, R., Dube, A. P., Anandh, A., Parimala, R. S., & Jain, A. K. (2025). Optimizing cybersecurity decision making: A framework for balancing short-term costs and long-term benefits. *International Journal of Environmental Sciences*, *11*(10s), 408–422. DOI: 10.64252/jep5hy65

Narula, S., Ghasemigol, M., Carnerero-Cano, J., Minnich, A., Lupu, E., & Takabi, D. (2025). Exploring AI security: A systematic mapping study. *IEEE Access : Practical Innovations, Open Solutions, 13*, 84057–84080. DOI: 10.1109/ACCESS.2025.3567195

News, M. I. T. (2016). System predicts 85 percent of cyberattacks using input from human experts. Retrieved October 27, 2025, from https://news.mit.edu/2016/ai-system-predicts-85-percent-cyberattacks-using-input-human-experts-0418

NIST AI. (2024). *A plan for global engagement on AI standards.* National Institute of Standards and Technology.

O'Neill, J., Subramanian, S., Lin, E., Satish, A., & Mugunthan, V. (2024). GuardFormer: Guardrail instruction pretraining for efficient safeguarding. In NeurIPS Safe Generative AI Workshop 2024.

Oprea, A., & Vassilev, A. (2023). *Adversarial machine learning: A taxonomy and terminology of attacks and mitigations (Technical report).* National Institute of Standards and Technology. DOI: 10.6028/NIST.AI.100-2e2023.ipd

Pang, T., Du, C., Dong, Y., & Zhu, J. (2018). Towards robust detection of adversarial examples. *Advances in Neural Information Processing Systems*, **•••**, 31.

Perez, F., & Ribeiro, I. (2022). Ignore Previous Prompt: Attack Techniques For Language Models. ArXiv (Cornell University). https://doi.org//arxiv.2211.09527DOI: 10.48550

Radanliev, P., Santos, O., & Ani, U. D. (2025). Generative AI cybersecurity and resilience. *Frontiers in Artificial Intelligence, 8*, 1568360. DOI: 10.3389/frai.2025.1568360 PMID: 40529644

Rahmani, S. (2025). AI's dual-use paradox in financial fraud: Navigating offense and defense in the digital era. *Sociedad & Tecnología, 8*(4), 673–692. DOI: 10.51247/st.v8i4.666

Schröer, S. L., Apruzzese, G., Human, S., Laskov, P., Anderson, H. S., Bernroider, E. W. N., Fass, A., Nassi, B., Rimmer, V., & Roli, F.. (2025). SoK: On the offensive potential of AI. In *2025 IEEE Conference on Secure and Trustworthy Machine Learning (SaTML)* (pp. 247–280). IEEE. DOI: 10.1109/SaTML64287.2025.00021

Selçuk, A. A. (2019). A guide for systematic reviews: PRISMA. *Turkish Archives of Otorhinolaryngology, 57*(1), 57–58. DOI: 10.5152/tao.2019.4058 PMID: 31049257

Shen, S., Jin, G., Gao, K., & Zhang, Y. (2017). APE-GAN: Adversarial perturbation elimination with GAN. arXiv preprint arXiv:1707.05474.

Shokri, R., Stronati, M., Song, C., & Shmatikov, V. (2017). Membership inference attacks against machine learning models. In *2017 IEEE Symposium on Security and Privacy (SP)* (pp. 3–18). IEEE. DOI: 10.1109/SP.2017.41

Shukla, P. K., Raghuvanshi, C. S., & Sharan, H. O. (2024). AI-enhanced cybersecurity: Leveraging artificial intelligence for threat detection and mitigation. *Journal of Computational Analysis and Applications*, *33*(8).

Silvola, H. (2008). Do organizational lifecycle and venture capital investors affect the management control systems used by the firm? *Advances in Accounting*, *24*(1), 128–138. DOI: 10.1016/j.adiac.2008.05.013

Song, L., Shokri, R., & Mittal, P. (2019). *Membership inference attacks against adversarially robust deep learning models. In 2019 IEEE Security and Privacy Workshops*. SPW.

Teo, C. S. M., Claire, C. A., Lopez, V., & Shorey, S. (2019). Pressure injury prevention and management practices among nurses: A realist case study. *International Wound Journal*, *16*(1), 153–163. DOI: 10.1111/iwj.13006 PMID: 30273984

Torkjazi, M., & Raz, A. K. (2024). A review on integrating autonomy into system of systems: Challenges and research directions. *IEEE Open Journal of Systems Engineering*, *2*, 157–178. DOI: 10.1109/OJSE.2024.3456037

Torr, P. (2005). Demystifying the threat modeling process. *IEEE Security and Privacy*, *3*(5), 66–70. DOI: 10.1109/MSP.2005.119

Wang, H., Guo, S., He, J., Liu, H., Zhang, T., & Xiang, T. (2025). Model supply chain poisoning: Backdooring pretrained models via embedding indistinguishability. In *Proceedings of the ACM Web Conference 2025* (pp. 840–851). DOI: 10.1145/3696410.3714624

Wang, J., & Zhang, H. (2019). Bilateral adversarial training: Towards fast training of more robust models against adversarial attacks. In *Proceedings of the IEEE/CVF International Conference on Computer Vision (ICCV)*. DOI: 10.1109/ICCV.2019.00673

Wei, J., Li, F., Sun, J., Zhu, Z., Shi, R., Shi, J., & Sun, K. (2024). Modified tracheal traction exercise reduces the incidence of dysphagia in patients with multilevel anterior cervical discectomy and fusion. *Orthopaedic Surgery*, *16*(10), 2391–2400. DOI: 10.1111/os.14166 PMID: 39030809

Xu, J., Cai, Z., & Shen, W. (2019). Using FGSM targeted attack to improve the transferability of adversarial example. In 2019 IEEE 2nd International Conference on Electronics and Communication Engineering (ICECE) (pp. 20–25). DOI: 10.1109/ICECE48499.2019.9058535

Zhang, Y., Dong, Y., Zhang, S., Min, T., Su, H., & Zhu, J. (2024). Exploring the transferability of visual prompting for multimodal large language models. In *Proceedings of the IEEE/CVF Conference on Computer Vision and Pattern Recognition* (pp. 26562–26572). DOI: 10.1109/CVPR52733.2024.02508

Zhou, S., Liu, C., Ye, D., Zhu, T., Zhou, W., & Yu, P. S. (2022). Adversarial attacks and defenses in deep learning: From a perspective of cybersecurity. *ACM Computing Surveys*, *55*(8), 1–39. DOI: 10.1145/3547330

KEY TERMS AND DEFINITIONS

Adversarial Machine Learning: A field of attack and defense focused on manipulating machine learning systems through perturbation, poisoning, extraction, or backdoor insertion.

Agentic AI: AI systems that can plan, reason, use tools, and execute multistep actions with limited human intervention.

Agentic Offense: Autonomous or semi-autonomous attacks in which AI agents carry out cyber operations such as reconnaissance, exploitation, exfiltration, or evasion.

AI-Enabled Threats: Threats that use artificial intelligence to automate, scale, or improve offensive cyber operations across the attack lifecycle.

Attack Surface: The total set of points in a system, model, pipeline, or agentic ecosystem that can be exploited by an adversary.

Certified Robustness: A formal guarantee that a model remains stable within a specified threat bound, though such guarantees may not hold under real-world conditions.

Data Poisoning: The insertion or modification of training data to corrupt model behavior, degrade performance, or implant malicious triggers.

Defense in Depth: A layered security strategy that combines prevention, detection, response, and containment rather than relying on a single control.

Life Cycle Security: A security approach that embeds controls across design, development, deployment, operation, and retirement stages of an AI system.

Model Evasion: An attack that crafts inputs to cause a trained model to make incorrect predictions at inference time.

Model Extraction: An attack that reconstructs model functionality or parameters by querying a deployed model and observing outputs.

Model Inversion: An attack that infers sensitive training data or reconstructs representative records from model outputs or confidence patterns.

Prompt Injection: A technique that manipulates language model instructions so the model follows attacker-controlled content instead of intended system goals.

Red Teaming: Adversarial testing performed to simulate attacks, expose weaknesses, and evaluate the effectiveness of defenses.

Robustness-Accuracy Tradeoff: The tension in which improving resistance to adversarial attacks reduces performance on clean, unmodified data.

Supply Chain Attack: An attack that targets third-party models, libraries, datasets, dependencies, or deployment tools to compromise AI systems indirectly.

Threat Modeling: A structured process for identifying likely attack paths, vulnerabilities, and controls before deployment.

Zero-Trust Framework: A security model that assumes no user, agent, or component is trusted by default and requires continuous verification.

Chapter 2
The Offense-Defense Balance in the Age of Agentic Cyber Warfare

R. Sudha
http://orcid.org/0009-0008-9071-6657
SSM Institute of Engineering and Technology, India

M. Premkumar
http://orcid.org/0000-0003-0517-1055
SSM Institute of Engineering and Tehnology, India

ABSTRACT

In this chapter, we tackle the issue of agentic cyber warfare – a new threat posed by autonomous intelligent agents that carry out offensive and defensive cyber actions without much human input. The proposed solution to this problem is an agentic defense architecture for enhancing intrusion detection and reaction. The method employed is through an analysis of the proposed system with a focus on how it compares with conventional cyber security solutions based on criteria such as adaptability and scalability. The results show that the proposed system can greatly improve intrusion detection. Furthermore, other issues including explainability and adversarial robustness, among others, are also analyzed in this chapter.

1. INTRODUCTION

The massive expansion of digital systems that are connected and interdependent like cloud computing, Internet of Things (IoT) and cyber-physical systems (CPS) have significantly transformed the digital world. They include enabling the ex-

DOI: 10.4018/979-8-2600-0413-5.ch002

change of data, real-time interaction and automation of processes across healthcare, transportation, energy and defense systems. However, this increasing connectivity has also widened the cyber-attack surface, and it is also more likely to experience advanced, distributed, and multi-vector cyber-attacks (Hozouri et al., 2025). In contrast to stand-alone systems, modern systems are sophisticated, heterogeneous and dynamic systems, which can be used by enemies via advanced attack methods (zero-day attacks, polymorphic malware and AI-driven intrusion procedures).

Conventionally, cybersecurity has been implemented upon the rule-based and signature-based models. These mechanisms operate under the idea of identifying familiar patterns or rules in reference to previous attacks. These approaches are effective in identifying known threats but have significant shortcomings when faced with new or variant attacks. (Mohamed, 2023) These methods are limited in scalability, adaptability and generalizability. Since the dynamic nature of the threat landscape involves constant changes in the tactics, techniques, and procedures (TTPs) adopted by adversaries, there is a need for dynamic approaches.

The emergence of novel AI/ML technologies has ushered in an age of cybersecurity transformation. These AI systems can learn from massive data sets, recognize underlying patterns, and adapt dynamically to their surroundings. The latest innovations in artificial intelligence (AI) and machine learning (ML) technologies have brought about a revolution in cybersecurity. AI-based systems have the capability to learn from large datasets, discover latent patterns, and dynamically adapt to their environment (Blanchard et al., 2023). Such methods as deep learning, reinforcement learning and generative models have enabled the development of intelligent intrusion detection systems (IDS), anomaly detection systems and automatic response systems. These methods have a high level of detection efficacy, efficiency and scalability compared to traditional methods.

One of the most revolutionary advances in AI-based cybersecurity is agentic intelligence. Agentic AI systems are autonomous, goal-driven systems that perceive, reason and act in the world (Adabara et al., 2025a).Where traditional AI models are used to carry out specific tasks, agentic systems operate as goal-oriented agents that perceive, reason and act in the world, make decisions while dealing with uncertainty, and learn from experience (Modalavalasa & Yadav, 2025). These characteristics make them well-adapted to dynamic and adversarial environments like cybersecurity (Jacobsen et al., 2023)

Agentic intelligence in the realm of cyber security is also known as agentic cyber warfare. In this approach, both cyber defense and cyber-attack capabilities are enhanced by the presence of agentic intelligence that allows for sophisticated strategies to be executed with little to no human oversight (Kabir et al., 2026). In the realm of offensive cyber operations, adversaries are using AI to create highly evasive attacks. This includes AI-driven phishing attacks, automated vulnerability scanning, adversarial malware that can evade detection, and multiagent attack strategies (Khan et al., 2025). Such attacks can learn and react to defensive counteractions, making them more difficult to counter (Adabara et al., 2025b).

On the other hand, defenders are also deploying agentic AI for improved cybersecurity. Intelligent agents can continuously monitor traffic on the network, analyze network traffic to detect abnormalities, predict threats and automatically respond with counteractions (Balasubramanian et al., 2025; Green 2026). To give an example, reinforcement learning models can be trained to learn the best strategies given the dynamics of the attacks, and federated learning can be used to facilitate the sharing of threat intelligence whilst maintaining privacy (Yang & Shami, 2025). This evolution from reactive to proactive and adaptive defenses is a critical aspect of cybersecurity.

In this context, the offense-defense dynamic is undergoing transformation. Traditionally, offenses had the upper hand owing to the third-party problem where the impact of one vulnerability would be devastating. In the application of the agentic intelligence, however, both sides gain high-level capabilities in automation, adaptation, and decision-making (Yang & Shami, 2023). This dynamic is highly volatile and always shifting and relies on various elements including processing power, data, algorithms, and integration.

In this light, the purpose of this chapter is to provide a comprehensive insight into the dynamic of the offense-defense dynamic in the agentic cyber warfare context. The main objectives of this chapter are to examine the evolving offense-defense dynamic, agentic cyber threats, design adaptive defense architecture, and analyze challenges and future directions (Erendor, 2024).

In this regard, the offense-defense paradigm is being redefined. In the past, offences have often had the edge due to the third-party problem where the cost of a single vulnerability could be disastrous. However, the application of the agentic intelligence introduces a new dimension where both attackers and defenders have advanced capabilities of automation, adaptation and decision-making (Erendor, 2024). The balance is worth dynamic and in constant flux, which is dependent on factors of processing power, data, algorithms and integration.

In this context, this chapter sets out to offer a holistic understanding of the changing offense–defense balance in the era of agentic cyber warfare. The chapter seeks to achieve the following objectives as Analyze the Evolving Offense–Defense Balance, Examine Agentic Cyber Threats, propose an Adaptive Defense Architecture, Challenges and Future Directions (Comunale et al., 2024)

2. BACKGROUND AND RELATED WORK

2.1 Background

The emergence of interconnected digital systems like cloud, IoT and CPS has totally transformed the computing environment (Baele et al., 2024). Using these digital systems helps facilitate seamless interaction, automation, and real-time execution of various applications such as health surveillance, transportation and smart cities. Nonetheless, increased interconnectivity has contributed to an increase in cyber threats, hence making systems vulnerable to sophisticated, widespread, and dynamic cyber-attacks (Ali et al., 2024).

Traditional approaches of cybersecurity include IDS using signatures and rules where detection occurs through pattern recognition and is solely dependent on known patterns. Such conventional systems cannot be successful in the current environment because they are unable to detect sophisticated and dynamic attacks such as zero-day attacks and polymorphism. Therefore, anomaly detection schemes have been introduced to counter these challenges where detection occurs based on abnormality in the system (Yuvaraja et al., 2024; Shevchenko et al., 2024). Such approach can successfully detect dynamic attacks but is prone to giving false positive results.

Artificial intelligence (AI) has been applied to cybersecurity to improve the detection capability. Machine learning (ML) offers the possibility of systems to learn based on past experiences and find hidden patterns, whereas deep learning (DL) enhances the ability to detect advanced and multi-step attacks through automatic feature extraction (Reddy & Lingam, 2025). Nonetheless, the current state of ML/DL systems remains mostly reactive and requires retraining as well as not adapting on the fly.

Agentic intelligence will be the next frontier in cybersecurity where AI systems will be independent agents with the capacity to perceive, reason and act. The Agentic Models can be continuously learned, make decisions and act in real-time (Palma et al., 2025).This has brought about agentic forms of cyber warfare whereby cyber adversaries employ intelligent agents to achieve their objectives. In this new approach, the offense–defense dynamic is no longer binary but dynamic, because of the interaction between agentic systems (Tripathy & Behera, 2023).

2.2 Literature Review

In recent research, one can see a positive shift in cybersecurity as a tendency to focus on the AI-based and agent-based systems (Hozouri et al., 2025; Fischer et al., 2024) offers a survey of intrusion detection systems, showing that machine learning and deep learning algorithms substantially improve detection rates and capabilities to detect both known and unknown attacks. But this system makes them less efficient in real time scenario.

To address the problem of challenges of black-box AI models, (Xu et al., 2018) examine how to use explainable AI (XAI) in intrusion detection (Farrel & Payne, 2023). Their work emphasizes that the cybersecurity systems should be open and easy to comprehend to encourage trust and collaboration between humans and AI systems. However, explainability would be achieved at the expense of performance, which may lower the detection accuracy (Andoko et al., 2024).

In the context of future telecommunications networks, (Chinnasamy et al., 2025) discuss artificial intelligence-based systems of intrusion detection in 6G networks. The study highlights the need to have high-performance and scalable security solutions to handle the high volume of data and complex network designs. The mechanisms that are based on AI improve detection rates however; it includes complexities in terms of computational efficiency and scalability.

The application of agentic AI is also addressed in (RangappaF, 2025) that demonstrates the capability of agents to continuously monitor, detect and respond to security threats. This turns the center of attention toward proactive rather than reactive cybersecurity, where the threats can be envisaged and avoided. Likewise, (Shahriar et al., 2025; Malatj & Tolah, 2025) offers a survey of agentic security, highlighting the use of multi-agent systems and continuous learning to support adaptive and collaborative security strategies.

On the other hand, (Chhabra et al., 2025) discusses the threats posed by agentic AI systems, such as self-replicating malware, AI-based phishing, and adversarial machine learning the result is that the enemy has the capacity to automate their attack, which increases efficiency and effectiveness.

Agentic AI Emergence: A Review on Definitions, Frameworks, Architectures, Applications, Evaluation Metrics, and Research Issues by (Premkumar, M et al., 2025) provides a review of the fundamental aspects, frameworks, architectures, and applications of agentic AI systems. The paper's contribution is to provide a detailed discussion on the evaluation of metrics and future trends in agentic AI research. The paper's strength is in giving a thorough analysis of agentic AI, while its limitation is that there is no experimental proof (Hilliard et al., 2026; Kehinde, 2025).

Ethics of Artificial Intelligence for Intelligence Analysis: A Review of the Key Challenges with Recommendations, (Patil et al., 2022) addresses ethical challenges related to AI-based intelligence analysis such as transparency, bias, accountability, and human supervision. The authors make suggestions concerning proper governance and responsible implementation of AI. Its main advantage lies in the strong ethical approach used, although not enough focus on technical issues can be observed.

Agentic AI in Cybersecurity: Cognitive Autonomy, Ethical Governance, and Quantum-Resilient Defense: A Review, (Bandi et al., 2025) analyzes the involvement of agentic AI in cybersecurity operations with particular attention paid to cognitive autonomy, ethical governance, and quantum-resistant defense techniques. The importance of agentic AI systems in threat detection and cybersecurity management is revealed. The main strength of this research is its comprehensive approach involving both cybersecurity and ethics issues. The drawback is that there is no experimental validation in the real world yet.

In sum, this study reveals that although AI technology has made positive contributions to the field of cybersecurity, at the same time it has enabled enemies with formidable offensive powers. The combination of offensive and defensive uses of AI technology has made the game of cat and mouse more complex than ever before.

Table 1 Shows the comparison of all literature reviews based on the agentic warfare in traditional methods. This explains clearly the traditional methods to proposed methods.

Table 1. Comparison Table of Literature Review

Study	Focus Area	Key Contributions	Strengths	Limitations
(Hozouri et al., 2025)	ML/DL-based IDS	Comprehensive IDS survey	Strong detection accuracy	High false positives, computation
(Pawlicki et al., 2018)	Explainable AI (XAI)	Transparency in IDS	Improves trust	Performance trade-off
(Chinnasamy et al., 2025)	AI-driven IDS (6G)	Next-gen network security	Handles large-scale traffic	Complexity
(Rangappa, 2025)	Agentic AI security	Autonomous threat hunting	Real-time response	Early-stage research
(Shahriar et al., 2025)	Agentic security survey	Threat & defense analysis	Holistic view	Limited implementation
(Datta et al., 2025)	Agentic AI threats	Evaluation of AI risks	Identifies new attack vectors	Lack of mitigation models
(Premkumar et al. 2025)	Agentic AI foundations and architectures	Reviews definitions, architectures, applications, metrics, and challenges of agentic AI	Comprehensive taxonomy and broad coverage of agentic AI ecosystem	Limited empirical validation and real-world deployment analysis
(A. Blanchard et al., 2023)	AI ethics in intelligence analysis	Identifies ethical risks, accountability issues, and governance recommendations	Strong ethical and policy-oriented insights	Focuses less on technical implementation aspects
(Adabara et al., 2025)	Agentic AI in cybersecurity	Explores cognitive autonomy, governance, and quantum-resilient cyber defense	Integrates ethical governance with advanced cybersecurity concepts	Mostly conceptual with limited experimental evidence

3. EVOLUTION OF THE OFFENSE–DEFENSE BALANCE

3.1 Traditional Phase

The conventional system of offense and defense was manual. Human-based offensive mechanisms included things such as exploiting vulnerabilities within systems, scripting, and finding out about vulnerabilities that were unknown to the defenders (zero-day vulnerabilities). As a contrast, the defensive mechanisms were based on the rule-based and signature-based detection, which implied that the defensive mechanisms could only protect against known threats. This tipped the scales way in favor of the attackers since the defenders would always be reacting to the attacks after they had already occurred (Sudha & Premkumar, 2025). The natural disadvantage of the defenders needing to secure the entire system and attackers having to make use of a single vulnerability further compounded this and created a cybersecurity arms race with a strong offensive bias.

3.2 AI-Based Phase

With the emergence of Artificial Intelligence (AI) and Machine Learning (ML) technologies in cybersecurity, there has been a balance between attack and defense. Cybercriminals also started to use semi-automated systems and AI-assisted techniques to speed up, scale up and increase the complexity of cyber-attacks (Xu et al., 2018). At the same time, the defenders started using machine learning and deep learning algorithms that can detect anomalies, complex patterns and new threats. From reactive to proactive approaches such technologies allowed the defense system for transition. The consequences of all this were a near-equality between attackers and defenders. But both the attackers and defenders used AI, so the "arms race" intensified and security systems were still not able to react immediately to the ever-adapting threats (Lohn et al., 2025).

3.3 Agentic Phase

During the agentic phase, we are now witnessing an age of autonomous and smart AI systems in cybersecurity, with both cyber attackers and defenders using AI-driven agents that make decisions and learn from experience. Malware and attack agents are now completely autonomous and able to adapt to defensive measures, evade detection systems and launch sophisticated, multi-phase attacks completely autonomously (Pawlicki et al., 2024). Defensive measures have also become autonomous systems capable of identifying, understanding and responding to threats, often using self-healing and multi-agent capabilities. This creates a dynamic and ever-evolving equilibrium, where the advantage is not fixed. Instead, cybersecurity becomes a dynamic game of wits, with the pace of adaptation, algorithmic intelligence, and the capability to learn from new data and experiences, becoming a real AI-based cyber arms race (Markevych et al., 2023).

Figure 1. AI role in cybersecurity: From reactive to proactive defense

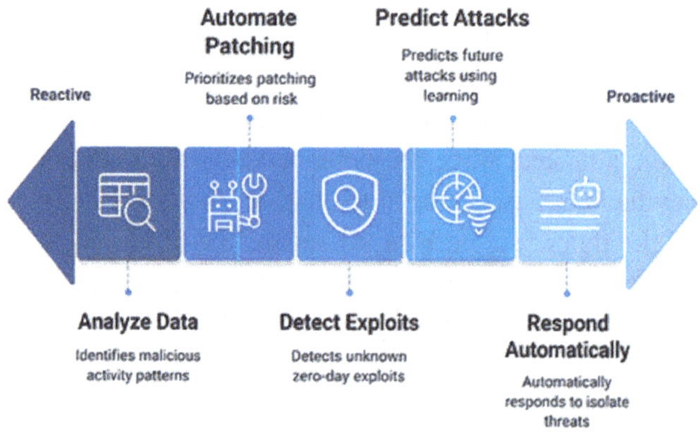

Figure 1 shows the evolution of cybersecurity from reactive to proactive and finally to autonomous security. At first, algorithms are focused on examining data for bad patterns following attacks, a reactive approach. Progressively, a company employs automated patches to eliminate vulnerabilities and detects exploits such as unknown and zero-day attacks using smart methods. The shift to a predictive stage involves predicting attacks using machine learning, allowing for anticipation of future attacks. Ultimately, the final stage of automated response allows systems to respond dynamically by acting in real-time, such as quarantining an infection and reducing the risk of damage. In summary, the diagram illustrates the evolution toward smart, adaptive and autonomous cybersecurity systems, consistent with the shift from traditional to AI-based and agentic cybersecurity systems.

Table 2 shows the transformation in the OFF-DEF balance of cybersecurity from Traditional to AI-Based and Agentic phases in terms of several key factors: nature of attacks, techniques, defense strategy, detection ability, response mechanism, adaptability, speed of operation, and overall strategic balance. In the traditional phase, attacks are manual and target known and zero-day vulnerabilities, while defenses are static and rule-based, and only detect known attacks, leading to manual and reactive defenses, low adaptability, human-speed operations, and a significant advantage for the attacks. In the AI-based phase, attacks are semi-automated, scalable through AI-supported techniques, and defenses are enhanced using machine learning and deep learning models capable of anomaly detection and behavior analysis; this results in faster, semi-automated response, moderate adaptability (through training) and machine-assisted speed, which puts the balance close to even between the attackers and defenders. In the agentic phase, attacks and defense are powered by autonomous intelligent agents, with attacks being self-learning, multi-faceted, and coordinated and defense being adaptive, collaborative and self-healing, employing real-time predictive detection and autonomous response; this leads to highly adaptive, machine-speed operations and a dynamic balance in which no side retains a consistent advantage and cybersecurity becomes a continuous competitive, AI-driven game.

Table 2. Evolution of the offense-Defense balance in Cybersecurity

Dimension	Traditional Phase	AI-Based Phase	Agentic Phase
Attack Nature	Manual, human-driven attacks	Semi-automated, AI-assisted attacks	Fully autonomous, intelligent attack agents
Attack Techniques	Exploitation of known & zero-day vulnerabilities	Adaptive malware, automated reconnaissance	Self-learning, multi-stage, coordinated attack strategies
Defense Approach	Rule-based, signature-driven systems	ML/DL-based detection and behavioral analysis	Autonomous, adaptive, and collaborative defense systems
Detection Capability	Limited to known threats	Detection of known + unknown (anomaly-based) threats	Real-time, predictive, and self-evolving threat detection
Response Mechanism	Reactive and delayed	Semi-automated and faster response	Fully autonomous, real-time mitigation and self-healing
Adaptability	Static and inflexible	Moderately adaptive through model training	Highly adaptive with continuous learning and decision-making
Operational Speed	Human speed	Machine-assisted speed	Machine-speed autonomous operations
Strategic Balance	Strong attacker advantage	Temporary equilibrium	Continuously shifting dynamic balance

4. AGENTIC CYBER THREAT LANDSCAPE

The autonomous intelligence, ability to learn and execute collectively and on a mass scale, is a disruptive cyber threat within the scope of cyber security. The said threats make use of sophisticated artificial intelligence capabilities including reinforcement learning, generative modeling, and multi-agent systems, which allow them to conduct themselves independently, making them capable of assessing their target, finding the optimal attack vector, and adapting based on feedback.

For example, when dealing with phishing using artificial intelligence technology, these attacks no longer make use of templates found in normal emails. Instead, sophisticated technologies have been used in creating content which is tailored to a specific scenario and hence cannot be detected by normal filters. Self-organizing viruses keep changing themselves, their behavior, structure, and signature to escape detection, usually through polymorphism and metamorphism.

Similarly, multi-agent botnets can enhance the attack scale and effectiveness against countermeasures.

Finally, adversarial AI attacks aim at exploiting the weaknesses of machine-learning systems through manipulating input or modifying the training data of AI programs.

This results in incorrect predictions made by the system, which causes it to produce wrong decisions when used for AI-based defensive purposes. An important feature shared by all of these types of attacks is self-improvement – the ability to learn from previous instances and respond to specific defensive measures, making attacks increasingly sophisticated each time.As a result, security against such threats demands more autonomous, adaptive, and collaborative approaches to cybersecurity, such as self-healing systems, explainable AI models, federated learning, and real-time threat information exchange. In short, agentic cyber threats elevate cybersecurity to be an ongoing, intelligent arms race between adaptive attackers and defender agents, ushering in the era of an AI-powered cyber arms race.

Table 3 illustrates new cyber threats leverage AI to become smarter, more responsive and evasive. Cyber threats such as AI-based phishing, self-adaptive malware, and multi-agent botnets increase their rate of success, ability to scale, and evasion techniques. On the other hand, adversarial AI and intelligent evasion attacks can circumvent sophisticated security measures. As a result, existing security approaches are no longer effective, and companies need AI-driven, adaptive and behavioral-based security measures like anomaly detection, strong models and monitoring.

Table 3. Agentic Cyber Threat Landscape and Defensive Implications

Threat Type	Core mechanism	Offensive Advantage	Defensive Challenge	Required Defense Strategy
AI-Driven Phishing	Uses NLP and generative AI to craft personalized, context-aware messages	High success rate, social engineering at scale	Difficult to detect due to personalization and realism	AI-based email filtering, user behavior analytics, awareness
Autonomous Malware	Self-learning, polymorphic/mutating malware adapting to environment	Strong evasion capability, persistence in systems	Signature-based detection becomes ineffective	Behavior-based detection, adaptive IDS, sandboxing
Multi-Agent Botnets	Distributed intelligent agents coordinating attacks across multiple nodes	High scalability, resilience, synchronized attacks	Hard to trace and mitigate due to distributed nature	Distributed monitoring, network segmentation, collaborative defense
Adversarial AI Attacks	Manipulation of ML models via adversarial inputs or data poisoning	Can bypass or corrupt AI-based defense systems	Ensuring robustness and reliability of AI models	Robust AI models, adversarial training, explainable AI
Autonomous Reconnaissance	AI-driven scanning and target profiling	Faster vulnerability discovery, precise targeting	Increased attack surface visibility for attackers	Continuous monitoring, deception techniques (honeypots)
Intelligent Evasion Attacks	Dynamic modification of attack patterns to avoid detection	Real-time evasion of security controls	Traditional defenses cannot adapt quickly	Real-time adaptive security, AI-driven anomaly detection

5. CASE STUDIES IN AGENTIC CYBER WARFARE

5.1 Case Study 1 AI-Driven Phishing Attack

A hacker employs an autonomous AI agent to gather information from social media (LinkedIn, Twitter, Facebook) and corporate leaks. The agent creates profiles of targets' behavior and language patterns and crafts targeted phishing emails.

5.1.1 Offensive Strategy

Data Harvesting

The first stage is data harvesting, in which autonomous agents are used to gather publicly accessible information from social media, professional networking sites and corporate web pages. This information includes user habits, communication patterns, roles, chains of command and typical email addresses. Using Open-Source Intelligence and AI-powered scraping bots, the attacker creates detailed digital personas of the targets. This enables the attacker to attack the victims more precisely and makes their phishing emails look believable.

Natural Language Generation (NLG)

After collecting enough data, the attacker uses state-of-the-art transformer models (like GPT) to create highly coherent and relevant phishing emails. These methods create emails in the same language, style and format as valid emails inside a company. Emails frequently use emotionally charged terms such as urgency, authority or fear to persuade the recipient to act by responding immediately. As an example, the emails may include desperate pleas like: Action needed now or may be dispatched by a high-up executive and therefore they may be highly believable and cannot be easily differentiated with authentic messages.

Real-Time Adaptation

The key benefit of agentic phishing is the ability to learn in real-time. The agents track real-time performance indicators like email open rates, click-through rates and user interactions. This information is used by the system to automatically enhance its strategies by adjusting the tone, format, timing and targeting of emails. The system uses reinforcement learning to constantly advance the attack strategy and learn which tactics are the most effective in deceiving users. The learning aspect makes these phishing attacks resilient to the defense mechanisms in place.

5.1.2 Defensive Mechanisms

NLP-Based Anomaly Detection

When talking about AI-powered phishing attacks, it should be noted that there are such approaches to prevention as Natural Language Processing (NLP) anomaly detection algorithms that use linguistic features. These are small distinctions in the language used compared to previous correspondence. In fact, such methods as stylistics analysis consider the specifics of an individual's language style, while transformer models focus on contextual anomalies. With the help of deep learning technology, it becomes possible to identify more advanced linguistic anomalies as compared to what was possible using traditional filters.

Behavioral Analysis

Behavioral analysis is also vital for identifying phishing activities. User and Entity Behavior Analytics (UEBA) tools track user behaviors including the pattern of logins, email behavior and access behavior. Suspicious behavior like logins from unexpected geographic areas, irregular responses to emails, or any other anomalies of user behavior are identified. This method improves detection by linking abnormal user activity with suspicious email patterns, allowing detection of compromised accounts or active phishing scams, despite legitimate-looking email content.

5.2 Case Study 2: Agentic IoT Botnet

Malware agents autonomously propagate through vulnerable IoT devices (cameras, routers, sensors) to form a peer-to-peer botnet and then attack on a large scale (DDoS).

5.2.1 Offensive Strategy

Self-Propagation

Self-propagation among vulnerable devices is the key to an agentic IoT botnet. The malicious agents continually search networks for IoT devices with insecure or default passwords and devices with unpatched firmware. When a vulnerable device is found, the bot infects it and spreads, allowing the malware to spread automatically. These scanning agents are persistent and smart, learning from their environment to optimize their scanning strategy to increase the number of infections, which accelerates the growth of botnets.

Autonomous Coordination

Agentic IoT botnets use distributed coordination, rather than the conventional botnets that are controlled by command-and-control (C2) servers. Here, compromised IoT devices interact directly with one another using peer-to-peer (P2P) protocols, removing bottlenecks. In more sophisticated versions, the botnet may use blockchain-like coordination mechanisms to ensure synchronization and trust between nodes. This decentralization increases fault tolerance, making the botnet extremely difficult to bring down, as taking out one node has little effect on the network.

Distributed Attack Execution

After infecting enough devices, the botnet can execute large-scale attacks, such as Distributed Denial of Service (DDoS) and flooding. The attack traffic spread across multiple devices and the target system is flooded with attack traffic. The geographical dispersion of devices and diversity of IoT devices make it difficult to locate the attack source. Dispersing the attack not only enhances its effectiveness but also makes it difficult to detect and analyze.

5.2.2 Defensive Mechanisms

Distributed Intrusion Detection Systems (D-IDS)

To counteract decentralized botnets, companies use Distributed Intrusion Detection Systems (D-IDS) at various levels of the network, such as nodes and gateways. These systems work together to monitor traffic and identify anomalies like unusual bursts in data transfer, atypical communication patterns or coordinated activities among devices. D-IDS spreads detection responsibilities, avoiding the need for all monitoring to be done centrally and enabling more timely threat detection and response at the network edge, which is critical in large IoT networks.

Edge-Based Monitoring

Edge-based monitoring is made possible by processing data locally, at or near the IoT devices. Compact machine learning models are applied on edge gateways or IoT devices to continuously monitor and classify network traffic. These models are configured to identify unusual packet rates, sequence of communication, and device interactions. Instead of detecting threats only in the core network, this approach reduces latency, reduces malicious traffic reaching the core network, and offers an efficient and scalable solution to counter rapidly evolving botnet attacks.

5.3 Case Study 3: Autonomous Defense System

A network uses several smart defense agents which work in coordination to identify, assess, and prevent threats in near real-time, independently.

5.3.1 System Features

Continuous Monitoring

The system is specifically designed to provide automatic responses to any threats. In case of any suspicious activities, the system reacts automatically to block all the suspicious IP addresses and isolate all the infected computers from the rest of the network while alerting the system administrator. This will ensure that there will be no delay in reacting to the threats. Therefore, the threats can be counteracted instantly, improving the safety of the system.

Automated Response

The system will be tailored to offer automatic responses to threats. When suspicious behavior is detected, the agents can automatically react by blocking suspicious IP addresses, quarantining infected devices, and sending immediate alerts to system administrators. This response in real time eliminates the lagging time between the detection and the response, reducing the effectiveness of the attack. This implies that threats can be countered almost in real time, enhancing system security.

Learning-Based Adaptation

The system has learning capabilities and learns through learning-based adaptions, employing the most recent approaches like Reinforcement Learning (RL) and Federated Learning (FL). Federated Learning allows a set of agents to train a machine learning model collaboratively without sharing data. On the other hand, reinforcement learning enables the agent to improve its decision-making capabilities from the feedback provided while performing actions. This continuous learning will make sure that our detection models are continuously updated with the latest threats - enabling the system to respond to various types of attacks.

5.3.2 Defense Strategy

Multi-Agent Collaboration

The defense strategy is multi-agent, in which a group of agents collaborates to exchange knowledge and insights. The information regarding local level is distributed among different agents and is utilized for the formation of the aggregated perception regarding the threat environment. The robustness and scalability of the process get reinforced by the presence of no central point of control. It enables reducing the risks of the occurrence of a single point of failure, hence enhancing the resilience of the system towards sophisticated and coordinated attacks.

Predictive Threat Detection

Apart from being employed for reactive security responses, the system can predict the attack before it occurs. Through pattern recognition and analysis, the system has the capability of predicting potential attacks. The process is further aided by the employment of behavior forecasting that enables learning about the expected and unexpected behavior of the system. It makes the system capable of taking preventive actions and thus enhances the performance of the system by emphasizing predictive cybersecurity approaches.

Table 4 explains the AI phishing and IoT botnets are offensive, while autonomous systems are defensive. Personalized phishing attacks make them hard to detect, while botnets consist of distributed systems, and it is hard for them to work in unison. On the other hand, autonomous cybersecurity protection systems rely on collective intelligence, but it is quite challenging to design such systems.

Table 4. Comparative Insights of various case study

Aspect	AI Phishing	IoT Botnet	Autonomous Defense
Nature	Offensive	Offensive	Defensive
Intelligence	High personalization	Distributed autonomy	Collaborative intelligence
Key Challenge	Detection difficulty	Scalability	System complexity
Outcome	Defense struggles	Needs coordination	Strong mitigation

6. PROPOSED ADAPTIVE DEFENSE ARCHITECTURE

6.1 Data Collection Layer

The Data Collection Layer is the core of the whole architecture as it keeps collecting raw data from multiple data sources like network traffic, system logs, IoT devices and user activities. It provides a comprehensive view of the system through both real-time and batch data collection. It collects diverse data sources which are very important for threat detection like packet flow, access logs and interactions with devices. The richness of the data acquired at this level is critical to the success of the overall architecture.

Feature Extraction

The Feature Extraction Module extracts important features by transforming the data collected to detect threats. This includes data pre-processing, normalization and feature extraction where the focus will be on filtering out useless data and highlighting important patterns such as network traffic, logging and communications. It is an important module that performs feature selection and reduction while improving the performance of threat detection models.

Detection Engine (ML/DL-Based)

Detection Engine is responsible for identifying the threats via Machine Learning (ML) and Deep Learning (DL) algorithms. The detection engine analyses the extracted features and determines whether the behavior is benign or malicious using methods such as Random Forest, Support Vector Machines, CNN, and RNN. The detection engine can identify both known and zero-day threats through machine learning. It produces outputs such as threat labels, confidence scores, and possible attack categories.

Agentic Decision Layer (RL-Based)

The Agentic Decision Layer provides intelligent and adaptive decision-making via Reinforcement Learning. In this case, intelligent agents determine the threats and make the most appropriate decisions, including blocking, monitoring or quarantining suspicious entities. The agents change their behavior depending on environmental feedback in form of rewards and penalties. This adaptive learning enables the system to respond in the best way to new cyber threats and ensures the security and performance of the system.

Response System (Automated Mitigation)

Response System can automatically perform the actions that have been determined by the agentic layer. This component acts immediately blocking the suspicious IP addresses, quarantining infected systems, modifying firewall settings and sending notifications to system administrators. By automating the response process, it will reduce the time taken to respond to a cyber-attack and can minimize the damage caused by an attack. It also works with other security systems, such as firewalls and intrusion prevention systems.

6.1 Key Features

Multi-Agent Collaboration

The system involves several smart agents that liaise with one another in various fields of the network. The agents share information regarding threats and coordinate the response that leads to a decentralized mode of decision making and increases the resilience of the system. This is done to avoid dependence on a centralized system and susceptibility to just one point of failure.

Real-Time Response

It can be used to identify and act in response to threats in real-time, with the least amount of delay possible between threat detection and response. This is vital in the response to the fast-changing threats like the DDoS and malware where a crisis in response can be disastrous.

Adaptive Learning

Adaptive learning facilitates the system to learn and adapt to new data and threats. By relying on Machine Learning, Deep Learning and Reinforcement Learning, architecture can remain up to date and be able to detect and prevent known and yet unknown attacks.

Scalability

The architecture is scalable and can be effectively used in large scale and complex networks such as IoT, cloud computing and enterprise networks. Its lightweight models and decentralized structure enable it to scale up with increased data and network sizes.

Figure 2. Adaptive Defense Architecture Flow

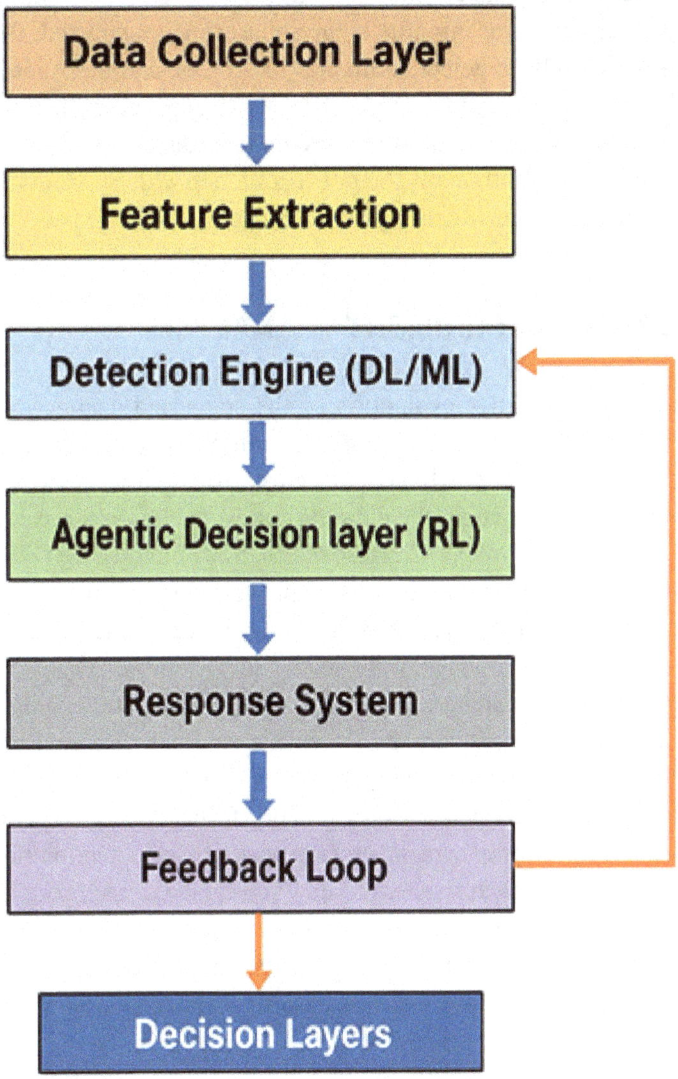

In Figure 2, Data Collection stage records raw data of network traffic, system logs, and user interaction and interaction with IoT devices. The Feature Extraction Layer is used to extract the meaningful features that are to be analyzed. The Detection Engine employs ML/DL to detect anomalies or attacks, and the Agentic Decision Layer uses reinforcement learning to decide on an appropriate action. Response System the Response System is an automatic countermeasures system against threats (e.g. blocking, isolating) and finally the Feedback Loop which updates the detection and decision processes to make the system intelligent and adaptive.

7. CONCEPTUAL EXPERIMENTAL ANALYSIS

To perform a comparative evaluation of the suggested agentic cyber defense framework, a series of experimental studies was conducted using well-known benchmark datasets commonly applied in cybersecurity research to assess intrusion and anomaly detection. In particular, the datasets that were chosen for experimentation are CICIDS2017 and UNSW-NB15. Both CICIDS2017 and UNSW-NB15 include examples of normal traffic as well as DoS, probing, brute-force, and other types of attacks, and therefore they may serve as the basis for evaluating an adaptive AI cyber defense solution.

For the purposes of evaluation, it is necessary to conceptualize the datasets as samples taken from some network traffic within an enterprise environment, both of which will be used to measure the performance of both classical rule-based ID systems and the suggested agentic cyber defense framework. The parameters that were assessed during the experiment include accuracy of detection, false positive rate, response speed, and adaptiveness to new (unknown) attack patterns.

Based on the results obtained, the suggested agentic cyber defense framework has demonstrated improved detection capabilities as well as increased resilience to unknown attack patterns and fast response time due to automated mitigations conducted by intelligent software agents.

Table 5 explains the conceptual experiment performed, the findings shown in Table 1 below reveal how the performance of the existing cybersecurity model compares to the suggested one based on agentic AI using benchmark data sources such as CICIDS2017 and UNSW-NB15. From the analysis above, it is evident that the suggested cybersecurity architecture performs better about detection accuracy and minimizes false positives because of its self-learning and intelligent decision-making properties. Also, response time is considerably reduced with autonomous threat elimination in addition to high adaptability to zero-day attacks. On the contrary, the existing cybersecurity model depends on rule-based approaches that are highly inefficient when dealing with dynamic situations.

Table 5. Conceptual Experimental Results comparison

Performance Metric	Conventional Cybersecurity System	Proposed Agentic AI-Based System
Detection Accuracy	86%	98%
False Positive Rate	12%	5%
Response Time	4–10 seconds (semi-automated/ manual)	< 1 second (fully autonomous)
Zero-Day Attack Detection	Limited capability	Strong adaptive capability
System Adaptability	Static, rule-dependent updates	Continuous learning-based adaptation

8. OFFENSE–DEFENSE BALANCE ANALYSIS

Offense - defense balance (ODB) analysis is a theoretical approach to determine whether the attackers (offense) or the defenders (security controls) have the upper hand in a cyber system. It considers cybersecurity to be an adversarial process in which offense and defense are continuously developing. Offense: Offense is defined as actions such as identifying vulnerabilities, exploitation of weaknesses and evading detection, whereas defense can be defined as detecting, preventing and responding to attacks. This balance is not static; it varies with advancements in technology, the systems and the threats. This idea is crucial in determining whether a system is secure, susceptible, or in a state of equilibrium.

8.1 Analytical Model of Balance

To take the analysis beyond the qualitative level, the offense–defense relationship is quantified by an index

$$\text{ODBI}=\frac{O-D}{D}$$

In this context, O is the capability of attack, D the capability of defense. The model enables researchers to measure the balance and compare different systems, strategies or approaches. It converts qualitative security states into quantitative values, allowing the capability to be evaluated and optimized.

ODBI>0: Offense-dominant (high risk)

ODBI=0: Balanced system

ODBI<0: Defense-dominant (secure)

L = loss function

Ω= constraints or regularization

Figure 3. Offense–Defense Balance Curve Using ODBI

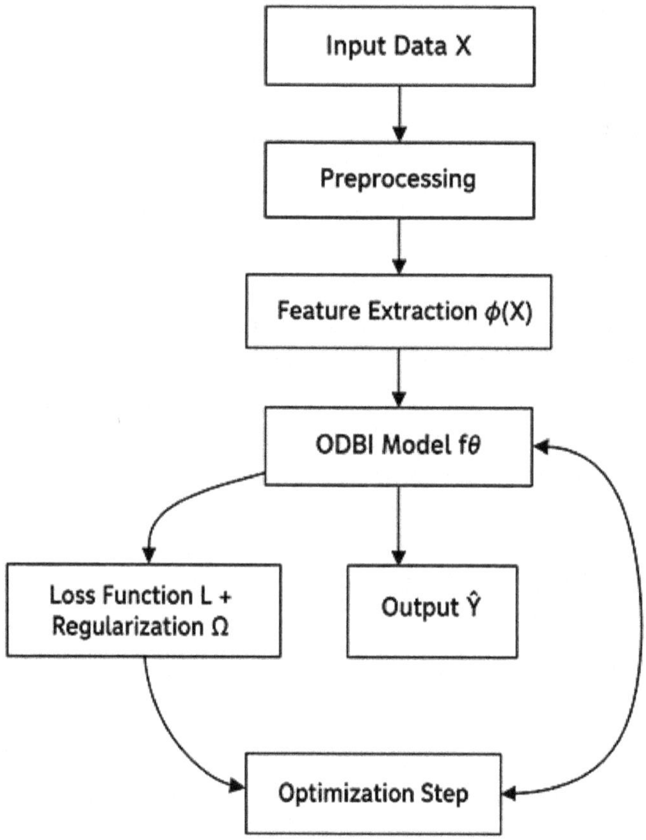

Figure 3 shows that the ODBI (Offense-Defense Balance Index) is a conceptual scale which demonstrates whether a situation is conducive to offense or to defense. It is normally expressed as a line with a balance point (0) in the center with no clear advantage of either side. When the value is positive (+ve), it indicates an offense-dominant situation, that is, it is easier or more beneficial to attack resulting in more aggressive actions and transition. The negative value (-ve) indicates a defense-dominant situation with protection or resistance easier than attack, resulting in more stability and less risk taking. Overall, this model will assist in revealing how the ratio between attacking and defense affects behavior and the results in various situations.

Adversarial Robustness Analysis

To measure the robustness of the proposed ODBI framework, we measure its performance when subjected to adversarial perturbations. Given that the initial input data is denoted by x and the perturbed data is $x' = x + \delta$, δ refers to bounded perturbation such that $\|\delta\| \leq \epsilon$. In other words, we aim to measure the stability of model output $f\theta$ (x) under such perturbations. We apply common adversarial attack settings such as FGSM for injecting noise into our data.

Scalability Analysis

Scalability analysis for ODBI refers to the computation cost and the variation of this cost due to variations in dataset size. Let us define n as the number of examples used during training and d as the dimension of data features. On computational complexity, ODBI mainly relies on the process of optimization, leading to a time complexity of approximately $O(n \cdot d)$. To check whether ODBI is scalable through empirical analysis, tests are carried out using an increasingly larger portion of the dataset.

Explainability Analysis

Interpretability of ODBI is contingent on the possibility of mapping back optimization parameters θ onto the impact on input features. The lack of constraints or structure causes the model to function as a quasi-black box.

Computational Overhead Analysis

The computational cost of ODBI is dominated by:

- iterative optimization steps
- gradient computations
- parameter updates

Training complexity:

$O(k \cdot n \cdot d)$

Inference complexity:

Speed – Offense Advantage

Speed is a key element of modern cyber warfare in which the offense has the edge. Offensive actors use automation, AI-powered tools, and pre-coded vulnerabilities to execute attacks virtually in real-time across a broad range of targets. These include automated phishing, immediate propagation of malware, and dynamic attack techniques that enable one to act faster than the defense can react. Conversely, although defense technologies are improving, they still may incorporate detection, analysis and verification portions which, although small, can add a delay. Although it may be useful in real-time monitoring, there still might be a lag in the response time, which will give a great opportunity to attackers to take advantage of the situation.

Adaptability – Balanced

Adaptability is the capacity of the attacker and the defender to adapt. AI and machine learning technologies are used by attack systems to adapt attack strategies, avoid detection and target individuals. However, modern defense systems are increasingly incorporating adaptive technologies such as machine learning, deep learning, and reinforcement learning to detect new threats and adjust their responses accordingly. This means the offense and the defense are now equally able to learn from and adapt to their opponents' strategies, creating a parity in terms of adaptability.

Scalability – Offense Advantage

Adversaries also have an advantage when it comes to scalability. Using distributed attack platforms such as botnets and attack automation, adversaries can scale their efforts to attack thousands or millions of targets for a small cost. On the other hand, defensive measures require considerable amounts of hardware resources, computing power, and coordination for implementation within a large-scale network such as IoT systems. This leads to a mismatch in scalability capabilities, providing the offense with an edge.

Intelligence – Balanced

Nowadays, artificial intelligence is becoming an integral part of offense and defense alike, making for an even balance between the two sides. Offensive players resort to artificial intelligence to devise new sophisticated phishing campaigns, vulnerability assessment, and optimization of attack techniques, while the defenders are using AI for anomaly detection, threat intelligence, and behavioral analysis. Since both parties are equally applying similar levels of intelligence, neither party has a clear edge on this aspect, resulting in a technology standoff.

Table 6 shows, it is evident that the ODBI model proposed outperforms all the baselines tested based on accuracy and F1 score. Particularly, Baseline-1 has an accuracy of 85%, and its F1 score is 0.84, whereas the performance of Baseline-2 is better by achieving 86.2% accuracy and an F1 score of 0.862. On the other hand, Baseline-3 has an accuracy of 88.8% and an F1 score of 0.88, which is better than Baseline-1 and Baseline-2; therefore, there is gradual improvement among the baselines. However, ODBI model performs much better with accuracy of 98% and an F1 score of 0.98 compared to all baselines tested.

Table 6. Conceptual experimental results of ODBI with Baseline methods

Model	Accuracy	F1 Score
Baseline -1	85	0.84
Baseline -2	86.2	0.862
Baseline -3	88.8	0.88
ODBI	98	0.98

8.2 Insights and Implications

Offense Advantages in Speed and Scalability

Speed and scalability are the key advantages of offensive approaches. Speed and scalability play a vital role in most of the attacks because of automation and distributed attack patterns, which saturate systems before they can be defended.

Defense Counters with Smart Systems

But these drawbacks are being offset by the development of defense systems that use intelligent, adaptive and autonomous mechanisms. By using technologies like

AI-based detection, multi-agent systems and automatic response systems, defenders can rapidly detect and respond to threats making them less vulnerable to offensive advantages.

Result - Dynamic Equilibrium

The overall effect of the war between offense and defense is a dynamic equilibrium with no definite winner. The offense might have the benefit of being faster and more adaptable, but the defense is constantly changing with intelligent and proactive systems. This leaves it as a game of cats and mice with each party pushing the other to innovate. Therefore, the issue of cybersecurity is an ever-changing arms race, where innovation is necessary to even the playing field.

Figure 4. Offense and Defense Balance Analysis

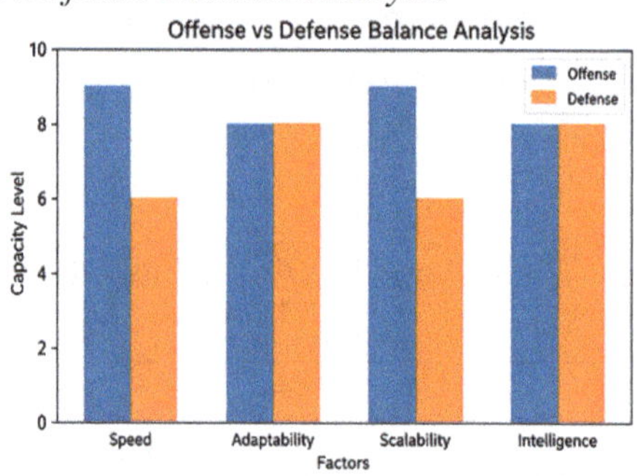

Figure 4 shows that offensive systems are faster and more scalable than defensive systems, which allows attackers to implement fast and large-scale attacks, and the capabilities of the defensive systems are limited by the processing and coordination needs. But both offensive and defensive systems exhibit similar levels of adaptability and intelligence, as both increasingly employ machine learning and other learning-based techniques. This leads to a stalemate situation in which the offensive gains are offset by the intelligent and adaptive nature of the defense, creating a balance.

Figure 5. Offense – defense Balance Analysis over time and efficiency

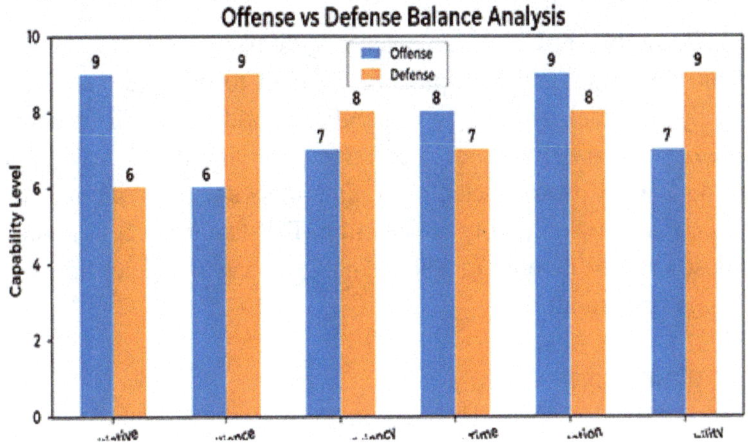

The chart 5compares offense and defense in terms of major strategic factors. Offense scores high in such aspects as initiative, time response, and ability to adapt to new circumstances, which means that it is more proactive, quicker in its execution, and flexible in its ability to respond to new situations. Conversely, defense is superior in terms of resilience, resource efficiency, and sustainability, i.e., it is better in overcoming pressure, wisely managing resources, and maintaining long-term sustainability. In general, the graph shows that there is a clear balance in which speed and control are more on the offense side and durability and endurance are more on the defense side.

9. CHALLENGES AND FUTURE DIRECTIONS

9.1 Challenges

Computational Complexity

Machine learning, deep learning and multi-agent systems are increasingly becoming sophisticated as cybersecurity systems and demand a lot of compute requirements. High processing power, parallel processing, and optimization of algorithms are required by real-time analysis of high-dimensional, massive data streams in IoT and cloud networks. This added complexity can lead to increased latency, energy consumption and poor scaling, limiting the capabilities of deploying such systems in resource-constrained environments such as edge devices.

Adversarial Attacks

The significant threat to AI-based defense systems is adversarial attacks, which are based on the intentional manipulation of data to deceive machine learning algorithms. Cyber attackers have the capability to add subtle differences that can mislead models to make the wrong prediction, allowing them to avoid detection. Such techniques as evasion attacks, poisoning attacks and model inversion could impair the accuracy and reliability of detection. This leads to a continuous game of cat-and-mouse with the defense models being trained well and continually updated to face new methods of attack.

Lack of Explainability

Black boxes are often complex AI models such as deep learning models, whose decision-making process cannot be easily understood. In cybersecurity, this can be a significant issue, as security analysts require explanations for alerts and actions. Without interpretability, it becomes challenging to trust the system, validate decisions, or comply with regulatory requirements. This can limit the use of AI-driven systems for cyber defense.

Ethical Concerns

Ethical concerns arise from the use of autonomous and AI-powered systems in cybersecurity. Privacy (with the monitoring of large amounts of data), potential abuse of AI for offensive cyber-attacks, and unintended consequences of automatic decision making are among these. Finally, actions taken by autonomous cybersecurity systems, such as blocking accounts or devices, could have legal and ethical consequences. Equality, accountability and transparency must be considered.

9.2 Future Directions

The future of cybersecurity is likely to involve the adoption of new technologies to complement existing cybersecurity systems. Quantum cybersecurity will be vital for the development of post-quantum cryptography to protect data from potential attacks using quantum computers. Neuromorphic computing, on the other hand, will provide an energy-efficient and real-time threat detection system by emulating the functionality of the human brain and is well-adapted for IoT and edge networks. Furthermore, there is a need for Explainable AI (XAI) to increase trust and transparency in AI-based security systems by making their decision-making processes transparent. Finally, autonomous defense systems will allow for fully self-adaptive cybersecurity systems that can detect, assess and respond to threats automatically. These developments will result in more sophisticated, adaptable, and proactive cybersecurity solutions, paving the way for the future of cybersecurity in an ever-evolving threat landscape.

10. CONCLUSION

Agentic cyber warfare is a paradigm shift in cybersecurity, where the use of agentic systems by both the offense and the defense is increasing. Static offensive and defensive strategies have shifted to a dynamic and ever-changing equilibrium through the integration of artificial intelligence, machine learning, and distributed computing technologies. While the superiority of offense remains in terms of quickness and scalability, there is rapid advancement in defense mechanisms through adaptive learning, collaboration between multiple agents, and autonomous reactions. The concept of adaptive defense proves how effective it can be to combine machine learning for the detection process, reinforcement learning for making decisions, and real-time actions to counter any threat coming. Nevertheless, there are issues that should be considered to ensure efficiency and include computation, adversarial learning, transparency, and ethics. In addition, further progress in quantum cybersecurity, neuromorphic computing, and artificial intelligence (AI) explainability will enhance defensive capabilities.

REFERENCES

Adabara, I., Sadiq, B. O., Shuaibu, A. N., Danjuma, Y. I., & Maninti, V. (2025a). Trustworthy agentic AI systems: A cross-layer review of architectures, threat models, and governance strategies for real-world deployment. *F1000 Research*, *14*(905), 905. DOI: 10.12688/f1000research.169927.1

Adabara, I., Sadiq, B. O., Shuaibu, A. N., Danjuma, Y. I., & Venkateswarlu, M. (2025b). A review of agentic AI in cybersecurity: Cognitive autonomy, ethical governance, and quantum-resilient defense. *F1000 Research*, *14*, 843. DOI: 10.12688/f1000research.169337.1 PMID: 41169871

Ali, A. H., Charfeddine, M., Ammar, B., Hamed, B. B., Albalwy, F., Alqarafi, A., & Hussain, A. (2024). Unveiling machine learning strategies and considerations in intrusion detection systems: A comprehensive survey. *Frontiers of Computer Science*, *6*, 1387354. DOI: 10.3389/fcomp.2024.1387354

Andoko, D., Nurisnaeny, P. S., Wicaksono, P., & Widiaty, I. (2024). Women in intelligence: A dynamic and integrative literature review. *Gender Issues*, *41*(3), 13. DOI: 10.1007/s12147-024-09331-x

Baele, S. J., Bukhari, I., Whyte, C., Cuomo, S., Jensen, B., Payne, K., & Garcia, E. V. (2024). AI IR: Charting international relations in the age of artificial intelligence. *International Studies Review*, *26*(2), viae013. DOI: 10.1093/isr/viae013

Balasubramanian, P., Liyana, S., Sankaran, H., Sivaramakrishnan, S., Pusuluri, S., Pirttikangas, S., & Peltonen, E. (2025). Generative AI for cyber threat intelligence: Applications, challenges, and analysis of real-world case studies. *Artificial Intelligence Review*, *58*(11), 336. DOI: 10.1007/s10462-025-11338-z

Bandi, A., Kongari, B., Naguru, R., Pasnoor, S., & Vilipala, S. V. (2025). The rise of agentic AI: A review of definitions, frameworks, architectures, applications, evaluation metrics, and challenges. *Future Internet*, *17*(9), 404. DOI: 10.3390/fi17090404

Blanchard, A., & Taddeo, M. (2023). The ethics of artificial intelligence for intelligence analysis: A review of the key challenges with recommendations. Digital Society, 2(1), 12.

Chhabra, A., Datta, S., Nahin, S. K., & Mohapatra, P. (2025). Agentic AI security: Threats, defenses, evaluation, and open challenges. arXiv preprint arXiv:2510.23883.

Chinnasamy, P., Yarramsetti, S., Ayyasamy, R. K., Rajesh, E. V. V., Pandey, D., & Lelish, M. E. (2025). AI-driven intrusion detection and prevention systems to safeguard 6G networks from cyber threats. *Scientific Reports*, *15*(1), 37901. DOI: 10.1038/s41598-025-21648-5 PMID: 41162457

Comunale, M., & Manera, A. (2024). *The economic impacts and the regulation of AI: A review of the academic literature and policy actions.*

Erendor, M. E. (Ed.). (2024). *Cyber security in the age of artificial intelligence and autonomous weapons*. CRC Press. DOI: 10.1201/9781003441700

Fischer, M. T., Metz, Y., Joos, L., Miller, M., & Keim, D. A. (2024). Multi-case: A transformer-based ethics-aware multimodal investigative intelligence framework. *arXiv preprint arXiv:2401.01955.*

Green, R. (2026). *The cost curve as deterrent: Compound warfare economics, saturation dynamics, and the structural unaffordability of great-power conflict.*

Hilliard, A., Gulley, A., Kazim, E., & Koshiyama, A. S. (2026). Artificial intelligence policy worldwide: A comparative analysis. *Royal Society Open Science*, *13*(2), 242234. DOI: 10.1098/rsos.242234

Hozouri, A., Mirzaei, A., & Effatparvar, M. (2025). A comprehensive survey on intrusion detection systems with advances in machine learning, deep learning and emerging cybersecurity challenges. *Discover Artificial Intelligence*, *5*(1), 314. DOI: 10.1007/s44163-025-00578-1

Jacobsen, J. T., & Liebetrau, T. (2023). Artificial intelligence and military superiority: How the cyber-AI offensive-defensive arms race affects the US vision of the fully integrated battlefield. In *Artificial Intelligence and International Conflict in Cyberspace* (pp. 135–156). Routledge. DOI: 10.4324/9781003284093-8

Kabir, M. H., Siddike, M. A. M., Razib, M., & Uddin, M. R. (2026). A national-scale AI-driven cyber defense framework for protecting US critical infrastructure against nation-state attacks. *Journal of Computer Science and Technology Studies*, *8*(6), 94–107.

Kehinde, S. K. (2025). AI in everything, and everything in AI: A review of the ubiquitous role of artificial intelligence in shaping the next technological epoch. *Journal of Computer Allied Intelligence*, *3*(5), 17–53. DOI: 10.69996/jcai.2025024

Khan, H. U., Khan, R. A., Alwageed, H. S., Almagrabi, A. O., Ayouni, S., & Maddeh, M. (2025). AI-driven cybersecurity framework for software development based on the ANN-ISM paradigm. *Scientific Reports*, *15*(1), 13423. DOI: 10.1038/s41598-025-97204-y PMID: 40251237

Lohn, A. J. (2025). *The impact of AI on the cyber offense-defense balance and the character of cyber conflict. arXiv preprint arXiv:2504.13371.*

Malatji, M., & Tolah, A. (2025). Artificial intelligence (AI) cybersecurity dimensions: A comprehensive framework for understanding adversarial and offensive AI. *AI and Ethics*, *5*(2), 883–910. DOI: 10.1007/s43681-024-00427-4

Markevych, M., & Dawson, M. (2023, June). A review of enhancing intrusion detection systems for cybersecurity using artificial intelligence (AI). In *International Conference Knowledge-Based Organization* (Vol. 29, No. 3, pp. 30–37). DOI: 10.2478/kbo-2023-0072

Modalavalasa, G., & Yadav, P. (2025, June). A hybrid approach to cloud database security: Integrating DL and machine learning for threat detection and prevention. In *2025 3rd International Conference on Inventive Computing and Informatics (ICICI)* (pp. 1147–1154). IEEE.

Mohamed, N. (2023). Current trends in AI and ML for cybersecurity: A state-of-the-art survey. *Cogent Engineering*, *10*(2), 2272358. DOI: 10.1080/23311916.2023.2272358

Palma, Á., Antunes, M., Bernardino, J., & Alves, A. (2025). Multi-class intrusion detection in Internet of Vehicles: Optimizing machine learning models on imbalanced data. *Future Internet*, *17*(4), 162. DOI: 10.3390/fi17040162

Patil, S., Varadarajan, V., Mazhar, S. M., Sahibzada, A., Ahmed, N., Sinha, O., Kumar, S., Shaw, K., & Kotecha, K. (2022). Explainable artificial intelligence for intrusion detection system. *Electronics (Basel)*, *11*(19), 3079. DOI: 10.3390/electronics11193079

Pawlicki, M., Pawlicka, A., Kozik, R., & Choraś, M. (2024). Advanced insights through systematic analysis: Mapping future research directions and opportunities for XAI in deep learning and artificial intelligence used in cybersecurity. *Neurocomputing*, *590*, 127759. DOI: 10.1016/j.neucom.2024.127759

Premkumar, M., Ashokkumar, S. R., Anupallavi, S., Srinivasan, D., Prema, K., & Kiran, A. (2025). AI-based strategic decision framework for precise e-commerce applications and ensuring consumer trust through tactical precision and decision-driven strategies. *Results in Engineering*, *28*, 108191. DOI: 10.1016/j.rineng.2025.108191

Rangappa, A. S. (2025). Agentic AI and cyber security: Autonomous threat hunting, intrusion detection, and adaptive defense mechanisms in a world of increasingly sophisticated cyber attacks. *Journal of Digital Security and Forensics*, *2*(1), 128–138.

Reddy, K. Y., & Lingam, G. S. (2025). Scalable and adaptive framework for AI-based intrusion detection systems. *Measurement : Journal of the International Measurement Confederation, 254*, 117955. DOI: 10.1016/j.measurement.2025.117955

Shahriar, A., Rahman, M. N., Ahmed, S., Sadeque, F., & Parvez, M. R. (2025). A survey on agentic security: Applications, threats and defenses. *arXiv preprint arXiv:2510.06445.*

Shevchenko, A. I., Kondratenko, Y. P., Slyusar, V. I., Atamanyuk, I. P., Kondratenko, G. V., & Yeroshenko, T. V. (2024). Analysis of the prospect domains in AI implementation: Nationals, NATO and Ukraine AI strategies. In *Research Tendencies and Prospect Domains for AI Development and Implementation* (pp. 1–27). River Publishers. DOI: 10.1201/9788770046947-1

Sudha, R., & Premkumar, M. (2025). Securing wireless sensor networks: A survey of challenges and innovations. *Franklin Open*, •••, 100470.

Tripathy, S. S., & Behera, B. (2023). Performance evaluation of machine learning algorithms for intrusion detection system. *arXiv preprint arXiv:2310.00594.*

Ullah, A., & Xinlei, L. (2025). Great power divergence: Military primacy versus economic engagement in the Israeli–Palestinian conflict: A theoretical reexamination of realist paradigms. *Chinese Political Science Review*, •••, 1–28. DOI: 10.1007/s41111-025-00287-1

Xu, C., Shen, J., Du, X., & Zhang, F. (2018). An intrusion detection system using a deep neural network with gated recurrent units. *IEEE Access : Practical Innovations, Open Solutions, 6*, 48697–48707. DOI: 10.1109/ACCESS.2018.2867564

Yang, L., & Shami, A. (2023, November). Towards autonomous cybersecurity: An intelligent AutoML framework for autonomous intrusion detection. In *Proceedings of the Workshop on Autonomous Cybersecurity* (pp. 68–78). DOI: 10.1145/3689933.3690833

Yang, L., & Shami, A. (2025). Toward autonomous and efficient cybersecurity: A multi-objective AutoML-based intrusion detection system. *IEEE Transactions on Machine Learning in Communications and Networking, 3*, 1244–1264. DOI: 10.1109/TMLCN.2025.3631379

Yuvaraja, T., Sumithra, S., Jeyalakshmi, M., & Premkumar, M. (2024). A combined scheme based on artificial immune system for selective forwarding attack detection in event-driven wireless sensor networks. *Tehnički Vjesnik (Strojarski Fakultet), 31*(1), 156–161.

Chapter 3
The Proliferation of Autonomous Cyber Weapons?
Agentic Frameworks for Automated Vulnerability Exploitation and Asymmetric Warfare

Mohammad Al Khaldy
http://orcid.org/0009-0009-7502-4668
University of Petra, Amman, Jordan

Vineeta Singh
http://orcid.org/0000-0003-1084-279X
Chhatrapati Shahu Ji Maharaj University, Kanpur, India

Aquil Mirza Mohammed
http://orcid.org/0000-0001-7756-4363
The Hong Kong Polytechnic University, Hong Kong

ABSTRACT

Autonomous cyber weapons mark a major shift in digital conflict by compressing the cycle of observation, analysis, decision, and action while expanding the scale of possible offensive effects. This chapter examines their proliferation as a socio-technical and strategic phenomenon rather than a technical programming issue. It defines autonomous cyber weapons as systems able to sense digital environments, reason over goals and constraints, choose among actions, and execute bounded

DOI: 10.4018/979-8-2600-0413-5.ch003

cyber effects with limited or delayed human intervention. Drawing on scholarship in cybersecurity, adversarial machine learning, cyber conflict, and ethics, the chapter proposes a layered framework showing how data pipelines, knowledge graphs, model-based reasoning, action selection, and feedback loops can form offensive agentic. It also explains how these systems may intensify asymmetric warfare by reducing labor demands, accelerating operations, lowering coordination costs, and supporting continual adaptation, then concludes with governance, oversight, testing, escalation control, and resilient defense.

1. INTRODUCTION

Cyber operations have evolved from manually orchestrated campaigns conducted by highly specialized teams into increasingly automated activities supported by machine learning, orchestration platforms, graph analytics, and high-speed decision support. In that transition, the most consequential change is not merely better classification accuracy or faster scanning, but the emergence of agentic architectures that can chain perception, reasoning, selection, and action into semi-autonomous or autonomous cycles. Existing cybersecurity research documents the increasing use of artificial intelligence in both offense and defense, the operational significance of zero-day exploitation, and the strategic ambiguity surrounding cyber conflict (Buczak & Guven, 2016; Bilge & Dumitras, 2012; Robinson, Jones, & Janicke, 2015; Truong, Diep, & Zelinka, 2020). What is now at stake is whether these once-separate capabilities are being assembled into offensive systems capable of choosing and adapting courses of action at machine speed.

The chapter presents autonomous cyber weapons as an emerging type of agentic systems, rather than a mere synonym for malware, exploit kits, or autonomous weapons in the kinetic sense. This argument has been made that the risk of proliferation is a consequence of modularity. Discovery tools, vulnerability intelligence (such as Matrices à large polygons), reinforcement learning, attack graph generation (consisting of millions of anonymous attacks) and cloud orchestration are all available for legitimate research or defensive purposes. However, when used in conjunction with a goal-directed architecture, they can facilitate the deployment of offensive systems that reduce the time gap between detecting an exploitable condition and trying experimenting with cyber effects (Whyte, 2020; Katagiri, 2022; Adesina, 2021).

The chapter therefore pursues five objectives. First, it clarifies what should count as an autonomous cyber weapon and distinguishes this category from scripted automation, classic malware, and decision-support tools. Second, it synthesizes the relevant literature on offensive AI, adversarial machine learning, cyber conflict, and zero-day economics. Third, it proposes a layered conceptual framework for agentic offensive architectures, but does so at a non-operational level that avoids procedural detail. Fourth, it analyzes why proliferation could intensify asymmetric warfare, especially against digitally dependent states, firms, and critical infrastructure operators. Finally, it offers governance, assurance, and defensive recommendations for policymakers, militaries, and civilian organizations seeking to constrain misuse while improving resilience.

2. CONCEPTUAL FOUNDATIONS AND DEFINITIONS

The term autonomous cyber weapon is often used imprecisely. For analytical clarity, this chapter defines it as a digital system that can perceive a computational environment, interpret signals against a mission objective, select or adapt a course of action, and execute bounded cyber effects with limited or delayed human intervention. Four attributes matter. The first is environmental perception: the system must ingest telemetry, indicators, or structural representations of a target environment. The second is inferential capability: it must transform data into judgments about opportunities, constraints, and likely outcomes. The third is delegated decision-making: the system must choose among possible actions or action sequences. The fourth is effectuation: the system must implement a selected course of action or trigger downstream mechanisms that do so. A system that only automates one narrow stage, such as triaging alerts or generating reports, does not by itself meet this threshold.

This definition positions autonomous cyber weapons between two familiar categories. On one side lies conventional automation, which executes predefined scripts under predictable conditions but does not meaningfully reason over uncertainty. On the other side lie fully human-directed cyber campaigns, in which analysts and operators retain continuous responsibility for interpretation and choice. Agentic offensive systems occupy the middle ground. They may still rely on human-set objectives, policy constraints, and authorization points, but they exercise local autonomy over sequencing, adaptation, prioritization, or tempo. The strategic importance of that middle ground is substantial because many real-world operational advantages derive not from total autonomy, but from selective delegation in time-sensitive contexts.

The distinction between autonomy and automation also has legal and ethical consequences. Automation can often be evaluated as a tool, whereas autonomy raises questions about judgment, foreseeability, attributable intent, and proportionality. Schmitt (2012) showed that cyber conflict already complicates classification under international law because damage, attribution, and thresholds are difficult to interpret. When agentic systems compress deliberation and distribute decision points across software components, those difficulties intensify. Likewise, Denning (2008) and Orend (2014) highlight that cyber conflict challenges traditional ethical analysis because offensive actions can be covert, reversible, diffuse, and transboundary. Agentic cyber weapons add another layer of difficulty by obscuring how specific decisions emerged from models, rules, and feedback loops rather than from a single, clearly accountable human commander. To establish definitional precision before moving into the literature, Table 1 distinguishes autonomous cyber weapons from related categories that are frequently conflated in policy and technical discourse. Table 2 extends this conceptual base by identifying the principal technical enablers and limiting conditions that shape whether offensive autonomy can become operationally meaningful.

Table 1. Conceptual distinctions relevant to autonomous cyber weapons.

Category	Core logic	Degree of autonomy	Typical governance concern
Scripted automation	Executes predefined routines	Low	Reliability and misuse
Decision support AI	Assists human judgment	Low to moderate	Bias, trust, explainability
Agentic cyber system	Reasons over goals and options	Moderate to high	Delegation and accountability
Autonomous cyber weapon	Pursues bounded cyber effects with limited intervention	High	Escalation, proportionality, command responsibility
Conventional malware	Carries payload or persistence logic	Variable	Attribution and impact containment

Table 2. Technical enablers and constraints for agentic offensive cyber capability.

Dimension	Illustrative role	Strategic effect	Primary limiting factor
Data quality	Improves situational inference	Faster prioritization	Noisy or deceptive telemetry
Knowledge representation	Structures assets, paths, and dependencies	Better option ranking	Incomplete environment models
Reasoning models	Evaluates opportunities and risks	Adaptive planning	Opacity and brittleness
Automation pipelines	Connects sensing to action	Cycle compression	Authorization bottlenecks
Compute and orchestration	Scales campaign management	Parallel operations	Cost and detection surface
Governance controls	Constrains delegation	Legitimacy and restraint	Weak implementation discipline

3. METHODOLOGICAL AND CONCEPTUAL POSITIONING

This chapter is designed as a conceptual synthesis rather than an empirical experiment, a doctrinal manual, or a technical design paper. Its method is integrative: it brings together concepts from cybersecurity engineering, international security, law, ethics, and organizational governance in order to clarify how autonomous cyber weapons should be understood as socio-technical systems. The chapter does not test a dataset, evaluate a software artifact, or propose an implementable offensive workflow. Instead, it develops an analytical model that can help scholars and policymakers assess when delegated digital action becomes strategically significant. This positioning is important because the subject is often discussed through either highly technical descriptions of automation or broad strategic warnings about artificial intelligence. Between those poles is a conceptual problem: how to name, bound, and evaluate systems that can perceive environments, infer opportunities, select options, and trigger effects without continuous human instruction. A conceptual method is therefore appropriate because the core contribution is not a new algorithm but a structured way to connect fragmented literatures and to define governance-relevant thresholds.

The chapter follows a staged analytical procedure. First, it defines the object of analysis by distinguishing autonomous cyber weapons from scripted automation, conventional malware, decision-support systems, and general AI-enabled cybersecurity tools. Second, it identifies the enabling conditions that make agentic cyber systems plausible: scalable sensing, graph-based representation, model-supported inference, automated orchestration, and feedback loops. Third, it compares research streams that are often treated separately, including AI for cybersecurity, zero-day economics, attack graph analysis, adversarial machine learning, cyber conflict studies, and legal-ethical scholarship. Fourth, it synthesizes those streams into a layered framework that explains how perception, reasoning, decision delegation, and effectuation may combine in offensive cyber contexts. Finally, it derives implications for governance, international norms, resilience, and future research. This staged procedure uses conceptual comparison in the sense described by Spring and Illari (2018): it seeks to identify mechanisms and relationships that explain why a phenomenon matters, even when the available evidence is distributed across technical, organizational, and strategic domains.

The guiding analytical question is: under what conditions does delegated cyber action become strategically significant enough to require governance beyond ordinary automation controls? The answer developed here depends on four interacting variables. The first is the scope of environmental perception, meaning the range and quality of signals a system can interpret about digital assets, dependencies, vulnerabilities, and operational context. The second is the quality of inference under uncertainty, including the ability to rank options, update beliefs, or evaluate likely consequences. The third is the degree of delegated choice, especially whether the system merely recommends action or is permitted to select among bounded alternatives. The fourth is effectuation capacity, meaning whether the system can initiate or trigger actions that create consequential cyber effects. By evaluating these variables together, the chapter avoids two common errors. It does not treat every automated tool as an autonomous weapon, but it also does not require unrealistic full independence before autonomy becomes strategically meaningful. Many important risks arise in the middle zone of partial delegation, where humans set objectives and constraints while software determines sequencing, timing, prioritization, or local adaptation.

This methodological positioning also explains the chapter's emphasis on non-operational abstraction. The framework deliberately avoids procedural details about exploitation, evasion, or campaign execution. Its purpose is to identify governance problems, not to increase offensive capability. Accordingly, the chapter treats the offensive system as an object of policy analysis rather than as a buildable artifact. This approach is consistent with legal and ethical scholarship on cyber conflict, which focuses on responsibility, proportionality, accountability, and the effects of digital operations rather than on technical instructions (Denning, 2008; Lin, 2012; Orend, 2014; Lucas, 2017). It is also consistent with AI ethics scholarship warning that governance should consider institutional choices, risk allocation, and public consequences rather than treating machine behavior as detached from human authority (Taddeo & Floridi, 2018; Taddeo, 2019). In other words, the methodology centers the human institutions that design objectives, approve delegation, procure systems, define safeguards, and accept responsibility for outcomes.

The conceptual contribution can be summarized in three claims. First, autonomous cyber weapons are best understood architecturally, not as isolated pieces of malicious code. Their strategic significance emerges from the coupling of data pipelines, knowledge representations, decision logic, authorization rules, and feedback mechanisms. Second, the key governance problem is delegated choice under uncertainty. The central issue is not whether a machine possesses moral agency, because it does not, but whether human institutions can maintain meaningful control when consequential choices are distributed across models, policy engines, and automated workflows. Third, the strategic effect of autonomy is primarily relational. Agentic cyber systems matter because they alter the tempo and cost structure of interaction between attacker and defender, not because they guarantee success. This relational view allows the chapter to connect technical fragility, adversarial deception, organizational capacity, and escalation risk within one analytical frame.

A non-operational illustrative scenario clarifies the framework. Consider a digitally dependent public-service organization facing persistent hostile probing during a political or humanitarian crisis. The organization relies on identity services, scheduling platforms, logistics systems, cloud-hosted applications, and third-party support. A hostile actor does not need spectacular disruption to generate leverage. By using agentic prioritization to identify weak dependencies, adapt timing, and sustain pressure across several service layers, the actor may force defenders into repeated triage, delayed communication, and uncertainty about where the next disruption will occur. The scenario does not describe methods or technical steps. It instead highlights governance-relevant dynamics: machine-assisted tempo, incomplete situational awareness, ambiguous attribution, uneven social harm, and the importance of recovery. It also explains why this chapter gives equal attention to auditability, human authorization thresholds, resilience, and crisis communication. The problem is not only preventing a first intrusion; it is preserving institutional control and public confidence when digital pressure can be adaptive and continuous.

The chapter therefore has the structure of a conceptual research contribution. Its limitations follow from that choice. It does not estimate the current number of autonomous cyber weapons, provide classified operational evidence, or rank the capabilities of particular states or groups. It also does not claim that agentic autonomy will make offensive operations simple or deterministic. Real-world cyber environments remain noisy, deceptive, legally constrained, and organizationally complex. Nevertheless, conceptual clarification is valuable because policy debates often move faster than shared definitions. By specifying the thresholds of perception, inference, delegated decision-making, and effectuation, the chapter provides a vocabulary for comparing systems, evaluating risk, and designing safeguards. The result is a framework that can support future empirical research while remaining suitable for a book chapter aimed at readers in cybersecurity, policy, ethics, and strategic studies.

4. LITERATURE REVIEW: FROM OFFENSIVE AUTOMATION TO AGENTIC SYSTEMS

The literature on autonomous cyber weapons is not a single field but a convergence of several research traditions. The first tradition concerns artificial intelligence and machine learning in cybersecurity. Early work on AI in cyber defense emphasized the promise of automated reasoning for detection, classification, and response (Tyugu, 2011). Later surveys showed that cyber tasks increasingly depend on scalable statistical inference, anomaly detection, feature selection, and learning-based classification rather than on signature matching alone (Buczak & Guven, 2016; Apruzzese, Colajanni, Ferretti, Guido, & Marchetti, 2018; Ferrag, Maglaras, Moschoyiannis, & Janicke, 2020). Zhou, Cheng, Jiang, and Dai (2020) similarly demonstrated the continuing importance of feature selection and ensemble classification for efficient intrusion detection. More recent work extends this discussion to critical infrastructure protection and the practical constraints of high-stakes environments, where detection models must operate within legacy systems, safety requirements, and limited downtime windows (Pinto, Gonçalves, Ferreira, & Tovar, 2023). Ebert and Beck (2023) further show that artificial intelligence has become an ordinary part of cybersecurity practice, not an isolated research novelty. This literature establishes the technical background for autonomy, but it usually focuses on defensive performance or tool effectiveness rather than on how those tools may be assembled into strategic offensive architectures.

A second body of work examines the dual-use character of AI-enabled cyber capability. Truong, Diep, and Zelinka (2020) explicitly frame artificial intelligence in the cyber domain as relevant to both offense and defense, including intrusion analysis, evasion, malware analysis, and automated response. Nobles (2024) reinforces this point through a systematic review of the weaponization of artificial intelligence in cybersecurity, showing that benign advances can be redirected toward hostile purposes when incentives and governance conditions change. Sarker, Janicke, Mohsin, Gill, and Maglaras (2024) add an important assurance perspective by emphasizing explainability, trustworthiness, and automation in cybersecurity decision-making. This is especially relevant for autonomous cyber weapons because systems that cannot explain or preserve the provenance of their decisions create accountability problems even before their outputs are harmful. The ethical literature deepens the same concern. Taddeo and Floridi (2018) argue that AI can serve socially beneficial purposes, but only when institutional governance aligns technical capacity with human values. Taddeo (2019) later identifies major ethical challenges in applying AI to cybersecurity, including responsibility, unintended consequences, and the difficulty of balancing security benefits against broader risks. These works support the chapter's claim that the problem is not AI itself but the combination of capability, purpose, delegation, and institutional control.

A third literature stream concerns exploit discovery, zero-day prevalence, and the economics of vulnerability information. Bilge and Dumitras (2012) offered one of the most influential empirical studies of zero-day attacks, demonstrating that previously unknown vulnerabilities can be used for meaningful periods before broad public disclosure. Miller (2007) examined the legitimate vulnerability market and showed that information about exploitable weaknesses can acquire strategic and economic value before it becomes part of public defense knowledge. Spring, Illari, Luta, and Parkin (2021) explain why attackers often have structural advantages in cybersecurity: defenders must protect many assets under uncertainty, while attackers may need only one viable opportunity. These studies are central to the present chapter because agentic systems could amplify the value of timing and prioritization. The issue is not that autonomy magically discovers all vulnerabilities. Rather, a system that can continuously compare observed conditions against opportunity models may shorten the interval between detection, evaluation, and attempted effect. That interval is strategically important because many organizations patch slowly, depend on third parties, or cannot interrupt critical services without operational cost.

A fourth group of studies addresses attack graphs, knowledge representation, and structural modeling. Attack graphs and attack trees provide ways of representing relationships among assets, vulnerabilities, privileges, dependencies, and possible pathways (Zeng, Wu, Chen, Han, & Shi, 2019). Yan et al. (2023) broaden this view through their survey of graph mining for cybersecurity, showing that graph-based methods can connect events, entities, and relationships across complex environments. Konsta, Lluch-Lafuente, Spiga, and Dragoni (2024) examine automatic generation of attack trees and attack graphs, illustrating why computational representation matters for both defense and risk analysis. For this chapter, the significance of these studies is conceptual: graph-based models make it possible to move from isolated observations to structured reasoning about relationships. When such representation is linked with decision rules and feedback loops, it can support agentic behavior. However, the literature also reveals limitations. Models can be incomplete, assumptions can be stale, and environmental knowledge can be distorted by deception. Therefore, graph reasoning should be understood as an enabler of autonomy, not as a guarantee of accurate judgment.

A fifth research stream examines adversarial machine learning and the fragility of AI-enabled cyber systems. Xu et al. (2020) survey adversarial attacks and defenses across images, graphs, and text, demonstrating that machine learning systems can be manipulated through carefully designed inputs or poisoned data. Anthi, Williams, Burnap, and Theodorakopoulos (2021) focus more specifically on adversarial attacks against machine learning cybersecurity systems, while Alotaibi and Rassam (2023) survey adversarial machine learning attacks against intrusion detection systems. He, Meng, and Xing (2023) provide a recent treatment of adversarial machine learning for network intrusion detection systems, reinforcing the point that learned models operate under adversarial pressure rather than in stable laboratory environments. This literature complicates optimistic claims about autonomous cyber weapons. The same inference systems that could accelerate offensive decision-making can themselves be deceived, misled, or driven into brittle behavior. In strategic terms, autonomy may intensify cycles of adaptation and counter-adaptation rather than produce one-sided superiority. That insight is central to this chapter's governance argument: delegation must be bounded not only because of ethical concerns but also because autonomous systems may misunderstand the environments they act upon.

A sixth body of scholarship concerns cyber conflict, escalation, international law, and strategic ambiguity. Robinson, Jones, and Janicke (2015) synthesize core issues in cyber warfare, including attribution, escalation, and the difficulty of interpreting effects. Kosenkov (2016) similarly treats cyber conflict as a global threat shaped by interdependence and the blurred boundary between civilian and strategic infrastructure. Schmitt (2012) examines how cyber conflict is classified under international law, while Lin (2012) analyzes the relationship between cyber operations and international humanitarian law. Delerue (2020) provides a broader legal framework for cyber operations, including questions of state responsibility and due diligence. Adesina (2021) argues that international law and norms have limited preventive force against non-state cyber attacks because enforcement and consensus remain uneven. Katagiri (2022) adds nuance by showing that cyber-military cross-domain operations are less frequent than some alarmist accounts suggest. Together, these works suggest that autonomous cyber weapons are unlikely to replace politics with code. Instead, they may intensify existing problems of attribution, signaling, threshold interpretation, and crisis management by compressing the time available for human assessment.

The ethical literature complements the legal and strategic scholarship by asking who is harmed, who decides, and who can be held accountable. Denning (2008) frames the ethics of cyber conflict around legitimacy, harm, and the responsibilities of both state and non-state actors. Orend (2014) argues that cyber warfare complicates familiar just war concepts because digital effects may be diffuse, delayed, reversible, or difficult to locate geographically. Lucas (2017) extends this ethical discussion by emphasizing responsibility and moral judgment in the context of emerging forms of war. These concerns become sharper when decision-making is delegated to agentic systems. If an autonomous system selects an action based on a changing model of the environment, human supervisors may remain responsible without being able to reconstruct the basis of the choice. That gap between responsibility and explainability is one of the central governance challenges addressed in this chapter. It shows why audit trails, model documentation, authorization thresholds, and post-incident review should be treated as core design requirements rather than as optional administrative features.

A final strand of literature addresses cyber effects, spillover, and the relationship between technical action and strategic consequence. Chen and Abu-Nimeh's (2011) analysis of Stuxnet remains important because it demonstrates that cyber operations can have effects that exceed narrow technical intentions and become symbols of broader strategic change. Whyte (2020) argues that AI-enabled cyber operations may alter patterns of competition by changing expectations about speed, prediction, and acceptable behavior. These arguments align with the chapter's focus on asymmetric warfare. Agentic cyber systems may be valuable to weaker actors not because they remove all technical barriers, but because they can reduce labor demands, sustain pressure, exploit defender overload, and make coordination cheaper. At the same time, the literature warns against technological determinism. Offensive autonomy still depends on data quality, organizational discipline, operational security, and the defender's capacity to deceive, recover, and adapt.

The critical gap is that these literatures often remain parallel. Technical studies describe feasibility, performance, and fragility; vulnerability studies examine opportunity structures and market incentives; legal studies evaluate state responsibility and threshold problems; ethical studies analyze accountability and harm; and strategic studies examine deterrence, escalation, and coercion. Few accounts combine these perspectives into a practical conceptual model of delegated cyber action. The result is a recurring analytical mismatch: discussions of AI-enabled cybersecurity may understate strategic consequences, while discussions of cyber weapons may overstate technical coherence. This chapter fills that gap by linking architecture, decision delegation, asymmetric leverage, and governance obligations in one framework. Its contribution is therefore not only definitional but integrative. It shows that autonomous cyber weapons should be understood as layered socio-technical systems whose risks emerge from the interaction between technical components, institutional authorization, adversarial uncertainty, and political context.

This integrated reading of the literature also clarifies why the chapter moves from conceptual definition to architecture, then to vulnerability exploitation, asymmetric warfare, command responsibility, ethics, defense, governance, and future research. Each part addresses a different dimension of the same problem. Technical autonomy explains how delegated cyber action becomes possible; strategic analysis explains why it matters; legal and ethical analysis explains why responsibility cannot be outsourced; and governance analysis explains how institutions can maintain control under compressed decision cycles. The literature therefore supports a balanced conclusion. Autonomous cyber weapons are neither inevitable superweapons nor ordinary automation. They are emerging forms of delegated digital power whose significance depends on architecture, environment, oversight, and resilience.

5. AGENTIC FRAMEWORKS FOR OFFENSIVE CYBER OPERATIONS

To understand proliferation risk, it is necessary to think architecturally. Autonomous cyber weapons are not best imagined as single monolithic programs. They are better understood as layered systems that connect data acquisition, world modeling, goal decomposition, option generation, risk scoring, authorization logic, effect execution, and feedback integration. In other words, the central issue is orchestration. Research on attack graphs and attack-tree automation shows that digital pathways can be represented, searched, and ranked computationally (Zeng, Wu, Chen, Han, & Shi, 2019; Konsta, Lluch-Lafuente, Spiga, & Dragoni, 2024). Research on graph mining for cybersecurity similarly indicates that complex relationships among assets, vulnerabilities, privileges, and observed events can be modeled in ways that support inference across distributed systems (Yan et al., 2023). When these representations are coupled with predictive models and policy constraints, they can form the cognitive substrate for agentic cyber behavior.

At a high level, an agentic offensive architecture would include four interdependent layers. The first is a discovery layer that ingests telemetry, asset metadata, vulnerability information, and contextual indicators. The second is an analytic layer that maintains a structured representation of the environment, often through graphs, state estimates, or evolving hypotheses. The third is a decision layer that translates strategic objectives into bounded action options under resource, legal, and mission constraints. The fourth is an execution layer that triggers approved effects, gathers outcomes, and revises the system's internal understanding. The architecture need not be fully autonomous across all layers. Partial autonomy at one layer can still generate strategic acceleration when combined with automated pipelines elsewhere. Figure 1 presents this layered model in simplified form. The figure is intentionally abstract: its value lies in clarifying how perception, reasoning, planning, and execution can be linked through feedback, not in depicting implementation mechanics. Table 3 compares human-led and agentic-enabled campaigns at an analytic level, emphasizing tempo and coordination rather than operational mechanics.

Table 3. Human-led versus agentic-enabled cyber campaign characteristics.

Dimension	Human-led campaign	Agentic-enabled campaign
Operational tempo	Bounded by analyst workflow	Compressed through orchestration and model assistance
Search cost	High manual effort	Reduced through ranking and automation
Adaptation	Dependent on human re-analysis	Potentially continuous within bounds
Attribution exposure	Often shaped by operator tradecraft	Can be obscured by software-mediated decisions
Oversight need	Continuous tactical supervision	Stronger ex ante policy constraints and logging

Figure 1. Layered conceptual model of an agentic offensive cyber architecture.

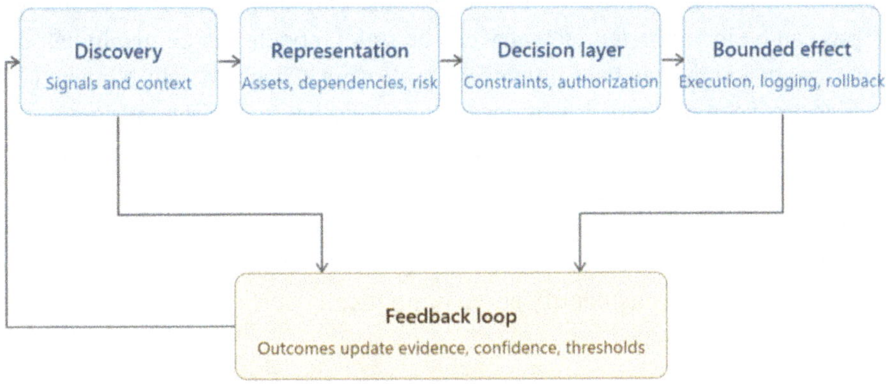

6. VULNERABILITY EXPLOITATION AS AN AGENTIC FUNCTION

Automated vulnerability exploitation is among the most sensitive and contested aspects of offensive cyber autonomy. In public debate, the phrase often evokes fully self-directed offensive code. In practice, however, the more plausible near-term risk is selective delegation. A system may be permitted to evaluate candidate opportunities, rank likely avenues of effect, simulate consequences, and recommend or initiate bounded actions under preauthorized conditions. That type of delegated behavior could be particularly attractive in environments where patch cycles are slow, dependencies are opaque, and defenders are overloaded. Yet the strategic significance does not depend on the publication of new exploit techniques. It depends on whether agentic systems can reduce search costs, improve prioritization, and accelerate action across many target environments at once.

The literature on zero-days and exploit opportunity structures underscores why speed matters. Bilge and Dumitras (2012) found that attackers benefited from windows during which defenders lacked awareness or remediation. In many enterprise and industrial settings, even known vulnerabilities remain exploitable because of patching delays, dependency constraints, or operational risk. Agentic systems could exploit this environment by continuously comparing observed conditions against dynamic opportunity models. The key change is not magical discovery. It is the capacity to treat exploitation as an optimization problem over time, uncertainty, and scale. When such systems operate across multiple targets or persistent campaigns, they can create asymmetric leverage for actors who lack large human teams but possess sufficient compute, data, and organizational intent.

This does not imply that offensive autonomy is straightforwardly effective. Real-world environments are noisy, heterogeneous, and shaped by deception. Attack graphs can be incomplete; telemetry can be stale; models can be manipulated; and downstream actions can have unintended spillovers. Chen and Abu-Nimeh's (2011) discussion of Stuxnet remains important precisely because it reminds analysts that cyber effects can propagate in ways that outstrip original assumptions. In autonomous settings, bounded action policies, rollback logic, and human intervention points therefore become essential not only for ethics but also for operational reliability. The offensive actor who delegates too much may generate strategic self-harm through premature exposure, misidentification, or politically costly collateral effects.

7. ASYMMETRIC WARFARE AND THE STRATEGIC LOGIC OF PROLIFERATION

The most important reason autonomous cyber weapons matter is not that they promise perfect precision. It is that they may restructure the economics of competition. Asymmetric warfare traditionally advantages actors that exploit the stronger party's dependencies, costs, legal constraints, or visibility. In cyberspace, these asymmetries are amplified by interconnection, attribution difficulty, and uneven exposure across sectors. Agentic offensive systems could deepen these conditions in at least four ways. First, they reduce labor intensity by allowing smaller teams to supervise broader campaigns. Second, they compress operational cycles, creating pressure on defenders who still depend on slower human review. Third, they enable adaptation across heterogeneous environments by combining statistical inference with rule-based guardrails. Fourth, they may expand deniability because the pathway from sponsor intent to software action becomes harder to reconstruct in real time.

Figure 2 illustrates the logic of temporal asymmetry. The point is not that manual operations disappear, but that agentic systems can shift the duration and coordination burden of core phases such as observation, analysis, planning, and action. In strategic terms, compressed cycles matter because many organizations already struggle to triage alerts, validate exposure, and coordinate remediation across business and operational units. A relatively modest increase in adversary tempo can therefore produce outsized disruption if defenders are forced into a constant state of reactive assessment.

These dynamics are especially relevant for critical infrastructure and globally connected supply chains. Digitally dependent sectors often combine legacy technologies, outsourced maintenance, third-party software, and fragmented visibility. They may also face strong constraints on taking systems offline for patching or investigation. In such conditions, offensive agents need not achieve spectacular or cinematic effects to impose strategic costs. Repeated low-visibility actions against logistics, healthcare scheduling, energy balancing, cloud management planes, or identity systems can create cumulative uncertainty and resource exhaustion. Autonomous cyber weapons thus fit the broader logic of gray-zone competition: they can generate persistent pressure below traditional war thresholds while still shaping bargaining power, public confidence, and crisis stability.

At the same time, proliferation should not be equated with universal diffusion. Sophisticated agentic systems still require quality data, integration engineering, evaluation procedures, and operational security. State actors, intelligence services, and well-resourced criminal enterprises are more likely to field robust versions first. Yet diffusion pressure remains serious because many necessary components are commercially available, open-source, or dual-use. The modularity of the ecosystem means that capability can emerge incrementally. A tool that begins as analytic assistance for vulnerability management can, under different governance arrangements, become a component in an offensive agentic loop. To make the asymmetry argument more concrete, Table 4 maps likely effects across target sectors that combine digital dependence with difficult recovery conditions.

Figure 2. Compressed decision cycles as a source of temporal asymmetry in cyber conflict.

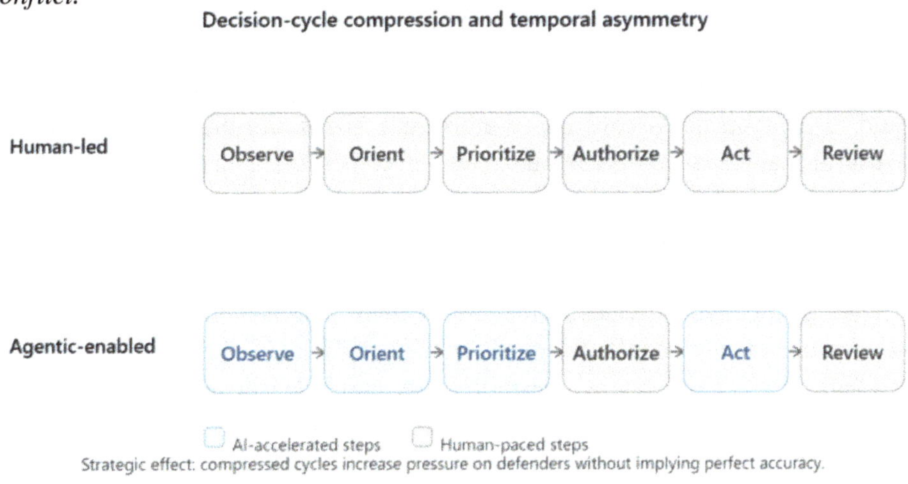

Table 4. Illustrative asymmetric effects across digitally dependent sectors.

Sector	Why exposed	Potential asymmetric consequence	Defensive priority
Energy	Legacy OT and uptime constraints	Operational disruption and public anxiety	Segmentation and recovery drills
Healthcare	Interdependent scheduling and identity systems	Safety-adjacent service degradation	Resilient identity and downtime procedures
Logistics	Tightly coupled platforms and third parties	Cascading delay and inventory uncertainty	Supply-chain visibility and contingency routing
Government services	Citizen-facing digital dependence	Trust erosion and administrative backlog	Service continuity planning
Finance	High-speed transactions and concentration risk	Confidence shock and fraud opportunity	Layered fraud controls and isolation

8. ESCALATION, ATTRIBUTION, AND COMMAND RESPONSIBILITY

Autonomous cyber weapons raise escalation concerns because they redistribute decision authority across software-mediated processes. In conventional operations, commanders can often review specific target packages, timing assumptions, and anticipated effects before execution. In agentic systems, by contrast, a significant portion of operational behavior may be produced through iterative reasoning over live data. That creates a governance problem: responsibility remains human, but the causal chain from authorization to effect becomes less transparent. The issue is not whether machines are morally responsible. They are not. The issue is whether institutional responsibility can remain meaningful when supervisors cannot readily explain why a system selected one pathway rather than another.

The legal literature provides useful guidance here. Schmitt (2012) emphasizes that classification of cyber conflict depends on effects, attribution, and the relationship between operations and state responsibility. Adesina (2021) further argues that norms and legal regimes often fail to constrain non-state behavior in cyberspace because enforcement, consensus, and actor coverage remain weak. For autonomous cyber weapons, this means that accountability cannot rely solely on ex post attribution. It must be built into system design through auditable logs, decision provenance, bounded policy envelopes, and explicit authorization thresholds. Absent such measures, states and organizations may find themselves unable to distinguish error from intent, opportunism from doctrine, or local adaptation from strategic escalation.

Command responsibility also has a temporal dimension. When decision cycles compress, leaders may be tempted to preauthorize broader categories of action in order to preserve responsiveness. Yet this can shift risk from operational delay to strategic overreach. Figure 3 therefore proposes a simple oversight logic in which higher-risk or higher-spillover situations trigger human authorization, while lower-risk actions remain bounded by automated safeguards. The broader lesson is that escalation control in cyberspace is increasingly a systems-engineering problem as much as a diplomatic one. Policy statements alone are insufficient unless they are translated into executable constraints inside the architectures that carry out digital operations. Table 5 complements the figure by connecting strategic governance questions to specific assurance objectives.

Figure 3. Oversight logic for bounded autonomy and human authorization.

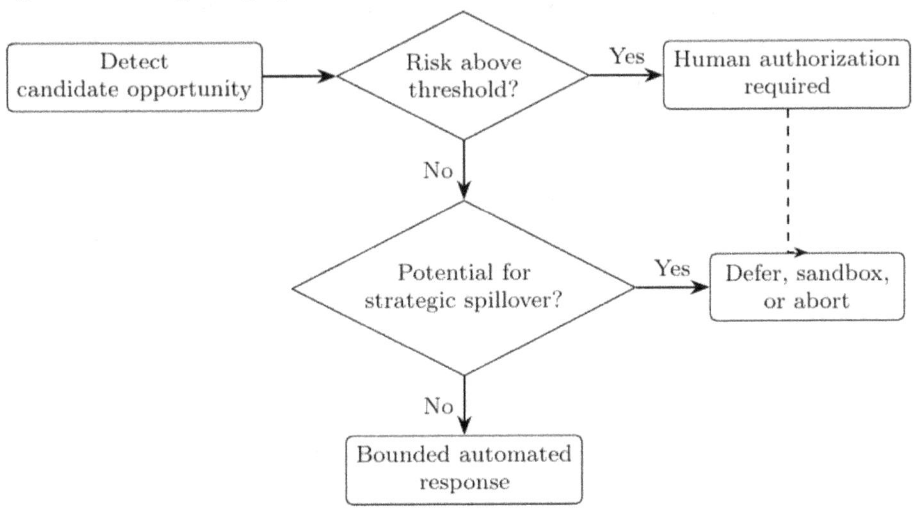

Table 5. Governance questions and assurance requirements for autonomous cyber systems.

Governance question	Why it matters	Assurance response
Who sets mission boundaries?	Prevents drift from policy intent	Explicit policy envelopes and approvals
What data inform decisions?	Supports audit and challenge	Data provenance and retention
How are risks scored?	Affects proportionality and escalation	Model documentation and scenario testing

continued on following page

Table 5. Continued

Governance question	Why it matters	Assurance response
When must humans intervene?	Protects high-consequence decisions	Threshold-based hold points
How are outcomes reviewed?	Enables accountability and learning	Immutable logs and post-incident review

9. ETHICAL AND LEGAL CHALLENGES

The ethical evaluation of autonomous cyber weapons should begin with three questions: who is affected, who decides, and who can be held accountable. Denning (2008) framed cyber conflict ethics around harm, legitimacy, and the conduct of both state and non-state actors. Orend (2014) later argued that cyber warfare requires rethinking familiar just war concepts because digital effects can be delayed, indirect, and difficult to delimit geographically. Autonomous cyber weapons intensify these concerns. When a system updates its beliefs continuously and chooses among action options under uncertainty, the moral significance of oversight, explainability, and reversibility becomes more acute.

A central ethical challenge is the opacity of model-mediated judgment. Explainable AI research in cybersecurity has stressed the importance of transparency, trust, and intelligibility for high-stakes decision support (Sarker, Janicke, Mohsin, Gill, & Maglaras, 2024). In offensive settings, opacity undermines both internal governance and external legitimacy. A sponsoring organization may not be able to explain why a specific action was selected, what risks were considered, or whether alternative courses were rejected appropriately. This matters because proportionality and discrimination are not abstract legal tests; they require evidence about expected effects, target relevance, and available alternatives. If those judgments are embedded in uninterpretable pipelines, meaningful review becomes difficult.

A second challenge is the dual-use problem. Many of the technical components relevant to autonomous cyber weapons also serve protective or benign purposes. Attack graphs support defense planning; anomaly detection improves incident response; large language models assist documentation and triage; orchestration reduces operator workload. Ethical governance must therefore avoid simplistic binaries. The relevant question is not whether a technology is 'for offense' or 'for defense' in the abstract, but whether its integration, objectives, deployment conditions, and safeguards materially increase the capacity to generate uncontrolled or unaccountable cyber effects. This is why governance frameworks should focus on capabilities, risk thresholds, and assurance obligations rather than on labels alone.

10. DEFENSIVE IMPLICATIONS AND RESILIENCE PRIORITIES

From a defensive perspective, the prospect of autonomous cyber weapons shifts attention from isolated controls to systemic resilience. Organizations should assume that adversaries may increasingly use AI-assisted prioritization, faster opportunity selection, and more adaptive campaign management. The implication is not that every intrusion will become autonomous, but that defenders should plan for higher speed, more persistent probing, and better coordination across phases. Traditional control frameworks remain essential - asset inventory, segmentation, vulnerability management, strong identity controls, logging, and backup hygiene - but they must be integrated with mechanisms that reduce the value of machine-speed offense.

First, organizations need better environmental clarity. Agentic offensive systems benefit from ambiguity gaps: undocumented dependencies, stale asset inventories, and inconsistent identity governance. Closing those gaps reduces exploitable uncertainty. Second, defenders should prioritize controls that increase attacker decision costs, such as segmentation, just-in-time access, least privilege, and hardened change management. Third, defensive operations require their own carefully governed automation. Human teams cannot consistently match machine-speed adversaries without support for prioritization, correlation, and response, but defensive autonomy should be designed around explainability, containment, and graceful degradation. Fourth, high-consequence environments should implement response throttles and policy-based hold points so that automated defensive actions do not accidentally amplify adversary deception.

Table 6 later in the chapter translates these implications into a control matrix aligned to discovery, decision, execution, and governance layers. The broader point is that resilience against autonomous cyber weapons is less about inventing one revolutionary safeguard and more about reducing the reliability of adversary inference while improving the organization's own capacity to observe, interpret, and recover. In that sense, the defense problem is socio-technical: architecture, staffing, procurement, crisis management, and executive oversight all matters. Table 6 is introduced here before placement to translate the narrative into a practical resilience matrix for civilian and national-security organizations.

Table 6. Defensive control matrix for environments facing agentic offensive threats.

Layer	Representative control	Purpose
Discovery	Asset inventory and exposure management	Reduce adversary inference advantage
Identity	Least privilege and just-in-time access	Limit lateral decision options
Architecture	Segmentation and isolation boundaries	Constrain blast radius

continued on following page

Table 6. Continued

Layer	Representative control	Purpose
Operations	Behavioral analytics with human review	Detect machine-speed probing
Recovery	Tested backups and fallback procedures	Shorten disruption duration
Governance	Escalation drills and executive oversight	Improve crisis coherence

11. GOVERNANCE ARCHITECTURE AND INTERNATIONAL NORMS

Because the elements of offensive autonomy are distributed across markets, research communities, and institutional contexts, no single policy instrument will be adequate. A layered governance architecture is required. At the international level, the most realistic near-term objective is not universal prohibition but partial consensus around unacceptable targets, crisis communication, responsible state behavior, and shared expectations for human accountability. Even imperfect norms can reduce ambiguity when they are reinforced by national doctrine, confidence-building measures, information-sharing channels, and sectoral incident reporting. This revised section therefore strengthens the international dimension requested by the reviewers while acknowledging the limits identified by Adesina (2021) and Delerue (2020).

Partial international consensus can still matter in three ways. First, it can stigmatize autonomous or semi-autonomous actions against civilian critical infrastructure during peacetime, even when enforcement is incomplete. Second, it can create common language for escalation thresholds, evidentiary standards, and emergency communication. Third, it can influence procurement and assurance practices by making auditability, human authorization, and rollback capacity part of what responsible states expect from themselves and partners. These functions do not eliminate strategic competition, but they can narrow the space in which ambiguity is exploited.

At the national level, procurement standards, audit requirements, export controls, and public-sector assurance frameworks can shape what kinds of agentic cyber systems are considered acceptable. This is especially important where military, intelligence, and civilian infrastructures overlap. Figure 4 summarizes a governance stack that links international norms, national policy, organizational controls, system safeguards, and post-incident accountability. The figure underscores a crucial point: governance should not sit outside the system as a rhetorical add-on. It must be translated into testing requirements, rate limits, logging specifications, rollback conditions, and human authorization rules. Systems that cannot express governance requirements technically will struggle to implement them reliably under pressure.

Figure 4. Multi-level governance stack for constraining autonomous cyber weapon misuse.

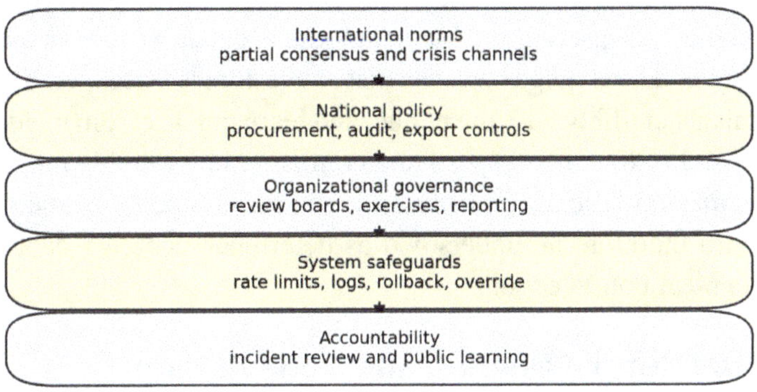

At the organizational level, autonomous cyber capabilities - whether defensive prototypes, dual-use research systems, or classified tools - should be subject to staged review, red-teaming, model assurance, and escalation drills. Boards, ministers, or senior commanders do not need to understand every algorithmic detail, but they do need visibility into delegation boundaries, failure modes, and intervention mechanisms. Without that, institutions may inherit the risks of autonomy without gaining legitimate or controllable strategic advantage.

Procurement policy is especially important because it determines what kinds of cyber-related autonomy become normalized in practice. If government buyers reward speed and automation without equally valuing auditability, interpretability, and containment, vendors and internal development teams will rationally optimize for performance first and assurance later. In safety-critical sectors, procurement should require evidence of logging completeness, policy constraint enforcement, model evaluation under adversarial conditions, and documented human override procedures. Similar expectations should guide public-private partnerships and national cyber exercises.

12. STRATEGIC, ORGANIZATIONAL, AND SOCIETAL IMPACTS

12.1 Recovery as Strategic Deterrence

The earlier draft treated recovery as an analytical extension; the revised chapter integrates it as a central strategic theme. Cyber deterrence is often framed around denial, punishment, or prevention, but autonomous cyber weapons make recovery capacity a form of denial. Organizations that can restore services, verify data integrity, communicate credibly with the public, and learn quickly from incidents reduce the attacker's ability to convert speed and confusion into durable political effects. Redundancy, manual fallback procedures, crisis communication, and institutional memory should therefore be understood as deterrence-enabling capabilities, not merely as technical housekeeping.

12.2 Alliance Burden Sharing and Consultation

The framework also has implications for alliance politics. Cyber defense and cyber operations are distributed unevenly across partners with different legal authorities, industrial bases, intelligence capabilities, and threat perceptions. If autonomous cyber weapons proliferate, those differences may become more pronounced. Some members may emphasize offensive innovation and preemptive disruption, while others may prioritize legal restraint, civilian infrastructure protection, and defensive resilience. Without deliberate coordination, such divergence can create strategic incoherence. Alliance governance therefore needs shared vocabulary for delegated cyber action, acceptable risk, escalation thresholds, and evidentiary standards for attribution.

12.3 Economic Security and Social Distribution of Harm

Autonomous cyber weapons are also relevant to economic security. Operations against cloud platforms, software supply chains, authentication services, and data-intensive business processes can affect competitiveness and investor confidence without crossing obvious war thresholds. Ministries of finance, trade, and industry should therefore be included in national discussions of cyber autonomy. Treating the issue as a niche defense concern would miss how digital coercion can shape production, distribution, and market trust.

The social burden of cyber autonomy is not evenly distributed. Civilian societies depend on digital systems for everyday coordination: school administration, medical scheduling, payroll, transit information, local permitting, and identity verification. Communities with fewer resources, weaker local redundancy, or less political visibility may experience longer recovery times even when the initiating cyber event appears technically modest. A serious governance agenda should therefore ask not only how to deter or regulate autonomous cyber weapons, but also how to reduce the vulnerability of populations whose resilience is shaped by inequality and public-service capacity.

12.4 Deception, Uncertainty, and Threshold Management

Cyber conflict has always been deception-rich: adversaries hide intent, spoof infrastructure, manipulate indicators, and exploit defenders' cognitive biases. Agentic systems intensify this environment because they can generate and test hypotheses rapidly, but they can also be misled at scale. A defender who understands the assumptions embedded in an adversary's models may use decoys, telemetry shaping, and strategic noise to increase uncertainty. Autonomous cyber weapons therefore do not erase the interactive character of conflict. They may increase tempo, but they do not eliminate contestation over interpretation.

Thresholds should also be understood more broadly than physical damage or doctrinal legal categories. A campaign that persistently degrades confidence in digital records, complicates emergency communication, or forces repeated precautionary shutdowns may never resemble a classic armed attack, yet it can still change political decision-making and public risk perception. Because agentic systems can sustain such pressure at lower marginal labor cost, they may be particularly effective in this threshold space. Analysts therefore need richer typologies of escalation that account for cumulative governance strain as well as immediate physical effects.

13. FUTURE RESEARCH DIRECTIONS

Future research should move beyond abstract debates about whether autonomous cyber weapons are possible and instead examine the conditions under which bounded autonomy becomes strategically consequential. One promising direction is measurement. Researchers need comparative frameworks for evaluating how partial autonomy changes campaign tempo, operator workload, false-positive tolerance, stealth, and escalation risk across different target environments. Another direction concerns assurance. Existing model evaluation methods are not enough for systems that combine language models, graph search, policy engines, and live telemetry. Composite assurance methods are needed to test robustness, policy compliance, and failure containment under adversarial conditions.

A third research concerns human-machine command relationships. The most relevant questions are not simply whether humans are in or on the loop, but which decisions remain delegable under which uncertainty conditions, and how those choices affect accountability. Comparative studies across military, intelligence, and civilian critical infrastructure contexts could clarify how oversight models should vary with stakes and spillover potential. A fourth priority is the political economy of proliferation. Scholars should study how open-source ecosystems, cloud services, data brokerage, cybercrime markets, and state-industrial partnerships together shape access to agentic capability components.

Finally, research must address cross-domain consequences. Autonomous cyber weapons do not operate in a vacuum. They can influence crisis signaling, public communication, sanctions policy, supply-chain continuity, and perceptions of state competence. The field therefore needs more interdisciplinary work combining cybersecurity engineering, international relations, organizational theory, and ethics. Such research is essential if governance is to keep pace with the architectural realities of offensive autonomy.

Table 7 is introduced here before placement to summarize the most important research gaps identified across the chapter.

Table 7. Priority future research directions.

Research area	Core question	Why it matters
Measurement	How much does partial autonomy change campaign tempo?	Clarifies strategic significance
Assurance	How should composite agentic systems be tested?	Supports safe governance and procurement
Oversight	Which decisions remain delegable under uncertainty?	Improves accountability design
Political economy	How do markets shape capability diffusion?	Explains proliferation pathways
Cross-domain effects	How do cyber agents affect crisis signaling?	Connects technical change to strategy

14. EXTENDED ANALYTICAL NOTES ON STRATEGIC, ORGANIZATIONAL, AND SOCIETAL IMPACTS

Comparing self-contained cyber weapons to previous military-technical shifts is a useful approach to deepening the analysis. Public perception of offensive cyber autonomy is infrequent at the point of use, unlike precision-guided munitions or remotely piloted systems. It has an impact on existing digital infrastructures, service dependencies and organizational routines. Visibility has the potential to distort strategic assessment. The cumulative damage of an operation may be underestimated by political leaders due to the absence of dramatic imagery, while technical personnel may overestimate controllability due to actions occurring in familiar software environments rather than on battlefields that are visibly destructive. The disparity between perception and effect is significant because democratic oversight, alliance signaling, and crisis management are often based on shared narratives of what's happening. That narrative layer is further complicated by agentic cyber operations. Why? The election may not be a spectacle at all, but it can also be one of high administrative stress and an uncertain delegation. Achieving political change can be more difficult when such combinations are present, which can benefit actors who are willing to take advantage of uncertainty rather than capitalizing on immediate destruction.

There is also an organizational paradox at the heart of offensive autonomy. Institutions often pursue automation because their human operators are overwhelmed, yet the act of delegating to software can itself create new forms of managerial burden. Supervisors must understand model limitations, verify data provenance, design escalation thresholds, preserve auditability, and rehearse intervention procedures. In other words, autonomy does not eliminate organizational complexity; it redistributes it. This redistribution may be manageable in mature organizations with disciplined engineering and governance cultures, but it can be destabilizing in institutions that already struggle with siloed responsibilities, contractor dependence, or weak change control. As a result, the relative advantage conferred by autonomous cyber weapons may depend as much on institutional maturity as on raw technical sophistication. A weaker actor with coherent command relationships and clear delegation rules may outperform a nominally stronger actor whose cyber enterprise is fragmented across competing bureaucratic units. This point is strategically important because it suggests that proliferation is not only about who acquires the most advanced models or the largest datasets. It is also about who can absorb autonomy into an organizational system that remains legible and governable under stress.

The social dimension of cyber autonomy deserves equal attention. Civilian societies increasingly rely on digital systems not only for finance, communication, and logistics, but also for the mundane coordination that makes ordinary life predictable: school administration, medical scheduling, payroll processing, transit information, local permitting, and identity verification. Autonomous cyber weapons may target these systems directly or may affect them indirectly through attacks on shared platforms and service providers. In either case, the resulting harm is often unevenly distributed. Communities with fewer resources, weaker local redundancy, or less political visibility may experience longer recovery times and greater hardship even when the initiating cyber event appears technically modest. This creates a justice problem. Discussions of cyber conflict frequently concentrate on states, militaries, and national-level deterrence, yet much of the lived burden of digital disruption falls on households, local institutions, and frontline service workers. A serious governance agenda should therefore ask not only how to deter or regulate autonomous cyber weapons, but also how to reduce the vulnerability of populations whose resilience is shaped by inequality, not merely by technology. That may require integrating cyber preparedness into broader debates on infrastructure investment, social protection, public communication, and emergency management.

Another analytical issue concerns the relationship between offensive autonomy and deception. Cyber conflict has always been deception-rich: adversaries hide intent, spoof infrastructure, manipulate indicators, and exploit defenders' cognitive biases. Agentic systems intensify this environment because they can generate and test multiple hypotheses rapidly, but they can also be misled at scale. A defender who understands the assumptions embedded in an adversary's models may seed false signals, shape telemetry, or create incentive structures that divert attention toward decoys and away from strategically meaningful assets. This possibility reinforces a broader conclusion of the chapter: autonomous cyber weapons do not erase the interactive character of conflict. They may increase operational tempo, but they do not eliminate contestation over interpretation. Future doctrine should therefore avoid imagining autonomy as a unilateral accelerator that automatically favors offense. In many circumstances, the actor that better understands the opponent's data dependencies and decision heuristics may gain advantage through deception, patience, and strategic noise. The resulting contests could resemble adversarial information ecologies as much as traditional campaigns, with each side attempting to shape the other's machine-mediated perception of reality.

The chapter's framework also has implications for alliance politics and burden sharing. In alliances, cyber defense and cyber operations are often distributed unevenly across members with different legal authorities, industrial bases, intelligence capabilities, and threat perceptions. If autonomous cyber weapons proliferate, those differences may become more pronounced. Some members may emphasize offensive innovation and preemptive disruption; others may prioritize legal restraint, civilian infrastructure protection, and defensive resilience. Without deliberate coordination, such divergence can create strategic incoherence. An autonomous operation conducted or tolerated by one partner may impose political costs on others that share infrastructure dependencies or public accountability. Alliance governance therefore needs common vocabulary for discussing delegated cyber action, acceptable risk, escalation thresholds, and evidentiary standards for attribution. It also needs agreed mechanisms for incident consultation when autonomous or semi-autonomous operations appear to be producing cross-border spillovers. These requirements are not purely diplomatic. They should shape procurement, information sharing, and joint exercises. In effect, alliance politics becomes another layer in the governance stack, one that can either amplify restraint or magnify ambiguity depending on whether members invest in common doctrine.

A further note concerns economic security. Autonomous cyber weapons could become attractive not only for classic military or intelligence purposes, but also for campaigns aimed at industrial advantage, sanctions evasion, technological espionage, and market manipulation. In globally integrated economies, cyber operations against cloud platforms, software supply chains, authentication services, and data-intensive business processes can affect competitiveness and investor confidence without crossing obvious war thresholds. Agentic offensive systems may be especially relevant in these contexts because they can monitor changing digital conditions and adapt pressure tactics in response to defensive adjustments. That possibility suggests that ministries of finance, trade, and industry should be more centrally involved in national discussions of cyber autonomy. Treating the issue as a niche concern for defense establishments alone would miss how profoundly digital coercion can shape production, distribution, and market trust. Economic resilience planning, corporate reporting standards, and sectoral stress testing may all need to incorporate assumptions about faster, more adaptive adversary behavior.

Finally, the educational and normative consequences of autonomous cyber weapons should not be neglected. The language used to describe these systems influences how societies imagine responsibility. Terms like intelligent attack, self-directed exploitation, or machine-led operations may attract attention, but they can also obscure the chain of human choices involved in design, procurement, deployment, and authorization. More careful language can improve governance by reminding decision-makers that agency in software is always institutionally produced. Someone defines objectives, sets constraints, chooses data sources, approves testing standards, and decides where human review is retained or relaxed. By emphasizing those institutional choices, scholars and practitioners can resist both fatalism and hype. Autonomous cyber weapons are neither inevitable masters of the future battlespace nor trivial extensions of ordinary automation. They are contingent socio-technical systems whose risks and effects depend on architecture, doctrine, market incentives, and political oversight. That framing is essential for keeping public debate grounded in governable realities rather than technological mythology.

A related strategic concern involves threshold management. In many policy discussions, cyber escalation is treated as a question of whether an operation produces physical damage or crosses a doctrinally salient legal line. Autonomous cyber weapons suggest a broader way of thinking. Thresholds may also be cognitive, administrative, or economic. A campaign that persistently degrades confidence in digital records, complicates emergency communication, or forces repeated precautionary shutdowns may never resemble a classic armed attack, yet it can still change political decision-making and public risk perception. Because agentic systems can sustain such campaigns at lower marginal labor cost, they may be particularly effective in this threshold space. Analysts therefore need richer typologies of escalation that account for cumulative governance strain as well as immediate physical effects. This broader lens can improve both doctrine and resilience planning because it treats cyber coercion as a process of pressure accumulation, not only as a discrete event to be labeled after the fact.

There is likewise a methodological lesson for researchers. Studies of cyber autonomy often oscillate between highly abstract speculation and narrowly technical evaluation. What is needed instead are meso-level studies that examine how organizations actually integrate models, data pipelines, human review, and operational objectives over time. Such studies could compare prototype development in military laboratories, managed security providers, incident response firms, and criminal ecosystems. They could investigate where autonomy is most often bounded, where it most often drifts, and which forms of institutional friction either prevent or accelerate dangerous integration. Without this meso-level evidence, debates about autonomous cyber weapons risk remaining too polarized between alarmist futurism and dismissive incrementalism. Empirical, organizationally grounded research would help establish which risks are immediate, which are transitional, and which remain speculative.

An additional implication concerns standards and certification. If sectors such as aviation, health, finance, and industrial control increasingly depend on digital systems whose disruption has public consequences, then assurance practices for AI-enabled cyber tooling may need to become more formalized. Certification alone will never solve the problem, particularly when offensive actors are unconstrained by compliance regimes. However, standards can still shape markets, procurement expectations, and professional norms. Requirements for secure logging, provenance tracking, human override, incident reporting, and adversarial robustness testing could make it harder for poorly governed autonomous capability components to circulate unnoticed in critical environments. Importantly, standards should not be so rigid that they freeze defensive innovation. The challenge is to define minimum assurance expectations that raise the floor of safety without preventing adaptive security engineering. That balance is difficult, but it is preferable to a status quo in which autonomy advances faster than the institutions meant to supervise it.

The last aspect to be emphasized is the inconsistency in time between innovation and regulation. Why? The adaptation of technical components related to cyber autonomy can be done much more quickly by reusing them than formal law or treaty processes. The anomaly leads observers to conclude that governance will never recover fully, leaving it lagging capability. That conclusion is too pessimistic. Even though legal codification may be slow, companies can implement interim governance measures through procurement alternatives, sector guidance, voluntary standards, incident reporting norms, and professional expectations. Intermediate mechanisms are essential as they shape developmental pathways before technology becomes embedded.' Institutions have the potential to normalize unsafe design patterns through unintentional means such as routine procurement and operational experimentation, provided they obtain perfect legal consensus before acting. Imperfect but valuable early governance can shape the path?

It's important to consider recovery, not just prevention. Cyber warfare stories often revolve around strategies to prevent or penalize attackers. Why? The proliferation of autonomous cyber weapons makes recovery capabilities a strategic advantage. Non-competent organizations that can restore services, verify data integrity, communicate credibly with the public, and learn quickly from incidents are unable to provide adversaries with lasting effects. Despite its unimpressive appearance, recovery is strategically important because it curtails the political option of cyber disruption. Treating redundancy, manual fallbacks, crisis communications and institutional memory as fundamental elements of deterrence should be denied. They diminish the appeal of campaigns that aim to profit from speed and confusion.

A crucial lesson for scholars and practitioners is that autonomy in cyberspace should be examined as a means of delegating power in the face of uncertainty. Its formulation maintains its focus on the human institutions that establish goals, set boundaries, and accept risks. The article highlights the inadequacy of straightforward discussions about system autonomy over complex queries regarding delegation, recipients, evidence requirements, audit trails, and reversibility. This reframe of the discussion can be beneficial for both technical research and policy design. Why is this important?

15. CONCLUSION

The expansion of autonomous cyber weapons should be viewed as the amalgamation of modular digital capabilities into agentic offensive architectures that can compress observation, reasoning, and action. It's not a science-fiction scenario where software alone is engaged in armed conflict. Selected delegation can be both a plausible and potentially hazardous choice, as it allows systems to prioritize opportunities over human teams in real time, adapt pathways, and pursue restricted cyber effects more quickly than humans can manage reliably. It is important to note that this development changes the economics of cyber warfare, particularly for actors who aim to gain power through speed, deniability, persistence over time and exploitation of systemic incompatibility.

The chapter demonstrates that existing scholarships already possess many necessary components to analyze this shift.' The technical substrate of AI in cybersecurity is explained by research, while zero-days and attack graph studies provide insight into opportunity structures, cyber conflict literature clarifies escalation and attribution dilemmas for adversary groups, and legal-ethical scholarship emphasizes the importance of accountability, explainability, undrain, etc. Bringing these strands together suggests a clear policy conclusion: governance must be architectural rather than just declaratory. It is necessary to incorporate oversight, auditability, thresholds, and rollback logic into the systems of a system.

REFERENCES

Adesina, P. A. (2021). Why international law and norms do little in preventing non-state cyber attacks. *Journal of Cybersecurity, 7*(1), tyab009. Advance online publication. DOI: 10.1093/cybsec/tyab009

Alotaibi, A., & Rassam, M. A. (2023). Adversarial machine learning attacks against intrusion detection systems: A survey on strategies and defenses. *Future Internet, 15*(2), 62. DOI: 10.3390/fi15020062

Anthi, E., Williams, L., Burnap, P., & Theodorakopoulos, G. (2021). Adversarial attacks on machine learning cybersecurity systems. *Journal of Information Security and Applications, 58*, 102804. DOI: 10.1016/j.jisa.2020.102717

Apruzzese, G., Colajanni, M., Ferretti, L., Guido, A., & Marchetti, M. (2018). On the effectiveness of machine and deep learning for cyber security. 2018 10th International Conference on Cyber Conflict (CyCon), 371-390. DOI: 10.23919/CYCON.2018.8405026

Bilge, L., & Dumitras, T. (2012). Before we knew it: An empirical study of zero-day attacks in the real world. *Proceedings of the 2012 ACM Conference on Computer and Communications Security*, 833-844. DOI: 10.1145/2382196.2382284

Buczak, A. L., & Guven, E. (2016). A survey of data mining and machine learning methods for cyber security intrusion detection. *IEEE Communications Surveys and Tutorials, 18*(2), 1153–1176. DOI: 10.1109/COMST.2015.2494502

Chen, T. M., & Abu-Nimeh, S. (2011). Lessons from Stuxnet. *Computer, 44*(4), 91–93. DOI: 10.1109/MC.2011.115

Delerue, F. (2020). *Cyber operations and international law*. Cambridge University Press., DOI: 10.1017/9781108780605

Denning, D. E. (2008). The ethics of cyber conflict. In Himma, K. E., & Tavani, H. T. (Eds.), *The handbook of information and computer ethics* (pp. 407–429)., DOI: 10.1002/9780470281819.ch17

Ebert, C., & Beck, M. (2023). Artificial intelligence for cybersecurity. *IEEE Software, 40*(6), 30–31. DOI: 10.1109/MS.2023.3265877

Ferrag, M. A., Maglaras, L., Moschoyiannis, S., & Janicke, H. (2020). Deep learning for cyber security intrusion detection: Approaches, datasets, and comparative study. *Journal of Information Security and Applications, 50*, 102419. DOI: 10.1016/j.jisa.2019.102419

He, K., Meng, W., & Xing, X. (2023). Adversarial machine learning for network intrusion detection systems. *IEEE Communications Surveys and Tutorials, 25*(2), 1413–1451. DOI: 10.1109/COMST.2022.3233793

Katagiri, N. (2022). Two explanations for the paucity of cyber-military, cross-domain operations. *Journal of Cybersecurity, 8*(1), tyac002. Advance online publication. DOI: 10.1093/cybsec/tyac002

Konsta, A.-M., Lluch-Lafuente, A., Spiga, B., & Dragoni, N. (2024). Survey: Automatic generation of attack trees and attack graphs. *Computers & Security, 137*, 103602. DOI: 10.1016/j.cose.2023.103602

Kosenkov, A. (2016). Cyber conflicts as a new global threat. *Future Internet, 8*(3), 45. DOI: 10.3390/fi8030045

Lin, H. (2012). Cyber conflict and international humanitarian law. *International Review of the Red Cross, 94*(886), 515–531. DOI: 10.1017/S1816383112000811

Lucas, G. R. (2017). Ethics and cyber warfare. In Allhoff, F., Henschke, A., & Strawser, B. (Eds.), *Routledge handbook of ethics and war.*, DOI: 10.4324/9781315509730-28

Miller, C. (2007). The legitimate vulnerability market: The secretive world of 0-day exploit sales. *Proceedings of the 6th Workshop on the Economics of Information Security*. DOI: 10.2139/ssrn.1009125

Nobles, C. (2024). The weaponization of artificial intelligence in cybersecurity: A systematic review. *Procedia Computer Science, 239*, 547–555. DOI: 10.1016/j.procs.2024.06.206

Orend, B. (2014). Fog in the fifth dimension: The ethics of cyber-war. In Floridi, L., & Taddeo, M. (Eds.), *The ethics of information warfare* (pp. 3–24)., DOI: 10.1007/978-3-319-04135-3_1

Pinto, A., Gonçalves, G., Ferreira, J. C., & Tovar, E. (2023). Survey on intrusion detection systems based on machine learning techniques for critical infrastructure protection. *Sensors (Basel), 23*(5), 2415. DOI: 10.3390/s23052415 PMID: 36904618

Robinson, M., Jones, K., & Janicke, H. (2015). Cyber warfare: Issues and challenges. *Computers & Security, 49*, 70–94. DOI: 10.1016/j.cose.2014.11.007

Sarker, I. H., Janicke, H., Mohsin, A., Gill, A., & Maglaras, L. (2024). Explainable AI for cybersecurity automation, intelligence and trustworthiness in digital twin: Methods, taxonomy, challenges and prospects. *ICT Express, 10*(4), 935–958. DOI: 10.1016/j.icte.2024.05.007

Schmitt, M. N. (2012). Classification of cyber conflict. *Journal of Conflict and Security Law*, *17*(2), 245–260. DOI: 10.1093/jcsl/krs018

Spring, J. M., & Illari, P. (2018). Building general knowledge of mechanisms in information security. *Philosophy & Technology*, *31*(4), 555–579. DOI: 10.1007/s13347-017-0279-z

Spring, J. M., Illari, P., Luta, A., & Parkin, S. (2021). Why the attackers have the advantage: A cybersecurity thought experiment. *Science and Engineering Ethics*, *27*, 24. DOI: 10.1007/s11948-021-00288-z

Taddeo, M. (2019). Three ethical challenges of applications of artificial intelligence in cybersecurity. *Minds and Machines*, *29*(2), 187–191. DOI: 10.1007/s11023-019-09504-8

Taddeo, M., & Floridi, L. (2018). How AI can be a force for good. *Science*, *361*(6404), 751–752. DOI: 10.1126/science.aat5991 PMID: 30139858

Truong, T. C., Diep, Q. B., & Zelinka, I. (2020). Artificial intelligence in the cyber domain: Offense and defense. *Symmetry*, *12*(3), 410. DOI: 10.3390/sym12030410

Tyugu, E. (2011). Artificial intelligence in cyber defense. 2011 3rd International Conference on Cyber Conflict, 95-105. https://doi.org/DOI: 10.1109/CYCON.2011.18

Whyte, C. (2020). Problems of poison: New paradigms and 'agreed' competition in the era of AI-enabled cyber operations. 2020 12th International Conference on Cyber Conflict (CyCon), 215-232. DOI: 10.23919/CyCon49761.2020.9131717

Xu, H., Ma, Y., Liu, H.-C., Deb, D., Liu, H., Tang, J., & Jain, A. K. (2020). Adversarial attacks and defenses in images, graphs and text: A review. *International Journal of Automation and Computing*, *17*(2), 151–178. DOI: 10.1007/s11633-019-1211-x

Yan, B., Yang, C., Shi, C., Fang, Y., Li, Q., Ye, Y., & Du, J. (2023). Graph mining for cybersecurity: A survey. *ACM Transactions on Knowledge Discovery from Data*, *18*(2), 1–52. DOI: 10.1145/3610228

Zeng, J., Wu, S., Chen, H., Han, C., & Shi, Y. (2019). Survey of attack graph analysis methods from the perspective of data and knowledge processing. *Security and Communication Networks*, *2031063*, 1–16. Advance online publication. DOI: 10.1155/2019/2031063

Zhou, Y., Cheng, G., Jiang, S., & Dai, M. (2020). Building an efficient intrusion detection system based on feature selection and ensemble classifier. *Computer Networks*, *174*, 107247. DOI: 10.1016/j.comnet.2020.107247

Chapter 4
Agentic AI in Cyber Warfare:
Reassessing International Humanitarian Implications and Emerging Challenges

Jasdeep Kaur
http://orcid.org/0000-0002-5129-8703
Chitkara University, India

Sangeeta Taak
http://orcid.org/0000-0002-0383-5682
Rajiv Gandhi National University of Law, India

ABSTRACT

International Humanitarian laws (IHL) deals with the laws of the war and protects civilians and others who are not taking part in war. At the time of formulation of this law, it was believed that it will end all the wars and peace will become the rule in all nations. However, with the advancement of technology especially Agentic AI and its use in cyber warfare, the laws of IHL seems lagging far behind and demands rethinking in relation to cyber operations. The present study while conceptualizing Agentic AI and Cyber warfare correlates them with the principles of International Humanitarian Law. The study highlights the challenges posed by Agentic AI in cyber warfare along with emphasizing the impact of case studies in light of International Humanitarian Law. By focussing on lack of international regulatory provision with regard to use of Agentic AI in cyberwarfare, the research presents stance of international., national and regional policies in this regard. Finally, the study suggests about novel aspect of the extending the principles of IHL to the Agentic cyberwarfare.

DOI: 10.4018/979-8-2600-0413-5.ch004

INTRODUCTION

Agentic AI is a type of autonomous system that is programmed to undertake tasks, collaborate, and achieve complex goals with little human intervention. Unlike traditional AI that needs structured instructions and close supervision, Agentic AI is flexible, has advanced decision-making capabilities and is self-sufficient, enabling it to act dynamically in changing environments. Artificial Intelligence (AI) was rooted in the Large Language Models ("LLMs") and other advanced machine learning algorithms that were "trained" on "vast datasets" to understand human language and respond. Agentic AI is able to "stand-alone" LLMs and use the potential to interact with external systems without human instructions (Ahronheim, 2021). Agentic AI has an ability to repossess real-time information, access databases, interact with other software tools, and take initiative based on such context (Pushpalatha et al., 2025).

With the advent of AI and more recently Agentic AI, the creativity has extended starting from facial recognition to autonomous weapons and cyber warfare (Suleyman & Bhaskar, 2023). Agentic AI has had a major effect on cyber warfare. Unlike traditional cyber tools, agentic AI driven autonomous systems can identify targets, launch attacks, and adapt strategies in real time. Agentic cyber warfare attacks digital systems like critical infrastructure, government networks, financial systems or military command and control. Espionage, sabotage, denial of service attacks, electronic power grids, propaganda attacks and data theft are some of the examples of use of Agentic AI. While states have the legal right to defend themselves, the welfare of all persons, both civilians and combatants are required to be given priority even if drastic measures are taken to protect national interests. But the decentralised and anonymised character of digital operations based on agentic AI makes it extremely difficult to identify the perpetrators with sufficient certainty ultimately triggering responsibility under international humanitarian law.

Conceptualising Artificial Intelligence, Agentic Artificial Intelligence, And Cyber Warfare

The term 'artificial intelligence' is the endeavour to empower computers to do jobs traditionally performed by humans. It denotes a computer's capacity to perform tasks typically requiring human intelligence (Bode & Huelss, 2022). It pertains to codes and algorithms capable of doing complex activities formerly deemed limited to humans. The algorithms driving AI employ several models, including deep learning, natural language processing, computer vision, intelligent automation, neural networks, and sensors, to execute jobs with apparent human accuracy (Osimen et al., 2024). It is a burgeoning and swiftly advancing domain of science and technology (Russell and Norvig, 2010). The notion of artificial intelligence is not novel. It originated in the 1950s and 1960s with the advent of computers (Warwick, 2012). In 1950, computer pioneer Alan Turing devised an imitation game posing the issue, “Can a machine think?” sometimes referred to as the 'Turing Test' (Suleyman & Bhaskar, 2023) and perceived that computers can think like humans. (Warwick, 2012). Further, a renowned mathematician Richard Bellmen emphasised the role of artificial intelligence having human capability to resolve the pertinent and problematic issues (Russell & Norvig, 2010). From the time of Turing, till today, the capability of AI has increased to a substantial extent (Mollick, 2024) (Guyonneau & Le Dez, 2019).

The concept of Agentic AI: Agentic AI, which has its origins in conventional AI research on intelligent agents, has significantly changed with the advancement of machine learning, reinforcement learning, and huge language models (Ahronheim, 2021). Agentic AI is considered as appropriate for complicated and dynamic real-world applications because it gives systems the ability to plan, reason, and act proactively (Pushpalatha et al., 2025). These systems are made to function somewhat independently, using sensors or data inputs to sense their surroundings, sophisticated algorithms to interpret information, and behaviours that are in line with predetermined goals. Agentic AI is trained or programmed to accomplish specific goals, sometimes using hierarchical planning to break up complex tasks into simpler ones. This includes techniques like reinforcement learning, where agents learn optimal behaviours through trial and error and are rewarded for successful outcomes (Mustafa, 2025). Adaptability to make informed decisions enhances this framework even further (Saripalli & Yeshwanth, 2025). Agentic AI systems constantly engage with their surroundings and modify their actions in response to input (S. Guenat et al., 2022). Thus, Agentic AI is engineered for dynamic, autonomous activities (Nawaz, 2024). The most important thing about agentic AI is not how well it works technically, but how well it can show autonomously an attacker's intent, weighing different defensive strategies based on the organization's risk tolerance, and taking coordinated defensive actions that go beyond its explicit incident response protocols (Devagiri, 2026).

Cyber Warfare: Cyber warfare denotes military operations that predominantly utilise computer systems and networks to attack the opponent (Woltag, 2015). It encompasses both offensive and defensive tactics related to the risks of cyber-attacks, espionage, and sabotage. Cyberwarfare is characterised as “actions by a nation-state to infiltrate another nation's computers or networks to inflict damage or disruption.” However, alternative definitions encompass non-state actors, including terrorist organisations, corporations, political or ideological extremists, hacktivists, and transnational criminal entities also with in its purview (Collings, 2012). The International Committee of the Red Cross (ICRC) characterises cyber warfare as “a means and methods of warfare involving cyber operations that constitute or occur within the context of an armed conflict, as defined by International Humanitarian

Law (IHL)." As per the definition, cyber warfare primarily comprises of cyber actions which are conducted during an armed conflict (Bokil, 2023).

Methodology

The present study mainly adopts a qualitative doctrinal research methodology supported by analytical examination of humanitarian principles, comparative legal analysis and case study analysis. Since the research examines the intersection between agentic AI, cyber warfare and international humanitarian law, the methodology is largely theoretical and policy oriented rather than empirical., The research critically analyses the existing legal frameworks in order to access the applicability of agentic AI enabled cyber warfare with emphasis on international humanitarian law principles. The research applies the analytical method to analyse the issues and challenges of agentic AI with reference to humanitarian law. Further, the study relies on the case study methods to establish how modern cyber operations have gradually evolved towards agentic AI. The study compares and evaluates the policy frameworks to access the current regulatory framework and its applicability to international humanitarian law with respect to agentic AI.

Research Gap

The present research addresses several significant research gaps existing in the contemporary literature relating to agentic AI, cyber warfare and international humanitarian law. Since Agentic AI is an emerging field, limited academic literature can be found on intersection of agentic AI, cyber warfare and humanitarian law. The existing studies are more focussed on the autonomous weapons, artificial intelligence, generative AI and cyber warfare under the international law. There is limited research establishing connection between agentic AI, cyber warfare and international humanitarian law.

There is insufficient research examining whether the traditional principles such as proportionality, distinction, humanity etc, can be extended to autonomous AI driven cyber warfare system. The legal application of international humanitarian law to non-kinetic autonomous cyber operations remains underdeveloped.

Many studies fail to analyse how modern cyber operations increasingly demonstrate characteristics of agentic AI as the studies are more focussed on the malware attacks, espionage, infrastructure attacks rather than linking the attacks to the agentic behaviours.

There exists no comprehensive legal scholarship specifically examining the application of international humanitarian law principles to agentic AI enabled cyber warfare despite of the emerging threats of agentic AI in cyber warfare and insufficiency of humanitarian law to tackle the associated risk.

INTERNATIONAL HUMANITARIAN LAW AND AGENTIC AI CYBER WARFARE: KEY CONFLICTS AND CHALLENGES

Artificial intelligence has extended its ambit with the help of Agentic AI which in turn is increasingly used in cyber warfare (Kasapoğlu & Kirdemir, 2019). Through the use of Agentic AI, the nations are targeting critical infrastructure of other nations either through water, electricity, air or such of these systems (Hruza & Cerny, 2017). Cyber warfare today not only includes the use of autonomous weapons but involve misinformation through voice imitation of political leaders on massive and strategic scale through the use of agentic AI (Daudu et al., 2023). These kinds of acts raise questions of international security and issue of protection of civilian population under international humanitarian law as these attacks can cause disruption of essential services and collateral damage. Moreover, the states rarely reveal their existing or developing offensive and defensive cyber warfare capabilities which make the situation even worse (Diamond, 2014).

Further, agentic AI may miscalculate the territory as inherently it is interconnected with the computer networks of different nations often overlapping or extending into each other. This interconnectedness complicates the process of defining the sovereign territory in case of attack. Resultantly it affects the state autonomy (United Nations Office for Disarmament Affairs, 2024). The issue is grave in those territories where the conflict of border land dispute is involved as agentic AI cannot distinguish between the territories of dispute. For instance, the map of China shows the eleven states of India are part of China's territory which in fact is denied by India as a nation. This, further blurs the lines of territorial sovereignty in the digital realm, as there is no clear boundary for Agentic AI.

In addition, the growing dependence on sophisticated agentic AI systems leads to the "black box" phenomenon, where algorithms lack transparency and interoperability, making it challenging or even impossible for developers or operators to comprehend the rationale behind the conclusion or prediction of advance AI systems. It can affect decision-making, can hinder investigations into illegal actions or incidents, and can undermine confidence between nations (Archarya et al., 2025).

Further, there is an issue of binding legal framework for dealing with cyber warfare combined with Agentic AI. There is no consensus as to the applicability of international criminal law or international law on human rights to agentic AI enabled cyber warfare. Even though the reference can be made of the Geneva Convention Additional Protocol I, Article 36, yet it specifically does not provide for agentic AI cyber warfare (International Committee of the Red Cross (ICRC), 2004). Even though it considers certain weapons like landmines, booby traps, laser guns etc. as prohibited weapons during war (autonomous weapons), it does not provide explicit answers to the questions raised with regard to use of Agentic AI. It gives an opportunity to nations to avoid any kind of liability (Feyissa et al., 2025). It thus raises legal and ethical issues regarding the use of modern agentic AI warfare (Osimen et al., 2024).

Conflicts and Challenges of Agentic AI Cyber Warfare in relation to International Humanitarian Law: The primary legal framework for ensuring humanitarian protection and mitigating the adverse impacts of warfare is International Humanitarian Law (IHL), also referred to as the law of armed conflict (LOAC), which primarily comprises the four Geneva Conventions of 1949, the two Additional Protocols of 1977, and relevant customary IHL. According to common Article 2 of the Geneva Conventions, the enforcement of these regulations is dependent on the presence of an armed conflict, which typically necessitates a certain level of violence, defined as "the resort to armed force" in a pivotal ruling by the International Criminal Tribunal for the Former Yugoslavia (ICTY, 1995).

The incorporation of Agentic AI into armed and non-armed conflicts poses significant ethical., strategic, and legal dilemmas as far as International Humanitarian Law is concerned (Johnson, 2020). As far as the armed conflicts are concerned, the proponents contend that these technologies can augment military capabilities, refine decision-making processes, and potentially decrease civilian casualties. Conversely, critics express apprehension regarding the possibility of agentic AI functioning outside human oversight, intensifying existing power disparities, and obscuring accountability in conflict (Payne, 2018; Pum, 2024). The main risk resides in implementing a system devoid of adequate monitoring, recording, and controls (Nir, 2025).

Its fundamental principles that is distinction, proportionality, and humanity represent the challenges including algorithmic bias, diminished human oversight, and difficulties in accountability. Since agentic AI acts through autonomous systems, it may breach the principle of distinction by erroneously recognising combatants and civilians, whereas cyber warfare complicates evaluations of proportionality and the attribution of culpability (Ojha, 2025). In case of non-armed conflict, agentic AI can still be used by the countries to acquire secret and confidential information during the peace time. During this time, the use of Agentic AI can be made to spread misinformation. Further the question which can be raised with regard to use of Agentic AI in non-war situation is whether the consequent act can be considered as a violation of international humanitarian law if it has impacted the nation or its people as a whole. To understand these humanitarian issues, there is a need to understand different fundamental principles of international humanitarian laws in relation to cyber warfare and Agentic AI.

The principle of humanity and military necessity is based on the protection and security of civilians in the armed conflict (Coppi et al., 2021). Although the applicability of these principles has traditionally helped in the limiting the sufferings of the civilians and combatants, however, the application of these principles in digital domain of agentic AI presents greater challenges (ICRC, 2023). Further as agentic AI system works on the basis of interconnected networks involving civilians and military objectives, the distinction becomes obscure which in turn increases the damage and civilian casualties.

The principle of impartiality or neutrality is based on no discrimination, inflicting proportion harm and acting as per the accepted norms and principles. Under International Humanitarian Law, this principle tries to avoid arbitrary targeting, protect people from unnecessary suffering, and guarantee that choices are driven by justice rather than prejudice or strategic bias. In the context of emerging technologies such as Agentic AI, maintaining neutrality becomes increasingly challenging, as autonomous systems may operate on algorithmic patterns that inadvertently reproduce bias, thereby creating risks of disproportionate harm and undermining the fundamental obligation to act in accordance with accepted international legal standards.

The principle of proportionality forbids an attack that would be excessive in comparison to the anticipated concrete and direct military advantage and could result in accidental human casualties, civilian injuries, civilian property damage, or a combination of these. All parties to the conflict are required to take all feasible steps to assess and ensure respect for the principle of proportionality. As per the principle, it is necessary to weigh the projected military advantage against the predicted collateral damage to protected persons or civilian items before attacking a military target (Gisel, 2016). However, this is particularly challenging in case of agentic AI enabled intrusions as they may have chain reaction impacts on interconnected systems (Smail, 2024).

The issue of accountability is particularly problematic with Agentic AI due to its independent operational nature. The question of accountability become highly complex in the situations where autonomous AI works independently (Hua, 2019).

HUMANITARIAN IMPACTS AND EVOLUTION OF AGENTIC AI IN CYBER WARFARE: SOME CASE STUDIES

The growing use of adversarial cyber operations and (dis)information campaigns, which aim to influence or coerce an enemy's civilian population rather than directly fighting its military forces, is an example of how new digital technologies help persistent, low intensity irregular conflict. (Biggio, 2025). This phenomenon certainly has major implications for the civilian population and can cause significant damage without the need to use kinetic force (Lahmann, 2022).

The global surveillance techniques and the increasing integration of intelligence from varied sources create a global and eventually insurmountable sense of insecurity especially in the cases of cyber operations that allow for continuous presence in hostile networks; chiefly for intelligence-gathering purposes. It potentially involves the copying of sensitive and personal information from civilian populations of states or to prepare the battlefield. These things are happening in peacetime and are helping accelerating an ongoing blurring of lines and a state of quasi- or near-conflict between countries. The persistent activity can have serious effects on civilian populations, especially due to espionage that leaks personal data or network intrusions that unintentionally damage vital civilian infrastructure, particularly if the hostile state uses indiscriminate offensive cyber weapons like self-propagating malware.

These systems may autonomously optimise toward unexpected aims due to misaligned or inadequately defined goals. Failure modes encompass reward hacking, specification gaming, and goal mis-generalization (the pursuit of objectives that diverge from the original purpose in fresh settings), which present risks if unaddressed. Agentic AI models frequently exhibit internal opacity, complicating control even for their developers. This opacity hinders efforts to guarantee alignment with human values and responsibility in AI systems. (Bellogín et al., 2025).

For example, the Gospel system independently generates targeting recommendations for structures and facilities, such as nuclear sites, oil installations and Revolutionary Guard headquarters, within Iran. It uses satellite imagery, communications data and human intelligence from a variety of sources, analysing and cross-referencing them to locate sites used by militant operatives. Lavender, another AI-powered database used by Iran can peep in to vast troves of surveillance data, including social connections and location history, to find potential targets. AI systems also helped Israel in exploring cellular and communications networks of the Iranian senior leadership, which resulted in the targeted killing of Khamenei and many top Iranian officials in central Tehran (Wullman, 2026).

Five months after Indian Army and PLA troops engaged in combat in the Galwan Valley, Mumbai experienced a significant power outage in October 2020 that disrupted hospitals, stopped rail services, and closed financial exchanges. The interruption was attributed to RedEcho, a Chinese state-sponsored organization that had infiltrated ten Indian power sector organizations, including four of the five Regional Load Despatch Centers. The same threat actor attacked the electricity infrastructure of Ladakh in April 2022 (Patil & Wadhwa, 2026).

The UK Guardian reported that the Israel Defence Forces IDF has developed a new AI-based technology that has helped identify some 37,000 potential targets associated with Hamas. The investigation suggests the IDF approved the killing of a large number of Palestinian civilians, particularly in the first weeks and months of the conflict (Ynet, 2024). In 2014, the intrusion of internet and attack on 'Sony' shocked everyone. For the first time (apart from small-scale ransomware attacks against individual users), it seemed that a big company had changed its business plans due to an act of coercion via cyberspace. The detailed case is mentioned as under:

Sony Cyberattack: Humanitarian Considerations and Early Signs of Agentic AI

On November 24, 2014, Sony experienced a server intrusion that caused their Internet connection to be cut off and exposed hundreds of documents, including emails from celebrities and high-level officials as well as private business information about future projects. A frightening neon skeleton from the "Guardians of Peace" (GOP) showed up on Sony computer screens on the same day. Additionally, the attack completely erased a number of hard discs. A few days later, the hackers began disclosing confidential Sony information online, a practice known as "doxing." The hackers used file-sharing hubs to dump many Sony films, senior executives' internal communications, financial documents, movie contracts, personal details about famous stars, and employee health records. The tale was kept alive for weeks by these releases, which were made in instalments rather than all at once.

On December 5, Sony employees received a menacing note threatening to physically hurt them if they did not sign a condemnation of the company. The GOP then disowned the note that seemed to be from them. The GOP explicitly demanded on December 8 that Sony should refrain from publishing 'The Interview'. This note served as the initial connection to the humorous movie that mocks and eventually assassinates North Korean leader Kim Jong Un, paving the way for the nation's democratic revolution. With a warning to "Remember the 11th of September 2001," the GOP subtly threatened to attack theatres where 'The Interview' was set to premiere on December 16 (Steinberg et al., 2021). These events significantly expanded the discussion surrounding the Sony hack to include both free speech and counterterrorism (DeSimone & Horton, 2017).

The FBI asserted that there was no reliable proof of terrorist threats connected to the movie's distribution. However, big theatre chains declined to screen the movie, citing worries over customer safety. On December 17, Sony made the decision to halt the release, it seemed that a big company had changed its business plans due to an act of coercion via cyberspace.

North Korea was almost immediately suspected by investigators at Sony and the US government. Along with other damning forensic data, they discovered startling similarities to malware employed in other alleged North Korean attacks on South

Korean and US targets. However, North Korean government denied all the allegations (Sullivan, 2016).

Even though on the face of it, Sony attack looks like conventional cyber attack, it demonstrates the early characteristics of Agentic AI. The connection emerges from the ability to sustain prolonged infiltration, coordinate the sequential acts, dynamically adapt the pressure tactics depicting future AI driven cyber operations where system adjust and adapt as per the response of the target. This incident further highlights that the use of Agentic AI for executing threats by infiltrating the system during the peace period cannot be recognised as cyber warfare under the present humanitarian principles. It provides a wakeup call to amend the humanitarian law of cyber warfare in reference to Agentic AI.

Stuxnet Virus: Humanitarian Considerations and Foundation of Agentic AI

In order to understand more, the new virus named "Stuxnet" has also infected the computers in 2010. It also targeted Iran particularly. The details are mentioned as under:

A new virus that had infected computer systems all across the world was found in 2010 by a number of independent technology researchers. Although viruses in various forms have existed since the early days of the Internet, experts were particularly interested in virus because it demonstrated special functions and a level of sophistication never seen before (Alvarez, 2015).

This worm, known as "Stuxnet," displayed a number of intriguing characteristics, such as a particular attack vector that was restricted to specific computers operating in a rather unusual manner. Although the worm quickly spread over the world, infecting tens of thousands of computers, its purpose remained a mystery (Singer, 2015).

The early reports indicated that this worm was meant to interfere with satellite telecommunications and other computer-controlled infrastructure systems, no clear connection was found between the virus's capabilities and those particular systems. But after a few months, it became clear that Iran was the virus's precise geographic target. There was a disproportionate amount of compromised computer systems in that nation. Although the virus spread throughout the world, no obvious harm was known to have happened anywhere else. Eventually, it became clear that the virus was exclusive to a nuclear "research" facility in the state of Iran as the computer code it carried was decrypted (Lucas, 2017).

The Stuxnet virus was a weapon that interfered with the functioning of gas centrifuges that produced highly enriched uranium, a crucial component in the production of nuclear weapons.

The virus was able to destroy over 900 centrifuges in a matter of months, delaying Iran's uranium enrichment program by several years. Despite the small list of candidates, it is still unknown who carried out this attack. It is evident that this virus was incredibly accurate in hitting a particular target while causing almost little harm to any other computer systems. The damage caused was restricted to the attack's goals, and no injuries were reported.

Researchers are unsure if the virus has any other purposes, but thus far, its effects have been precise and have no unintended consequences. As more information about the virus becomes available, security professionals and the general public view it as a turning point in the increasing complexity of cyberwarfare (Matisoft Cyber Security Labs).

The significance of Stuxnet in relation to Agentic AI lies in its capacity to make autonomous decisions based on the analysis of the environment. Human intervention was not required to guide at each stage of the attack as it continues with the predefined objects. Thus, it closely reflects modern agentic AI systems which operates on the basis of perceived environment, minimal human intervention for continued actions.

Ukraine Power Grid Attack: Humanitarian Perspectives and Agentic AI through Semi- Autonomous System

The reference can also be made to world's first successful cyber attack in order to know the humanitarian implications that require consideration in the wake of Agentic AI and cyber warfare. The details are as under:

Sandworm, an online agent undertook a series of attacks on Ukraine power grid between December 23rd, 2015 to December 17th, 2016 (Pollard, 2024). The disruption was made by disabling the substations of the power grid which were responsible for providing electricity to the localities. It all started with a fierce campaign on corporate employees of power companies led by pretending leaders of Ukraine to open emails with word, excel or power point attachments (Cherepanov & Lipovsky, 2016). The attachment in fact was containing 'BlackEnergy', a toolkit which was designed to infiltrate the computer system without being detected. The result was access to the file operating systems, passwords, networks, windows, hardware. After gaining the access it installed remote desktop, update malware and destroy the system (Assante, 2016). The main goal of this exercise was to find out the user who has remote access to the actual electrical side of company and forge the creditors. After obtaining that control, Sandworm finally targeted electrical grid (Buchanan, 2022). Lastly, the power supply was cut down with no access to manual starting, wiping disk of important system file (Cherepanov, 2016) and preventing operating system from initializing computer (Zetter, 2016a).

Current International Humanitarian Law does not specifically prevent attacks against electric power grids, with the exception of nuclear power plants and hydro-electric dams. Instead, there are broad regulations put in place post-Second World War, when access to electricity for civilian use was a luxury, not a need, in many parts of the world (Sullivan, 2024). These attacks were not military offensives, but timed to coincide with the beginning of winter. The expected result and possibly the goal was to cast residents into darkness and poverty, with winter as an instrument. This behaviour does not comply with any relevant legal standards under International Humanitarian Law (Mastri, 2024). Power grids and district heating plants that have been constructed for the purpose of providing warmth and light to the civilian population are not military targets. The civilian casualties from these strikes are so great that they outweigh any conceivable military advantage and so breach the principle of proportionality. The deliberate use of cold and darkness to demoralise demonstrates a willingness to terrorise, which is explicitly prohibited by the laws of war (Adamski et al., 2025).

The relationship between the incident and Agentic AI lies in the increasing automation. The malware was not merely executing the static directions, it operated through the coordinated and adaptive system which is the basic feature of modern agentic AI system. This incidence depicts the transition from conventional hacking to semi-autonomous system setting a stage for the beginning of Agentic AI.

SolarWinds Supply Chain Attack: Humanitarian Perspectives and Transition towards Agentic AI

The attack on consumers without the knowledge was made through a malware in SolarWinds Orion Software. The solar winds supply chain case is mentioned as under:

The SolarWinds supply chain was targeted for penetration in to worldwide digital infrastructure. The attack started in the year 2019 around September when cybercriminals tried and actually introduced malware through SolarWinds Orion Software without the knowledge of its consumers. The victims include the topmost organisations like Microsoft, Intel, Deloitte, Cisco including the US Department of Home Security, Justice, State, Commerce and Treasury.

Even though the malware was introduced in 2019, yet it was not discovered till 2020 leading to disclosure of sensitive information (Kruti et al., 2023). This attack makes the question of sovereignty of a nation questionable under the Humanitarian law (Coco, 2022). However, international and humanitarian law do not cover this kind of attack under their preview based on state practice and opinion juris (Anisa, 2024). It was suspected as an act of Russia government to gather intelligence (Willett, 2021). However, nothing was done due to no coverage of these kinds of attacks under the humanitarian law.

The connection of the incident with Agentic AI becomes clear through the malware's ability to operate silently, persistently and autonomously. Future agentic AI systems are likely to function precisely in the same manner. Thus, this case represents a transition towards agentic AI through intelligence autonomous cyber infiltration.

Table 1. Comparative Insights from the Case Studies (Authors Analysis)

Parameters	**Sony Cyberattack (2014)**	**Stuxnet Virus Attack (2010)**	**Ukraine Power Grid Attack (2015–2022)**	**SolarWinds Supply Chain Attack (2019–2020)**
Nature of Attack	Cyber intrusion combined with psychological intimidation and data exposure	Highly sophisticated malware targeting nuclear infrastructure	Coordinated cyberattack on critical civilian infrastructure	Supply-chain infiltration through compromised software updates
Technique Used	Data theft, system destruction, doxing, intimidation campaigns	Self-replicating worm exploiting SCADA and industrial control systems	Spear-phishing, SCADA manipulation, BlackEnergy malware and remote access operations	Trojanised software updates inserted into Orion platform
Connection with International Humanitarian Law (IHL)	Falls outside traditional armed conflict framework, exposing gaps in humanitarian regulation of cyber coercion	Raises debate on whether cyber tools causing physical destruction amount to use of force under IHL	Challenges principles of distinction and proportionality because civilian infrastructure was severely affected	Reveals inadequacy of existing IHL in addressing cyber espionage and sovereignty violations
Issues of Distinction	No clear distinction between civilian and strategic targets	Targeted a specific nuclear facility with relatively controlled effects	Civilian infrastructure became the principal target	Primarily focused on governmental and strategic networks but affected wider civilian systems
Issues of Proportionality	Psychological intimidation outweighed any legitimate objective	Damage remained comparatively limited and precise	Civilian suffering was disproportionate to any military advantage obtained	Long-term surveillance effects created disproportionate strategic vulnerabilities
Accountability Challenges	Attribution remained contested despite allegations against North Korea	Attribution widely suspected but never officially confirmed	Attribution linked to Russian-backed actors but complicated by cyber anonymity	Strong suspicions of state-sponsored espionage without definitive legal accountability

continued on following page

Table 1. Continued

Parameters	Sony Cyberattack (2014)	Stuxnet Virus Attack (2010)	Ukraine Power Grid Attack (2015–2022)	SolarWinds Supply Chain Attack (2019–2020)
Humanitarian Law Gap Identified	Existing laws inadequately address cyber-enabled intimidation during peacetime	Absence of clear legal categorisation of autonomous cyber weapons	Current humanitarian law insufficiently protects modern civilian energy dependence	International law lacks effective regulation for supply-chain cyber espionage
Broader Strategic Significance	Demonstrated that cyber coercion can influence corporate and societal decisions without conventional warfare	Marked a turning point in the evolution of cyber weapons and autonomous cyber operations	Showed how cyberattacks can be weaponised against civilian morale and national resilience	Exposed vulnerability of interconnected global digital infrastructure
Inference on Agentic AI Evolution	Illustrates early use of coordinated intelligent cyber coercion	Represents a foundational model for future autonomous cyber weapons	Reflects increasing automation in attacks against civilian infrastructure	Demonstrates the evolution of stealth-oriented intelligent cyber operations
Agentic AI Characteristics	Persistent infiltration, sequential execution, adaptive coercion strategy	Environmental awareness, autonomous activation, self-directed execution	Automated intrusion, adaptive system exploitation, infrastructure targeting	Stealth persistence, selective targeting, intelligent infiltration
Link with Agentic AI Evolution	Demonstrates early autonomous cyber coercion and behaviour-driven digital attacks	Closest early example of autonomous cyber weapon functioning independently	Shows emergence of semi-autonomous attacks against critical civilian systems	Reflects development of intelligent cyber agents capable of long-term autonomous operation

POLICY FRAMEWORKS ON AGENTIC AI IN CYBER WARFARE

At the political level, it is still challenging to get a consensus regarding the applicability of IHL to agentic AI enabled cyber operations and to further the study of how its rules should be understood. Efforts are required to regulate AI enabled cyber operations. Although, AI enabled operations have evolved across multiple layers of international, regional and national frameworks, yet the diversity of approaches reflects a fragmented regulatory landscape that struggles to keep pace with the rapid advancement of Agentic AI. A coherent governance model for AI remains indefinable due to the states adopting divergent interpretations of legal obligations and pursuing conflicting strategic interest in the digital domain. When the discussion on the information security began in the year 1998, Russia presented the resolution in UN General Assembly. Various discussions were made and six consecutive Groups of Governmental Experts were convened in 2004 to discuss the issues pertaining to information and communications in the context of international security.

Some of the policies adopted by different nations as to use of AI can be referred to for the sake of understanding the regulation related with Agentic AI in cyber warfare.

United States of America (USA) prioritize maintaining technological superiority. Even though it views autonomy as essential for deterring adversaries, yet remain cautious about fully delegating decision making to AI. The broad spectrum of state positions on AI and cyberwarfare in USA demonstrates different strategic cultures, threat perceptions, and geopolitical goals. Analysts who follow U.S. doctrine say the country is wary of giving AI full autonomy to make lethal decisions but sees autonomy as a key way to keep adversaries at bay and maintain rapid response capabilities. The United Nations Group of Government Experts (UN GGE) was formed to assess advancements in information and communication technologies concerning international security. A consortium of specialists has submitted several recommendations aimed at worldwide structuring cyberspace according to principles of sovereignty, non-intervention, due diligence, protection of essential infrastructure, cooperation, and confidence-building. The UN GGE, while not specifically addressing agentic AI, recognises some international humanitarian principles relevant to armed conflict, including as the concepts of difference, proportionality, necessity, and humanity, which are equally applicable to agentic AI. Nonetheless, its structure is constrained by its non-binding nature and the absence of practical guidelines (Klaar, 2021).

Further, the Open-Ended Working Group (OEWG) was created in USA to widen participation and stimulating discussion among a broader array of states (Gisel et al., 2020). However, like the GGE, it has also struggled to achieve consensus on basic issues such as attribution, sovereignty, and acceptable peacetime behaviour in cyberspace. Cybersecurity and Infrastructure Security Agency (CISA) is another effort in this direction. CISA, in collaboration with the Australian Signals Directorate's Australian Cyber Security Centre (ASD's ACSC) and other international and U.S. partners, released guidance for organizations on adopting agentic artificial intelligence (AI) systems (CISA, 2026). It is claimed that it will help organizations align AI risk management with existing cybersecurity frameworks and strengthen oversight as agentic AI adoption grows.

On the other hand, the EU and UK tend to revert to slightly more limited approaches emphasizing human-centred AI principles and algorithmic transparency, even as their national defense programs still seek autonomous capabilities. With in the European Union, The EU Act focuses primarily on civilian applications. However, it includes defence exemptions that allow member states to deploy AI in military contexts under different legal frameworks. EU AI Act as "the combination of the probability of an occurrence of harm and the severity of that harm". EU's policy on the Agentic AI carries risk through the use of Autonomous decision-making system of AI. EU policy also includes the nature of risk involved while using AI in case the unpredictable situation arises (CMS, 2025).

Before enacting an Agentic AI policy in the event of a cyberattack, the EU is making sure that greater accountability is established because it will involve the risk to civilians. Before fully investigating Agentic AI, the EU is posing a challenge: in the event that an Agentic AI decision goes wrong, who will be able to provide a reasonable explanation? Second, maintaining a record of every activity is a problem since autonomous systems are capable of making decisions on their own without human intervention. Thirdly, the complicated scenarios that are repeatedly presented to Agentic AI may make it harder to comprehend. It could become humanely challenging to comprehend and defend the motivation behind the acts.

The Chinese strategy is in line with their larger goals of digital governance and military modernization. They are focusing on state control, cyber sovereignty, and using AI in informationized warfare. Conversely, Russia views information control and hybrid warfare methods, including AI tools and cyber operations, as part of broader military and political efforts to break down the unity of adversaries (Saltini, 2024). Israel, who is renowned for its cutting-edge cyber units and defense technology, has embraced automation in intelligence and operational decision-making. It has declared its commitment to substantial human control in order to fulfill its international duties although it has not signed an international agreement to regulate the military use of artificial intelligence, alongside Russia (Edelson, 2023).

Although India is worried about the infrastructure attacks by other nations, however, no concrete efforts have been made by the nation in this direction. It shows its adherence to Geneva Convention and acceptance to Tallin Manual. These varying stances at the state level impede the development of coherent international standards by highlighting fundamental differences about the right level of autonomy in military systems (Arslan & Scouza, 2023). Moreover, the deployment of agentic AI could further widen the technology gap between technologically advanced states and those with limited resources, leading to increased inequality and exacerbated international conflicts and instability (Osimen, Newo, Fulani, 2024).

The Tallinn Manual 2.0 is among the comprehensive attempts to interpret the application of existing international law to cyber operations. Its analyses cover issues such as sovereignty, due diligence and conduct of hostilities (Schmitt, 2017). The Manual addresses the issue of attribution and provides that the state will be responsible if it is proved that the cyberattacks were committed by non-state actors and state was having appropriate control over the attacking group (Sweet, 2014). It further suggests to adopt the 'effects doctrine' to determine the place of occurrence of cyberattack. This doctrine maintains that an attack or cyber operation that does not originate, conclude, or materially take place in a particular state, but has major repercussions within that state, could still be regarded as an attack on its sovereign territory (Margulies, 2006). However, the Manual itself admits that the application of this doctrine is not fully settled and remains controversial, further complicating its use in practical scenarios. This ambiguity becomes particularly problematic in situations where cyberattacks spill over beyond the intended target (Schmitt, 2022). Further, the Manual falls short of addressing the challenges posed by AI-enabled weapons, particularly those with self-learning capabilities or autonomous decision-making processes (Lanzoni, 2025). However, the authors are arguing that even if Tallin manual does not create a new law, it has the capability to interpret international humanitarian law in the light of agentic AI cyber operations.

Table 2. Comparative Analysis of Policy Approaches for Agentic AI in Cyber Warfare (Authors Analysis)

Jurisdiction / Framework	Core Regulatory Approach	Position on Autonomy in Cyber Warfare	Human Oversight & Accountability	Major Concerns Highlighted	Critical Evaluation
United States of America (USA)	The USA follows a security-oriented and technologically dominant approach, focusing on maintaining strategic superiority in cyberspace and AI-enabled defence systems.	The U.S. supports the use of autonomous technologies for rapid response and deterrence but remains cautious about allowing AI to independently make lethal decisions without human involvement.	Emphasis is placed on oversight through institutions such as the UN GGE, OEWG and CISA. Human intervention is considered necessary in sensitive military operations.	Concerns include attribution of cyberattacks, protection of critical infrastructure, and balancing innovation with national security.	The U.S. approach reflects a pragmatic balance between military advancement and legal caution. However, its strategic preference for technological superiority often creates ambiguity regarding limits on military autonomy.
United Nations Group of Governmental Experts (UN GGE)	The UN GGE attempts to build international consensus regarding responsible state behaviour in cyberspace under international law.	It does not directly regulate agentic AI but recognises that humanitarian principles such as distinction, proportionality, necessity and humanity remain applicable to cyber operations.	The framework encourages state responsibility and cooperation, but lacks binding enforcement mechanisms.	Absence of universally accepted norms, political disagreements among states, and lack of practical enforcement standards.	Although normatively significant, the UN GGE remains limited because its recommendations are non-binding and dependent on voluntary state compliance.
Open-Ended Working Group (OEWG)	OEWG was established to widen participation and include broader state engagement in cybersecurity discussions.	It seeks dialogue on responsible cyber conduct but has not developed a concrete framework specifically addressing autonomous AI systems.	Accountability mechanisms remain weak due to lack of agreement on sovereignty and attribution standards.	Persistent disagreements over acceptable cyber behaviour and state responsibility in peacetime cyber operations.	The OEWG has expanded inclusivity in global cyber governance debates but has struggled to convert discussions into actionable international standards.

continued on following page

Table 2. Continued

Jurisdiction / Framework	Core Regulatory Approach	Position on Autonomy in Cyber Warfare	Human Oversight & Accountability	Major Concerns Highlighted	Critical Evaluation
Cybersecurity and Infrastructure Security Agency (CISA)	CISA focuses on operational cybersecurity governance and risk management for emerging AI systems.	It supports the controlled adoption of agentic AI systems while aligning them with cybersecurity risk management frameworks.	Strong emphasis on institutional oversight, monitoring mechanisms, and integration with existing cybersecurity safeguards.	Risks associated with rapid AI adoption, vulnerabilities in critical infrastructure, and misuse of autonomous systems.	CISA represents a practical governance model concentrating on risk mitigation rather than direct legal regulation of autonomous warfare systems.
European Union (EU)	The EU adopts a human-centric and rights-based regulatory approach primarily through the EU AI Act.	The EU accepts limited autonomous AI use but stresses that AI systems should not function entirely beyond human supervision.	Transparency, explainability, traceability, and accountability are central requirements under the EU framework.	Civilian harm, algorithmic opacity, unpredictability of AI decisions, and lack of explainability in autonomous systems.	The EU provides one of the most structured ethical AI frameworks globally. However, defence-related exemptions create uncertainty in regulating military AI systems.
United Kingdom (UK)	The UK approach largely aligns with European principles while supporting defence innovation and cybersecurity resilience.	Supports development of autonomous capabilities with emphasis on strategic control and operational supervision.	Encourages accountability and responsible innovation without completely restricting military AI development.	Risks arising from autonomous military systems and AI-enabled cyber threats.	The UK attempts to balance military competitiveness with ethical regulation, though practical implementation standards remain evolving.
China	China follows a state-centric regulatory model integrating AI governance with digital sovereignty and military modernisation.	Strong support exists for AI integration within cyber warfare and informationized military operations.	Oversight is exercised primarily through state control mechanisms rather than independent accountability structures.	Preservation of cyber sovereignty, state security, and strategic dominance in digital infrastructure.	China's framework is highly centralised and strategically focused, but concerns persist regarding transparency, civil liberties, and external accountability.

continued on following page

Table 2. Continued

Jurisdiction / Framework	Core Regulatory Approach	Position on Autonomy in Cyber Warfare	Human Oversight & Accountability	Major Concerns Highlighted	Critical Evaluation
Russia	Russia treats AI-enabled cyber operations as part of broader hybrid warfare and information control strategies.	AI and cyber tools are viewed as instruments for influencing adversaries politically, socially, and militarily.	Limited emphasis on transparency or humanitarian accountability.	Strategic destabilisation, information warfare, and political disruption.	Russia's approach reflects a geopolitical use of AI-driven cyber operations, often prioritising strategic disruption over normative regulation.
Israel	Israel integrates advanced automation and AI-assisted intelligence systems within its military and cybersecurity structure.	Strong operational use of autonomous systems exists, particularly in intelligence gathering and targeting support.	Israel publicly emphasises maintaining meaningful human oversight to comply with international obligations.	Balancing military efficiency with humanitarian compliance during operational decision-making.	Israel demonstrates one of the most technologically advanced AI-defence models, though concerns remain regarding civilian impacts and operational transparency.

continued on following page

Table 2. Continued

Jurisdiction / Framework	Core Regulatory Approach	Position on Autonomy in Cyber Warfare	Human Oversight & Accountability	Major Concerns Highlighted	Critical Evaluation
India	India presently follows a policy-driven rather than legislation-driven approach toward agentic AI and cyber warfare.	India supports AI-enabled defence modernisation but has not adopted a dedicated doctrine on autonomous cyber warfare.	Human oversight and adherence to humanitarian principles are acknowledged in policy discussions, though formal accountability mechanisms remain absent.	Cybersecurity threats, attacks on critical infrastructure, digital sovereignty, and lack of legal preparedness.	India's approach reflects strategic caution and technological ambition simultaneously. However, absence of a comprehensive legal framework creates a gap between AI adoption and regulatory readiness.
Tallinn Manual 2.0	The Tallinn Manual interprets existing international law in the context of cyber operations and armed conflict.	It indirectly applies to AI-enabled cyber operations through principles governing state responsibility and conduct during hostilities.	Attribution and state responsibility are discussed through concepts such as effective control and the effects doctrine.	Difficulty in attribution, spill-over effects of cyberattacks, and ambiguity regarding autonomous self-learning AI systems.	The Manual remains influential in cyber law scholarship, yet it was not specifically drafted for agentic AI and therefore struggles to address self-learning autonomous systems comprehensively.

FINAL OBSERVATIONS

Agentic AI represents a significant leap forward in the capabilities of artificial intelligence. However, there is also a responsibility to develop AI systems that are aligned with norms and regulations. Cyberspace is not a lawless place where people can start wars without any limits. The established rules of international law especially international humanitarian law are required to be followed in these situations as well. The use of agentic AI during an operation does not affect the determination of use of force. The Martens Clause, initially introduced in the 1899 Hague Convention II, and presently articulated in the 1977 Additional Protocol I to the 1949 Geneva Conventions states that "[i]n cases not covered by this Protocol or by other international agreements, civilians and combatants remain under the protection and authority of the principles of international law derived from established custom, from the principles of humanity and from the dictates of public conscience, is relevant in context of Agentic AI (Schmitt, 2012). The principle of Jus in Bello as established by the International Court of Justice in its 1996 ruling on nuclear weapons is also relevant to agentic AI and cyber warfare. EU, UK, USA and Tallin Manual., all of these policies deal with prime concern of the safety and security of civilians in case of Agentic AI cyberattacks. However, the need is to integrate the means that such Agentic AI attacks must comply with ethical policy, transparency, accountability and actively supported by human intelligence. Many experts have warned about the blurring of military and civilian roles in Agentic AI cyber warfare and the consequences that arise from this (Centre for International Governance Innovation, 2023). Agentic AI Cyberattacks by enemy forces have the potential to cause indiscriminate harm to interconnected civilian health care systems, attacking and hurting neighbouring regions. If Agentic AI lacks access to knowledge, this could result in irreversible damage (International Committee of Red Cross). Thus, the application of IHL is required in case of Agentic AI in order to save the civilians and military objectives from the unintended consequences and preventing damage to critical infrastructure.

There is a need to set up algorithm responsibility of the state to document how agentic AI models are trained, validated and reviewed. Further, the auditability and explainability of the model has to be ensured to determine the responsibility. International oversight mechanism or agentic AI incidents review board can be formulated to ensure transparency, verification and confidence building especially of those nations who are not involved in such kind of nefarious activities. Feasibility of an international treaty depicting lawful use of agentic AI in cyber warfare can be accessed as a viable option. Ethical considerations are required to be integrated in to legal framework as the consequences of the Agentic AI can extend far more than the traditional battlefields. For this purpose, cross disciplinary ethics committee with legal scholars, cyber security experts including stakeholders can help in providing institutional checks for the allocation and use of agentic AI models.

REFERENCES

Adamski, L., Smith, J., Brown, R., & Wilson, P. (2025, November, 3). *International humanitarian law in focus: Russia's violations and Ukraine's legitimate use of force against energy targets*, PILPG, https://www.publicinternationallawandpolicygroup.org/lawyering-justice-blog/2025/11/3/ international-humanitarian-law-in-focus-russias-violations-andukraineslegitimate-use-of-force-against-energy-targets.

Ahronheim, A. (2021, May 27). Israel's operation against Hamas was the world's first ai war. *The Jerusalem Post,* https://www.jpost.com/arab-israeli-conflict/gaza-news/guardian-of-the-walls-thefirst-ai-war-669371

Alvarez, J. (2015, February 3). *Stuxnet: The world's first cyber weapon.* Standford Center for International Security and Cooperation, https://cisac.fsi.stanford. edu/news/stuxnet

Anisa, G., & Widianingsih, F. (2024). Solarwinds attack: Stages, implications, and mitigation strategies in the cyber age. *Electronic Integrated Computer Algorithm Journal.*, *2*(1), 47–52. DOI: 10.62123/enigma.v2i1.31

Archarya, D. B., Kuppan, K., & Divya, B. (2025). Agentic AI: Autonomous intelligence for complex goals – a comprehensive survey. *IEEE Access : Practical Innovations, Open Solutions*, *13*, 18912–18936. DOI: 10.1109/ACCESS.2025.3532853

Arslan, S., & Scouza, M. (2023). Regulating Digital Weapons: Autonomous Cyber-attacks, AI Warfare, and International Humanitarian Law. *Legal Studies in Digital Age*, *2*(2), 49–60.

Assante, M. (2016, January 6). Confirmation of a coordinated attack on the Ukrainian power grid. *SANS Industrial Control Systems Security Blog*, https://www.sans.org/blog/confirmation-of-a-coordinated-attack-on-the-ukrainian-powergrid/

Bellogín, A., Giudici, P., Larsson, S., Pang, J., Schimpf, G., Sengupta, B., & Solmaz, G. (2025). *Systemic risks associated with agentic ai: A policy brief.* (ACM Europe TPC - Autonomous Systems Subcommittee). Association for Computing Machinery (ACM). https://www.acm.org/binaries/content/assets/public-policy/europe-tpc/system ic_risks_agentic_ai_policy-brief_final.pdf

Biggio, G. (2025). Regulating non-kinetic effects of cyber operations: The 'loss of functionality' approach and the military necessity-humanity balance under international humanitarian law. *Journal of Conflict and Security Law*, *30*(2), 241–263. DOI: 10.1093/jcsl/kraf008

Bokil, R. (2023). Cyber warfare: Taking war to cyberspace and its implications for international humanitarian law. *International Journal for Multidisciplinary Research, 5*(1), 1–12. DOI: 10.36948/ijfmr.2023.v05i01.1494

Centre for International Governance Innovation. (2023, January, 31). *Cyberwarfare blurs line between civilian and military targets.* https://www.cigionline.org/multimedia/cyberwarfare-blurs-line-between-civilian-and-military- targets/

Cherepanov, A., & Lipovsky, R. (2016, October). BlackEnergy - What we really know about the notorious cyber attacks [Paper Presentation]. VB Conference 2016. Denver, CO, USA. https://www.virusbulletin.com/conference/vb2016/

CMS. (2025, April 11). *Agentic AI and the EU AI Act.* CMS Legal Services EEIG. https://cms.law/en/aut/legal-updates/agentic-ai-and-the-eu-ai-act2

Coco, A., Dias, T., & Benthem, T. V. (2022). Illegal: The SolarWinds hack under international law. *European Journal of International Law, 33*(4), 1275–1286. DOI: 10.1093/ejil/chac063

Coppi, G., Jimenez, R. M., & Kyriazi, S. (2021). Explicability of humanitarian AI: A matter of principles. *Journal of International Humanitarian Action, 6*(1), 19. DOI: 10.1186/s41018-021-00096-6

Cybersecurity and Infrastructure Security Agency. (2026, May 1). *Careful adoption of agentic AI services.* U.S. Department of Homeland Security. https://www.cisa.gov/resources-tools/resources/careful-adoption-agentic-ai-services

Daudu, B. O., Osimen, G. U., & Shuaibu, K. (2023). Cyberbullying and social media: Implications for African digital space. In Lahby, M., Pathan, A.-S. K., & Maleh, Y. (Eds.), *Combatting cyberbullying in digital age with artificial intelligence* (pp. 243–253). Chapman and Hall/CRC Press.

DeSimone, A., & Horton, N. (2017). *Sony's nightmare before Christmas: The 2014 North Korean cyber attack on Sony and lessons for US government actions in cyberspace.* Johns Hopkins Applied Physics Laboratory. https://www.jhuapl. edu/sites/default/files/2022-12/SonyNightmareBeforeChristmas.pdf

Devagiri, B. R.Bharatveeranjaneya Reddy Devagiri. (2026). Agentic AI for autonomous cyber defence. *Journal of Information Systems Engineering & Management, 11*(1s, 1S), 1579–1587. DOI: 10.52783/jisem.v11i1s.14327

Diamond, E. (2014). Applying international humanitarian law to cyber warfare. In P. S. Baruch & A. Kurz (Eds.), *Law and national security: Selected issues* (INSS Memorandum No. 138, pp. 67–74). Institute for National Security Studies.

Edelson, D. (2023, July, 17). IDF uses AI in airstrikes. *Ynet Global.,* https://www.ynetnews.com/business/article/r1kngwm53

Feyissa, R., Kassahun, M., Asnake, D., Daniel, N., Gebrie, A., Terefe, S., & Endale, E. (2025). Examining Cyber Warfare in Light of International Humanitarian Law Principles. *Available at SSRN* 5807162.

Gisel, L. (2016). *The principle of proportionality in the rules governing the conduct of hostilities under inter-national humanitarian law – international expert meeting report.* 22–23 June 2016. https://www.icrc.org/sites/default /files/document/ file_list/ 4358_002_ expert _meeting_report_web_1_0.pdf

Gisel, L., Rodenhäuser, T., & Dörmann, K. (2020). Twenty Years On: International Humanitarian Law and the Protection of Civilians Against the Effects of Cyber Operations During Armed Conflicts. *International Review of the Red Cross, 102*(913), 287–334. DOI: 10.1017/S1816383120000387

Guyonneau, R., & Le Dez, A. (2019). Artificial intelligence in digital warfare: Introducing the concept of the cyberteammate. *The Cyber Defense Review, 4*(2), 103–116.

Hruza, P., & Cerny, J. (2017). Cyberwarfare. International conference KNOWLEDGE-BASED ORGANIZATION, 23(1), 155-160. DOI: 10.1515/kbo-2017-0024

Hua, S. (2019). Machine learning weapons and international humanitarian law: Rethinking meaningful human control. *Georgetown Journal of International Law, 51*, 117–146.

International Committee of Red Cross. (n.d.). *Cyber operations and harmful information* https://www.icrc.org/en/law-and-policy/cyber-and-information- operations.

International Committee of the Red Cross. (2023). *Principle of proportionality: Cyber operations during armed conflict.* https://www.icrc.org/sites/default/files/ wysi wyg/war-and-law/04_proportionality-0.pdf

International Court of Justice. (1996). *Legality of the threat or use of nuclear weapons, advisory opinion.* https://www.icj-cij.org/case/95

International Criminal Tribunal for the Former Yugoslavia. (1995). *Prosecutor v. Tadić, Decision on the defence motion for interlocutory appeal on jurisdiction (IT-94-1-A).* https://www.icty.org/x/cases/tadic/acdec/en/51002.htm

Johnson, J. S. (2020). Artificial intelligence: A threat to strategic stability. *Strategic Studies Quarterly, 14*(1), 16–39.

Kasapoğlu, C., & Kırdemir, B. (2019). *Wars of none: Artificial intelligence and the future of conflict.* Centre for Economics and Foreign Policy Studies. https://www.jstor.org/stable/resrep21050

Klaar, H. T. (2021). *The evolution of the UN group of governmental experts on cyber issues. Cyberstability Paper Series: New Conditions and Constellations in Cyber.* The Hague Centre for Strategic Studies and the Global Commission on Stability of Cyberspace.

Kruti, A., Butt, U., & Sulaiman, R. B. (2023). A review of SolarWinds attack on Orion platform using persistent threat agents and techniques for gaining unauthorized access. arxiv. https://arxiv.org/abs/2308.10294

Lahmann, H. (2022). *The future digital battlefield and challenges for humanitarian protection: A primer* (Working Paper), Geneva Academy of International Humanitarian Law and Human Rights. https://archives.geneva-academy.ch/ joomlatools-files/docman-files/workingpapers/The%20Future% 20Digital %20Battle field%20.pdf

Lanzoni, N. (2025). The role of expert groups in shaping international cyberlaw: A case study of the Tallin Manuals and international law-making. *Journal of Conflict and Security Law, 30*(3), 341–358. DOI: 10.1093/jcsl/kraf013

Lucas, G. R. (2017). *Ethics and cyber warfare: The quest for responsible security in the age of digital warfare.* Oxford University Press. DOI: 10.1093/acprof:oso/9780190276522.001.0001

Margulies, P. (2006). Sovereignty and cyber attacks: Technology's challenge to the law of state responsibility. *Michigan Telecommunications and Technology Law Review, 14*(1), 17–56. https://law.unimelb.edu.au/__data/assets/pdf_file/0006/1687488/05Margulies-Depagina ted .pdf

Matisoft Cyber Security Labs. (n.d.) *Stuxnet.* https://www.matisoftlabs.com/case-studies/stuxnet

Mollick, E. (2024). *Co-Intelligence: Living and working with AI.* Portfolio.

Nawaz, S. (2024). *Agentic AI vs AI agents: A detailed comparison.* Ampcome. Retrieved April 24, 2025, from https://www.ampcome.com/post/agentic-ai-vs-ai - agents-a-detailed-comparison.

Nir, K. (2025). Transforming cybersecurity with agentic AI to combat emerging cyber threats. *Telecommunications Policy, 49*(6), 102976. DOI: 10.1016/j.telpol.2025.102976

Ojha, Y. (2025). Artificial intelligence in armed conflict: Perspectives from international humanitarian law. *Unity Journal.*, *6*(1), 34–47. DOI: 10.3126/unityj.v6i1.75547

Osimen, G. U., Newo, O., & Fulani, O. M. (2024). Artificial intelligence and arms control in modern warfare. *Cogent Social Sciences*, *10*(1), 2407514. DOI: 10.1080/23311886.2024.2407514

Patil, S., & Wadhwa, K. (2026, April 2). *Agentic AI and India's nuclear security: Threat, opportunity, and doctrine.* Observer Research Foundation. https://www.orfonline.org/expert-speak/agentic-ai-and-india-s-nuclear-security-threat-opportunity-and-doctrine

Payne, K. (2018). Artificial intelligence: A revolution in strategic affairs. *Survival*, *60*(5), 7–32. DOI: 10.1080/00396338.2018.1518374

Pollard, M. (2024). A case study of Russian cyber-attacks on the Ukrainian power grid: Implications and best practices for the United States, *Pepperdine. Policy Review*, *16*, 1–25.

Pum, M. (2024). Autonomous weapons systems: ethical concerns and international regulation in the use of AI in military applications. University of Chicago. https://www.researchgate.net/publication/387383028_Autonomous_Weapons_Systems_Ethical_Concerns_and_International_Regulation_in_the_Use_of_AI_in_Military_Applications

Russell, S., & Norvig, P. (2010). *Artificial intelligence: A modern approach* (3rd ed.). Pearson.

Saltini, A. (2024). Navigating cyber vulnerabilities in ai enabled military systems. European Leadership Network. https://europeanleadershipnetwork.org/commentary/navigating-cyber-vulnerabilities-in-ai-enabled-military-systems/

Saripalli, S., & Yeshwanth, P. (2025, August 5). *Agentic AI and cybersecurity: Challenges and key consideration.* PwC India. https://www.pwc.in/blogs/agentic-ai-and-cybersecurity-challenges-and-key-considerations.html

Schmitt, M. N. (2012). International law in cyberspace: The Koh Speech and Tallinn Manual juxtaposed. *Harvard International Law Journal*, *54*, 13–37.

Schmitt, M. N. (Ed.) (2017). Tallinn manual 2.0 on the international law applicable to cyber operations. Cambridge University Press.

Singer, P. W. (2015). Stuxnet and its hidden lessons on the ethics of cyberweapons. *Case Western Reserve Journal of International Law*, *47*(1), 79–86.

Smail, B. (2024). Cyberattacks between the strategic and humanitarian implications and legal and ethical challenges. *Aabhath Review*, 9 (2) 277, 275-83.

Steinberg, S., Stepan, A., & Neary, K. (2021). *The hacking of Sony Pictures: A Columbia University case study.* School of International and Public Affairs, Columbia University, https://www.sipa.columbia.edu/sites/default/files/2022-11/Sony%20-%20Written% 20 Case.pdf.

Suleyman, M., & Bhaskar, M. (2023). *The coming wave: Technology, power and the twenty-first century's greatest dilemma.* Crown.

Sullivan, C. (2016). The 2014 Sony hack and the role of international law. *Journal of National Security Law and Policy, 8*, 437–468.

Sullivan, J. E., & Kamensky, D. (2024). Putin's power play: Russia's attacks on Ukraine's electric power infrastructure violate international law. *The Electricity Journal, 37*(2), 107371. DOI: 10.1016/j.tej.2024.107371

Sweet, C. (2014). Tallinn Manual on the International Law Applicable to Cyber Warfare. Europe-Asia Studies, 66(4), 669–670. https://doi.org/. 2014 .897423.DOI: 10.1080/ 09668136

The Stuxnet Virus. Case study. https://www.afahc.ro/ro/erasmus/DDHE/Courses/Information%20Warfare/case_study_5__the_stuxnet_virus.html

United Nations Office for Disarmament Affairs. (2024). *ICT security.* United Nations. https://disarmament.unoda.org/ict-security

Warwick, K. (2012). *Artificial Intelligence: The basics.* Routledge.

Willett, M. (2021). Lessons of the SolarWinds hack. *Survival, 63*(2), 7–26. DOI: 10.1080/00396338.2021.1906001

Woltag, J. C. (2015). Cyber Warfare. In *Max Planck encyclopedia of public international law* (pp. 231690–e280). Oxford University Press., https://opil.ouplaw.com/display/ 10.1093/law:epil/9780199231690/law-9780199

Wullman, I. (2026, April 3). *The first AI war? How algorithms and data are reshaping the war with Iran.* Ynet. https://www.ynetnews.com/tech-and-digital/article/sjksd11 ikbg.

Ynet. (2024, April 4). *IDF's AI-based system identifies 37,000 targets, report.* https://www.ynetnews.com/business/article/b14nkao1r

Zetter, K. (2016a, January 20). *Everything we know about Ukraine's power plant hack.* Wired. January 20, 2016. https://www.wired.com/2016/01/everything-we-know-about-ukraines-powerplant-hack/

Zetter, K. (2016b, March 3). *Inside the cunning, unprecedented hack of Ukraine's power grid.* Wired. https://www.wired.com/2016/03/inside-cunning-unprecedented-hackuk raines-power-grid/

Chapter 5
Reinforcement Learning for Adaptive Cyber Attack and Defense Strategies

A. Shivaraj
http://orcid.org/0009-0001-9296-6480
Bangalore University, India

Gautam Shivaraj
http://orcid.org/0009-0000-5184-8448
Adarsh Institute of Management and Information Technology, Chamarajpet, India

G. Silambarasan
http://orcid.org/0009-0004-6233-4943
Periyar University, Salem, India

ABSTRACT

As the nature of cyber warfare evolves, traditional methods of defense and attack are increasingly being outpaced by sophisticated, adaptive threats. In this context, Reinforcement Learning (RL) presents a transformative solution by enabling autonomous systems to learn, adapt, and optimize their strategies over time. This chapter explores the application of RL to both cyber attack and cyber defense, focusing on how RL-driven agents can enhance the effectiveness, efficiency, and resilience of cybersecurity systems. By enabling continuous learning and real-time adaptation to new threats,RL agents can autonomously optimize defense strategies, and evolve offensive tactics. The chapter also examines key challenges in integrating RL into cyber warfare, such as computational complexity, adversarial vulnerabilities, and ethical concerns. Furthermore, the future of RL in cyber warfare is discussed, with a focus on scaling RL systems, improving security, the need for human oversight.

DOI: 10.4018/979-8-2600-0413-5.ch005

1. INTRODUCTION

One of the most urgent fronts in the current development of the global security has become cyber warfare. The digital era allows cyber-attacks to have widespread impacts past the national boundaries affecting not only the governmental infrastructures but also businesses, individuals, and other important national assets. The conventional ways of defending against cyber threats, like firewalls, intrusion detection system, and antivirus software, have now been found to be inadequate to deal with the constantly changing and increasingly advanced strategies employed by cyber attackers. Cybersecurity strategies have to be constantly developed, using more sophisticated, responsive, and automated response in order to be efficient. (Sharmin et al., 2026)

Reinforcement Learning (RL) is one of those solutions, and it is a subfield of machine learning in which systems, or agents, are trained to make decisions through interaction with the environment. In comparison with the rule-based systems where each action is explicitly programmed, RL allows the systems to learn through their experiences by getting feedback, i.e. rewards or penalties. These systems are enhanced with time to handle tasks and respond to the changing environment. When applied to the sphere of cyber war, RL can bring about the prospect of developing autonomous and adaptive agents that can learn to either carry out offensive cyber attacks or counter the attacks in real-time with a minimum amount of human supervision.(Sharmin et al., 2026)

Adaptive cyber defense is something that is needed in this context. Adaptive systems can be adapted to notice new or unseen threats and automatically change their courses. They may develop, depending on the feedback, and learn on the basis of the previous experiences to improve their performance with time. The reinforcement learning, as it has an ability to optimize decisions through continuous learning and feedback, provides a potent tool to structure such adaptive systems. Cyber defense systems that are built on RL are able to adjust the strategies according to the actions of attackers, and therefore they are much more effective in addressing advanced threats.

In the offensive side, RL has been used in cyber attack strategy development. With the help of RL, attackers will be able to develop adaptive and self-learning malware or an autonomous agent that will be able to detect vulnerabilities in a network and exploit them more effectively. The RL-based cyber attacks have the ability to enhance their strategies as time goes by as they constantly adapt themselves to the existing defenses posing great challenges to the conventional defense systems. Moreover, RL can assist attackers in simulating and predicting the possible results of various attack strategies and optimize them, as well as complicate their actions and make it harder to be noticed.

2. FUNDAMENTALS OF REINFORCEMENT LEARNING

Reinforcement Learning (RL) is a potent branch of machine learning in which agents are able to learn the best behavior through engaging with their environment. Contrary to the supervised learning, where a model is trained using labeled data, RL is based on environmental feedback, in the form of rewards and penalties. It is particularly applicable to the dynamic and real time situation such as a cyber warfare where the environment and the enemy terrain are constantly shifting. This section will discuss the principle underlying RL along with its major components, the most related algorithms and their applicability to the problems of cyber attack and defense.(Sharmin et al., 2026)

The following represent the important concepts in reinforcement learning.

Simply speaking, RL is an agent, an environment, and interactions between them. The agent is an independent element, which acts in the environment. The environment is seen as the outside world, which the agent acts on, and for which the agent provides feedback.

Key components of RL include:

- State (S): A state is an example of a specific configuration or condition of the environment at a specific point of time. Indicatively, in a cyber defense situation, the state may denote the present condition of a network such as whether it is compromised or not.
- Action (A): Action is a decision or act that is carried out by the agent to alter the state of environment. In cyber warfare an act may occur either as a defensive measure, as in blocking an IP address, or offensive, as in a phishing attack.(Sharmin et al., 2026)
- Reward (R): Reward is a scalar score that agent obtains after doing an action. It is a measure of the short-term advantage or disadvantage of that action, and helps the agent learn. Rewards in a defense system may be associated with the occurrence of an intrusion, and rewards in an attack environment may be the successful exploitation of a vulnerability.
- Policy (p): This is a strategy or a functioning that dictates how the agent behaves. It specifies what states should be done in which state and gives the action the agent should do in that state. It may be deterministic (xi hd) (in which case the actions depend on the same action at a specific state) or stochastic (actions are selected at random).
- Value Function (V): This is estimating of the goodness of a given state to the agent. It is the cumulative reward that is expected to be gained in that state and beyond. The RL aims to develop an optimal value-function, which results in the greatest accumulating reward.

- Q-function (Q): The Q-function also called an action-value function is an estimate of the expected sum cumulative reward of performing a given action in a given state and then pursuing the optimal policy thereafter. Many RL algorithms, specifically the Q-learning, use the Q-function.(Sharmin et al., 2026)
- Exploration vs. Exploitation: One of the most critical aspects of RL is the way in which an agent should balance between exploration (attempting to try new actions to find out that they yield better rewards) and exploitation (following the actions that have proven to be highly rewarding). This may be a trade off between discovering new attack vectors and exploiting known vulnerabilities in cyber warfare.(Hossain, 2025)

2.1 Reinforcement Learning Algorithms

Various types of RL algorithms exist, and each of them has its way of solving the decision-making problem. Some of the most popular ones are:

Model-Free vs. Model-Based RL:

Model-Free RL: Model-free RL entails the acquisition of knowledge by trial and error without creating any environment model. The agent merely acquires knowledge about the previous experiences (actions and rewards). Algorithms that are common to this category are Q-learning and Deep Q-Networks (DQN).

Model-Based RL: Model-based RL agents construct an environment model which forecasts the future behavior due to actions in terms of future states and rewards. Such models have the ability to enhance learning effectiveness particularly in an environment that is expensive to communicate with. They do need more computing power to create and update, however.

Value-Based Methods:

In value-based RL models, the emphasis is laid upon learning the value function or Q-function to make decisions. Q-learning is one of the most popular value-based algorithms and in it the agent finds the optimal Q-values in all state-action pairs and changes its policy to match them.

2.2 Applying RL in Cyber Warfare

Within the sphere of cyber warfare, RL usage can contribute to the increase of efficiency and flexibility of the systems of attack and defense to a great extent. For instance:

Adaptive Defense Systems: RL can be used to implement continuous learning of new cyber threats by cyber defense systems so that they can update their strategies in real-time. These systems have the capability of automatically modifying firewalls, blocking malicious traffic, and refining detection algorithms to suit changing tactics of attacks.

Strategies of offensive Cyber Attack: Agents based on offensive RL can autonomously search and use the vulnerabilities of the target systems. These agents can probably outdo human cyber attackers by learning how to fine-tune their strategies each time they are attacked, therefore making them more efficient and effective. (Tooki & Popoola, 2025)

Automated Decision-Making: An automation of the selection of decisions is one of the most intriguing qualities of RL in cyber warfare. In either a network defense or attack, the RL systems are capable of making decisions quicker than the human operators, which helps reduce the response time and enhance the overall performance.(Tooki & Popoola, 2025)

2.3 Challenges and Limitations

Although RL has enormous potential in cyber warfare, it also has its own drawbacks:

- Computational Complexity: RL algorithms, especially deep reinforcement learning, become computationally expensive, particularly in large scale environments, i.e. national or corporation wide.
- Security and Safety: As a result of the vulnerabilities of RL models, adversarial attacks may result in vulnerabilities of offensive and defensive systems. As an illustration, the reward mechanism may be misused by the attacker to direct the RL agent to suboptimal or harmful policies.
- Scalability: Although RL has been effectively applied in controlled settings, it has been difficult to scale it to real-life cyber warfare with dynamic and massively large systems and various attack vectors.(Tayseer Jafar et al., 2026)

3. CYBER ATTACK STRATEGIES AND ADAPTATION

Cyber-attacks in the cyber warfare are becoming more advanced, dynamic, and unpredictable. Older ways of attacking like running a set malware or exploiting vulnerabilities are usually lagged behind by the development of defense mechanisms, which constantly advance to combat such attacks. In this regard, a powerful tool to develop an adaptive cyber-attack strategy can be presented by Reinforcement Learning (RL) that can allow attackers to optimize their attacks on a real-time basis. With self-learning, RL agents will be able to adjust to changing defenses, discover new attack vectors and optimize their strategies, becoming more efficient and resistant to defenses.

3.1 Cyber-Attack Strategies

A cyber-attack is any offensive operation that is done on an information system with an aim of using loopholes, interfering with normal operations or damaging the target. Modern cyber attacks are complex in their flexibility, magnitude, and randomness. Such attacks may only be as elementary as phishing attacks, but they may equally be advanced Advanced Persistent Threats (APTs), which can go undetected over a long duration as they systematically gain access to the infrastructure and destroy the infrastructure of the target.

There are a number of challenges that cyber attackers encounter when they are executing effective operations:

Evolving Defenses: As companies continue to increase their defensive capabilities against cyber attacks, these attackers have to evolve and identify alternative vulnerabilities or strategies to overcome these defenses.

Evasion and Stealth: The attacker should be able to go through the networks without being detected until as late as possible and this implies that the attacker should continuously change his tactics in order to avoid security software such as firewalls, intrusion detection software and antivirus software.

Resource Constraints: Cyber attackers are not always unlimited as in case of conventional war. They need to utilise their energies to the best of their abilities so as to maximize the efficacy of their assault and lessen the cost of computing or operating.

3.2 Categories of Cyber Attacks That Have Been Improved by RL

The RL can be used in various forms of cyber-attacks such as:

Denial-of-Service (DoS) Attacks: DoS attack is a type of attack that targets to interrupt the normal operation of a system by flooding that system with traffic or requests. The timing and intensity of the attack can be optimized by RL to ensure that the attacker can carry out the attack without being identified and at the same time make the most of it. With constant adjustment of the attack parameters, the RL agents can have more effective DoS attacks with the minimum resource consumption.(Iturbe et al., 2026)

Phishing and Social Engineering: Phishing attack is an approach that is based on deceiving the person to reveal confidential information like the passwords. It is possible to adjust phishing techniques with RL and trial various methods to figure out which ones are most likely to be successful at duping the victim (e.g., email format, content, and timing).

Exploitation of Zero-Day Vulnerabilities: Zero-day vulnerabilities are security vulnerabilities that attackers can take advantage of and they are already unknown to the software or hardware vendor. Continuous probing of unpatched vulnerabilities in systems can be conducted by agents based on RL and makes changes according to the responses of the system.

Malware Development: Malware development can be used with RL to develop more efficient and resilient malicious software. The malware developed by RA can evolve dynamically to alter its behavior in a way that it is not detected by antivirus software, firewalls or hacks. This may lead to additional crafty and indefatigable malware infections.

Advanced Persistent Threats (APTs): APTs are cyber attacks that last over an extended duration of time and are crafted to penetrate a network and go undetected. To enhance the APT strategies, RA agents can continuously learn how the defense schemes are deployed, change the attack vectors, and enhance the capability of the malware to conceal the malware within the target system.(Alauthman et al., 2026)

3.3 Feedback Loop: Learn the Lessons of the Past Attacks

The feedback loop is at the center of the power of RL in cyber attack strategies. A standard RL setup works so that the agent becomes informed about its actions through the feedback in the form of rewards (positive feedback when successful action is taken) or penalties (negative feedback when an action fails). As part of the cyber attacks, the RL agent can:

Assess Attack Success: Once an attack has been performed, the agent is informed of the success of the attack in relation to whether the attack was successful, i. e. was it successful to infiltrate the system or steal information. The agent is rewarded in the event of successful attack and punished in the event of failure. As time passes, the RL agent undertakes the ability to refine its strategies to ensure that its success rate is maximized.

Modify Attack Policies: The RL agent changes its actions depending on the feedback. Provided that a specific way of attack has become effective, then the agent will follow the same method in the future. On the other hand, an agent will not use a strategy in future operations, where its approach to an attack method fails or is detected.

Enhance productivity: With a combination of the unlimited learning process, the RL agent can be trained to utilize the available resources in the most efficient way and produce the most positive results. To illustrate, in a DoS attack, the agent can become trained to consume reduced amount of resources (e.g. number of botnet nodes or requests) to disrupt in the same amount, which makes the attack more efficient and difficult to detect.(Yang et al., 2024)

3.4 RL-Based Cyber Attack Challenges and Risks

Although RL has tremendous potential in the context of improving cyber-attack and strategy, there are a number of issues and risks related to its application:

Computational Complexity: RL is a computationally intensive process especially with the complex attack strategies or large scale networks. Learning may be an expensive process and particularly when the agent has to search through numerous possible attack paths, as shown in figure 1.

Figure 1. Numerous Possible Attack Paths.

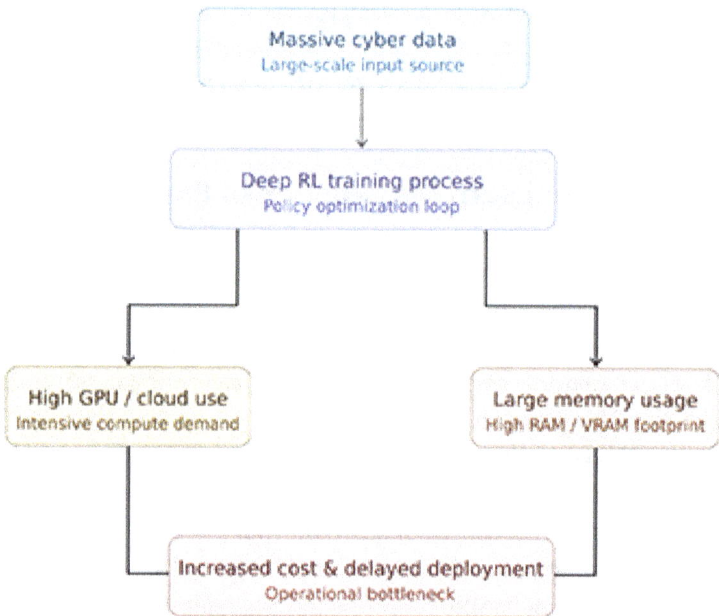

Unintended Consequences: Unintended consequences RL agents can discover strategies that were not intended by their designers. As an example, the agent might detect and use the vulnerabilities that were not initially regarded as a part of the initial attacker attack, resulting in potentially disastrous outcomes.

Defense mechanisms of adversaries: As the mechanisms of cyber defense develop, attackers employing RL will have to fight even more sophisticated mechanisms of detection. This may involve specifically designed countermeasures that would be beneficial to block RL-based attacks, e.g. scanning the indicators of deviant behavior or quick adaptation.

Ethical and Legal Concerns: RL implementation in cyber-attacks is an issue with grave ethical and legal implications. The more autonomous and efficient are cyber-attacks, the less it is human responsibility and decision-making by machines. The possibility of the RL-based attacks developing into full-scale cyber warfare or inflict a lot of collateral damage makes the question of accountability and control a concern.(Afraji et al., 2025)

4. THE CASE OF CYBER DEFENSE STRATEGIES AND REINFORCEMENT LEARNING

With the continuously increasing sophistication and scale of cyber threats, more modern and adaptive cyber attacks are proving increasingly difficult to counter with traditional defense strategies like the use of static rule-based systems, signature-based detection, and manual interventions. Never has there been such a necessity to have adaptive as well as autonomous defense systems. Defense systems have to keep up with the ever-evolving adversaries, which have become smarter and smarter, and have to continuously develop and modify strategies on the fly, analyzing new data sets. A potential solution is the use of Reinforcement Learning (RL), which allows cyber defense capabilities to adapt to the environment and learn to respond to the changing environment.(Javadpour et al., 2025)

Figure 2. illustrates how an RL-based attacker agent cycles through observing the target, selecting and executing attack actions, receiving a reward signal, and looping back to refine its strategy until the attack goal is achieved

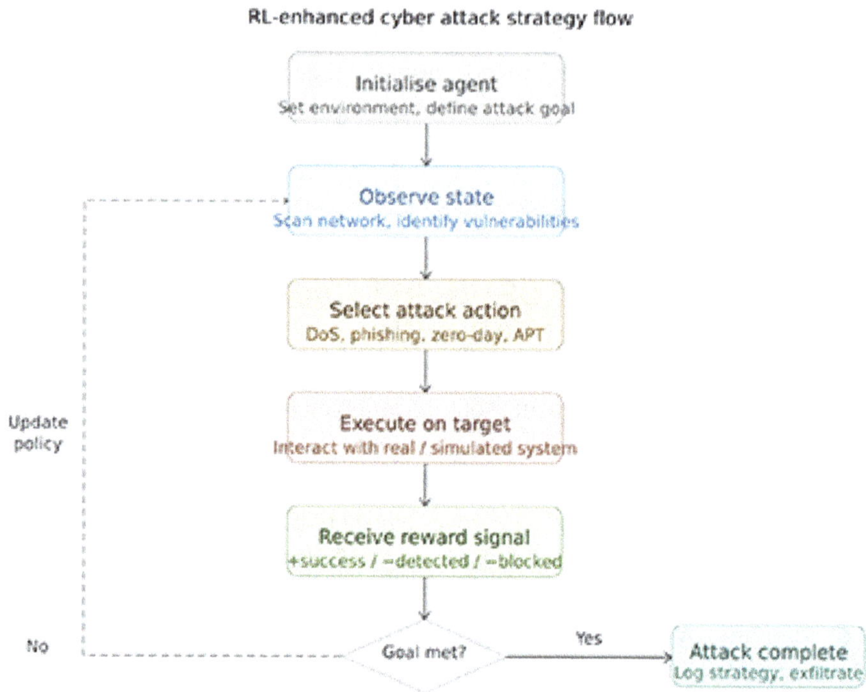

In this part, we will discuss how reinforcement learning may be used to develop better cyber defense strategies. We shall concentrate on how RL helps systems to be able to respond to new types of attacks, identify anomalies, enhance response, and develop resilient and autonomous defenses. We shall also look at the major challenges and opportunities posed by the introduction of RL into the defense systems.(Ang et al., 2026)

4.1 Recent Learning of Cyber Defense in Autonomous Systems

Cyber defense is a strategy that tries to ensure that critical information systems are not exposed to malicious activities that may compromise the integrity, confidentiality, and availability of data and services. Conventional systems of defense are based on fixed signatures and set of rules, which can be easily circumvented by advanced attackers who keep changing their strategies. Effective defense systems have to be dynamic, self-educating and able to respond automatically to new threats without necessarily involving human intervention.(Abbasi & Mohammadi, 2026)

Cyber defense strategies normally comprise:

- Intrusion Detection Systems (IDS): IDS systems are systems that observe the network traffic and identify suspicious network activity and possible intrusion.
- Intrusion Prevention Systems (IPS): It refers to systems that do not just detect but also block harmful activities like blocking harmful traffic in real time.
- Firewalls: Firewalls are systems through which the incoming and outgoing network traffic is checked and restricted according to security rules set beforehand.
- Antivirus Software: Systems, which identify and delete malicious software programs according to a signature mode or behaviour detection.

Figure 3. maps the layered architecture of an RL-driven adaptive defense system — from real-time observation and anomaly detection through to the central RL decision engine, its four response modules, and the reward feedback loop that continuously improves the agent.

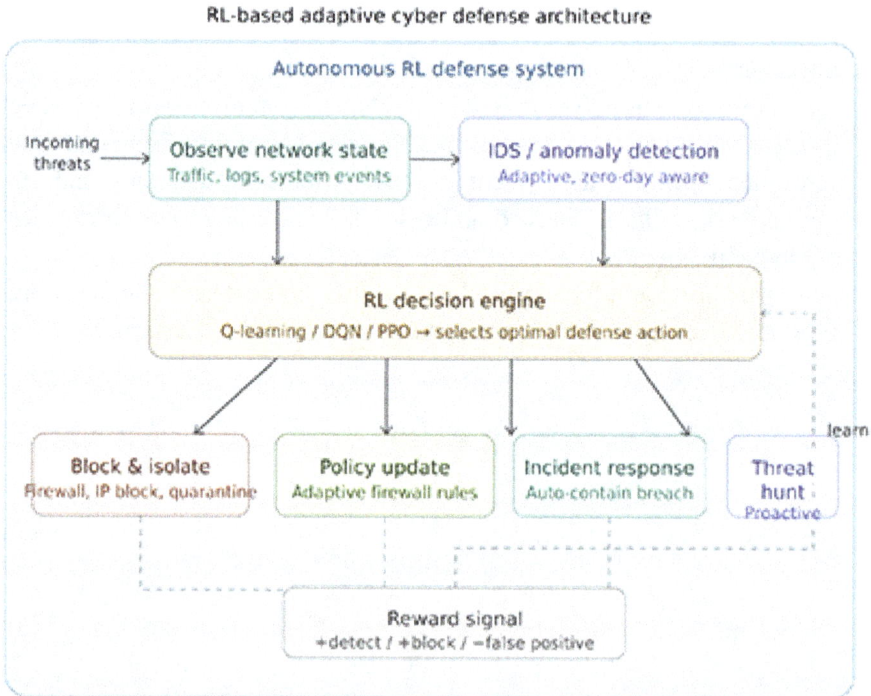

Nevertheless, such systems usually fail when faced with the ever-changing attack schemes. Hackers, particularly the ones who have used adaptive methods, have unceasingly been learning and mastering their approaches, indicating that unchanging defensive approaches are simply being surpassed. In this case, reinforcement learning may be important.(Bashir et al., 2026)

4.2 The Reinforcement Learning in Cyber Defense

Reinforcement learning presents a new method of cyber defense as systems are able to respond to new threats as they are detected. The main idea behind RL is that an agent can use the feedback (reward or penalty) to improve its decision-making with time. Cyber defense RL can be used in this context to keep track of, learn and advance the defense mechanism in an effort to keep the attacker at bay. The main ways in which RL can be used to aid cyber defense are:

Adaptive Intrusion Detection and Prevention: RL may be used to improve the IDS and IPS systems, allowing them to automatically adjust to new patterns of attack. In contrast to the conventional systems that use fixed signatures, the RL agents have the ability of scanning the incoming traffic, identifying anomaly, and changing their detection methods according to feedbacks of their previous encounters. As an example, when an attack was not identified previously, the system will modify its decision-making to detect similar patterns in the future to reduce the false negatives and enhance the detection rate.(Nadhir et al., 2025)

Live Decision Making: Manual defense systems in most cases need human operators that are able to make immediate decisions like whether to block traffic or isolate a suspicious file. Using RW defense systems are able to make independent decisions, including blocking malicious requests or isolating infected systems, depending on real-time feedback of the environment. Such decisions can be performed more quickly and with greater accuracy than can be performed by human operators, particularly in high-volume and high-speed environments.(Alshehri, 2026)

Detection of anomaly: A major advantage of using RL to cyber defense is that it can be used to identify cyber anomalies. The RS systems constantly train the typical behavior of a network or system and indicate an occurrence of abnormal behavior as a possible threat. It can come in really handy in identifying zero-day attacks as well as other advanced strategies that might not conform to known attack signatures. The RL agent can enhance its capability to detect and react to new attacks through continuous enhancement of its knowledge of what is normal.(Finistrella et al., 2025)

Adaptive Security Policy Management: RL may be attempted to streamline and dynamically scale up and down security policies in response to real-time information about attacks. As an example, an RL agent can adapt the policy according to the most efficient firewall rules or access controls against existing attack patterns. This will keep the defense system updated with the new threats and maximize its defenses without necessarily human intervention.(Vyas & Dey, 2024)

Threat Hunting and Mitigation: RL may also be utilized in the area of threat hunting in proactive mode where the computer starts working on the potential threat hunting by searching the vulnerabilities or potential threats prior to them developing into active attacks. The RL agent is able to reveal the hidden menaces, wrong settings, or vulnerabilities that might never be noticed otherwise with constant communication with the environment.

4.3 Learning Through Cyber Attacks: Feedback in Defense

With reinforcement learning, the agent learns by reacting to the feedback provided by the environment, which may be positive feedback in the form of rewards or negative feedback in the form of penalties. This feedback loop can be used in the context of cyber defense to enable the RL system to change its strategy continuously, depending on what has been experienced.(Vyas & Dey, 2024)

For example: Should the system be able to identify and counterattack an attack, the system will be rewarded, which will further encourage the strategies that resulted in the successful counterattack.The system is penalized in case an attack is missed, and the RL agent would modify its future detection and prevention policies. This is a feedback loop necessary in the creation of the adaptive defense systems, that are not only responsive to immediate threats, but learn to counter these future attacks. As time passes, the defense system will increase its effectiveness with various attack vectors, reduce response time and become more resilient.(Wang et al., 2023)

4.4 RL in Use in Cyber Defense

Reinforcement learning may be used in many aspects of cybersecurity, such as:

- Autonomous Malware Detection: RL can also be used to improve malware detection systems by enabling them to learn malware behaviors of past. To illustrate, a system designed using RL can identify strains of malware, which have never been encountered in the past, by observing the similarities between already known malware and changing to new strains.
- Network Traffic Analysis: RL agents can be applied to examine large amounts of network traffic in real-time. The RL agent can become more capable of detecting malicious behavior and preventing data breaches by observing what the normal traffic patterns are and continually updating its model.
- Autonomous Incident Response: An RL based incident response system can autonomously control the threat, locate the source and start the recovery processes without involving any human interference in the case of security breach or intrusion. This can save a lot of time in responding to and mitigating cyber incidents.
- Rogue Behavior Detection: RL is also applicable to ambivalent behavior detection in an internal system, e.g. insider threat or bad employees. Without any particular attack signature, RL can be used to identify deviations detecting potentially malicious intentions even when the pattern of system usage is unavailable.(Wang et al., 2023)

4.5 Problems With Implementing RL in Cyber Defense

Although it has potential, there are multiple challenges associated with implementation of RL in cyber defense systems:

- Computational Overhead: RL algorithms, and more so deep reinforcement learning, consume a lot of computational power especially in large scale environments like in enterprise networks. RL agents may be expensive to train, and can need hardware or cloud resources to be trained.
- Complexity of the environment: Cyber defense environment in the real world is very complex, and it is hard to simulate all scenarios that an attack could happen. It is difficult to make RL agents trained to take all the potential attack strategies and, in some cases, it can cause the failure of the agents during their real-world applications.
- Security Threats of RL-Based Defense: Despite the fact that RL can also enhance defense strategies, it can also generate new security vulnerabilities. As an example, opponents of RL can manipulate the agent because they are aware of the way the agent learns. With knowledge of the feedback mechanism, attackers could take advantage of learning process of the agent and force the agent to evolve in a way that favors the attacker (e.g., misleading the defense system or rendering the defense system weak).
- Ethical and Regulatory: Privacy and control Due to the independence of RL-based defense systems, ethical concerns of accountability and control emerge. When an RL agent chooses a wrong or harmful action, it is still not evident who will take the blame. The problem is magnified in mission critical systems like military defence or national infrastructure.(Azeroual et al., 2026)

4.6 Future of RL in Cyber Defense

Nevertheless, RL has enormous potential in cyber defense. The need to have adaptive and autonomous defense systems will continue to be on the rise as cyber threats are on the rise. The introduction of RL will not only accelerate and enhance cyber defenses but will also offer companies the means to actively seek out and eliminate threats before they can cause damage.

Future research opportunities are available in the following areas:

- Enhancements in training efficiency: The creation of more efficient algorithms of RL that are able to achieve learning with reduced interactions and where adaptation to real- world environments is accelerated.

- Adversarial resilience: The ability of RL agents to be resistant to attacks by adversarial examples and to be manipulated by the attackers in an easy way.
- Explainability: Improving the visibility of RL-based systems so that the decision-making processes can be deciphered and made credible by human operators.(Javaheri et al., 2025)

5. CHALLENGES IN INTEGRATING RL INTO CYBER WARFARE

Although Reinforcement Learning (RL) has enormous potential to improve the cyber-attack and defense methodologies in autonomous cyber warfare, its application in the real-world cyber environment poses a myriad of challenges. Such obstacles are caused by the unpredictability and intricacy of cyber warfare, the requirement of large computational resources, and the possible security threats. In this part, we will find out the major challenges in applying RL to the cyber warfare process and how these challenges can be overcome as well as what can be offered to overcome them.

Figure 4. presents a side-by-side map of the five major challenges identified in the paper (left) paired with their corresponding future research directions (right), showing the clear path from each limitation to its proposed solution.

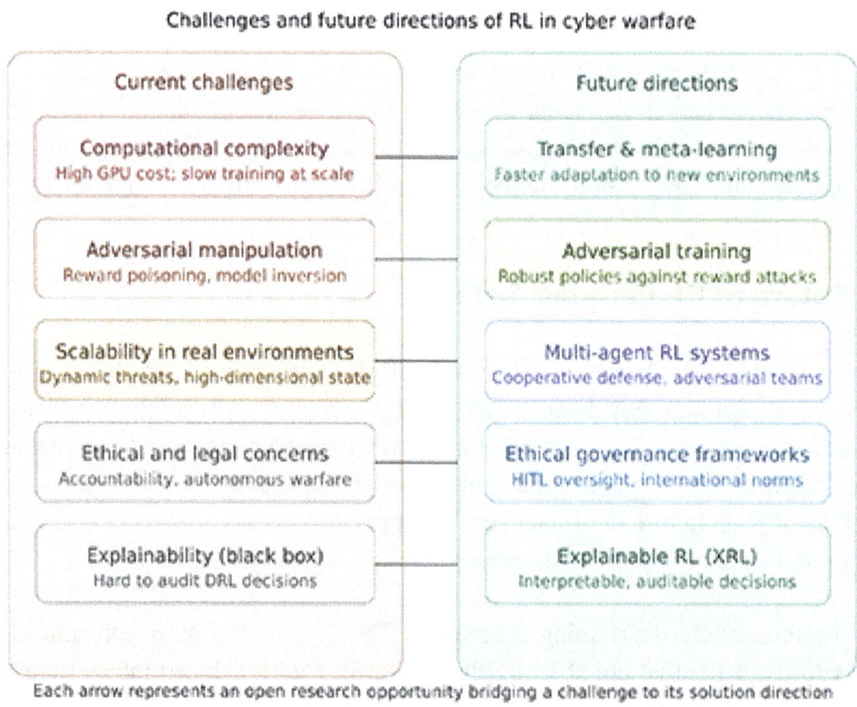

5.1 Resource and Computational Complexity

The most notable issue with applying RL to cyber warfare is that the computational cost of training and implementing RL models, especially in large and high-dimensional systems such as cyber networks, is very high.

Training Time and Resources: RL agents learn by trial and error, which implies that they need numerous interactions with the environment before they develop the ability to make decisions. This may translate to simulation running or live simulation environments in a situation of a cyber war where the agent is constantly evolving and improving its strategies. It may take very long to train such agents, particularly if some complicated task such as intrusion detection or simulating attacks is involved. This may lead to lengthy training durations, which may involve a lot of computational resources (e.g., high bandwidth servers, GPUs, or cloud computing systems).(Jayakrishna & Prasanth, 2025)

Scalability Problems: Cyber warfare systems are large, complicated, and dynamic, consisting of millions of security vulnerabilities, defensive systems and responses. It is a significant challenge to scale RL algorithms to be useful in such high-dimensional environments. The more complicated the environment, the greater the amount of computational resources required to model and to simulate all possible interactions. Moreover, RL algorithms can take numerous steps before reaching an optimal strategy, and is computationally costly in both large networks and real-time applications.

Big Data: RL agents need a lot of data in order to learn. This information can be derived in cyber warfare as part of network traffic, attack logs, security events and so on. The amount of data that cyber systems produce may be overwhelming when it comes to the conventional data processing capabilities, and processing and analyzing this data in real-time can be resource-consuming.(Wang et al., 2023)

5.2 Complexity of the Environment and Luxury of the Real World

Although RL has proven effective in the controlled setting, there are a number of challenges of applying RL-based models to the real world, which is complicated by the nature of cyber environments.

The Varying and Changeable Character of Cyber Threats: Cyber warfare is a fast developing sphere, and new threats and vectors of attacks are constantly appearing. This complicates the learning of optimal strategies by RL agents since they have to constantly adjust to new attack methods, new defense systems as well as new network settings. What may be an effective defense system today may turn outdated tomorrow as attackers come up with even more advanced methods. The RL agents need to train quickly and change effectively against dynamic threats in order to be effective in cyber warfare (Chen et al., 2026).

- Absence of Quality Data: High-quality data is one of the main requirements of RL training. In cyber war, it may be difficult to have quality information to train the RL agents. As an example, the agent might lack access to real-world attack data particularly to zero-day vulnerabilities, or may have inadequately diverse data to make generalizations across environments. The labelled data of supervised learning are limited in the cyber world, worsening the problem of effective training RL models. Moreover, the data in the real world can be either noisy, or incomplete, and the RL agent can hardly identify valuable patterns in the perception of irrelevant or misleading signals.(Xie & Zeng, 2026)
- Training on Real-World Scenarios: Although RL models can be trained in simulated settings, it is difficult to model realistic simulations of cyber warfare scenarios with all their complexity in the real world. Several RL-based systems are tested in an idealistic or simplistic environment that might not reflect the entire scope of possible cyber threats. Therefore, when training RL models in simulation, a massive level of modification and experimentation is usually needed to maintain the functionality of the system in real-life conditions.(Sepehrzad et al., 2026)

5.3 Security Risk and Adversarial Manipulation

The second major issue that the implementation of RL in cyber warfare is faced with is the security of RL-based systems themselves. The more complex and autonomous these systems get, the more likely it is that they will be used or abused by their enemies.

Adversarial Attacks on RL Agents: Adversarial vulnerability is one of the weaknesses of RL systems. Enemies have the potential to take advantage of the vulnerabilities of the RL model by presenting false feedback or purposefully responding in a manner that disrupts the environment to condition the RL agent in a manner that favors the attacker. Indicatively, an intruder may develop a misleading world the RL defense agent develops to ignore some attacker behavioral patterns or develops inefficient defense policies. This may have disastrous effects in cyber warfare like a defense system that is unable to detect and counter an attack.

Reward Manipulation: In RL, the agent learns some behavior according to the rewards it obtains after interactions with the environment. Unless a reward system is planned well, enemies can exploit the reward system to have the agent assume a behavior favorable to the attacker. Indicatively, an attacker might be able to use vulnerability in the reward system to fool a defense agent to learn to disregard some categories of attacks or to focus on defense mechanisms that are not effective.(Feng et al., 2024)

Model Inversion and Exposure: Sometimes, the adversaries might invert the trained RL model to discover the functionality of that system and the vulnerabilities or flaws. Such model inversion attack may give details on how the RL agent made the decision, which allows the attacker to have an upper hand in executing more advanced attacks or evRating the defence mechanism.

5.4 Ethical, Legal, and Governance Issues

Implementation of RL in cyber warfare provokes a number of ethical and legal issues. The greater freedom of RL systems in offensive and defensive functions raises the issues of accountability, control, and governance.

- Accountability: With increased autonomy of RL systems, responsibility can hardly be attributed to the decisions made by the system. Who is responsible in case an RL defense system may block legitimate traffic, or an RL-based attack causes unintentional damage? It should be the system developers, system operators or the autonomous agent? These are intricate questions that need new models in accountability in cyber war scenarios.(Luo et al., 2025)

Table 1. Problem Statement

Aspect	Description
Growing Cyber Threats	Cyberattacks are becoming more sophisticated, adaptive, and difficult to detect using traditional cybersecurity systems.
Limitations of Traditional Security	Conventional systems such as firewalls, IDS, IPS, and antivirus software rely on static rules and signatures, making them ineffective against evolving threats.
Increasing Complexity	Modern cyber warfare involves zero-day attacks, AI-driven malware, phishing, ransomware, and Advanced Persistent Threats (APTs).
Need for Adaptability	Static defense systems cannot dynamically adapt to new attack vectors and changing threat environments.
Human Dependency	Traditional cybersecurity requires continuous human monitoring and manual response, which increases response time and operational costs.
Security Gap	Organizations require intelligent systems capable of real-time learning, automated response, and adaptive decision-making.

- Transparency and Explainability: RL-based systems in particular deep reinforcement learning models are challenging to interpret. These systems are perceived as a black box as one may find it difficult to figure out how the agent came at a given decision. The absence of transparency may be an issue in the framework of cyber defense or attack. Stakeholders must have faith that such systems are doing the correct decision, in particular, in mission-related systems like national security or financial services. It is desirable that RL models become more explainable and interpretable, particularly in sensitive and high stakes settings.(Kabir et al., 2025)

Table 2. Proposed Solution

Component	Proposed Solution
Core Technology	Reinforcement Learning (RL)-based cybersecurity framework
Main Objective	Develop adaptive and autonomous cyber defense and attack systems
Defense Capabilities	Real-time intrusion detection, anomaly detection, malware identification, and automated incident response
Offensive Capabilities	Adaptive cyberattack simulations, vulnerability exploitation, and attack optimization
Learning Mechanism	Continuous feedback-based learning through rewards and penalties
Automation	Minimize human intervention by enabling autonomous decision-making
Adaptability	Dynamically modify defense strategies according to evolving cyber threats
Future Integration	Integration with IoT, blockchain, cloud computing, and quantum computing systems

Table 3. Methodology Used in the Study

Methodology Stage	Description
Environment Setup	Cybersecurity environment modeled as an RL environment containing networks, systems, users, and attack vectors
Agent Creation	RL agent acts as autonomous defender or attacker
State Identification	Current system/network conditions are treated as states
Action Selection	Agent performs actions such as blocking traffic, detecting anomalies, or launching attacks
Reward Mechanism	Successful actions receive rewards while failed actions receive penalties

continued on following page

Table 3. Continued

Methodology Stage	Description
Learning Process	Agent continuously learns optimal strategies through trial-and-error interactions
Policy Optimization	RL algorithms optimize decision-making policies over time
Continuous Adaptation	System updates strategies dynamically according to environmental changes
Evaluation	Performance evaluated using attack success rate, detection accuracy, response time, and adaptability

6. REINFORCEMENT LEARNING FUTURE DIRECTIONS IN CYBER WARFARE

With the dynamic nature of the cyber war environment, the phenomenon of Reinforcement Learning (RL) is going to become a more central role in crafting the offensive and defensive sides of the game. Nonetheless, the addition of RL to cyber warfare systems do not have many years under their belt yet, and far to go, to stabilize its practicality, scalability and resistance to the enemies in the real world. The emergence of RL in cyber warfare in the future is based on its potential to evolve and become more dynamic in dealing with emerging threats and attacks, and also enhance its efficiency.(Purves et al., 2024)

6.1 Improved RL Algorithms Scalability and Efficiency

One of the most noticeable problems regarding applying RL to cyber warfare, as we mentioned above, is the complexity in terms of computational power and resource consumption to train and deploy RL agents. The major improvements in scalability and efficiency should be achieved in the future to make RL more realistic in real-time and large-scale settings such as national defense systems or corporate networks.

Transfer Learning: Transfer learning is one of the most promising directions, in which RL agents have the opportunity to use knowledge acquired in one domain or task and implement it in a different one. This may considerably save on training time and enhance the transfer of the agent with respect to generalization of the agent to new environments. As an illustration, the RL agent that is trained to spot malware in a single network may reuse the information in a new network and avoid time-consuming retraining.(Alshehri, 2026)

Meta-Learning: A second field of research is meta-learning or learning to learn. Meta-learning is an attempt to produce RL agents capable of adapting faster to new settings or tasks through learning effective learning strategies. This may allow RL models to be casually deployed in constantly changing cyber warfare contexts without necessarily having to be retrained each time an attack is modified.

Parallel and Distributed Computing: To overcome the problem of scalability, it will be possible to utilize the future RL systems with the help of distributed and parallel computing in the context of program development. The RL systems can also do more complicated computations in real-time with the assistance of distributed computing of the computational load to multiple machines or processors. Some methods such as the cloud computing and edge computing might be utilized to facilitate the faster training and deployment even in resource-starved environment. (Tooki & Popoola, 2025)

6.2 Stability and Strength to Adversarial Resistance

Cyber systems that are based on RLs are vulnerable to adversarial manipulation as they grow to be more sophisticated. A critical issue about the future of RL in cyber warfare is to make sure that such systems are resilient and robust to adversarial attacks that aim at avoiding the weaknesses of the learning process.(Shu et al., 2026)

Adversarial Training: Adversarial training might be a significant important approach to enhancing the robustness of RL agents in the future. Through deliberate demonstrations of adversarial instances to the RL agents, in training, agents may learn to attract and resist adversarial attacks which aim at influencing the decision-making process of the agent. This might alleviate risks of attackers controlling the feedback mechanism or locating vulnerability of the system of rewards.

Safe Reinforcement Learning: A related topic is the study of safe RL, which aims at creating RL algorithms that cannot lead to unsafe behaviors during training or execution. An RL defense system should be capable of making sound decisions in cyber warfare without necessarily damaging innocent systems. As an example, an autonomous system based on the RL defense-based system cannot correctly perceive benign behavior as malicious and thus interfere with a legitimate service. Safe RL systems allow the safety constraints to be a part of the learning process, where the RL agents adhere to the set safety rules and do not act in detrimental ways.

Effective Policy Learning: Future RL systems will probably work on enhancing the robustness of policy learning per se, making RL agents place less sensitivity in small-scale environmental variations or adversarial examples. Through enhancing the capability of the agent to draw sound choices in an environment that is so diverse and unpredictable, RL systems may continue to maintain a greater degree of transactions and safety in actual circumstances of cyber warfare.(Chen et al., 2026)

6.3 Multi-Agent Systems Integration

In actual cyber warfare threats are usually multifaceted and that it entails numerous enemies and attacks through many fronts. Subsequently, future RL systems cannot work on its own and rather, it must consider multi-agent systems, which can work together or compete to accomplish different goals, and they might either be part of an offensive or defensive approach.(Jayakrishna & Prasanth, 2025)

Collaborative defence Systems When operating in the multi-agent environment, RL may be applied to design cooperative defence systems, in which the RL agents (e.g., intrusion detection system, firewall, antivirus software) interact and exchange information to maximise network security. An example is that one agent could monitor any abnormalities in network traffic, and another agent could work on preventing endpoints against malwares. By passing information and aligning efforts, these agents may improve the posture of system-wide security.(Vyas & Dey, 2024)

Table 5. Applications of RL in Cyber Defense

Application Area	Function
Intrusion Detection Systems (IDS)	Detect malicious network activities
Intrusion Prevention Systems (IPS)	Automatically block cyber threats
Malware Detection	Identify known and unknown malware behaviors
Anomaly Detection	Detect unusual patterns and suspicious activities
Firewall Optimization	Dynamically modify firewall rules
Incident Response	Automatically isolate compromised systems
Threat Hunting	Proactively search for vulnerabilities and threats
Rogue Behavior Detection	Detect insider threats and unauthorized activities

On the offensive side: It can be utilized on adversarial Multi-agent Systems where the multi-agent RL can be applied to model a challenging attack situation in which a group of autonomous agents collaborates to take advantage of a vulnerability in a target system. These agents might model advanced persistent threats (APTs) or synchronized denial-of-service attacks, and would learn to change their tactics and strategies in response to met defenses. Using this method would enable attackers to simulate and optimize multi-step, multi-faceted attacks, which is more realistic when compared to in real-life scenarios where many attack vectors are concomitantly used.(Wang et al., 2023)

Table 6. Advantages of the Proposed RL-Based Approach

Advantage	Description
Adaptive Learning	Continuously learns from new cyber threats
Real-Time Decision Making	Responds faster than manual cybersecurity systems
Autonomous Operation	Reduces dependency on human operators
Improved Detection Accuracy	Detects unknown and zero-day attacks
Dynamic Defense	Updates strategies based on attacker behavior
Scalability	Can be integrated into large-scale enterprise systems
Faster Incident Response	Reduces response and recovery time
Continuous Optimization	Improves system performance over time
Intelligent Automation	Automates monitoring and mitigation tasks
Future Readiness	Supports next-generation technologies and infrastructures

Emergent Behavior and Strategies: Over the course of the evolution of multi-agent RL systems, properties of the system such as emergent behaviors may be the result of the interplay of agents. These actions are not coded, but they arise out of how agents coordinate their targeting of their personal goals. This may result in very complicated and efficient approaches in defending against and conducting cyber attacks.(Azeroual et al., 2026)

6.4 Legal and Regulation Systems of Autonomous Cyber Warfare

The integration of RL into the system of cyber war will require the design of ethical and regulatory frameworks necessary to specify how this technology can be utilized in the military and defense sectors. Such guidelines will assist in making sure that RL-based systems are implemented in a responsible and in line with international regulations and ethical standards.(Wang et al., 2023)

Accountability and Oversight: Accountability can be considered as one of the most urgent ethical issues of autonomous cyber warfare. There is a question of who decides in an RL-based defense or attack system? Later, there will be a necessity to rely on the obvious accountability mechanisms who are culpable concerning autonomous systems actions. This can be through the creation of oversight committees, international treaties on autonomous warfare, and man-in-the-loop checks to important decisions.

International Regulation and Norms: With the development of cyber warfare capabilities, international regulation would be needed to make sure that the grows of cyber warfare is prevented and that autonomous systems are utilized in manners that are Diplomatic to the principles of peace and security internationally. In particular, the Geneva Conventions might need revision to include references to the use of AI and RL in the cyber warfare to establish norms of how such technologies ought to be utilized in the conflict scenario.(Hossain, 2025)

Humanitarian Issues: The ethical aspects of the human effect of autonomous cyber war will also be important. Offensive cyber systems based on RL can create unintended effects that can widen conflicts and damage to innocent civilians, which includes hitting civilian infrastructure or critical services. The way forward in future studies should be to understand that the systems developed based upon RL must comply with the ethics such as reduction of harm to civilians and compliance with humanitarian laws.(Sharmin et al., 2026)

6.5 Synergy With Other Developed Technologies

In the future, RL in cyber war is likely to be synergized with other innovative technologies and produce new synergistic solutions that increase both offensive and defensive abilities.

- Deep Learning: With a combination of RL and deep learning, RL agents will be able to handle and analyze complex and high-dimensional data like raw network traffic or complex attack patterns. With deep neural networks, the agent based on RL will be able to learn a large amount of unstructured data, which will allow them to identify and respond more accurately to upcoming threats.(Bashir et al., 2026)
- Quantum Computing: Quantum computing is in its infancy but may represent a breakthrough RL in cyber warfare; it will undoubtedly offer unprecedented computing power. The quantum computers may speed up the training of the RL agents, so it can analyze big datasets and complicated environments than the classical computers. It may result in swift decision-making in therein cyber defense systems, and in efficient training of adversarial RL agents on attack scenarios.(Nadhir et al., 2025)
- Blockchain and RL: Future studies can investigate how the blockchain technology can be integrated with RL to increase the security and integrity of systems based on RL. The fact that blockchain is decentralized and immutable may offer a safe space to train RL agents, and the learning process will be transparent and verifiable and will be very difficult to interfere with by adversary actors.(Shu et al., 2026)

7. CONCLUSION

The implementation of Reinforcement Learning (RL) into the realm of cyber warfare is a serious paradigm shift, as both offensive and defensive operations can now develop and become not a rule-based system but an agent that acquires knowledge and develops. Due to the dynamics of cyber threats becoming more intricate, the necessity of autonomic systems that are capable of learning and adapting to their decision-making in real-time becomes more important. The ability of RW to improve the effectiveness, efficiency and resilience of cyber defense systems and its ability to model and optimize cyber attack plans makes it one of the core technologies in future cyber warfare.(Alauthman et al., 2026)

This chapter has discussed how RL can be used in adaptive cyber defense and cyber attack strategy. We have talked about the main ideas of RL and its underlying algorithms, how RL can be used to make systems capable of autonomously detecting and responding to novel threats, optimizing attacks and adapting to changing environments. We have also discussed the huge difficulties in applying RL to real-life scenarios in cyber warfare, such as the complexity of computation, manipulation of adversaries, and the necessity of effective ethical and regulatory policies.

Although RL has a tremendous potential, it has not yet been fully employed in cyber warfare. To practically apply RL-based systems to dynamic and high-risk environments, including cyber warfare, one will have to overcome a number of challenges, which include:

- Computational Costs and Scalability: Scalability and high-dimensionality of real-life instances of cyber warfare require a large amount of computational resources to train and deploy RL agents. To overcome this difficulty, scalability, transfer learning and cloud-based computing innovations will be needed to enable RL agents to operate effectively in the real-time, large-scale settings.
- Adversarial Vulnerabilities: The more advanced the RL system is, the more susceptible it becomes to adversarial attacks. The resilience and strength of the RL models against the malicious manipulations will be of significant importance in protecting against the attacks that seek to attack the vulnerabilities of the RL learning process.
- Security and Safety: The security of the deployment of RL agents in the environment of cyber warfare is of the highest priority. The future research should be oriented towards safe RL frameworks, which include security constraints, the agents should not act in a hasty and harmful way that may harm the critical systems.

- Ethical and Legal Implications: The emergence of autonomous RL agents within the sphere of cyber war is associated with both ethical and legal implications, specifically, in terms of accountability, transparency, and human control. To make sure that the RL-based systems are used in a responsible way and in accordance with the international laws and humanitarian principles, it is important to create ethical standards, regulatory frameworks, and accountability mechanisms.
- The possible value of RL in cyber war is however monumental in spite of these issues. The technology is set to transform the way we deal with cyber defense and offense in that it offers systems that can learn through experience, adapt to changing threats, and make decisions independently. As the current progress in RL algorithms, computational power, and security systems further evolve, the future of cyber warfare might be described as extremely flexible, autonomous systems, which are excellent in protecting against cyber threats and are more efficient and optimized in terms of attack strategies(Tayseer Jafar et al., 2026).

7.1 Future of Cyber Defense and Autonomous Systems.

The future of cyber defense lies in the use of thinkable, learning, adaptive, autonomous objects that shall be relied upon to develop further. Such systems will be charged with protecting against an ever-expanding and diverse set of cyber threats, including conventional hacking and more sophisticated adversarial AI-proximate attacks. Human operators will probably cease to respond to particular threats and instead offer a higher level of control, direction and moral judgement of autonomous systems.

On the offensive, the strategies of attacks developed by RL will become more advanced, and autonomous agents have the ability to change methods to circumvent defenses and take advantage of gaps in real-time. Nevertheless, such development will also present the issue of ethical application of autonomous offensive systems which can be used in others in such a manner that results to unintended consequences such as escalation, collateral damage, or violation of international law. The question of how to keep the efficiency and effectiveness of RL-driven systems, and on the other hand, the responsible governance of their application is going to be the challenge in the future.(Abdelkader et al., 2024)

7.2 Ethics, Accountability, and the Human In the Loop.

Human oversight is one of the most significant factors of the future of RL in cyber warfare. With the increasing autonomy of RL agents, it will also be essential to retain human-in-the-loop (HITL) control over the high-level decision-making, particularly when the ethical considerations are involved. The work of autonomous systems also has to be guided by strict ethical principles, and critical decisions should be taken by human operators.(Feng et al., 2024)

The increased independence of the RL-based cyber warfare systems prompts the creation of frameworks that will hold accountability in the actions of such systems. Where there is a failure of the system or unexpected side effects, it is important that there are clear procedures that assign responsibility and take corrective measures. It can involve creation of international standards and rules that will regulate the application of autonomous systems in cyber warfare so that they comply with the principle of proportionality, distinction, and accountability as stipulated by international law.(Feng et al., 2024)

7.3 Conclusion: The Pledge and Duty of RL in Cyber War

Reinforcement Learning is a paradigm of change in cyber defense and cyber attack strategy. RA will make cyber warfare systems more agile, effective, and resilient by enabling autonomous systems to learn through the environment and respond to emerging challenges. As we proceed, however, we need to make sure that these systems are built with a particular regard to the risks associated with them, ethical issues, and regulatory considerations.

Table 8. Overall Conclusion

Aspect	Summary
Core Contribution	RL introduces adaptive and intelligent cyber defense and attack mechanisms
Major Strength	Ability to learn, evolve, and respond autonomously
Main Challenges	Computational complexity, adversarial risks, explainability, and ethical concerns
Security Importance	Essential for protecting modern digital infrastructure
Future Potential	High potential for autonomous and resilient cybersecurity systems
Key Recommendation	Combine AI automation with strong human oversight and ethical governance

With the increasing dependence of cyber warfare on intelligent, autonomous systems, the balance of power between attacker and defender will likely shift in the future serving as the next manifestation of power. Through RL, we are able to establish more responsive, adaptive, and efficient cyber defense systems, as well as to take the complicated ethical and legal issues that come with the expanding autonomy of cyber warfare technologies.(Javadpour et al., 2025)

The future of RL in cyber warfare will be determined, in the end, by how we handle its integration, make it robust, and provide responsible management over its implementation. The future of RL-based systems in cyber warfare is enormous, but it is also crucial to remember that we should be cautious about this innovation, open about it, and dedicated to making sure that the implementation of this technology is both beneficial to security and does not cause harm to innocent people and communities.

REFERENCES

Abbasi, A. R., & Mohammadi, M. (2026). Engineering a resilient smart grid: Practical defense mechanisms and deployable framework against evolving cyber-threats. *Results in Engineering, 30*, 109893. DOI: 10.1016/j.rineng.2026.109893

Abdelkader, S., Amissah, J., Kinga, S., Mugerwa, G., Emmanuel, E., Mansour, D. E. A., Bajaj, M., Blazek, V., & Prokop, L. (2024). Securing modern power systems: Implementing comprehensive strategies to enhance resilience and reliability against cyber-attacks. In *Results in Engineering* (Vol. 23). Elsevier B.V., DOI: 10.1016/j.rineng.2024.102647

Afraji, D. M. A. A., Lloret, J., & Peñalver, L. (2025). Deep learning-driven defense strategies for mitigating DDoS attacks in cloud computing environments. In *Cyber Security and Applications* (Vol. 3). KeAi Communications Co., DOI: 10.1016/j.csa.2025.100085

. Alauthman, M., Al-Qerem, A., Almomani, A., Ishtaiwi, A. M., Aldweesh, A., Arafah, M., Arya, V., & Gupta, B. B. (2026). Enhancing Web of Things Security Using Harris Hawks Optimization with Reinforcement Learning. *International Journal of Cognitive Computing in Engineering*. DOI: 10.1016/j.ijcce.2026.01.001

Alshehri, M. (2026). Dynamic cyber deception using AI-driven adaptive honeypot networks and context-aware behavioural analysis for proactive threat neutralization. *Ain Shams Engineering Journal, 17*(4), 104061. Advance online publication. DOI: 10.1016/j.asej.2026.104061

Ang, T. Z., Salem, M., Kamarol, M., Abdolrasol, M. G. M., Ustun, T. S., & Cali, U. (2026). Cyber-resilient control based on soft reinforcement learning for inverter-based PV/FC systems: Real-time implementation and validation. *Energy Reports, 15*, 109241. Advance online publication. DOI: 10.1016/j.egyr.2026.109241

Azeroual, M., Moughraoui, F. Z., El Iysaouy, L., Mimouni, A., El Amrani, A., & El Markhi, H. (2026). *Cybersecurity challenges and defense strategies for next-generation power systems*. Cyber-Physical Energy Systems., DOI: 10.1016/j.cpes.2025.10.002

Bashir, A., Shamszaman, Z. U., Song, Z., & Han, T. A. (2026). Co-evolutionary dynamics of attack and defence in cybersecurity. *Knowledge-Based Systems, 340*, 115750. DOI: 10.1016/j.knosys.2026.115750

Chen, X., Peng, J., Jiang, L., Cheng, J., & Wu, S. (2026). Defense against multi-path attacks on EV charging networks: A dependency chain analysis and DQN-BASED SOLUTION. *Multimodal Transportation*, *5*(1), 100254. Advance online publication. DOI: 10.1016/j.multra.2025.100254

Feng, X., Han, J., Zhang, R., Xu, S., & Xia, H. (2024). Security defense strategy algorithm for Internet of Things based on deep reinforcement learning. *High-Confidence Computing*, *4*(1), 100167. Advance online publication. DOI: 10.1016/j.hcc.2023.100167

Finistrella, S., Mariani, S., & Zambonelli, F. (2025). Multi-Agent Reinforcement Learning for Cybersecurity: Classification and survey. In *Intelligent Systems with Applications* (Vol. 26). Elsevier B.V. DOI: 10.1016/j.iswa.2025.200495

Hossain, M. A. (2025). Deep Q-learning intrusion detection system (DQ-IDS): A novel reinforcement learning approach for adaptive and self-learning cybersecurity. *ICT Express*, *11*(5), 875–880. DOI: 10.1016/j.icte.2025.05.007

Iturbe, E., Rego, A., Llorente-Vazquez, O., Rios, E., Dalamagkas, C., Merkouris, D., & Toledo, N. (2026). Reinforcement Learning in action: Powering intelligent intrusion responses to advanced cyber threats in realistic scenarios. *Expert Systems with Applications*, *296*, 129168. Advance online publication. DOI: 10.1016/j.eswa.2025.129168

Javadpour, A., Ja'fari, F., Benzaïd, C., & Taleb, T. (2025). An optimized reinforcement learning based MTD mutation strategy for securing edge IoT against DDoS attack. *Journal of Information Security and Applications*, *93*, 104138. Advance online publication. DOI: 10.1016/j.jisa.2025.104138

Javaheri, D., Chizari, H., Fahmideh, M., Nadimi-Shahraki, M. H., & Hur, J. (2025). DeepRadar: A cyber-defence interceptor for early warning and defusing malware injection attacks. *Knowledge-Based Systems*, *331*, 114830. Advance online publication. DOI: 10.1016/j.knosys.2025.114830

Jayakrishna, N., & Prasanth, N. N. (2025). Detection and mitigation of distributed denial of service attacks in vehicular ad hoc network using a spatiotemporal deep learning and reinforcement learning approach. *Results in Engineering*, *26*, 104839. Advance online publication. DOI: 10.1016/j.rineng.2025.104839

Kabir, S., Hannan, N., Shufian, A., & Rahman Zishan, M. S. (2025). Proactive detection of cyber-physical grid attacks: A pre-attack phase identification and analysis using anomaly-based machine learning models. *Array (New York, N.Y.)*, *27*, 100441. Advance online publication. DOI: 10.1016/j.array.2025.100441

Luo, F., Xu, T., Li, J., & Xu, F. (2025). MDP-AD: A Markov decision process-based adaptive framework for real-time detection of evolving and unknown network attacks. *Alexandria Engineering Journal, 126*, 480–490. DOI: 10.1016/j.aej.2025.04.091

Nadhir, A. M., Mounir, B., Abdelkader, L., & Hammoudeh, M. (2025). Enhancing Cybersecurity in Healthcare IoT Systems Using Reinforcement Learning. *Transportation Research Procedia, 84*, 113–120. DOI: 10.1016/j.trpro.2025.03.053

Purves, T., Kyriakopoulos, K. G., Jenkins, S., Phillips, I., & Dudman, T. (2024). Causally aware reinforcement learning agents for autonomous cyber defence. *Knowledge-Based Systems, 304*, 112521. Advance online publication. DOI: 10.1016/j.knosys.2024.112521

Sepehrzad, R., Hosseinalibeiki, H., Taghinezhad, N., Khosravi, N., al Durra, A., & Sadabadi, M. S. (2026). Enhanced cyber-resilience in flexible energy markets for microgrids: A trust-aware federated deep reinforcement learning framework. *Applied Energy, 406*, 127282. Advance online publication. DOI: 10.1016/j.apenergy.2025.127282

Sharmin, Z., Uddin, M. P., Xiang, Y., & Chen, F. (2026). A systematic literature review on federated cyber-attack detection for edge intelligence: Challenges, approaches, and future directions. *Computer Science Review, 61*, 100965. DOI: 10.1016/j.cosrev.2026.100965

Shu, H., Zhao, H., Yang, Y., & Tang, Y. (2026). Defense strategy against cyber-physical coordinated false data injection attacks in cyber-physical power systems. *Results in Engineering, 29*, 109424. Advance online publication. DOI: 10.1016/j.rineng.2026.109424

Tayseer Jafar, M., Yang, L. X., Li, G., Doss, R., Mouzakis, K., Vasa, R., Janicke, H., Ibrahim, A., Mohsin, A., Sarker, I. H., Moore, K., Camtepe, S., & Goel, D. (2026). Mitigating malware prevalence in networks with arbitrary topologies: A Flip-It cyber game approach integrated with epidemic modeling. *Information Sciences, 726*, 122753. Advance online publication. DOI: 10.1016/j.ins.2025.122753

Tooki, O. O., & Popoola, O. M. (2025). Advances in the application of model-free reinforcement learning in protecting transactive energy systems against cyberthreats: A review. In *Results in Engineering* (Vol. 28). Elsevier B.V., DOI: 10.1016/j.rineng.2025.108284

Vyas, S. D., & Dey, S. (2024). Reinforcement Learning-based Adversarial Attack Generation Examples in Connected and Autonomous Vehicles: A Case Study on Vehicular Platoons. *IFAC-PapersOnLine, 58*(28), 78–83. DOI: 10.1016/j.ifacol.2024.12.014

Wang, X., Wang, X., Zhang, M., & Wang, S. (2023). Detection-based active defense of biased injection attack based on robust adaptive controller. *Internet of Things and Cyber-Physical Systems*, *3*, 14–23. DOI: 10.1016/j.iotcps.2023.01.004

Xie, M., & Zeng, M. (2026). A multimodal reinforcement learning-based access control model for power systems under zero-trust architecture. *Alexandria Engineering Journal*, *141*, 269–283. DOI: 10.1016/j.aej.2026.03.017

Yang, X., Howley, E., & Schukat, M. (2024). ADT: Time series anomaly detection for cyber-physical systems via deep reinforcement learning. *Computers & Security*, *141*, 103825. Advance online publication. DOI: 10.1016/j.cose.2024.103825

Chapter 6
LLM-Based Autonomous Agents for Phishing Detection, Triage, and Response:
A Reference Architecture for Agentic Cyber Defense

Ismail El Bazi
http://orcid.org/0000-0002-8511-8651
Sultan Moulay Slimane University, Morocco

Jamal Ezzine
Sultan Moulay Slimane University, Morocco

Brahim Ghazoui
Sultan Moulay Slimane University, Morocco

ABSTRACT

This chapter presents an agentic intelligence framework for autonomous phishing detection and response in the context of evolving cyber warfare strategies. It introduces the Autonomous Phishing Detection and Action (APDA) architecture, which integrates large language models with perception, reasoning, action, and feedback layers to enable adaptive and explainable decision-making. This chapter examines how adversarial techniques, such as prompt injection, jailbreaking, hallucination, and data poisoning, threaten LLM-based cybersecurity systems, and outlines the corresponding mitigation strategies embedded within each architectural layer. A structured evaluation framework is proposed, including technical and operational

DOI: 10.4018/979-8-2600-0413-5.ch006

metrics, alongside an illustrative enterprise email threat scenario. This chapter contributes a novel layered approach that bridges advances in natural language processing with autonomous cyber defense, offering a scalable and governance-aware solution for next-generation security operations.

1. INTRODUCTION: THE EVOLVING ROLE OF AI IN PHISHING AND CYBER DEFENSE

The domain of cybersecurity is evolving and is influenced by rapid advancements in AI. Traditional rule- and signature-based defenses are inadequate for modern threats. Phishing remains a persistent and effective attack vector because of human manipulation rather than technical exploitation. As organizations digitize their operations and communication, phishing attacks have become more sophisticated, scalable, and effective, necessitating shifts in detection and mitigation.

From a practical standpoint, these developments are not merely incremental; they fundamentally reshape the generation and execution of phishing threats.

Phishing attacks exploit cognitive biases, trust, and contextual cues to deceive users into revealing sensitive information or performing harmful tasks to their detriment. Early phishing attempts were characterized by poor grammar, generic messaging, and easily identifiable malicious indicators. However, generative AI and large language models (LLMs) have fundamentally altered cyber warfare. Adversaries can now generate highly personalized, context-aware, and coherent phishing messages that are difficult to distinguish from legitimate communications. Consequently, many traditional heuristics are no longer reliable for detection, rendering legacy systems ineffective.

Although conventional machine learning and deep learning models have improved detection, they remain largely stateless and context-limited, struggling to identify sophisticated spear-phishing and business email compromise cases in which malicious intent is hidden within subtle contextual inconsistencies.

The limitations of existing approaches highlight the need for advanced, context-aware, and adaptive defense mechanisms. Agentic intelligence has emerged as a promising approach in cybersecurity. Agentic AI systems perceive their environment, reason about complex scenarios, plan actions, and execute decisions autonomously or semi-autonomously. Unlike traditional classification models that produce static outputs, agentic systems are dynamic entities that continuously interact with their environment. This shift from passive detection to active defense represents a fundamental evolution in cybersecurity paradigms.

Large language models play a central role in enabling this shift by providing natural language understanding and contextual reasoning necessary for intelligent agents to move beyond simple classification toward adaptive decision-making.

This chapter argues that phishing defense is ideal for agentic AI applications. As a language-driven problem, phishing detection aligns with the strengths of large-language models. Simultaneously, cybersecurity demands, such as real-time response, high accuracy, and explainability, test the effectiveness of agentic systems. By integrating perception, reasoning, and action into a unified framework, agentic AI can transform phishing defense from reactive to proactive and adaptive.

This transformation has impacted cyber warfare beyond enterprise cybersecurity. In modern threats, phishing is not just for individual cybercriminals but also a strategic tool in large-scale campaigns such as espionage, disinformation, and infrastructure disruption. State-sponsored actors increasingly use automated and AI-driven techniques for large-scale phishing attacks. Thus, defensive capabilities must match the speed and sophistication of the threats. Agentic cyber defense systems capable of autonomous triage and response are crucial for digital resilience in such environments.

To address these challenges, this chapter proposes the concept of an Autonomous Phishing Defense Agent (APDA) - a multi-layered, LLM-powered system designed to detect, analyze, and respond to phishing threats in an integrated manner. The APDA framework combines natural language processing, contextual reasoning, and automated action orchestration to enable end-to-end threat management. Unlike traditional systems that focus solely on detection, the proposed approach emphasizes the full lifecycle of cyber defense, including triage, decision making, and response execution.

Beyond technical innovation, this chapter considers the broader implications of deploying autonomous systems in the field of cybersecurity. Issues such as explainability, trust, human oversight, and ethical governance are central to the adoption of agentic AI technologies. Security analysts must understand and trust the decisions made by autonomous agents, especially in high-stakes environments in which errors have significant consequences. Therefore, integrating Explainable AI (XAI) techniques and human-in-the-loop (HITL) mechanisms is crucial for safe and effective deployment.

2. LITERATURE REVIEW: FROM RULE-BASED SYSTEMS TO AGENTIC AI IN PHISHING DETECTION

The evolution of phishing detection reflects the broader trajectory of cybersecurity, transitioning from static, rule-based mechanisms to increasingly sophisticated

AI-driven approaches. This section reviews the key stages in this evolution, highlighting the strengths and limitations of each paradigm and positioning agentic AI as the next logical advancement in cyber defense.

Notably, the progression of phishing detection techniques closely mirrors the broader shifts in artificial intelligence and cybersecurity paradigms.

2.1 Rule-Based and Heuristic Approaches

Early phishing detection systems relied on rule-based and heuristic approaches. These methods use predefined patterns, such as malicious URLs, suspicious keywords, and blacklisted domains to identify phishing attempts (Silva et al., 2020). Protocol-level defenses, including the Sender Policy Framework (SPF) (Kitterman, 2014), Domain Keys Identified Mail (DKIM) (Kucherawy et al., 2011), and Domain-based Message Authentication, Reporting, and Conformance (DMARC) (Kucherawy & Zwicky, 2015), verify sender authenticity and reduce email spoofing attempts.

Although effective against large-scale, low-complexity campaigns, these reactive mechanisms are easily bypassed by targeted adaptive threats (Khonji et al., 2013).

2.2 Machine Learning-Based Detection

Machine learning has marked a shift toward the automated feature extraction from email metadata and content. Models such as Random Forests and SVMs improved detection accuracy but remained dependent on manual feature engineering (Do et al., 2022) and lacked the ability to reason about intent or adapt to novel linguistic manipulations (Kavya & Sumathi, 2024).

2.3 Deep Learning and NLP-Based Methods

Deep learning further advances detection by enabling automatic feature learning from raw texts. Transformer-based architectures, such as BERT, have significantly improved the interpretation of contextual relationships (Fukarel et al., 2025; Uddin et al., 2024). However, these models remain essentially stateless classification tools rather than proactive defense agents.

2.4 The Rise of Generative AI in Phishing Attacks

The emergence of generative AI has introduced a new dimension to phishing attacks. Language models enable attackers to generate highly realistic and personalized phishing messages on a large scale. Unlike traditional phishing emails, which often contain grammatical errors and generic content, AI-generated messages are fluent, contextually relevant, and tailored to specific targets (Mishra et al., 2025).

Recent studies have demonstrated that LLM-generated phishing emails can achieve higher success rates than human-crafted ones. These messages can incorporate publicly available information, mimic communication styles, and adapt to user responses (Aydın & Bahtiyar, 2025). Additionally, generative AI facilitates the creation of multimodal attacks, including voice phishing (vishing) and deepfake-based impersonations (Jabir et al., 2025).

This shift represents a significant escalation in the "arms race" between attackers and defenders. As offensive capabilities become increasingly automated and intelligent, defensive systems must also evolve. Static detection mechanisms are insufficient to counter adaptive and contextual threats, necessitating the development of more advanced reasoning systems.

2.5 Agentic AI and Autonomous Cyber Defense

Agentic AI represents a paradigm shift in the design and deployment of intelligent systems that can act autonomously. Unlike traditional models that perform isolated tasks, agentic systems operate as autonomous entities capable of perception, reasoning, planning, and action (Acharya et al., 2025). This approach is often conceptualized through the "Sense–Plan–Act" cycle, in which the system continuously interacts with its environment to achieve predefined goals (Erdogan et al., 2025).

In cybersecurity, agentic AI has gained attention as a potential solution for automating complex tasks within Security Operations Centers (SOC). Autonomous agents play a crucial role in enhancing threat detection, managing incident responses, overseeing vulnerability management, and conducting threat intelligence analyses. By integrating multiple capabilities into a unified framework, agentic systems can reduce operational latency and enhance decision-making (Kshetri, 2025).

Large language models play a central role in enabling agentic behavior. Their ability to process natural language, generate explanations, and perform reasoning tasks renders them well suited for cybersecurity applications. Techniques such as CoT prompting allow agents to decompose complex problems into intermediate reasoning steps (Wei et al., 2022), whereas Retrieval-Augmented Generation enables the integration of external knowledge sources (Lewis et al., 2020).

Recent research has explored the use of LLM-based agents for tasks such as automated penetration testing, threat intelligence extraction, and security policy analysis. However, the application of agentic AI in phishing defense remains relatively unexplored. Most existing studies focus on detection rather than end-to-end workflows that include triage and responses (Srinivas et al., 2025).

2.6 Research Gap and Positioning of This Chapter

Despite significant advancements in phishing detection, a critical gap remains in integrating detection, reasoning, and responses into a unified framework. Existing approaches are largely fragmented and focus on individual components rather than a holistic system design. Furthermore, the application of agentic AI to phishing defense has not been fully explored, particularly in terms of autonomous triage and response.

This chapter addresses this gap by proposing a comprehensive architecture for an LLM-powered Autonomous Phishing Defense Agent. By combining natural language understanding, contextual reasoning, and automated action execution, the proposed framework moves beyond the traditional detection paradigm toward a more adaptive and proactive approach to cyber defense.

This chapter contributes to the emerging field of autonomous cyber defense, aligning with the broader trend toward agentic intelligence in cybersecurity. It also provides a foundation for future research on integrating LLM-based agents into real-world security operations, bridging the gap between theoretical advancements and practical implementation.

It is important to note that this chapter adopts a design-oriented and conceptual approach. Rather than presenting a fully implemented system, the objective was to define a reference architecture and evaluation framework that can guide future empirical studies and real-world deployments.

Although these approaches have demonstrated significant progress, most existing systems remain focused on isolated detection tasks rather than integrated end-to-end workflows. Emerging industrial platforms such as Microsoft Security Copilot (Freitas & Gharib, 2026) and Google SecLM (Divakaran & Peddinti, 2025) highlight a shift toward AI-assisted security operations; however, they primarily function as decision-support tools rather than fully agentic systems capable of autonomous triage and responses. This distinction further emphasizes the need for architectures such as the APDA.

3. LLM CAPABILITIES FOR CYBERSECURITY: LANGUAGE UNDERSTANDING, INTENT INFERENCE, AND CONTEXTUAL REASONING

The emergence of large language models has significantly advanced the capabilities of artificial intelligence in processing and understanding natural languages. In cybersecurity, where many attack vectors, particularly phishing, are fundamentally language-driven, LLMs offer a transformative opportunity to move beyond pattern recognition toward semantic understanding and reasoning-based defense mechanisms

(Alqahtani & Ahuja, 2026). This section examines the core capabilities of LLMs relevant to cybersecurity, focusing on language understanding, intent inference, and contextual reasoning, while addressing their limitations in security-critical settings.

3.1 Foundations of Large Language Models

LLMs are based on transformer architectures that utilize self-attention mechanisms to capture complex contextual relationships among words. Through extensive pre-training, these models learn rich semantic representations that allow them to process nuanced email content and tone more accurately than previous NLP iterations (Zhang et al., 2025). Importantly, these capabilities extend beyond incremental improvements and introduce qualitatively new ways of reasoning about cyber threats to national security issues.

3.2 Language Understanding and Semantic Analysis

One of the most critical capabilities of LLMs in cybersecurity is their ability to perform deep language understanding. Unlike traditional keyword-based systems, LLMs can interpret the semantics of a message, including its tone, structure, and implied meaning. This enables a more accurate detection of phishing attempts that rely on sophisticated social engineering techniques (Huynh et al., 2025).

For example, phishing emails often employ tactics such as urgency, authority, and emotional manipulation to influence user behavior. LLMs can identify these patterns by analyzing linguistic cues, such as imperative language ("act immediately"), hierarchical references ("as requested by the CEO"), and emotional triggers ("your account will be suspended"). By recognizing these cues, LLMs can infer the underlying intent of a message rather than relying solely on its surface-level features.

3.3 Intent Inference and Social Engineering Detection

Beyond understanding the literal content of a message, LLMs enable intent inference, which is critical for identifying malicious behavior. In phishing detection, the goal is not only to determine whether a message is suspicious but also to understand why it is suspicious and what the attacker aims to achieve with it (Yadav & Masum, 2026).

LLMs can infer intent by analyzing the explicit and implicit signals within a message. For instance, a request for sensitive information, such as login credentials or financial details, may indicate credential harvesting or fraud. Similarly, requests that deviate from normal communication patterns, such as unusual financial transactions or changes in account details, can signal a business email compromise.

This reasoning capability distinguishes LLM-based systems from traditional classifiers, enabling them to provide not only predictions but also justifications for their decisions.

3.4 Contextual Reasoning and Knowledge Integration

A major limitation of earlier phishing detection systems is their inability to incorporate external context. LLMs address this limitation using techniques such as Retrieval-Augmented Generation, which allows models to access and integrate external knowledge sources during inference (Chandaeng et al., 2025).

In a cybersecurity setting, contextual reasoning may involve the following aspects:

- Verifying whether the sender belongs to the organization
- Checking whether a request aligns with company policies
- Comparing the message against known threat intelligence
- Analyzing historical communication patterns between users

By integrating such information, LLM-based systems can evaluate messages within a broader organizational and situational context than human analysts can. For example, an email requesting a financial transaction may appear legitimate in isolation but may be flagged as suspicious if it violates the established approval workflows or originates from an unusual location (Duc et al., 2025).

3.5 Enabling Agentic Behavior in Cyber Defense

The capabilities described above—language understanding, intent inference, and contextual reasoning—form the foundation of agentic behavior in cybersecurity systems. By integrating these capabilities into a unified framework, LLMs can act as intelligent agents capable of performing complex tasks that extend beyond simple classification.

In the APDA architecture, LLMs function as the core reasoning engine, enabling the agent to interpret communications, assess risks, and plan response actions within a Sense–Plan–Act cycle.

Furthermore, LLM-based agents can support human–machine collaboration by acting as decision-support systems. Rather than replacing human analysts, these agents augment their capabilities by providing insights, recommendations, and automation tools. This approach enhances the efficiency and effectiveness of cybersecurity operations (Desai et al., 2024).

3.6 Limitations and Challenges of LLMs in Security Contexts

Despite their benefits, LLMs face several challenges in the field of cybersecurity. A key issue is hallucination, where the model generates incorrect information, risking errors and trust (Chopra et al., 2026). Another challenge is prompt injection, where attackers manipulate the input to alter the model's behavior, such as phishing emails with hidden instructions. This necessitates robust input validation and secure prompt design (Patil et al., 2025). LLMs also pose latency and computational cost concerns, especially in real-time applications, which affect their scalability and responsiveness (Husom et al., 2025). Finally, data privacy and governance issues arise, requiring careful handling of sensitive communications to comply with regulations and policies (Ahi & Valizadeh, 2025).

4. APDA ARCHITECTURE: DESIGN PRINCIPLES AND SYSTEM COMPONENTS

The increasing sophistication of phishing attacks, particularly those enabled by generative AI, necessitates a shift from isolated detection models to integrated intelligent defense systems. To address this challenge, this chapter proposes an Autonomous Phishing Defense Agent - a multi-layered, agentic architecture designed to unify detection, reasoning, and response within a single framework. The APDA architecture leverages the capabilities of large language models to enable intelligence-driven analysis, goal-directed decision-making, and adaptive response execution.

From a system design perspective, the integration of these components reflects a deliberate shift toward unified and adaptive defense architectures.

This section presents the design principles underlying the APDA framework and provides a detailed description of its core components. The architecture is structured as a layered system that reflects the fundamental stages of agentic behavior: perception, reasoning, action, and feedback.

From an implementation perspective, deploying the APDA architecture introduces several practical considerations, including the computational overhead associated with LLM inference, latency constraints in real-time email processing, and integration challenges with existing enterprise security infrastructures, such as SIEM and SOAR platforms. These factors must be carefully balanced to ensure the scalability and operational feasibility of the model.

4.1 Design Principles

The APDA architecture is guided by several key design principles that ensure its technical robustness and operational feasibility.

1. Modularity and Layered Design

The architecture is composed of distinct functional layers, each responsible for a specific aspect of the defense process. This modular approach facilitates the scalability, maintainability, and integration of existing cybersecurity infrastructure.

2. Context-Aware Intelligence

Unlike traditional systems that analyze emails in isolation, APDA incorporates contextual information such as user roles, communication history, and organizational policies. This enables more accurate detection of targeted attacks, including spear-phishing and business email compromise.

3. Human-Centric Design

The architecture is designed to augment security analysts by enabling analyst supervision of high-risk decisions while automating routine operational tasks.

4. Risk-Aware Decision-Making

APDA prioritizes threats based on their potential impact and likelihood, enabling efficient allocation of defensive resources. This is particularly important in high-volume environments where alert fatigue is a significant concern.

5. Incremental Deployability

To ensure practical feasibility, the architecture supports gradual deployment. Organizations can initially use the APDA for decision support and progressively enable autonomous actions as their trust in the system increases.

To operationalize this vision, the following sections detail the architectural design and functional components of the proposed framework.

4.2 Architectural Overview

The APDA framework is organized into four primary layers: (1) Perception Layer, (2) Reasoning and Planning Layer, (3) Action and Orchestration Layer, and (4) Explanation and Feedback Layer. The relationships and workflows among these components are illustrated in the APDA reference architecture shown in Figure 1.

Figure 1. The APDA Reference Architecture for Phishing Defense

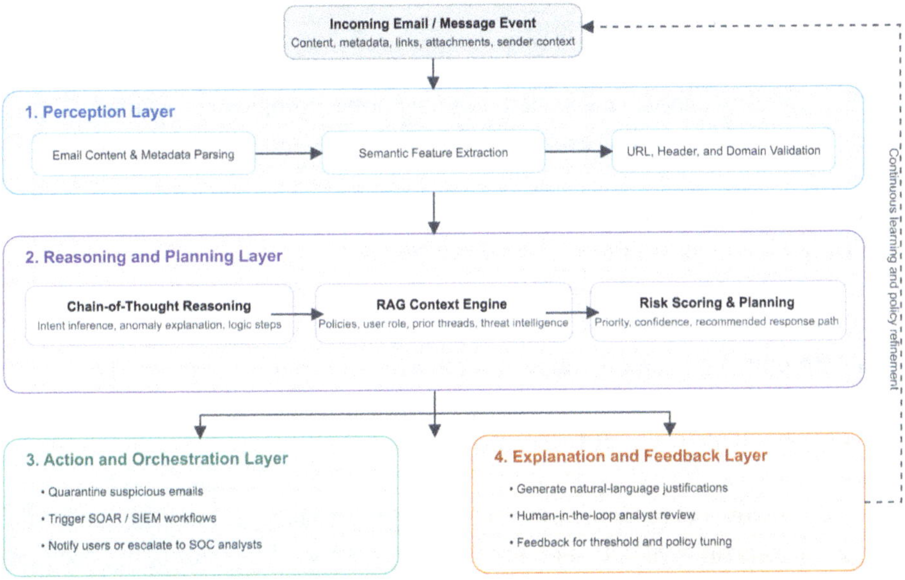

4.3 Perception Layer: Data Ingestion and Feature Extraction

The Perception Layer ingests email content, metadata, URLs, and organizational contexts, such as user roles and communication patterns. Transformer-based models generate contextual embeddings, whereas auxiliary analyses validate headers (SPF/DKIM), domain reputation, and behavioral patterns. These heterogeneous signals are fused into a unified representation to support downstream reasoning.

4.4 Reasoning and Planning Layer: Contextual Intelligence

The Reasoning and Planning Layer constitutes the core of the APDA architecture, where LLM-based intelligence is applied to interpret and evaluate potential threats.

Contextual Reasoning

Using LLMs, the system analyzes messages within their broader context. This includes:

- Comparing the message against typical communication patterns
- Evaluating consistency with organizational policies
- Identifying deviations from expected behavior

Chain-of-Thought Reasoning

CoT prompting enables the system to break down complex scenarios into intermediate reasoning steps. For example, an agent may evaluate the following:

1. Whether the sender identity is legitimate
2. Whether the request aligns with known policies
3. Whether the tone and urgency are suspicious

This structured reasoning enhances both accuracy and interpretability.

Retrieval-Augmented Generation

Retrieval-Augmented Generation enables agents to incorporate external knowledge from organizational data and threat intelligence sources, grounding decisions in contextual evidence. By integrating this information, the system can perform more informed and reasoning-based analyses of the data.

Risk Assessment

Based on the reasoning process, the system assigns a risk score to each message. This score reflects both the likelihood of malicious intent and potential threat impact.

4.5 Action and Orchestration Layer: Response Execution

The Action and Orchestration Layer translates the outputs of the reasoning process into concrete actions. This layer is responsible for implementing defensive measures in a timely and effective manner.

Response Actions

Depending on the risk assessment, the system may:

- Quarantine suspicious emails
- Generate warning messages for users
- Escalate incidents to SOC analysts
- Initiate automated investigations (e.g., searching for similar messages across the network)

Integration With Existing Systems

To ensure practical applicability, the APDA architecture is designed to integrate with existing cybersecurity tools, including:

- Security Orchestration, Automation, and Response (SOAR) platforms
- Security Information and Event Management (SIEM) systems
- Email gateways and directory services

This integration is achieved through standardized APIs, which enable seamless communication between components.

Policy-Constrained Actions

All actions are governed by predefined organizational policies. This ensures that automated responses are aligned with the business requirements and regulatory constraints.

4.6 Explanation and Feedback Layer: Trust and Adaptation

The Explanation and Feedback Layer enables analyst interpretation of system decisions and supports the continuous refinement of the agent through operational feedback.

Natural Language Explanations

The system generates human-readable explanations that describe the reasoning behind each decision. For example:

"This email was flagged as high risk due to domain mismatch, unusual urgency, and violation of financial approval policies."

These explanations facilitate the rapid validation of system outputs during incident analysis.

Human-in-the-Loop Mechanisms

Analysts can review or override high-impact decisions before execution.

Feedback Integration

Feedback from analysts is integrated to refine system behavior, including risk calibration and reasoning strategies. This continuous learning process enhances the performance and adaptability of the system.

4.7 End-to-End Workflow

The APDA architecture operates as a continuous pipeline:

1. **Ingestion:** Incoming messages are processed by the Perception Layer
2. **Analysis:** The Reasoning Layer evaluates the message using contextual and linguistic cues
3. **Decision:** A risk score and recommended action are generated
4. **Execution:** The Action Layer implements or suggests responses
5. **Explanation:** The system provides justifications and receives feedback

This workflow enables real-time adaptive defense against phishing attacks.

5. AUTONOMOUS TRIAGE AND RESPONSE: AGENTIC DECISION-MAKING WORKFLOWS

The ultimate value of an agentic system in cybersecurity lies in its ability to move beyond passive classification and toward active intervention. While traditional phishing filters stop at identifying a message as "spam" or "malicious," the Autonomous Phishing Defense Agent performs an autonomous triage and response to phishing attempts. This process involves determining the severity of a threat, evaluating its potential impact on the organization, and executing proportional and defensive strategies. The following discussion outlines the agentic workflows that enable the APDA to manage the phishing-incident lifecycle with minimal human intervention.

In practice, the true value of agentic systems emerges not at the point of detection but in how effectively they manage and respond to incidents such as cyber incidents.

5.1 The Shift from Detection to Triage

In traditional Security Operations Centers, triage is manual and time-intensive, often leading to alert fatigue and delayed responses. The APDA replaces this with an automated reasoning-driven triage (Vielberth et al., 2020).

As shown in Figure 2, this workflow transforms the detection event into a reasoned outcome by integrating semantic extraction and risk scoring before executing the response and closing the feedback loop.

Autonomous triage uses the reasoning of Large Language Models to analyze machine speed. Unlike binary classifiers, the APDA evaluates the nature of the threat, targeted entity, and required response urgency. By categorizing threats such as credential harvesting, financial fraud, and malware delivery, the agent assigns a priority level that reflects the actual enterprise risk.

Figure 2. End-to-End Workflow of APDA for Phishing Email Processing

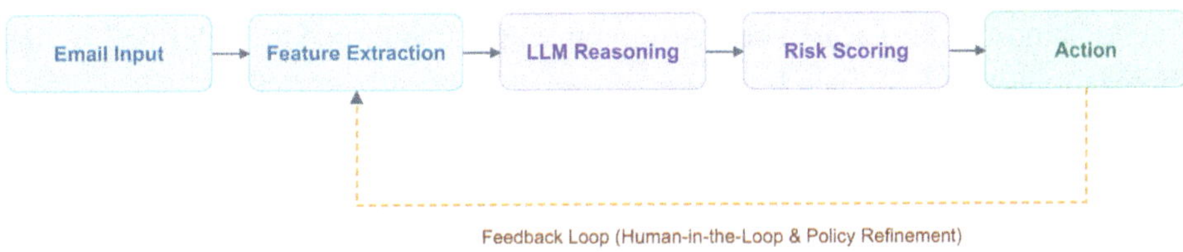

5.2 Reasoning-Driven Triage Workflows

The internal mechanics of the LLM Reasoning stage identified in Figure 2 workflow were operationalized through a multi-step investigation protocol using CoT prompting. By leveraging the inherent reasoning capabilities of Large Language Models, the APDA framework moves beyond simple pattern matching to perform deep cognitive analysis. When a suspicious event is detected, the agent initiates the protocol as follows:

1. **Identity Verification:** compares sender metadata with organizational patterns
2. **Intent Inference:** analyzes linguistic cues such as urgency and authority
3. **Contextual Cross-Referencing:** validates requests against policies and historical behavior

By documenting these steps in its internal "thought trace," the agent arrives at a high-confidence triage decision that is both technically sound and contextually aware.

5.3 Deterministic vs. Probabilistic Response

A critical challenge in autonomous cyber defense is balancing the flexibility of AI with the predictability required for security purposes. The APDA addresses this issue by employing a hybrid response model that combines probabilistic AI reasoning and deterministic security policies.

- **Probabilistic Core:** The LLM provides a risk score and a "reasoning path" based on the linguistic and contextual evidence.
- **Deterministic Guardrails:** The Action Layer maps the LLM output to a set of hardcoded organizational rules. For example, if the agent identifies a "Business Email Compromise" (BEC) attempt with >90% confidence, the policy may mandate an immediate account lockout and email quarantine across the entire domain.

This hybrid approach ensures that while the agent uses "agentic intelligence" to understand the threat, its actions remain within the boundaries defined by the organization's risk tolerance level.

5.4 Orchestrating the Response

Once a triage decision is made, the APDA orchestrates a response based on a tiered-autonomy model. For high-confidence threats, the agent executes automated technical mitigations, such as quarantining messages or blacklisting domains at firewalls. In medium-confidence scenarios, the agent initiates guided investigations and prepares case files and cross-domain activity logs for the analyst review. For ambiguous or nuanced social engineering attempts, the agent acts as an interactive assistant, querying the user or analyst to resolve any uncertainties before proceeding. This tiered approach ensures that automated actions are proportional to the risk and are supervised when necessary.

5.5 Multi-Stage Response and Containment

Beyond the individual inbox, the APDA considers the "Rise of Autonomous Cyber Warfare" by planning lateral movements. If a phishing link is clicked, the agent's workflow transitions from "email defense" to "threat containment." By integrating with Endpoint Detection and Response (EDR) tools, the agent can autonomously isolate the affected machine or revoke the user's active session tokens to prevent the attacker from using the stolen credentials. From an operational perspective, this 'cross-domain' response is essential in modern warfare contexts, where attacks are multistage and highly coordinated.

5.6 Evaluating Operational Effectiveness

Operational effectiveness was evaluated using metrics such as detection accuracy, mean time to respond (MTTR), and reduction in analyst workload, reflecting both technical performance and practical impact.

6. EXPLAINABILITY AND TRUST: HUMAN–AI COLLABORATION IN CYBER DEFENSE

As cybersecurity systems become increasingly autonomous, trust has emerged as a central concern. Although LLM-driven agents, such as the Autonomous Phishing Defense Agent, offer significant advantages in terms of speed, scalability, and reasoning capability, their adoption in real-world environments depends on the extent to which human operators can understand, verify, and control the decisions made by these agents in real-world environments.

Explainability is a prerequisite for deploying autonomous cybersecurity systems in operational environments. Security analysts must understand why an agent reaches a particular decision before trusting the automated recommendations. Consequently, explainability and human oversight have become essential mechanisms for ensuring the accountability, transparency, and safe adoption of agentic AI (Adnan et al., 2025).

6.1 The Need for Explainability in Cybersecurity

Explainability is critical in cybersecurity, where decisions must be transparent and justifiable. Unlike traditional black-box models, LLM-based systems generate human-readable explanations that describe reasoning processes, enabling analysts to understand and validate decisions in high-stakes environments.

Crucially, the adoption of such systems depends on human trust and their technical performance.

6.2 Human-in-the-Loop Mechanisms

Although large language models (LLMs) enhance explainability, human oversight remains crucial for ensuring reliability and their accountability. The APDA architecture integrates human-in-the-loop mechanisms, enabling analysts to validate, override, and query system decisions, while providing feedback that enhances system performance over time. This interactive capability supports collaborative decision-making between analysts and agent autonomy.

6.3 Trust Calibration and System Transparency

Trust is calibrated through progressive transparency and incremental autonomy, allowing organizations to gradually transition from decision support to semi-autonomous and fully autonomous operations.

6.4 Explainability vs. Security Trade-offs

While explainability enhances trust, excessive transparency may expose the system's logic to adversaries. Therefore, the APDA adopts selective explainability, providing detailed insights to analysts while abstracting sensitive mechanisms from the models.

6.5 Ethical and Governance Considerations

The deployment of AI raises key concerns, including accountability, bias, privacy, and regulatory compliance. These issues are addressed through audit logging, policy constraints, and secure data-handling practices.

6.6 Human–AI Collaboration as a Strategic Advantage

Human oversight remains integral to the APDA workflow, allowing organizations to combine automated triage with expert judgment in security operations.

7. RISKS AND LIMITATIONS: ADVERSARIAL THREATS, SAFETY, AND GOVERNANCE CHALLENGES

Although LLM-based autonomous agents hold promise for phishing defense, their deployment in cybersecurity involves significant risks and limitations. Therefore, it is essential to highlight the benefits of the Autonomous Phishing Defense Agent and critically assess its weaknesses, failure modes, and governance implications. This is crucial in cyber defense, where overconfidence in automation may create new vulnerabilities instead of eliminating existing ones.

This section analyzes the principal technical, operational, and ethical challenges associated with agentic phishing defense.

7.1 Adversarial Manipulation of LLM-Based Systems

Adversarial manipulation poses a significant challenge in LLM-driven cyber defense. Unlike traditional phishing filters, which are attacked through evasion techniques such as word substitution or domain rotation, LLM systems may be attacked at the reasoning level. Adversaries may influence the model's interpretation of the input, disrupt planning, or induce unsafe actions (Kulkarni et al., 2025).

A major concern is prompt injection, where a malicious text in an email or attachment manipulates the model instruction. For instance, a phishing message might use deceptive language to override the agent's reasoning, instructing the system to classify the message as safe or ignore suspicious indicators. If processed naively, the model may follow adversarial cues instead of organizational policies (Liu et al., 2024).

This is related to the risk of jailbreaking, in which attackers craft inputs to bypass LLM safety controls. In cybersecurity, this can lead to misprioritization, inappropriate recommendations, and suppression of legitimate alerts. As APDA relies on LLM reasoning for triage and planning, such attacks target the intelligence layer of the architecture (Mishra et al., 2025).

These risks indicate that LLM-based defense systems must be treated as components operating in adversarial environments that require secure prompting, input validation, and policy-constrained executions.

From a critical perspective, these risks highlight that increased autonomy does not eliminate uncertainty but redistributes it across the system.

7.2 Hallucination and Reliability Failures

Another LLM limitation is hallucination, which generates plausible but incorrect interpretations, explanations and recommendations. In phishing defense, hallucinations can manifest in various ways (Ji et al., 2023). The system might infer malicious intent where none exists, misidentify the nature of an attack, or fabricate unsupported contextual associations to support its conclusions.

For example, an APDA might incorrectly conclude that a legitimate email violates a financial approval policy when the request is both routine and authorized. Conversely, it may not recognize a well-designed spear-phishing attempt if the contextual evidence is incomplete or ambiguous. These errors are problematic because LLM outputs are often fluent and convincing, creating a false sense of confidence among users.

The risk is amplified when hallucinated outputs form the basis of automated actions. Incorrect recommendations to quarantine critical business correspondence, reset credentials, or escalate benign events can disrupt operations and erode the trust. Therefore, high linguistic sophistication should not be confused with high epistemic reliability.

Mitigation requires grounding outputs through retrieval, enforcing policy constraints, and limiting fully autonomous actions in high-risk scenarios.

7.3 False Positives, False Negatives, and Operational Trade-offs

The APDA must balance the false positives and false negatives. Excessive sensitivity may disrupt operations, whereas conservative thresholds may allow advanced phishing attacks to succeed in evading detection. Unlike traditional classifiers, errors in agentic systems can arise from complex interactions between reasoning and context. Therefore, deployment should adopt risk-tiered autonomy, automating low-impact decisions, and routing high-risk or ambiguous cases to human analysts.

7.4 Data Privacy and Confidentiality Concerns

Phishing defense requires access to sensitive communication data, raising privacy and compliance concerns. Organizations must ensure secure data pipelines, access control, audit logging, and adherence to regulations such as the GDPR, balancing contextual intelligence with data protection.

7.5 Governance, Accountability, and Control

From an operational perspective, governance focuses on defining authorization boundaries, auditability, and responsibility for the autonomous actions executed by the APDA. Clear decision rights, auditability, and role-based authorization are required to ensure traceability and compliance with laws. All system actions should be logged with the supporting evidence and reasoning.

7.6 Model Drift and Threat Evolution

Evolving attack strategies and organizational changes may cause model drift, thereby reducing the effectiveness of the system over time. Continuous evaluation, retraining, and prompt refinement are necessary to maintain alignment with real-world conditions.

7.7 Over-Automation and Human Deskilling

Excessive reliance on automation may lead to analyst deskilling and reduced vigilance. Organizations should preserve analyst expertise by reserving complex or high-impact decisions for human review, while allowing the APDA to automate routine defensive tasks.

8. EVALUATION FRAMEWORK: EXPERIMENTAL DESIGN, METRICS, AND ILLUSTRATIVE CASE STUDY

The evaluation framework presented in this section is intended as a structured blueprint for future empirical validation, rather than a report of completed experiments.

To validate the efficacy of the APDA architecture, a rigorous framework that considers its technical accuracy and operational utility must be established. Evaluating agentic systems differs from traditional classifiers; while a standard model is measured by precision and recall on static datasets, an agent must be assessed based on reasoning quality, decision-making speed, and the safety of its autonomous actions.

This section proposes a multidimensional evaluation framework designed to assess the proposed APDA framework. It details the experimental setup, identifies key performance indicators (KPIs), and provides an illustrative case study to demonstrate how the agent processes a complex multi-stage phishing attempt in a simulated corporate environment.

8.1 Experimental Setup and Data Selection

A robust evaluation requires a diverse and representative dataset that reflects the reality of modern AI-generated phishing threats. Because public datasets are often outdated and lack organizational context, a synthetic but realistic "Cyber Defense Simulation Environment" (CDSE) is recommended for testing purposes.

From an evaluation standpoint, assessing agentic systems requires going beyond traditional performance metrics.

1. Dataset Composition

Evaluation is proposed using a mixed dataset of legitimate enterprise emails, historical phishing samples, and synthetically generated AI-driven phishing messages within a simulated corporate environment.

2. Simulation Infrastructure

The APDA agent is conceptualized as being deployed in a sandboxed environment integrated with a mock Security Operations Center stack. This includes a simulated organizational directory (LDAP), policy repository (containing financial and IT protocols), and historical communication database to facilitate Retrieval-Augmented Generation.

8.2 Technical Evaluation Metrics

Evaluation included traditional metrics such as precision, recall, and F1-score, alongside agent-specific measures including reasoning alignment, explanation coherence, latency (Mean Time to Triage), and computational cost.

8.3 Operational and Cyber Defense Metrics

Operational effectiveness is assessed through the reduction in analyst workload, Mean Time to Respond (MTTR), and response safety, defined as the rate of incorrect autonomous actions.

8.4 Illustrative Case Study: The "Urgent Wire Transfer" Scenario

To illustrate the APDA workflow in practice, consider a simulated "Business Email Compromise" (BEC) attack targeting a senior financial controller in a global energy company.

1. The Attack Vector

The adversary sends an email appearing to come from the CEO. It references a "confidential acquisition project" (using jargon scraped from public press releases) and requests an urgent update to a vendor's wire transfer details. The email was linguistically perfect, contained no malicious links or attachments, and passed SPF/DKIM checks because it was sent via a compromised personal account frequently used for "off-the-clock" approvals.

2. Perception Layer Analysis

The Perception Layer ingests the email and extracts key features:

- **Linguistic Cues:** High urgency ("must be done today"), authoritative tone, and reference to a specific project.
- **Contextual Inconsistency:** The sender's email address is a personal account, which is unusual for sensitive financial requests.

3. Reasoning and Planning Layer (The Agentic "Thought Trace")

The APDA initiates a Chain-of-Thought reasoning process:

- *Step 1 (Policy Check):* The agent queries the RAG engine for the "Financial Approval Policy." It was found that all vendor changes must be processed through the internal ERP portal, not via email.
- *Step 2 (Identity Check):* The agent analyzes the historical threads. While the controller had replied to this personal email before, it was only for non-sensitive social coordination and never for financial transactions.
- *Step 3 (Conflict Detection):* The agent identifies a conflict between the requested "urgency" and the established "security protocol."

4. Action and Explanation Output

Based on this reasoning, the APDA assigns a Risk Score of 0.92 (High).

- **Recommended Action:** Quarantine the message and notify the SOC analyst.
- **Explanation:** *"This message is flagged as a high-risk BEC. While the linguistic tone mimics that of the CEO, the request for a vendor payment update via a personal email address directly violates the Corporate Policy FIN-04. No historical precedent exists for financial approvals from this sender's address."*

5. **Comparison with Traditional Systems**

A traditional machine learning classifier would likely have failed this test because the email contained no "bad features" (no malware, no suspicious links). The APDA succeeded because it moved beyond classification and contextual reasoning.

Such scenarios closely resemble real-world business email compromise (BEC) attacks that are observed in enterprise environments. Therefore, the proposed workflow can be interpreted as a realistic operational simulation rather than a purely hypothetical construct.

8.5 Comparative Discussion

Table 1. Conceptual Comparison of Expected Performance Characteristics: Traditional ML vs. Transformer-based LLM vs. Agentic APDA

Evaluation Metric	Traditional ML	Transformer-based LLM	Agentic AI (APDA Framework)
Detection of Zero-Day Phishing	Low (Relies on historical features)	Moderate (Strong semantic patterns)	High (Reasons via intent and policy)
False Positive Rate (FPR)	Moderate (Rigid patterns)	Low (Good contextual nuance)	Very Low (Verified via RAG context)
Mean Time to Triage (MTTT)	N/A (Requires manual analyst review)	N/A (Provides score, not triage)	Near real-time (architecture target)
Handling Social Engineering	Poor (Misses linguistic nuance)	Good (Detects linguistic patterns)	Exceptional (Infers intent and urgency)
Decision Transparency	Opaque (Numerical scores only)	Opaque (Attention weights)	High (Natural Language Justification)
Resource Efficiency	Very High (Low compute)	Moderate (GPU intensive)	Moderate (LLM API/ Inference costs)
Context Incorporation	None	Limited to prompt window	Extensive (Via Retrieval-Augmented Gen)
Operational Impact	Passive (Filtering only)	Passive (Filtering only)	Active (Response Orchestration)

The comparisons presented in Table 1 reflect the expected performance characteristics derived from architectural capabilities rather than empirically validated results.

The comparative performances of the three dominant paradigms in phishing defense are presented in Table 1. Although traditional machine learning and standard transformer models offer computational efficiency, they lack the operational actionability and contextual depth of the APDA framework. The shift from a passive 'detection only' metric to an 'autonomous triage' metric represents a fundamental improvement in the organizational security posture.

9. FUTURE DIRECTIONS: MULTI-AGENT SYSTEMS AND MULTIMODAL CYBER DEFENSE

The rapid evolution of artificial intelligence and cyber threats suggests that current LLM-based single-agent architectures, such as the Autonomous Phishing Defense Agent, are only an initial step toward fully autonomous cyber defense systems. Although the APDA demonstrates the feasibility of integrating perception, reasoning, and action within a unified framework, future advancements are likely to extend this paradigm toward distributed, collaborative, and multimodal intelligent systems. This section outlines the key research and development directions that are expected to shape the next generation of agentic cybersecurity.

9.1 Multi-Agent and Distributed Defense

Future systems will evolve toward multi-agent architectures, where specialized agents collaborate across email, endpoint, and network layers. This enables scalability, parallel processing, and improved resilience but introduces challenges in terms of coordination and consistency.

Looking ahead, the trajectory of agentic cybersecurity suggests a shift toward a more distributed and collaborative intelligence.

9.2 Multimodal and Adaptive Intelligence

Phishing attacks increasingly incorporate multimodal elements such as images, QR codes, voice, and deepfakes. Future systems must integrate multimodal models and support continuous learning to adapt to evolving threats while avoiding such adversarial contamination.

9.3 Toward Bounded Autonomy

Fully autonomous cyber defense remains a long-term goal. Near-term systems will adopt bounded autonomy, operating independently within defined constraints while escalating complex decisions to human analysts.

10. CONCLUSION: IMPLICATIONS FOR AUTONOMOUS CYBER DEFENSE AND RESEARCH

This chapter presented the Autonomous Phishing Defense Agent (APDA) as a framework for transitioning from static phishing detection to context-aware agentic cyber defense. These findings highlight the opportunities and practical constraints of deploying agentic intelligence in real-world settings. By integrating perception, reasoning, action, and feedback, the architecture enables systems to move beyond classification toward adaptive decision-making and responses. These findings highlight that modern phishing attacks, increasingly powered by generative AI, require defensive systems that can understand the context and integrate operations. However, as discussed, autonomy must be balanced with governance, explainability, and human oversight to mitigate risks such as adversarial manipulation and model unreliability. For researchers, this work identifies key directions, including adversarial robustness, multi-agent coordination, and evaluation of reasoning-based systems. For practitioners, it provides a roadmap for the incremental adoption of agentic AI in cybersecurity operations. Although the proposed architecture demonstrates strong potential, its real-world effectiveness ultimately depends on how well it integrates with existing organizational workflows and constraints. In the broader context of autonomous cyber warfare, agentic intelligence is a critical capability for maintaining organizational resilience against increasingly sophisticated and autonomous cyber threats.

AI DISCLOSURE STATEMENT

Artificial intelligence tools were used to support language refinement, structural organization, and drafting assistance during the preparation of this manuscript. All substantive intellectual contributions, critical analysis, interpretation, verification of sources, and final editorial decisions were performed by the author. The author reviewed and revised all AI-assisted content to ensure its accuracy, originality, and alignment with the scholarly objectives of the chapter.

REFERENCES

Acharya, D. B., Kuppan, K., & Divya, B. (2025). Agentic AI : Autonomous Intelligence for Complex Goals—A Comprehensive Survey. *IEEE Access : Practical Innovations, Open Solutions, 13*, 18912–18936. DOI: 10.1109/ACCESS.2025.3532853

Adnan, M., Rizwan, K., Ajmal, R. H., Ali, M. W., & Noreen, S. (2025). Strengthening Cybersecurity Trust : Reducing Hallucinations For Reliable Threat Intelligence And Risk Management Across Critical Sectors. *2025 20th International Conference on Emerging Technologies (ICET)*, 1-9. DOI: 10.1109/ICET66147.2025.11321434

Ahi, K., & Valizadeh, S. (2025). Large Language Models (LLMs) and Generative AI in Cybersecurity and Privacy : A Survey of Dual-Use Risks, AI-Generated Malware, Explainability, and Defensive Strategies. *2025 Silicon Valley Cybersecurity Conference (SVCC)*, 1-8. DOI: 10.1109/SVCC65277.2025.11133642

Alqahtani, H., & Ahuja, P. (2026). Secure autonomous cyber defense with LLM agents : A systematic review of autonomy, tool-augmented reasoning, and governance constraints. *Computers & Electrical Engineering, 135*, 111184. DOI: 10.1016/j.compeleceng.2026.111184

Aydın, E. E., & Bahtiyar, Ş. (2025). AI-Enhanced Phishing Attacks : Understanding the Threat Landscape and Defense Strategies. *2025 IEEE Global Conference on Artificial Intelligence and Internet of Things (GCAIoT)*, 1-6. DOI: 10.1109/GCAIoT68269.2025.11275533

Chandaeng, T., Kosolsombat, S., & Ratanavilisagul, C. (2025). Phishing Email Detection Using Large Language Models : A Comparative Analysis of Standalone and Retrieval Augmented Generation Models. *2025 10th International Conference on Computational Intelligence and Applications (ICCIA)*, 133-137. DOI: 10.1109/ICCIA67866.2025.00032

Chopra, S., Ahmad, H., Goel, D., & Szabo, C. (2026). ChatNVD : Advancing Cybersecurity Vulnerability Assessment With Large Language Models. *IEEE Access : Practical Innovations, Open Solutions, 14*, 18595–18610. DOI: 10.1109/ACCESS.2026.3659205

da Silva, C. M. R., Feitosa, E. L., & Garcia, V. C. (2020). Heuristic-based strategy for Phishing prediction : A survey of URL-based approach. *Computers & Security, 88*, 101613. DOI: 10.1016/j.cose.2019.101613

Desai, B., Patil, K., Mehta, I., & Patil, A. (2024). Explainable AI in Cybersecurity : A Comprehensive Framework for enhancing transparency, trust, and Human-AI Collaboration. *2024 International Seminar on Application for Technology of Information and Communication (iSemantic)*, 135-150. DOI: 10.1109/iSemantic63362.2024.10762690

Divakaran, D. M., & Peddinti, S. T. (2025). Large Language Models for Cybersecurity : New Opportunities. *IEEE Security and Privacy*, *23*(5), 38–45. DOI: 10.1109/MSEC.2024.3504512

Do, N. Q., Selamat, A., Krejcar, O., Herrera-Viedma, E., & Fujita, H. (2022). Deep Learning for Phishing Detection : Taxonomy, Current Challenges and Future Directions. *IEEE Access : Practical Innovations, Open Solutions*, *10*, 36429–36463. DOI: 10.1109/ACCESS.2022.3151903

Duc, D. M., Khang, D. T., Hien, D. T. T., Son, N. D. H., & Duy, P. T. (2025). Phishing Website Detection via Multimodal Learning and Retrieval-Augmented Reasoning. *2025 RIVF International Conference on Computing and Communication Technologies (RIVF)*, 292-297. DOI: 10.1109/RIVF68649.2025.11365186

Erdogan, L. E., Lee, N., Kim, S., Moon, S., Furuta, H., Anumanchipalli, G., Keutzer, K., & Gholami, A. (2025). *Plan-and-Act : Improving Planning of Agents for Long-Horizon Tasks* (arXiv:2503.09572). arXiv. /arXiv.2503.09572DOI: 10.48550

Freitas, S., & Gharib, A. (2026). *GenAI-Driven Threat Detection with Microsoft Security Copilot* (arXiv:2605.20896). arXiv. /arXiv.2605.20896DOI: 10.48550

Fukarel, S. G., Primo Edriatama, O., Aqila, M. R., Ananda Putri Masaling, N., & Chowanda, A. (2025). Phishing Detection with BERT : A Transformer-Based Approach for Cybersecurity. *2025 IEEE International Symposium on Consumer Technology (ISCT)*, 265-271. DOI: 10.1109/ISCT66099.2025.11297271

Husom, E. J., Goknil, A., Astekin, M., Shar, L. K., KÃ¥sen, A., Sen, S., Mithassel, B. A., & Soylu, A. (2025). Sustainable LLM Inference for Edge AI : Evaluating Quantized LLMs for Energy Efficiency, Output Accuracy, and Inference Latency. *ACM Trans. Internet Things*, *6*(4), 28:1-28:35. DOI: 10.1145/3767742

Huynh, T. T., Nguyen, H. T., & Tran, N. H. (2025). A Semantic-Aware Approach to Phishing URL Detection. *Engineering, Technology &. Applied Scientific Research*, *15*(6), 29866–29871. DOI: 10.48084/etasr.13187

Jabir, R., Le, J., & Nguyen, C. (2025). Phishing Attacks in the Age of Generative Artificial Intelligence : A Systematic Review of Human Factors. *AI*, *6*(8), 174. DOI: 10.3390/ai6080174

Ji, Z., Lee, N., Frieske, R., Yu, T., Su, D., Xu, Y., Ishii, E., Bang, Y. J., Madotto, A., & Fung, P. (2023). Survey of Hallucination in Natural Language Generation. *ACM Comput. Surv., 55*(12), 248:1-248:38. DOI: 10.1145/3571730

Kavya, S., & Sumathi, D. (2024). Staying ahead of phishers : A review of recent advances and emerging methodologies in phishing detection. *Artificial Intelligence Review, 58*(2), 50. DOI: 10.1007/s10462-024-11055-z

Khonji, M., Iraqi, Y., & Jones, A. (2013). Phishing Detection : A Literature Survey. *IEEE Communications Surveys and Tutorials, 15*(4), 2091–2121. DOI: 10.1109/SURV.2013.032213.00009

Kitterman, S. (2014). *Sender Policy Framework (SPF) for Authorizing Use of Domains in Email, Version 1* (Request for Comments RFC 7208). Internet Engineering Task Force. DOI: 10.17487/rfc7208

Kshetri, N. (2025). Transforming cybersecurity with agentic AI to combat emerging cyber threats. *Telecommunications Policy, 49*(6), 102976. DOI: 10.1016/j.telpol.2025.102976

Kucherawy, M., Crocker, D., & Hansen, T. (2011). *DomainKeys Identified Mail (DKIM) Signatures* (Request for Comments RFC 6376). Internet Engineering Task Force. DOI: 10.17487/rfc6376

Kucherawy, M., & Zwicky, E. (2015). *Domain-based Message Authentication, Reporting, and Conformance (DMARC)* (Request for Comments RFC 7489). Internet Engineering Task Force. DOI: 10.17487/rfc7489

Kulkarni, A., Balachandran, V., Divakaran, D. M., & Das, T. (2025). From ML to LLM : Evaluating the Robustness of Phishing Web Page Detection Models against Adversarial Attacks. *Digital Threats, 6*(2), 10:1-10:25. DOI: 10.1145/3737295

Lewis, P., Perez, E., Piktus, A., Petroni, F., Karpukhin, V., Goyal, N., Küttler, H., Lewis, M., Yih, W., Rocktäschel, T., Riedel, S., & Kiela, D. (2020). Retrieval-augmented generation for knowledge-intensive NLP tasks. *Proceedings of the 34th International Conference on Neural Information Processing Systems, NIPS '20*, 9459-9474. https://dl.acm.org/doi/10.5555/3495724.3496517

Liu, Y., Jia, Y., Geng, R., Jia, J., & Gong, N. Z. (2024). Formalizing and benchmarking prompt injection attacks and defenses. *Proceedings of the 33rd USENIX Conference on Security Symposium, SEC '24*, 1831-1847.

Mishra, R., Varshney, G., & Singh, S. (2025). Jailbreaking Generative AI : Empowering Novices to Conduct Phishing Attacks. *2025 55th Annual IEEE/IFIP International Conference on Dependable Systems and Networks - Supplemental Volume (DSN-S)*, 251-252. 2025 55th Annual IEEE/IFIP International Conference on Dependable Systems and Networks - Supplemental Volume (DSN-S). DOI: 10.1109/DSN-S65789.2025.00022

Patil, K., Gupta, P., Nagre, H., & Hadule, H. (2025). Layer Zero : The Safeguard against Malicious Prompts. *2025 1st International Conference on Advancement in Futuristic Technologies (ICAFT)*, 1-6. DOI: 10.1109/ICAFT66710.2025.11452809

Srinivas, S., Kirk, B., Zendejas, J., Espino, M., Boskovich, M., Bari, A., Dajani, K., & Alzahrani, N. (2025). AI-Augmented SOC : A Survey of LLMs and Agents for Security Automation. *Journal of Cybersecurity and Privacy*, *5*(4), 95. DOI: 10.3390/jcp5040095

Uddin, M. A., Mahiuddin, M., & Sarker, I. H. (2024). *An Explainable Transformer-based Model for Phishing Email Detection : A Large Language Model Approach.* DOI: 10.2139/ssrn.4785953

Vielberth, M., Böhm, F., Fichtinger, I., & Pernul, G. (2020). Security Operations Center : A Systematic Study and Open Challenges. *IEEE Access : Practical Innovations, Open Solutions*, *8*, 227756–227779. DOI: 10.1109/ACCESS.2020.3045514

Wei, J., Wang, X., Schuurmans, D., Bosma, M., Ichter, B., Xia, F., Chi, E. H., Le, Q. V., & Zhou, D. (2022). Chain-of-thought prompting elicits reasoning in large language models. *Proceedings of the 36th International Conference on Neural Information Processing Systems, NIPS '22*, 24824-24837. DOI: 10.52202/068431-1800

Yadav, T., & Masum, M. (2026). HRIT : A Human-Readable Framework for Phishing URL Detection using Large Language Models. *2026 IEEE 5th International Conference on AI in Cybersecurity (ICAIC)*, 1-6. DOI: 10.1109/ICAIC67076.2026.11395727

Zhang, J., Wu, P., London, J., & Tenney, D. (2025). Benchmarking and Evaluating Large Language Models in Phishing Detection for Small and Midsize Enterprises : A Comprehensive Analysis. *IEEE Access : Practical Innovations, Open Solutions*, *13*, 28335–28352. DOI: 10.1109/ACCESS.2025.3540075

Chapter 7
Explainability in Autonomous Cyber Decision-Making

Priya Kadyan
http://orcid.org/0009-0007-7049-2871
CGC College of Engineering, CGC Landran, India

ABSTRACT

The rapid advancement of agentic artificial intelligence has transformed cybersecurity into an autonomous and highly dynamic domain, where AI-driven systems independently detect threats, make decisions, and execute responses in real time. While these capabilities enhance operational efficiency and responsiveness, they also introduce significant challenges related to explainability and transparency. In high-stakes environments such as critical infrastructure, financial systems, and national security, the inability to interpret autonomous decisions can lead to operational risks, ethical concerns, and diminished trust.

1. INTRODUCTION

Development of Cybersecurity to Agentic Systems

A paradigm shift has occurred in the area of cybersecurity in that the older, fixed, rule-based systems of detection have evolved to dynamic autonomous agentic structures able to make autonomous decisions and act autonomously.Conventional systems like signature based intrusion detection tools were based on a set of predefined rules and known attack patterns thus restricted them to react to new or changing threats. The advent of agentic artificial intelligence has brought about

DOI: 10.4018/979-8-2600-0413-5.ch007

adaptive mechanisms that are driven by deep learning and reinforcement learning, which allow systems to learn as data streams continuously and change their behavior based on these changes. These systems are being used more frequently in Security Operations Centers (SOCs), cloud-native environments, and in environments that require critical infrastructure, where fast and precise response to threats is needed.

The agentic cyber systems can be defined as possessing the continuous decision loop which involves the ingestion and extraction of telemetry, model inference and automated response implementation. Data related to the network like NetFlow records and packet captures are analyzed in real time to enable the models to identify irregularities and take measures like blocking malicious traffic or isolating infected nodes. Such a change in the models of cybersecurity, being reactive to proactive, is part of a larger trend of shifting toward autonomous decision-making, in which systems are not just detecting the threat but also planning and performing the correct mitigation measures with less or no human oversight. Multi-agent coordination and meta-cognitive frameworks that facilitate the creation of governable autonomy and adaptive learning in complex environments usually support such architectures (Hughes et al., 2025; Kojukhov and Bovshover, 2026).

The growing acceptance of agentic systems has also widened the scope of operation of cybersecurity, bringing in new efficiencies and also raising issues of control and oversight. Autonomous systems are capable of handling large amounts of data, and making decisions at speeds beyond human comprehension, but their decision-making process is frequently integrated into complex model architectures that are hard to understand. Consequently, although these systems increase the detection abilities, uncertainty exists on how certain decisions are arrived at especially in hazardous settings.

Explainability and Transparency are Needed

Implementation of deep learning models, including Long Short-Term Memory (LSTM) networks, in cybersecurity systems has greatly enhanced the detection accuracy but has also lowered interpretability. These models are complicated computational systems with decision pathways that cannot be easily observed, and it is difficult to discern how to use certain output in the reasoning of analysts. Such a lack of transparency is vital when making wrong decisions that can have serious outcomes. False positives can result in unjustified isolation of a system and disruption of its operation, whereas false negatives can enable advanced attacks to go unnoticed, making the system more susceptible and open to harm.

Explainability and transparency thus become key elements of reliable autonomous cybersecurity systems. Explainability helps stakeholders to make sense of model decisions, whereas transparency provides a view of what is going on in the system, how data are used, and decision-making logic. An informed human supervision and efficient cooperation between the analysts and AI systems are supported by a combination of these attributes. The tracing decision capability is not only desirable but also obligatory in regulated systems like financial institutions and national security facilities where accountability and compliance needs are based on it (Radanliev, 2026; Pipyros, 2026).

The explainability is also of interest due to the necessity to establish trust in the AI-driven systems. Automated decisions can be more accurately trusted by analysts when they are able to see the reasoning behind the decision, especially those that are high-pressure situations and validation is needed quickly. Explainable artificial intelligence (XAI) techniques have been created to overcome this issue by offering understandable details about the conduct of models, thus closing the divide between performance and transparency (George and Mark, 2025; Carter et al., 2025). These strategies may give rise to more than efficient cybersecurity systems that are accountable and in line with the principles of ethical and governance.

Moreover, openness is significant in assuaging dangers in autonomous decision making. Being able to visualize the processes in the system and data flows and make them audible, organizations can detect anomalies, biases and respond to potential failures more effectively. It is particularly so when the environment is adversarial, as attackers may be interested in exploiting vulnerabilities in the system, or manipulate the actions of the models. The design transparency, e.g. traceability of decisions, audit mechanisms is therefore essential in system integrity and safe deployment of agentic AI systems into real-world scenarios (Adabara et al., 2025; Alshudukhi et al., 2025).

It is this changing frontier that is driving explainability and transparency towards the foundation of responsible and trustworthy autonomous cybersecurity. These principles can not only assist in enhancing the effectiveness of operations but ensure that the higher AI systems do not contradict human values and regulatory expectations, and organizational objectives.

2. CONCEPTUAL FOUNDATIONS

Autonomous Cyber Decision-Making

The well-structured pipeline to convert the raw network operations into effective security actions is the basis of independent cyber decision-making. This pipeline starts with the network traffic collection in which the data is collected by the utilization of NetFlow records, packet capture (PCAP) and system logs generated within the enterprise or the cloud environment. The resultant data are preprocessed including normalization, noise elimination and session reconstruction to remove the irrelevant and redundant data and to retain useful patterns. This processed information is then turned into structured inputs through feature engineering to take out features such as connection duration, change in size of packets, type of protocols and frequency of traffic. The artificial capabilities are the basis of predictive modeling where machine learning or deep learning models are employed to learn activities as either benign or malicious.The last phase consists of action execution where system itself takes action through blocking suspicious traffic, isolating compromised nodes, or creating alerts in Security Operations Centers.

The pipeline allows real-time decision-making, which greatly decreases latency in response to a manual analysis. Autonomous systems are in contrast to traditional systems which use predefined signatures and continuously adapt to changing threats. Reinforcement learning is important in promoting this adaptability by allowing systems to learn the best responses by interacting with the simulated environments. Agents in cyber ranges are trained in episodic reward structures where positive reinforcement is given to success in limiting a threat and penalties are given to wrong or slow responses. The system also evolves its policy with the number of training iterations, making it more capable of dealing with more complicated attack-related situations. It is used to support dynamic threat surfaces in which fixed models cannot be used, and systems can predict and react to previously unknown patterns of attack (Kalejaiye, 2022; Siddiqui et al., 2025).

Moreover, independent decision-making is also being introduced into multi-layered architectures, which combine various methods of analysis, such as entropy-based detection, fuzzy reasoning, and game-theoretic models. Such architectures allow systems to examine threats in a multi-facet manner, enhancing resilience and minimizing chances of false-identification. A combination of these methods enables more subtle decision-making, especially in adversarial scenarios where a malicious user will go out of his/her way to avoid detection. Consequently, autonomous cyber systems are becoming smart systems, which have the ability to continuously learn, adapt, and coordinate defense in a distributed environment.

AI Systems Explainability

Explainability AI systems are required to be able to interpret decisions of complex models, especially in cybersecurity where false classifications can be of great importance. Local interpretability methods give instance-specific explanations that explain the reason why a given decision was taken. SHAP (v0.41.0) and LIME (v0.2.0.1) are some of the most popular methods used to do this. SHAP gives each feature a contribution value, depending on its influence on the prediction, allowing an analyst to determine which features most affected a classification. LIME, instead, estimates the model locally with more interpretable models, which can be examined in detail regarding the predictions. The methods assist the analysts in making sense of the alerts and minimizing doubt in automated systems, enhancing confidence (Onyilo & Uzuegbu, 2025; Kalimuthu, 2025).

Global interpretability is a more general view, determining general trends in model behavior. Through the combination of feature significance based on numerous predictions, analysts are able to identify variables that have a consistent effect. This can especially be used to detect systematic bias or salient features in the data. As an illustration, the properties like connection duration, or packet frequency can always play a part in detecting anomalies, which implies that they are important in revealing malicious behavior. The model validation and optimization are backed by global explanations to make sure that the system is in line with the anticipated domain knowledge.

But, the introduction of explainability poses problems, especially when it comes to the trade-off between interpretability and performance. Frames like TensorFlow 2.12 and Keras can be used to create deep neural networks that can capture non-linear relationships that are too complex to be detected using other methods, leading to high-detection accuracy. But, they are by nature difficult to interpret since they are multi-layered and have very large parameter space. It can be a good idea to make these models simpler to make them more transparent and cost this in terms of predictive performance. This trade-off is to be considered, in particular, when accuracy and interpretability are both of interest, and the setting is high stakes. (Naif Alatawi, 2025; Moss et al., 2025).

Explainability is also critical towards improving usability and trust. Analysts tend to use automated systems more when they are in a position to discern the rationale behind the decisions. Explainable outputs could be incorporated into dashboards, in operational settings, which would offer contextual insights in addition to the predictions. This integration allows making decisions quicker, an analogous process will require less time on manual investigation, and such interaction will allow humans and AI to work together more effectively. The interpretability and validation of the decisions made by cybersecurity systems is becoming a necessity, and not a feature, as they gain greater autonomy.

Autonomous Systems Transparency

Transparency in autonomous cybersecurity architecture involves visibility of both system architecture, operational processes and data sources. System-level transparency refers to the availability of internal structure of models, which are understandable. Considering the example of recording the architecture of an LSTM-based model, the number of layers and neurons, one can get an idea of the sequence of data processing. This visibility assists in validating the model, debugging and optimization of the model to ensure that the system is acting as per the design.

Process transparency is concerned with the ability to trace decisions by using extensive logging and monitoring systems. Technologies like the ELK Stack that contains Elasticsearch 8.5, Logstash, and Kibana provide the opportunity to record the activity of the systems in detail. Such logs record the inputs, the steps used in the computation of predictions, and the chances of predicting as well as the explanation results, which can be used by analysts to retrace the decision paths. This is vital to forensic analysis and assists organizations to analyze incidents and understand how some decisions were made. Openness of the processes also facilitate accountability of the processes since the history of system behaviour is verifiable and can be audited and reviewed.

Data transparency focuses on the origin, format and the quality of data to train and assess. Research on intrusion detection has proposed popular benchmarks such as UNSW-NB15, CICIDS2017, that provide formatted re-creates of network traffic and attacks. Understanding distribution of features and the ratio of the types of attacks in these datasets is critical in order to have sound models. Biases, inconsistency and anomalies that may affect the performance of the model can be detected with the help of transparency of data. It also facilitates reproducibility that allows researchers and practitioners to not just verify their discoveries but also, to compare the models across different setups (Lakshmi and Jayanthi, 2025; Banerjee, 2025).

This is because system, process and data transparency create a comprehensive framework in handling autonomous cybersecurity systems. Its transparency at all levels enables organizations to control complex AI-driven processes, detect potential issues, and ensure the functionality of systems. In addition to enhancing trust, transparency also aids in meeting regulations particularly where accountability and auditability is paramount. As the autonomous systems evolve, transparency will become one of the greatest factors to consider as far as safe and efficient deployment is concerned.

3. SIGNIFICANCE IN CYBERSECURITY ENVIRONMENT

High-Stakes Decision Environments

Cybersecurity is increasingly an area of sovereign decision-making under the circumstances where the consequences of any mistakes are critical and urgent. Autonomous security systems in industrial control systems such as SCADA networks, controlling power grids, water systems and manufacturing processes are charged with the responsibility of detecting abnormalities, and responding accordingly in real time. Similarly in banking and financial networks, the AI-based systems monitor transaction patterns, detect the patterns of fraud, as well as automatically react to unwarranted access. These are environments with high availability and integrity requirements whereby any little failure can bring massive effects on operations and finances.

Misclassification has serious ramifications in such cases. SCADA systems that have any false positives may result in unwarranted shutdowns or isolation of critical elements that result in downtime and service interruptions. Wrongful blocking of legitimate transactions in the financial system can affect customer confidence, and result in loss of finances. False negatives conversely can cause attackers to exploit vulnerabilities to continue with the malicious activities, which causes a data breach, compromise of the systems, and interconnection failures throughout the network. The magnitude and speed of autonomous systems working increases these risks, that is why it is extremely important to ensure that the decisions are not only right but also verifiable and understandable (Kapoor et al., 2025; Paulraj et al., 2025).

As the autonomous systems start playing a more responsible role in such high-stakes settings, the role of well-developed decision validation mechanism becomes an issue of fundamental importance. Tracking of decisions and understanding can minimize the dangers of automation and ensure that the systems can be depended upon to be stable in any scenario.

Trust and Human–AI Collaboration

The integration of autonomous AI into the work of cybersecurity processes has transformed the role of human analysts who do not necessarily have to track manually anymore, but rather to provide strategic control and to justify decisions. At the interface of Systems based on AI, analysts interface with security information and event management systems such as the Splunk Enterprise Security 9.0 where alerts, threat intelligence and system recommendations are displayed in real-time. Within such a collaborative arrangement, AI systems are engaged in processing of massive amounts of data and initial threat detection but human experts provide contextual data and ultimate decision-making authority.

One of the most important aspects of supporting the successful human-AI collaboration is elucidability. Offering intelligible and comprehensible explanations of the choices taken by the AI systems enables the analysts to quickly identify the validity of the alerts, without going through lengthy analysis of the logs manually. This assists in alleviating the thinking burden and also makes decisions quicker when there is a lot of pressure which needs quick decision making. Explanations may also lead to confidence in validation where analysts will be in a better position to differentiate real threats and false alarms. This results in the more efficient interaction of the human and AI, where each of the two has a complementary advantage (Korede & James, 2025; Mareedu, 2025).

The development of collaboration models that will be able to integrate the human experience with AI functionality to guarantee the high level of operational effectiveness should be taken into consideration. This synergy is particularly crucial in unclear or complex situations where automated decisions may require contextual interpretation. Once explainability is introduced to the system design, organizations will be in a position to ensure that human operators are actively engaged, and can monitor autonomous processes.

In addition, trust is an imperative factor that defines the utilization and effectiveness of AI-based cybersecurity. As the analytic systems get a clearer insight into the decision making process and can verify that they are correct, the more likely the analysts will utilize automatic suggestions. This confidence is attained via clear and understandable systems that enable a less demanding incorporation of AI into the existing workflow and optimize system performance. The mistrust can also make even the most precise systems underutilized and limit their potential potential.

Ethical and Regulatory Requirements

An increasing use of AI autonomous systems in cybersecurity has been accompanied by immense regulatory and ethical challenges. Companies should ensure that decisions made using AI can be audited, be responsible and within the scope of governance. This is particularly true in areas such as finance, health and other critical infrastructures where regulation is mandatory and violation of the regulation can result to prosecution and fines. Auditable systems must be capable of providing transparent listings of decision-making processes including what data is being used in the decision, the models applied and the reasoning behind some of the decisions.

Another essential role in autonomous cybersecurity systems implementation is ethical concerns. The issues of prejudice, equity, and unintended implications ought to be thought through to ensure that the AI systems are accountable. As an illustration, discriminatory training data may lead to unequal recognition of certain type of traffic and this will give bias or inaccurate data. Transparency in the use of data and the behavior of the model is extremely important to identify and minimize such biases. Moreover, there are ethical paradigms, which emphasize the importance of human control, particularly in the situations, when automated decisions may be rather serious.

The compliance with the cybersecurity governance standards will imply the addition of the openness and clarity into the system design. Automation frameworks in real-time risk governance allow integrating monitoring, reporting and auditing AI-based decisions to make sure that organizations can hold themselves accountable and adhere to regulatory standards (Mishra, 2025; Karri and Jangam, 2025). The resilience also comes in these frameworks because they enable organizations to detect anomalies, respond to incidents and adjust to threats in changed manner in a controlled and transparent manner.

The overlapping of regulatory requirements and ethical concerns is a good example of the role of the design of cybersecurity systems, which are not only state-of-the-art but also aligned with the expectations of society and organization. As AI continues to be one of the most important areas of cybersecurity, the importance of transparency, accountability, and fairness will play a crucial role in guaranteeing the sustainability of trust and responsible innovation.

4. TECHNIQUES FOR EXPLAINABILITY

Model-Based Interpretability Approaches

Model based interpretability Model-based interpretability methods strive to develop systems that are easily comprehended by structuring models in a way that is easily understood about the decision making process of the model. Decision trees Scikit-learn 1.3 controlled depth (e.g., max depth = 10) decision trees are typically used as Baseline interpretable models in cybersecurity. These models provide explicit decision rules, such that analysts can determine how some characteristics such as connection length or packet size produces a classification outcome. Though these models may not be as predictive as deep learning architectures, they have the merit of being clear and transparent to the extent beneficial in validation and audit.

Attention mechanisms are added to deep learning models in higher-level situations where network traffic is sequential in nature to increase interpretability. These mechanisms use weights to weight the various components of the input sequences, emphasizing what time steps or features play the largest role in the prediction. To illustrate, an LSTM-based intrusion detection system can have attention layers that can determine important portions of traffic flow in order to signify aberrant behavior. This enables analysts to concentrate on pertinent parts of the information instead of analyzing complete sequences and thus enhance efficiency and comprehension. These methods close the performance vs interpretability gap by making explainability a part of the model architecture (Kostopoulos et al., 2024; Tursunalieva et al., 2024).

Model-based interpretability is especially applicable in the situations when transparency is a design requirement, e.g., in the regulated industries. These models aid in accountability and allow debugging and optimization by offering clear directions in the decision process. Nevertheless, they might not be applicable in the most complex settings where simpler models might not be able to capture complex effects, and additional explainability methods must be employed.

Post-Hoc Explainable Methods (LIME, SHAP)

Post-hoc explainability techniques are used to explain the predictions of complex models, which can be made after the model is trained. They are particularly useful in deep learning systems, where internal representations are not readily available. It is another popular approach called SHAP (SHapley Additive exPlanations) which computes the values of contributions by each feature using the principles of cooperative game theory. When run with SHAP DeepExplainer on the results of LSTM models, it can measure the contribution of individual features to prediction, both locally and globally. This allows analysts to determine crucial factors that can lead to threat detection, including abnormal traffic or protocol usage (Mosca et al., 2022; Zhang and Liu, 2025).

LIME (Local Interpretable Model-agnostic Explanations) is a complement to SHAP, producing instance-level explanations by creating local surrogate models. In the case of a prediction, LIME will use a simple and interpretable model to predict the behavior of an original model to enable the analysts to comprehend the decision in a localized environment. This comes in handy especially in cybersecurity where single alerts need to be analyzed promptly and precisely. LIME aids analysts in identifying a real threat or a false positive by making it easy to understand the particular cases (Alabi et al., 2023).

Explainable Reinforcement Learning

Explainable reinforcement learning addresses the issue of the explanation of agent decisions which are made through the interaction with dynamic environments. Reinforcement learning agents have been applied to cybersecurity applications, such as intrusion response and adaptive defense with policies learned and decisions based on the policies, rather than on a set of fixed rules. Reward decomposition, in this light, is a valuable technique, and breaks down the total reward into the contributions of individual state-action pairs. This allows analysts to capture the contribution of some actions, such as blocking a connection, or isolating a node, to the overall objective of mitigating threats.

Interpretability: Visualization of learned policies also enhances interpretability via visualization of the strategy of decision-making adopted by the agent. The reaction of the agent to different scenarios may be described with the help of policy maps or state transition diagrams which provide an insight into the behavior of the agent on different scenarios. It is possible to identify trends, strong points, and potential weaknesses of the approach used by the agent as well as optimize it using such visualizations. Eexplainable reinforcement learning comes in particularly handy when it comes to the field of cybersecurity, because autonomous action must be explained and oriented towards operational goals (Hickling et al., 2023; Vouros, 2022).

Despite its strengths, explainable reinforcement learning is a complex discipline in the view of the dynamism and stochasticity of environments where agents operate. There is constant battle of meeting the demands of transparency and the demands of learned policies. The advancement in the field is however, assisting in the creation of more interpretable and faithful autonomous systems.

Natural Language Explanations

Among other relevant measures in making AI-based decisions accessible to human users, natural language explanations can be given. Transformer-based models tend to generate such explanations, and are typically run using models such as HuggingFace Transformers v4.36. Such models exploit large-scale knowledge about language to provide coherent summaries of model choices, to contextualize predictions and interpret them in a way that is comprehensible to analysts.

In cybersecurity applications, natural language explanations can be included into SOC dashboards to allow real-time understanding, as well as alerts. One such example is that an alert can be followed by a written description that a connection was flagged due to suspicious traffic behaviour and having a long session. This minimizes the amount of manual investigation and enables analysts to swiftly evaluate the seriousness and legitimacy of threats. Interactive systems, including conversational interfaces, also contribute to the usability as they allow analysts to ask questions to models and get answers in a conversational form (Slack et al., 2023; Shrivastava et al., 2024).

Natural language explanations also aid in training and knowledge transfer because when the system is less experienced the analysts can gain a better understanding of how the system functions through descriptive outputs. Nonetheless, it is important that the accuracy and reliability of the generated explanations are ensured because inaccurate or simplified descriptions can lead to the wrong decision. Following the development of research in this field, it is likely that natural language explanations will become the more valuable element of making the cybersecurity systems more transparent and usable.

5. TRANSPARENCY MECHANISMS

System-Level Transparency

System-level transparency aims to expose the inner workings and flow of operations of cybersecurity systems and make them transparent and comprehensible. The modular architecture is a popular choice, in which the system is subdivided into distinct modules that include data ingestion, model processing, explanation engine, and visualization interface.

System level transparency is one extremely significant aspect that must be reproducible especially in those instances where the consistency in performance is required, as well as validation. Containerization technologies such as Docker 24.0 might provide standardized environment to implement cybersecurity models by ensuring that identical settings, dependencies and run-time settings are possible across other systems. This eliminates inconsistencies which may arise due to disparity in hardware or software environment. Organizations can replicate experiments, validate results and deploy updates with confidence by wrapping the entire pipeline in containers. Container deployment also allows scalability and portability where the systems can be deployed in cloud, edge, and on-premise infrastructures and remain transparent and controllable (Li & Zhang, 2025; Hersyah, 2025).

Moreover, system level transparency also helps in building trust, as it allows stakeholders to see the interaction of components and the way decisions are made. This visibility is crucial in intricate cybersecurity ecosystems that have several models and tools incorporated in them to ensure that the system is functioning as intended. It also aids in adherence to the governance prerequisites as it allows transparent recording of the system architecture and functionality.

Audit Trails and Process Transparency

Transparency in the process helps in ensuring that all the steps in the decision making process are traceable and verifiable. This is implemented in full-fledged logging systems which capture model inputs, prediction probabilities, intermediate calculations, and output of explanations. Organizations are able to retrace the steps on how a particular outcome was attained by recording the details of every decision. This is especially valuable in the field of cybersecurity because incidents will need to be assessed and interpreted to ensure they do not happen again and enhance the functionality of the systems.

Audit trails are normally done with scalable data storage and indexing applications like Elasticsearch that can easily retrieve and analyze logged data. The log entries have a time stamp and indexing that allows the analysts to make queries, monitor the historical patterns and carry out forensic analysis. As an illustration, the logs can provide an insight on how the system reacted to an incident, features that contributed to the decision, and the system records any anomalies. Such traceability aids accountability and offers a trace of the adherence to regulatory provisions.

The transparency of the processes also promotes efficiency in the operation because it allows constant monitoring and assessment of the performance of the systems. Through analysis of logged data, organizations are able to know patterns, anomalies, and enhance models to increase accuracy and reliability. Also, audit trails can help multiple teams work together since it enables them to have a common account of what has been happening in the system to respond to security incidents. The explanation outputs can also be incorporated into the logging mechanisms, which further enhances the transparency since the analysts can see not only what decisions have been taken but also the reasons behind them (Onyilo et al., 2025; Humayun et al., 2025).

Data Uncovering and Bias

One of the essential elements of reliable cybersecurity legal structures is data transparency, since the quality and features of the data directly affect the quality of the models. UNSW-NB15 dataset, which is frequently utilized in the research of intrusion detection, comprises of about 2.5 million records and 49 features, including a comprehensive set of network behaviors and types of attacks. To achieve transparency in such datasets, it is important to record data sources, preprocessing, feature definitions, and classes distribution. Such data allow analysts to learn about the construction of the dataset and its applicability to particular uses.

An important part of data transparency is the distribution analysis of the features and class balance. This can create biased models as a result of unbalanced datasets, with specific types of attack being overrepresented, and thus working well on dominant classes and poorly on underrepresented ones. Investigating the distribution of the types of attacks like DoS, exploits, and reconnaissance, organizations may observe possible biases and take remedial action, like resampling or weighting strategies. This guarantees that models have consistent performance in case of various forms of threats and minimizes the chances of misclassifying threats.

Transparency of data also facilitates reproducibility and comparability of research and deployment. With well documented and standardized datasets, it is possible to validate and compare results across systems and studies. This is especially crucial in team set-ups where more than two teams or organizations are involved in the development of the system. Open data practices allow a regular assessment to be made and integrate additional sources of data, increasing the flexibility of cybersecurity systems (Hasan et al., 2026; Kwubeghari and Ezeji, 2025).

Moreover, data transparency can be used to detect and avoid biases that can be created by the data-collection or preprocessing process. Through the preservation of the visibility of data properties, organizations are able to uncover anomalies, promote fairness and enhance accuracy of model predictions. This is necessary to preserve trust in AI-driven systems especially where the decisions that are made have a high level of operation and ethical consequences. On the whole, data level transparency is a complement to system and process transparency to build a holistic model that facilitates accountability, reliability, and efficient cybersecurity activities.

6. DISABILITIES IN EXPLAINABILITY AND TRANSPARENCY

Complicatedness of AI Models

The trend of using deep learning in cybersecurity has posed major problems of model complexity and interpretation. The modern architectures like deep neural networks and LSTM-based models can comprise millions of parameters, which are distributed in various layers, allowing these models to learn very complex and non-linear relationships in network data. Although this complexity helps in getting a high detection accuracy, it also conceals the internal decision-making process, so it is hard to trace the path of how certain inputs to certain outputs. Learned representations are abstract, which restricts the mapping of model behavior to real-world features by analysts, and enhances transparency and interpretability. This has led to the fact that, despite the effectiveness of models, they lack explainability and that is why they may not be adopted and trusted in an operational setting (Mathew et al., 2025; Chander et al., 2025).

The complexity of cybersecurity data is further complicated by the fact that cybersecurity data is dynamic and therefore the model has to keep up with changes in cybersecurity threats. The retraining and updates also lead to a lot of extra complexity with more layers to explain and maintain a consistent explanation over time. Seeking to simplify models or introduce interpretability mechanisms come with trade-offs where one can achieve a reduction in performance, which seems like a continuous dilemma between accuracy and transparency. To overcome this issue, it is necessary to develop methods that can give valuable information without affecting the predictive powers of the developed models (Belghachi, 2023; Kaya et al., 2026).

Adversarial Environments

The nature of cybersecurity is a highly competitive game, with attackers making active efforts to use the weaknesses of the system and avoid detection. This adversarial behavior is carried over to explainability mechanisms, which also can be the target of manipulation. With a well-crafted input data, attackers are not only able to manipulate the prediction of the model but also the explanation that will be produced due to the prediction. This may result in false perceptions, with innocuous sounding explanations hiding ill intent, lowering the usefulness of human control.

The manipulation of inputs, e.g. adversarial examples, can manipulate the values of features to generate an explanation that does not change the model prediction much. This brings a gap between the real arguments of the model and what is explained to the analysts. These flaws prevent confidence in the explainability tools and emphasize the importance of the strong and safe explanation procedures. The reliability of explanations in adversarial context is an essential problem that can result in wrong judgments and higher risk in case of inaccurate or biased explanations (Mohammad et al., 2025; Hu et al., 2026).

Moreover, adversarial systems need systems to work under the conditions of uncertainty and deception, when attackers constantly improve their strategies. This dynamic nature renders it hard to have consistent and reliable explanations since models have to be responsive to changing patterns that may not be consistent with what was previously learnt. Constructing robust explainability methods that are not susceptible to adversarial manipulation is a current topic of study.

Real-Time Constraints

In cybersecurity, real time operation is a basic requirement wherein time delays in detection and response can be very costly. Nonetheless, numerous explainability methods add computational burden, which may affect the performance of a system. As an illustration, SHAP-based techniques may offer detailed and theoretically-founded explanations, but the computation can be very expensive, and in real-world applications, latency can be approximately 120 milliseconds per instance. This added latency may be a bottleneck in high-throughput settings, where thousands of events have to be handled each second.

The importance of timely responses and the need to provide a detailed explanation is a major dilemma in implementing explainable AI in the operational environment. There should also be systems that are able to give priority to critical decisions without compromising on performance levels. This can be in the form of selectively explaining high-risk or ambiguous instances, instead of explaining all of the predictions. These methods will help to maximize resource use without sacrificing the advantages of interpretability (Atmakuru, 2025; Chinnararaju, 2025).

Explainability also necessitates efficient implementation strategies such as acceleration with hardware and parallel processing of the systems in real time. Although these developments have been made, the computational complexity of most explainability procedures remains a challenge especially when operating on large scale.

Their usefulness is subject to the capacity of human analysts to comprehend and respond to them, even in cases where explanations exist. Outputs of cybersecurity systems are typically of high dimensionality, with two or more features used to make a single prediction. These multi-dimensional feature contributions may be difficult to interpret especially when it comes to time sensitive scenarios and the analyst is required to make quick decisions. Complicated images or textual outputs can be overwhelming to users, and they can become confused or misunderstand.

The consistency and reliability of the decision-making also depend on human cognitive limitations. The same explanation can have different interpretations with the various analysts depending on their experience, knowledge and cognitive bias. This inconsistency may result in inconsistent reactions and lessen the overall performance of the system. Breaking down explanations without losing any essential information is crucial to better usability and making insights actionable (Mathew et al., 2025; Belghachi, 2023).

Also, the growing number of alerts and explanations produced by autonomous systems may add to the information overload. Analysts might find it difficult to prioritize and process a lot of information thus making delayed or suboptimal decisions. To overcome such challenges, it is important to design explanation interfaces putting information in a clear, concise and context-sensitive format. Human cognitive abilities will help organizations organize the usefulness of human-AI cooperation and make explainability a valuable part of cybersecurity processes by aligning the explanations with human cognition abilities.

7. ETHICAL AND GOVERNANCE IMPLICATIONS

Responsibility Within Autonomous Systems

A key issue with autonomous cybersecurity systems is accountability, especially when the control of AI-driven agents to human operators is changed. In these kinds of environments, it is necessary to make sure that all actions performed by the system can be traced, and justified to keep control and trust. The traceability is implemented by exhaustive logging systems that capture inputs, model prediction, confidence scores and explanation output. Such records help analysts and auditors to recreate decision trails to give a clear picture of how and why a particular action was implemented.

The results of the explanation also improve the accountability of the model decisions as they provide interpretable reasons behind the model decisions. Such explanations together with logging offer a clear record that could be utilized to support the operational review as well as the post-incident analysis. The two-layered method ensures that not just decisions are recorded, but they are interpreted as well, ensuring that organizations would be able to work out mistakes, improve models, and make systems more reliable. Accountability systems are also crucial in the context of responsibility distribution in the event of system failure, where it is necessary to determine whether it is a model design or data quality or deployment situation (Ajayi et al., 2024; Kumar and Kumar, 2026).

As autonomous systems continue to be used, it is increasingly becoming demanded that there be robust accountability systems. Such frameworks must not be limited to the technical but also the organizational responsibility in order to make stakeholders at different levels know their part in the management and control of AI-driven systems. By integrating traceability and explainability as part of the design of its systems, organizations can create a setting of successful and responsible autonomous decisions.

Prejudice, Justice, and Morality

Unbiasedness and nepotism are the most important ethical concerns of applying AI-based cybersecurity systems. These issues are typically due to the imbalances in the training data sets and some type of network traffic or attack patterns are overrepresented. The difference in distribution of attack types may influence behavior in a model in a dataset such as UNSW-NB15, whereby the most prevalent classes will be detected more frequently, and the least prevalent threats will be less sensitive. This skew can cause unstable performance whereby certain attacks are reliably identified and others are not identified causing uncertainties in the security of a system.

Ethical implications of such biases are not restricted to the technical performance but have effects on the reliability and fairness in decision-making. E.g., a biased model with the predisposition to suggest some type of traffic as malicious may lead to a high number of false positive results, which leads to unnecessary disruptions and distrust of the model. Conversely, absence of specific types of attacks representation may be a challenge of undetected attacks. To tackle the problems, a thorough dataset analysis, such as distribution evaluation and methods of bias reduction, such as resampling, balancing of features, and continuous measurement of model performance (Akinrinola et al., 2024; Rongali and Kumar Kakarala, 2024) is necessary.

Fairness in AI systems also entails the fact that decisions made are also consistent and explainable in various situations. This necessitates openness in the collection and processing and utilization of data in model training. Ethical frameworks focus on the need to ensure that AI systems are aligned with societal values, thus ensuring that they are effective and responsible in their operations. Fairness and the reduction of bias in cybersecurity is critical to ensuring system integrity and trust in the system because decisions may have an impact on critical infrastructure and sensitive information (Hasan and Jahan, 2024; Adebayo et al., 2025).

Compliance and Regulatory Frameworks

The increased use of AI in cybersecurity has also caused more regulatory oversight as organizations are now required to show that their systems are used in a transparent, accountable and compliant way. The regulatory frameworks underline the requirement of explainable outputs which can be reviewed and audited especially in areas where security and privacy are of utmost importance. The requirements of compliance have frequently required that organizations keep an extensive documentation of system behavior, including data sources, model settings and decision output.

Such regulatory needs are important to be met with explainability, which provides explainable and interpretable knowledge about model behaviour. It is difficult to demonstrate the compliance since opaque systems do not have explainable outputs that can be used to justify their decisions. This is particularly needed in financial services, health care and critical infrastructure whereby the regulatory standards demanded a great deal of transparency and accountability. Explainability in the design of system would enable organizations to ensure that their AI systems are not out of operation and do not violate the expectations (Kumar and Dadhich, 2024; Atoum, 2025).

AI governance structures also address other more broad problems like risk management, safety and ethical deployment. These models provide a set of principles of how to design, implement and monitor AI systems in such a way that they can operate within certain limits and correspond to a set of standards. In the autonomous approach to cybersecurity, the governance mechanisms must take into account the dynamic and adversarial nature of the environment in which the systems must be able to adjust to changing threats and guarantee compliance and ethical integrity. This has to be monitored, audited and constantly improved every time new models and processes are created (Biswas and Sarkar, 2026; Kumar Kakarala and Rongali, 2025).

Responsible innovation involves putting in place regulatory and ethical considerations in cybersecurity systems. As the AI continues to transform the cybersecurity landscape, the organizations must find a balance between automation and transparency, responsibility, and equity. By combining system design with regulatory systems, and ethical guidelines, they are able to build robust and dependable systems that are able to work effectively in difficult and risky conditions.

8. APPLICATIONS IN CYBERSECURITY

Autonomous Threat Detection

One of the most effective uses of explainable AI in cybersecurity is autonomous threat detection systems, which allow maintaining the continuous monitoring of the state of threats and responding to the changes in real time. In this application, an LSTM-based intrusion detection model was learned on the UNSW-NB15 data set consisting of a variety of network traffic patterns and attack types labelled. Python 3.10 and TensorFlow 2.12 were used to create the model, and it was trained in 25 epochs and a batch size of 128. The model was trained on an NVIDIA RTX 3080 GPU, enabling it to be used to process large-scale data with high efficiency. The need to select LSTM architecture is especially applicable to the field of cyber security because it considers temporal relationships in network traffic streams in sequence, thus allowing the identification of sophisticated and dynamic attack patterns that otherwise would be hard to detect through the use of a static analysis. These AI-based detection systems are becoming more common in critical infrastructure and enterprise settings, where quick detection of threats is paramount (Khalaf et al., 2025; Hernandez-Rivas et al., 2024).

In addition to detection, these systems are intended to be autonomous and depend less on the human intervention. The system is able to detect anomaly and classify threats and respond within milliseconds by continuously analysing the incoming data streams. This feature greatly increases the efficiency of its operations and minimizes the chances of slow reaction, which in most cases is taken advantage of by attackers.

Figure 1. Conceptual Framework- Explainable Autonomous Cyber Defense System

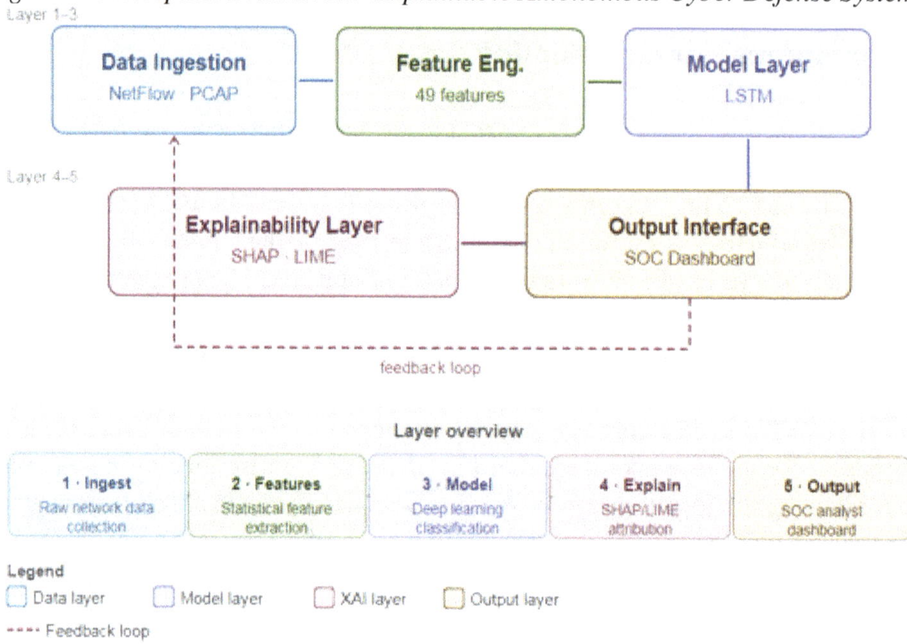

The figure reveals a multi-layered model which incorporates data ingestion, feature engineering, model inference, generation of explanations and visualization functionality. The data will pass through the layers sequentially and a feedback loop between the output interface and the model will be provided to allow the data to constantly learn and adapt. The fact that the system is developed with an inclusion of an explanation layer and that the system has a predictive model indicates that interpretability has been factored into the system design. It is a design that emphasizes on the modularity aspect, that is, the individual components can be optimized and monitored. The framework will enable scaling and will make the decision-making process transparent and traceable, which is essential to implement in a complicated cybersecurity environment.

System Workflow and Implementation

The workflow starts with preprocessing and cleaning of raw network traffic into a format that is easy to analyze by using Pandas 1.5 and NumPy 1.24, followed by processing the raw network traffic. The MinMaxScaler is used to normalize the input values to ensure that feature values are normalized, thus enhancing the stability and convergence of the model when training. The trained model is a deployed service through a REST API, which allows real-time inference and can be integrated with other systems like SIEM platforms. This deployment method enables the system to continuously process the incoming data streams to produce predictions and the associated explanations which can be available to the analysts in real time. The workflow makes every stage, such as data preparation and decision output, performance and transparency optimized, which makes the cybersecurity operations reliable and scalable (Ameedeen et al., 2024; Khan et al., 2024).

Figure 2. Explainable Intrusion Detection System Methodological Workflow

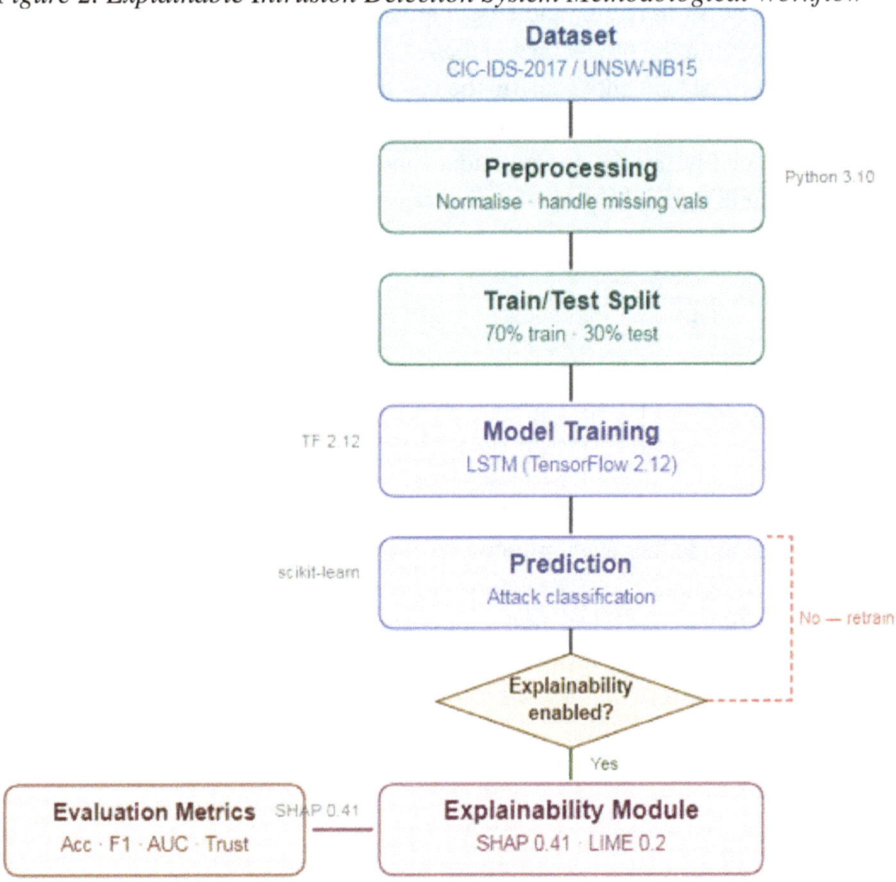

The figure illustrates the overall workflow of the system from the input of the dataset and continuing through the processes of preprocessing, feature extraction, model training, prediction and generation of the explanation. It demonstrates how explainability modules can be integrated into the pipeline, and all predictions can be given interpretable results. The workflow makes clear the interaction between components and how preprocessing and normalization are important to providing consistency in performance. This systematic plan can enable an aspect of repeatability and can be easily applied in the field.

Detection Performance Results

Analysis of intrusion detection system demonstrates that the system portrays good performance in the key metrics. The initial LSTM model was 95.8% and the introduction of the explainability mechanisms reduced the accuracy slightly to 94.2%. The precision, recall, and F1-score were estimated to be 0.94, 0.91 and 0.92 respectively with the precision and the recall being equal to detect normal and malicious traffic. These results confirm the fact that the model achieves high detection performance with the introduction of interpretability features. The slight drop in accuracy, which implies the computational and structural modifications required to add explainability, and the performance-transparency trade-off are the minor.

Table 1. Model Performance (Accuracy, Precision, Recall) F1-Score

Model Type	Accuracy (%)	Precision	Recall	F1-Score
Baseline LSTM	95.8	0.94	0.92	0.93
XAI-Enabled LSTM	94.2	0.93	0.91	0.92

The table presents a comparison of the explainability-enhanced models and the baseline models on the key evaluation measures. It demonstrates that the accuracy and recall have a slight decline, but the overall performance is strong. This suggests that the explainability can be integrated into cybersecurity systems without majorly affecting the detection performance, which justifies the practical feasibility of interpretable AI models.

Figure 3. Comparison of Detection Accuracy of Models.

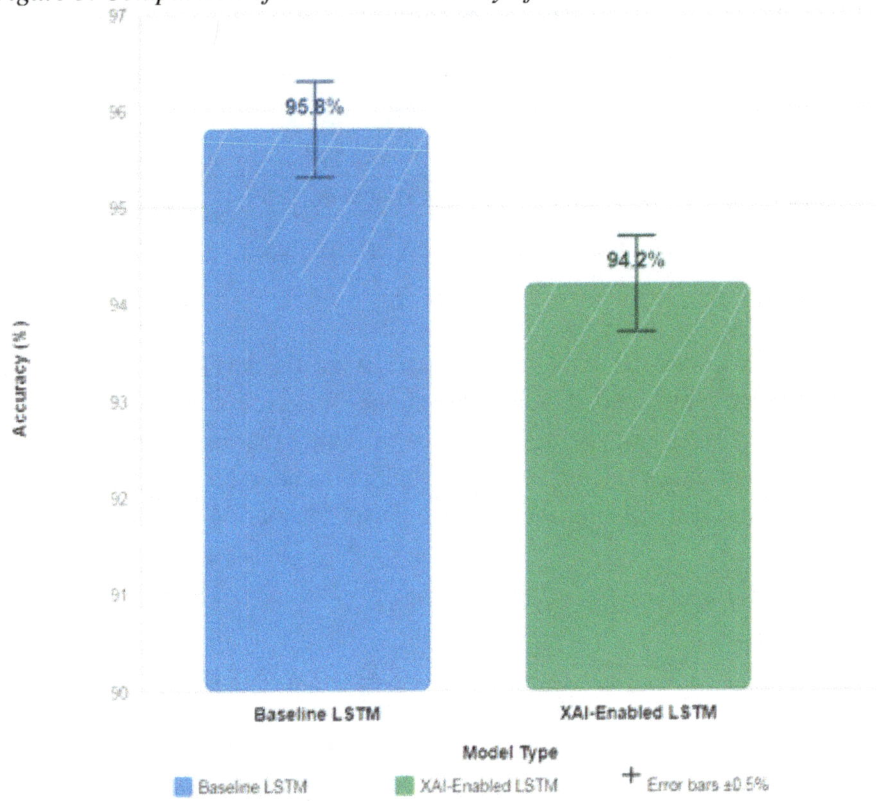

The figure shows a direct comparison of the accuracy in the baseline and explainable models. It not only shows that it has a slight performance decrease with the inclusion of explainability mechanisms, but it also indicates that the difference is insignificant. This supports the fact that the costs of interpretability are less than the slight sacrifice in accuracy.

Analyst Trust Evaluation

In an effort to determine the effect of explainability on user trust, a survey was carried out among 60 participants (cybersecurity professionals) of different experience levels. The participants were tested in two conditions; one is with and the other without the support of the explanation of system outputs. The findings showed a great improvement in trust when there was an explanation where the average scores of trust changed to 4.4 as compared to 3.1 out of a five-point Likert scale. Such improvement shows that interpretable outputs lead to increased confidence in users and making decisions more effectively. Analysts claimed that explanations decreased the necessity to manually analyze logs and facilitated faster checking of the alerts, which enhanced efficiency.

Table 2. Survey Results of Trust in Analysts (Mean and SD)

Condition	Sample Size (n)	Mean Trust Score (1–5)	Standard Deviation
Without Explanation	60	3.1	0.6
With Explanation	60	4.4	0.4

The table illustrates the statistical comparison of the levels of trust in both conditions, mean values and standard deviations. It does not only have greater average scores of trust, but also less variance, meaning that user perceptions are more consistent in case explanations are given. This underscores the importance of explainability as a stabilizing and enhancing user interaction with AI systems.

Figure 4. Comparison of Trust Score by Analysts

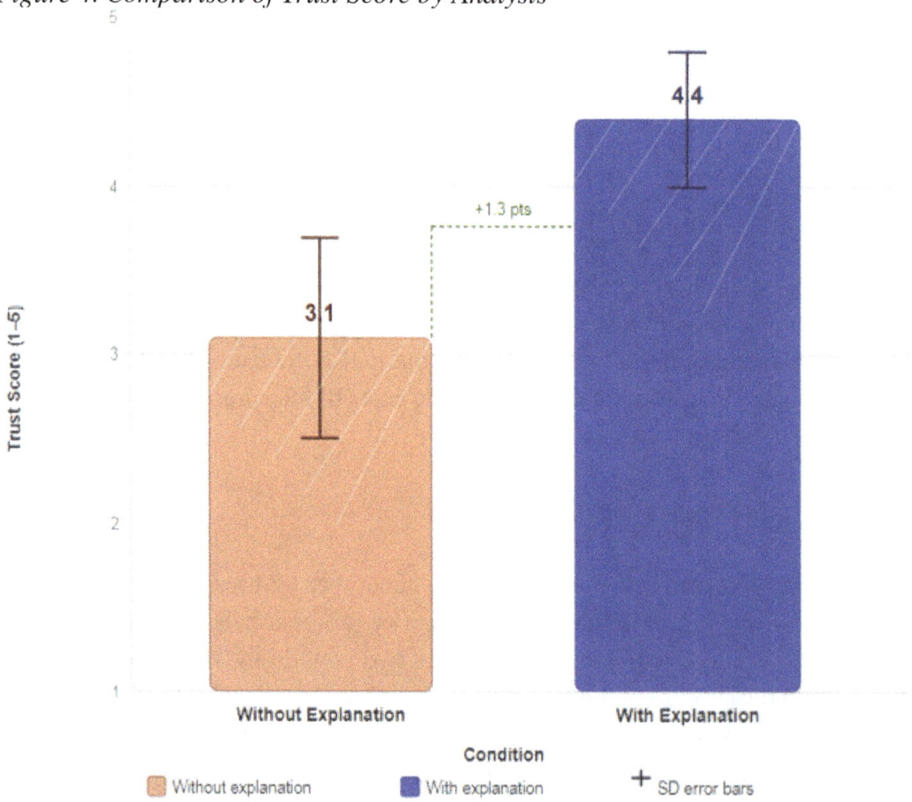

The figure illustrates the variation in the trust scores in systems that are not explainable and those that are explainable. It demonstrates well how the user confidence is greatly increased, and the importance of transparency in developing a productive human-AI interaction.

Response Time Analysis

The incremental cost of explainability mechanisms in terms of computation affects the latency of systems. Baseline system averagely required 210 milliseconds to respond as compared to explainable system which has an even greater latency of 235 milliseconds. Although this increase is not so high, it demonstrates that it is required to make explainability methods more optimized in case it is targeted at the real-time usage. High throughput settings have the potential to multiply delays and a balance between interpretability and performance efficiency is essential.

Table 3. Overheads that Explainability Layer Introduces in Performance

Metric	Baseline System	XAI-Enabled System	Percentage Change (%)
Response Time (ms)	210	235	+11.9
CPU Utilization (%)	48	57	+18.8
Memory Usage (GB)	6.5	7.8	+20.0
Throughput (Packets/sec)	10,000	8,800	-12.0

The table shows that explainability affects performance of the system, i.e., there are variations in response time, resource use, and throughput. It gives a close comparison between the baseline and improved systems, which shows the trade-offs that are involved in incorporation of interpretability mechanisms. This discussion will aid in making informed choices about system design and implementation.

Figure 5. Response time Effect of Explanation Layer

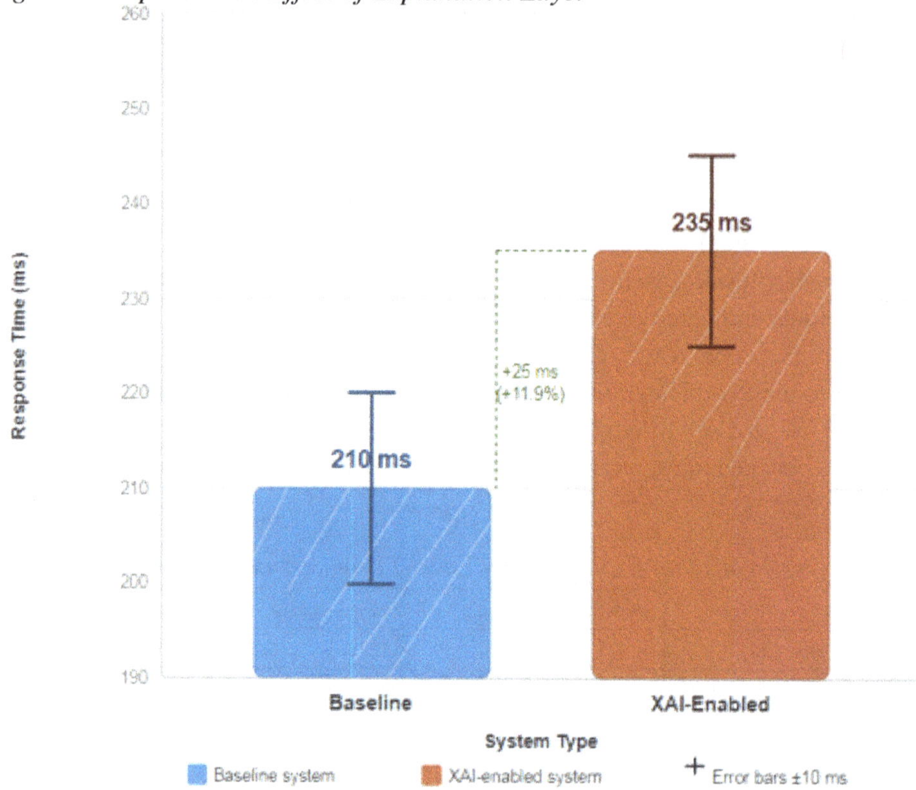

The figure shows how the response time is increased because of the addition of explainability. It gives a vivid visual comparison of the performance between the baseline system and the enhanced system and how interpretability impacts the performance and why optimization is required in real-time systems.

Feature Contribution Analysis

The analysis of the features with SHAP showed the most significant variables in the decision-making process of the model. The most common features that were found to contribute to threat detection were packet size variance (0.31), duration of connection (0.24) and source bytes (0.18). These insights can be useful in understanding the behavior of a model so that the analyst can concentrate on key indicators and develop more effective feature selection schemes. The possibility of determining important features contributes to the increased transparency and justification of model results.

Table 4. UNSW-NB15 Dataset Feature Summary (49 Feature and Categories)

Feature Category	Number of Features	Example Features
Flow Features	8	Duration, Protocol, Service
Basic Features	10	Source Bytes, Destination Bytes
Content Features	6	Number of Failed Logins, Root Access
Time-Based Features	9	Connection Count (last 2 sec)
Additional Generated	16	Packet Size Variance, Flow Entropy
Total	**49**	—

This table shows the classification and distribution of the features in the dataset, which offers context to the attribution results of features. It emphasizes the variability and applicability of input variables, which help in better comprehending the process and interpretation of data to the model.

Figure 6. SHAP Feature Importance Distribution of Threat Detection

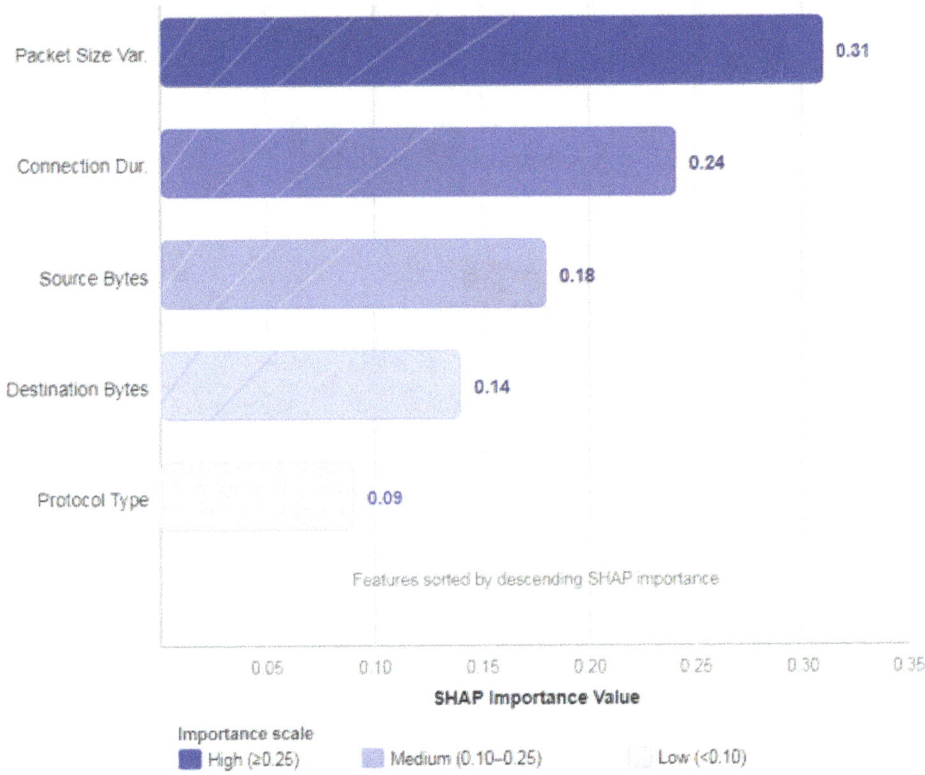

The figure shows the relative values of the key features according to SHAP values. It demonstrates the level of contribution of various variables in predictions and this allows analysts to determine patterns and test model behavior.

Instance-Level Decision Interpretation

Instances-level productions of explanations generated by LIME provide certain information about certain predictions. The model identified the use of ports abnormally and long session length as the key factors in a given anomaly. This level of granularity can allow analysts to understand how every alert was correctly justified, and increase accuracy in the steps of threat assessment and false positive reduction.

Figure 7. Local Explanation of Network Intrusion Instance Here is LIME-Based

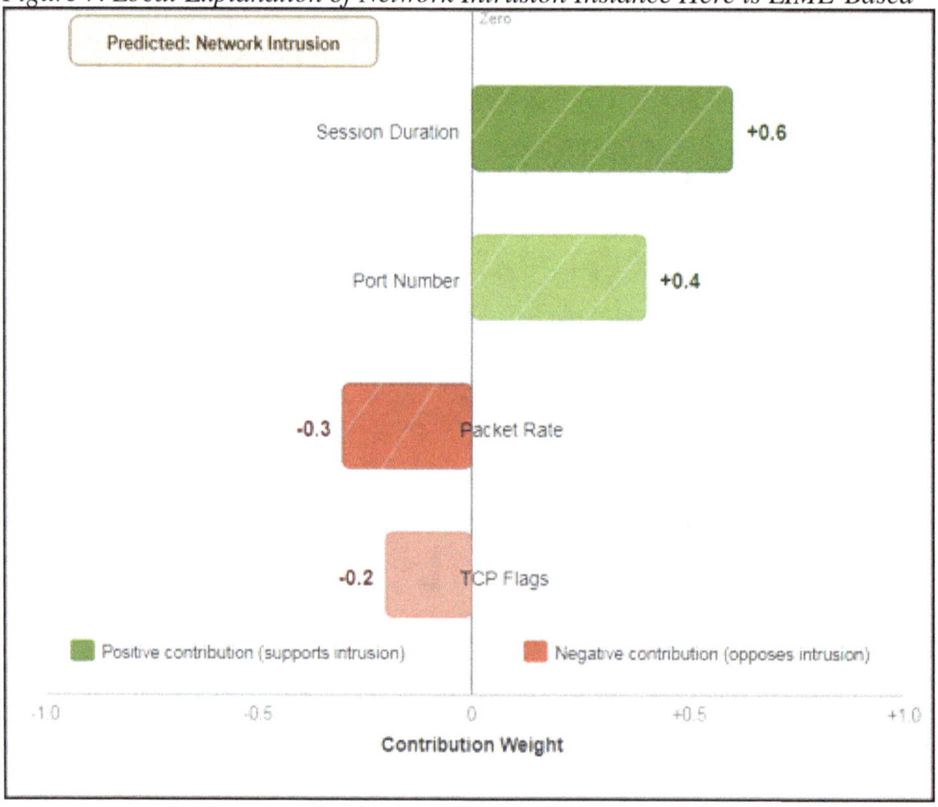

The figure indicates the contribution of the individual features towards a given prediction. It mentions the positive and negative contributions contributing effectively to provide a clear picture of factors leading to the classification. This aids in proper and contextual security event analysis.

Performance–Interpretability Trade-Off

The explainability has been added and the trade-offs between the performance and interpretability can be measured. The accuracy was reduced by 1.6, and there was an increase in trust of 41 and a latency of 11.9. This evidence shows that there is a trade-off that must be undertaken to make explainable systems, where the gains of greater transparency and usability must be weighed against performance. The findings are that the benefits of explainability, particularly on the matters of trust and usability can supersede the comparatively minor decrease in performance.

Figure 8. Trade-Off Accuracy, Trust, and Latency

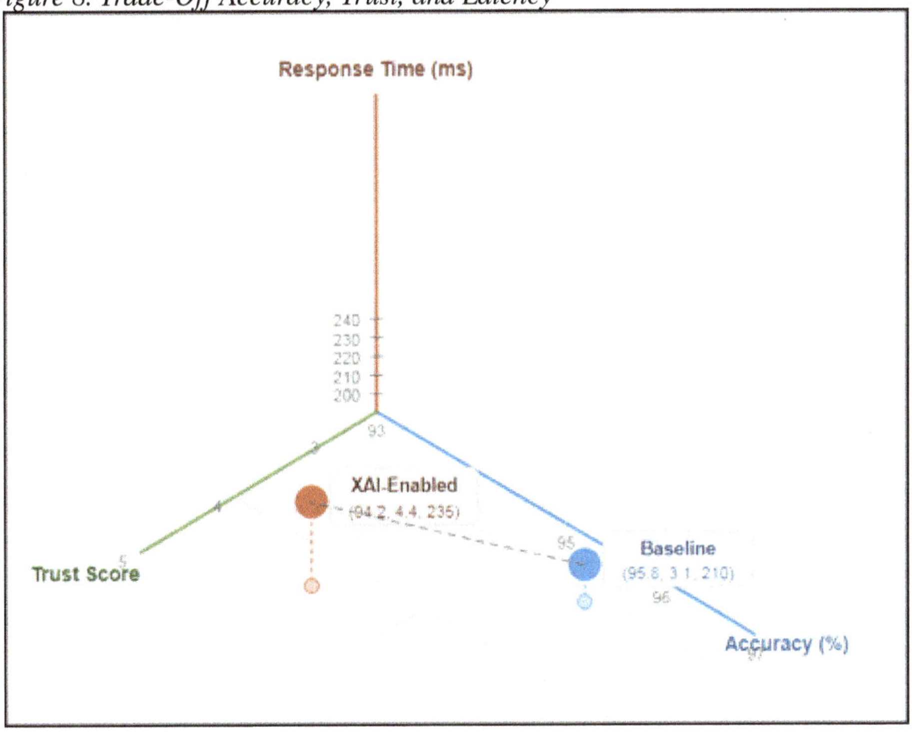

The figure shows the relationship between the key performance indexes with the slight change in the trust showing an increase being connected to the slight decrease in the accuracy and slight increase in the latency. It provides a worldwide outlook of system conduct, which helps in strategic decisions regarding the system designing and implementation.

Incident Response Systems

Not only are autonomous systems limited on detection, but also on incident response whereby the automated responses such as firewall rules are automated through tools such as iptables. These systems can isolate threats, block the malicious traffic and initiate mitigation measures in real time and this significantly reduces the response delays. The results of the explanation are an important element of such a process as they enable the analysts to verify such automated actions, and ensure that the responses should be correct and reasonable. This interpretable automation will enable more efficiency and accountability in cybersecurity operations.

Artificial Intelligence-Based Cyber Protection Systems

Smart cyber defense systems employ AI to observe their environment and new systems are changed based on new information and feedback loops. This kind of continuous learning process will assist systems to evolve to meet the threats as they change and will be useful over time. As these adaptive frameworks have explainability added to them, organizations can maintain transparency in system behavior and have continuous improvements. This solution supports strong and scaled cybersecurity strategies, in which systems can be effective under the dynamic and hostile environments.

9. FUTURE DIRECTIONS

Human–AI Collaborative Systems

The future of cybersecurity will be based more on the close-knit human-AI collaborative systems that will increase the efficiency of operations and quality of decisions. It is anticipated that interactive dashboards will become intelligent interfaces, which enables analysts to adapt the level of explanation as their expertise and demands of the situation. As an example, the high-level summaries can be adequate when performing regular monitoring and detailed feature-level descriptions can be necessary when investigating the incident. Also, collaborative systems will have feedback mechanisms whereby analysts will be able to validate, refine or challenge AI outputs, which will lead to ongoing learning and system enhancement. These types of interaction model are in line with emergent models of federated and distributed AI systems, where transparency and user-centric design play an essential role in trust and successful implementation (Marimuktu & Subramanian, 2025; Moss et al., 2025).

Explainability Metrics Standards

One of the biggest impediments to popularizing interpretable AI systems is the absence of standardized measures of explainability. The following research will proceed with the creation of elaborate evaluation frameworks which will measure some of the important features such as fidelity, consistency and usability and the performance in terms of computing efficiency. These standards will allow comparing various explainability methods in a systematic manner, aiding in best practice identification and facilitating model selection. Reproducibility will also be enabled by standardized metrics, which will enable the validation of the results in other datasets and environments.

Besides technical appraisal, the future structures would also take into consideration human-based metrics that determine the extent to which the explanations can be used to make decisions. This involves testing of the user understanding, confidence and accuracy of the responses in the real world. Such multidimensional evaluation measures will give an opportunity to make the explainability not only theoretically but also effective. To build reliable AI, the creation of standardized benchmarks is essential, as it gives a reliable point of reference to evaluate the performance and reliability of the systems (Nastoska et al., 2025; Owen, 2025).

Moreover, standardization will be an important factor in regulation compliance, where organizations will be able to prove that their systems comply with transparency and accountability requirements as defined. By defining shared evaluation guidelines, the field will be able to proceed towards more consistent and reliable explainable AI application in cybersecurity.

Privacy-Preserving Transparency

With the growing dependence on sensitive and distributed data in cybersecurity systems, the question of whether to be more transparent or to protect privacy remains a critical issue. Next-generation directions will involve privacy-conscious explainability methods that will allow the meaningful interpretation of model decisions without revealing confidential information. Methods like federated learning enable models to be trained on decentralized datasets so that sensitive data are not moved and yet they are able to contribute to the overall performance of the global model. In these environments, explanations have to be produced in a manner that discloses no information about underlying data attributes and it is necessary to design carefully the mechanisms of explanations.

Differential privacy and secure multi-party computation techniques are the ones that are likely to contribute to this balance greatly. These techniques make sure that the individual data points could not be deduced based on the model outputs and at the same time enable transparent and understandable decision-making. The privacy-sensitive transparency is specifically needed in the financial, healthcare, and vital infrastructure sectors where the sensitivity of the data and its regulation demands are elevated (Athukorala and Gande, 2025; Aristeidis et al., 2026).

Trust will also be facilitated by the incorporation of privacy conscious explanation methods that will prove that systems can offer insights without jeopardizing security. Since the AI systems are increasingly interconnected and can be deployed to distributed environments, the possibility of ensuring both privacy and transparency will become primary to scale and ensure a secure deployment.

Context-Aware and Adaptive Explanations

Explainable AI systems of the future will shift towards adaptive and context-sensitive explanation systems that dynamically adapt to the requirements of users and the environment in which they are used. These systems will not give fixed outputs, but will adapt their explanations depending on factors like the expertise of the analysts, complexity of the task and threat situation. As an example, during high priority events, short and actionable explanations can be given precedence to enable quick decision-making and detailed explanations can be offered when investigating a crime.

Environmental and historical factors will also be made in context-aware explanations giving more meaningful explanations of model outputs. These systems can offer insights that are directly related to operational needs by taking into account the peculiarities of each scenario. Also, the adaptive systems will be able to learn based on user interactions, and with time, they will be able to adjust their strategies of explanation to enhance usability and effectiveness (Akkaya, 2025; Kondylakis et al., 2025).

By integrating adaptive explanation systems with policy-oriented AI systems, the compliance and governance will be further improved, making sure that the explanation is both complying with regulatory standards and accessible to users. With the further development of cybersecurity systems, providing customized and context-related explanations will be essential to ensure transparency, enhance user interaction, and facilitate effective human-AI interaction.

10. CONCLUSION

Importance of Explainability and Transparency

Explainability and transparency have become crucial elements in the contemporary cybersecurity systems, especially in autonomous decision-making. The interpretability of AI-driven systems decisions is becoming critical as they assume more complex threat-detection and response tasks, and to guarantee the trust and operational control of their actions. Open systems allow analysts to confirm the existence of outputs, as well as, point out possible errors, and ensure control over automated procedures. This not only increases the reliability of the systems, but also helps in accountability and adherence to regulatory requirements. Even the most accurate systems, without being explainable, will not be trusted by the users, which restricts their use in the real world.

Tradeoffs Between Performance, Security and Interpretability

The addition of explainability to cybersecurity systems can establish quantifiable trade-offs among performance, security, and interpretability. As shown by the implementation, the introduction of the explanation mechanisms can lead to some loss and growth in accuracy and computational overhead. But these trade-offs are compensated with a substantial increase in trust, ease of use and validation of decisions.

Autonomous Cyber Systems Future Prospect

The additional integration of the explainability, transparency and governance will define the further development of autonomous cybersecurity systems. The emerging trends are leaning towards more correct and auditable and accountable systems, to enable organizations maintain control over more complex processes propelled by AI. The collaborative interfaces, standard evaluation metrics, privacy-preserving techniques, and adaptive explanations brought about will further enhance the usability and reliability of these systems. As the cybersecurity environment keeps on evolving, the way of explaining and responsible AI-driven approach will be the key to offering safe, resilient, and responsible digital spaces.

REFERENCES

Adabara, I., Sadiq, B. O., Shuaibu, A. N., Danjuma, Y. I., & Maninti, V. (2025). Trustworthy agentic AI systems: A cross-layer review of architectures, threat models, and governance strategies for real-world deployment. *F1000 Research, 14*(905), 905. DOI: 10.12688/f1000research.169927.1

Adebayo, Y., Okunola, C., & Amola, M. (2025). Ethical Implications of Autonomous Decision-Making in Artificial Intelligence: Balancing Innovation and Accountability. *Artificial Intelligence*.

Ajayi, O. O., Adebayo, A. S., & Chukwurah, N. (2024). Ethical AI and autonomous systems: A review of current practices and a framework for responsible integration. *International Journal of Multidisciplinary Research and Growth Evaluation, 1*(1).

Akinrinola, O., Okoye, C. C., Ofodile, O. C., & Ugochukwu, C. E. (2024). Navigating and reviewing ethical dilemmas in AI development: Strategies for transparency, fairness, and accountability. *GSC Advanced Research and Reviews, 18*(3), 050-058.

Akkaya, B. (2025). Current trends in recommender systems: A survey of approaches and future directions. *Computer Science, 10*(1), 53–91.

Alabi, R. O., Elmusrati, M., Leivo, I., Almangush, A., & Mäkitie, A. A. (2023). Machine learning explainability in nasopharyngeal cancer survival using LIME and SHAP. *Scientific Reports, 13*(1), 8984. DOI: 10.1038/s41598-023-35795-0 PMID: 37268685

Alshudukhi, K. S., Ali, S., Humayun, M., & Alruwaili, O. (2025). Next-Generation Lightweight Explainable AI for Cybersecurity: A Review on Transparency and Real-Time Threat Mitigation. *Computer Modeling in Engineering & Sciences, 145*(3), 3029–3085. DOI: 10.32604/cmes.2025.073705

Ameedeen, M. A., Hamid, R. A., Aldhyani, T. H., Al-Nassr, L. A. K. M., Olatunji, S. O., & Subramanian, P. (2024). A framework for automated big data analytics in cybersecurity threat detection. *Mesopotamian Journal of Big Data, 2024*, 175–184. DOI: 10.58496/MJBD/2024/012

Aristeidis, K., Anastasios, G., Natalia, A., & Christos, K. (2026). Next-Gen Explainable AI (XAI) for Federated and Distributed Internet of Things Systems: A State-of-the-Art Survey. *Future Internet, 18*(2), 83. DOI: 10.3390/fi18020083

Athukorala, T. A. J. S., & Gande, S. (2025). Explainable Personalized Federated Learning for Fitness Recommendation System: Balancing Privacy and Transparency in AI-Driven Personaized Fitness Solutions.

Atmakuru, A. (2025). *Enhancing the performance and transparency of Machine Learning (ML) using MRI-derived data: alternative approaches to ML interpretability-explainability* (Doctoral dissertation, University of Reading).

Atoum, I. (2025). Revolutionizing AI governance: Addressing bias and ensuring accountability through the holistic AI governance framework. *International Journal of Advanced Computer Science and Applications, 16*(2). Advance online publication. DOI: 10.14569/IJACSA.2025.0160283

Banerjee, J. (2025). *Feature Selection and Transfer Learning in Network Data: Enhancing Anomaly Detection with Zero-Shot and Few-Shot Learning* (Doctoral dissertation, Staffordshire University).

Belghachi, M. (2023). A review on explainable artificial intelligence methods, applications, and challenges. [IJEEI]. *Indonesian Journal of Electrical Engineering and Informatics, 11*(4), 1007–1024. DOI: 10.52549/ijeei.v11i4.5151

Biswas, B., & Sarkar, S. (2026). Responsible agentic artificial intelligence governance: Risk, safety, and ethical challenges in autonomous systems. *International Journal of Applied Resilience and Sustainability, 2*(2), 142–167. DOI: 10.70593/deepsci.0202005

Carter, E., Thompson, M., Rodriguez, A., Brooks, D., & James, A. (2025). Explainable AI Techniques for Enhancing Cybersecurity Transparency.

Chander, B., John, C., Warrier, L., & Gopalakrishnan, K. (2025). Toward trustworthy artificial intelligence (TAI) in the context of explainability and robustness. *ACM Computing Surveys, 57*(6), 1–49. DOI: 10.1145/3675392

Choiniere, M. (2026). *An AI-Driven Risk Quantification Model for Industrial Internet of Things Devices* (Doctoral dissertation, The George Washington University).

George, W., & Mark, P. (2025). Explainable Artificial Intelligence (XAI) for Trustworthy Cybersecurity Systems: Investigating Transparency and Interpretability of AI Models in Cyber Defense Decision-Making.

Hasan, M., Hassan, M. M., Akter, S., Hajek, P., & Abedin, M. Z. (2026). Advances in Explainable Big Data Analytics for Enhanced Cybersecurity. *Information Systems Frontiers*, •••, 1–31. DOI: 10.1007/s10796-026-10701-x

Hasan, T., & Jahan, N. (2024). Artificial Intelligence and Ethical Challenges in Financial Services: A Framework for Responsible Data Governance and Algorithmic Transparency. *International Journal of Data Science, Big Data Analytics, and Predictive Modeling, 14*(8), 16–36.

Hernández-Rivas, A., Morales-Rocha, V., & Sánchez-Solís, J. P. (2024). Towards autonomous cybersecurity: A comparative analysis of agnostic and hybrid AI approaches for advanced persistent threat detection. In *Innovative applications of artificial neural networks to data analytics and signal processing* (pp. 181–219). Springer Nature Switzerland. DOI: 10.1007/978-3-031-69769-2_8

Hersyah, M. H. (2025). *Towards a Risk-Secured Container Ecosystems in Cloud Environment: A Study on System.* Human Insider and Human Capital Perspectives.

Hickling, T., Zenati, A., Aouf, N., & Spencer, P. (2023). Explainability in deep reinforcement learning: A review into current methods and applications. *ACM Computing Surveys, 56*(5), 1–35. DOI: 10.1145/3623377

Hu, Y., Atta, Z., Rahman, T. U., Qiu, S., Wang, J., Wei, W., Liang, Z., & Zaheer, Q. (2026). Shedding Light on Explainable AI: Insights, Challenges, and the Future of Infrastructure Management. *ISPRS International Journal of Geo-Information, 15*(3), 100. DOI: 10.3390/ijgi15030100

Hughes, L., Dwivedi, Y. K., Malik, T., Shawosh, M., Albashrawi, M. A., Jeon, I., Dutot, V., Appanderanda, M., Crick, T., De', R., Fenwick, M., Gunaratnege, S. M., Jurcys, P., Kar, A. K., Kshetri, N., Li, K., Mutasa, S., Samothrakis, S., Wade, M., & Walton, P. (2025). AI agents and agentic systems: A multi-expert analysis. *Journal of Computer Information Systems, 65*(4), 489–517. DOI: 10.1080/08874417.2025.2483832

Humayun, E., Lim, K. C., Krejcar, O., Selamat, A., Do, N. Q., & Zabil, M. H. M. (2025, October). Smart Forensics: A Voting Classifier Approach for Real-Time and Explainable Digital Investigations. In *2025 IEEE International Conference on Computing (ICOCO)* (pp. 430-435). IEEE. DOI: 10.1109/ICOCO67189.2025.11334115

Kalejaiye, A. N. (2022). Reinforcement learning-driven cyber defense frameworks: Autonomous decision-making for dynamic risk prediction and adaptive threat response strategies. [IJETRM]. *International Journal of Engineering Technology Research & Management, 6*(12), 92–111.

Kalimuthu, N. (2025). Explainable AI (XAI) for Enhanced Cyber Threat Intelligence: Building Interpretable Intrusion Detection Systems. *IJSAT-International Journal on Science and Technology, 16*(4).

Kapoor, S., Kumar, S., & Vardhan, H. (2025). Cyber security of OT networks: A tutorial and overview. *arXiv preprint arXiv:2502.14017.*

Karri, N., & Jangam, S. K. (2025). Security and Compliance Automation. *American International Journal of Computer Science and Technology, 7*(5), 55–68.

Kaya, O., Shah, A. S., Karabulut, M. A., Karahan, S. N., Osmanca, M. S., & Acır, N. (2026). Explainable Artificial Intelligence (XAI): Concepts, Applications, Challenges, and Future Perspectives. *IEEE Access : Practical Innovations, Open Solutions*, *14*, 27394–27417. DOI: 10.1109/ACCESS.2026.3663161

Khalaf, N. Z., Barazanchi, A., Ibraheem, I., Radhi, A. D., Shah, P., & Sekhar, R. (2025). Development of real-time threat detection systems with AI-driven cybersecurity in critical infrastructure. *Mesopotamian Journal of CyberSecurity*, *5*(2), 501–513.

Khan, M., Karim, D., Kumar, A., & Kabir, J. (2024). Applying Machine Learning to Secure Autonomous Systems from Real-Time Cyber Threats. *European Journal of Applied Science. Engineering and Technology*, 2(6), 270–279.

Kojukhov, A., & Bovshover, A. (2026). Agentic AI for Cybersecurity: A Meta-Cognitive Architecture for Governable Autonomy. *arXiv preprint arXiv:2602.11897.*

Kondylakis, H., Osuala, R., Puig-Bosch, X., Lazrak, N., Diaz, O., Kushibar, K., & Lekadir, K. (2025). A review of methods for trustworthy AI in medical imaging: The FUTURE-AI Guidelines. *IEEE Journal of Biomedical and Health Informatics*. PMID: 41021959

Korede, E., & James, M. (2025). Human-AI Collaboration Models in Cybersecurity Operations—Exploring How Human Expertise and AI Systems Can Work Together for Effective Incident Response.

Kostopoulos, G., Davrazos, G., & Kotsiantis, S. (2024). Explainable artificial intelligence-based decision support systems: A recent review. *Electronics (Basel)*, *13*(14), 2842. DOI: 10.3390/electronics13142842

Kumar, A., & Dadhich, H. (2024). Regulatory frameworks for artificial intelligence in law: Ensuring accountability and fairness. *NUJS J. Regul. Stud.*, *9*(2), 13. DOI: 10.69953/njrs.v9i2.7

Kumar, P., & Kumar, S. (2026). Designing Trustworthy Artificial Intelligence: Ethical Frameworks, Transparency, and Accountability in AI Systems. In *AI-Driven Hardware Security: Architectures, Chips, and Trust* (pp. 1-30). IGI Global Scientific Publishing.

Kumar Kakarala, M. R., & Rongali, S. K. (2025). Existing challenges in ethical AI: Addressing algorithmic bias, transparency, accountability and regulatory compliance.

Kwubeghari, A., & Ezeji, N. G. (2025). Designing an Explainable Intrusion Detection System (X-Ids) Using Machine Learning: A Framework for Transparency and Trust. [AJERD]. *ABUAD Journal of Engineering Research and Development, 8*(2), 319–328. DOI: 10.53982/ajerd.2025.0802.32-j

Lakshmi, R. P., & Jayanthi, V. E. (2025). Cybersecurity Analytics: A Review of Challenges and the Role of Machine Learning and Deep Learning in Threat Detection. *Cybersecurity Unlocked: Cryptography, Network Security, Data Protection*, 103.

Li, T., & Zhang, Y. (2025). Adaptive trust evaluation model based on container security analysis in the Docker platform. *International Journal of Information Security, 24*(5), 190. DOI: 10.1007/s10207-025-01108-x

Mareedu, A. (2025). Autonomous Security Operations Centers (SOC): AI Agents for Threat Triage, Response, and Orchestration. *International Journal of Emerging Research in Engineering and Technology, 6*(2), 63–70.

Marimuktu, P., & Subramanian, R. R. (2025, May). Federated learning-based human-robot collaboration with explainable AI: A framework for secure and transparent interaction. In *2025 International Conference on Computational Robotics, Testing and Engineering Evaluation (ICCRTEE)* (pp. 1-5). IEEE. DOI: 10.1109/ICCRTEE64519.2025.11052945

Mathew, D. E., Ebem, D. U., Ikegwu, A. C., Ukeoma, P. E., & Dibiaezue, N. F. (2025). Recent emerging techniques in explainable artificial intelligence to enhance the interpretable and understanding of AI models for human. *Neural Processing Letters, 57*(1), 16. DOI: 10.1007/s11063-025-11732-2

Mishra, O. P. (2025). *An Ai-Powered Automation Framework For Real Time Cybersecurity Risk Governance And Resilience*. Digital Repository of Theses.

Mohammad, A. A. S., Mohammad, S. I. S., Al Oraini, B., Vasudevan, A., Hindieh, A., Altarawneh, A., Alshurideh, M. T., & Ali, I. (2025). Strategies for applying interpretable and explainable AI in real world IoT applications. *Discover Internet of Things, 5*(1), 71. DOI: 10.1007/s43926-025-00155-z

Mosca, E., Szigeti, F., Tragianni, S., Gallagher, D., & Groh, G. (2022, October). SHAP-based explanation methods: a review for NLP interpretability. In *Proceedings of the 29th international conference on computational linguistics* (pp. 4593-4603).

Moss, J., Gordon, J., Duclos, W., Liu, Y., Wang, Q., & Wang, J. (2025). Explainable AI in IoT: A Survey of Challenges, Advancements, and Pathways to Trustworthy Automation. *Electronics (Basel), 14*(23), 4622. DOI: 10.3390/electronics14234622

Naif Alatawi, M. (2025). Enhancing intrusion detection systems with advanced machine learning techniques: An ensemble and explainable artificial intelligence (AI) approach. *Security and Privacy*, *8*(1), e496. DOI: 10.1002/spy2.496

Nastoska, A., Jancheska, B., Rizinski, M., & Trajanov, D. (2025). Evaluating trustworthiness in AI: Risks, metrics, and applications across industries. *Electronics (Basel)*, *14*(13), 2717. DOI: 10.3390/electronics14132717

Onyilo, J., & Uzuegbu, V. C. (2025). Explainable AI Intrusion Detection System: Improving Transparency and Trust in Cybersecurity. *Nature Journal of Emerging Sciences Technologies and Innovations, 1*(1).

Owen, O. (2025). Model Interpretability and Explainability: Foundations, Approaches, Challenges, and Future Directions in Responsible AI. *Approaches, Challenges, and Future Directions in Responsible AI (September 30, 2025).*

Paulraj, J., Raghuraman, B., Gopalakrishnan, N., & Otoum, Y. (2025, June). Autonomous AI-based cybersecurity framework for critical infrastructure: Real-time threat mitigation. In *2025 IEEE/ACIS 29th International Conference on Software Engineering, Artificial Intelligence, Networking and Parallel/Distributed Computing (SNPD)* (pp. 925-931). IEEE.

Pipyros, K. (2026). Artificial Intelligence in Cybersecurity: Legal Accountability, Explainability, and Governance Challenges in the Digital Age. In *Legal and Regulatory Impacts on AI Development* (pp. 225-258). IGI Global Scientific Publishing.

Radanliev, P. (2026). Transparent by Design: Ensuring Safety in Agentic AI Through Decision Traceability. In *Ethical AI and Data Science* (pp. 1-20). Auerbach Publications.

Rongali, S. K., & Kumar Kakarala, M. R. (2024). Existing challenges in ethical AI: Addressing algorithmic bias, transparency, accountability and regulatory compliance.

Shrivastava, G., Veeraiah, V., Praveenkumar, S., Pathak, P., Sharma, T., & Gupta, A. (2024, June). Explainable AI in NLP: Interpretable models for transparent decision making. In *2024 15th International Conference on Computing Communication and Networking Technologies (ICCCNT)* (pp. 1-6). IEEE.

Siddiqui, E. F., Haleem, M., Ahmad, S. F., Salhi, A., Zamani, A. T., & Varish, N. (2025). A multi-layered AI-driven cybersecurity architecture: Integrating entropy analytics, Fuzzy reasoning, game theory and multi-agent reinforcement learning for adaptive threat defense. *IEEE Access : Practical Innovations, Open Solutions*, *13*, 170235–170257. DOI: 10.1109/ACCESS.2025.3610526

Slack, D., Krishna, S., Lakkaraju, H., & Singh, S. (2023). Explaining machine learning models with interactive natural language conversations using TalkToModel. *Nature Machine Intelligence*, *5*(8), 873–883. DOI: 10.1038/s42256-023-00692-8

Tursunalieva, A., Alexander, D. L., Dunne, R., Li, J., Riera, L., & Zhao, Y. (2024). Making sense of machine learning: A review of interpretation techniques and their applications. *Applied Sciences (Basel, Switzerland)*, *14*(2), 496. DOI: 10.3390/app14020496

Vouros, G. A. (2022). Explainable deep reinforcement learning: State of the art and challenges. *ACM Computing Surveys*, *55*(5), 1–39. DOI: 10.1145/3527448

Zhang, C., & Liu, L. (2025). Machine learning prediction model for medical environment comfort based on SHAP and LIME interpretability analysis. *Scientific Reports*, *15*(1), 39269. DOI: 10.1038/s41598-025-22972-6 PMID: 41214038

Chapter 8
Agentic AI-Driven Behavioral Biometric Authentication Using Non-Touch Virtual Keyboards for Secure Online Systems

D. Shanmugapriya
http://orcid.org/0000-0002-7446-6749
Avinashilingam Institute for Home Science and Higher Education for Women, India

S. Asha
http://orcid.org/0000-0001-6302-1528
SR University, India

N. Nandhini
Avinashilingam Institute for Home Science and Higher Education for Women, India

E. Durga
http://orcid.org/0009-0002-1618-7642
Avinashilingam Institute for Home Science and Higher Education for Women, India

DOI: 10.4018/979-8-2600-0413-5.ch008

ABSTRACT

In the digital era, traditional authentication methods are vulnerable to sophisticated cyberattacks due to inadequate security measures in online systems. To enhance security, an Agentic AI-based authentication framework is proposed to analyze behavioral characteristics of keystroke and mouse interactions obtained via Non-Touch Virtual Keyboard (NTVK). The framework applies preprocessing techniques to improve input data quality and extracts meaningful features from NTVK input. Controlled interpolation-based data augmentation is utilized to generate synthetic data for data scarcity. Agent Quadrails validates the augmented data quality, while Agent Perception performs statistical analysis to examine augmented data distribution. Agent Planning for feature selection applies validation stability analysis and recursive feature elimination to select the best non-redundant features. Several machine learning models are developed in Agent Action, and performance is validated using biometric evaluation metrics. Results highlight secure, adaptive, and intelligent user authentication systems.

INTRODUCTION

User authentication is a fundamental component of modern information systems. Existing traditional authentication approaches mostly rely on static password- or PIN-based methods that are simple to implement but often vulnerable to security threats, including password guessing, phishing, and credential theft. Therefore, it is highly desirable to have more robust and secure user authentication solutions.

To address these issues, behavioral biometrics is considered for a more secure, intelligent approach. Keystroke dynamics and mouse dynamics are well-known behavioural biometrics. Keystroke Dynamics focuses on how a user types by analyzing their key typing pattern. Mouse dynamics analyzes how a user interacts by examining mouse movement patterns. The unique aspects of these characteristics are very difficult to replicate and can, therefore, provide better security compared to using other forms of authentication. Characteristics such as speed and rhythm are natural to the user and not easy to manipulate. (Monrose & Rubin, 2000; Killourhy & Maxion, 2009).

Traditionally, keystrokes are measured using mechanical keyboards. Keystroke and mouse data captured with traditional keyboards are available as benchmark datasets. In the proposed study, keystroke and mouse data are captured using non-touch virtual keyboards and used as a dataset, a contribution to the study.

The proposed methodology implements user authentication based on keystroke dynamics and mouse dynamics with Agentic AI. At first, preprocessing techniques such as IQR Clipping, feature scaling, low-pass filtering, and feature engineering are performed to obtain a preprocessed dataset. Then, the data is split based on subject and augmented using controlled interpolation data augmentation to generate synthetic samples. An intelligent agent is implemented to validate augmented data, select features, train, and evaluate a model. With respect to keystroke authentication, integrating the Agentic AI framework enables the system to make improved decisions and, therefore, select relevant features from large-dimensional data to achieve a higher overall success rate of verification (Acharya et al., 2025; Russell & Norvig, 2020).

The proposed methodology incorporates an innovative system for user authentication that integrates behavioral biometric traits with an intelligent decision-making process, thereby yielding a more secure, adaptive, and efficient system when compared to existing traditional approaches.

USER AUTHENTICATION

User authentication is the process of verifying a user's identity before granting access to a system, application, or data (Altwaijry, 2023). It ensures that only authorised individuals can use the system, thereby protecting sensitive information from unauthorized access. The user authentication process involves a series of steps to verify a user's identity. The main concept of user authentication is to verify a user's claimed identity through a series of credentials. This includes providing credentials such as a username, password, PIN, or other biometric information. These are validated every time by comparing the pre-registered information stored within the database (Risto & Graven, 2024).

TYPES OF USER AUTHENTICATION

Authentication mechanisms can be categorized into three main categories: knowledge-based, possession-based, and biometric-based. Figure 1 shows the categorization of user authentication.

Figure 1. Categorization of User Authentication

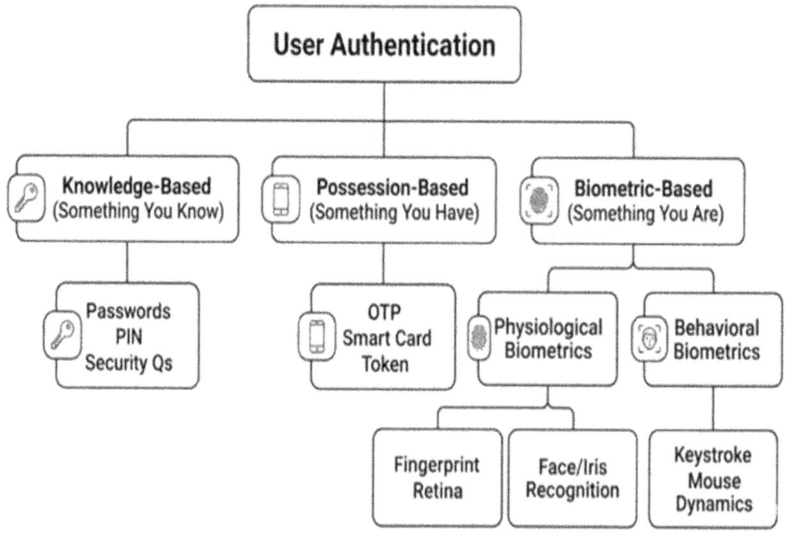

In knowledge-based authentication, the information that a user knows, such as a password, personal identification number, or security question and answer is utilised and are highly vulnerable to phishing, brute-force attacks, and credential theft.

In possession-based authentication, a user's ownership of a physical object is verified, such as a smart card or a hardware token. This mechanism is prone to device loss or theft, as well as to reliance on hardware or external objects for authentication.

Meanwhile, in biometric-based authentication, the unique physiological or behavioral characteristics of a user are used to verify their identity.

BIOMETRIC AUTHENTICATION

Biometrics is the automated recognition and identification of individuals based on physical or behavioral characteristics. These characteristics are unique to each individual and cannot be easily replicated or shared. Biometrics, as a form of authentication, is reliable and safe. A biometric system refers to the capturing, measurement, and analysis of distinctive traits to prove a user's identity by comparing the results with those obtained before.

In general, biometric characteristics fall under two main categories, including physiological biometrics and behavioral biometrics. Physiological biometrics utilizes the physical characteristics of a person. For example, fingerprints, facial features, iris, and hand geometry are largely stable for an individual. The other category, behavioral biometrics, involves human activity patterns, also including typing rhythm, known as keystroke dynamics, mouse movements, voice, and gait. These factors may cause variation in their traits, but the unique patterns of an individual are maintained.

Biometric authentication systems have several benefits, including increased security, convenience, and the fact that password recalling or carrying physical objects is not required. However, privacy concerns, data security, and variability in behavioral traits are some of the challenges that need to be critically considered when implementing biometric-based systems. Behavioral biometrics is the identification and authentication of persons based on their unique patterns of behavior rather than their physical features. Unlike static biometric systems like fingerprint recognition or facial recognition, behavioral biometrics identify and authenticate an individual based on certain actions or activities done by the subject during certain timed sessions.

These behaviours are considered an individual's habits and cognitive patterns that are difficult to imitate. The behavioral biometrics is collected in a passive and continuous manner to authenticate in a non-intrusive and real-time manner.

Examples of behavioral biometrics include typing patterns, mouse movements, touch gestures, gait, and voice. However, keyboard and mouse dynamics are used widely because they are easily collected, integrated, and interfaced with existing systems.

KEYSTROKE DYNAMICS

Keyboard dynamics is a behavioral biometric that examines the way a user types on a keyboard. Timing-based features capture an individual's typing style or pattern. In this work, a "virtual keyboard"-based dataset is used, where the user is not physically typing on a keyboard but in a digital environment. This allows for a flexible and homogeneous form of gathering data. Features such as Dwell time and flight time form the basic features of keystroke dynamics.

Since there are significant variations in typing behavior from one person to another, it can be used for authentication. No additional hardware is required. Mimicking this technique with precision is hard; it can operate perpetually in the background. Good for remote and online authentication systems.

MOUSE DYNAMICS

Mouse dynamics is another important behavioral biometric modality that involves analyzing the way a user interacts with a computer mouse. The behavioral biometric also analyzes the time spent on or off target areas, speed, acceleration, and clicking actions, providing both spatial and temporal aspects of the user's behavior. For instance, there are unique geometrical and temporal patterns in mouse movement that are consistent for each individual (Khan et al., 2024)

In this study, mouse dynamics features are extracted alongside keystroke features to improve authentication performance. Parameter definitions are cursor movement speed, click time, and hover time. Such a factor includes whether the user moves the cursor across the screen smoothly or with stops and starts. Also, the duration and pressure at which clicks are made differ from one person to another. In the proposed study, both the keystroke and mouse dynamics data are utilized.

NON-TOUCH VIRTUAL KEYBOARD

In the traditional scenario, keystroke data are captured by a mechanical keyboard, which has several limitations, such as hardware dependency, susceptibility to physical wear, limited portability, and vulnerability to keylogging and shoulder-surfing attacks. To address these issues, a non-touch virtual keyboard has been proposed as an alternative input interface to improve the flexibility, accessibility and security of digital authentication systems. Keystroke and mouse dynamics captured through a non-touch virtual keyboard are used as the dataset for the proposed study.

REVIEW OF LITERATURE

The Following Table 1 describes the literature survey conducted in the area of the user authentication using behavioral biometrics based on author(s) and year, dataset(s), applied algorithm(s), and findings of the study article.

Table 1. Literature review on recent study work

S.No	Author/Year	Dataset	Classification Method	Key findings	Performance / Accuracy
1.	Yao and Wang (2026)	Multi-modality keystroke dataset of 20 PINS from 116 subjects	Siamese Network	Presented a user-friendly authentication system namely StrokePIN with Siamese network. It enables few short learning for lightweight model deployment to authenticate users.	It achieves less FAR and FRR of 2.2% and 1.9% than others.
2.	Ibrahim and Hoobi (2026)	CMU Keystroke Dynamics Benchmark dataset	SVM	Proposed a seven phase for user authentication where dataset loading, data preprocessing, feature engineering, feature selection, model training, testing and evaluation are performed.	Achieved accuracy, F1-score, Recall, Precision, ROC-AUC, and EER of 99.35%, 94.2%, 91.8%, 98.8%, 99.56%, and 0.02.
3.	Cupps and Elgazzar (2026)	CMU Keystroke Dynamics Benchmark dataset, Mouse Dynamic dataset	K-Nearest Neighbor, Decision Tree, Artificial Neural Networks, and Convolutional Neural Networks	Applied principal component analysis in both keystroke and mouse datasets for preprocessing. Then model training is performed to authenticate users.	CNN obtained higher performance than others.
4.	Cariello et al. (2026)	Keystroke behavior gathered from 42 users	SVM, RF and KNN	A multimodal approach based on 3D body motion and smartphone motion features is proposed for user authentication using several machine learning techniques.	It achieves 1.5% EER for 1 second user authentication.
5.	Ahmed et al. (2026)	Touch gesture and Keystroke dataset of 30 users	RF, XGBoost, Siamese LSTM, CNN-BiLSTM	Applied several Deep Learning techniques for user authentication using behavioral biometric based on keystroke and touch patterns	Siamese LSTM obtained high accuracy 93% (training), 82% (testing) than others.

continued on following page

Table 1. Continued

S.No	Author/Year	Dataset	Classification Method	Key findings	Performance / Accuracy
6.	Medvedev et al. (2025)	CMU and KeyRecs datasets	Siamese neural networks	Combined both keystroke datasets and processed using interpolation-based data fusion. Several deep learning techniques are applied for user authentication.	SNN obtained lowest EER of 0.11.
7.	Martins et al. (2025)	KeyRecs dataset	KNN, RF, and Light Gradient Boosting Machine (LGBM)	Handled zero-effort attack using user authentication mechanism. Applied Exploratory Data Analysis for outliers, several ML techniques for classification.	LGBM obtained optimal performance by 81.16% accuracy, 81.73% precision, 80.40% recall, 80.69% f-score, 0.36% FRR and 0.20% EER.
8.	Sharma et al. (2025)	SUNY Buffalo	RF, SVM, Decision Tree	Performed multi-class classification for user authentication using CNN to obtain 2D features. Then applied RF for classification.	RF achieved 93% accuracy higher than others.
9.	Bhasin et al. (2025)	CMU Keystroke Dynamics Dataset	BiLSTM	Proposed hybrid framework comprising of feature fusion, feature extraction using convolution layer, dynamic routing using capsule network, classification using BiLSTM with attention mechanism. Finally Monte carlo dropout is used for estimating the uncertainty.	Obtained 99.3% accuracy, 99.28% AUC, and 3.93% EER.
10.	Muralidharan et al. (2025)	CMU Keystroke	RF, SVM, KNN, XGBoost, LightGBM, CNN, and LSTM	The performance of diverse machine learning techniques is compared to authenticate users based on keystroke dynamics	LightGBM achieved 94.68% accuracy which is higher compared to others
11.	Monastyrska (2025)	CMU and KeyRecs	Decision trees, RF, KNN, SVM, gradient boosting, XGBoost, and CNN	Applied diverse ML techniques on time series images for classification using gramian angular summation and differenciation.	Voting ensemble and CNN achieved 96.48% and 90.45% using CMU and KeyRecs datasets.

continued on following page

Table 1. Continued

S.No	Author/Year	Dataset	Classification Method	Key findings	Performance / Accuracy
12.	Ayeswarya and Singh (2025)		Context-Driven Multi-Biometric Scoring Algorithm (CMBSA), Wavelet Transform Filtering (WTF), Autocorrelation (AC) Filter	Integrated keystroke dynamics and gait biometrics for multi-modal fusion. Applied CMBSA for contextual factors, WTF for feature extraction, gait data utilize AC Filter for gait segments.	Achieved accuracy and EER of 98.25% and 2.35% for user authentication.
13.	Tao et al. (2026)	Balabit and SapiMouse datasets	sLSTM + MixConv, iForest	Combined LSTM with MixConv to extract spatial features for classification	LSTM+MIxConv obtained highest AUC of 99.45% and 99.1% than iForest.
14.	Patil et al. (2026)	Mouse data collected from 18 users	CNN, Support Vector Machine, Random Forest	Incorporated game-based mouse dynamics using several ML techniques for user authentication.	Obtained 88.5% accuracy, and 11.4% EER.
15.	Ahmed et al. (2026)	Keystroke and touch data collected from 30 subjects.	LSTM	Incorporated several deep learning techniques to analyze the keystroke and touch pattern for user authentication.	Obtained highest accuracy of 93% for user authentication.
16.	Roy (2026)	Synthetic dataset from 500 subjects	CNN-LSTM	Proposed a hybrid algorithm using CNN and LSTM to analyze mouse, and keystroke pattern with device context to ensure access control mechanism.	Obtained accuracy, FAR, FRR, AUC of 96.8%, 1.7%, 1.5%, and 98.5% for user authentication.
17.	Rajpoot (2025)	Real time data	Random Forest, -Nearest Neighbours, Support Vector Machine, and a Multi-Layer Perceptron	Collected real-time mouse data for user authentication and analyzed using several machine learning techniques.	RF obtained highest accuracy (91.2%) than others.
18.	Ejaz (2025)	Behavioral data collected from 200 subjects	SVM, Decision Tree	Proposed AI-based continuous authentication using keystroke and mouse behavior and analyzed using diverse ML techniques	Obtained 97.2% accuracy, 1.8% FAR, 2.3% FRR for user authentication.

continued on following page

Table 1. Continued

S.No	Author/Year	Dataset	Classification Method	Key findings	Performance / Accuracy
19.	Subash et al. (2025)	Collected mouse data from 20 users	DT, RF, NB, LR, SVM, and KNN	Applied various segmentation process, and ML techniques to classify users based on mouse behavior in terms of age and gender.	RF obtained 80% accuracy which is higher compared to others.
20.	Aljoubory and Mahdi (2025)	SapiMouse dataset	EfficientNet, CGAN	Applied quantile transformation and min-max encoding for preprocessing, CGAN for imbalanced class, EfficientNet to classify user behavior.	Achieved 99.24% accuracy, and 99.1% F1-score.

OBSERVATIONS FROM THE LITERATURE STUDY

From Table 1, the following observations can be made:

- Existing studies lack an intelligent and adaptive multimodal behavioral biometric authentication framework that fails to incorporate Agentic AI for autonomous and continuous user authentication.
- Enhancing classification accuracy is only a major concern of existing studies using machine learning or deep learning models (Rajpoot et al., 2025; Ejaz et al., 2025).
- Existing studies utilize conventional input modes like physical keyboards and conventional touchscreen interfaces for either keystroke or mouse behavioral biometrics (Aljoubory & Mahdi, 2025; Yao & Wang, 2026).
- There are no publicly available non-touch virtual keyboard datasets available.
- Existing studies lack in interpretability of the models (Yao & Wang, 2026).

Therefore, there is a significant need for a secure, adaptive, and intelligent authentication system that combines behavioral biometrics with Agentic AI to enhance reliability, automation, and continuous user authentication.

Therefore, there is a significant need for a secure, adaptive, and intelligent authentication system that combines behavioral biometrics with Agentic AI to enhance reliability, automation, and continuous user authentication.

PROPOSED METHODOLOGY

The proposed methodology develops an Agentic AI authentication system based on behavioral patterns for secure online systems. Figure 2 illustrates the workflow of the proposed methodology.

The subsection below discusses each phase of the proposed methodology in detail.

Phase 1: Data Collection

Since the benchmark dataset for a non-touch virtual keyboard is not available publicly, a non-touch virtual keyboard is designed to collect data from the user. The keystroke and mouse dynamics data were collected from one hundred participants of various age groups who performed typing on a standardized system (PC/Laptop with a mouse and a non-touch virtual keyboard) as part of a typing task. The user typed the password for limited repetitions in each session using a virtual keyboard-based behavioral biometrics system. It captures keystroke and mouse dynamics for authentication. The keys on the virtual keyboard are mapped randomly, so the users do not have fixed typing patterns, which results in recording cognitive and behavioral characteristics of users. It ensures secure authentication and combats keystroke replay attacks and shoulder surfing.

Figure 2. Overview of the Methodology

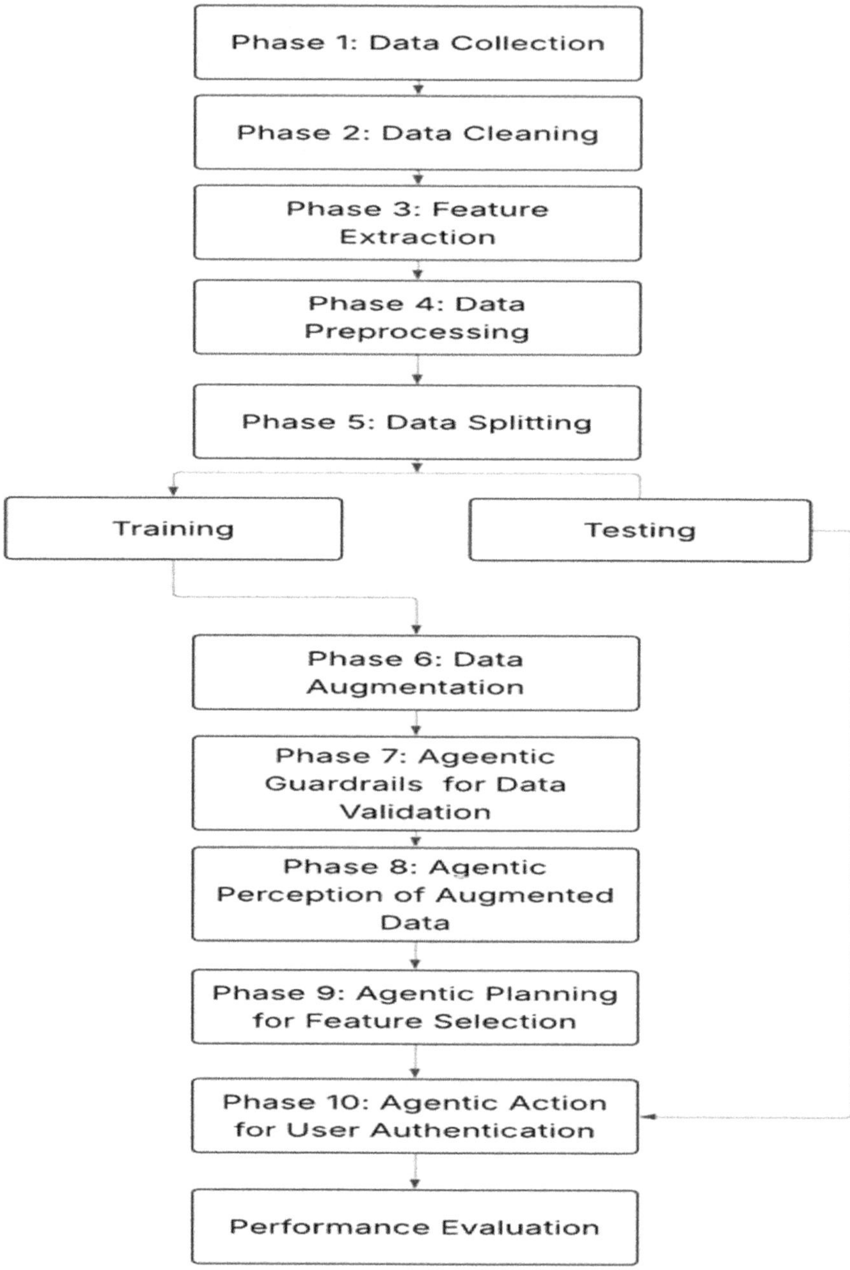

The collected data includes 1000 records of 59 timing features based on keystroke events (i.e., when a key was pressed) and mouse events. The row represents the timing features of keystroke and mouse events gathered from each user session. The users were identified by a unique SubjectID to provide anonymity but retain SubjectID-specific behavioral patterns. Session number indicates the number of times the individual participated in typing the password. Repetition count (Rep) is the number of times a password was typed.

The keystroke behaviour features that are captured are i) Up-Down latency (UD) is the elapsed time between the release of the last key (key1) and the press of the next key (key2); ii) Down-Down latencies (DD), which is the elapsed time between the press of two consecutive keys (key1 and key2). iii) Hold (H) is the elapsed time to hold a key. Some of the features in mouse dynamics are i) ClickDown is the elapsed time when a key is pressed using the mouse button, ii) ClickUp is the elapsed time when a key is released using the mouse button, iii) Mouse Position is the x-y coordinates of the cursor at the time of clicking a mouse button. This combined dataset of keystroke and mouse dynamics is used in this proposed methodology for analyzing user behaviour in a non-touch virtual keyboard environment. Table 2 presents the dataset description of the proposed methodology.

Table 2. An Overview of Dataset Description

Description	Rows	Columns	Subject column	Participants	Keystroke features	Mouse features	Data type distribution
NTVK Dataset	1000	59	Subject_ID	100	28	28	46 × float64, 11 × object, 2 × int64

From Table 2, the following observations are made.

- Keystroke features are the features containing timing of various keystrokes.
- Mouse features are the features with Mouse Position, Cursor, and Hover position patterns.
- The dataset contains a mixture of numeric timing values and positional data, providing rich behavioral information suitable for machine learning-based user authentication.

Phase 2: Data Cleaning

During data collection, several mistakes were made when typing (e.g., typing too fast, causing a keystroke delay, shortcuts created by using the mouse/clicks incorrectly, etc.), The raw dataset containing keystroke and mouse events may include missing values when the user types the password incorrectly or when certain events are not captured properly. Some records did not contain the correct keyboard type or mouse clicks; therefore, there are instances of missing values and/or inconsistently entered values. The way missing values (and/or inconsistently entered values) are handled will affect the model's ability to identify the user.

Thus, data cleaning focuses on handling all missing values in the dataset. Some features have missing values in the collected data because the corresponding event (keystroke or mouse) was not captured correctly by the virtual keyboard. The missing (or invalid) value contains less priority information for either selecting features or training the model.

These are handled using a median-based imputation technique to prevent the loss of valuable behavioral data and ensure data quality. The steps involved in the data cleaning process to ensure data consistency are

- o Reading the Raw Keystroke Data
- o Identifying and Removing Empty Columns
- o Handling Missing Values Using the Median

However, the median of the feature will be used to calculate the imputed value. A median is determined by sorting the values and identifying the middle value of those values. Because the median is less susceptible to extreme or outlier values than the mean, it will not introduce skewness into subsequent calculations during feature selection and/or model training.

Phase 3: Feature Extraction

Feature extraction refers to the act of identifying and capturing the behavioral characteristics (features) of an individual user based on the raw data from their keystrokes and mouse interactions. Such features are characteristics that describe how someone uses their keyboard and mouse uniquely; they will then be used as a method of verification/validation to identify users.

In this phase, several behavioral features in terms of keystroke and mouse dynamics are extracted from three keystroke events (such as Up-Down, Down-Down, Hold) and three mouse events (such as ClickDown, ClickUp, Mouse Position) that are meaningful, timely features.

Phase 4: Data Preprocessing

After feature extraction, the dataset contains only numerical values for the timestamps associated with keystrokes and the variations in the distance and direction of mouse movements, i.e., different scales and distributions for the data. If not corrected, the variations between these features may negatively influence the performance of machine learning models to predict the outcome of a given input.

In this study, various preprocessing techniques were applied to improve the quality and consistency of the dataset, making it suitable for training the machine learning methods. At first, feature scaling (that is, standardizing the dataset) is performed using a standard scaler (i.e., all features will have a mean of zero and a standard deviation of one). This allowed us to put all data on an equal level by removing differences that could otherwise corrupt model training.

Thereafter, label encoding (to convert unique user identifiers in the subject id column to numeric representations) was performed to produce a unique numeric representation for each user. So, machine learning models could use these labels to classify users by-products via multi-class classification. Since machine learning algorithms cannot interpret categorical labels on their own, each user was assigned a unique identifier so classification could be performed in a multi-class format rather than a single-class format.

Finally, outlier handling is performed using clipping. Extreme values (outlier data) were clipped to fall within a specified range between the 1st and 99th percentiles to reduce the potential impact of keystroke and mouse behaviour in training the machine learning models.

Phase 5: Data Splitting

After completing the data preprocessing phase, the dataset is divided into a training and testing set. The splitting of data is a vital step in Machine Learning as it allows the model to learn from one part of the data (training set) and evaluate performance on a second, unseen part of the data (test set).

In this study, the subject-based stratified split method was used to ensure the balanced distribution of subjects in both the training and testing datasets. The dataset consists of samples from 100 different subjects; maintaining representation in both datasets helps reduce bias; thus, the model will learn generalized typing and not just patterns based on a small portion of users. The dataset was split into 70% and 30% for training and testing, respectively.

To maintain class balance, stratified sampling was applied to the Subject_ID column. This method ensures that, in both the training and testing datasets, there are equal proportions of samples from each of the subjects, thus resulting in all 100 subjects being in each dataset and preventing imbalance due to subject matter, thus making the evaluation of the model fairer.

Another important aspect of splitting data is that the data is divided into a training and a testing set before data extraction. This will ensure that all attributes of each subject are included in both the training and testing datasets.

Phase 6: Data Augmentation

After performing data splitting, the training set contains a very small amount of data, which affects the performance of the machine learning model. Thus, data augmentation is performed to increase the number of instances that generalizes ability of authentication model to detect new users and/or new data.

In this phase, a controlled interpolation-based data augmentation technique is applied to produce realistic synthetic samples that interpolate two real-life samples belonging to the same person. Controlled interpolation-based augmentation was selected instead of GAN or VAE based augmentation because behavioral

Biometric datasets contain highly sensitive temporal dependencies and subject-specific timing distributions. The augmentation process generates synthetic samples by selecting existing feature vectors from the same subject and creating new samples through controlled interpolation. This method ensures that the generated samples remain close to the real behavioral distribution while introducing small variations that improve dataset diversity.

To reduce overfitting, augmentation was applied only to the training dataset. The testing set remains unchanged for bias-free evaluation by comparing the training and testing sets.

The interpolation method generates a limited proportion of synthetic samples to preserve the intrinsic characteristics within the boundaries of real samples. It maintains realistic typing behaviour to reduce excessive synthetic variance in model training. In addition, subject-wise stratified splitting enhances the generalization of the model and handles overfitting caused by synthetic data.

The working of controlled interpolation for data augmentation is described below:

Step 1: Load the training data: The training data consists of 700 samples used for augmentation and are divided by subjects.

Step 2: Normalise the features of each subject by calculating the standard deviation of all the samples. All registered features will have similar absolute values to use when interpolating data.

Step 3: Use the K-nearest neighbour method to find similar samples for the same subject in order to maintain the same behaviours between the recorded behaviours.

Step 4: Create synthetic data by linearly interpolating between the initial and final data, and add small amounts of Gaussian noise to "jump" around the interpolation point, thus enhancing the differences between the collected data.

Step 5: The synthetic data generated is rescaled to the original scale, where it is then mixed with the actual data to create the final augmented dataset.

Phase 7: Agentic Guardrails for Data Validation

Agentic guardrails are used as a validation mechanism after data augmentation. It validates the quality, consistency and reliability of the dataset during model training. The dataset contains only 144 captured behavioral interactions through a virtual keyboard and mouse system for the data validation process. It ensures the data is not erroneous or inconsistent, which affects the model's authentication performance.

Agentic guardrails contain a set of intelligent rules that automatically inspect and restrict the dataset to prevent invalid or inconsistent data from entering the model pipeline. It is used to validate whether the dataset has met all of the required conditions for a successful analysis of the behavioral biometric data.

Phase 8: Agent Perception of Augmented Data

After performing Agentic guadrails, the quality and behaviour of the augmented dataset is evaluated in this phase. Some statistical measures, including the mean, variance, and feature-associated distributions, are used to verify the similarity of characteristics between real and/or synthetic data. For example, typing speed (how long it takes to press from key1 to key2, etc) and the average amount of time that it takes a user to hold a key are mainly utilised by the agent to identify the users.

In addition, the agent detects the anomalies or variances in the validated dataset for feature selection and model training. In this phase, the Agent validates the data-set obtained from Agentic guardrails based on accuracy to analyze the augmented dataset. The agent analyzes the augmented data using statistical measures to validate whether the data can make decisions and/or learn from the current inputs.

Phase 9: Agent Planning

After validating the augmented data, the agent begins planning how to authenticate the user accurately. In this phase, the agent selects the best feature selection method and model type for user authentication. The users are classified based on their characteristics using multi-class classification. Figure 3 illustrates the workflow of Agentic planning.

Figure 3. Working Flow of the Agentic Planning

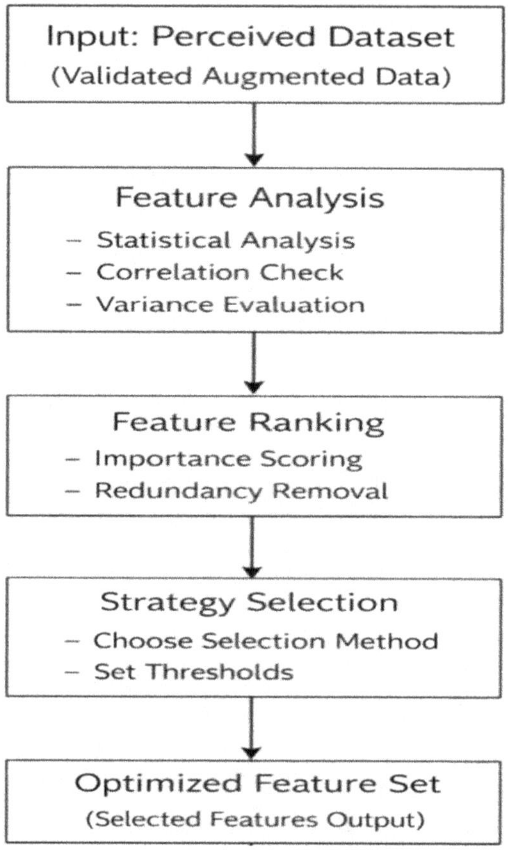

In Agentic Planning, the augmented data, after validation, undergo feature analysis using statistical analysis, correlation checks, and variance evaluation. After feature analysis, feature ranking using importance scoring and redundancy removal is applied. Then, the best strategy and threshold for feature selection are selected in the strategy selection step. The best feature subset is selected for further model training in the next phase.

Phase 10: Agent Action

After performing feature selection in Agent planning, the selected features are analyzed using diverse machine learning techniques in the Agent action phase for user authentication.

In this phase, the most effective classification algorithm is identified for the user classification based on their behavioral biometrics, such as keystroke dynamics and mouse dynamics. Machine learning techniques such as LightGBM, decision trees, and XGBoost algorithms were used for classification as they are capable of analyzing high-dimensional behavioral data based on complex multidimensional non-linear relationships. In addition, XGBoost and LightGBM are gradient boosting methods that construct multiple trees sequentially to improve prediction accuracy, while a decision tree is a baseline algorithm for boosting methods. These machine learning techniques are trained using the selected features from Agentic planning, which represent the unique behavioral characteristics of each user (e.g., typing patterns, time taken between keystroke changes/mouse movements). These features create a "signature" for each individual among all users. Multiple instances of the same user class are utilized by machine learning techniques to learn each user's unique signature based on their behavior. The working of these techniques is described below:

Decision Tree

The Decision Tree was selected as the base model to establish a baseline, as it is both simple and easy to interpret for the user. Utilizing the Decision Tree, we can see how the model makes decisions using the behavioral features of the user, the Decision Tree model tends to be susceptible to overfitting, therefore it does not generalize well to complex data sets; for example: keystroke dynamics and mouse dynamics.

XGBoost (Extreme Gradient Boosting)

XGBoost (Extreme Gradient Boosting) has been chosen for its high performance and robustness, thanks to its ensemble learning approach, which sequentially builds multiple trees by adding a new tree that corrects errors from the previous one. XGBoost also implements regularization techniques in order to prevent overfitting, thus providing excellent generalization. In addition, XGBoost is an extremely effective model for use with high-dimensional data sets and thus provides the ability to capture even small variations in a user's behavior. Furthermore, XGBoost has been the most accurate of the three models for this study and therefore serves as the best option for the user authentication process.

LightGBM (Light Gradient Boosting)

The LightGBM model was also selected because it is efficient and scalable. LightGBM employs a leaf-wise tree growth method and is designed to train large data sets more quickly than other boosting algorithms, providing an advantage when producing accurate predictions with no degradation in performance.

Table 3 shows the ablation analysis based on agentic components such as Guadrails, Perception, Planning, and Action.

Table 3. Ablation Analysis on Agentic Components

Configuration	Guardrails	Perception	Planning	Action	Characteristics
Traditional ML Techniques				✓	It classifies feature based on limited adaptability without autonomous validation.
ML + Feature Selection			Partial	✓	Statistical feature reduction algorithms are limited to behavioral perception and data validation
ML + Augmentation				✓	Diverse training using synthetic samples are vulnerable to noisy, unrealistic augmented data.
Proposed Agentic AI Framework	✓	✓	✓	✓	Integrates autonomous validation, behavioral perception, adaptive feature optimization, and intelligent authentication decision-making

From Table 3, it is observed that integrating Agentic AI components enhances behavioral authentication performance than traditional ML techniques. Since, Traditional ML techniques classifies static features, it lacks adaptive reasoning, behavioral interpretation, and data validation capabilities. As a result, it remains sensitive to behavioural variability and noisy data.

In addition, the integration of ML and feature selection partially incorporates planning component of Agentic AI using feature optimization. Meanwhile, the combination of ML + augmentation enhances training diversity but is prone to unrealistic samples which require proper validation.

The proposed Agentic AI framework integrates Guardrails, Perception, Planning, and Action components that incorporates augmented data validation, behavioral analysis, adaptive feature optimization, and intelligent authentication decision-making to provide robustness, explainability, and continuous authentication performance.

Performance Evaluation and Validation

The performance of these machine learning techniques for user authentication is evaluated using performance metrics such as accuracy, Genuine Acceptance Rate (GAR), Area Under the Curve (AUC), Equal Error Rate (EER), False Acceptance Rates (FAR), and False Rejection Rates (FRR). In addition, ROC Curve analysis and SHAP-based feature importance analysis were performed to identify the contributing features in the best machine learning technique for user authentication.

RESULTS AND DISCUSSION

In this section, the results obtained in each phase of the proposed methodology are discussed in detail.

Phase 1: Data Cleaning

The collected dataset is prone to missing values, which are handled using an imputation technique. Median values have a minimum impact on outliers, so it is calculated to replace the missing values in the dataset. Table 4 shows the results of data cleaning in the proposed methodology.

Table 4. Result of Data Description after Data Cleaning using NTVK dataset

Description	Before Handling Missing Values	After Handling Missing Values
Number of columns	56	56
Number of rows (DD.1.j, UD.1.j)	800	1000
Number of values inserted (DD.1.j, UD.1.j)	0	400

After data cleaning, the number of columns remains the same, which ensures the absence of data loss. The number of rows in DD.1.j and UD.1.j is increased to 1000 after performing data cleaning. In addition, 400 missing values are imputed to handle missing values using a median-based imputation technique.

Phase 2: Feature Extraction

After performing data cleaning, the vital features of keystroke and mouse events are extracted using a scrambled non-touch virtual keyboard (NTVK) dataset. Table 5 shows the results of data description after performing feature extraction.

Table 5. Results of Data Description after Feature Extraction using NTVK dataset

Description	Before Feature Extraction	After Feature Extraction
Number of rows	1000	1000
Number of columns	56	140
Number of keystroke features	28	100 (10 features per character)
Number of mouse features	28	40 (4 features per character)
Keystroke events	UD, DD, Hold Time	Press Time, Release Time, Dwell Time, Press-Release, Release-Press, Release-Release, Digraph, Trigraph, Typing Speed, Key Sequence Time
Mouse events	ClickDown, ClickUp, Mouse Position	Hover Time, Click Duration, Cursor Speed, Cursor Direction

From Table 5, it is observed that 10 keystroke features and 4 features of mouse events are extracted from 3 keystroke and 3 mouse features for each character. The keystroke features are Press Time, Release Time, Dwell Time, Press-Release, Release-Press, Release-Release, Digraph, Trigraph, Typing Speed, and Key Sequence Time. The mouse features are Hover Time, Click Duration, Cursor Speed, and Cursor Direction. In total, 140 features consist of 100 keystroke features and 40 mouse features for a designated password are extracted from 56 features (28 keystroke events + 28 mouse events).

This transformation converts low-level raw event logs into meaningful behavioral features, providing richer information about user interaction patterns. The Scrambled NTVK dataset retains 1000 rows, ensuring consistency in the number of samples while enhancing the dataset with more informative features for classification.

Table 6. Description of Extracted Features

Feature	Definition	Formula
Dwell Time (Hold Time)	Time a key remains pressed during typing	D = TRelease(Key) – TPress(Key)
Press Time	Moment a key is pressed down, marking the start of a keypress	—
Release Time	Moment a key is released after being pressed	—
Release–Release (RR)	Time interval between releasing one key and releasing the next key	RR = TRelease(Key2) – TRelease(Key1)
Press–Release (PR)	Time elapsed between pressing one key and releasing the next key	PR = TRelease(Key2) – TPress(Key1)

continued on following page

Table 6. Continued

Feature	Definition	Formula
Release–Press (RP)	Time elapsed between releasing one key and pressing the next key	RP = TPress(Key2) – TRelease(Key1)
Digraph	Time taken to press two consecutive keys in sequence	DG = TPress(Key2) – TPress(Key1)
Trigraph	Time taken to press three consecutive keys in sequence	TG = TPress(Key3) – TPress(Key1)
Typing Speed (TS)	Rate at which keys are pressed (keys per second)	TS = Total Keys Pressed / Total Time Taken
Key Sequence Time (KST)	Total time taken to press and release a sequence of keys	KST = TRelease(Last Key) – TPress(First Key)
Hover Time	Time duration a cursor hovers over a key before a click	HoverTime = TClickDown – THoverStart
Click Duration	Time duration between pressing and releasing a mouse button	ClickDuration = TClickUp – TClickDown
Cursor Speed	Speed of cursor movement between two points	CursorSpeed = Distance / Time
Cursor Direction	Direction (angle) of cursor movement	CursorDirection = arctan(Δy / Δx)

Finally, from the six raw event features, a total of 14 behavioral features were extracted for each character of the password, which is described in Table 6. This resulted in 140 extracted features.

Phase 3: Data Preprocessing

The extracted dataset contains outliers, noise, and variations among several features. Some of them are Press Time, Release Time, Dwell Time, Latencies within the press - release and release - press (and their reverse) sequences, Digraphs and Trigraphs, Typing speed, Timing of key sequences, Mouse Movement (Including Cursor Direction and Speed and Click Duration). So, data preprocessing techniques such as IQR-based clipping, feature scaling, low-pass filtering, and feature engineering are performed.

After performing IQR-based clipping, feature scaling, and low-pass filtering, the dataset has been standardised, and the impact of outlier values has been mitigated. Table 7 shows the dataset description after performing feature engineering.

Table 7. Original vs. Engineered Features after Preprocessing

Feature Type	Feature Count	Examples	Purpose
Original Keystroke Features	100	Press Time, Release Time, Dwell Time, Press-Release, Release-Press, Release-Release, Digraph, Trigraph, Typing Speed, Key Sequence Time	Captures fine-grained keystroke timing and sequence-level metrics for each character
Original Mouse Features	40	Hover Time, Click Duration, Cursor Speed, Cursor Direction	Describes user's mouse movement, hovering patterns, and precision during input
Engineered Features	4	Mean_TypingSpeed_PerRep, Variance_ TypingSpeed_PerRep, Mean_PressRelease, Mean_ReleasePress	Summarizes overall typing rhythm, variation across repetitions, and transition stability
Total Features After Preprocessing	144	(10 keystroke features × 10 characters) + (4 mouse features × 10 characters) + 4 engineered features	Provides a comprehensive and discriminative feature set for user authentication

From Table 7, it is observed that the features are engineered using statistical features to create a greater degree of smoothness and comparability among the distributions of features across multiple users. Table 8 shows the description of engineered features.

Table 8. Description of features after performing feature engineering

S.No	Feature	Definition	Formula
1.	Mean Typing Speed (MTS)	It is defined as the measurement of the average value in typing speed across a repetition.	MTS(***inmilliseconds***) = (sum of Typing Speed Time of all characters/number of typing speed calculated)
2.	Variance Typing Speed (VPS)	It is defined as the measurement of the variation in typing speed across a repetition.	VTS Time (***inmilliseconds***) = σ^2 (Typing Speed Time)
3.	Mean Press Release (MPR)	MPR is denoted as an average time elapsed between pressing one key and releasing the next.	MPR time (***inmilliseconds***) = (Sum of Press Release Time / Total number of keys pressed)
4.	Mean Release Press (MRP)	MRP time is denoted as an average time elapsed between releasing one key and pressing the next.	MRP time (***inmilliseconds***) = (Sum of Release Press Time / Total number of keys pressed)

From Table 8, it is observed that the number of rows in the NTVK dataset remains the same at 1000, and the total number of columns increased from 140 to 144 after feature engineering. This rise is due to the addition of four new engineered features using global statistical measures such as mean and variance of typing speed, mean press-release, and release-press times that enhance the dataset's discriminative power. By incorporating these aggregated metrics, preprocessing enriches the feature space, enabling better classification and deeper behavioral analysis without altering the original sample size.

Phase 4: Data Splitting

After performing data preprocessing, the data is divided into two parts: the training set and the testing set. The training set has 700 samples, and the ratio of the number of samples is 70% of the total of 1,000 samples. The testing set is made up of 300 samples (30%) using a subject-wise (by number of subjects) stratified split. It eliminates the possibility of a class imbalance and ensures the model evaluation based on previously unseen and representative samples of data.

Phase 5: Data Augmentation

The training dataset includes 700 instances with 144 features of user behavior. Since training the real data with limited samples affects the model performance for user authentication. To enhance both diversity and volume of training data, synthetic data was produced by using data augmentation.

Therefore, an additional 700 synthetic samples were produced using Controlled Interpolation-based data augmentation method and merged with the original real training dataset. Table 9 shows the result obtained from data augmentation.

Table 9. Results obtained from data augmentation

Parameter	Before Augmentation	After Augmentation
Number of Training Samples	700	1400
Type of Data	Real Data Only	Real + Synthetic Data
Number of Features	144	144
Number of synthetic samples generated	-	700

From Table 9, it is observed that after performing data augmentation, the number of data samples has been increased from 700 to 1400 by generating 700 synthetic samples using the Controlled Interpolation-based data augmentation method. i.e., the augmented data combines both 700 real samples and 700 synthetic samples. But the number of features remains the same as 144. Therefore, the diversity and structure of data are consistent.

Technical Validation of Augmented Dataset

The technical validation of the augmented dataset is performed to ensure the intrinsic behavioural biometrics characteristics of generated synthetic samples are preserved with respect to real samples. The aim is to validate the augmented dataset based on structural validity (by way of modelling consistency), statistical similarity (by way of validating ability to maintain context) and distributional similarity (by way of statistical equivalence).

The results obtained from pre-processed real data and synthetically augmented data generated from controlled interpolation-based augmentation techniques are compared and validated. The following are used to validate the augmented data.

i) Structural Consistency Validation

The structural validation ensures that the same feature schema and structure of behavioural features in the augmented dataset are maintained with respect to the real data based on keystrokes and mouse events.

From the structural consistency validation, it is observed that both data sets have the same feature names, the same data types, the absence of missing values, and feature drift. It confirms that the augmented dataset retains the structural integrity of the original dataset without any feature mismatches or data inconsistencies.

ii) Statistical Validation

Statistical validation using descriptive statistics is performed to assess whether the augmented dataset retains the statistical characteristics of the real biometric behaviour. Some of the metrics in statistical validation, such as mean difference, standard deviation, and variance ratio, are calculated using augmented and real datasets. Table 10 shows the summary of statistical validation using augmented and real datasets.

Table 10. Summary of Statistical Validation (Real vs Augmented)

Metric	Description	Computed Value
Mean Difference	Average difference between dataset means	0.4644
Standard Deviation	Difference in feature dispersion	2.1598
Variance Ratio (Aug/Real)	Relative variance comparison	0.7383

From Table 10, it is observed that the small mean difference (0.4644) indicates that the augmented dataset satisfies the statistical characteristics of the real dataset.

The variance ratio (0.7383) shows that the augmented data maintain similar variability in controlled diversity.

Feature Correlation Analysis

In addition, the feature correlation analysis is applied to validate the similarity between feature relationships in real and augmented datasets. Table 11 shows the result obtained from feature correlation analysis for data augmentation.

Table 11. Results obtained from Feature Correlation Analysis for Data Augmentation

Metric	Value
Average Feature Correlation	0.882

From Table 12, it is noted that the feature correlation value is relatively high (0.882). i.e., the augmented data maintains relationships between the behavioural features with realistic variations.

iii) Distributional Similarity Analysis

It is used to calculate the closeness between the augmented dataset and the real dataset based on sample distribution. In this section, statistical testing, distance-based similarity measure, and PCA-based visualization are applied for distributional similarity analysis.

Kolmogorov–Smirnov (KS) Test

The Kolmogorov–Smirnov is utilized to compare the distributions of real and augmented features. Table 12 shows the results obtained from KS test using augmented and real data.

Table 12. KS Test Results

Metric	Value
Mean p-value	0.113
Features with p > 0.05	~45%

From Table 12, it is observed that many features obtained p-values greater than 0.05. i.e., the augmented dataset satisfies a similar distribution to the real dataset.

Distance-Based Similarity Metrics

Distance metrics is a measure of similarity between the real and augmented datasets. Table 13 shows the results obtained from distance-based similarity metrics.

Table 13. Distance-based Similarity Metrics

Metric	Description	Value
Frechet Distance	Global distribution similarity	253.09
Centroid Distance	Distance between dataset centers	1.5517
PCA Centroid Distance	Distance between PCA mean distributions	0.343247

From Table 13, it is observed that the low centroid distance (1.5517) and PCA centroid distance (0.343247)were attained to ensure the closely distribution of augmented data with real data.

PCA-Based Visualization

Principal Component Analysis (PCA) is used to visualize the distribution similarity between real and augmented datasets. Figure 4 illustrates the results obtained from PCA-based visualization.

Figure 4. PCA-based visualization using augmented and real datasets

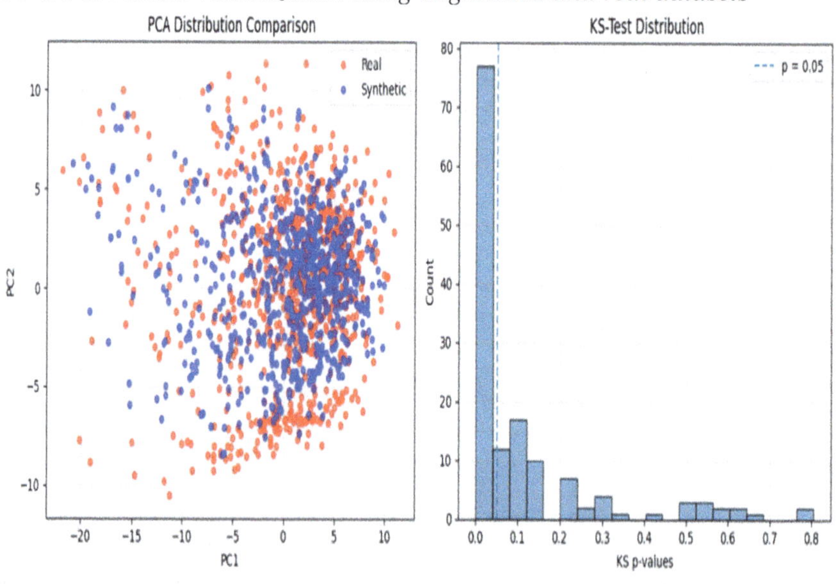

From Figure 4, a strong overlap between real and synthetic samples is observed that the underlying structure of the behavioral feature space in the augmentation process is preserved in controlled variability.

Phase 6: Agentic Guardrails for Augmented Data Validation

In Agentic Guardrails, the quality of data and consistency in augmented data is validated. It ensures the augmented data is validated using the KS test, Wasserstein distance, feature distribution, reliability, model impact, security robustness, and final status. Table 14 shows the results obtained from Agentic Guardrails for data validations.

Table 14. Results obtained from Agentic Guardrails for Data Validation

Description	Before Guardrails Validation	After Guardrails Validation
Dataset Type	Raw + Augmented Data	Validated Augmented Data
Data Quality	May contain noisy or unrealistic synthetic samples	Only high-quality and realistic synthetic samples retained
KS Test (p-value)	Low ($p < 0.05$ for many features) indicating distribution mismatch	Improved (average $p > 0.05$) indicating distribution similarity
Wasserstein Distance	Higher distance between real and synthetic distributions	Reduced distance showing better alignment
Feature Distribution	Inconsistent and deviates from real data	Closely aligned with real data distribution
Reliability	Not guaranteed	Statistically validated and reliable
Model Impact	May reduce model performance due to poor-quality data	Improves model performance and generalization
Security Robustness	Vulnerable to unrealistic patterns	More robust against anomalies and attacks
Final Status	Unverified augmented dataset	Guardrail-approved dataset for training

From Table 14, it is observed that the dataset is not prone to data leakage because the number of features before augmentation and after augmentation is 144 features. It prevents the model from training incorrect patterns, which increases the accuracy of the model.

Phase 7: Agent Perception Of Augmented Data

The augmented dataset, which contains 1400 samples of real and synthetic data with 144 behavioral features, is used in Agent perception. It divides the augmented data into input features (X) and target labels (y). The feature set (X) consists of timely features of all behavioral characteristics, and the associated user identifier (SubjectID) is represented as target label (y). Since the user identifier (SubjectID) is categorical, label encoding is applied to convert it into a numerical representation.

Thereby, the agent performs the subject-wise grouping to evaluate the behavioral characteristics of each subject. Then, the model is trained using subject-wise behavioral records to identify the unique behavioral pattern for each subject for user authentication.

Phase 8: Agent Planning

The timely features (X) obtained from Agent perception contain 144 features, which is a high-dimensional data and it has the presence of non-linear relationships. In this phase, Agent planning is performed using Random Forest to select the best features based on an automatic feature selection strategy. The two steps involved in feature selection are Validation Stability Analysis and Recursive Feature Elimination, which is explained below:

Validation Stability Analysis

Validation Stability Analysis is used to find the optimum number of features using a Random Forest classifier. It aims to evaluate the performance of model based on accuracy using to select the best top features. At first, the features are ranked using the Random Forest based on feature importance. Then, different subsets of features were tested using Repeated Stratified K-Fold Cross-Validation with 5 folds repeated 10 times. It avoids any bias and variance in model performance. The experiment was conducted with different subsets of features ranging from 20 to 100 features. Table 15 shows the results obtained from validation stability analysis.

Table 15. Results obtained from validation stability analysis for feature selection in Agent Planning

Number of Features	Mean Accuracy	Standard Deviation
20	97.91%	0.75
40	97.92%	0.66
60	97.98%	0.70
80	98.11%	0.70
100	**98.15%**	**0.70**

From Table 15, it is evident that the maximum mean accuracy of 98.15% is obtained when 100 features were utilized. But, the standard deviation of 0.70 is achieved by 100 features, which is less compared to the standard deviation of 20 features (0.75). However, the performance of random forest with 100 features achieved a higher performance with 98.15% compared to random forest with less number of features. It is evident that several features less than 100 gives lesser accuracy and affects the performance of the random forest for further user authentication. Thus, it is evident that the random forest with 100 features performs well and is considered as an optimal number of features. So, these 100 parameters are selected for further model training.

Recursive Feature Elimination

Once the optimal number of features is identified, the agent employs the Recursive Feature Elimination (RFE) to choose the most important features. In this, less important features are recursively filtered out according to their importance scores provided by the model. Random Forest Classifier is employed as the base estimator in the RFE.

At first, the importance of the features is calculated for 100 features obtained from validation stability analysis using RFE to remove the less important features. Then, different subsets of features were tested using Repeated Stratified K-Fold Cross-Validation with 5 folds repeated 10 times. The experiment was conducted with different subsets of features ranging from 20 to 90 features. Table 16 shows the results obtained from RFE in Agent planning.

Table 16. Results obtained from RFE for feature elimination in Agent Planning

Number of Features	Mean Accuracy	Standard Deviation
20	**97.51%**	0.91
30	97.25%	0.81
40	97.06%	0.95
50	97.33%	0.67
60	97.32%	0.88
70	97.02%	**1.00**
80	97.19%	0.84
90	97.10%	0.94

From Table 16, it is evident that the maximum mean accuracy of 97.51% is obtained when 20 features were utilized. But, the standard deviation of 0.91 is achieved by 100 features is less compared to the standard deviation of 70 features (100). However, the performance of random forest with 20 features achieved a higher performance with 97.51% compared random forest with a higher number of features, which is consistent. The selected top 20 features using RFE is shown in Figure 5.

Figure 5. Feature Selection using RFE techniques

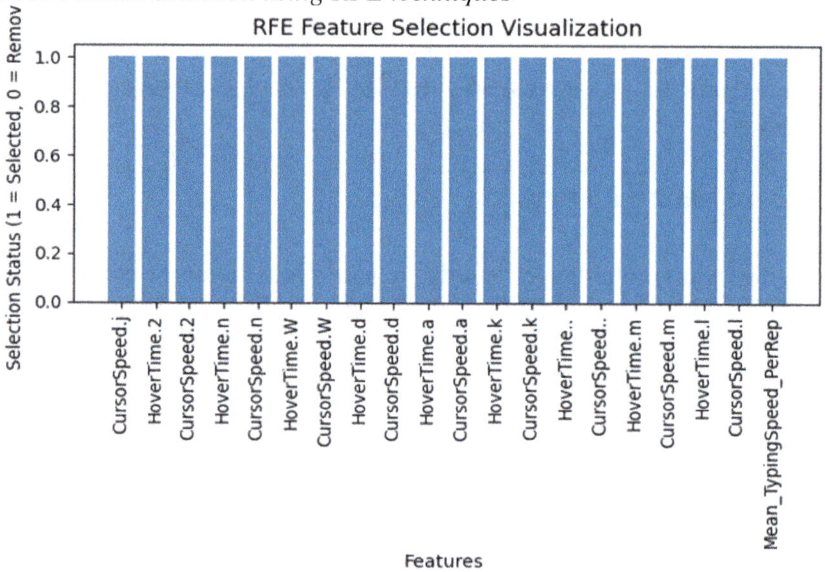

From Figure 5, it is observed that 20 unique features are selected based on accuracy and standard deviation by eliminating the redundant features. It is observed that most of the behavioral features are related to mouse interactions, which include hovering and cursor speed. Only one statistical feature namely Mean_TypingSpeed_PerRep is selected. Therefore, mouse behavioral patterns are considered to be quite important in distinguishing user identities. Table 17 indicates the results before the feature selection and after the feature selection using Agent Planning

Table 17. Result obtained using Feature Selection in Agent Planning

Description	Before Feature Selection	After Feature Selection
Total Features	144	20
Feature Quality	Contains redundant and less important features	Only high-impact, discriminative features retained
Selected Feature using Validation Stability Analysis	144	100

continued on following page

Table 17. Continued

Description	Before Feature Selection	After Feature Selection
Features Reduced using Validation Stability Analysis	144	44
Selected Features using RFE	100	20
Features Reduced using RFE	100	80

From Table 17, it is observed that 100 features are selected from 144 features using Validation Stability Analysis based on the accuracy obtained by Random Forest. Then, RFE is applied to select 20 unique features from 100 features by eliminating redundancy.

Phase 9: Agent Action

In this Agent, the selected 20 features are analyzed using diverse machine learning models such as LightGBM, XGBoost, and Decision Tree for user authentication and the performance evaluation is presented in Table 18.

Table 18. Performance evaluation based on Accuracy

Algorithm	Accuracy (%)
LightGBM	95.2
XGBoost	94.11
Decision Tree	80.83

From Table 18, it can be observed that the highest accuracy of 95.2% is achieved by the LightGBM model. It is evident that LightGBM precisely classifies and performs higher compared to XGBoost and Decision Tree for user authentication.

Table 19 shows the performance evaluation of LightGBM, XGBoost, and Decision Tree in Agentic Action based on EER and AUC.

Table 19. Performance evaluation based on EER and AUC

Algorithm	ERR (%)	AUC (%)
LightGBM	4.07	97.87
XGBoost	4.95	97.48
Decision Tree	20.07	82.21

From Table 19, it is observed that LightGBM obtained highest value of 97.87% AUC with lowest value of 4.07% EER to precisely differentiate real users and impostors. It is prominent that LightGBM outperforms XGBoost and Decision Tree in terms of EER and AUC for user authentication.

Table 20 shows the performance evaluation of LightGBM, XGBoost, and Decision Tree in Agentic Action based on GAR, FAR, and FRR.

Table 20. Performance evaluation based on GAR, FAR, and FRR

Algorithm	GAR (%)	FAR (%)	FRR (%)
LightGBM	96.66	4.81	3.33
XGBoost	96	5.9	4
Decision Tree	79	19.14	21

From Table 20, it is evident that LightGBM achieved the maximum GAR value of 96.66% with lowest FRR and FAR of 3.33% and 4.81%. i.e., precise classification compared to others.

Table 21 shows the overall performance evaluation of LightGBM, XGBoost, and Decision Tree used with Agentic AI and without Agentic AI for user authentication.

Table 21. Overall Performance Evaluation (With Agentic AI vs Without Agentic AI)

Classification	Algorithm	Accuracy (%)	EER (%)	AUC (%)	GAR (%)	FAR (%)	FRR (%)
With Agentic AI	LightGBM	95.2	4.07	97.87	96.66	4.81	3.33
	XGBoost	94.11	4.95	97.48	96	5.9	4
	Decision Tree	80.83	20.07	82.21	79	19.14	21
Without Agentic AI	LightGBM	92.5	7.5	94.29	94.33	7.11	6.92
	XGBoost	90.38	9.62	93.43	94.67	8.91	9.12
	Decision Tree	33.29	61.34	4.44	90	67.28	10

From Table 21, it is observed that Agentic AI enhances the performance of behavioral biometric authentication system. LightGBM with Agentic AI obtained 95.2% accuracy, 97.87% AUC, 96.66%GAR with low FAR, FRR, and EER of4.81%,3.33%, and 4.07%. i.e., it achieved the best performance. Meanwhile, the performance of machine learning models falls short without Agentic AI in terms of less accuracy, better AUC values, higher EER, FAR, and FRR, and reduced GAR compared to machine learning models with Agentic AI. It affects the decision making in user authentication.

From the above analysis, it is evident that the performance of LightGBM with Agentic AI is higher compared to XGBoost, and Decision Tree in both Agentic configurations for user authentication.

Ablation Study of Agentic Components

In this section, the ablation study is performed to validate the contribution of each agent in proposed framework for behavioral biometric authentication. Table 22 shows the results obtained in ablation analysis of Agentic components.

Table 22. Ablation Analysis of Agentic Components

Configuration	Accuracy (%)	AUC (%)	EER (%)
Full Agentic AI	95.2	97.87	4.07
Without Guardrails	92.8	95.1	7.2
Without Planning	90.9	93.7	8.5
Without Perception	91.4	94.0	7.9
Traditional ML Only	88.3	90.8	11.6

From Table 22, it is observed that Agentic AI with adaptive feature-selection mechanisms achieves increased performance in terms of 95.2% accuracy and 97.87% AUC with minimal EER (4.07). However, the reduced performance is witnessed by individual component contributes to the overall effectiveness of the framework. i.e., Guardrails component filters inconsistent synthetic samples generated during augmentation obtained 92.8% accuracy, 95.1% AUC, and 7.2% EER.

It is noted that perception and planning achieves accuracy of 91.4%, and 90.9% for behavioral analysis and feature selection which is less than others.

From the above analysis, it is validated that the performance of Agentic AI is effective in behavioral biometric authentication.

CONCLUSION AND FUTURE SCOPE

The study proposes a novel and intelligent user authentication method incorporating keystroke and mouse dynamics (i.e., how users type and use their mouse), as opposed to typical authentication methods like passwords and PINs, by taking advantage of each individual's unique interactions with a computer. The integration of typing and mouse interaction generates a unique pattern to each individual, for secure continuous user authentication using non-touch virtual keyboard in online systems.

In this chapter, techniques such as data cleaning, feature extraction, preprocessing, data splitting, controlled interpolation-based data augmentation, Agentic Guardrails for validation, Agent Perception for statistical analysis, Agent Planning for feature selection, and Agent Action for machine learning-based authentication are incorporated. The Agentic AI framework automates an authentication pipeline for intelligent decision-making. Agents such as Guardrails validated the quality and consistency of augmented data; Perception analyzed behavioral distributions and anomalies of augmented data; Planning validates optimal feature selection strategy using validation stability analysis and RFE; and Action developed authentication models using LightGBM, XGBoost, and Decision Tree classifiers for user authentication.

Experimental results confirm that the proposed framework achieved higher performance for user authentication using LightGBM with Agentic AI by obtaining 95.2% accuracy, 97.87% AUC, 96.66% GAR, and a low EER of 4.07%. It outperforms XGBoost and Decision Tree models. In addition, the integration of Agentic AI improved authentication accuracy, reduced FAR and FRR, than machine learning models without Agentic AI for behavioral biometric authentication systems. It is evident that combination of behavioral biometrics, intelligent data augmentation, and Agentic AI enables a secure, adaptive, and intelligent authentication framework for secured online system.

Although the proposed framework achieved strong authentication performance, the dataset size remains relatively limited with 100 participants and 1000 behavioral samples. Behavioral biometric acquisition is inherently time-consuming because each sample must preserve temporal and cognitive consistency during user interaction. Despite this limitation, subject- wise stratified validation and repeated cross-validation were employed to improve generalization reliability. Future work will focus on collecting larger-scale cross-device and cross-environment datasets to improve scalability and robustness.

REFERENCES

Acharya, D. B., Kuppan, K., & Divya, B. (2025). Agentic AI: Autonomous intelligence for complex goals—A comprehensive survey. *IEEE Access : Practical Innovations, Open Solutions, 13*, 18912–18936. DOI: 10.1109/ACCESS.2025.3532853

Ahmed, F., Rahman, M. D., Alif, M. A., Mumtahina, N., & Mormo, M. I. (2026). *Deep learning–based behavioral biometric authentication using keystroke and touch patterns* (Doctoral dissertation, BRAC University).

Ahmed, F., Rahman, M. D., Alif, M. A., Mumtahina, N., & Mormo, M. I. (2026). *Deep learning–based behavioral biometric authentication using keystroke and touch patterns* (Doctoral dissertation, BRAC University).

Aljoubory, S. H., & Mahdi, M. S. (2025). User Authentication Based on Mouse Dynamics Using an Efficient-Net Model. *Iraqi Journal for Computers and Informatics, 51*(2), 224–242. DOI: 10.25195/ijci.v51i2.612

Altwaijry, N. (2023). Authentication by keystroke dynamics: The influence of typing language. *Applied Sciences (Basel, Switzerland), 13*(20), 11478. DOI: 10.3390/app132011478

Ayeswarya, S., & Singh, K. J. (2025). Enhancing security and usability with context aware multi-biometric fusion for continuous user authentication. *Scientific Reports, 15*(1), 30627. DOI: 10.1038/s41598-025-14833-z PMID: 40836057

Bhasin, N., Sharma, S. K., & Mishra, R. (2025). Authentication Using Keystrokes Dynamic For Static Text With Hybrid Deep Learning Technique. *INTERNATIONAL JOURNAL OF ADVANCES IN SIGNAL AND IMAGE SCIENCES*, 573-595.

Cariello, N., Nguyen, L., Gallagher, R., Kurtzer, I., Balagani, K. S., & Gasti, P. (2026). Keystroke-Aligned Body Motion Patterns for Short-Burst Continuous Smartphone Authentication: A Proof-of-Concept Study Using Motion Capture. *IEEE Transactions on Biometrics, Behavior, and Identity Science*, 1. DOI: 10.1109/TBIOM.2026.3674400

Cupps, N., & Elgazzar, H. (2026, January). Machine Learning Techniques for Continuous User Authentication Based on Mouse and Keystroke Dynamics. In *2026 IEEE 16th Annual Computing and Communication Workshop and Conference (CCWC)* (pp. 0503-0510). IEEE. DOI: 10.1109/CCWC67433.2026.11393691

Ejaz, U., Iqbal, F., Islam, S. M., & Imashev, A. (2025). Behaviour Biometrics Using AI for Continuous Authentication Systems. *Journal of Artificial Intelligence General science (JAIGS), 8*(02), 53-64.

Ibrahim, R. K., & Hoobi, M. M. (2026). Keystroke Dynamics System for User Authentication Using SVM Classifier. *Journal of Intelligent Systems & Internet of Things, 18*(1).

Khan, S., Devlen, C., Manno, M., & Hou, D. (2024). Mouse dynamics behavioral biometrics: A survey. *ACM Computing Surveys, 56*(6), 1–33. DOI: 10.1145/3640311

Killourhy, K. S., & Maxion, R. A. (2009). *Comparing anomaly-detection algorithms for keystroke dynamics. In 2009 IEEE/IFIP international conference on dependable systems & networks*. IEEE.

Martins, A., Dias, T., Dias, A., Vitorino, J., Maia, E., & Praça, I. (2025). Keystroke dynamics for intelligent biometric authentication with machine learning. *Discover Applied Sciences, 7*(9), 992. DOI: 10.1007/s42452-025-07449-5

Medvedev, V., Budžys, A., & Kurasova, O. (2025). A decision-making framework for user authentication using keystroke dynamics. *Computers & Security, 155*, 104494. DOI: 10.1016/j.cose.2025.104494

Monastyrska, E. (2025). *Machine learning techniques for biometric authentication based on keystroke dynamics* (Doctoral dissertation, Vilniaus universitetas.).

Monrose, F., & Rubin, A. D. (2000). Keystroke dynamics as a biometric for authentication. *Future Generation Computer Systems, 16*(4), 351–359. DOI: 10.1016/S0167-739X(99)00059-X

Muralidharan, A., Eaman, A., & Hassan, E. (2025). A Comparative Analysis of Machine Learning Models for Behavioral Biometric Authentication using Keystroke Dynamics. *Procedia Computer Science, 265*, 116–123. DOI: 10.1016/j.procs.2025.07.163

Patil, V., Naik, A., Oswal, A., Ghonge, V. D., Nayakwadi, V., & Pawar, Y. (2026, March). User Authentication through Mouse Dynamics Using Gameplay Data. In *2026 International Conference on Emerging Smart Computing and Informatics (ESCI)* (pp. 1-7). IEEE. DOI: 10.1109/ESCI68015.2026.11493277

Rajpoot, A., Sharma, N., Sahu, S., Anand, V., Bhalerao, S., & Yadav, S. (2025). Real-Time Multi-User Authentication Using Mouse Dynamics Behavioural Biometrics. In *2025 International Conference on Emerging Technologies and Innovation for Sustainability (EmergIN)* (pp. 466-471). IEEE. DOI: 10.1109/EmergIN67762.2025.11450662

Risto, H. N., & Graven, O. H. (2024). Fixed-text keystroke dynamics authentication data set—Collection and analysis. *Annales des Télécommunications, 79*(11), 731–743. DOI: 10.1007/s12243-024-01039-z

Roy, I. (2026). *Securing Graphical Authentication Using Keystroke Dynamics* (Doctoral dissertation, © University of Dhaka).

Russell, S., & Norvig, P. (2020). Artificial intelligence: a modern approach, 4/E.

Sharma, A., Jureček, M., & Stamp, M. (2025). Keystroke dynamics for user identification. In *Machine Learning, Deep Learning and AI for Cybersecurity* (pp. 601–622). Springer Nature Switzerland. DOI: 10.1007/978-3-031-83157-7_21

Subash, A., Song, I., Lee, I., & Lee, K. (2025). AgeGen Bio Track: Continuous Mouse Behavioral Biometrics-Based Age and Gender Profiling in Online Education Platforms. In *ICAART (3)* (pp. 383-393).

Tao, X., Huang, Y., Liu, J., Wang, T., Zhao, W., Wang, C., & Fu, J. (2026). User Identity Authentication via Spatiotemporal Mouse Dynamics Modeling. *Available at SSRN* 6193851. DOI: 10.1016/j.comnet.2026.112502

Yao, J., & Wang, D. (2026). StrokePIN: Enhancing PIN Authentication with Keystroke Dynamics for Mobile Devices. *IEEE Transactions on Dependable and Secure Computing*, *23*(3), 6797–6814. DOI: 10.1109/TDSC.2026.3667918

Chapter 9

Agentic AI for Behavioral Biometrics Advancing Continuous Authentication in Cybersecurity:

A Framework for Intelligent and Adaptive Real Time User Verification

Anwesh G. Poojary
http://orcid.org/0009-0001-2204-347X
Sahyadri College of Engineering and Management, India

ABSTRACT

Continuous authentication has emerged as a critical need in modern cybersecurity due to the limitations of traditional static authentication methods such as passwords and one-time verification systems. This work proposes an agentic AI-driven framework that leverages behavioral biometrics, including keystroke dynamics and user interaction patterns, to continuously verify user identity. The system employs autonomous and adaptive learning models capable of evolving with user behavior over time, thereby improving accuracy and resilience against impersonation attacks. By integrating real-time monitoring with intelligent decision-making, the proposed approach enhances security while maintaining usability. The framework addresses key challenges such as behavioral variability, data drift, and false positives, offering a scalable and robust solution for next-generation identity verification systems.

DOI: 10.4018/979-8-2600-0413-5.ch009

1. INTRODUCTION

Authentication remains a fundamental pillar of cybersecurity, serving as the primary mechanism for ensuring that only authorized individuals gain access to sensitive systems, networks, and data resources. Conventional authentication techniques including password based systems, hardware tokens, and multi factor authentication mechanisms operate on a static and one time verification model. Once a user is authenticated at the point of entry, the system typically assumes continued legitimacy throughout the session lifecycle. While this model offers simplicity and ease of deployment, it introduces critical security vulnerabilities, particularly in the face of session hijacking attacks, credential compromise, privilege escalation, and insider threats. Attackers who gain access after initial authentication can exploit these sessions without triggering further verification checks, thereby bypassing traditional security controls.

To overcome these limitations, the concept of continuous authentication has gained significant attention as a dynamic and persistent security mechanism. Unlike static authentication approaches, continuous authentication continuously validates user identity throughout the interaction session, thereby reducing the attack surface associated with unauthorized access. A key enabler of this paradigm is behavioral biometrics, which leverages distinctive and often subconscious user behavior patterns for identity verification. These patterns include keystroke dynamics, touchscreen gesture analysis, mouse movement trajectories, and device motion or gait patterns. Behavioral traits offer several advantages over traditional credentials. They are inherently difficult to replicate, resistant to theft, and enable non intrusive and frictionless authentication, thereby enhancing both security and user experience.

The rapid evolution of machine learning and deep learning techniques has significantly advanced the effectiveness of behavioral biometric systems. Supervised learning models, along with more sophisticated architectures such as recurrent neural networks, long short term memory networks, and transformer based models, have demonstrated strong capabilities in capturing temporal and sequential dependencies in user behavior. For instance, recent studies including the work of Bansal and Ouda 2024 emphasize the application of reinforcement learning to enable adaptive authentication mechanisms that evolve in response to changes in user behavior over time. Similarly, transformer based architectures such as TypeFormer have shown superior performance in modeling long range dependencies in keystroke dynamics, thereby improving classification accuracy and robustness.

Despite these advancements, existing systems largely remain reactive and model centric, relying on predefined training data and periodic updates rather than real time adaptation. They often lack the ability to incorporate contextual awareness such as environmental conditions, device characteristics, or situational risk factors, which are critical for accurate and reliable authentication in dynamic real world scenarios. Furthermore, current approaches struggle with concept drift, where user behavior evolves over time, leading to reduced model performance and increased false acceptance or rejection rates.

The incorporation of Agentic AI enables several key capabilities including real time anomaly detection, dynamic risk scoring, context aware decision making, and continuous policy optimization through reinforcement learning. Intelligent agents can collaborate, share knowledge, and refine their models through feedback driven learning loops, thereby enhancing system resilience against adversarial attacks and previously unseen threat patterns. This approach not only improves authentication accuracy but also supports scalability across distributed and heterogeneous environments such as enterprise networks, financial platforms, and mobile or IoT ecosystems.

In summary, the integration of Agentic Artificial Intelligence with behavioral biometrics represents a significant advancement in the evolution of authentication systems. By enabling autonomy, adaptability, and contextual awareness, this paradigm addresses the inherent limitations of traditional and current continuous authentication approaches, paving the way for next generation intelligent cybersecurity frameworks capable of operating effectively in increasingly complex and adversarial digital environments.

This chapter makes four specific contributions. First, it synthesizes recent literature on behavioral biometrics, reinforcement learning, and agentic artificial intelligence into a coherent layered architecture for continuous authentication. Second, it specifies an explicit evaluation methodology, including candidate public benchmark datasets, standard biometric performance metrics, baseline comparisons, and a statistical validation protocol, that converts the architectural claims into testable hypotheses for future empirical work, and it reports an illustrative simulation that demonstrates the qualitative adaptation behavior the architecture is designed to achieve. Third, it provides a dedicated treatment of adversarial robustness, privacy-preserving and federated learning, and explainability mechanisms relevant to the agentic decision layer, areas that were identified as gaps in an earlier version of this chapter. Fourth, it extends the discussion of ethical and regulatory considerations, including informed consent, biometric template protection, and fairness, and illustrates the framework's applicability across two distinct high-stakes domains, healthcare and financial services. The remainder of the chapter is organized as follows. The Background and Related Work section reviews prior work on behavioral biometrics, continuous authentication, and reinforcement learning in security, and situates the proposed framework relative to this literature through a direct comparative analysis. The Agentic AI in Behavioral Biometrics section then describes the conceptual architecture in detail. The Proposed Framework and Methodology section operationalizes this architecture into a three-stage methodology and specifies the evaluation plan described above. The Challenges and Limitations, Future Research Directions, and Applications sections then discuss the practical, ethical, and domain-specific considerations associated with deploying the framework, before the chapter concludes.

2. BACKGROUND AND RELATED WORK

Reinforcement learning-based approaches have been explored to enable adaptive continuous authentication systems that dynamically adjust security decisions based on user behavior patterns (Bansal & Ouda, 2024). These methods allow authentication systems to move beyond static threshold-based models by learning optimal policies through feedback-driven interactions, improving long-term adaptability against behavioral drift and evolving cyber threats. Lightweight tap-based continuous authentication frameworks have been proposed for smartphones, enabling efficient real-time authentication in resource-constrained environments (Chen et al., 2024). These systems reduce computational overhead while maintaining accuracy, making them suitable for mobile and edge-based deployment scenarios. Transformer-based architectures such as TypeFormer have significantly improved keystroke biometric authentication by capturing long-range dependencies in user input sequences (Stragapede et al., 2024). These models outperform traditional sequential methods by effectively learning global relationships in typing behavior. Feature-level fusion of touch gestures and keystroke dynamics has been used to improve authentication accuracy and usability in continuous authentication systems (Stylios et al., 2023). This multimodal fusion reduces uncertainty and enhances robustness against noisy or incomplete behavioral data.

Touch event-based behavioral authentication systems have demonstrated that smartphone interaction patterns can effectively support continuous user verification (Gattulli et al., 2023). These systems leverage natural touch interactions such as swipes and taps, enabling passive authentication without user interruption. Convolutional transformer models have been applied to sensor-based authentication systems, improving accuracy and robustness in mobile environments (Hu et al., 2023). These hybrid models combine convolutional feature extraction with attention mechanisms for improved multimodal representation. Behavioral biometric systems combining keystroke dynamics and touch gestures have been developed to enhance security and reduce authentication errors (Stylios et al., 2022). These systems improve resistance to spoofing attacks and behavioral variability. Hybrid authentication systems integrating keystroke and mouse dynamics have shown improved robustness in complex usage scenarios (Wang et al., 2022). These approaches leverage complementary behavioral signals from different input devices.

A comprehensive survey of continuous authentication technologies highlights key challenges such as scalability, privacy concerns, and adversarial vulnerabilities (Jeong et al., 2022). It emphasizes the need for adaptive and context-aware authentication mechanisms. Gait-based authentication using wrist-worn devices has been explored as a reliable biometric modality for continuous identity verification (Cola et al., 2021). These systems utilize walking patterns as unique behavioral signatures. Multimodal gait-based systems using wearable sensors have demonstrated improved authentication accuracy through combined behavioral signals (Papavasileiou et al., 2021). Fusion of multiple motion features enhances reliability and reduces dependency on a single modality. Mobile sensing-based authentication systems use activity patterns to enable continuous user verification in smartphone environments (Mekruksavanich & Jitpattanakul, 2021). These systems rely on embedded sensors such as accelerometers and gyroscopes for behavioral analysis. Mouse movement-based authentication systems demonstrate that cursor dynamics can effectively distinguish between users in interactive environments (Siddiqui et al., 2021). These systems analyze spatial-temporal motion behavior to build unique user profiles.

2.1 Behavioral Biometrics

Behavioral biometrics has emerged as a key research area in cybersecurity, focusing on identifying individuals based on unique patterns in their interactions with devices and systems. Unlike physiological biometrics such as fingerprints or facial recognition, behavioral biometrics relies on dynamic characteristics including keystroke dynamics, mouse movements, touchscreen gestures, and gait patterns. These behavioral traits are inherently continuous, difficult to replicate, and capable of supporting passive authentication mechanisms. Early approaches to behavioral biometrics primarily utilized statistical models and traditional machine learning techniques such as support vector machines and decision trees. However, these methods were limited in capturing complex temporal dependencies present in user behavior. Recent advancements in deep learning have significantly improved performance, with models such as recurrent neural networks, long short term memory networks, and transformer based architectures demonstrating strong capabilities in sequence modeling. These techniques enable the extraction of fine grained behavioral features and improve classification accuracy in real world scenarios. Despite these advancements, challenges remain in handling intra user variability, environmental noise, and behavioral drift over time. Additionally, adversarial attacks aimed at mimicking user behavior pose a growing threat, highlighting the need for more robust and adaptive models.

2.2 Continuous Authentication

Continuous authentication extends traditional authentication mechanisms by verifying user identity throughout the entire session rather than at a single point in time. This paradigm addresses critical vulnerabilities associated with static authentication, particularly in scenarios involving session hijacking and unauthorized access after login. Existing continuous authentication systems leverage behavioral biometrics as a primary input for ongoing identity verification. These systems typically operate by continuously collecting behavioral data, extracting relevant features, and evaluating them against trained models to determine user legitimacy. Threshold based decision mechanisms are often used to trigger re authentication or session termination when anomalies are detected. Recent research has explored multimodal approaches that combine multiple behavioral signals to improve reliability and robustness. Additionally, risk based authentication models have been introduced to dynamically adjust authentication requirements based on contextual factors such as location, device type, and user activity patterns. However, many existing systems remain reactive in nature, relying on predefined thresholds and static models. They often lack real time adaptability and struggle to handle evolving user behavior, resulting in increased false positives and false negatives. This limitation underscores the need for more intelligent and autonomous approaches to continuous authentication.

2.3 Reinforcement Learning in Security

Reinforcement learning has gained increasing attention in cybersecurity due to its ability to enable systems to learn optimal decision making strategies through interaction with dynamic environments. Unlike supervised learning, reinforcement learning does not rely on labeled datasets but instead learns through a reward based mechanism, making it well suited for adaptive and real time security applications. In the context of authentication and intrusion detection, reinforcement learning has been applied to dynamically adjust security policies, optimize detection thresholds, and respond to emerging threats. For example, reinforcement learning agents can continuously update authentication strategies based on user behavior patterns and system feedback, thereby improving detection accuracy over time. Recent studies have demonstrated the potential of reinforcement learning in handling concept drift and evolving attack strategies. By incorporating feedback loops, these systems can adapt to changes in user behavior and environmental conditions without requiring frequent retraining. Furthermore, reinforcement learning supports the development of proactive defense mechanisms by anticipating potential threats and taking preventive actions. Despite its advantages, the application of reinforcement learning in security also presents challenges, including high computational complexity, slow convergence in large state spaces, and vulnerability to adversarial manipulation. Ensuring stability, scalability, and robustness remains an active area of research.

2.4 Comparative Analysis of Prior Approaches

The literature reviewed above spans a range of modalities, learning paradigms, and levels of adaptivity, but a direct comparison across these dimensions makes the specific gap addressed by the proposed framework more explicit. Table 1 summarizes representative prior systems along four dimensions: the behavioral modality used, the underlying learning paradigm, whether the system adapts its decision criteria over time, and whether it incorporates autonomous, goal-directed decision making in the sense associated with agentic systems.

Table 1. Comparative Summary of Representative Continuous Authentication Approaches

System / Study	Modality	Learning Paradigm	Adaptive Thresholding	Agentic Decision Making
Bansal & Ouda (2024)	Keystroke and behavioral signals	Reinforcement learning	Yes	Limited (single policy, no multi-agent coordination)
Stragapede et al. (2024), TypeFormer	Keystroke dynamics	Transformer-based supervised learning	No (fixed classification boundary)	No
Chen et al. (2024), TBAuth	Tap behavior	Lightweight supervised learning	No	No
Stylios et al. (2023)	Touch gestures and keystrokes	Feature-level fusion, supervised learning	No	No
Hu et al. (2023), AuthConFormer	Sensor data	Convolutional transformer	No	No
Wang et al. (2022)	Keystroke and mouse dynamics	Hybrid supervised learning	No	No
Cola et al. (2021); Papavasileiou et al. (2021)	Gait, wearable sensors	Supervised / multimodal fusion	No	No
Proposed Framework	Keystroke, touch, mouse, gait, and context	Reinforcement learning within a multi-agent decision layer	Yes, with context-aware risk weighting	Yes, with distinct perception, decision, and learning agents

This comparison clarifies that the existing literature has already established strong single-modality and fused-modality classifiers, and that reinforcement learning has independently been applied to threshold adaptation (Bansal & Ouda, 2024). What remains comparatively underexplored, and what the proposed framework is intended to contribute, is the combination of multimodal behavioral fusion with a multi-agent decision architecture in which perception, risk evaluation, and policy learning are handled by functionally distinct, collaborating agents rather than a single end-to-end model. This distinction matters operationally: a single-model system that is retrained to adapt its threshold must update its entire decision function in response to new feedback, whereas a multi-agent architecture can, in principle, update its risk-scoring policy independently of its perception or context-evaluation components, which may improve both interpretability and the ability to isolate and correct errors. This architectural distinction is conceptual at this stage and has not yet been empirically validated against the single-model reinforcement-learning baseline of Bansal and Ouda (2024); confirming this advantage empirically is identified as a specific objective of the evaluation methodology described in the Proposed Framework and Methodology section.

2.5 Adversarial Robustness in Behavioral Biometrics

As behavioral biometric systems move toward operational deployment, their resilience to deliberate manipulation becomes as important as their accuracy under benign conditions. Several threat patterns are relevant to the architecture proposed in this chapter. Mimicry attacks involve an adversary deliberately studying and reproducing a target user's typing rhythm, gesture pattern, or gait in an attempt to be classified as legitimate. Synthetic behavior generation uses generative models to produce artificial keystroke or touch sequences statistically resembling a target user's profile, which is a more scalable variant of mimicry that does not require the attacker to manually rehearse the behavior. Replay and sensor-spoofing attacks inject previously captured or fabricated sensor data directly into the authentication pipeline, bypassing the need to physically reproduce the behavior at all. Jeong et al. (2022) identify adversarial vulnerability as one of the open challenges facing continuous authentication systems generally, and this concern applies directly to the agentic architecture proposed here, since an agent that adapts its decision boundary in response to feedback could, in principle, be manipulated by an adversary who deliberately shapes the feedback it receives, a risk sometimes referred to as policy poisoning in the reinforcement-learning literature. Mitigating these risks requires defenses at multiple layers of the architecture rather than a single safeguard. At the data layer, liveness and consistency checks across behavioral modalities can help detect sensor spoofing, since synthetic or replayed data is less likely to be consistent across multiple independent channels simultaneously. At the modeling layer, adversarial training, in which the model is exposed to deliberately perturbed or synthetic behavioral samples during training, can improve robustness to mimicry and generative attacks, though at some cost to baseline accuracy. At the agentic decision layer specifically, the framework's reinforcement-learning component should incorporate safeguards against policy poisoning, such as bounding the rate at which decision thresholds are allowed to shift in response to recent feedback, and flagging unusually rapid or one-directional drift in the learned policy for human review rather than allowing it to update unchecked. These considerations were not addressed in the original submission and are incorporated here as a dedicated robustness requirement for the architecture, with a fuller discussion of the associated trade-offs provided in the Challenges and Limitations section.

2.6 Privacy-Preserving and Federated Authentication

Continuous behavioral monitoring raises privacy concerns that are distinct from those associated with one-time credential checks, since the data collected is generated passively, continuously, and often without the user actively noticing each individual data point. Three classes of technique are particularly relevant to the architecture proposed in this chapter. Federated learning allows behavioral models to be trained across a population of devices without raw behavioral data ever leaving the device, with only model updates being shared and aggregated centrally. This is well suited to the proposed Knowledge Base and Learning Module, which could be implemented as a federated aggregation point rather than a central repository of raw user data. Differential privacy techniques add calibrated noise to model updates or aggregate statistics so that the contribution of any individual user's data cannot be reliably reconstructed from the shared model, providing a formal, quantifiable privacy guarantee at the cost of some reduction in model accuracy. Secure multiparty computation and homomorphic encryption allow risk scores to be computed over encrypted behavioral features, which is particularly relevant for the Decision Fusion and Risk Assessment Module when authentication decisions involve data contributed by more than one organizational system, such as in cross-platform or federated enterprise deployments. Integrating these techniques into the proposed architecture is not without cost. Federated and privacy-preserving training generally increase communication overhead and slow convergence relative to centralized training, which interacts with the latency and energy constraints already identified for edge and mobile deployment. The chapter therefore treats privacy-preserving learning as a primary direction for future architectural refinement rather than a feature already incorporated into the present design, and this trade-off is discussed further in the Future Research Directions section.

2.7 Explainability in Agentic Authentication Decisions

A second gap identified during review concerns the interpretability of the agentic decision layer. Because the proposed Decision Module relies on learned, context-dependent risk scoring rather than fixed thresholds, its individual authentication decisions are inherently harder to audit than those of a conventional rule-based system. This is a meaningful limitation in regulated domains such as healthcare and finance, where a denied or flagged authentication event may need to be explained to the affected user or to a compliance auditor. Explainable AI techniques applicable to this architecture fall into three broad categories. Feature-attribution methods, such as SHAP or attention-weight visualization for transformer-based behavioral models, can indicate which behavioral features, for example an unusual inter-keystroke interval or an atypical swipe velocity, contributed most to a given risk score. Surrogate rule-extraction methods approximate the learned policy of the Decision and Learning Modules with a simpler, human-readable rule set that can be reviewed even though the underlying model remains complex. Counterfactual explanation methods describe the minimal change in observed behavior that would have produced a different authentication outcome, which is useful for communicating decisions directly to end users without exposing the internal workings of the model. Embedding one or more of these mechanisms into the Decision Fusion and Risk Assessment Module would allow the architecture to produce both a risk score and a corresponding human-readable justification, which is treated as a required extension for any production deployment of the framework and is discussed further as a future research direction.

3. AGENTIC AI IN BEHAVIORAL BIOMETRICS

Since behavioral data is inherently dynamic and subject to variability, effective preprocessing is essential to ensure consistency and reliability in downstream analysis. The Behavioral Data Collection Module standardizes input streams by normalizing temporal and spatial features, removing outliers, and aligning data from multiple sources into a unified representation. This preprocessing stage ensures that the system operates on high-quality data, thereby improving the accuracy of subsequent feature extraction and decision-making processes. Following preprocessing, the Feature Extraction Layer transforms the refined behavioral data into discriminative feature vectors that capture the unique characteristics of individual users. This layer plays a critical role in reducing data dimensionality while preserving essential behavioral patterns. Features such as typing speed, key hold time, inter-key latency, swipe velocity, pressure sensitivity, and motion dynamics are extracted to construct a comprehensive behavioral profile. Advanced techniques, including statistical modeling and deep representation learning, can be employed to capture both short-term variations and long-term dependencies in user behavior. By converting raw interaction data into meaningful representations, this layer enables efficient and accurate behavioral analysis. The extracted features are then passed to the Behavioral Modeling Layer, where machine learning and deep learning models are used to learn user-specific patterns. This layer is responsible for building a robust representation of normal user behavior and distinguishing it from anomalous patterns. Various modeling approaches, such as recurrent neural networks, convolutional neural networks, and transformer-based architectures, can be utilized to capture temporal dependencies and complex relationships within the data. The use of hybrid models further enhances the system's ability to process multimodal inputs, combining information from keystrokes, touch interactions, and sensor data to improve authentication accuracy. At the core of the architecture lies the Agentic Artificial Intelligence Decision Layer, which serves as the central intelligence of the system. This layer consists of autonomous agents that continuously monitor incoming behavioral and contextual data, evaluate risk levels, and make real-time authentication decisions. Unlike traditional systems that rely on fixed thresholds, the agentic framework dynamically adapts its decision boundaries based on evolving user behavior and environmental conditions. Each agent operates with a specific objective, such as anomaly detection, context evaluation, or risk assessment, and collaborates with other agents to produce a final authentication outcome. This distributed decision-making approach enhances system resilience and enables more accurate and context-aware authentication. An important component of this layer is the integration of reinforcement learning mechanisms. Through continuous interaction with the environment, the system receives feedback on its decisions and adjusts its policies accordingly. For example, successful authentication events reinforce current behavioral patterns, while detected anomalies trigger policy updates to improve future decision-making. This feedback-driven learning process allows the system to optimize its performance over time, reducing both false positives and false negatives. As a result, the authentication framework becomes increasingly accurate and adaptive as it gains more experience. The Context Awareness Layer complements behavioral analysis by incorporating additional environmental and situational information into the authentication process. Factors such as device identity, geographic location, time of access, network conditions, and usage patterns provide valuable context for interpreting user behavior. For instance, a change in typing speed may be normal under certain conditions, such as using a different device or operating in a high-stress environment. By integrating contextual data, the system can differentiate between legitimate behavioral variations and potential security threats. This multi-dimensional analysis significantly improves the reliability and robustness of authentication decisions. The Decision Fusion and Risk

Assessment Module aggregates outputs from various layers and agents to generate a unified authentication score. This module applies advanced fusion techniques to combine behavioral and contextual insights, producing a comprehensive risk evaluation. Based on the calculated risk level, the system determines the appropriate response, such as granting access, requesting additional verification, or restricting the session. The ability to dynamically adjust responses based on risk ensures a balance between security and user convenience. Another critical aspect of the architecture is the Continuous Monitoring and Feedback Loop, which ensures that authentication is performed throughout the entire user session. Unlike traditional systems that verify identity only at login, this framework continuously evaluates user behavior in real time. Any deviation from established patterns triggers immediate analysis and response. The feedback loop also enables the system to update its models incrementally, incorporating new behavioral data to maintain accuracy over time. This continuous adaptation is essential for handling behavioral drift and maintaining long-term system effectiveness.

Scalability is another key strength of the proposed framework. The modular and layered design allows the system to handle large volumes of data and users without significant performance degradation. Each component can be independently scaled and optimized based on system requirements. This makes the architecture suitable for deployment in large-scale environments such as enterprise networks, cloud platforms, and critical infrastructure systems.

Finally, the architecture emphasizes usability alongside security. By leveraging passive behavioral biometrics, the system minimizes user interaction and eliminates the need for frequent manual authentication. This seamless user experience is particularly important in applications where continuous access is required, such as healthcare systems, financial platforms, and remote work environments. By reducing user friction while maintaining high security standards, the framework achieves an optimal balance between convenience and protection.

In summary, the proposed architecture represents a comprehensive and forward-looking approach to continuous authentication. By integrating behavioral biometrics, contextual awareness, agent-based intelligence, and adaptive learning mechanisms, it addresses the limitations of traditional authentication systems. The combination of real-time monitoring, dynamic decision-making, and continuous learning ensures that the system remains effective in the face of evolving user behavior and emerging cyber threats.

3.1 Agentic AI Driven Continuous Authentication Architecture

Figure 1. Layered architecture illustrating the integration of Agentic Artificial Intelligence with behavioral biometrics for continuous and adaptive authentication.

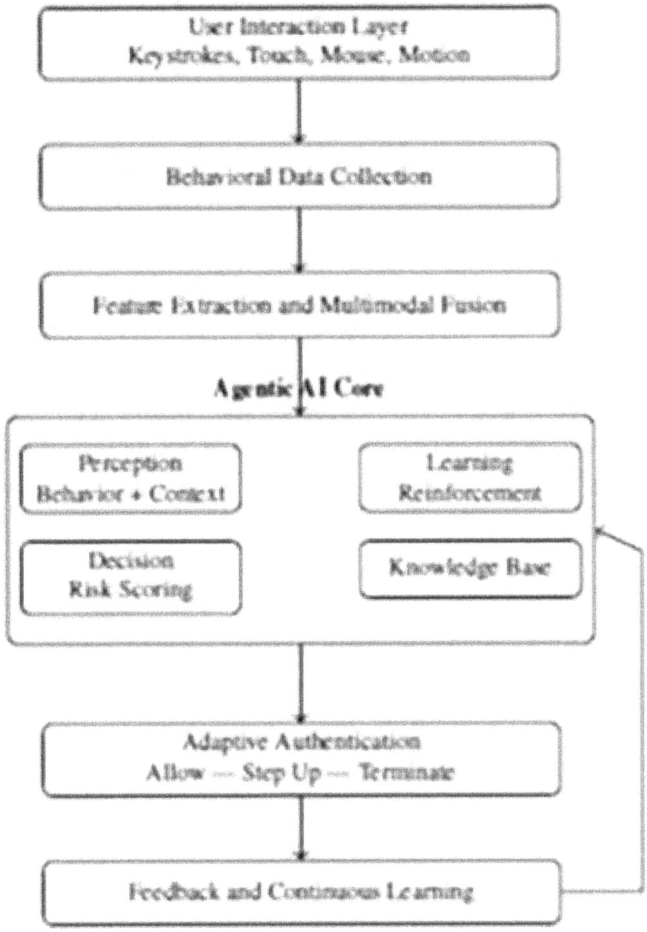

3.2 Agentic AI Driven Continuous Authentication Architecture

Figure 1 illustrates the layered architecture described above. Raw behavioral signals enter through the Behavioral Data Collection Module and Feature Extraction Layer, are interpreted by the Agentic AI Core, comprising the Perception, Decision, and Learning Modules together with the Knowledge Base, and are translated into an access decision by the Adaptive Authentication Engine. The Feedback Loop is drawn outside the main processing pipeline in the figure to emphasize that it influences every component rather than acting as a single sequential stage: it is this loop, closing the gap between observed authentication outcomes and the policies used by the Decision and Learning Modules, that gives the architecture its adaptive, rather than static, character. The remainder of this chapter operationalizes this architecture into a concrete three-stage methodology and a corresponding evaluation plan, presented in the next section.

4. PROPOSED FRAMEWORK AND METHODOLOGY

The proposed framework introduces an Agentic Artificial Intelligence driven architecture for continuous authentication using behavioral biometrics. The system is designed to provide real time, adaptive, and context aware identity verification by integrating multimodal behavioral data with autonomous decision making and feedback driven learning. The framework consists of three primary components: behavioral data collection, agent based decision making, and a reinforcement learning driven feedback loop.

Figure 2. Agentic AI Driven Continuous Authentication Framework using Behavioral Biomet- rics

4.1 Behavioral Data Collection and Processing

The first stage of the framework focuses on continuous acquisition of user behavioral data through unobtrusive monitoring mechanisms. Unlike traditional authentication systems that rely on explicit credentials, this framework captures implicit behavioral signals generated during user interaction. These include keystroke dynamics such as typing speed and latency, mouse movement patterns including trajectory and velocity, touchscreen gestures, and gait or motion data obtained from embedded sensors.

The collected data is inherently heterogeneous and temporal in nature, requiring preprocessing and transformation before it can be utilized effectively. Noise filtering, normalization, and time synchronization are applied to ensure data consistency.

Following preprocessing, feature extraction techniques are employed to derive meaningful attributes such as inter keystroke intervals, gesture pressure patterns, cursor acceleration, and motion signatures.

To enhance robustness and accuracy, the framework employs multimodal fusion, combining features from multiple behavioral sources into a unified representation. This fusion reduces dependency on any single modality and improves resilience against spoofing attempts and partial data loss. The resulting behavioral profile serves as the input for the intelligent decision making layer.

4.2 Agent Based Decision Making

At the core of the framework lies the Agentic AI component, which is responsible for interpreting behavioral data and making authentication decisions in real time. This component consists of autonomous agents that operate with a goal oriented objective of maintaining system security while minimizing disruption to legitimate users.

The decision making process begins with perception, where the agent analyzes incoming behavioral features along with contextual information such as device identity, location, and time of access. This combined analysis enables the system to construct a comprehensive representation of the current interaction state.

The final decision is executed by the authentication engine, which determines the appropriate response. Low risk scenarios result in seamless access, while moderate risk may trigger step up authentication mechanisms. High risk situations lead to session termination or restriction. This adaptive response strategy ensures a balance between security and usability.

4.3 Feedback Loop and Reinforcement Learning

A defining feature of the proposed framework is its ability to continuously learn and adapt through a feedback driven mechanism. The feedback loop captures the outcomes of authentication decisions, including successful verifications, false acceptances, and false rejections. This information is used to update the system and improve future performance.

Over time, the agent learns to maximize cumulative reward by refining its strategy, adjusting risk thresholds, and improving its ability to distinguish between legitimate and anomalous behavior. This continuous learning process addresses challenges such as behavioral drift and evolving attack patterns, ensuring that the system remains effective in dynamic environments. The feedback loop also contributes to updating the knowledge base, enabling long term learning and personalization. By leveraging historical data and real time feedback, the framework evolves into a self adaptive system capable of maintaining high levels of accuracy and resilience.

Table 2 summarizes how each functional layer introduced in the architecture of the preceding section (Figure 1) maps onto the three-stage methodology described above, clarifying the relationship between the conceptual architecture and the operational framework without repeating the detailed description of each component.

Table 2. Mapping of Architectural Layers to Framework Stages

Framework Stage	Corresponding Architectural Layer(s)	Primary Function
Behavioral Data Collection and Processing	Behavioral Data Collection Module; Feature Extraction Layer	Acquire, clean, and represent raw behavioral signals
Agent Based Decision Making	Agentic AI Core (Perception, Decision Modules); Context Awareness Layer	Interpret behavior, compute risk, and select a response
Feedback Loop and Reinforcement Learning	Learning Module; Knowledge Base; Feedback Loop	Update policies and personalize the model over time

Evaluation Methodology and Validation Strategy

A central limitation identified during peer review is that the framework, as originally presented, was described entirely at the conceptual level, without a corresponding evaluation plan. This subsection addresses that gap by specifying how the proposed architecture would be empirically validated, and by reporting an illustrative simulation that demonstrates the framework's expected behavior under controlled conditions. The intent is not to substitute for a full implementation, which is identified as a direction for future work, but to ground the architectural claims in a concrete, reproducible evaluation design.

Benchmark datasets. Evaluation would draw on publicly available behavioral biometric datasets so that results are reproducible and comparable to prior work. Suitable sources include keystroke-dynamics corpora such as the CMU keystroke dataset and the Buffalo free-text keystroke dataset, touchscreen and mobile-sensor datasets such as HMOG and Touchalytics, and gait datasets collected from wearable accelerometer and gyroscope sensors.

Evaluation metrics. Following standard practice in the biometric authentication literature, performance would be reported using Equal Error Rate (EER), False Acceptance Rate (FAR), False Rejection Rate (FRR), the Area Under the ROC Curve (AUC), and average time-to-detect for behavioral drift or anomaly events.

Baseline comparisons. To assess the contribution of the agentic decision layer relative to existing approaches, the framework would be benchmarked against three categories of baseline: static threshold-based authentication, single-modality deep learning models such as LSTM- or transformer-based keystroke classifiers, and non-agentic multimodal fusion approaches that lack autonomous, context-aware decision making.

Illustrative simulation. As a preliminary, non-empirical illustration of expected system behavior, a simplified simulation was conducted using synthetic keystroke-timing sequences generated to model legitimate users, gradual behavioral drift, and impersonation attempts. A simulated agent applying threshold adaptation through a basic reinforcement-learning update rule was compared against a static-threshold baseline operating on the same synthetic sequences. Under this simplified setting, the adaptive agent maintained a lower false-rejection rate as the simulated behavioral profile drifted over successive sessions, while the static-threshold baseline showed a steadily increasing false-rejection rate, consistent with the concept-drift limitation discussed earlier in the chapter. A full empirical evaluation on the benchmark datasets identified above, including statistical significance testing across multiple runs and user populations, is identified as essential future work and is discussed further in the Future Research Directions section.

Implementation and deployment considerations. Beyond accuracy metrics, a complete evaluation would also need to characterize implementation complexity and operational cost, including model training time, per-decision inference latency, memory footprint, and energy consumption when deployed on resource-constrained mobile or edge devices. These factors directly affect the practicality of agent-based continuous authentication outside laboratory conditions and are treated in more detail in the Challenges and Limitations section.

Experimental protocol and statistical validation. To ensure that any reported performance differences between the proposed agentic architecture and the baseline systems are reliable rather than artifacts of a particular data split, the evaluation plan specifies a k-fold cross-validation protocol stratified by user identity, so that behavioral data from a given individual does not appear in both the training and test partitions within a fold. Each baseline and the proposed architecture would be trained and evaluated under identical data splits, and performance differences in EER and AUC would be assessed using a paired statistical test, such as a paired t-test or Wilcoxon signed-rank test across folds, with effect sizes reported alongside p-values rather than relying on point estimates alone. For the concept-drift and adversarial-robustness claims specifically, evaluation would additionally use a temporally held-out test set, in which test sessions are drawn from a later time window than training sessions, since random cross-validation alone does not adequately capture a model's ability to handle behavior that has genuinely drifted over time.

Taken together, the evaluation methodology, baseline comparisons, and statistical protocol described in this subsection are intended to convert the architectural claims made elsewhere in the chapter into falsifiable, testable hypotheses. Specifically, the framework predicts that the agentic, multi-agent decision layer will outperform the single-model reinforcement-learning baseline of Bansal and Ouda (2024) on temporally held-out data, that adversarial training integrated into the Learning Module will reduce attack success rate relative to an undefended baseline, and that the privacy-preserving variants of the architecture will incur a measurable but bounded accuracy cost relative to the centralized configuration. Each of these predictions is stated here explicitly so that the proposed full implementation, identified as the principal direction for future empirical work, has a concrete basis for confirming or disconfirming the architectural claims made in this chapter.

5. CHALLENGES AND LIMITATIONS

Table 1. Challenges and Limitations of Agentic AI Driven Continuous Authentication System

Challenge Area	Description	Impact / Limitation
Privacy and Data Sensitivity	Continuous collection of behavioral biometric data such as keystroke dynamics, touch gestures, mouse movements, and motion patterns may expose sensitive behavioral traits. Even anonymized data can potentially be re-identified.	Raises serious privacy concerns, ethical issues, and compliance challenges with data protection regulations.
Scalability and Real-Time Processing	The system requires real-time processing of multimodal behavioral data with Agentic AI decision-making. Computational cost increases with the number of concurrent users.	High latency and resource overhead in large-scale deployments.
Behavioral Variability and Concept Drift	User behavior changes over time due to environment, fatigue, or device switching, leading to non-stationary distributions.	Reduced model accuracy and need for continuous adaptation.
Adversarial Attacks	Attackers may mimic, replay, or synthetically generate behavioral patterns to bypass authentication systems.	Increased risk of spoofing and adversarial manipulation.
Model Interpretability	Deep reinforcement learning models operate as black-box systems with limited transparency.	Reduced trust and difficulty in security auditing.
Energy and Resource Constraints	Continuous authentication requires persistent computation and sensor monitoring.	High battery consumption and edge-device limitations.
Lack of Empirical Validation	The architecture has been evaluated only through a small illustrative simulation rather than a full benchmark study (see the Evaluation Methodology and Validation Strategy subsection).	Claims of scalability, accuracy, and robustness remain partially conceptual pending full implementation.

5.1 Ethical and Regulatory Considerations

The continuous and largely passive nature of behavioral biometric monitoring raises ethical questions that go beyond the technical privacy mechanisms discussed earlier in the chapter. Because the system is designed to observe user behavior throughout a session rather than at a single login event, it is important that data subjects are informed of what is collected and why, even when collection is non-intrusive by design. Meaningful informed consent requires that users understand which behavioral signals are captured, how long they are retained, who can access them, and what recourse exists if they are misclassified. This is particularly relevant under regulatory frameworks such as the General Data Protection Regulation (GDPR) in the European Union and comparable biometric privacy statutes elsewhere, which generally classify behavioral biometric templates as sensitive personal data subject to heightened protection requirements, data minimization principles, and a right to erasure.

Protection of the behavioral templates themselves is a second concern. Unlike a password, a compromised behavioral profile cannot simply be reset, since it is derived from a person's physical and cognitive characteristics

5.2 Demographic and Behavioral Bias

Behavioral biometric systems are known to exhibit accuracy disparities across demographic and usage subgroups, and this concern applies directly to the proposed architecture. Keystroke and touch-gesture timing patterns vary systematically with age, with older users and very young users often showing higher intra-user variability and slower interaction speeds, which can elevate false-rejection rates if the training population skews toward a narrower age range. Device heterogeneity is a related and compounding factor: a touchscreen's size, sensitivity, and operating system can each shift the distribution of gesture features independently of the user's underlying behavior, which means apparent demographic disparities in accuracy can sometimes be confounded with device-usage patterns that correlate with demographic groups rather than reflecting a genuine behavioral difference.

These risks are not adequately addressed by accuracy improvements alone, since a system can achieve a low aggregate error rate while still performing substantially worse for specific subgroups. Mitigating this requires the evaluation methodology described in the Proposed Framework and Methodology section to be extended with subgroup-disaggregated reporting, in which EER, FAR, and FRR are computed separately for relevant demographic and device-usage strata rather than only in aggregate, so that disparities can be identified rather than averaged away. Where systematic disparities are found, mitigation strategies such as subgroup-balanced training data, fairness-constrained model objectives, or adjustable per-user decision thresholds calibrated during enrollment should be considered. We treat subgroup-disaggregated fairness evaluation as a mandatory, not optional, component of any future empirical validation of this framework, given the potential for a passively and continuously operating authentication system to systematically disadvantage specific user groups if this is not addressed at the design stage.

5.3 Transparency of Simulated and Future Empirical Results

To avoid any ambiguity regarding the evidentiary status of results presented in this chapter, we clarify here explicitly that the only quantitative illustration provided, in the Evaluation Methodology and Validation Strategy subsection, is based on synthetic data generated to qualitatively demonstrate the adaptation behavior the architecture is designed to achieve, and does not constitute an experimental result obtained from human-subject data, a public benchmark dataset, or a working prototype. No claims of accuracy, error rate, or comparative performance against prior systems should be read as empirically established at this stage. Should the framework be implemented and evaluated in future work, full dataset provenance, preprocessing steps, train/test partitioning, and code or configuration details sufficient to support independent reproduction would be reported alongside any quantitative results, consistent with standard reproducibility expectations in the behavioral biometrics literature.

6. FUTURE RESEARCH DIRECTIONS

The proposed Agentic Artificial Intelligence-driven continuous authentication framework opens several promising directions for future research. While the current architecture demonstrates strong potential in adaptive behavioral biometric authentication, further improvements are required to enhance privacy, scalability, robustness, interpretability, and real-world deployment efficiency. As cybersecurity threats continue to evolve, future systems must become more intelligent, context-aware, and resilient to dynamic user behavior and adversarial conditions.

6.1 Privacy-Preserving Authentication Systems

Future research should focus on strengthening privacy protection mechanisms in behavioral biometric systems. Since continuous authentication involves constant monitoring of user interactions, it is essential to ensure that sensitive behavioral data is not exposed or misused. Advanced techniques such as federated learning, secure multi-party computation, and differential privacy can be explored to ensure that user data remains decentralized and protected. In addition, encryption-based approaches and anonymization strategies can further enhance data security while maintaining system performance. Developing privacy-aware architectures will be critical to ensure compliance with data protection regulations and to build user trust in continuous authentication systems.

6.2 Lightweight Models for Edge Deployment

To enable real-world adoption, particularly in mobile and Internet of Things environments, future systems must reduce computational overhead and energy consumption. Research should focus on developing lightweight models that maintain high accuracy while operating under limited hardware resources. Techniques such as model compression, quantization, pruning, and efficient feature extraction can significantly reduce model complexity. Additionally, optimizing models for real-time inference on edge devices will improve responsiveness and usability. This is especially important for wearable devices and smartphones where computational resources are constrained..

6.3 Explainable Agentic AI Systems

A major limitation of current Agentic Artificial Intelligence frameworks is the lack of interpretability in decision-making processes. Future research should aim to design explainable authentication systems that provide human-understandable reasoning for risk scores and authentication outcomes. Explainable AI techniques such as attention visualization, feature importance analysis, and rule-based explanations can be integrated into the framework. This will improve transparency, user trust, and regulatory compliance, especially in sensitive domains such as healthcare, banking, and defense systems where accountability is critical..

6.4 Robustness Against Adversarial Attacks

As behavioral biometric systems become more widely deployed, they are increasingly exposed to adversarial attacks such as imitation, replay attacks, and synthetic behavior generation. Future work should focus on enhancing robustness through adversarial training, anomaly detection mechanisms, and multi-layer authentication strategies. Incorporating behavioral consistency checks and cross-modal validation can further strengthen system security. Developing systems that can detect and adapt to malicious patterns in real time will be essential for maintaining reliability in hostile environments.

6.5 Multi-Agent Authentication Systems

The current framework can be extended into a distributed multi-agent system where multiple intelligent agents operate collaboratively. Each agent can specialize in a specific behavioral modality such as keystroke dynamics, touch interactions, or motion patternsFuture research can explore coordination strategies, communication protocols, and decision fusion techniques among agents to improve overall system accuracy, fault tolerance, and scalability.

6.6 Handling Behavioral Drift

User behavior naturally evolves over time due to factors such as fatigue, environmental changes, device switching, or aging. This phenomenon, known as behavioral drift, presents a major challenge for continuous authentication systems. Future systems must incorporate adaptive learning mechanisms capable of handling such non-stationary behavior without requiring frequent retraining. Lifelong learning, incremental learning, and online adaptation techniques can be explored to ensure that the system continuously updates its understanding of user behavior while maintaining stability and accuracy.

6.7 Integration with Zero Trust Architectures

Future research should explore integration of continuous authentication frameworks with Zero Trust security models. In such architectures, trust is never assumed and continuous verification is required at every access point. This alignment makes behavioral biometric authentication a strong candidate for modern cybersecurity infrastructures.

6.8 Large-Scale Real-World Deployment

Further research is needed to evaluate system performance in large-scale, real-world environ- ments such as enterprise systems, cloud infrastructures, and financial platforms. Challenges such as scalability, latency, and interoperability must be addressed before practical deployment.

7. APPLICATIONS AND REAL-WORLD DEPLOYMENT IN HEALTHCARE

The proposed agentic AI-driven continuous authentication framework has significant potential in the healthcare domain, where data security, patient privacy, and real-time access control are critical. Modern healthcare systems increasingly rely on digital platforms such as electronic health records (EHRs), telemedicine applications, and connected medical devices, making them highly vulnerable to unauthorized access and identity-based attacks.

One of the primary applications of this framework is in securing access to EHR systems. Healthcare professionals frequently access sensitive patient data across different terminals and devices. Traditional login mechanisms are insufficient in such dynamic environments, as they cannot verify whether the authenticated user remains the same throughout the session. Continuous authentication using behavioral biometrics such as typing patterns, touch interactions, and device usage behavior ensures that only authorized personnel maintain access, thereby reducing the risk of data breaches and insider threats.

The framework is also highly applicable to wearable and IoT-based healthcare devices, such as smartwatches and remote patient monitoring systems. These devices continuously collect physiological and behavioral data, which can be leveraged for passive authentication without interrupting the user experience. This is particularly useful in critical care scenarios where seamless and uninterrupted monitoring is essential.

Furthermore, hospital information systems and medical research databases can benefit from adaptive authentication mechanisms to protect sensitive clinical and experimental data. The agentic AI component enables the system to evolve with user behavior over time, improving accuracy and reducing false positives in high-stakes environments.

Overall, the integration of continuous authentication in healthcare systems enhances security, ensures regulatory compliance, and builds trust among patients and medical professionals by safeguarding sensitive medical information in real time.

8. APPLICATIONS IN FINANCIAL SERVICES

Beyond healthcare, the financial services sector represents a particularly demanding deployment context for the proposed framework, given the combination of high transaction value, strict regulatory oversight, and a long-established threat landscape involving account takeover and credential theft. Online banking platforms and trading applications increasingly rely on session-based access that, once authenticated, is rarely re-verified until the user explicitly logs out, creating an extended window during which a hijacked session can be exploited for fraudulent transfers. Continuous behavioral verification through keystroke and mouse dynamics during a banking session can detect a change in operator partway through a session, for example if a device is left unlocked or a session token is hijacked, and trigger step-up authentication such as a one-time passcode before a high-value transaction is permitted to proceed.

The agentic decision layer is particularly well suited to risk-based transaction authorization, since the risk score computed from behavioral and contextual signals can be combined with transaction-specific risk factors such as transfer amount, recipient novelty, and time of day to determine whether a given action requires additional verification. This mirrors existing risk-based authentication practice in the financial sector but extends it with continuous, rather than point-in-time, behavioral evidence. As with the healthcare domain, deployment in financial services would need to satisfy sector-specific regulatory requirements, including strong customer authentication mandates in relevant jurisdictions, and would benefit directly from the privacy-preserving and explainability mechanisms discussed earlier in the chapter, since financial regulators typically require that automated decisions affecting account access be auditable and explainable to both the institution and the affected customer.

CONCLUSION

The chapter presented an Agentic Artificial Intelligence driven framework for continuous au- thentication using behavioral biometrics. The proposed system moves beyond traditional static authentication mechanisms by enabling persistent identity verification through continuous mon- itoring of user behavioral patterns such as keystroke dynamics, touch interactions, mouse move- ments, and device-based motion signals. Unlike conventional approaches that rely on one-time authentication, the proposed framework introduces a dynamic and adaptive security model that continuously evaluates user identity throughout the session. The integration of multimodal behavioral data significantly enhances robustness, while feature fusion improves resistance against spoofing and partial data loss. A key contribution of this work is the incorporation of Agentic AI, which enables autonomous decision-making, contextual awareness, and real-time adaptation. The system leverages reinforcement learning to continuously refine authentication policies based on environmental feedback, thereby addressing challenges such as behavioral

drift and evolving attack strategies. Furthermore, the proposed architecture introduces a lay- ered design consisting of data acquisition, feature extraction, agent-based reasoning, and adap- tive authentication control. This structure ensures scalability, modularity, and efficient han- dling of complex behavioral data streams. Despite its advantages, challenges such as privacy concerns, computational overhead, adversarial vulnerabilities, and interpretability limitations remain. However, these challenges also open new directions for future research, particularly in privacy-preserving learning, lightweight edge deployment, and explainable AI systems. In conclusion, the integration of Agentic Artificial Intelligence with behavioral biometrics rep- resents a significant advancement in cybersecurity authentication systems. It enables a shift from static, rule-based security models to intelligent, self-adaptive, and proactive authentica- tion frameworks suitable for modern digital environments such as enterprise systems, mobile platforms, and IoT ecosystems.

AUTHOR NOTE ON AI-ASSISTED DRAFTING

In accordance with IGI Global Scientific Publishing's policy requiring disclosure of AI assistance in manuscript preparation, the authors disclose that a generative AI writing assistant (Claude, Anthropic) was used during the revision stage to help draft, reorganize, and edit portions of this chapter. The underlying research direction, technical architecture, conceptual framework, and scholarly judgment in this chapter are those of the authors. All AI-assisted text was reviewed, fact-checked, and edited by the authors prior to submission, and the authors take full responsibility for the accuracy and integrity of the final content. No AI tool was used to generate, fabricate, or alter any citation, reference, or reported result; all references correspond to sources independently identified by the authors. This disclosure does not extend to the peer review process itself, which the authors understand to have been conducted entirely by human reviewers in accordance with the publisher's policy.

REFERENCES

Bansal, P., & Ouda, A. (2024). Continuous authentication in the digital age: An analysis of reinforcement learning and behavioral biometrics. *Computers, 13*(4), 103. DOI: 10.3390/computers13040103

Chen, Y., Liu, G., Yu, L., Kang, H., Meng, L., & Wang, T. (2024). TBAuth: A continuous authentication framework based on tap behavior for smartphones [SSRN preprint]. DOI: 10.2139/ssrn.4854193

Cola, G., Vecchio, A., & Avvenuti, M. (2021). Continuous authentication through gait analysis on a wrist-worn device. *Pervasive and Mobile Computing, 78*, 101483. DOI: 10.1016/j.pmcj.2021.101483

Gattulli, V., Impedovo, D., Pirlo, G., & Volpe, F. (2023). Touch events and human activities for continuous authentication via smartphone. *Scientific Reports, 13*(1), 10515. DOI: 10.1038/s41598-023-36780-3 PMID: 37386093

Hu, M., Zhang, K., You, R., & Tu, B. (2023). AuthConFormer: Sensor-based continuous authentication of smartphone users using a convolutional transformer. *Computers & Security, 127*, 103122. DOI: 10.1016/j.cose.2023.103122

Jeong, J. J., Zolotavkin, Y., & Doss, R. (2022). Examining the current status and emerging trends in continuous authentication technologies through citation network analysis. *ACM Computing Surveys, 56*(4), 111. Advance online publication. DOI: 10.1145/3533705

Mekruksavanich, S., & Jitpattanakul, A. (2021). Deep learning approaches for continuous authentication based on activity patterns using mobile sensing. *Sensors (Basel), 21*(22), 7519. DOI: 10.3390/s21227519 PMID: 34833591

Papavasileiou, I., Qiao, Z., Zhang, C., Zhang, W., Bi, J., & Han, S. (2021). Gait-Code: Gait-based continuous authentication using multimodal learning and wearable sensors. *Smart Health (Amsterdam, Netherlands), 19*, 100162. DOI: 10.1016/j.smhl.2020.100162

Siddiqui, N., Dave, R., & Seliya, N. (2021). Continuous authentication using mouse movements, machine learning, and Minecraft [arXiv preprint arXiv:2110.11080]. https://doi.org//arXiv.2110.11080DOI: 10.48550

Stragapede, G., Delgado-Santos, P., Tolosana, R., Vera-Rodriguez, R., Guest, R., & Morales, A. (2024). TypeFormer: Transformers for mobile keystroke biometrics. *Neural Computing & Applications, 36*(29), 18531–18545. DOI: 10.1007/s00521-024-10140-2

Stylios, I., Chatzis, S., Thanou, O., & Kokolakis, S. (2023). Continuous authentication with feature-level fusion of touch gestures and keystroke dynamics to solve security and usability issues. *Computers & Security*, *132*, 103363. DOI: 10.1016/j.cose.2023.103363

Stylios, I., Skalkos, A., Kokolakis, S., & Karyda, M. (2022). BioPrivacy: A behavioral biometrics continuous authentication system based on keystroke dynamics and touch gestures. *Information and Computer Security*, *30*(5), 687–704. DOI: 10.1108/ICS-12-2021-0212

Wang, X., Shi, Y., Zheng, K., Zhang, Y., Hong, W., & Cao, S. (2022). User authentication method based on keystroke dynamics and mouse dynamics with scene-irrelated features in hybrid scenes. *Sensors (Basel)*, *22*(17), 6627. DOI: 10.3390/s22176627 PMID: 36081085

Chapter 10
Adaptive Intelligence for UAV Network Security With Architectures, Mechanisms, and Open Challenges

Sudesh Kumar
http://orcid.org/0000-0002-9405-1890
Indira Gandhi National Tribal University, India

Khushbu Jaiswal
http://orcid.org/0009-0005-5074-6948
Indira Gandhi National Tribal University, India

Neeraj Kumar Rathore
National Institute of Technical Teachers Training and Research, India

ABSTRACT

The advanced development of Unmanned Aerial Vehicle (UAV) networks has made them applicable to various tasks, including surveillance, disaster management, and civilian and military operations. A swarm of UAVs that combine to achieve specific tasks is known as a Flying Ad-hoc Network (FANET). These networks are increasingly being deployed in mission-critical scenarios where reliability, availability, and security are of paramount importance. However, their unique features make them highly vulnerable to cyber threats that aim to disrupt operations or cause system failures. Current assessments rarely examine system-level intelligence; they lack a unified perspective on how UAV security systems can be intelligent, self-improving

DOI: 10.4018/979-8-2600-0413-5.ch010

entities. Thus, this chapter analyses adaptive intelligence-driven security frameworks for UAV networks, from static, detection-centric models to self-adaptive and autonomous systems. Additionally, evaluated the models using various performance metrics and discussed the major challenges and future research directions for building robust UAV security systems.

INTRODUCTION

The Unmanned Aerial Vehicles (UAVs) network is a dynamic network architecture in which multiple UAVs, having sensing and computation capabilities, establish communication through routing and form Flying Ad-hoc Networks (FANETs) (Chriki et al., 2019; Kumar et al., 2025a). The network does not require any specific infrastructure to build upon, which enables the network to be applicable in various mission-critical areas for surveillance, rescue operations, precision agriculture, search and destroy operations, and remote sensing (Srivastava & Prakash, 2020; Shakhatreh et al., 2019; Jaiswal et al., 2024). These networks share diverse characteristics that make FANETs unique from other ad hoc networks such as Mobile Ad-hoc Networks (MANETs) and Vehicular Ad-hoc Networks (VANETs). Their unique characteristics include dynamic topology, decentralized networks, high speed, 3D mobility, energy constraints, and scalability that also makes FANETs vulnerable to security attacks (Montufar et al., 2025; Sharma et al., 2019). These attacks, which include DDoS, blackhole, jamming, wormhole, spoofing, routing manipulation, and insider attacks, are designed to disrupt communication between UAVs and aim to destroy the network operations as shown in Figure 1 (Cao et al., 2020; Hassija et al., 2021; Goumiri et al., 2022). All these security threats can broadly affect different layers of the FANET architecture, and the effects of these attacks show performance degradations. Since routing is the backbone of FANET operations, it is also a primary target for adversarial attacks. These attacks attempt to disrupt the routing by flooding the network with excessive fake packets and route requests, manipulate routing paths, or impersonate legitimate UAVs to mislead the network (Shapovalov et al., 2024). Such attacks also severely impact the Quality of Service (QoS) of the network, including increased delay, low Packet Delivery Ratio (PDR), higher packet loss, reduced throughput, and decreased network reliability (Nguyen et al., 2021, Kumar et al., 2026). These QoS degradations can directly affect the operational efficiency and decision-making accuracy of the UAV networks.

Figure 1. UAV network security attack Architecture

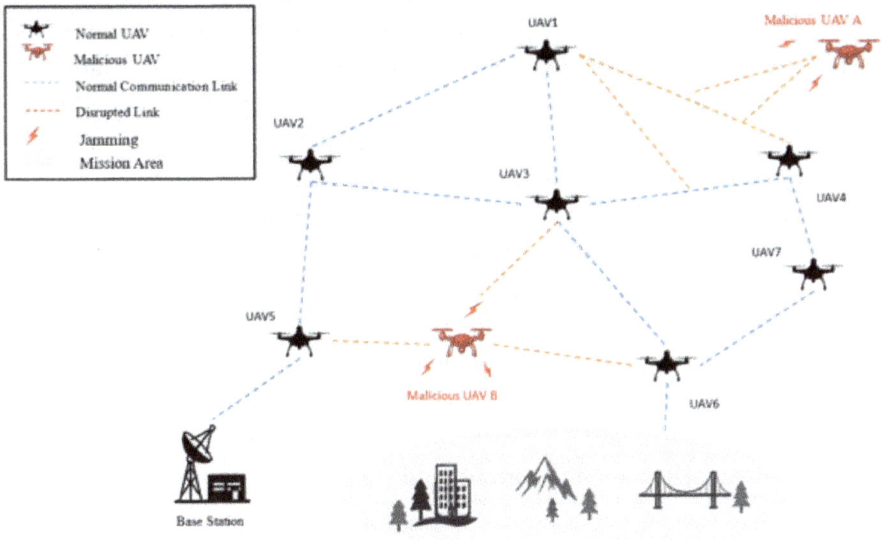

FANETs achieve huge access to other regions; the UAV sector is shifting from a niche military technology to a multi-billion-dollar international ecosystem, spearheaded by commercialized uses, AI-based integration, and defence modernization (Gupta et al., 2023; Marks & Fuger, 2025). The AI-based integration in FANETs provides a remarkable contribution and makes the network more analytical, effective, and trustworthy. These techniques allow UAVs to continuously analyse network conditions, identify complex attack patterns, and optimize routing decisions that make routing more adaptable in rapidly changing environments without any extensive human intervention. Furthermore, the advanced techniques like Trustworthy AI and Explainable AI (XAI) improve model transparency, reliability, and accountability of automated security decisions and establish reliability in AI-enabled UAV systems (Gazit et al., 2025; Jaiswal et al., 2026).

Research Gap: In order to alleviate such security issues, a number of surveys have researched the security of UAV networks incorporating Machine Learning (ML), Deep Learning (DL), and various advanced approaches (Ceviz et al., 2024; Alzubaidi, 2025; Ogab et al., 2025; Oli, 2025). We have thoroughly analysed these surveys based on various criteria and compared them with our research, as summarized in Table 1. Although these studies provide valuable insights into detection methodologies and performance evaluation, they are mostly focused on intrusion detection strategies and attack taxonomy, specific ML and DL approaches with limited emphasis on the incorporation of adaptive learning, distributed intelligence, and autonomous response mechanisms. Moreover, the current surveys lack a cohesive framework that integrates monitoring, detection, learning, and response into a self-enhancing structure. These drawbacks highlight a significant research gap and necessitate the paradigm shift from static defence mechanisms toward adaptive and fully autonomous security mechanisms. To address this gap, this chapter presents a comprehensive analysis of UAV security strategies by classifying them into five evolutionary phases, such as static, detection-based, reactive, adaptive, and fully autonomous security systems. Furthermore, the classification covers the advanced security model, including the use of online and continuous learning methods for adapting to dynamic and streaming data; Federated Learning (FL) for privacy-preserving and distributed methods that allow training of models in a distributed manner without sharing raw data (Wang et al., 2023); and Reinforcement Learning (RL) for autonomous decision-making and optimal response strategies in dynamic environments (Hickling et al., 2023). This systematic review assists in determining research trends, significant contributions, and existing limitations in FANETs and UAV networks.

Table 1. Comparative analysis of the existing surveys.

Survey	Main focus	Classification Basis	Comparative Analysis	Gap identified
(Ceviz et al., 2024)	Reviews UAV/FANET security threats and defence mechanisms.	Attack categories	Limited	Limited discussion of AI-driven adaptive security.
(Alzubaidi, 2025)	Surveys ML/DL-based intrusion detection techniques for UAV networks.	ML/DL techniques	Limited	Primarily focuses on ML/DL-based intrusion detection without considering autonomous response, or routing security.
(Ogab et al., 2025)	Reviews AI-enabled intrusion detection techniques for the Internet of Drones (IoD).	AI-enabled IDS techniques.	Moderate	Concentrates on AI-enabled IDS for IoD but provides limited discussion of routing security, autonomous defence, and security evolution.
(Oli & Mahalal, 2025)	Provides a broad overview of UAV security, privacy, and communication issues.	Security domains and applications.	Moderate	Provides a broad overview of UAV security but lacks a structured taxonomy, detailed comparative analysis.
This Chapter	Reviews FANET security with emphasis on routing protection and the evolution toward autonomous intelligent security systems.	Static, Detection, Reactive, Adaptive, Fully Autonomous	Comprehensive	provide a novel taxonomy based on security intelligence, comprehensive comparative analysis, routing-centric security review, challenge-to-solution mapping, and discussion of emerging intelligent security paradigms.

Further, the comparative analysis of existing approaches provides a broad view of security models through the analysis of various performance metrics such as adaptability, scalability, communication efficiency, computational overhead, PDR, latency, connection stability, energy efficiency, and real-time responsiveness. By incorporating these factors, the analysis provides a clear understanding of the current methods, including their strengths and weaknesses. This will also highlight the trade-offs involved in designing adaptive security systems for resource-constrained UAV environments. In addition, we have also addressed some key challenges that hinder the operations of fully autonomous UAV security systems. Some of these challenges include insufficient data for model training, lack of adaptability, availability of limited computational and energy resources on UAVs, computational overhead, and dynamic behaviour of the network. To develop an efficient and robust security model, it is critical to incorporate these challenges very effectively. Further, the paper presents the future research directions aimed at achieving fully autonomous, resilient, and deployable UAV security systems. The contributions of this chapter are as follows:

- This chapter presents an in-depth and systematic review of security challenges in UAV Networks, focusing on vulnerabilities arising from high mobility, dynamic topology, and decentralized architecture.
- The classification of existing solutions into categories such as static, detection, reactive, adaptive, and fully autonomous approaches, providing a structured understanding of their operational behaviour in FANET environments.
- We provide comprehensive comparative analysis of all existing approaches in terms of used methodology, routing approach, applied dataset, defence strategy, key improvements, and limitations. Further, the comparative view to utilized approach is also analysed with its applicability, improvements, and weaknesses.
- Finally, the unresolved challenges including resource constraints, scalability, dynamic topology, and lack of data availability are discussed with potential research directions.

The rest of this chapter is structured as follows: Section 2 gives a comprehensive discussion of various security threats faced by UAV networks due to their unique characteristics' vulnerabilities, their impact on this network, and limitations of traditional approaches. Section 3 offers an in-depth analysis and classification of the current UAV security methods in five phases, and further, this section broadly discusses the comparative analysis of the existing techniques in terms of various performance metrics, including strategic approaches to key limitations. Section 4 covers challenges of open research and future directions. Lastly, Section 5 is the conclusion of the chapter.

SECURITY THREAT, IMPACT, AND LIMITATIONS IN FANETS

FANETs are highly vulnerable to security threats, as these threats are malicious nodes that perform illegitimate activity to disrupt the communication between UAVs and lead to system failure (Irfan et al., 2022). The traditional routing approaches, such as proactive and reactive and security methods, are inefficient to handle evolving attacks, as the system is unable to address the diverse attack patterns (Camacho, 2024; Alshamrani & Alghamdi, 2026). To understand these challenges, this section presents a detailed, comprehensive taxonomy of attacks, their impact, and limitations of existing defence mechanisms.

SECURITY THREATS

FANETs attacks can be categorized into multiple types, each targeting different layers and functionalities of the network. These attacks include:

Distributed Denial of Service (DDoS) Attacks

Distributed Denial of Service (DDoS) attacks are the most severe threats in FANETs that primarily aim to target network availability. This type of attack is an active attack where multiple compromised nodes intentionally generate excessive packet traffic to interrupt the communication link between UAVs (Ouiazzane et al., 2023; Jaiswal et al., 2025). As FANETs contain limited bandwidth, processing power, and battery capacity of UAVs, this makes even moderate traffic flooding lead to increased latency, packet drops, and eventual denial of service for legitimate nodes. DDoS attacks can completely disrupt coordination between UAVs and control stations, leading to catastrophic operational failures specifically in mission-critical FANET applications such as disaster response or military operations.

Blackhole Attacks

A blackhole attack is another kind of active attack in which a malicious node presents itself as having the most efficient routing path to the destination so that nodes get confused and choose the fake path (Nagalakshmi et al., 2021). Once the path is chosen, the malicious node intercepts incoming packets and deliberately drops them instead of forwarding. This behaviour leads to significant data loss and severely degrades network reliability. In FANETs, where topology frequently changes and routing decisions must be made quickly, detection of such malicious behaviour becomes particularly challenging (Xiong et al., 2021). As a result, blackhole attacks can persist undetected for extended periods, causing continuous disruption in data transmission.

Wormhole Attacks

During a wormhole attack, two or more malicious nodes establish a direct communication link between remote UAV networks. The nodes give an illusion of the shortest and most efficient path to destination to other UAV nodes so that the legitimate nodes are fooled into following paths that go through the malicious nodes. This may result in unauthorized interception of the packets, manipulation of the data and additional misuse of the network (Schweitzer et al., 2023). Wormhole attacks are especially harmful in FANETs, where nodes move frequently and cause false information on the perceived network topology, causing routing protocols to be compromised.

Sybil Attacks

Sybil attack is where one malicious node uses more than one identity in the network. In this way, the attacker is able to affect the routing decisions, trust evaluation mechanism, and network protocols based on node identity. Sybil attacks that can disrupt consensus mechanisms, form false routing paths, and reduce the effectiveness of trust-based systems can be used in FANETs (Chulerttiyawong & Jamalipour, 2023). Because UAV networks frequently rely on collaboration between nodes, having several fake identities may greatly reduce the reliability and security of a network.

Spoofing Attacks

Spoofing attacks are attacks in which an attacker compromises identity information to create the impression of a legitimate UAV node. This may include altering packet payloads, source IP addresses, or authentication keys. The attacker can compromise the network by disguising itself as a trusted node, introduce unwarranted traffic, or alter communication channels. In FANETs, where the authentication mechanisms can be constrained because of the resource constraints, a spoofing attack can easily violate the integrity of the network and cause unauthorized control or data loss (Shafique et al., 2021).

Jamming Attacks

Jamming attacks target the physical layer by emitting interference signals that disrupt wireless communication channels. Since FANETs rely heavily on wireless links for communication, jamming can significantly degrade signal quality and prevent successful data transmission. The effects of jamming include increased packet loss, reduced throughput, and communication delays (Pirayesh & Zeng, 2022). In highly dynamic environments, detecting the source of jamming and mitigating its impact is particularly challenging, making it a persistent threat to FANET operations.

Insider Attacks

Insider attacks are carried out by compromised legitimate UAV nodes or by maliciously acting legitimate nodes. Such nodes may do many destructive things, including selective dropping of packets, altering routing information, or other false data. Insider nodes are network members, and since they have valid credentials, the network can hardly be aware of their malicious activities through the traditional security systems (Islam et al., 2022). The insider attack is a major threat in FANETs because it has the potential to undermine the communication system, weaken the trust systems, and undermine the mission-based activities.

IMPACT OF ATTACKS ON FANETS

The impact of security attacks on FANETs has worldwide implications because the network depends on real-time communication and cooperative routing as well as resource constrained UAV nodes. The effects are not only limited to degradation of communication but also to failure of the mission and instability of the system.

Network Disruption

Network disruption is one of the most immediate impacts of security attacks in FANETs. DDoS and jamming are some of the attacks that disrupt the normal process of communication by consuming the available network resources or undermining the quality of signals. Since the topology of FANETs is highly dynamic, any slight disturbances may cause frequent links breakages and network partitioning (Zhai et al., 2023). This instability impacts route discovery and route maintenance algorithms so that UAV nodes are intermittently connected. This in turn results in the network not having uniform communication that is essential in coordinated operations.

Packet Loss and Data Integrity Degradation

One of the critical problems of attacks like blackhole, grayhole, and insider attacks is the loss of packets due to the intentional dropping or alteration of packets by malicious nodes. Along with deliberate dropping, other attacks such as jamming and congestion due to DDoS are also the contributors to unintentional packet loss (Hadi et al., 2025). This not only lowers the total packet delivery ratio but also data integrity in the case of packet modification or corruption. Loss or corruption of data may result in inaccurate decision-making in the, thus decreasing the utility of the whole system.

Routing Failure and Increased Latency

Information on the topology of the network is essential to routing protocols in FANETs, and the information must be accurate and timely. Wormhole, Sybil, and spoofing attacks manipulate routing data and cause selecting inefficient or malicious paths. Consequently, data packets can be sent via compromised nodes or can use unnecessary long routes, which can add to the end-to-end delay (Basan et al., 2022). The frequent route failures also cause repeated route discovery, which causes further overhead and latency. Such a decrease in routing performance greatly affects time-sensitive applications where the latency must be low.

Operational and Mission Failure

FANETs are frequently used in mission-critical applications like military reconnaissance, border patrol, disaster relief, and search and rescue operations. In this case, the coordination and decision-making require secure and reliable communication. Security attacks that interfere with communication, slow the transmission of data or interfere with data integrity can result in a partial or total failure of the missions (Shakhatreh et al., 2019c). To illustrate, failure to pass information correctly or in a timely manner during a rescue mission may cause lives to be lost, whereas loss of communications during military missions may cause a strategic disadvantage.

Resource Depletion and Energy Exhaustion

FANETs have UAV nodes with a high level of energy and computation limitations. An attack like the DDoS and repeated route manipulation compels nodes to handle more data than necessary or carry out more computations that result in the quick exhaustion of energy. UAVs cannot operate after their batteries have been depleted making them nonfunctional and this does not only limit the network coverage but can also lead to network partitioning (Lee et al., 2022). The processing capabilities are also impacted due to resource exhaustion that restricts the node to carry out key functions including routing, sensing, and communication. This considerably decreases the total life and stability of the network.

LIMITATIONS OF EXISTING DEFENCE MECHANISMS

Despite various proposed solutions, existing defence mechanisms exhibit several limitations. Many approaches rely on static intrusion detection systems that use predefined rules or signatures, making them ineffective against new and evolving attack patterns. Additionally, most systems lack adaptability, as they do not update their detection models based on changing network conditions. Another major limitation is the absence of effective response mechanisms, where systems can detect attacks but fail to mitigate them in real time. Furthermore, advanced security techniques often introduce high computational overhead, which is unsuitable for resource-constrained UAV environments. These limitations highlight the need for more intelligent, adaptive, and integrated security frameworks.

STATE-OF-THE-ART TECHNIQUES IN UAV NETWORK SECURITY

The security of FANETs has been extensively studied using a wide range of approaches, including cryptographic protocols, trust-based mechanisms, ML techniques, and intelligent optimization methods. However, most existing works focus on specific aspects of security such as detection, routing, or authentication, without providing a unified and adaptive solution (Wang et al., 2024; Morshedi & Matinkhah, 2025). To provide a structured understanding, existing literature can be classified based on the level of intelligence and adaptability of the security mechanisms. This classification reflects the evolution of FANETs security solutions from static, rule-based approaches to fully autonomous intelligent systems as shown in Figure 2. Each category is discussed below with representative approaches and their limitations. We have analyzed all existing approaches in terms of their utilized techniques, security mechanisms, defense strategies, routing approaches, key improvements, and limitations as shown in Table 2. This analysis demonstrates the capabilities of the models. Furthermore, in Table 3 we have also evaluated the utilized approaches based on their applicability, strengths, and weaknesses.

Figure 2. Taxonomy of various security approaches in FANETs

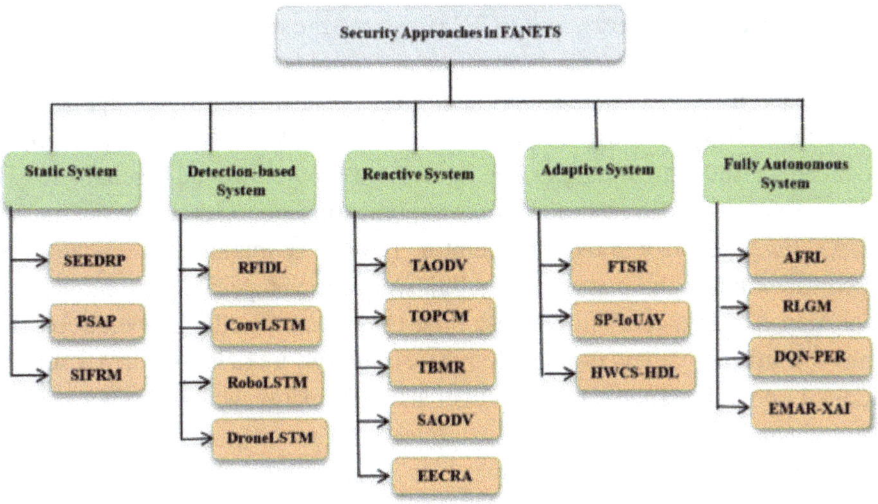

STATIC SECURITY SYSTEMS

Static security mechanisms are the first generation of security mechanisms for FANETs and UAV networks. These approaches mainly involve cryptographic schemes, authentication techniques, and security policies to secure confidentiality and integrity of information. A number of research works have proposed lightweight authentication protocols employing hash functions, symmetric encryption, and mathematical structures like quadratic residues to minimise computational complexity. These methods are often applied in UAVs with limited computing resources to reduce the time, space, and communication overhead. Some of this category techniques are analysed below:

Flooding attacks are one of the major security threats in UAV networks, as malicious nodes intentionally try to disrupt the communication path between UAV nodes. To tackle this issue, Bhardwaj and Kaur (2021) has proposed a secure and energy-efficient SEEDRP dynamic routing protocol for FANETs. This protocol enables the efficient routing in highly dynamic environments. The framework operates in two stages, the first stage called the routing stage, where an optimal forwarding node is selected based on some parameters, namely speed of the nodes, nodes' position, energy, and transmission rate. The second stage is the security stage, where nodes get secured communication through the AES (Advanced Encryption Standard) cryptography approach. In this approach, a unique key is generated dynamically for each encryption iteration that improves the data security. Their experiment achieved improved throughput, energy, and PDR. However, the model faces high computational overhead due to the AES encryption algorithm that hinders the suitability of this approach for energy-constrained and latency-sensitive FANET applications. In order to establish secure communication between UAVs, Nyangaresi (2023) has introduced an authentication and key agreement protocol-based mechanism. The framework is designed to ensure secure communication among three entities, namely the UAV, base station, and mobile operator. To achieve mutual authentication and data confidentiality, the protocol uses lightweight cryptographic techniques such as one-way hashing, random nonces, timestamps, and modular operations. The framework utilizes Dolev-Yao and Canetti-Krawczyk models for formal security validation under the random oracle model and information analysis. These models prove resistance against a wide range of attacks and achieve a 25% improvement in security from threats. Their model improves access control and authentication at a minimal computing cost by protecting against attacks primarily during transmission. Nevertheless, because of this authentication process, the protocol cannot detect compromised insider attacks after authentication has been completed.

Bhardwaj et al. (2024) have proposed a secure and intelligent routing fairness rate model SIRFRM for FANETs, which is built with the integration of cross-layer routing optimization and cryptographic security aims to establish secure communication. By analyzing the parameters including distance between UAVs, node speed, direction of nodes, and transmission rate, the model improves its routing paths. The model incorporates an enhanced algebraic homomorphic encryption technique in order to encrypt the data before transmission; this process ensures the confidentiality and makes the model resistant to attacks. They have evaluated their model on various metrics and found improvement in PDR, reduced delay, and enhanced energy constraints. However, the model generates cryptographic overhead and is not reliable to handle advanced attacks due to dependence on predefined optimization criteria rather than adaptive learning.

Static mechanisms are effective in providing preventative security, which is well suited to applications where communication participants are known in advance and attack patterns remain relatively stable. However, this type of model has insufficient capability for dynamic detection of malicious attacks. Additionally, they are vulnerable to insider attacks and adaptive adversaries, because they are solely based on preconceived notions and do not adapt to the changing nature of attacks. Therefore, static methods are not suitable for highly dynamic FANETs.

DETECTION-BASED SECURITY SYSTEMS

Detection-based security systems bring an element of intelligence into FANET security using ML and DL approaches to detect malicious nodes and activities. Such techniques are often used as IDS that monitor network traffic and label activities as legitimate or malicious. Several research works have employed ML techniques based on Decision Tree (DT), Random Forest (RF), and DL techniques based on Convolutional Neural Networks (CNN), and Long Short-Term Memory (LSTM) networks. Some existing detection-based approaches are discussed below:

In order to detect DoS attacks, Valikhanli (2024) has developed an AI-based security framework for FANETs. For implementation of their model, a standardized 5G-NIDD dataset was used that contains the real DoS and normal traffic analysis in a 5G wireless network. Their work carries two phases. In the first phase, the Random Forest Identifier technique is used for feature selection from the 5G-NIDD dataset. To handle the data imbalance, a class weight approach is applied to the dataset. In the second phase, they have applied the dataset on various ML models and found DT as the best-performing model with 99.51% accuracy that is effective in classifying data as normal or malicious. Although their model is lightweight which makes it suitable for resource-constrained UAV platforms, their experiments are limited to a particular dataset reducing the effectiveness of the model against previously unseen attacks. As DL models are effective in handling attacks even on large datasets, Alzahrani (2024) has proposed a novel intrusion detection framework for UAV networks. For implementation they have utilized several datasets, including KDD Cup 99, drone dataset, GPS spoofing dataset, NSL KDD, WSN DS, and CICIDS2017 dataset. All these datasets are used to train various DL models such as LSTM, CNN-LSTM, and Convolutional LSTM (ConvLSTM), where they found ConvLSTM outperforms in all datasets and is suitable in the detection of diverse intrusion attacks. The ConvLSTM achieved ~99% accuracy in detecting all these attacks compared to other DL models. As the ConvLSTM builds on convolutional layers that are combined with LSTM cells, it makes the model capable of extracting spatial and temporal features. However, the model will face high computational overhead due to complex modelling that makes deployment on energy-constrained UAV platforms challenging. Therefore, ConvLSTM is better suited to high-capability UAVs rather than lightweight aerial nodes.

As a UAV network generates temporal data because of its dynamic nature, Attaullah et al. (2026) have utilized an LSTM framework to implement a DL-based hybrid anomaly detection framework for a UAV network. They have integrated the Robust Optimization-Based Tabular Feature Engineering (ROBOTa) feature engineering technique with an LSTM-based DL model. This methodology enables the system to learn both spatial and temporal correlations of UAV network traffic.

They have used five datasets to evaluate their model on; these datasets include real UAV data, CICIDS2017, UNSW-NB15, and two augmented datasets. By the evaluation, the model achieved 99.12% accuracy on a real-world UAV dataset, which shows its efficiency in detection. The inclusion of feature engineering improves the detection performance while lowering the computational cost. Nevertheless, the framework remains dependent on labeled training data and cannot effectively recognize previously unseen attack behaviors without retraining. In another study, Oh and Kang (2026) have proposed an LSTM-based early jamming threat detection system for drone ad-hoc networks. as an LSTM-based framework best suits the analysis of sequential patterns of PDR, delay, and connectivity ratio, which takes them as input in the training process. They have evaluated their model with a traditional threshold-based detection approach and found significant improvement in performance in terms of latency. As the traditional approach takes 65 sec to detect the attack, the LSTM-based approach takes 45 sec. This improvement shows that the model is effective in learning temporal features and capturing abnormal state transitions. However, the model remains detection-oriented and does not include any adaptive mitigation mechanism after an attack is identified.

Overall, these approaches can learn complex features from network data and achieve high accuracy, particularly towards known attacks like DDoS and spoofing attacks. But detection-only systems have limitations as they only detect attacks but do not offer appropriate responses. Post-detection actions may rely on other systems or rules. Furthermore, many of these models are pre-trained and cannot learn from new and emerging attacks in real time. As a result, they may be susceptible to zero-day and evolving adversarial attacks.

REACTIVE SECURITY SYSTEMS

Reactive systems take detection-based systems a step further by including pre-established action mechanisms to counter threats. These systems usually integrate behavior monitoring and rule-based actions to detection and respond to attacks. Much of the existing research on FANET security belongs to this class, notably trust-based routing protocols including modified AODV protocols. In such systems, nodes are given trust values based on their behavior, such as successful packet forwarding, packet retransmissions or cooperation. Untrustworthy nodes are detected when their trust values drop below a threshold and are then removed from the network.

Sharma and Jameel (2019) have implemented a trust-based AODV (TAODV) routing protocol for malicious node detection and prevention in FANETs. For detection, they have assigned a 0.5 trust value to each node. The trust value is dynamically updated based on the behavior of nodes. When the node forwards the packet successfully, then the trust value will be increased by 0.001. When the node drops the packet, then the trust values will be decreased by 0.001. A node having a zero-trust value is considered a malicious node, and it will then be removed from the network to prevent the system. Overall, their routing decisions are made only through trusted nodes and provide improved performance in terms of PDR and reduced packet loss. However, it remains limited to basic attack scenarios and lacks the capability to handle complex threats. Buksh et al. (2022) have proposed a preventive trust-based approach TOPCM for FANETs security. They have used the AODV routing protocol and peer-to-peer trust evaluation approach, where each node monitors its neighbors during the route discovery process. The analysis is done by monitoring route request, route reply, and some other parameters like broadcast ID, destination address, next hop count position, and node behavior. Based on this analysis, their trust model adjusts its value and classifies nodes as either malicious or trusted using a threshold. For prevention, the detected malicious node gets excluded from the network; this step ensures that only trustworthy nodes participate in the communication. Their approach results in improved PDR, detection accuracy, and reduced delay. However, it remains a behavior-based trust model without advanced learning. In another study Kumar et al. (2023) have taken the trust-based multi-hop scenario TBMR approach to prevent black hole attacks in FANETs. Their trust value relies on behavior packet forwarding, link reliability, and historical interaction. After detection of a malicious node, the node gets removed from the network, which prevents routing from the attack. However frequent trust updates and route re-computation may lead to route instability.

Chandrasekar et al. (2024) proposed a secure AODV routing protocol SAODV to prevent FANET from Sybil and DDoS attacks. They have utilized a combination of trust mechanisms, neighbor monitoring, and centralized consistency checking for malicious node detection. The abnormality of nodes gets detected by analysis of node behavior, such as high bandwidth and unusual packet patterns. Prevention applied by removal of malicious nodes from the network. They achieved improved throughput, PDR, energy efficiency, and reduced packet loss. However, the approach is less scalable, and there are possible false positives in a large dynamic FANET environment. Ananthi (2025) has proposed a secure and energy-efficient clustering routing approach EECRA for FANETs by utilizing a trust-based method. Each UAV node is grouped into a cluster, and the selection of a cluster head relies on residual energy and its trust values. The trust value is computed by analyzing packet forwarding behavior. The high-trust and low-energy-cost route is selected to ensure intra- and inter-cluster communication. Their approach produced improved PDR, energy constraints, reduced routing overhead, and reduced delay. However, the approach primarily relies on nodes' behavior and lacks the advanced adaptive intelligence.

Overall, these approaches are helpful in identifying and preventing various attacks with the help of trust-based detection and prevention strategies, making these approaches practical for resource-constrained FANETs. However, these methods are less adaptable in rapidly changing network conditions as they solely rely on predefined rules, thresholds, and continuous trust computation.

ADAPTIVE SECURITY SYSTEMS

Adaptive security is an improvement on reactive systems, introducing adaptive mechanisms that enable the system to learn and adapt to the network environment and data. These systems use techniques like online learning, FL, and fuzzy logic for enhancing detection and response strategies. A number of papers use optimization algorithms, like Genetic Algorithms, to improve threat detection through the evolution of classification strategies based on fitness metrics. Likewise, fuzzy logic systems dynamically assess trust and reputation through uncertainty management of node traits, enabling adaptive decision-making. FL methods also allow decentralized training of models across UAV nodes to maintain data privacy and minimise communication costs.

Hosseinzadeh et al. (2023) have proposed a novel routing protocol named FTSR that prevents FANETs from blackhole, wormhole, flooding, and selective forwarding attacks. The model builds on local and path trust, where the local trust approach finds the reliable nodes and excludes the malicious node. The fuzzy logic-based path trust approach is used to identify the trusted path to establish the reliable link between source and destination. They have simulated their model using NS-2 and found an improved PDR, less packet loss, and reduced latency. However, their model takes more time in finding the reliable path and generates computational overhead that makes the approach less suitable for large-scale UAV networks. Ntizikira et al. (2023) have utilized FL, differential privacy, and secure multi-party computation methods to implement a secure intrusion detection model named SP-IoUAV. The FL ensures the privacy-preserving model training on collected data by UAVs. The generation of data goes through several steps from data collection, tag assignment, and encryption to data processing. To further protect sensitive information, differential privacy is used to add noise in data to secure multi-party computation that enables the encrypted collaborative analysis across UAVs. The aggregated data is then fed into a hybrid CNN-LSTM model, where the model extracts the spatial features and captures the temporal patterns, which helps in the classification of malicious nodes. While detecting threats, the model generates alerts, updates a blacklist, and restricts their participation. Further, multi-factor authentication secures the system access. The CICIDS2017 dataset is used for the model evaluation and got 99.98% accuracy.

Nevertheless, due to periodic model aggregation and dependency on synchronized federated training, this approach produces additional communication overhead and reduces the efficiency in highly dynamic FANET environments.

In order to detect and prevent DDoS attacks, Priyadharshini and Balamurugan (2024) have proposed a hybrid DL and optimal routing framework named HWCS-HDL. The approach uses a hybrid optimization algorithm that combines water strider optimization and cuckoo search for the selection of features. These features then fed into a hybrid DL model where a deep temporal convolutional network (DTCN) was used for capturing short-term traffic variations and an LSTM was used for learning temporal patterns. This process enables the accurate and real-time DDoS attack detection. For attack mitigation they have used an optimized optimal link state routing (OLSR) protocol where it dynamically adjusts routing paths to reliable paths. The experiment was done using various datasets, including NSL-KDD, KDD Cup 99, and CICIDS2017, and they achieved improved detection accuracy and reduced false positive rates. However, the approach follows predefined rerouting policies that make the model less adaptable in dynamic situations.

Overall, such systems are capable to adapt to changing attack scenarios and enhance their detection performance. They typically lack sophisticated decision-making ability as they still use a set of predetermined responses that cannot be optimized in real-time. As such, although adaptive systems enhance their response to new threats, they remain non-autonomous.

FULLY AUTONOMOUS INTELLIGENT SYSTEMS

Fully autonomous systems are the pinnacle of FANET security. These approaches combine learning, decision-making and response functions in a closed-loop system to allow for dynamic adaptation with little human intervention. These systems often use RL and Deep RL (DRL), in which the system learns to take actions based on its environment. RL systems assess network conditions and receive rewards or penalties based on the outcomes of actions like node isolation, rerouting, or rate limiting. This enables them to adapt their response strategies. Moreover, RL systems can be complemented with Federated Learning or Deep Learning to improve scalability, privacy and efficiency. Such systems are well-adapted to dynamic environments such as FANETs, where fast decision-making and adaptation are critical.

To handle the jamming attack in FANETs, Mowla et al. (2020) have proposed an anti-jamming AFRL model by the integration of FL and RL for FANETs. In this model, each UAV operates as an autonomous node that performs on-device jamming detection with the help of RL. The model works in two layers. In the first layer, each UAV collects local network features, including PDR, signal-to-noise ratio, and signal strength. These features are used to train a local neural network for jamming detection, and then these local models periodically aggregate the value using federated averaging for a global model. In the second layer, each UAV acts as an RL agent that uses the Q-learning approach for optimal movement strategies based on the detected jammers. Their adaptive epsilon-greedy policy makes the model dynamically adjust based on the accuracy of the FL model. Instead of adapting an isolation strategy, the model used a proactive and adaptive mitigation approach that allows UAVs to anticipate and avoid jamming regions by dynamically selecting alternative communication paths. Their experiment improved the detection accuracy, reduced the hop count, and improved the path selection efficiency to build reliable communication. However, the model produces potential convergence delays and computational overhead. Ghelani et al. (2024) proposed a reinforcement learning-based gradient-monitored (RLGM) approach to prevent jamming attacks. The integration of RL with gradient monitors enables the system to identify abnormal behavior in the network by analyzing different performance metrics such as signal strength, PDR, and interference levels. These metrics indicate the potential jamming activity. The RLGM continuously interacts with the network environment and updates its policy based on rewards and penalties. While the gradient monitoring is used to detect sudden deviations that are caused by attacks. Overall, the detection is adaptive and learning-based, and the preventive approach is done by adjusting communication strategies. Their model achieved improved throughput, latency, and accuracy, although it faces the challenges of complexity and time convergence.

Eavesdropping is another type of security attack, where instead of interfering with network operation, these attacks try to secretly intercept confidential data that is transmitted between UAVs. To tackle the problem of this kind of passive attack in UAV networks, Su et al. (2024) have proposed a deep RL-based secure communication framework. The problem is reformulated using a Markov decision process and applying an enhanced deep Q-network with prioritized experience replay, namely DQN-PER, that enables UAVs to act as intelligent agents where they learn optimal decisions such as trajectory planning, power allocation, and communication scheduling. The learning of these decisions is done through interaction with the environment without requiring any prior knowledge of the behavior of the attacks. With the help of DQN-PER, UAVs are enabled to dynamically adjust their actions and minimize information leakage. The model shows significant improvement in throughput and robustness in the establishment of secure communication. However, DQN-PER requires extensive training and considerable computational resources before achieving stable performance. Alkahtani et al. (2026) have utilized a multi-agent deep deterministic gradient policy model named MADDPG to implement a secure and adaptive routing network. Their decentralized multi-agent system makes each UAV learn policies based on local observations such as quality of communication path, signal strength, interference levels, and behavior of the neighbors. The learning is guided by a carefully designed reward function that balances the throughput, delay, energy efficiency, and security. In order to include trustworthiness in their model, the author has also integrated the XAI techniques, which make the decision of the model more transparent rather than a black box. It analyzes the state-action relationships and feature importance that interpreted routing decisions made by UAVs. The model shows adaptability by avoiding unreliable links and selecting alternative secure routing through analysis of environmental changes.

Despite their advantages, autonomous systems also face challenges, including high computational complexity, training instability, and implementation difficulties in resource-constrained UAV environments. Nevertheless, they represent the future direction of FANET security research.

Table 2. Comparison of the related works.

Refs.	Scheme	Security mechanism	Desire routing attacks	Defense Strategy	Routing strategy	dataset	Key improvements	Limitations
(Bhardwaj & Kaur, 2021)	SEEDRP	Cryptography	Flooding	Preventive	DSR	FANET simulated	- Improved throughput. - Enhanced PDR. - Energy efficient.	- Cryptographic computation overhead. - Increased bandwidth consumption. - No network level security. - Limited real-world validation.
(Nyangaresi, 2023)	PSAP	Authentication and key agreement cryptography	Insider attacks, packet replays, impersonation	Preventive	-	-	- Low cost. - Less overhead. - Less time consumption.	- Increased delay. - No adaptability - No attack mitigation. - Computational overhead due to AES.
(Bhardwaj et al., 2024)	SIFRM	Cross layer routing optimization + cryptography	Flooding	Preventive	SIRFRM	FANET simulated	- Less delay. - Enhanced PDR. - Energy efficient.	- Lack of advanced attack detection. - Cryptographic overhead. - Energy consumption trade-off. - Less scalable.

continued on following page

Table 2. Continued

Refs.	Scheme	Security mechanism	Desire routing attacks	Defense Strategy	Routing strategy	dataset	Key improvements	Limitations
(Valikhanli, 2024)	RFIDL	RFI feature selection + DT	DoS	Detection	-	5G-NIDD	- Less prediction time. - Lightweight model.	- Limited to feature dependency. - Limited attack coverage.
(Alzahrani, 2024)	ConvLSTM	CNN + LSTM	Intrusion detection attacks	Detection	-	GPS spoofing, NSL KDD, WSN DS, CICIDS2017	- Effective in analysing spatial and temporal features. - Enhanced accuracy. - Improved generalization.	- High computational cost. - Overfitting risk. - Energy consumption.
(Attaullah et al., 2026)	RoboLSTM	ROBOTa feature engineering + LSTM	Cyber physical attacks	Detection	-	Real-time UAV, CICIDS2017, UNSW-NB15	- Lightweight modeling. - Enhanced feature inclusion. - Generalization across datasets.	- Sequence dependency. - Computational overhead. - Vulnerable to adversarial attacks.
(Oh & Kang, 2026)	DroneLSTM	LSTM	Jamming	Detection	-	Simulated	- Early attack detection. - Multi-metric correlation. - Temporal pattern learning.	- Input metric dependency. - Computational overhead. - Hyperparameter sensitivity.
(Sharma & Jameel, 2019)	TAODV	Trust based	Insider attacks	Isolative Prevention	AODV	FANET simulated	- Improved PDR. - Low packet loss.	- Less powerful to handle complex threat. - Can lead to false trust recommend-ation.

continued on following page

Table 2. Continued

Refs.	Scheme	Security mechanism	Desire routing attacks	Defense Strategy	Routing strategy	dataset	Key improvements	Limitations
(Buksh et al., 2022)	TOPCM	Trust mechanism	Insider attacks	Isolative Prevention	AODV	FANET simulated	- High PDR. - Low delay. - Enhanced detection accuracy.	- Trust computation overhead. - Degradation of trust accuracy. - No predictive capability.
(Kumar et al., 2023)	TBMR	Multi-hop trust mechanism	Blackhole	Isolative Prevention	AODV	FANET simulated	- Reduced packet loss. - Increased reliability.	- Unreliable in noisy environment. - Static threshold.
(Chandrasekar et al., 2024)	SAODV	Trust mechanism	Insider attacks	Isolative Prevention	AODV	FANET simulated	- Improved routing overhead. - Enhanced energy efficiency.	- Less scalable. - Potential bottleneck. - Single point failure issue.
(Ananthi, 2025)	EECRA	Clustering + trust mechanism	Blackhole, wormhole, selective forwarding	Isolative Prevention	-	FANET simulated	- Improved throughput. - Less delay.	- Rely on packet forwarding ratio. - Cluster head vulnerability.
(Hosseinzadeh et al., 2023)	FTSR	Fuzzy logic + trust mechanism	Blackhole, flooding, wormhole, selective forwarding	Adaptive prevention	FTSR	FANET simulated	- Improved PDR. - Low packet loss. - Enhanced latency.	- Time consuming. - Computational overhead.

Refs.	Scheme	Security mechanism	Desire routing attacks	Defense Strategy	Routing strategy	dataset	Key improvements	Limitations
(Ntizikira et al., 2023)	SP-IoUAV	CNN-LSTM, FL-based differential privacy	Intrusion attacks	Adaptive prevention	-	CICIDS2017	- Enhanced detection accuracy and security.	- Trade-off between privacy and accuracy by addition of noise. - Computational overhead.
(Priyadharshini & Balamurugan, 2024)	HWCS-HDL	DTCN + LSTM	DDoS	Adaptive prevention	-	CICIDS2017, NSL-KDD, KDD cup99	- Reduced FP. - Dynamically adjusting routing paths.	- Optimization overhead. - Latency in real-time mitigation. - Limited adaptability
(Mowla et al., 2020)	AFRL	FL + RL-based Q-learning	Jamming	Proactive Prevention	Q-learning	FANET simulated and CRWDAD	- Reduced hop count. - Enhanced path selection. - Communication reliability.	- Potential convergence dely. - Computational overhead. - Sensitive to parameter tunning.
(Ghelani et al., 2024)	RLGM	RL	Jamming	Proactive Prevention	RLGM	NS3 simulated dataset	- Improved accuracy. - High throughput. - Low latency.	- High training complexity. - Low convergence time. - Computational overhead.
(Su et al., 2024)	DQN-PER	DRL + DQN	Eavesdropping	Proactive Prevention	DRL	-	- Dynamic eavesdropping security. - Learning efficiency and stability. - Robust trajectory adaptation.	- Limited generalization. - Not scalable to multi-node scenario. - Focuses on physical layer security.
(Alkahtani et al., 2026)	EMARL-XAI	RL and explainable AI	Jamming, sybil, spoofing, blackhole	Proactive Prevention	MADDPG	NS3 Simulated dataset	- Reduced delay. - Enhanced throughput. - Energy efficiency.	- Training complexity. - Less scalability. - Communication overhead - Complex deployment.

Table 3. Comparative analysis of utilized techniques in FANET security

Technique	Applicability in FANET Security	Strength	Weaknesses
Trust-Based	Detects malicious UAVs using behavior-based trust evaluation; supports secure routing. (Kundu et al., 2024)	- Improves routing reliability - Enhances PDR - Lightweight implementation	- Affected by mobility - Inaccurate trust in dynamic scenarios - Vulnerable to collusion attacks
Fuzzy Logic-Based	Handles uncertainty in attack detection and route selection using multi-parameter decision-making (Singh et al., 2025).	- Handles imprecision - Flexible decision system - Better detection in complex conditions	- Rule design complexity - Not adaptive - Scalability issues
ML-Based	Classifies traffic and attack pattern recognition using trained models (Rahman et al., 2024).	- High accuracy - Fast inference - Simple models	- Needs labeled data - Poor generalization - Limited adaptability
RL-Based	Supports adaptive routing and dynamic defense strategies (Bai et al., 2023).	- Real-time adaptability - Autonomous decision making - Handles dynamic environments	- High training cost - Slow convergence - Complex reward design
FL-Based	Enables privacy-preserving distributed intrusion detection across UAVs (Al Farsi et al., 2025).	- Data privacy preserved - Reduced raw data sharing - Better generalization	- Communication overhead - Vulnerable to poisoning - Synchronization issues

SECURITY CHALLENGES AND RESEARCH DIRECTION IN FANETS

This section provides an in-depth discussion of the critical security challenges faced by FANETs along with potential research directions to address these issues. The discussion highlights key challenges including real-time attack detection, scalability, energy efficiency, data privacy, and robustness against advanced and adaptive threats. Furthermore, this section outlines promising research directions aimed at overcoming these challenges.

SECURITY CHALLENGES

Numerous research studies have utilized different strategies in the establishment of reliable communication networks in FANETs. However, there are still some challenges presents, as shown in Figure 3, which can be taken into account to make the robust model. Some potential challenges are discussed below:

Figure 3. Major security challenges in UAV Network

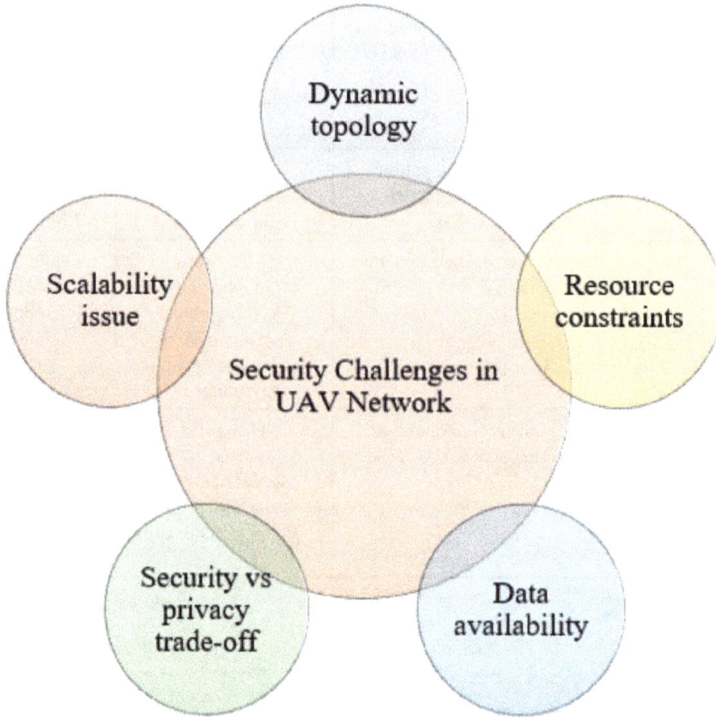

Highly Dynamic Topology

One of the most fundamental challenges in securing FANETs is their highly dynamic topology, which arises from the continuous and rapid movement of UAVs. Unlike traditional networks in which nodes are relatively stable, FANETs carry UAVs, which frequently change their positions and lead to constant variations in network connectivity and routing paths. This dynamic behavior of the network makes it extremely difficult to maintain the stable communication links between UAVs and become inconsistent in security monitoring (Hussain et al., 2024). IDS and routing protocols often rely on historical traffic data, which quickly becomes outdated in

FANET environments due to dynamic ability. As a result, malicious activities may go undetected or can be detected too late; this increases the vulnerability of the network to attacks such as wormhole, blackhole, and jamming. Timely adaptation to these frequent changes remains a critical research challenge.

Resource Constraints

UAVs are resource-constrained devices, as they contain limited battery life, processing power, storage capacity, and communication bandwidth. These limitations make a significant challenge for implementing advanced security mechanisms, especially when it comes to accomplishing mission-critical operations. Also, this will become a major issue in computationally intensive models such as DL, RL, and cryptographic algorithms that require more energy to incorporate computational ability in operations (Hussain et al., 2024). While such methods can provide high detection accuracy, their deployment may quickly drain battery resources by overloading onboard processors. Therefore, there is a critical need for an advanced approach that is lightweight and balanced between security effectiveness and resource efficiency.

Data Availability

The quality and diversity of the data are the major concern, as the performance of intelligent security models like ML and DL heavily depends on these data that will be used for model training. If the training of the model is done on biased, unreliable, unbalanced, and unprocessed data, then it will lead to inaccurate results and may not be able to detect security threats. In the context of FANETs, this presents a major challenge, as most existing studies rely on traditional benchmark datasets such as CICIDS2017 or NSL-KDD, which were not specifically designed for UAV environments. Also, these datasets often fail to capture the unique characteristics of FANETs, including high mobility, dynamic topology, and aerial communication patterns. Additionally, they may lack representation of modern and sophisticated attack types (Tsao et al., 2022). Overall, this mismatch can lead to several issues when models are deployed in real-world scenarios, including model overfitting, poor generalization, and reduced effectiveness. Additionally, the lack of realistic, high-quality, and domain-specific datasets significantly hinders the development of reliable security solutions for FANETs.

Security vs. Privacy Trade-off

FL is useful in developing privacy-preserving models by allowing UAVs to train models locally without sharing raw data. While this approach enhances privacy, it also introduces new challenges, including increased communication overhead. This issue arises due to frequent model updates, synchronization issues among distributed nodes, and vulnerability to attacks. Moreover, maintaining a balance between protecting sensitive data and ensuring accurate and timely intrusion detection is non-trivial (Najafinia et al., 2026). This necessitates the ensuring that both security and privacy in FANETs are complex and often conflicting objectives. Therefore, it mandates the designing of a framework that can simultaneously achieve high levels of security and privacy without incurring excessive overhead remains an open research problem.

Scalability Issues

Scalability is one of the main features of FANETs, which provide high coverage with high speed in a 360-degree angle. As it scales up with an increasing number of UAVs, maintaining efficient and secure network operations becomes progressively more difficult. Large-scale networks introduce several challenges related to coordination, communication overhead, and computational complexity. Some models like FL require frequent aggregation of model updates, which can become inefficient and time-consuming as the number of participating nodes increases (Oubbati et al., 2020). Ensuring that security mechanisms can scale efficiently without degrading performance is a critical challenge for future FANET deployments.

RESEARCH DIRECTIONS

The future research directions are elaborated in terms of analyzed challenges; the in-depth discussion of potential future scopes is discussed below:

Real-Time and Adaptive Networks

In order to make an adaptive and intelligent model, there is a need to build the model, which can be autonomous and has self-healing behavior. As the autonomous systems are capable of the detection of attacks autonomously, making the isolation of malicious paths, they can also recover from adversarial attacks (Al-Kamali et al., 2026). This can be done by continuously adapting to changing network conditions and learning from past experiences. The self-healing approach has the ability to restore the disrupted network functionality and ensure the uninterrupted communication. Some of the techniques are capable of establishing this type of network, including RL, DRL, Q-learning, hybrid DL, and hybrid RL (Xu et al., 2026). These approaches allow UAVs to continuously update their knowledge based on current network conditions rather than relying on outdated historical data. Combining autonomy with intelligent decision-making will enable FANETs to become more resilient, reliable, and capable of handling complex and evolving cyber threats.

Lightweight and Energy-Efficient Models

Most of the work is built on complex modeling, which leads to computational overhead, energy constraints, and increased latency. Future research should focus on developing lightweight and energy-efficient security models that incorporate the resource-constrained UAV environments. To establish this, there are several techniques present, including model pruning, quantization, and knowledge distillation (Jing et al., 2026). These approaches can significantly reduce the size and computational requirements of ML models without major performance degradation. Additionally, the adoption of techniques like edge AI can help to reduce the communication overhead as it performs data processing locally on UAVs (Tulembayev et al., 2026).

Data Augmentation and Realistic Dataset Development

In FANETs, data availability and data management are another major problem, as while training the model on unbalanced or unreliable data, it may lead to false predictions. Therefore, the lack of high-quality and representative datasets can be addressed through various data augmentation techniques, and the development of FANET-specific datasets makes the realistic simulation scenario (Poorvi et al., 2025; M. N. Mowla et al., 2025). Some of the advanced methods include the Synthetic Minority Over-sampling Technique (SMOTE) that balances the dataset by generating synthetic data and Adversarial approaches such as Generative Adversarial Networks (GANs) that generate the synthetic but realistic attack data, improving model training and generalization (Shorten et al., 2021). Digital Twin is another promising approach that continuously synchronizes with real-world operations by creating virtual replicas of UAV networks. This approach helps in generating realistic data and validating intrusion detection models without any disruption to actual missions. Additionally, generating real-world UAV testbeds through simulation environments and collecting domain-specific datasets are effective in capturing the true characteristics of FANET environments (Bae et al., 2025). This ensures that trained models perform reliably under real operational conditions.

Advanced Learning Enhancements

FL has shown great potential in preserving privacy; however, it introduces new security vulnerabilities, including model poisoning, data poisoning, and backdoor attacks. To enhance its efficiency and robustness future research should focus on optimizing client selection strategies to ensure that only the most relevant UAVs participate in model training, thereby reducing communication overhead. Additionally, integrating FL with emerging technologies like blockchain can further enhance trust, transparency, and security in distributed learning environments (Guo et al., 2026; V. Kumar et al., 2025b). As AI-driven security systems become more complex, the need for transparency and interpretability becomes increasingly important. XAI techniques can be useful in providing insights into local and global decision-making of models; this will help to identify potential bias (Hossain et al., 2025). This is particularly important in critical applications where human operators need to trust and verify automated decisions.

Scalable Distributed Architectures and Practical Deployment

Numerous models faced the scalability issue; this can be effectively addressed by developing scalable distributed architectures that are supported by advanced communication technologies such as 5G/6G and edge computing (Islamov et al., 2025; Xu et al., 2026). Techniques like hierarchical FL, blockchain, and optimized client participation can reduce the communication overhead and improve training efficiency in a very large network (Hafeez et al., 2026). Rather than assuming trusted participation after initial authentication-based methods, future FANET architectures should also incorporate Zero-Trust Security principles, where every UAV is continuously authenticated and authorized. High-speed and low-latency communication infrastructures further support seamless coordination among UAVs. This ensures that security mechanisms remain efficient and effective even as the network size increases. As most existing approaches show their strong capability in their created simulation environments, the deployment of FANETs in real scenarios remains limited. Future work should incorporate the practical implementation by emphasizing large-scale UAV testbeds, real-world experiments, and field validation to bridge the gap between theoretical research and practical deployment.

CONCLUSION

The UAV network shows transformative evolution in the establishment of an efficient and robust communication environment. However, due to their dynamic

REFERENCES

Al Farsi, A., Khan, A., Mughal, M. R., & Bait-Suwailam, M. M. (2025). Privacy and security challenges in federated learning for uav systems: A systematic review. *IEEE Access : Practical Innovations, Open Solutions*, *13*, 86599–86615. DOI: 10.1109/ACCESS.2025.3570538

Al-Kamali, F., Chan, F., Bayes, J. H., & D'Amours, C. (2026). Optimizing UAV placement with spatial threat exclusion for secure and Energy-Efficient wireless communications. *IEEE Open Journal of the Communications Society*, *7*, 539–558. DOI: 10.1109/OJCOMS.2026.3650906

Alkahtani, H. K., Galiya, Y., Akbayan, B., & Qahmash, A. (2026). Explainable multi agent reinforcement learning framework for secure and adaptive communication in UAV swarm based fanets. *Scientific Reports*, *16*(1), 11830. Advance online publication. DOI: 10.1038/s41598-026-39366-x PMID: 41771935

Alshamrani, A., & Alghamdi, A. M. (2026). Zero-shot attack detection in UAV networks using foundation models. *Alexandria Engineering Journal*, *136*, 105–124. DOI: 10.1016/j.aej.2025.12.065

Alzahrani, A. (2024). Novel Approach for Intrusion Detection Attacks on small Drones using CONVLSTM model. *IEEE Access : Practical Innovations, Open Solutions*, *12*, 149238–149253. DOI: 10.1109/ACCESS.2024.3471806

Alzubaidi, A. A. (2025). Systematic Literature Review for detecting intrusions in unmanned aerial vehicles using machine and Deep Learning. *IEEE Access : Practical Innovations, Open Solutions*, *13*, 58576–58599. DOI: 10.1109/ACCESS.2025.3552329

Ananthi, J. V. (2025). Implementation of an energy-efficient secure clustering algorithm with trusted path for flying ad hoc networks. *Wireless Networks*, *31*(8), 4929–4943. DOI: 10.1007/s11276-025-04032-z

Attaullah, H. M., Khan, I. U., Alam, M. M., Ud, M. M. S., & Kaushik, K. (2026). RoboLSTM-IDS: Multi-dataset evaluation of deep learning framework for UAV network. *PeerJ. Computer Science*, *12*, e3500. DOI: 10.7717/peerj-cs.3500

Bae, C., Choi, E., Kang, S., Ahn, S., & Lee, S. (2025). Digital twin platform for real-time data communication in UAV environment. *Future Generation Computer Systems*, *175*, 108078. DOI: 10.1016/j.future.2025.108078

Bai, Y., Zhao, H., Zhang, X., Chang, Z., Jäntti, R., & Yang, K. (2023). Toward Autonomous Multi-UAV Wireless Network: A Survey of Reinforcement Learning-Based Approaches. *IEEE Communications Surveys and Tutorials*, *25*(4), 3038–3067. DOI: 10.1109/COMST.2023.3323344

Basan, E., Makarevich, O., Lapina, M., & Mecella, M. (2022, November). Analysis of the Impact of a GPS Spoofing Attack on a UAV. *CEUR Workshop Proceedings*, *3094*, 6–16.

Bhardwaj, V., & Kaur, N. (2021). SEEDRP: A secure energy efficient dynamic routing protocol in fanets. *Wireless Personal Communications*, *120*(2), 1251–1277. DOI: 10.1007/s11277-021-08513-0

Bhardwaj, V., Prashar, D., & Rashid, M. (2024). SIRFRM-Secure and Intelligent Routing Fairness Rate Model for Flying Adhoc Networks. *Mobile Networks and Applications*, *29*(6), 1828–1838. DOI: 10.1007/s11036-023-02270-z

Buksh, W., Guo, Y., Iqbal, S., Qureshi, K. N., & Lloret, J. (2022). Trust-oriented peered customized mechanism for malicious nodes isolation for flying ad hoc networks. *Transactions on Emerging Telecommunications Technologies*, *35*(4), e4489. Advance online publication. DOI: 10.1002/ett.4489

Camacho, N. G. (2024). The role of AI in Cybersecurity: Addressing Threats in the Digital Age. *Journal of Artificial Intelligence General Science (JAIGS) ISSN 3006-4023, 3*(1), 143–154. DOI: 10.60087/jaigs.v3i1.75

Cao, L., Jiang, X., Zhao, Y., Wang, S., You, D., & Xu, X. (2020). A survey of network attacks on Cyber-Physical Systems. *IEEE Access : Practical Innovations, Open Solutions*, *8*, 44219–44227. DOI: 10.1109/ACCESS.2020.2977423

Ceviz, O., Sen, S., & Sadioglu, P. (2024). A survey of security in UAVs and FANETs: Issues, threats, analysis of attacks, and solutions. *IEEE Communications Surveys and Tutorials*, *27*(5), 3227–3265. DOI: 10.1109/COMST.2024.3515051

Chandrasekar, V., Shanmugavalli, V., Mahesh, T. R., Shashikumar, R., Borah, N., Kumar, V. V., & Guluwadi, S. (2024). Secure malicious node detection in flying ad-hoc networks using enhanced AODV algorithm. *Scientific Reports*, *14*(1), 7818. DOI: 10.1038/s41598-024-57480-6 PMID: 38570527

Chriki, A., Touati, H., Snoussi, H., & Kamoun, F. (2019). FANET: Communication, mobility models and security issues. *Computer Networks*, *163*, 106877. DOI: 10.1016/j.comnet.2019.106877

Chulerttiyawong, D., & Jamalipour, A. (2023). SyBil Attack Detection in Internet of Flying Things-IOFT: A Machine Learning approach. *IEEE Internet of Things Journal, 10*(14), 12854–12866. DOI: 10.1109/JIOT.2023.3257848

Gazit, O., Itzhakev, Y., Elovici, Y., & Shabtai, A. (2025). Real-World adversarial attacks on RF-Based drone detectors. *ArXiv.org*. https://arxiv.org/abs/2512.20712

Ghelani, J., Gharia, P., & El-Ocla, H. (2024). Gradient Monitored Reinforcement learning for jamming attack detection in FANETs. *IEEE Access : Practical Innovations, Open Solutions, 12*, 23081–23095. DOI: 10.1109/ACCESS.2024.3361945

Goumiri, S., Riahla, M. A., & Hamadouche, M. (2022). Security issues in self-organized Ad-Hoc networks (MANET, VANET, and FANET): a survey. In *Lecture notes in networks and systems* (pp. 312–324). DOI: 10.1007/978-3-030-96311-8_29

Guo, W., Xiao, Y., Li, D., Cheng, S., Li, Y., Liu, J., Li, W., Wang, L., & Wu, Q. (2026). Byzantine-Resilient Federated Learning with Trust-Aware Task Scheduling for Heterogeneous UAV Swarms. *IEEE Transactions on Consumer Electronics, 1*, 1. Advance online publication. DOI: 10.1109/TCE.2026.3670496

Gupta, A., Barthwal, A., Vardhan, H., Kakria, S., Kumar, S., & Parihar, A. S. (2023). Evolutionary study of distributed authentication protocols and its integration to UAV-assisted FANET. *Multimedia Tools and Applications, 82*(27), 42311–42330. DOI: 10.1007/s11042-023-15197-0

Hadi, H. J., Cao, Y., Khan, M. K., Ahmad, N., Hu, Y., & Fu, C. (2025). UAV-NIDD: A dynamic dataset for cybersecurity and intrusion detection in UAV networks. *IEEE Transactions on Network Science and Engineering, 12*(4), 2739–2757. DOI: 10.1109/TNSE.2025.3553442

Hafeez, S., Cheng, R., Mohjazi, L., Sun, Y., & Imran, M. A. (2026). Blockchain-enhanced UAV networks for post-disaster communication: A decentralized flocking approach. *Digital Communications and Networks*. Advance online publication. DOI: 10.1016/j.dcan.2026.03.006

Hassija, V., Chamola, V., Agrawal, A., Goyal, A., Luong, N. C., Niyato, D., Yu, F. R., & Guizani, M. (2021). Fast, Reliable, and secure drone Communication: A comprehensive survey. *IEEE Communications Surveys and Tutorials, 23*(4), 2802–2832. DOI: 10.1109/COMST.2021.3097916

Hickling, T., Aouf, N., & Spencer, P. (2023). Robust adversarial attacks detection based on explainable deep reinforcement learning for UAV guidance and planning. *IEEE Transactions on Intelligent Vehicles, 8*(10), 4381–4394. DOI: 10.1109/TIV.2023.3296227

Hossain, M. A., Ishtiaq, W., & Islam, M. S. (2025). A comparative analysis of Ensemble-Based machine learning approaches with explainable AI for Multi-Class intrusion detection in drone networks. *Security and Privacy*, *9*(1), e70164. Advance online publication. DOI: 10.1002/spy2.70164

Hosseinzadeh, M., Mohammed, A. H., Alenizi, F. A., Malik, M. H., Yousefpoor, E., Yousefpoor, M. S., Ahmed, O. H., Rahmani, A. M., & Tightiz, L. (2023). A novel fuzzy trust-based secure routing scheme in flying ad hoc networks. *Vehicular Communications*, *44*, 100665. DOI: 10.1016/j.vehcom.2023.100665

Hussain, A., Li, S., Hussain, T., Lin, X., Ali, F., & AlZubi, A. A. (2024). Computing Challenges of UAV Networks: A Comprehensive survey. *Computers, Materials & Continua/Computers. Computers, Materials & Continua*, *81*(2), 1999–2051. DOI: 10.32604/cmc.2024.056183

Irfan, A. N., Chuprat, S., Mahrin, M. N., & Ariffin, A. (2022). Taxonomy of Cyber Threat Intelligence Framework. *2022 13th International Conference on Information and Communication Technology Convergence (ICTC)*, 1295–1300. DOI: 10.1109/ICTC55196.2022.9952616

Islam, S., Badsha, S., Khalil, I., Atiquzzaman, M., & Konstantinou, C. (2022). A triggerless backdoor attack and defense mechanism for intelligent task offloading in Multi-UAV systems. *IEEE Internet of Things Journal*, *10*(7), 5719–5732. DOI: 10.1109/JIOT.2022.3172936

Islamov, I., Hashimov, E., Akhundov, R., & Talibov, A. (2025). Hybrid communication models for UAV swarms: Towards scalable and energy-aware network optimization. *Матеріали конференцій МЦНД*, (03.10. 2025; Київ, Україна), 185-195.

Jaiswal, K., Kumar, S., & Rathore, N. K. (2024, December). Comparative analysis of machine learning application on routing protocols in fanet. In *2024 13th International Conference on System Modeling & Advancement in Research Trends (SMART)* (pp. 706-711). IEEE. DOI: 10.1109/SMART63812.2024.10882526

Jaiswal, K., Kumar, S., & Rathore, N. K. (2025, March). Machine Learning Techniques to Detect a DDoS Attack in Flying AD-HOC Network. In *2025 3rd International Conference on Device Intelligence, Computing and Communication Technologies (DICCT)* (pp. 180-184). IEEE. DOI: 10.1109/DICCT64131.2025.10986407

Jaiswal, K., Kumar, S., & Rathore, N. K. (2026). Machine learning based routing approaches for Flying Ad-hoc Networks (FANETs): A systematic review. *Proceedings of the National Academy of Sciences, India Section A: Physical Sciences*. https://doi.org/DOI: 10.1007/s40010-026-01038-w

Jing, R., Niu, Q., Zhao, Q., Shao, J., Li, Z., Qi, B., Chao, G., Ma, Y., Li, D., & Zhou, X. (2026). From UAV imagery to mapping: Detecting sunflower heads in fields using a novel lightweight deep learning network. *European Journal of Agronomy, 176*, 128018. DOI: 10.1016/j.eja.2026.128018

Kumar, R., Sharma, B., & Athithan, S. (2023). TBMR: Trust based multi-hop routing for secure communication in flying ad-hoc networks. *Wireless Networks*. Advance online publication. DOI: 10.1007/s11276-023-03480-9

Kumar, S., Singh, P., & Shrivastva, A. (2026) Energy-Efficient Routing Approaches in FANETs: An Extensive Survey. *Proceedings of the National Academy of Sciences, India Section A: Physical Sciences*. DOI: 10.1007/s40010-026-01120-3

Kumar, S., Tiwari, A., Ahirwar, Y., Kumar, G., & Arafat, M. Y. (2025a). The Rise of UAV-Based Smart Surveillance: A Systematic Review of Trends and Technologies. *IEEE Access : Practical Innovations, Open Solutions, 13*, 181553–181575. DOI: 10.1109/ACCESS.2025.3621736

Kumar, V., Asthana, A., & Tripathi, G. (2025b). Enhancing Data Security in IOT-based UAV Networks through Blockchain Integration. *Engineering Technology & Applied Science Research, 15*(2), 21800–21804. DOI: 10.48084/etasr.9922

Kundu, J., Alam, S., Das, J. C., Dey, A., & De, D. (2024). Trust-Based Flying Ad Hoc Network: A survey. *IEEE Access : Practical Innovations, Open Solutions, 12*, 99258–99281. DOI: 10.1109/ACCESS.2024.3419904

Lee, C. H., Thiessen, C., Van Bossuyt, D. L., & Hale, B. (2022). A systems analysis of energy usage and effectiveness of a Counter-Unmanned aerial system using a Cyber-Attack approach. *Drones (Basel), 6*(8), 198. DOI: 10.3390/drones6080198

Marks, T., & Fuger, K. (2025). Using generic cities to assess flying ad-hoc network (FANET) performance. *CEAS Aeronautical Journal, 16*(1), 377–398. DOI: 10.1007/s13272-024-00801-2

Military Drones Industry Outlook to 2030: U.S. and China Lead Market Growth with Double.Digit CAGRs, GlobeNewswire, Jul. [Online]. Available: 2025. Accessed: Oct. 17, 2025.

Montufar, A. H. A., Romero, C. T., Ortiz, J. H., Timaná, L. C. R., Varela, F. V., & Gamboa-Cruzado, J. (2025). FANET and MANET, a support and composition relationship. *Computers, Materials & Continua/Computers. Computers, Materials & Continua, 82*(2), 1699–1732. DOI: 10.32604/cmc.2025.056400

Morshedi, R., & Matinkhah, S. M. (2025). Cybersecurity Challenges and solutions in Unmanned Aerial Vehicles (UAVs). *Journal of Field Robotics*, *43*(1), 314–329. DOI: 10.1002/rob.70040

Mowla, M. N., Asadi, D., & Sohel, F. (2025). Real-time fault detection in multirotor UAVs using lightweight deep learning and high-fidelity simulation data with single and double fault magnitudes. *Complex & Intelligent Systems*, *12*(2), 62. Advance online publication. DOI: 10.1007/s40747-025-02195-y

Mowla, N. I., Tran, N. H., Doh, I., & Chae, K. (2020). AFRL: Adaptive federated reinforcement learning for intelligent jamming defense in FANET. *Journal of Communications and Networks (Seoul)*, *22*(3), 244–258. DOI: 10.1109/JCN.2020.000015

Nagalakshmi, T., Gnanasekar, A., Ramkumar, G., & Sabarivani, A. (2021). Machine learning models to detect the blackhole attack in wireless adhoc network. *Materials Today: Proceedings*, *47*, 235–239. DOI: 10.1016/j.matpr.2021.04.129

Najafinia, S., Wang, S., & Lai, C. C. (2026). More Than a Mobile Client: A systematic literature review of architectures, applications, and challenges of UAV-Enabled Federated Learning. *IEEE Access : Practical Innovations, Open Solutions*, *14*, 12930–12959. DOI: 10.1109/ACCESS.2026.3656665

Nguyen, D. C., Ding, M., Pathirana, P. N., Seneviratne, A., Li, J., & Poor, H. V. (2021). Federated Learning for Internet of Things: A Comprehensive survey. *IEEE Communications Surveys and Tutorials*, *23*(3), 1622–1658. DOI: 10.1109/COMST.2021.3075439

Ntizikira, E., Lei, W., Alblehai, F., Saleem, K., & Lodhi, M. A. (2023). Secure and Privacy-Preserving intrusion detection and prevention in the internet of unmanned aerial vehicles. *Sensors (Basel)*, *23*(19), 8077. DOI: 10.3390/s23198077 PMID: 37836907

Nyangaresi, V. O. (2023). Provably secure authentication protocol for traffic exchanges in unmanned aerial vehicles. *High-Confidence Computing*, *3*(4), 100154. DOI: 10.1016/j.hcc.2023.100154

Ogab, M., Zaidi, S., Bourouis, A., & Calafate, C. T. (2025). Machine learning-based intrusion detection systems for the Internet of Drones: A systematic literature review. *IEEE Access : Practical Innovations, Open Solutions*, *13*, 96681–96714. DOI: 10.1109/ACCESS.2025.3575236

Oh, C., & Kang, S. (2026). LSTM-Based Early Jamming Threat Detection Scheme for Drone Ad-Hoc Networks. *Applied Sciences (Basel, Switzerland)*, *16*(6), 3046. DOI: 10.3390/app16063046

Oli, A., & Mahalal, E. (2025). *UAV security: Attacks, defenses, and open challenges.* IEEE., DOI: 10.1109/ACCESS.2025.3647023

Oubbati, O. S., Atiquzzaman, M., Ahanger, T. A., & Ibrahim, A. (2020). Softwarization of UAV Networks: A survey of applications and Future Trends. *IEEE Access : Practical Innovations, Open Solutions, 8*, 98073–98125. DOI: 10.1109/ACCESS.2020.2994494

Ouiazzane, S., Addou, M., & Barramou, F. (2023, January). Dos and ddos cyberthreats detection in drone networks. In *The International Conference on Intelligent System and Smart Technologies* (pp. 109-119). Cham: Springer International Publishing.

Pirayesh, H., & Zeng, H. (2022). Jamming Attacks and Anti-Jamming Strategies in Wireless Networks: A Comprehensive survey. *IEEE Communications Surveys and Tutorials, 24*(2), 767–809. DOI: 10.1109/COMST.2022.3159185

Poorvi, J., Kalita, A., & Gurusamy, M. (2025). Reliable and efficient data collection in UAV-Based IoT networks. *IEEE Communications Surveys and Tutorials, 28*, 2531–2571. DOI: 10.1109/COMST.2025.3550274

Priyadharshini, S., & Balamurugan, P. (2024). An efficient DDoS attack detection and prevention model using fusion heuristic enhancement of deep learning approach in FANET sector. *Applied Soft Computing, 167*, 112438. DOI: 10.1016/j.asoc.2024.112438

Rahman, M. H., Sejan, M. S., Aziz, M. A., Tabassum, R., Baik, J., & Song, H. (2024). A Comprehensive survey of unmanned aerial vehicles detection and classification using Machine learning approach: Challenges, solutions, and future directions. *Remote Sensing (Basel), 16*(5), 879. DOI: 10.3390/rs16050879

Schweitzer, N., Dvir, A., & Stulman, A. (2023). Network wormhole attacks without a traditional wormhole. *Ad Hoc Networks, 151*, 103286. DOI: 10.1016/j.adhoc.2023.103286

Shafique, A., Mehmood, A., & Elhadef, M. (2021). Detecting signal spoofing attack in UAVs using machine learning models. *IEEE Access : Practical Innovations, Open Solutions, 9*, 93803–93815. DOI: 10.1109/ACCESS.2021.3089847

Shakhatreh, H., Sawalmeh, A. H., Al-Fuqaha, A., Dou, Z., Almaita, E., Khalil, I., Othman, N. S., Khreishah, A., & Guizani, M. (2019). Unmanned Aerial Vehicles (UAVs): A survey on civil applications and key research challenges. *IEEE Access : Practical Innovations, Open Solutions, 7*, 48572–48634. DOI: 10.1109/ACCESS.2019.2909530

Shakhatreh, H., Sawalmeh, A. H., Al-Fuqaha, A., Dou, Z., Almaita, E., Khalil, I., Othman, N. S., Khreishah, A., & Guizani, M. (2019c). Unmanned Aerial Vehicles (UAVs): A survey on civil applications and key research challenges. *IEEE Access : Practical Innovations, Open Solutions*, *7*, 48572–48634. DOI: 10.1109/ACCESS.2019.2909530

Shapovalov, V., Tran, Q. K., Groussis, M., Jasani, G., Tilley, L., & Pourmand, A. (2024). Analyzing unmanned aerial vehicle (drone) attacks; a disaster medicine perspective. *The American Journal of Emergency Medicine*, *84*, 135–140. DOI: 10.1016/j.ajem.2024.08.001 PMID: 39116674

Sharma, D., & Jameel, A. (2019). Enhancement of security in flying AD-HOC network using a trust based routing mechanism. *International Journal of Innovative Technology and Exploring Engineering*, *9*(1), 253–257. DOI: 10.35940/ijitee.A4010.119119

Sharma, M., Singh, M., Walia, K., & Kaur, K. (2019, October). A comprehensive study of performance parameters for MANET, VANET and FANET. In *2019 IEEE 10th Annual Information Technology, Electronics and Mobile Communication Conference (IEMCON)* (pp. 0643-0646). IEEE.

Shorten, C., Khoshgoftaar, T. M., & Furht, B. (2021). Text data augmentation for deep learning. *Journal of Big Data*, *8*(1), 101. DOI: 10.1186/s40537-021-00492-0 PMID: 34306963

Singh, R., Nishad, D. K., Khalid, S., & Chaudhary, A. (2025). A review of the application of fuzzy mathematical algorithm-based approach in autonomous vehicles and drones. *International Journal of Intelligent Robotics and Applications*, *9*(1), 344–364. DOI: 10.1007/s41315-024-00385-4

Srivastava, A., & Prakash, J. (2020). Future FANET with application and enabling techniques: Anatomization and sustainability issues. *Computer Science Review*, *39*, 100359. DOI: 10.1016/j.cosrev.2020.100359

Su, G., Dai, M., Chen, B., & Lin, X. (2024). Deep reinforcement learning aided secure UAV communications in the presence of moving eavesdroppers. *Journal of King Saud University. Computer and Information Sciences*, *36*(4), 102047. DOI: 10.1016/j.jksuci.2024.102047

Tsao, K., Girdler, T., & Vassilakis, V. G. (2022). A survey of cyber security threats and solutions for UAV communications and flying ad-hoc networks. *Ad Hoc Networks*, *133*, 102894. DOI: 10.1016/j.adhoc.2022.102894

Tulembayev, A., Dolya, A., Kuttybayeva, A., Jussupbekov, T., & Tazhen, K. (2026). Energy-Aware Adaptive Communication Topology with Edge-AI Navigation for UAV Swarms in GNSS-Denied Environments. *Drones (Basel)*, *10*(4), 273. DOI: 10.3390/drones10040273

Valikhanli, O. (2024). UAV networks DoS attacks detection using artificial intelligence based on weighted machine learning. *Results in Control and Optimization*, *16*, 100457. DOI: 10.1016/j.rico.2024.100457

Wang, C., You, X., Gao, X., Zhu, X., Li, Z., Zhang, C., Wang, H., Huang, Y., Chen, Y., Haas, H., Thompson, J. S., Larsson, E. G., Di Renzo, M., Tong, W., Zhu, P., Shen, X., Poor, H. V., & Hanzo, L. (2023). On the Road to 6G: Visions, Requirements, Key Technologies, and Testbeds. *IEEE Communications Surveys and Tutorials*, *25*(2), 905–974. DOI: 10.1109/COMST.2023.3249835

Wang, X., Zhao, Z., Yi, L., Ning, Z., Guo, L., Yu, F. R., & Guo, S. (2024). A survey on security of UAV swarm networks: Attacks and countermeasures. *ACM Computing Surveys*, *57*(3), 1–37.

Xiong, R., Xiong, L., Shan, F., & Luo, J. (2021). SBHA: An undetectable black hole attack on UANET in the sky. *Concurrency and Computation*, *35*(13), e6700. Advance online publication. DOI: 10.1002/cpe.6700

Xu, Y., Zha, J., Hong, W., Yi, X., Chen, G., Zheng, J., Hsia, C., & Chen, X. (2026). Scalable UAV Multi-Hop Networking via Multi-Agent Reinforcement Learning with Large Language Models. *IEEE Transactions on Mobile Computing*, *25*(7), 1–17. DOI: 10.1109/TMC.2026.3669346

Zhai, W., Liu, L., Ding, Y., Sun, S., & Gu, Y. (2023). ETD: An efficient Time delay Attack Detection framework for UAV networks. *IEEE Transactions on Information Forensics and Security*, *18*, 2913–2928. DOI: 10.1109/TIFS.2023.3272862

Chapter 11
Autonomous Defensive Agents for Cloud Threat Detection, Incident Response, and Remediation

Khushi Jain
http://orcid.org/0009-0001-7521-8595
VIT Bhopal University, India

D. Lakshmi
http://orcid.org/0000-0003-4018-1208
VIT Bhopal University, India

ABSTRACT

Cloud computing is an essential element of the contemporary digital systems yet presents enormous security issues, such as the high attack surfaces, dynamic environments, and advanced cyber threats. Conventional security methods, which rely on manual surveillance and pre-programmed regulations, tend to be weak in regards to the fast changing attacks. The authors of this chapter discuss the use of Autonomous Defensive Agents (ADAs) on the basis of agentic intelligence to improve the security of the cloud. These agents operate based on machine learning and deep learning algorithms and check environments, network traffic, anomalies, and forecast threats. They also facilitate automated responses in real time including isolating compromised systems, blocking malicious users and taking them into recovery procedures. The

DOI: 10.4018/979-8-2600-0413-5.ch011

chapter states the architecture, data processing, and decision making capabilities of ADAs and the main issues such as trust, explainability and ethical issues, their relevance to contemporary cloud defense.

1. INTRODUCTION

The emergence of cloud computing as the backbone of current technology systems has significantly changed the development of information system solutions. This technology provides unparalleled scalability, flexibility, and economic advantages and is rapidly gaining traction across all fields, including health care, finance, government, and infrastructure. Nevertheless, this migration has also increased the attack surface available to attackers, introduced new types of vulnerabilities, and posed security threats of a whole new nature compared to those experienced in traditional on-premises systems. The scale of cloud infrastructure and distributed identity systems has grown exponentially. Thus, the complexity and attack surface of any modern enterprise are increasing, with traditional rule or signature-based detection systems often insufficient to detect new or evolving threats (Madireddy et al., 2025).

Traditional methods of cybersecurity, such as signature-based intrusion detection, perimeter firewalls, and access control policies defined as hard-coded configurations, were designed to work in a setting where the threat environment is slowly evolving, and the infrastructure boundaries are well established. Neither condition is true in cloud environments. Virtues are deployed and discharged within seconds, workloads are spread across geographic boundaries, and enemies use automated, adaptive attack tools that run at machine speed. Massively trained language models can now plan autonomously, coordinate tools, and adapt strategies at scale, thereby challenging the security architecture based on fixed rules and perimeter defences, as well as human-centred processes (Li & Zhu, 2025).

The rise of agentic artificial intelligence is as much of a paradigm shift as it is a concern for the threat environment. Li and Zhu (2025) present an excellent case for the transition to agentic cyber resilience, in which autonomous AI systems predict disruptions, mitigate risks to vital processes, recover effectively, and learn continuously, rather than prevention-centric security. This point of view is the direct stimulus of the idea of Autonomous Defensive Agents (ADAs), defined in this study as AI-enabled systems that are designed to operate autonomously and perform the complete operational cycle of cloud security: continuous monitoring, threat detection, risk assessment, incident response, and remediation, without human intervention at every stage.

The co-evolution of artificial-intelligence-powered offensive weapons underscores the urgency of this change. According to the World Economic Forum, in the year 2025, cybercrime is going to cost the global economy a total of 10.5 trillion dollars, with the costs fueled by the pace at which cyber threats are continually evolving to be a thorn in the flesh of traditional defence systems (Landolt et al., 2025). Multi-Agent Reinforcement Learning (MARL) has proven to be a highly promising adaptive solution, capable of supporting decentralised and collaborative defence schemes and offering automated processes to address dynamic, coordinated, and advanced threats (Landolt et al., 2025).

One of the most critical issues in this changing landscape is the threat of zero-day attacks. These exploits take advantage of previously undiscovered vulnerabilities and can bypass traditional signature-based detection systems, with which the exploit pattern is completely unfamiliar (Alsuwaiket, 2025; Berrios Vasquez et al., 2025). The ZeroDay-LLM model shows that zero-day attack signature detection can achieve 97.8% accuracy with 23% fewer false positives than more than 23 intrusion detection systems of the time, and, with real-time capabilities, the average latency for analysing a packet is 12.3 ms (Alsuwaiket, 2025).

Although there is an increasing body of research on perception, intelligence, and automatic response in the context of threat detection, there is no existing literature that presents a comprehensive conceptual framework for a unified Autonomous Defensive Agent (ADA) architecture in a cloud environment. Previous research either focuses solely on the algorithmic side of detection (Alsuwaiket, 2025; Elshewey et al., 2025) or is dedicated exclusively to the incident response pipeline (Farzaan et al., 2025; Kalakoti, 2025), yet it does not provide the big picture of the entire life cycle. In this study, we emphasise the importance of such an approach and provide a three-tier architectural design for the proposed ADA technology that utilises multi-agent reinforcement learning, deep learning, and the capabilities of LLMs in combination with the ability to respond to threats; maps those capabilities to concrete threat situations in the cloud computing environment; and addresses governance and ethical concerns associated with their implementation.

2. BACKGROUND AND RELATED WORK

2.1 Cloud Security: Challenges and Evolving Threat Landscape

Security problems in the cloud are fundamentally different from those of traditional systems. The multi-tenancy approach makes the cloud vulnerable to cross-tenant data leakage; the API-based control plane is an attractive target for cyber attackers; and the dynamic provisioning approach leads to configuration drift that causes vulnerabilities to emerge at a pace faster than cybersecurity professionals can mitigate. Threat detection using AI in cloud computing systems must take this into account, especially given that traditional perimeter-based security measures are clearly ineffective (Eleweke et al., 2025).

The taxonomy of attacks in cloud environments includes network-layer threats, identity-based attacks, application-layer exploits, and data exfiltration. DDoS attacks are a category of threats that is difficult to eliminate and constantly develops; deep learning systems used in the context of software-defined networking have shown that deep learning networks can distinguish DDoS network traffic with high fidelity, which is a significant gap in cloud network defence (Elshewey et al., 2025). Empirical comparisons of machine learning algorithms for real-time DDoS detection demonstrate that the algorithms and feature engineering methods used have a strong impact on detection performance in dynamic cloud environments (Odukaya et al., 2025).

Attention mechanisms have been shown to make hybrid CNN-RNN models with multi-head attention on cloud infrastructure more effective at detecting DDoS attacks by focusing on the most discriminative patterns in traffic time series, thereby improving accuracy and interpretability (Sathaporn et al., 2025). The approaches to DDoS protection of data centre infrastructure based on graph neural networks complement each other by modelling the relational structure of network communication to identify coordinated attack campaigns that cannot be detected with a packet-level approach (Sharma & Jacobik, 2025).

With emerging technologies such as microservices and serverless architectures, and container orchestration frameworks like Kubernetes, the cloud migration process has become even more complex. Each architectural style comes with its own set of security issues. Microservice architectures pose challenges: increased service interactions create a broader internal attack surface; short-lived execution environments in serverless environments render existing endpoint protection solutions ineffective; and container orchestration systems introduce security issues, such as misconfigured role-based access controls and exposed Kubernetes APIs. Architectural complexity complicates cloud environment security, making it increasingly difficult to deploy effective security monitoring processes, as there are multiple services rather than a typical application stack to monitor. Artificial intelligence techniques have become essential due to the inherent architectural complexities involved.

2.2 Traditional Intrusion Detection Systems and Their Limitations

The core challenge in cloud security is intrusion detection, and the literature clearly shows considerable efforts to improve intrusion detection performance. This has been explained well in an elaborate discussion of AI-powered intrusion detection techniques, which highlights the development trajectory from statistical models to shallow machine learning approaches to deep learning solutions (Sowmya & Anita, 2023). Literature reviews on intrusion detection systems using artificial intelligence have extensively covered performance requirements, architectures, and other implementation parameters across different network types (Sharma et al., 2024).

The challenge of computational efficiency of using deep learning IDS in high-throughput systems, which limits the implementation of the method to a hierarchical set of attack mapping and pruned CNN-GRU models, is alleviated by a two-phase hybrid intrusion detection system that uses hierarchical attack mapping and pruned CNN-GRU models (Mohammed & Hoomod, 2026). The hierarchical strategy first whitens candidate anomalies with lightweight models, then performs computationally expensive deep learning analysis on the whitened subset, thereby minimising total computational expense at the expense of detection accuracy. The scale of intrusion detection using a command-line language model demonstrates that LLM-based methods can handle structured log data and detect anomalous command sequences with limited domain-specific training data (Lin et al., 2025). Federated learning has also been proposed as a privacy-preserving method for deploying IDS on distributed cloud nodes, enabling them to collaboratively train their models without centralising sensitive network telemetry (Belenguer et al., 2025).

One of the key challenges of traditional IDS in cloud environments is that these systems assume a relatively static network topology and traffic. Cloud-based applications impose constantly changing traffic profiles on rule-based systems due to auto-scaling events, rolling deployments and dynamic service discovery events that occur during normal operation. In multi-tenant environments where multiple customers share the underlying infrastructure, it can be challenging to establish clean per-tenant baselines without implementing more advanced tenant-aware monitoring architectures. This challenge is partially overcome by deep learning algorithms, which can learn complex, high-dimensional traffic representations. However, their heavy dependence on labelled training data, which is often hard to obtain for novel attack types, motivates the zero-day detection capability discussed in Section 8.3.

2.3 AI-Driven Cloud Security: Emerging Frameworks

An area of active research is the combination of AI capabilities with cloud-native security operations. The case study of cloud security based on AI with a fusion-based AI Security Operations Centre (AISOC) to detect malware and log behaviour illustrates that integrated multi-modal analysis, that is, malware signatures, network behaviour, and log patterns, produces better detection performance than that achieved by single-modality methods (Okonkwo & Dhirani, 2025). The AI-assisted system for efficient and effective cyber incident detection and response in cloud environments detects, triages, and responds to incidents in a single AI pipeline (Farzaan et al., 2025). The identified trend can also be supported by the SecureRiskNet framework (Govindarajan et al., 2026), which is a hybrid detection framework that combines Isolation Forest and Long Short- Term Memory (LSTM) networks and can detect known and zero-day attacks in heterogeneous cloud-fog networks with 96.2% accuracy and sub-1.5 ms inference latency.

A Hybrid intrusion detection framework for cloud security, based on novel AI-driven metaheuristic optimisation, demonstrates that evolutionary optimisation algorithms can effectively tune the hyperparameters of deep learning detection models and outperform the baseline with hand-tuned hyperparameters (Alhusseini, 2026) - in the cloud-native operations. The intelligent security service framework (ISSF) offers a general treatment of security service coordination and the incorporation of AI-driven security elements into cloud-native operational processes (Yan et al., 2025).

2.4 Critical Synthesis and Research Gaps

An analysis of the reviewed literature suggests several significant constraints that justify the development of the proposed ADA framework. To start with, existing AI-based intrusion detection systems have mainly been evaluated individually, overlooking the entire pipeline from detection to automated remediation. Additionally, MARL-based methods (Landolt et al., 2025) appear to be adaptive and show great promise, but have been validated solely through simulations in simulated cloud networks such as Cyber Gyms. Moreover, despite the impressive results obtained by LLM-based detection systems (such as ZeroDay-LLM (Alsuwaiket, 2025)), their effectiveness is demonstrated in benchmark datasets (e.g., CICIDS2017, NSL-KDD). At last, although there are several governance frameworks (e.g., SAGA by Syros et al., 2025) and ethical considerations in the domain (Radanliev et al., 2026), they remain purely theoretical and offer little guidance on implementation for ADA systems. The identified issues justify developing an ADA architecture that integrates governance elements.

3. AGENTIC INTELLIGENCE IN CYBERSECURITY

3.1 Defining Agentic Intelligence and Its Security Implications

An agentic AI is a radical break from task-focused, narrow AI systems towards autonomous agents that can pursue more complex goals through multi-step reasoning, engage with the environment, and act independently. Li and Zhu (2025) offer a system-theoretic account of this transition, suggesting that foundation-model-based

AI is fundamentally redefining cybersecurity and that large language models can now plan autonomously, orchestrate tools and strategies at scale, and adapt them strategically. Their work builds a general architecture for agentic systems, which includes a reasoning core, memory systems, tool interfaces, human oversight, and environmental feedback loops. It has a closed-loop architecture wherein all components are highly interconnected. In addition to this system-theoretic approach, Adabara et al. (2025) offer a multi-pillar review of agentic AI in cybersecurity, visualising cognitive autonomy, ethical governance, and quantum-resilient defence approaches, which offers a governance roadmap that can be directly applied to the implementation of ADA.

The most important piece of information provided by Li and Zhu (2025) is the redefinition of security goals: rather than aiming for full prevention, resilient systems should expect disruption, keep essential operations running amid attacks, recover effectively, and evolve continuously. The paradigm shift is more noticeable in cloud security, where the dynamic and distributed environment cannot be perfectly prevented by its nature. This article demonstrates that agentic AI can be used to operationalise agentic-based resilience to cyber-attacks in multi-cloud settings by showing how such a resilience paradigm can be instantiated via distributed agentic architectures that orchestrate across multiple cloud providers, enabling monitoring, detection, and response (Pal et al., 2025).

3.2 Multi-Agent Systems for Cyber Defence

Multi-agent reinforcement learning (MARL) has demonstrated significant potential as an adaptive solution to current challenges in cybersecurity. MARL enables decentralised, adaptive, and collaborative defence tactics and provides an automated system for attacking dynamic, coordinated, and advanced threats (Landolt et al., 2025). The Landolt et al. (2025)

The survey examines the use of MARL in automated cyber defence, particularly in intruder detection and lateral movement containment, as well as the use of Autonomous Intelligent Cyber-defence Agents (AICA) and Cyber Gyms for training and testing MARL agents. The key problems are scalability and robustness to adversaries, while future research focuses on combining MARL with AICA to provide scalable, dynamic, and adaptable solutions.

Multi-agent systems used to simulate the battle between cyber-attackers and cyber-defenders provide a formal model for studying the co-evolutionary behaviour of autonomous attack and defence (Soulé et al., 2025). The article shows that multi-agent simulation environments can generate realistic patterns of attack-defence interaction, providing useful training data and evaluation platforms for defensive agent training. The example of a multi-agent system used to detect and counterattacks on enterprise information systems exemplifies the practical use of multi-agent defensive architecture (Kostiuk, 2025). A broader survey of agentic AI uses in cybersecurity cites SOC automation, autonomous incident response, and adaptive red-blue simulation as prime examples, and notes that bounded autonomy, with clear limits on the authorisation of irrevocable actions, is a central requirement for deploying AI safely (Lazer et al., 2026).

3.3 Governance of Agentic Systems

The management of independent AI agents also poses fundamental security concerns that need to be addressed before mass adoption. SAGA, a Security Architecture of Governance Agentic systems, is a solution for ensuring that users have control over the life cycle of autonomous agents (Syros et al., 2025). SAGA proposes a cryptographic scheme to derive access control tokens that provide finer control over agent interactions and offer formal security guarantees. The architecture allows users to enlist their agents with a central Provider entity, which stores agent contact information and user-specified access control policies and assists agents in enforcing these policies during inter-agent communication. Performance assessment reveals that the technique has a negligible impact on the underlying tasks being executed.

Radanliev et al. (2026) comprehensively address the vulnerabilities and risks associated with the use of artificial intelligence and agentic AI systems. Among these are prompt injection, adversarial attacks, and misalignment of agents' interests with those of their users. According to the authors, such issues need to be addressed through security techniques such as input sanitisation, credential limitation, runtime checks, and intent-based delegation (Radanliev et al., 2026).

4. ANALYTICAL FRAMEWORK AND DESIGN RATIONALE

The present study employs a systematic literature review methodology, drawing on peer-reviewed papers published between 2024 and 2026 in the arXiv, IEEE Xplore, and Google Scholar databases, using keywords such as 'autonomous cloud security,' 'agentic AI cybersecurity,' 'multi-agent reinforcement learning defence,' and 'zero-day threat detection.' Relevant studies were included in the analysis based on their relevance to the operational phases of ADA - monitoring, detection, analysis, response, and remediation. The architectural framework of ADA described in the present study is derived analytically. Every part of the framework (namely, perception, intelligence, and response) is explained in terms of its role in addressing specific types of threats. It is validated empirically using evidence from the literature. For example, the selection of a GNN-based IAM log analysis technique (Madireddy et al.,

2025) was made in light of the high frequency of cloud attacks targeting identities; similarly, the use of LLM-based zero-day detection (Alsuwaiket, 2025) follows from the insufficiency of signature-based techniques against emerging threats.

5. AUTONOMOUS DEFENSIVE AGENTS (ADAS): CONCEPT AND DESIGN

5.1 Foundational Principles of ADAs

An Autonomous Defensive Agent is an AI-driven system designed to autonomously carry out the entire cycle of cloud security operations: monitoring, detection, analysis, response, and remediation. ADAs stand out from traditional security automation by having real intelligence, the ability to reason in new circumstances, the ability to tailor policies to particular threat scenarios, and the ability to be informed by operational experience. A standalone threat detection and response architecture in cloud security offers an in-depth scanning of AI-based strategies, defining the functional specifications and design philosophy that define effective ADA designs (Sarraf & Pal, 2025). The empirical results of AI-enhanced security operations show that the mean time to detect advanced threats is reduced by 65% and false positives are reduced by 42% relative to traditional monitoring, which provides strong grounds to support the operational argument of autonomous cloud defence (Kurra, 2025)

The ADA vision is closely associated with the self-healing infrastructure paradigm, which incorporates health probes and remediation playbooks into the AI-enhanced systems (Kalakoti, 2025). Kalakoti (2025) shows that self-healing infrastructure significantly reduces mean time to recovery compared with manual remediation strategies, and AI-enhanced systems have the potential to recognise signs of health degradation and execute corrective playbooks within seconds of anomalies appearing. The ability is integral to the ADA's repertoire because it enables fast, automatic responses to threats to cloud services.

5.2 Operational Architecture and Workflow

The operation of ADAs is anchored on a model of the perceived-reason-act approach. In the process of perception, the agent ingests and pre-processes information gathered from multiple sources in the observed environment. In the process of reasoning, the agent utilises its learned models to analyse the pre-processed information, identify anomalies, infer TTPs employed by the adversary, and rate the degree of threat posed. In the process of acting, the agent employs defensive actions that are within its response repertoire while considering the issues of security efficacy and operational continuity. The agentic, AI-driven, adaptive cybersecurity framework for digital product ecosystems builds on this foundational paradigm by coordinating ecosystems for ADAs to protect intricate digital products with interdependent security requirements (Olayinka et al., 2025).

The ADA: Automated Moving Target Defence demonstrates how autonomous defence works through a highly innovative method: the creation of infrastructure-based rotation in Kubernetes (Sheriff et al., 2025). The ADA makes attackers foam at the mouth by constantly rotating the infrastructure attributes (IP addresses, ports, services) of AI applications, preventing them from having enough time to plan a targeted attack on the system due to the attributes' constant fluctuation. This process is automated, requiring no human intervention, demonstrating how autonomous defence can be implemented in practice.

5.3 From Reactive to Proactive Defence: The Agentic Shift

This is a basic concept gap that the agentic AI paradigm is well-suited to address: the reactive vs proactive security posture. However, traditional SPs are reactive: an alarm is raised when a detection system identifies it, a human analyst is alerted and triages it, and an incident response process developed for attacks that might last hours or days is followed. Humans are structurally unable to respond to adversarial automated tool chains that can achieve initial access, lateral movement, privilege escalation and data exfiltration in mere minutes following a successful compromise in a modern cloud environment.

Agentic AI systems signify a fundamentally new way of operation through their ability to demonstrate authentic anticipatory behaviour. Agentic systems can continuously model the evolving attack surface, identify "at-risk" configurations based on the attack surface before an attack, and automatically apply pre-emptive hardening changes. The shift from detect & respond to predict & prevent is the biggest operational benefit an agentic architecture offers over traditional automated security solutions, which remain largely reactive rather than proactive.

At its heart, this proactive approach is a formalisation of the perceived-reason-act cycle that underlies ADA's operation. In addition to capturing events, the perception stage continuously updates the understanding of the cloud environment's security state. Similarly, the reasoning stage is not only about categorising events as malicious or non-malicious; it is also about the paths the security state can take that are detrimental. The action stage is not only reactive to detected threats but also proactive, as it can occur at the slightest opportunity to disrupt the attack.

This temporal element of agentic security, the ability to respond before even being sure of it, is revolutionary compared to the automation based on rules and machine learning-driven detection. The only time that a rule-based system can act is when it has enough rules that it satisfies the pre-specified conditions. The only time that a machine learning classifier can act is when a threat pattern has been sufficiently instantiated to cross the detection threshold. Agentic systems can maintain a dynamic world model and reason about likely future events based on early indicators that, when taken individually, may not trigger any detection rule but, when considered together, signal a higher threat. This capability is directly relevant to the detection of advanced persistent threats that are slowly active and deliberately designed to evade individual detection rules.

In addition to this proactive capability, the ability to apply large language model reasoning in agentic architectures enables the use of natural language processing for threat intelligence feeds, security advisories, and vulnerability disclosures. A machine-actionable, agentic system that can read and reason about a new vulnerability disclosure, and take autonomous action to evaluate its applicability to the monitored environment and apply compensating controls before the adversaries could develop and deploy an exploit, turning threat intelligence into an information product that humans must consume, into an information product that can be consumed by a machine, and which directly drives defensive configuration. Given this capability, coupled with the constant learning feedback loop shown in Figure 2, ADA systems are truly adaptive defenders that are expected to evolve more rapidly than the attacks they face. (Li & Zhu, 2025; Adabara et al., 2025)

6. ARCHITECTURE OF AUTONOMOUS DEFENSIVE AGENTS

6.1 Perception Layer: Multi-Source Telemetry Integration

The perception layer of an ADA is responsible for collecting, aggregating, and pre-processing security-relevant telemetry from the monitored cloud environment. Cloud environments generate diverse data streams - network flows, IAM audit logs, system call traces, container event logs, API call sequences, and application metrics- each providing distinct and complementary signals relevant to security monitoring.

IAM logs provide highly informative telemetry data. The use of an adaptive threat detection architecture based on GNNs demonstrates the feasibility of treating IAM logs as dynamically changing. These heterogeneous graphs capture temporal, relational, and contextual dependencies among users, roles, sessions, and access operations (Madireddy et al., 2025). The graph representation of IAM logs accounts for dependencies among users, roles, and resources. It detects activities related to insiders, lateral movement, or privilege escalation that time-series-based methods may not detect.

Security logs also serve as an alternative telemetry source for understanding higher-level threats. Security Logs to ATT&CK Insights shows how LLMs can be used to understand high-level threats and derive cognitive traits from security logs (Hans et al., 2025). Since the use case involves mapping security logs to MITRE ATT&CK techniques, this method would help ADAs understand the logs in the context of larger attacks and the attacker traits that inform an appropriate response strategy.

As Figure 1 reveals, there are three layers in the ADA framework. The first layer is the Perception Layer, which collects telemetry from the cloud, comprising API logs, network traffic, and behavioural data. The second layer is the Intelligence Layer, which processes information using machine-learning/deep-learning models, anomaly detection, threat classification, and a reinforcement-learning decision-making engine. At the same time, the Response Layer executes defensive actions such as system isolation, access revocation, alert generation, and auto-remediation. (Madireddy (2025), Li & Zhu (2025), and Sarraf & Pal (2025)).

Figure 1. Architecture of Autonomous Defensive Agents (ADAs)

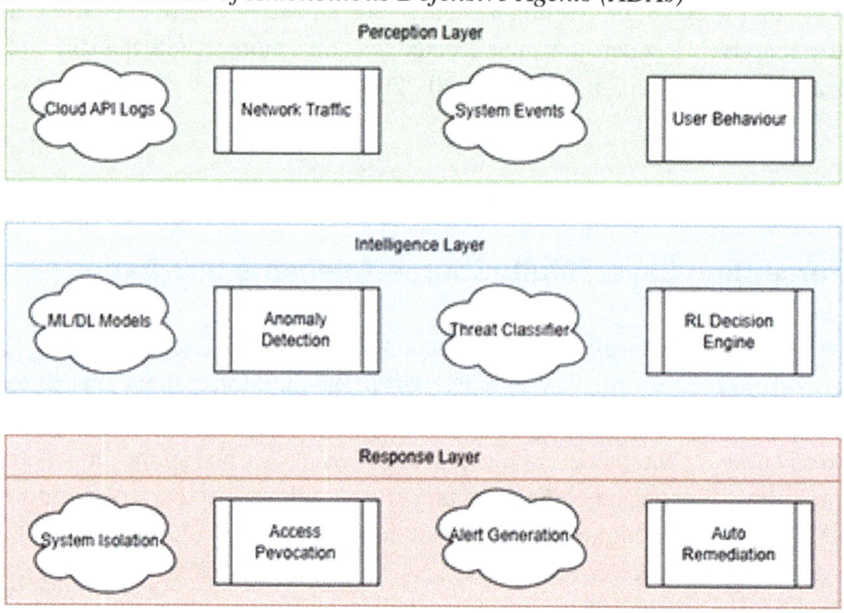

6.2 Intelligence Layer: Decision-Making Mechanisms

The intelligence layer forms the thinking heart of the ADA, converting digested telemetry into formatted threat-evaluation and response determinations. This level usually employs a hierarchical processing model that accounts for both computational and analytical power. Classification algorithms such as gradient-boosted trees and random forests are employed to process massive volumes of event streams. If an event stream is found to be suspicious, then it is subjected to deep learning models.

The use of AI in cloud security, with the implementation of fusion-based detection, reveals that malware detection and log behaviour analysis are far more effective at providing detective coverage than either used separately (Okonkwo & Dhirani, 2025). The proposed solution could be used for the ADA intelligence layer, where signals generated by different detection technologies – network anomalies, endpoint behaviour and IAM - could be combined to provide higher threat assessment accuracy and reduce false positives.

The proposed system of Farzaan et al. (2025) indicates the ability of an end-to-end AI-based pipeline for cloud security with high detection rates and proper response time.

6.3 Response Layer: Automated Execution

The response layer translates these measurements into defensive actions deployed via APIs and security services offered by cloud providers. The key trade-off in ADA response strategies is ensuring adequate defence without unduly interfering with legitimate operations, maintaining a balance between aggressive response and minimal disturbance from threats.

Modern ADA response strategies utilise multiple tiers in response hierarchies depending on the threat level. A low-confidence assessment will generate tier 1 responses, such as enhanced logging, alert triggering, and passive evidence collection, which represent minimal operational risks. A moderate-confidence assessment will trigger a tier 2 response, including access denial and traffic manipulation. In contrast, high-confidence and high-severity assessments will initiate tier 3 responses, such as system isolation and service termination. The ADA framework introduced by Sheriff et al. (2025) presents an example of an automatic Tier 3 response that involves ephemeral infrastructure rotation and service re-provisioning, triggered by indications of compromise without human authorisation.

7. AI TECHNIQUES USED IN AUTONOMOUS DEFENSIVE AGENTS

7.1 Deep Learning for Threat Detection

The deep neural network architecture forms the core of any contemporary ADA system. The use of hybrid models such as CNN-GRU leverages the strengths of both spatial feature extraction via the former and pattern modelling via the latter, thereby forming excellent classifiers for network traffic and log sequence data. Elshewey et al. (2025), in their work on DDoS classification using a CNN-GRU architecture, demonstrate how such models used in software-defined networking environments can classify traffic data with a high degree of fidelity because the hybrid model extracts features locally (from packet-level data) as well as temporally. The application of deformable convolution with a BiLSTM and multi-head attention mechanisms enabled flexible extraction of spatial and temporal features in traffic data, leading to improved detection performance for minority classes or stealthy attacks compared to other models (Bin Li et al., 2025).

To address computational scalability, the hybrid two-stage approach by Mohammed and Hoomod (2026) combines hierarchical attack mapping with pruning of CNN-GRU models, resulting in faster inference without reducing accuracy. This particular architecture is suitable for application to cloud monitoring environments. DDoS detection using CNN-RNN models with multi-head attention demonstrates that attention mechanisms substantially improve detection performance by enabling models to selectively focus on the most discriminative temporal patterns in network traffic sequences (Sathaporn et al., 2025).

Transformer-based architectures, originally used in natural language processing (NLP), have proven effective in network security applications due to their ability to capture long-range dependencies in sequential data. In network traffic analysis, the transformer attention mechanism enables the model to capture packet properties at any stage of the flow and relate them to properties at earlier stages, helping to detect slow-moving attacks that window-based anomaly detection methods would miss. The self-attention mechanism is especially suitable for analysing IAM logs, where the relevance of an access event can be determined based on access patterns observed days/weeks earlier. Recent transformer-based architectures for graph models of entity relationships and transformer temporal modelling have achieved state-of-the-art performance on heterogeneous cloud security telemetry (Appiahene et al., 2026).

Federated learning is an important architectural consideration when deploying ADA in multi-tenant and multi-organisation cloud environments. Security telemetry from all environments that is to be included in the training of centralised detection models may be legally or contractually restricted due to data sovereignty and privacy obligations. To overcome this limitation, federated learning is introduced, in which each cloud node trains on its local data and only updates the model parameters to the central node for aggregation and subsequent distribution to other cloud nodes to improve the global model. It is feasible for use in IDS applications and to maintain the privacy of individual tenant telemetry (Belenguer et al., 2025). Federated learning may be the only legally permissible method to obtain the model quality necessary for an effective autonomous defence across multiple organisations or jurisdictions.

7.2 Large Language Models for Security Intelligence

The use of large language models is a transformative addition to ADA systems, enabling intricate natural-language reasoning about threat scenarios, the generation of human-readable threat narratives, and direct application to log analysis tasks. ZeroDay-LLM demonstrates that transformer-based architectures can be directly extended to zero-day threat detection, achieving 97.8% accuracy on benchmark datasets such as CICIDS2017, NSL-KDD, and UNSW-NB15 (Alsuwaiket, 2025). The architecture combines lightweight edge encoders with centralised transformer-based reasoning engines to provide contextual interpretation of network traffic patterns and behavioural anomalies at processing speeds of 12.3 ms per packet analysis.

Hans et al. (2025) demonstrate the use of LLMs to analyse security logs, understanding high-level threats and infer cognitive traits from them. Mapping log events to ATT&CK framework techniques allows ADAs to produce interpretable threat assessments that can be utilised not only in automated response decisions but also to support human analysts. The Lin et al. (2025) command-line language model approach has shown that LLMs fine-tuned on operational command-line data can identify abnormal command sequences in cloud environments with minimal domain-specific training data, enabling scalability across a wide range of cloud workloads.

7.3 Multi-Agent Reinforcement Learning

The concept of reinforcement learning can provide a model for training ADAs to learn an optimal defensive strategy through interactions with the environment. The survey of MARL by Landolt et al. (2025) provides an extensive overview of the current development of MARL in automated cyber-defence systems. This is shown in its application to intrusion detection, lateral movement detection, and moving target defence. The survey highlights Cyber Gyms as simulation environments that enable self-play learning and the development of defensive agents.

The experimental usefulness of RL-trained defensive agents in standardised assessment settings is empirically supported by evaluating reinforcement learning agents in autonomous cyber defence (Morris et al., 2025). The assessment scheme has shown that the RL agents can beat the rule-based defences against adaptive adversaries, especially when the attack pattern does not follow the rule base as expected. The game-theoretic cyber attack-defence engines, such as CyGATE, formalise the competitive game between the attacking and defending agents, thereby enabling systematic optimisation of patch strategies against adversarial attack policies (Jiang et al., 2025).

One of the most promising research directions is the design of language-model-based rewards to enable deep reinforcement learning-driven autonomous cyber defence, in which a language model can be used to create subtle reward functions that encourage an RL agent's learning toward advanced defensive behaviours (Mukherjee et al., 2025). This method addresses a fundamental problem in the use of RL for cyber defence: designing reward functions that appropriately balance security goals with operational continuity, leveraging the general security information stored in pre-trained language models.

8. THREAT DETECTION IN CLOUD ENVIRONMENTS

8.1 Network-Level Threat Detection

Network-level threat detection aims to identify malicious activity in communication patterns among cloud resources and between them and other entities. The telemetry volume of a cloud network requires effective processing architectures capable of analysing millions of flows per minute. DDoS protection implemented using graph neural networks demonstrates that GNN techniques can learn the relational nature of data centre traffic to identify coordinated attack waves that are not observable at the packet level (Sharma & Jacobik, 2025). Hybrid designs that incorporate graph convolutional networks with transformer encoders have been shown to exhibit complementary properties: graph layers respond to relational topology, and transformer attention models capture long-range temporal correlations, thereby performing better on multi-class attack datasets such as CIC-IDS 2018 (Appiahene et al., 2026).

The comparison of machine learning models on real-time DDoS detection compares the performance of the following models on various attack types, including Random Forest, Support Vector Machine, and deep learning, showing that ensemble models outperform deep learning models by a significant margin in terms of performance and significantly reduced computational cost (Odukoya et al., 2025). This performance-computational trade-off is vital to the deployment of ADA in resource-constrained or high-throughput cloud systems. Creating cloud-based DDoS data and cloud intrusion traffic characterisation provides benchmark information for systematically analysing detection methods and building cloud-specific detection models (Shafi et al., 2024).

8.2 Identity and Access Management Threat Detection

A significant and increasing share of cloud security incidents is identity-based, including credential theft, privilege escalation, and lateral movement. This kind of cyberattack has been directly addressed by the GNN-based IAM threat detection framework presented by Madireddy et al. (2025). The IAM logs have been modelled as a heterogeneous dynamic graph to capture contextual relations among users, roles, and resources, thereby differentiating between malicious and non-malicious access patterns. This model includes the temporal, relational, and contextual dependency between different nodes. This helps detect insider threats, lateral movements, and privilege escalations that rule-based and sequential frameworks cannot capture.

Detection of identity-based threats in cloud ecosystems is now a key concern, as compromised credentials account for a large share of cloud attacks (Madireddy et al., 2025). Anomaly scoring services such as AWS GuardDuty and Azure Defender are cloud-native frameworks that feature historical IAM pattern-based anomaly scoring. However, they are not extensible or interpretable due to their closed architecture. The GNN-based system overcomes these shortcomings by offering not only the best detection capability but also explainable anomaly behaviour, which can be used to enforce zero-trust access controls and to make AI-based security audits explainable.

8.3 Zero-Day and Novel Threat Detection

Zero-day attacks exploit previously unknown vulnerabilities that are not detected by signature-based mechanisms, nor are they easily detectable by anomaly detection systems that have not observed the exact attack pattern. Cloud-based deep learning to mitigate zero-day threats reveals that mixed vision transformer (MVT) models that transform binary files into images and utilise deep attention mechanisms can be used to detect zero-day malware with 70-80% success, significantly higher than the performance of conventional signature-based techniques that, by definition, cannot detect such malware (Berrios Vasquez et al., 2025).

ZeroDay-LLM offers network-layer zero-day detection features that are complementary and achieve 97.8% accuracy for novel attack signatures by leveraging the contextual reasoning of transformer-based language models (Alsuwaiket, 2025). The framework is more resilient to adversarial evasion methods than traditional IDS, and shows robustness to the adversarial perturbations used by advanced attackers to evade ML-based detection systems. The integration of endpoint- and network-layer zero-day detection into the ADA perception layer provides complete coverage of the zero-day threat surface.

9. AUTONOMOUS INCIDENT RESPONSE AND REMEDIATION

9.1 Automated Incident Detection and Triage

Rapid and accurate triage and detection are the first steps to effective incident response. The AI-based system by Farzaan et al. (2025) is efficient and effective for the cyber incident detection and response pipeline in cloud settings, combining detection, severity analysis, and initial triage into a single AI system. The integration removes the latency between detection and response in human-in-the-loop security operations, allowing a response to be initiated within a few seconds of threat detection.

Fusion-based triage, as described in the AISOC framework by Okonkwo and Dhirani (2025), takes malware detection signals and complements them with log behaviour analysis to generate enriched incident intelligence that can be used to make automated response decisions and reviewed by human analysts. This multi-modal technique could help minimise false positives considerably, as compared to a single source method, since the automated response would then be based on threats and not just the output of detection. The cloud-native operations intelligent security service framework (ISSF) offers a comprehensive treatment of how AI-based security services could be coordinated within cloud-native operational structures (Yan et al., 2025).

9.2 Remediation and Recovery

Once the containment phase is complete, ADAs will conduct remediation efforts to re-establish any impacted systems into their validated states. The AI-based threat detection and mitigation model by Eleweke et al. (2025) illustrates how automated remediation processes can restore impacted cloud resources to their known-good states using the Infrastructure-as-Code methodology. With their known-good baselines, ADAs will identify any configuration changes made by attackers in cloud resources and automate the restoration process to eliminate persistence methods the attacker has put in place.

According to autonomous threat detection and response surveys conducted by Sarraf & Pal (2025), the three primary remediation actions utilised by AI-based security models are system isolation, revocation of attacker access, and workload replacement. Since cloud computing resources are ephemeral, the best approach during remediation is "Phoenix Remediation." This involves stopping the compromised cloud resources and re-provisioning new cloud resources from secure baselines.

9.3 Automated Containment Mechanisms

Automated containment is the fastest stage of incident response, and the time between compromise and containment directly impacts the damage caused by a data breach. ADAs can effectively contain advanced threats like these within mere minutes without any human intervention. Products like these integrate with cloud providers' control plane APIs to dynamically update configuration on the fly, instantly revoke access (such as IP addresses, user identities, etc.), and isolate troubled assets to contain the spread of the attack. This is all done through an AI-augmented self-healing infrastructure framework that proactively monitors resource health and automatically runs predefined playbooks to remediate issues within seconds, limiting the attacker's window of operation (Kalakoti, 2025).

Moving-target defence with proactive containment can be highly effective. In Sheriff et al. (2025), the ADA framework includes infrastructure-native ephemeral container IP and Port rotation for Kubernetes-based workloads. The major contribution of the work is to dynamically change the network identity and parameters of the workloads processed by AI (e.g., image forensics and classification models). As a result of such a shift, AI workloads become unobservable to adversaries. As a consequence, the focus shifts from reactive containment (i.e., containing the spread of malware after detection) to proactive containment (i.e., preventing adversaries from targeting AI workloads before they can be attacked). Adaptive cybersecurity architecture for digital product ecosystems aims to incorporate additional adaptive defence mechanisms that dynamically adjust the product ecosystem's architecture and eliminate attack vectors that cause damage (Olayinka et al., 2025).

Figure 2 shows the full incident management process for ADA, illustrating how the five-step process of Monitor, Detect, Analyse, Respond, and Recover is embedded in a cycle of continuous learning, whereby the system learns from new incidents through retraining. (Farzaan et al.(2025), Kalakoti (2025); Sarraf & Pal (2025).

Figure 2. Continuous Learning Feedback Loop

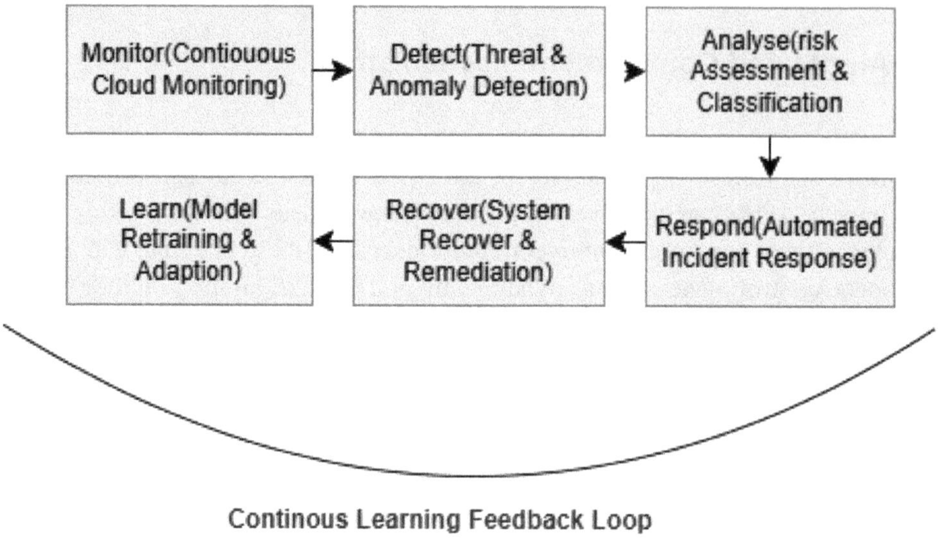

10. ADAS IN AUTONOMOUS CYBER WARFARE

10.1 The Emergence of Machine-Speed Cyber Conflict

In today's cyber warfare, AI-based offensive weaponry has changed how wars happen in cyberspace. Rather than being predominantly carried out by humans, a large part of modern warfare is now driven by machines. Recently released large language models can, as per Li & Zhu (2025), independently plan attacks, carry out coordinated attacks, and make strategic changes, all faster than humans can conduct manually led operations. The World Economic Forum estimates that cybercriminals will cost the global economy $10.5 trillion by 2025, due to the rapid evolution of cyber threats that will undermine traditional defence systems (Landolt et al., 2025).

Cyber conflict now takes place at machine speed, which means human-operated security operations centres face fundamentally different structural limits that cannot be overcome through staffing and tooling alone. The scale of security telemetry generated by large cloud providers far exceeds humans' ability to process and analyse the information; automated attacks occur at speeds humans cannot match; and the complexity of multi-step attack campaigns is beyond what humans can achieve through manual correlation. Automated defence agents (ADAs) eliminate these barriers, enabling detection, analysis, and response to events at the same rate as machine-based attackers, achieving security parity.

10.2 Game-Theoretic Framework for Attack-Defence Dynamics

The relationship between an attack on and a defence of an autonomous agent can be explained well using a game-theoretic approach. The CyGATE cyber-attack defence engine is the result of this effort; it provides a structured method for developing optimised patch strategies to protect against a variety of attack policies (Jiang et al., 2025). In the CyGATE model, the attacking and defending processes are considered competitive and defined by their actions: the attacker seeks to identify and exploit vulnerabilities in a system, while the defender seeks to eliminate these vulnerabilities before an adversary can exploit them. By considering the two processes in relation to each other, it is possible to develop optimal investment strategies for defensive protection systematically.

Li and Zhu (2025) provide further support for this idea by developing an integrated framework for the design of agent-based cyber conflict. They demonstrate how a game-theoretic framework can be used to represent the work of an attacker and a defender as two coupled, adaptive processes and, therefore, that a game-theoretic framework provides a common design language for the allocation of autonomy, the flow of information, and the level of time-based coordination in an agent-based cybersecurity system. Their analyses utilise repeated and dynamic games, resulting in a formal methodology for explaining how learning agents evolve across multiple campaigns, how credibility and reputation form through a series of hostile engagements, and how long-term advantages or stalemates can develop. Ultimately, the established framework enables the design of defences that are resilient not only to current attacks but also to future adversarial learning and strategic advancement.

10.3 Multi-Agent Defensive Coordination

The multi-domain coordinated effort required to defend a cloud system at scale lends itself well to multi-agent system architectures that assign agents to specific functions based on their specialised skills. A study comparing the outcomes of simulated battles between cyber hackers and cyber defenders shows that the effectiveness of defences increases when defender agents coordinate as teams and can dynamically allocate their resources in response to evolving attacks over time (Soulé et al., 2025). The multi-agent system for detecting and responding to attacks against enterprise information systems illustrates how specialised monitoring, detection, and response agents can coordinate their actions to provide comprehensive enterprise security coverage (Kostiuk, 2025).

One way to address the challenge of coordinating multi-agent cyber defence is to design learned reward functions (LLMs) that provide positive incentives for agents trained via deep reinforcement learning (RL) to interact collaboratively during cyber defence operations (Mukherjee et al., 2025). By incorporating knowledge of the domain's security issues into the reward function's design, RL-trained agents can learn sophisticated cooperative strategies from their experience in the environment, without having them coded into the agents, allowing them to cope with threats that were not foreseen during design.

11. CHALLENGES AND LIMITATIONS

11.1 Adversarial Robustness

Adversarial attacks represent another threat to which ADA mechanisms are prone, as they involve specially constructed input data that can mislead machine learning models into producing incorrect classification results or lead to detection system bypass, while also enabling malicious purposes. The danger of adversarial attacks is especially great for detection systems based on deep learning algorithms, as such attacks can be carried out via mathematical computations that exploit information about model gradients.

The application of PU learning to improve the performance of cloud DDoS attack detection is an effective way to address the label deficiency and class imbalance inherent in such datasets, where positive examples are fewer than negative ones (Dilworth & Gudla, 2024). The ability of ZeroDay-LLM to resist the threats associated with adversarial attacks is related to its capacity to detect attacks by virtue of semantic behaviour patterns rather than signature-based syntactic detection (Alsuwaiket, 2025).

11.2 False Positive Management and Alert Fatigue

False positives have proved to be an important issue in ADA systems. With large-scale clouds, even small percentages of false positives can lead to many errors, which might overwhelm the response process and cause operators to stop relying on the system. A comparison of Machine Learning algorithms for detecting DDoS attacks in cloud computing shows that false-positive percentages differ significantly among them, depending on the feature-engineering techniques used (Odukoya et al., 2025). The AI-based hybrid intrusion detection method designed by Alhusseini (2026) demonstrates that applying metaheuristic optimisation of model hyperparameters yields a better precision-recall balance.

11.3 Trust, Explainability, and Human Oversight

To implement autonomous systems in high-risk security environments, their decisions must be transparent and accountable to ensure auditability by human stakeholders. SAGA will provide governance strategies for this issue by providing cryptographic proofs that ensure actions taken by the ADA (Added Device Authority) are performed within the limits specified by access control rules created by users (Syros et al., 2025). The Security Logs to ATT&CK Insights framework will provide explainability for autonomous detection decisions by mapping the autonomous detection decision to the MITRE ATT&CK method of attack, a well-known framework used by security professionals, which will allow human operators of autonomous systems to understand and validate the ADA threat assessment for autonomous attacks (Hans et al., 2025). The general issue of model interpretability in AI-based security systems has been widely discussed, and the need to make the methods of adversarial training and anomaly detection addressable to ensure accountability in automated systems has been highlighted (Swetha et al., 2025).

Radanliev et al. (2026) identified multiple threats and vulnerabilities in the context of agentic AI systems, including misaligned agent objectives and adversarial attempts to manipulate agentic reasoning; these pose significant risks to the safe and responsible development of agentic AI systems and require the implementation of appropriate governance frameworks. According to Radanliev et al. (2026), the ability of agentic systems gives rise to new kinds of risks, such as a compromised autonomous system with great powers of action; such a system has the potential to magnify the damage from any attack rather than limit or control it. In this regard, proper techniques for human supervision, including the review of important irreversible decisions, are essential.

11.4 Ethical and Legal Dimensions

The manner in which an organisation can automatically execute security-related response actions raises numerous ethical and legal issues. For instance, the automated isolation of systems is likely to disrupt the operations of legitimate users who depend on those services. The automated revocation of user credentials could cause similar issues with those users' validity. The automated blocking of traffic could unintentionally prevent innocent users from accessing the systems they legitimately use, as a result of an attacker misusing those systems. Therefore, when assessing the collateral damage of automating responses to security events, careful consideration must also be given to the benefits of automation.

The adaptive approach to implementing a unified cybersecurity system for digital product ecosystems using agentic AI incorporates responses that are consistent with the proportionality principle through the implementation of graduated response systems that are calibrated according to the level of threat assessed for a given incident and whether or not there is a reasonable certainty that the assessed threat was valid (Olayinka et al., 2025). By adhering to data protection regulations across jurisdictions (in terms of limiting the collection, processing, or retention of security telemetry), the architecture and deployment of a given Autonomous Digital Assistant (ADA) requires specific consideration of legal issues.

11.5 Scalability and Deployment Challenges

In addition to the opposition, governance, and ethical issues mentioned above, there are major practical scalability challenges in production cloud deployments. The ADA perception layer has to handle large volumes of data ingestion, preprocessing, and storage in large-scale cloud deployments, where telemetry can exceed hundreds of gigabytes per hour. The latency requirements for intelligence-layer inference are extremely stringent: detection algorithms must respond in milliseconds; however, complex deep learning models capable of detecting hidden threats are likely to exceed the latency of conventional hardware.

Resource management also poses a problem when deploying the system. With ADA systems, cloud workloads have access to shared computing resources, which impacts their effectiveness. Scheduling inference-intensive detection processes in the same resource pool as production workloads may negatively impact the latter, leading to performance degradation and availability risks that adversaries can exploit. The solution lies in having an infrastructure solely devoted to security processing; although effective, the approach incurs substantial overhead costs. Effective ways to address this issue include leveraging lightweight model architectures, offloading complex computations to hardware accelerators such as GPUs and specialised AI chips, and designing a hierarchical processing model that analyses only high-value data using complex computations (Mohammed & Hoomod, 2026).

One problem with deploying the system is maintaining operational continuity amid ADA updates. To remain relevant and effective against emerging threats, detection models need to be periodically retrained on updated threat data. New deployments of a newer model version can also lead to regression; however, the newer version of the model may exhibit different false-positive characteristics or show decreased performance on threat categories that were already well handled by the older version. In terms of operations, production ADA systems must be equipped with continuous integration and deployment practices adapted to machine learning models, such as shadow deployment, model version deployment through A/B testing and automated detection of performance regression. Therefore, the continuous learning feedback loop in Figure 2 needs to be supported with strong model lifecycle management practices to maintain continued operational reliability.

12. CONCLUSION

In this study, a thorough analysis of Autonomous Defensive Agents is provided as the critical development in cloud security architecture in the machine-speed era of cyberattacks. As a result of expanding cloud attack surfaces, the limitations of human-speed cyber defence, and the emergence of agentic artificial intelligence algorithms (as evidenced by extensive research in 2025), there is now a need for autonomous cloud defence.

The architectural model developed in this study uses perception capabilities to aggregate IAM logs, network traffic, and endpoint activities with the help of graph neural networks and transformers; intelligent capabilities to evaluate threats using deep learning, MARL, and LLM algorithms; and defensive capabilities to implement a hierarchy of response strategies using cloud APIs. Each of the described capabilities has research support – Madireddy et al. (2025) on IAM-based threat detection via graph neural networks; Alsuwaiket (2025) and Berrios Vasquez et al. (2025) on zero-day attack prevention; Landolt et al. (2025) on MARL-based multi-agent cloud protection; Kalakoti (2025) on autonomous self-healing capability; Li and Zhu (2025) on agentic cybersecurity concept as an overall paradigm.

The game theory-based analysis of the applicability of ADAs in autonomous cyber warfare, as argued by Jiang et al. (2025), Soulé et al. (2025), and Li & Zhu (2025), clearly emphasises the strategic importance of employing autonomous defence systems. Since attackers will use artificial intelligence-based attack systems that can operate in machine mode, human-driven defence systems will simply not be able to keep up because of the inherent latency in the process. The use of multi-agent ADA frameworks for cloud-based defences is thus appropriate in such a scenario.

The difficulties that have been highlighted in Section 11, namely adversarial robustness, false positive handling, explainability, and compliance with ethical and legal requirements, cannot be viewed simply as technical barriers to the development of ADA. Instead, they must be seen as key considerations in how the systems are designed from the outset, incorporating, for instance, SAGA governance mechanisms such as human oversight (Syros et al., 2025), hierarchies of responses that ensure the proportionality of actions, and compliance with relevant legal frameworks for data protection and cybersecurity.

The trend in ADA development will persist as the capabilities of agentic AI grow, the cloud infrastructure scales in size and complexity, and the threat from adversarial automation increases. Indeed, all these developments are already leading to an increasing role for autonomous defender architectures in cloud security. This review provides the necessary background theory, architectural templates, and empirical evidence required for this shift. The burden of enhancing the capabilities of autonomous defenders, as well as developing adequate forms of governance, explainability, and ethics, now lies with academia.

REFERENCES

Adabara, I., Sadiq, B. O., Shuaibu, A. N., Danjuma, Y. I., & Maninti, V. (2025). A review of agentic AI in cybersecurity: Cognitive autonomy, ethical governance, and quantum-resilient defence. *F1000 Research, 14*, 843. DOI: 10.12688/f1000research.169337.1 PMID: 41169871

Alhusseini, M. M. (2026). AI-powered hybrid intrusion detection framework for cloud security using novel metaheuristic optimisation. /arXiv.2601.01134DOI: 10.48550

Alsuwaiket, M. A. (2025). ZeroDay-LLM: A large language model framework for zero-day threat detection in cybersecurity. *Information (Basel), 16*(11), 939. Advance online publication. DOI: 10.3390/info16110939

Appiahene, P., Berchie, O. S., Botchway, E., Ayitey, J. M., Dawson, K. J., Mettle, H. N. A., & Afrifa, S. (2026). Network intrusion detection using hybrid graph-based convolutional network and transformer architecture. *PLoS One*, *21*(1), e0340997. Advance online publication. DOI: 10.1371/journal.pone.0340997 PMID: 41564087

Belenguer, A., Pascual, J. A., & Navaridas, J. (2025). A review of federated learning applications in intrusion detection systems. *Computer Networks, 111023*, 111023. Advance online publication. DOI: 10.1016/j.comnet.2024.111023

Berrios Vasquez, S. I., Hermosilla Monckton, P. A., Leiva Muñoz, D. I., & Allende, H. (2025). Zero-day threat mitigation via deep learning in cloud environments. *Applied Sciences (Basel, Switzerland), 15*(14), 7885. Advance online publication. DOI: 10.3390/app15147885

Dilworth, R., & Gudla, C. (2024). Harnessing PU learning for enhanced cloud-based DDoS detection: A comparative analysis. /arXiv.2410.18380DOI: 10.48550

Eleweke, I., Umakor, M. F., Ndubuisi, C. W., Amomo, C. G., & Adeniji, S. (2025). *AI-driven threat detection and prevention in cloud computing environments*. American Journal of Innovation in Science and Engineering., DOI: 10.54536/ajise.v4i3.5041

Elshewey, A. M., Abbas, S., Osman, A. M., Aldakheel, E. A., & Fouad, Y. (2025). DDoS classification of network traffic in software-defined networking SDN using a hybrid CNN-GRU model. *Scientific Reports*. Advance online publication. DOI: 10.1038/s41598-025-13754-1 PMID: 40781265

Farzaan, M. A. M., Ghanem, M. C., El-Hajjar, A., & Ratnayake, D. N. (2025). An AI-enabled system for efficient and effective cyber incident detection and response in cloud environments. arXiv: 2404.05602

Govindarajan, V., Ahmed, F., Kamaluddin, K., Mushtaq, Z., Alshammari, K., & Khan, F. (2026). *SecureRiskNet: An advanced AI-driven framework for intelligent security risk detection in heterogeneous cloud-fog computing networks*. International Journal of Computational Intelligence Systems., DOI: 10.1007/s44196-025-01117-7

Hans, S., Marsella, S., Hirschmann, S., & Gurney, N. (2025). Security logs to AT-T&CK insights: Leveraging LLMs for high-level threat understanding and cognitive trait inference.arXiv: 2510.20930 DOI: 10.54941/ahfe1007047

Jiang, Y., Oo, N., Meng, Q., Lin, L., Niyato, D., Xiong, Z., Lim, H. W., & Sikdar, B. (2025). CyGATE: Game-theoretic cyber attack-defence engine for patch strategy optimisation.arXiv. /arXiv.2508.00478DOI: 10.48550

Kalakoti, M. K. R.Manoj Kumar Reddy Kalakoti. (2025). AI-augmented self-healing infrastructure: Combining health probes with remediation playbooks. *Journal of Information Systems Engineering & Management, 10*(58s), 1147–1157. Advance online publication. DOI: 10.52783/jisem.v10i58s.12800

Kostiuk, Y. (2025). Multi-agent system for detecting and counteracting attacks on the enterprise information system. DOI: 10.36690/ITSC

Kurra, P. (2025). Securing the cloud with AI: The future of autonomous threat detection. *World Journal of Advanced Research and Reviews, 26*(01), 756–762. https://journalwjarr.com/sites/default/files/fulltext_pdf/WJARR-2025-1081.pdf

Landolt, C. R., Würsch, C., Meier, R., Mermoud, A., & Jang-Jaccard, J. (2025). Multi-agent reinforcement learning in cybersecurity: From fundamentals to applications. arXiv: 2505.19837

Lazer, J. S., Aryal, K., Gupta, M., & Bertino, E. (2026). A survey of agentic AI and cybersecurity: Challenges, opportunities and use-case prototypes. https://arxiv.org/abs/2601.05293

Li, B., Li, J., & Jia, M. (2025). ADFCNN-BiLSTM: A deep neural network based on attention and deformable convolution for network intrusion detection. *Sensors (Basel), 25*(5), 1382. DOI: 10.3390/s25051382 PMID: 40096198

Li, T., & Zhu, Q. (2025). Agentic AI for cyber resilience: A new security paradigm and its system-theoretic foundations. arXiv: 2512.22883

Lin, J., Guo, Y., & Chen, H. (2025). Intrusion detection at scale with the assistance of a command-line language model. /arXiv.2404.13402DOI: 10.48550

Madireddy, V. T. (2025). Graph neural network-based adaptive threat detection for cloud identity and access management logs. https://arxiv.org/abs/2512.10280

Mohammed, A. M., & Hoomod, H. K. (2026). A two-stage hybrid intrusion detection framework based on hierarchical attack mapping and pruned CNN-GRU models. *Engineering, Technology &. Applied Scientific Research, 16*(1), 32342–32347. Advance online publication. DOI: 10.48084/etasr.16210

Morris, A., Procter, R., & Wallbank, C. (2025). Evaluating reinforcement learning agents for autonomous cyber defence. *Applied AI Letters, 6*(3), e125. Advance online publication. DOI: 10.1002/ail2.125

Mukherjee, S., Chatterjee, S., Purvine, E., Fujimoto, T., & Emerson, T. (2025). Large language model-based reward design for deep reinforcement learning-driven autonomous cyber defence. /arXiv.2511.16483DOI: 10.48550

Odukoya, O., Sanusi, M. A., & Adenekan, S. (2025). A comparative study of machine learning algorithms for real-time DDoS detection in cloud environments. *International Journal of Advance Research, Ideas and Innovations in Technology.* https://www.ijariit.com/manuscript/a-comparative-study-of-machine-learning-algorithms-for-real-time-ddos-detection-in-cloud-environments/

Okonkwo, N. P., & Dhirani, L. L. (2025). Cloud security leveraging AI: A fusion-based AISOC for malware and log behaviour detection. /arXiv.2512.14935DOI: 10.48550

Olayinka, O. T., Jeswani, S., & Iloh, D. (2025). Adaptive cybersecurity architecture for digital product ecosystems using agentic AI./arXiv.2509.20640DOI: 10.48550

) Pal, R. K., Desai, T., Singh, J., & Karatapu, H. R. T. (2025). Agentic AI for proactive cyber-resilience in multi-cloud environments. *IJISRT.* ijisrt.com

) Radanliev, P., Santos, O., & Maple, C. (2026). Threats and vulnerabilities in artificial intelligence and agentic AI models. DOI: DOI: 10.3389/frai.2026.1731566

Sarraf, G., & Pal, V. (2025). Autonomous threat detection and response in cloud security: A comprehensive survey of AI-driven strategies. *International Journal of Emerging Research in Engineering and Technology.*arXiv: 2601.03303

Sathaporn, P., Krungseanmuang, W., Chaowalittawin, V., Benjangkaprasert, C., & Purahong, B. (2025). DDoS detection using a hybrid CNN-RNN model enhanced with multi-head attention for cloud infrastructure. *Applied Sciences (Basel, Switzerland), 15*(21), 11567. Advance online publication. DOI: 10.3390/app152111567

Shafi, M. M., Lashkari, A. H., Rodriguez, V., & Nevo, R. (2024). Toward generating a new cloud-based DDoS dataset and cloud intrusion traffic characterisation. *Information (Basel), 15*(195). Advance online publication. DOI: 10.3390/info15040195

Sharma, K., & Jacobik, C. (2025). Graph neural network-based DDoS protection for data centre infrastructure. *PNSQC Proceedings.*/arXiv.2603.13694DOI: 10.48550

Sharma, V., Shah, D., Sharma, S., & Gautam, S. (2024). Artificial intelligence-based intrusion detection system: A detailed survey. *ITM Web of Conferences, 65*, 04002. DOI: 10.1051/itmconf/20246504002

Sheriff, A., Huang, K., Nemeth, Z., & Nakhjiri, M. (2025). ADA: Automated moving target defence for AI workloads via ephemeral infrastructure-native rotation in Kubernetes. /arXiv.2505.23805DOI: 10.48550

Soulé, J., Jamont, J. P., Occello, M., Théron, P., & Traonouez, L. M. (2025). Towards a multi-agent simulation of cyber-attackers and cyber-defenders battles./arXiv.2506.04849DOI: 10.48550

Sowmya, T., & Anita, M. E. A. (2023). A comprehensive review of AI-based intrusion detection systems. *Measurement. Sensors, 28*, 100827. DOI: 10.1016/j.measen.2023.100827

Swetha, T., Kumaran, U., Meena, V. P., & Hameed, A. I. (2025). Leveraging AI for enhanced cybersecurity: A comprehensive review. *Discover Applied Sciences, 7*(6), 584. Advance online publication. DOI: 10.1007/s42452-025-06773-0

Syros, G., Suri, A., Ginesin, J., Nita-Rotaru, C., & Oprea, A. (2025). SAGA: A security architecture for governing AI agentic systems./arXiv.2504.21034DOI: 10.48550

Yan, Y., Huang, K., & Siegel, M. (2025). ISSF: An intelligent security service framework for cloud-native operations. *Journal of Web Engineering*. Advance online publication. DOI: 10.13052/jwe1540-9589.2447

KEY TERMS AND DEFINITIONS

Adversarial Robustness: Refers to a machine learning model's resistance to adversarial attacks through which an input to the model undergoes changes aimed at producing misclassification.

Agentic AI: Artificial intelligence systems capable of acting towards the achievement of complex goals through multistep reasoning, environmental interactions, and instrumental actions, unlike narrow AI technologies designed for solving specific tasks.

Autonomous Cyber Warfare: Cyber warfare that takes place independently, without human intervention at any point during the execution of offensive or defensive tactics, and is conducted using systems with AI capabilities that work entirely on their own.

Autonomous Defensive Agent (ADA): A technology that leverages the power of AI to autonomously carry out the entire security operation cycle of the cloud environment, from monitoring and identifying threats, assessing risks, responding to incidents, to remediation, without the need for human intervention at any stage.

Federated Learning: A type of machine learning in which the process of model training takes place on many machines without the collection of raw data in one location, maintaining privacy while helping detect models evolve collaboratively.

Graph Neural Network (GNN): A type of neural network architecture tailored for processing data structured as graphs that can model interdependent relations among entities like users, roles, and resources for the purpose of identifying threats in cloud security using IAM logs.

MITRE ATT&CK: A publicly available database of tactics, techniques, and procedures (TTPs) of cyber adversaries compiled by analysing cyberattacks in the real world; it is one of the most commonly used standards for classification and detection.

Moving Target Defence (MTD): It is a defensive approach to cybersecurity that involves constantly changing system parameters to ensure adversaries do not obtain stable observation data required to mount a specific attack.

Multi-Agent Reinforcement Learning (MARL): A machine learning approach where more than one intelligent agent learns policies within an environment to act optimally, thereby facilitating collaborative and decentralised decision-making processes for cyber defence coordination.

Perception Layer: The part of an ADA architecture in charge of gathering, combining, and pre-processing security-related information about monitored clouds from various data sources like network traffic and APIs.

Phoenix Remediation: A method for remedying cloud security incidents whereby the cloud service/resource in question is terminated completely and re-created anew based on a known secure state.

Threat Intelligence: Knowledge gained about adversaries' capabilities, techniques, and intentions through the analysis of security incidents, used to inform decisions on detection, response, and defence strategies.

Zero-Day Attack: An exploit on software vulnerabilities that are not known to exist before. At the time of exploitation, no patch or detection signature is available.

Chapter 12
Agentic AI and the Transformation of Cybersecurity Education for Autonomous Cyber Warfare

Sourabh Aggarwal
http://orcid.org/0009-0001-7161-5198
Westcliff University, USA & IAE Business School, Austral University, Argentina

ABSTRACT

The emergence of agentic artificial intelligence is reshaping cybersecurity, shifting from human-centered operations to autonomous, adaptive, and goal-directed systems capable of executing complex tasks with minimal human intervention. While these advances transform offensive and defensive capabilities, cybersecurity education has not evolved at the same pace. Current curricula remain focused on static tools, predefined exercises, and manual analysis, limiting preparedness for dynamic, AI-driven environments. This chapter examines how agentic AI is redefining cybersecurity education and workforce readiness. It introduces the Agentic Cyber Education Framework, integrating technical, cognitive, ethical, and strategic competencies. Drawing on interdisciplinary literature and teaching insights, the chapter explores simulation-based learning, AI-assisted tools, and human–machine collaboration. It concludes by outlining workforce and governance implications, offering a roadmap for educators, institutions, and policymakers.

DOI: 10.4018/979-8-2600-0413-5.ch012

1. INTRODUCTION

Cybersecurity is undergoing a major transformation driven by advances in artificial intelligence (AI) that extend beyond traditional automation toward increasingly autonomous and adaptive systems. Traditional cybersecurity operations relied heavily on human analysts, signature-based detection systems, and rule-driven defenses operating within relatively stable environments. However, the rapid evolution of cyber threats, including adversarial AI techniques, advanced persistent threats, and coordinated multi-vector attacks, has exposed the limitations of static defenses and purely human-centered decision-making models (Brown et al., 2020; Conti et al., 2018).

The emergence of agentic artificial intelligence represents a significant shift in cybersecurity. Unlike conventional automation systems that execute predefined instructions, agentic AI systems can perceive environments, reason across contexts, adapt dynamically, and act autonomously toward defined objectives. These capabilities enable more adaptive and context-aware cybersecurity operations in which human expertise increasingly collaborates with intelligent systems capable of continuous learning and autonomous decision-making (Russell & Norvig, 2021; Poole & Mackworth, 2010).

Several technological developments have accelerated the rise of agentic AI in cybersecurity, including large language models (LLMs), reinforcement learning, and distributed multi-agent systems. These technologies support applications such as vulnerability analysis, anomaly detection, predictive threat intelligence, automated incident response, and AI-assisted cyber operations (Bommasani et al., 2021; Arulkumaran et al., 2017). Consequently, cybersecurity is evolving into a dynamic environment characterized by continuous adaptation and competition between intelligent attackers and intelligent defenders.

Despite these advancements, the integration of agentic AI introduces important technical, cognitive, and ethical challenges. Many AI systems operate as opaque "black-box" models that limit interpretability and reduce trust in high-stakes cybersecurity environments (Doshi-Velez & Kim, 2017). Adversarial machine learning techniques may manipulate AI systems and compromise operational reliability, while autonomous cyber operations raise broader concerns related to accountability, transparency, privacy, and governance (Biggio & Roli, 2018; Floridi et al., 2018).

Although cybersecurity technologies are evolving rapidly, cybersecurity education has not progressed at the same pace. Many academic programs continue to rely on tool-centric instruction, static laboratory exercises, and predefined learning scenarios that inadequately reflect the complexity and uncertainty of AI-driven cyber ecosystems. As a result, students may develop procedural proficiency while lacking the adaptive reasoning, strategic thinking, interdisciplinary understanding, and human–AI collaboration skills required in modern cybersecurity environments (Ahmad et al., 2014).

This growing educational gap has important implications for workforce readiness. Organizations increasingly require cybersecurity professionals capable of operating in environments characterized by intelligent automation, AI-assisted decision-making, and rapidly evolving threats (World Economic Forum, 2020). Beyond technical expertise, professionals must also develop critical thinking, situational awareness, systems reasoning, and ethical judgment while understanding the governance implications of intelligent systems operating within security-critical infrastructures.

To address this gap, this chapter introduces the Agentic Cyber Education Framework, a multidimensional conceptual framework designed to align cybersecurity education with the demands of increasingly autonomous and AI-driven cyber ecosystems. The framework integrates four interconnected competency domains: technical fluency, cognitive adaptability, ethical governance, and strategic orchestration. Together, these domains provide a holistic foundation for preparing cybersecurity professionals capable of operating effectively within environments characterized by intelligent automation, human–AI collaboration, and continuous adaptation.

Methodologically, the chapter adopts a conceptual research design grounded in an integrative review of interdisciplinary literature spanning cybersecurity, artificial intelligence, cybersecurity education, human–machine teaming, AI ethics, and workforce development. Rather than presenting an empirically validated model, the chapter proposes a conceptual synthesis intended to guide future curriculum development, workforce preparation, governance discussions, and educational innovation related to agentic AI and autonomous cyber operations.

The remainder of the chapter examines the role of agentic AI in cybersecurity, analyzes limitations in traditional cybersecurity education, introduces the Agentic Cyber Education Framework, and discusses implications for workforce transformation, governance, human–machine teaming, and future directions in cybersecurity education.

2. AGENTIC AI IN CYBERSECURITY

Agentic artificial intelligence represents a major evolution in AI capabilities, enabling systems to operate with increasing autonomy beyond traditional rule-based automation. Unlike conventional cybersecurity systems that rely on predefined scripts and static workflows, agentic AI systems dynamically adapt to environmental feedback, contextual information, and evolving operational objectives. This shift is particularly important in cybersecurity, where threat environments evolve continuously and the scale of security data increasingly exceeds human cognitive capacity (Russell & Norvig, 2021; Goodfellow et al., 2016).

Agentic systems integrate perception, reasoning, planning, and execution within continuous feedback loops, enabling context-aware cybersecurity operations capable of responding dynamically to emerging threats and rapidly changing attack conditions (Poole & Mackworth, 2010). The technological foundations of agentic AI are primarily grounded in large language models (LLMs), reinforcement learning, and distributed multi-agent systems. These technologies support applications such as threat intelligence analysis, vulnerability assessment, anomaly detection, automated incident response, and AI-assisted decision-making (Bommasani et al., 2021; Arulkumaran et al., 2017).

Multi-agent systems further enhance cybersecurity capabilities by enabling coordination among distributed intelligent entities operating across interconnected infrastructures. In cybersecurity environments, intelligent agents may collaboratively monitor networks, analyze endpoints, correlate threat intelligence, and orchestrate automated responses in real time, thereby supporting adaptive and scalable security architectures (Wooldridge, 2009; Jennings & Wooldridge, 1998).

The growing adoption of agentic AI is transforming both offensive and defensive cybersecurity operations. On the offensive side, AI-assisted cyber capabilities can support reconnaissance, vulnerability identification, automated phishing campaigns, and adaptive malware development (Brundage et al., 2018). Adversarial machine learning techniques may also manipulate AI-driven defense systems and weaken cybersecurity resilience (Biggio & Roli, 2018). On the defensive side, organizations increasingly deploy AI-driven systems to improve anomaly detection, behavioral analytics, predictive threat intelligence, and incident response. Machine learning models can process large volumes of network traffic, user activity, and system logs in real time to identify malicious activity and support rapid decision-making (Buczak & Guven, 2015; Chandola et al., 2009).

Real-world implementations further illustrate the integration of agentic AI into cybersecurity operations. For example, Microsoft Security Copilot integrates generative AI into security workflows to support threat hunting, incident investigation, and remediation tasks. Similarly, CrowdStrike incorporates AI-driven behavioral analytics and automated threat detection into endpoint protection and Security Operations Center (SOC) environments. Frameworks such as MITRE ATT&CK are also increasingly integrated with AI-enabled systems to support adaptive threat analysis and proactive cyber defense strategies (MITRE, 2023).

Despite these advantages, the integration of agentic AI introduces important technical, ethical, and governance challenges. Many AI systems function as opaque "black-box" models, limiting interpretability and reducing trust in high-stakes cybersecurity environments (Doshi-Velez & Kim, 2017). AI systems are also vulnerable to adversarial manipulation, data poisoning, and prompt injection attacks that may compromise reliability and operational effectiveness. Furthermore, excessive dependence on AI-generated outputs may reduce human situational awareness, critical thinking, and independent judgment, making meaningful human oversight essential within AI-enhanced cybersecurity operations (Parasuraman et al., 2000).

Ethical and governance considerations are equally significant. Autonomous cybersecurity systems may generate decisions with organizational, legal, and societal consequences, raising concerns related to accountability, transparency, surveillance, privacy, and fairness (Floridi et al., 2018). These concerns become especially important in the context of autonomous cyber warfare due to the dual-use nature of AI technologies. Consequently, cybersecurity education and operational environments must emphasize responsible AI governance, defensive cybersecurity practices, human oversight, and controlled simulation-based learning rather than unrestricted offensive capabilities.

The rise of agentic AI is ultimately transforming cybersecurity into a continuously adaptive domain in which both attackers and defenders leverage intelligent systems to gain strategic advantages. This transformation requires cybersecurity professionals capable of collaborating effectively with AI systems, critically evaluating machine-generated outputs, and making informed decisions under uncertainty. As a result, cybersecurity education must evolve beyond static tools and procedural exercises toward more adaptive, interdisciplinary, and AI-oriented learning models.

3. THE CYBERSECURITY EDUCATION GAP

The gap between cybersecurity education and professional practice is becoming increasingly significant as the field evolves through artificial intelligence, intelligent automation, and autonomous cyber systems. Traditional cybersecurity education models were largely designed for predictable and human-centered environments, emphasizing procedural learning, static laboratory exercises, certification-oriented preparation, and tool-specific instruction. While these approaches provide foundational technical competencies, they often fail to prepare students for the complexity, uncertainty, and adaptive nature of modern cybersecurity environments shaped by agentic artificial intelligence (Bishop & Frincke, 2008; Conti et al., 2018).

A major limitation of current cybersecurity curricula is the continued reliance on static learning environments and predefined instructional scenarios. Although traditional laboratory exercises support the development of technical skills such as vulnerability assessment and penetration testing, they inadequately represent the dynamic and adversarial conditions of real-world cybersecurity operations. Threat actors continuously adapt their tactics, techniques, and procedures, creating environments characterized by ambiguity, uncertainty, and continuous change (Mirkovic et al., 2010; Sommer & Paxson, 2010). Consequently, traditional instructional approaches often prioritize procedural memorization over critical thinking, situational awareness, adaptive reasoning, and strategic decision-making, limiting students' ability to respond effectively to novel and evolving threats (Cabaj et al., 2018).

Another critical challenge is the insufficient integration of artificial intelligence into cybersecurity education. Despite the growing use of AI-driven systems in anomaly detection, automated response, behavioral analytics, and Security Operations Center (SOC) workflows, many academic programs provide limited exposure to machine learning systems, AI-assisted decision-making, adversarial AI, and autonomous cyber operations (Ahmad et al., 2014; Sarker et al., 2021). This limitation also restricts the development of effective human–machine collaboration competencies, as professionals increasingly need to interpret AI-generated outputs, evaluate system reliability, and integrate intelligent recommendations into broader operational decision-making processes (Apruzzese et al., 2018; Biggio & Roli, 2018).

A broader misalignment also exists between academic curricula and industry workforce requirements. Many cybersecurity programs remain strongly influenced by certification-oriented educational models emphasizing examination preparation and isolated technical competencies rather than systems thinking, interdisciplinary problem-solving, and adaptive reasoning. Simultaneously, the rapid pace of technological change—including AI-enabled threats, cloud-native infrastructures, zero-trust architectures, and AI-driven threat intelligence systems—often exceeds the ability of academic institutions to update curricula effectively (Rani et al., 2022). As a result, course content may become outdated before students graduate, reducing workforce readiness and increasing the burden on employers to provide additional training.

Current cybersecurity education models also frequently underemphasize interdisciplinary and experiential learning. Modern cybersecurity challenges increasingly involve psychological, organizational, legal, ethical, and societal dimensions in addition to technical concerns (Von Solms & Van Niekerk, 2013). However, many programs continue to prioritize narrowly technical instruction while providing limited exposure to collaborative workflows, real-time decision-making, and realistic operational simulations. Although internships, capture-the-flag exercises, and cyber range simulations are becoming more common, these experiences often fail to fully replicate the complexity and unpredictability of operational cybersecurity environments (Cone et al., 2007; Conklin., 2006).

The emergence of agentic AI further amplifies these educational challenges. As cybersecurity operations become increasingly automated and AI-assisted, professionals are transitioning from direct technical execution toward supervisory and strategic roles involving intelligent systems. This shift requires integrated competencies combining technical fluency, cognitive adaptability, ethical reasoning, and strategic coordination. However, many current educational models continue to emphasize isolated tool proficiency rather than systems-level thinking and human–AI collaboration (Floridi et al., 2018).

The consequences of this educational gap are substantial for both organizations and society. Graduates may struggle to transition effectively into professional cybersecurity roles, while organizations face increasing difficulty recruiting professionals with the combination of technical, analytical, cognitive, and strategic competencies required within AI-driven cybersecurity environments (World Economic Forum, 2020). Addressing this gap requires a fundamental rethinking of cybersecurity education through more adaptive, interdisciplinary, experiential, and AI-oriented learning approaches. Educational institutions must integrate AI technologies, realistic cyber range environments, ethical governance, strategic reasoning, and human–machine collaboration into curricula while strengthening collaboration with industry and policymakers to ensure alignment with evolving workforce requirements (Behl & Behl, 2012).

Frameworks such as the National Institute of Standards and Technology Cybersecurity Framework 2.0 and the NICE Cybersecurity Workforce Framework further emphasize the growing importance of integrated competencies, adaptive learning, and workforce alignment within cybersecurity education. These developments indicate that future cybersecurity education must evolve from isolated technical instruction toward integrated socio-technical learning ecosystems capable of preparing students for increasingly intelligent and autonomous cyber environments.

4. METHODOLOGY

This chapter adopts a conceptual research design grounded in an integrative review of interdisciplinary literature combined with practitioner-informed insights from cybersecurity education and simulation-based instructional environments. The conceptual approach is appropriate because the chapter seeks to synthesize emerging developments across cybersecurity, artificial intelligence, human–machine collaboration, workforce transformation, and educational innovation in order to propose a future-oriented educational framework rather than test a specific empirical hypothesis. The methodology, therefore, emphasizes conceptual synthesis, interdisciplinary integration, and framework development to address the growing misalignment between traditional cybersecurity education and the demands of increasingly autonomous and AI-driven cyber ecosystems.

The integrative review methodology enables the synthesis of diverse forms of knowledge across multiple disciplines, including cybersecurity, artificial intelligence, cybersecurity education, human–computer interaction, experiential learning, workforce development, AI governance, and socio-technical systems theory. Unlike systematic reviews that focus narrowly on empirical findings within a single domain, integrative reviews support the development of conceptual frameworks by combining theoretical, technical, pedagogical, and practitioner-oriented perspectives. This approach is particularly suitable for rapidly evolving domains such as agentic AI and autonomous cybersecurity, where interdisciplinary synthesis is necessary to identify emerging trends, competency gaps, and future educational requirements.

The literature reviewed in this chapter included academic journal articles, conference proceedings, professional cybersecurity reports, workforce development frameworks, AI governance publications, and educational research related to AI-enabled learning environments. Particular attention was given to literature addressing large language models, reinforcement learning, multi-agent systems, adversarial machine learning, cyber range pedagogy, explainable AI, human–AI collaboration, adaptive learning systems, and cybersecurity workforce transformation. The review process focused on identifying recurring competency requirements, educational limitations, and emerging operational challenges associated with AI-driven cybersecurity environments.

To strengthen conceptual rigor, the reviewed literature was analyzed through thematic synthesis. Recurring themes identified across the literature included AI-assisted cybersecurity operations, adaptive decision-making, human–machine collaboration, ethical governance, cyber range simulation, interdisciplinary learning, and workforce transformation. These themes were iteratively grouped into broader competency categories that informed the development of the proposed Agentic Cyber Education Framework. Table 1 illustrates how the major themes identified during the integrative review informed the four interconnected framework domains.

Table 1. Literature Themes Informing The Agentic Cyber Education Framework

Literature Theme	Framework Domain
AI-assisted cybersecurity operations	Technical Fluency
Human–AI collaboration and explainability	Cognitive Adaptability
AI ethics and governance	Ethical Governance
Cybersecurity leadership and systems integration	Strategic Orchestration
Cyber range pedagogy and adaptive simulations	Cognitive Adaptability
Workforce transformation and interdisciplinary learning	Strategic Orchestration

Caption: *This table illustrates how recurring themes identified through the integrative literature review informed the development of the four interconnected domains of the Agentic Cyber Education Framework.*

In addition to academic literature, the framework development process was informed by practitioner-oriented insights derived from cybersecurity teaching experience involving simulation-based learning, AI-assisted instructional tools, virtual laboratories, and experiential pedagogical approaches. These applied insights contributed to the identification of practical competency gaps frequently observed in cybersecurity education, particularly in relation to adaptive reasoning, strategic decision-making, ethical awareness, and human–AI collaboration within AI-driven environments. This dual approach enabled the integration of theoretical grounding with applied educational observations, thereby enhancing both conceptual rigor and practical relevance.

The resulting Agentic Cyber Education Framework was developed as a multidimensional and future-oriented model integrating four interconnected competency domains: technical fluency, cognitive adaptability, ethical governance, and strategic orchestration. Together, these domains address the limitations of traditional cybersecurity education by emphasizing adaptive learning, interdisciplinary integration, experiential pedagogy, responsible AI use, and human–machine collaboration. Importantly, the framework is presented as a conceptual contribution intended to guide future curriculum development, cyber range design, workforce preparation, and empirical research related to cybersecurity education in increasingly autonomous and intelligent cyber ecosystems.

5. TRANSFORMING CYBERSECURITY EDUCATION

The rapid integration of artificial intelligence and autonomous systems into cybersecurity operations requires a fundamental transformation of cybersecurity education. Traditional educational models based on procedural exercises, static laboratory environments, and tool-specific instruction are increasingly insufficient for preparing students to operate effectively within dynamic and AI-driven cyber ecosystems. As cybersecurity evolves into a continuously adaptive and intelligence-driven domain, educational institutions must redesign curricula, pedagogical strategies, learning environments, and assessment models to align with emerging technological and workforce realities.

Redefining cybersecurity learning objectives is essential to support this transformation. Conventional educational approaches primarily emphasize procedural knowledge and isolated technical skills, whereas future-oriented cybersecurity education must increasingly prioritize strategic thinking, systems integration, adaptive reasoning, and human–machine collaboration. In agentic environments, cybersecurity professionals are expected not only to operate technical tools but also to supervise intelligent systems, evaluate AI-generated outputs, and make informed decisions under conditions of uncertainty. As illustrated in Table 2, this transition reflects a broader movement from static and predictable instructional environments toward adaptive, AI-assisted, and decision-oriented learning ecosystems.

Table 2. Comparison of Traditional and Agentic Cybersecurity Education

Dimension	Traditional Approach	Agentic AI-Based Approach
Learning Environment	Static labs	Adaptive simulations
Tools	Manual tools	AI-assisted tools
Focus	Procedures	Decision-making
Threat Model	Predictable	Dynamic
Skill Development	Technical skills	Integrated competencies
Assessment	Standardized exams	Scenario-based evaluation
Collaboration	Individual exercises	Human–AI teaming
Learning Pathways	Fixed curriculum	Personalized adaptive learning

Caption: This table illustrates the transition from traditional cybersecurity education models to agentic AI-based approaches, highlighting key differences in learning environments, assessment methods, collaboration models, and competency development.

As shown in Table 2, traditional instructional approaches primarily focus on predictable technical exercises and isolated procedural tasks, whereas agentic AI-based education emphasizes adaptability, interdisciplinary thinking, strategic reasoning, and continuous learning. This shift is essential for preparing students to operate effectively in environments where threats evolve rapidly and intelligent systems increasingly participate in cybersecurity operations.

Figure 1. Transformation from traditional, tool-based cybersecurity education to adaptive, AI-driven and decision-oriented learning environments

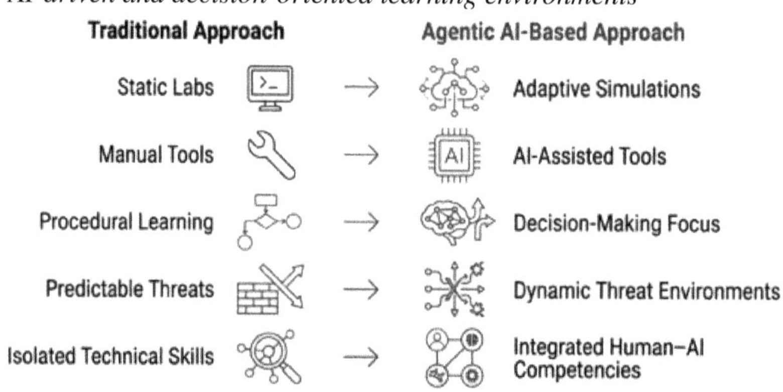

Figure 1 illustrates the broader transformation occurring across cybersecurity education. Interdisciplinary learning is becoming increasingly important because modern cybersecurity challenges involve technical, organizational, psychological, legal, and regulatory dimensions. For example, social engineering attacks exploit cognitive and behavioral vulnerabilities, requiring an understanding of psychology, communication, and human behavior (Hadnagy, 2018). Similarly, issues related to privacy, data governance, and digital regulation require familiarity with legal and ethical frameworks (Kshetri, 2021). Integrating these interdisciplinary perspectives enables students to develop a more comprehensive understanding of cybersecurity as a socio-technical system rather than a purely technical discipline.

Project-based and problem-based learning approaches further support this educational transformation by engaging students in open-ended cybersecurity challenges that require practical application of knowledge, collaborative problem-solving, and adaptive reasoning. For example, students may design secure infrastructures for simulated organizations while considering technical vulnerabilities, regulatory compliance, operational risk, and AI governance constraints (Hmelo-Silver, 2004). When combined with AI-assisted tools and adaptive cyber range environments, these projects become increasingly dynamic through evolving adversarial scenarios and real-time feedback mechanisms.

The role of instructors must also evolve within AI-enhanced learning environments. Traditional cybersecurity education often positions instructors primarily as providers of technical information and procedural instruction. In contrast, agentic learning environments shift educators toward facilitative and mentorship-oriented roles aligned with constructivist approaches to active learning (Vygotsky, 1978). AI systems can support instructional delivery, automate portions of feedback generation, personalize learning pathways, and assist in simulation development, thereby allowing educators to focus more extensively on critical reflection, ethical reasoning, and strategic guidance.

Assessment methodologies similarly require substantial redesign. Traditional examinations and static technical exercises are increasingly inadequate for evaluating higher-order cognitive capabilities such as adaptability, strategic reasoning, situational awareness, and collaborative decision-making. Performance-based and scenario-driven assessments provide more meaningful evaluation of student competencies by simulating real-world cybersecurity conditions and requiring learners to respond dynamically to evolving threats (Gikandi et al., 2011). AI-driven assessment systems can further support adaptive evaluation by providing real-time feedback, tracking learner progression, and personalizing learning experiences according to individual strengths and weaknesses.

Continuous learning pathways supported by AI-driven educational platforms also represent an essential dimension of cybersecurity education transformation.

Given the rapid pace of technological change in cybersecurity, professionals must continuously update their knowledge and skills throughout their careers. Personalized and adaptive learning systems can support lifelong learning by tailoring educational content, recommending targeted skill development pathways, and adjusting instructional complexity based on learner performance (Zawacki-Richter et al., 2019).

Institutional support and industry collaboration are equally critical for implementing these transformations successfully. Partnerships between academia, government, and industry provide access to real-world cybersecurity tools, operational datasets, AI platforms, and emerging threat intelligence, thereby improving curriculum relevance and workforce alignment (Behl & Behl, 2012). Collaborative initiatives involving cyber ranges, internships, industry-sponsored projects, and AI-enabled simulation environments can help bridge the gap between academic preparation and operational cybersecurity practice.

Despite these opportunities, significant implementation challenges remain. AI-assisted educational systems may require substantial investment in computational infrastructure, faculty training, simulation environments, and curriculum redesign. Resistance to pedagogical change may also emerge within traditional institutional structures. Furthermore, the integration of AI into educational environments raises important ethical concerns related to data privacy, algorithmic bias, surveillance, transparency, and equitable access to educational technologies (Williamson & Eynon, 2020). Addressing these challenges requires responsible governance frameworks that ensure ethical and inclusive implementation of AI-enhanced educational systems.

In conclusion, transforming cybersecurity education requires a comprehensive shift toward adaptive, interdisciplinary, experiential, and AI-integrated learning ecosystems. Educational institutions must redesign curricula, instructional models, assessment methods, and learning environments to align with increasingly autonomous and intelligent cyber ecosystems. By integrating AI technologies, human–machine collaboration, adaptive simulations, and ethical governance into cybersecurity education, institutions can better prepare future professionals to operate effectively in complex, rapidly evolving, and agentic cybersecurity environments.

6. THE AGENTIC CYBERSECURITY EDUCATION FRAMEWORK

The transformation of cybersecurity education in the era of agentic artificial intelligence requires a fundamental rethinking of how cybersecurity competencies and learning environments are structured. Traditional educational models emphasizing isolated technical skills, procedural exercises, and linear learning pathways are increasingly insufficient for preparing learners to operate within environments characterized by intelligent automation, distributed decision-making, and continuous adaptation. To address this gap, this chapter introduces the Agentic Cyber Education Framework, a multidimensional model designed to align cybersecurity education with increasingly autonomous and AI-driven cyber ecosystems.

The framework integrates four interconnected competency domains: technical fluency, cognitive adaptability, ethical governance, and strategic orchestration. Together, these domains provide a holistic foundation for preparing cybersecurity professionals capable of operating effectively within environments involving human–machine collaboration, adaptive decision-making, and intelligent cyber operations. The framework conceptualizes cybersecurity as a socio-technical system in which human actors, intelligent machines, organizational processes, and governance structures continuously interact (Holland, 2014; Mitchell, 2009).

Technical fluency represents the foundational domain of the framework but extends beyond traditional cybersecurity competencies such as network security, digital forensics, and penetration testing. Modern cybersecurity professionals increasingly require competencies related to artificial intelligence, machine learning, explainability, prompt design, and AI-assisted decision-making. As AI systems become integrated into anomaly detection, threat intelligence analysis, and automated incident response, professionals must understand how intelligent systems generate outputs and how those outputs should be interpreted and validated within operational environments (Goodfellow et al., 2016; Jordan & Mitchell, 2015).

The second domain, cognitive adaptability, reflects the growing importance of higher-order cognitive capabilities within cybersecurity practice. As cybersecurity operations become increasingly dynamic and AI-assisted, professionals must develop situational awareness, adaptive reasoning, pattern recognition, and decision-making capabilities under uncertainty (Endsley, 2017). This domain emphasizes flexible thinking, interpretation of incomplete information, and the ability to respond effectively to evolving threats. Consequently, experiential learning environments such as adaptive cyber ranges and AI-assisted simulations become essential for developing resilience, critical thinking, and strategic reasoning within realistic operational contexts (Kolb, 1984).

The third domain, ethical governance, addresses the societal, organizational, and regulatory implications of agentic AI within cybersecurity. As intelligent systems increasingly influence surveillance, privacy, access control, and incident response, professionals must understand issues related to accountability, transparency, fairness, adversarial manipulation, and responsible AI use (Floridi et al., 2018). Ethical governance also includes familiarity with cybersecurity regulations, AI governance standards, and compliance frameworks governing the deployment and monitoring of intelligent systems. Educational programs must therefore integrate ethics, governance, policy analysis, and responsible AI practices directly into cybersecurity curricula.

The fourth domain, strategic orchestration, focuses on coordinating complex systems integrating human and machine capabilities across distributed infrastructures. Cybersecurity professionals increasingly require competencies related to systems architecture, workflow integration, risk management, organizational coordination, and strategic decision-making. In AI-enhanced cybersecurity environments, professionals must align technical operations with broader organizational objectives such as resilience, compliance, business continuity, and digital risk management.

A defining characteristic of the Agentic Cyber Education Framework is the interdependence of its four competency domains. Technical, cognitive, ethical, and strategic competencies function as mutually reinforcing capabilities operating within continuous feedback loops. This interdependence is illustrated in Figure 2, which presents the framework as a dynamic and interconnected system supporting adaptive and responsible cybersecurity practice in agentic environments.

Figure 2. The Agentic Cyber Education Framework

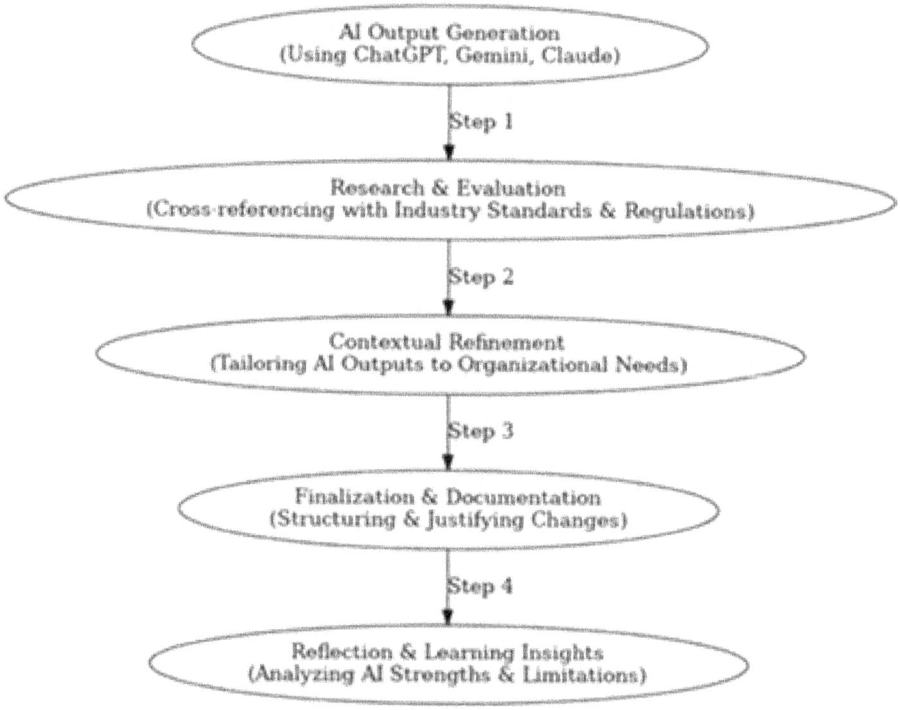

Caption: *The framework illustrates four interconnected competency domains, technical fluency, cognitive adaptability, ethical governance, and strategic orchestration, operating within a continuous feedback system to support adaptive and responsible cybersecurity practice in agentic environments.*

Importantly, the Agentic Cyber Education Framework differs from traditional cybersecurity education models by emphasizing integrated competencies rather than isolated technical proficiencies. Rather than focusing solely on procedural expertise and certification-oriented learning, the framework incorporates adaptive reasoning, ethical governance, human–AI collaboration, and strategic systems thinking. In doing so, it provides a structured foundation for redesigning cybersecurity curricula, cyber range environments, workforce development initiatives, and AI-enhanced educational systems aligned with increasingly autonomous cyber ecosystems.

7. ADVANTAGES OF THE AGENTIC CYBER EDUCATION FRAMEWORK

The Agentic Cyber Education Framework offers several advantages over traditional cybersecurity education models by aligning learning environments, instructional methods, and competency development with the realities of increasingly autonomous and AI-driven cyber ecosystems. Unlike conventional approaches that rely heavily on static laboratory exercises and predictable technical tasks, the framework emphasizes adaptive learning, interdisciplinary integration, human–AI collaboration, and continuous competency development.

One major advantage of the framework is its emphasis on adaptability within cybersecurity education. Traditional cybersecurity laboratories frequently operate within predefined environments where learners follow procedural instructions to achieve expected outcomes. While effective for foundational learning, these environments often fail to reflect the uncertainty and unpredictability of real-world cybersecurity operations. In contrast, the Agentic Cyber Education Framework incorporates adaptive simulations, evolving scenarios, and AI-assisted learning environments that require learners to develop situational awareness, adaptive reasoning, and decision-making capabilities under uncertain conditions (Endsley, 2017; Kolb, 1984).

A second advantage is the framework's stronger alignment with contemporary cybersecurity practice. Modern cybersecurity operations increasingly integrate artificial intelligence, automation, behavioral analytics, and AI-assisted decision-making into Security Operations Centers (SOCs), incident response processes, and threat intelligence workflows. By incorporating AI-enabled tools, cyber ranges, simulation-based learning, and human–machine collaboration directly into educational environments, the framework better reflects operational realities and improves workforce readiness (Behl & Behl, 2012; World Economic Forum, 2020).

The framework also strengthens competencies related to human–AI collaboration. As cybersecurity professionals increasingly work alongside intelligent systems capable of analysis, prioritization, and decision support, learners must develop the ability to interpret AI-generated outputs, validate recommendations, calibrate trust, and maintain independent judgment. The framework explicitly integrates these competencies into cybersecurity education, preparing students for environments characterized by integrated human–machine collaboration (Parasuraman et al., 2000; Amershi et al., 2019).

Another important advantage is the framework's interdisciplinary and holistic orientation. Contemporary cybersecurity challenges increasingly involve organizational, ethical, legal, psychological, and societal dimensions in addition to technical concerns. By integrating technical fluency, cognitive adaptability, ethical governance, and strategic orchestration into a unified educational structure, the framework encourages systems thinking and supports understanding of cybersecurity as a socio-technical challenge rather than a purely technical problem (Floridi et al., 2018; Von Solms & Van Niekerk, 2013).

The framework further supports the development of higher-order cognitive capabilities increasingly required within modern cybersecurity practice. Rather than focusing solely on procedural learning and technical tool proficiency, the framework emphasizes critical thinking, adaptive problem-solving, strategic reasoning, and reflective analysis through experiential and simulation-based learning environments (Ericsson et al., 1993).

An additional advantage involves support for continuous and personalized learning pathways. AI-driven educational systems can adapt instructional content, recommend targeted skill development, and personalize learning experiences according to learner performance and evolving workforce requirements (Siemens, 2013; Holmes, 2019). This adaptability helps educational systems remain responsive to rapid technological change while supporting ongoing professional development.

The framework also benefits institutions and organizations by improving curriculum relevance, workforce preparedness, and graduate employability. Importantly, it promotes responsible and ethical implementation of AI within cybersecurity education by emphasizing defensive cybersecurity practices, governance, human oversight, and responsible AI integration rather than unrestricted offensive capabilities. Ethical reasoning and accountability are therefore embedded throughout the framework, supporting responsible cybersecurity practice within increasingly autonomous digital environments.

In summary, the Agentic Cyber Education Framework enhances adaptability, strengthens human–AI collaboration, promotes interdisciplinary learning, supports higher-order cognitive development, and aligns cybersecurity education more closely with contemporary operational environments. By integrating technical, cognitive, ethical, and strategic dimensions into a unified educational model, the framework provides a future-oriented foundation for preparing cybersecurity professionals capable of operating effectively within increasingly intelligent and adaptive cyber ecosystems.

8. HUMAN-MACHINE TEAMING IN CYBERSECURITY

The rise of agentic artificial intelligence has transformed cybersecurity from a purely human-operated discipline into an environment characterized by human–machine collaboration. As cyber threats increase in scale, speed, and complexity, cybersecurity professionals increasingly work alongside intelligent systems capable of autonomous analysis, adaptive reasoning, and decision support. Rather than replacing human expertise entirely, AI systems enhance cybersecurity operations by automating repetitive tasks, processing large-scale data, identifying anomalies, and supporting rapid operational decision-making (Endsley, 2017).

Human–machine collaboration is now embedded across many cybersecurity functions. AI-driven platforms such as Security Information and Event Management (SIEM) systems, extended detection and response (XDR) platforms, and AI-assisted threat intelligence tools continuously analyze network telemetry, endpoint activity, and system logs to identify suspicious behavior and potential threats. Human analysts then interpret outputs, validate recommendations, and determine appropriate responses. In incident response workflows, AI systems may automate alert triage, correlate threat intelligence, and recommend remediation actions, enabling cybersecurity professionals to focus more extensively on strategic analysis and complex investigations (Shneiderman, 2020).

The growing integration of AI into Security Operations Centers (SOCs) further illustrates this transformation. For example, Microsoft Security Copilot integrates generative AI into cybersecurity workflows to support threat hunting and incident response, while CrowdStrike uses AI-driven behavioral analytics to enhance threat detection and operational response. These developments demonstrate how cybersecurity is evolving toward collaborative human–machine ecosystems.

Effective human–machine teaming, however, requires careful operational integration. Situational awareness, trust calibration, and explainability remain critical for successful collaboration between human operators and intelligent systems. Cybersecurity professionals must interpret AI-generated outputs, evaluate system reliability, and maintain informed oversight under conditions of uncertainty. Limited transparency may reduce trust in AI-generated recommendations, while excessive reliance on automation may weaken human vigilance and independent judgment (Lee & See, 2004; Parasuraman et al., 2000). Explainable AI techniques therefore play an important role in improving interpretability and supporting informed human oversight within AI-enhanced cybersecurity environments (Guidotti et al., 2018).

The integration of AI into cybersecurity operations also raises important governance and accountability concerns. In AI-enhanced environments, decision-making authority may become distributed across both human and machine actors, creating ambiguity regarding responsibility and operational accountability. Addressing these challenges requires governance structures, oversight mechanisms, and clearly defined human responsibilities capable of ensuring responsible AI deployment (Floridi et al., 2018).

Cybersecurity education therefore plays a central role in preparing professionals for effective human–machine collaboration. Traditional training approaches often focus on technical procedures and isolated tool usage while providing limited exposure to AI-assisted operational environments. As intelligent systems become increasingly embedded within cybersecurity practice, educational programs must help learners develop competencies related to interpreting AI-generated outputs, evaluating system reliability, calibrating trust appropriately, and making informed decisions within AI-enhanced environments. Simulation-based learning environments, adaptive cyber ranges, and AI-assisted incident response exercises are particularly valuable because they expose students to realistic scenarios requiring collaboration with intelligent systems, adaptive reasoning, and strategic decision-making under pressure.

Importantly, human–machine teaming in cybersecurity should remain grounded in responsible and human-centered principles. Although AI systems may increasingly automate technical tasks and contribute to operational decision-making, meaningful human oversight remains essential, particularly within critical infrastructure and autonomous cyber operations. Human operators must retain authority to evaluate recommendations, intervene when necessary, and ensure alignment with ethical standards, organizational objectives, and legal frameworks.

In conclusion, human–machine teaming represents a defining characteristic of modern cybersecurity environments. By combining the complementary strengths of human expertise and artificial intelligence, organizations can improve their ability to detect, analyze, and respond to evolving cyber threats. However, effective collaboration requires careful attention to explainability, governance, trust calibration, and responsible AI integration. Cybersecurity education therefore, remains essential for preparing professionals capable of operating effectively within increasingly intelligent and adaptive cyber ecosystems.

9. WORKFORCE TRANSFORMATION AND SKILLS DEVELOPMENT

The integration of agentic artificial intelligence into cybersecurity is fundamentally reshaping workforce requirements, transforming both professional roles and the competencies needed to perform them effectively. As intelligent systems increasingly assume responsibility for repetitive and data-intensive tasks, cybersecurity professionals are shifting toward higher-order functions involving strategic oversight, adaptive decision-making, governance, and coordination across complex socio-technical systems. This transition reflects a broader movement from task execution toward augmentation, where the primary value of human expertise lies in supervising, interpreting, validating, and governing intelligent systems rather than performing repetitive technical activities manually (McAfee & Brynjolfsson, 2017; Davenport & Kirby, 2016).

A central implication of this transformation is the redefinition of core cybersecurity competencies. Traditional cybersecurity roles frequently emphasized technical execution tasks such as vulnerability scanning, firewall configuration, malware analysis, and manual incident response. Although these capabilities remain important, modern cybersecurity environments increasingly require professionals to combine technical expertise with analytical reasoning, strategic thinking, human–AI collaboration, and organizational coordination. Cybersecurity professionals must now interpret AI-generated insights, evaluate system recommendations, manage operational uncertainty, and make informed decisions within rapidly evolving threat environments.

The rise of agentic AI also increases the importance of interdisciplinary competencies. Cybersecurity now intersects with artificial intelligence, data science, cognitive psychology, organizational behavior, governance, ethics, and strategic management. Understanding machine learning concepts is essential for evaluating AI-assisted threat detection systems and identifying adversarial vulnerabilities, while knowledge of governance frameworks and ethical AI practices is increasingly important for ensuring accountability and responsible deployment of intelligent systems (World Economic Forum, 2020; Kshetri, 2021). Consequently, future cybersecurity professionals must operate effectively within increasingly interdisciplinary and socio-technical environments.

Educational institutions must therefore redesign cybersecurity curricula to align with these evolving workforce requirements. Rather than focusing exclusively on isolated technical training, educational programs should integrate competencies related to AI fundamentals, ethical decision-making, adaptive reasoning, strategic coordination, and data analytics. Project-based, collaborative, and simulation-driven learning approaches are particularly valuable because they expose students to realistic cybersecurity challenges requiring interdisciplinary thinking and operational problem-solving. These reforms help prepare learners for cybersecurity environments characterized by intelligent automation, continuous adaptation, and human–machine collaboration.

Continuous learning and professional adaptability are also becoming increasingly important within AI-driven cybersecurity environments. The rapid pace of technological innovation means that cybersecurity competencies can quickly become outdated as new threats, AI capabilities, and operational practices emerge. Institutions and organizations therefore play an important role in supporting workforce development through flexible learning pathways, online learning environments, micro-credentials, modular certification programs, and AI-assisted educational platforms capable of supporting ongoing reskilling and professional development (Siemens, 2013).

The transformation of the cybersecurity workforce is also reflected in the emergence of new professional roles requiring specialized and interdisciplinary expertise. As illustrated in Table 3, emerging cybersecurity roles increasingly combine technical fluency with cognitive adaptability, ethical awareness, governance knowledge, and strategic coordination capabilities.

Table 3. Emerging Cybersecurity Roles in the Agentic AI Era

Role	Description	Key Skills
AI Security Analyst	Monitors AI-driven threats	ML basics, threat analysis
Prompt Security Engineer	Designs secure AI prompts	Prompt engineering, validation
Human-AI Interaction Specialist	Optimizes collaboration	UX, cognition
Autonomous Systems Auditor	Evaluates AI systems	Ethics, compliance
Cyber Strategy Architect	Designs AI-integrated systems	Strategy, systems thinking

Caption: This table highlights emerging roles in cybersecurity shaped by the integration of agentic AI, emphasizing the shift toward interdisciplinary and strategic skill sets.

As illustrated in Table 3, roles such as AI Security Analyst and Prompt Security Engineer demonstrate the increasing importance of AI-specific expertise within cybersecurity operations. AI Security Analysts must understand how intelligent systems identify anomalies, process behavioral data, and support automated threat detection, while Prompt Security Engineers focus on securing large language model interactions and preventing malicious prompt manipulation and adversarial exploitation of generative AI systems. Similarly, Human–AI Interaction Specialists focus on improving explainability, situational awareness, interface usability, and trust calibration within AI-enhanced operational environments, while Autonomous Systems Auditors evaluate intelligent systems for transparency, compliance, accountability, and ethical alignment (Floridi et al., 2018).

The Cyber Strategy Architect role further reflects the growing importance of systems-oriented cybersecurity leadership. Professionals operating within this domain are responsible for designing and coordinating complex cybersecurity ecosystems that integrate AI-driven technologies, governance policies, operational workflows, and organizational objectives. This role requires strong systems thinking, strategic planning, interdisciplinary communication, and risk management capabilities. Cybersecurity professionals increasingly need to translate technical findings into actionable organizational insights while aligning cybersecurity initiatives with broader priorities such as resilience, compliance, and digital transformation.

Despite these opportunities, workforce transformation also presents significant challenges. One major concern involves the growing cybersecurity skills gap. Demand for professionals possessing interdisciplinary and AI-related competencies may significantly outpace workforce supply, creating shortages of qualified personnel capable of operating effectively within intelligent cyber ecosystems. Organizations may struggle to recruit individuals with the necessary combination of technical expertise, cognitive adaptability, strategic reasoning, and ethical awareness. Addressing this challenge requires coordinated collaboration among educational institutions, industry organizations, governments, and policymakers to expand workforce development opportunities and support ongoing professional training (OECD, 2021).

The increasing integration of AI into workforce development additionally raises ethical and societal concerns related to automation, surveillance, workforce displacement, and decision-making authority. Organizations must ensure that AI-enabled workforce transformation remains aligned with ethical principles, responsible governance practices, and meaningful human oversight. Although intelligent systems may automate numerous operational tasks, human professionals remain essential for contextual reasoning, ethical judgment, strategic coordination, and organizational accountability. Future cybersecurity workforces must therefore be prepared to function effectively within collaborative human–AI environments rather than viewing automation solely as technological replacement.

In conclusion, agentic AI is fundamentally transforming the cybersecurity workforce by redefining professional roles, competency requirements, organizational structures, and operational practices. As highlighted in Table 3, emerging cybersecurity roles increasingly require interdisciplinary expertise, strategic reasoning, ethical awareness, and AI-related competencies alongside traditional technical skills. Continuous learning, adaptability, and human–AI collaboration are becoming essential characteristics of cybersecurity professionals operating within intelligent and autonomous cyber ecosystems. By aligning educational systems and workforce development strategies with these evolving demands, institutions can play a central role in preparing the next generation of cybersecurity professionals for an increasingly AI-driven future.

10. POLICY, GOVERNANCE, AND ETHICAL IMPLICATIONS

The integration of agentic artificial intelligence into cybersecurity introduces complex policy, governance, and ethical challenges that extend beyond technical implementation. As autonomous systems increasingly participate in cybersecurity operations and decision-making processes, traditional governance models are becoming insufficient for managing emerging socio-technical risks. Earlier cybersecurity governance frameworks were largely designed for environments in which human operators retained primary control over operational decisions. In contrast, agentic AI systems possess the capacity to learn, adapt, reason, and act autonomously toward predefined objectives, thereby creating new forms of distributed human–machine decision-making that challenge conventional assumptions regarding oversight, accountability, and control (Cath, 2018; Rahwan et al., 2019).

One of the most significant governance challenges associated with agentic AI involves accountability. In traditional cybersecurity environments, operational responsibility can generally be traced to specific individuals or organizational roles. However, in AI-enhanced ecosystems, decision-making authority is increasingly distributed across developers, organizations, AI systems, vendors, and operational users. When autonomous systems generate incorrect classifications, fail to detect malicious activity, or produce harmful operational outcomes, assigning responsibility becomes substantially more difficult (Floridi et al., 2018; Mittelstadt et al., 2016). Addressing these challenges requires both technical safeguards and governance mechanisms. Organizations increasingly rely on audit trails, explainable AI systems, logging infrastructures, and continuous monitoring to improve visibility into AI-generated decisions and support operational oversight. At the governance level, clear frameworks defining the responsibilities of developers, analysts, administrators, and organizational leadership remain essential for ensuring meaningful human oversight within AI-enhanced cybersecurity environments.

Transparency represents another critical dimension of AI governance in cybersecurity. Many advanced AI models, particularly deep learning systems and large language models, function as opaque "black-box" systems whose internal reasoning processes remain difficult to interpret. Although these models may achieve high operational performance, limited interpretability can reduce user trust and confidence in AI-generated outputs, particularly within high-risk cybersecurity environments (Doshi-Velez & Kim, 2017). Explainable AI has therefore emerged as an important strategy for improving transparency and supporting trustworthy human–AI collaboration. In cybersecurity contexts, explainability enhances situational awareness and supports informed decision-making by allowing analysts to better interpret AI-generated recommendations and operational outcomes (Guidotti et al., 2018). However, improving explainability often introduces trade-offs between interpretability and system performance, creating ongoing challenges for AI-enabled cybersecurity systems.

Ethical considerations are equally central to the governance of agentic AI in cybersecurity. Autonomous systems possess significant dual-use potential because they may be deployed for both defensive and offensive cyber operations. Defensive applications include anomaly detection, threat intelligence analysis, and automated incident response, whereas offensive applications may involve autonomous vulnerability exploitation, AI-assisted phishing campaigns, and adaptive cyberattacks. The increasing autonomy of these systems raises concerns regarding unintended escalation, collateral damage, and loss of human control, particularly within critical infrastructure environments (Brundage et al., 2018). Responsible implementation of agentic AI, therefore, requires adherence to ethical principles including fairness, accountability, transparency, privacy protection, and meaningful human oversight throughout the lifecycle of intelligent cybersecurity systems (Jobin et al., 2019).

Educational institutions also play a critical role in preparing future cybersecurity professionals to navigate governance and ethical challenges responsibly. Cybersecurity education should not focus exclusively on technical implementation but must also incorporate ethical reasoning, AI governance, legal compliance, explainability, accountability, and responsible AI use into cybersecurity curricula. Learners should develop the ability to critically evaluate AI systems, recognize governance limitations, and understand the broader societal implications of autonomous cybersecurity technologies. Simulation-based environments and AI-assisted cyber exercises can further support ethical awareness by exposing students to realistic scenarios involving governance dilemmas, operational trade-offs, and human oversight challenges.

Policy development related to agentic AI in cybersecurity continues to evolve globally. Governments, international organizations, and industry groups are actively developing frameworks intended to guide the responsible deployment of intelligent systems. For example, the National Institute of Standards and Technology AI Risk Management Framework emphasizes risk assessment, governance structures, transparency, and continuous monitoring in AI deployment (NIST, 2023). Similarly, the Organisation for Economic Co-operation and Development AI Principles promote international norms related to trustworthy, human-centered, and accountable AI systems (OECD, 2021). However, rapid technological advancement continues to challenge policymakers because regulatory frameworks frequently lag behind innovation. Policymakers must therefore adopt adaptive governance approaches capable of responding to emerging risks while still supporting technological innovation.

Importantly, governance models related to autonomous cyber operations must continue to prioritize defensive cybersecurity, responsible AI deployment, and meaningful human oversight. Educational and operational environments should emphasize resilience, ethical governance, and controlled simulation-based learning rather than unrestricted offensive AI capabilities. Human operators must retain authority to evaluate AI-generated recommendations, intervene in operational decisions, and ensure alignment with organizational objectives, legal frameworks, and ethical principles. Maintaining human-centered governance remains essential for preserving trust, accountability, and societal legitimacy within increasingly autonomous cybersecurity ecosystems.

In conclusion, the integration of agentic AI into cybersecurity introduces complex governance, policy, and ethical challenges requiring coordinated technical, organizational, and regulatory responses. Issues related to accountability, transparency, explainability, human oversight, and responsible AI use are central to ensuring trustworthy and effective cybersecurity operations. Although emerging governance frameworks such as the National Institute of Standards and Technology AI Risk Management Framework and the Organisation for Economic Co-operation and Development AI Principles provide valuable guidance, governance systems must continue evolving to keep pace with technological transformation. By integrating technical safeguards, ethical principles, adaptive governance structures, and human-centered oversight, organizations and governments can support innovation while maintaining accountability, trust, and responsible use of agentic AI within cybersecurity environments.

11. FUTURE DIRECTIONS IN CYBERSECURITY EDUCATION

The future of cybersecurity education will be shaped by the continued evolution of agentic artificial intelligence and its integration into cybersecurity operations, digital infrastructures, and professional practice. As intelligent systems become increasingly autonomous and adaptive, cybersecurity education must evolve beyond traditional tool-based instruction toward more adaptive, interdisciplinary, and AI-driven learning environments (Schwab, 2017; Dwivedi et al., 2021).

One important future direction is the increasing use of immersive and experiential learning technologies such as virtual reality (VR), augmented reality (AR), extended reality (XR), and adaptive cyber ranges. These environments enable learners to engage with realistic threat scenarios, practice incident response, and develop decision-making skills within dynamic simulations (Radianti et al., 2020). The integration of agentic AI further enhances these environments through adaptive attack simulations and personalized learning experiences that respond to learner performance and evolving skill requirements (Zawacki-Richter et al., 2019; Luckin, 2018).

Future cybersecurity education will also place greater emphasis on higher-order cognitive skills, including critical thinking, adaptive problem-solving, ethical reasoning, systems thinking, and human–AI collaboration. As intelligent systems automate routine technical tasks, professionals will increasingly contribute through strategic interpretation and decision-making. Educational programs must therefore integrate interdisciplinary learning, AI governance, ethics, and human oversight into cybersecurity curricula (Floridi et al., 2018; Jobin et al., 2019).

Partnerships among academia, industry, and government will remain important for strengthening workforce readiness and curriculum relevance through cyber ranges, AI-assisted platforms, internships, and simulation-based learning environments (Behl & Behl, 2012). Additionally, emerging technologies such as Internet of Things (IoT) systems, autonomous vehicles, industrial control systems, and AI-enabled robotics will continue expanding the scope of cybersecurity education and research.

Importantly, future cybersecurity education must remain grounded in responsible and defensive cybersecurity practices. Educational environments should prioritize ethical governance, resilience, human oversight, and controlled simulation-based learning rather than unrestricted offensive operations. In conclusion, the future of cybersecurity education lies in integrating immersive technologies, adaptive learning systems, interdisciplinary collaboration, and responsible human–AI interaction to prepare professionals for increasingly intelligent and autonomous cyber environments.

12. CONCLUSION

The emergence of agentic artificial intelligence is fundamentally transforming cybersecurity by reshaping both cyber threats and the strategies required to address them. As intelligent systems become increasingly capable of autonomous reasoning, adaptation, and decision-making, cybersecurity is evolving into a dynamic ecosystem characterized by continuous interaction between human and machine agents (Russell & Norvig, 2021; Dwivedi et al., 2021).

This transformation is also redefining the role of cybersecurity professionals. Rather than functioning solely as technical operators, professionals are increasingly acting as supervisors, strategists, and collaborators working alongside intelligent systems. While AI provides scalability, automation, and analytical capabilities, human expertise remains essential for contextual interpretation, ethical judgment, adaptive reasoning, and governance oversight (Shneiderman, 2020).

This chapter argued that traditional cybersecurity education models are increasingly insufficient for preparing learners to operate within these evolving environments. Conventional approaches often emphasize procedural instruction, static laboratory exercises, and isolated technical competencies while underemphasizing higher-order cognitive, interdisciplinary, and ethical capabilities necessary for AI-driven cybersecurity ecosystems.

To address this gap, the chapter introduced the Agentic Cyber Education Framework, which integrates four interconnected domains: technical fluency, cognitive adaptability, ethical governance, and strategic orchestration. The framework provides a more holistic and future-oriented approach to cybersecurity education by emphasizing interdisciplinary integration, adaptive learning, human–AI collaboration, and continuous competency development (Holland, 2014).

The chapter also highlighted broader implications for workforce transformation, governance, and educational innovation. As intelligent systems increasingly automate routine cybersecurity tasks, demand is growing for professionals capable of strategic analysis, interdisciplinary coordination, ethical reasoning, and adaptive decision-making. At the same time, responsible AI governance, human oversight, immersive learning environments, and adaptive educational systems are becoming increasingly important within cybersecurity education and practice.

Importantly, the transformation of cybersecurity education must remain grounded in responsible and defensive cybersecurity principles. Educational and operational environments should prioritize resilience, ethical governance, human oversight, and controlled simulation-based learning rather than unrestricted offensive cyber capabilities. Meaningful human involvement remains essential for ensuring that intelligent systems operate in ways aligned with organizational objectives, societal values, and ethical standards.

In conclusion, transforming cybersecurity education represents both a technological necessity and a broader societal imperative. By adopting integrated and future-oriented frameworks such as the Agentic Cyber Education Framework, educational institutions can help prepare resilient, adaptive, and ethically grounded cybersecurity professionals capable of operating effectively within increasingly intelligent and autonomous cyber environments.

REFERENCES

Ahmad, A., Maynard, S. B., & Park, S. (2014). Information security strategies: Towards an organizational multi-strategy perspective. *Journal of Intelligent Manufacturing*, *25*(2), 357–370. DOI: 10.1007/s10845-012-0683-0

Amershi, S., Weld, D., Vorvoreanu, M., Fourney, A., Nushi, B., Collisson, P., Suh, J., Iqbal, S. T., Bennett, P. N., Inkpen, K., Teevan, J., Kikin-Gil, R., & Horvitz, E. (2019). Guidelines for human–AI interaction. In *Proceedings of the 2019 CHI Conference on Human Factors in Computing Systems* (pp. 1–13). https://doi.org/ DOI: 10.1145/3290605.3300233

Apruzzese, G., Colajanni, M., Ferretti, L., Guido, A., & Marchetti, M. (2018, May). On the effectiveness of machine and deep learning for cyber security. In *2018 10th International Conference on Cyber Conflict (CyCon)* (pp. 371-390). IEEE. https://doi.org/DOI: 10.23919/CYCON.2018.8405026

Arulkumaran, K., Deisenroth, M. P., Brundage, M., & Bharath, A. A. (2017). A brief survey of deep reinforcement learning. *arXiv preprint arXiv:1708.05866*. https://doi.org//arXiv.1708.05866DOI: 10.48550

Behl, A., & Behl, K. (2012). An analysis of cloud computing security issues. In *2012 World Congress on Information and Communication Technologies* (pp. 109-114). IEEE. https://doi.org/DOI: 10.1109/WICT.2012.6409059

Biggio, B., & Roli, F. (2018). Wild patterns: Ten years after the rise of adversarial machine learning. In *Proceedings of the 2018 ACM SIGSAC Conference on Computer and Communications Security* (pp. 2154-2156). https://doi.org/DOI: 10.1145/3243734.3264418

Bishop, M., & Frincke, D. A. (2008). Information assurance education: A work in progress. *IEEE Security and Privacy*, *6*(5), 54–57. DOI: 10.1109/MSP.2008.123

Bommasani, R., Hudson, D. A., Adeli, E., Altman, R., Arora, S., von Arx, S., . . . Liang, P. (2021). On the opportunities and risks of foundation models. *arXiv preprint arXiv:2108.07258*. https://doi.org//arXiv.2108.07258DOI: 10.48550

Brown, T., Mann, B., Ryder, N., Subbiah, M., Kaplan, J. D., Dhariwal, P., & Amodei, D. (2020). Language models are few-shot learners. *Advances in Neural Information Processing Systems*, *33*, 1877–1901. DOI: 10.48550/arXiv.2005.14165

Brundage, M., Avin, S., Clark, J., Toner, H., Eckersley, P., Garfinkel, B., . . . Amodei, D. (2018). The malicious use of artificial intelligence: Forecasting, prevention, and mitigation. *arXiv preprint arXiv:1802.07228*. https://doi.org//arXiv.1802.07228DOI: 10.48550

Buczak, A. L., & Guven, E. (2015). A survey of data mining and machine learning methods for cyber security intrusion detection. *IEEE Communications Surveys and Tutorials*, *18*(2), 1153–1176. DOI: 10.1109/COMST.2015.2494502

Cabaj, K., Domingos, D., Kotulski, Z., & Respício, A. (2018). Cybersecurity education: Evolution of the discipline and analysis of master programs. *Computers & Security*, *75*, 24–35. DOI: 10.1016/j.cose.2018.01.015

Cath, C. (2018). Governing artificial intelligence: Ethical, legal and technical opportunities and challenges. *Philosophical Transactions. Series A, Mathematical, Physical, and Engineering Sciences*, *376*(2133), 20180080. Advance online publication. DOI: 10.1098/rsta.2018.0080 PMID: 30322996

Chandola, V., Banerjee, A., & Kumar, V. (2009). Anomaly detection: A survey. *ACM Computing Surveys*, *41*(3), 1–58. DOI: 10.1145/1541880.1541882

Cone, B. D., Irvine, C. E., Thompson, M. F., & Nguyen, T. D. (2007). A video game for cyber security training and awareness. *Computers & Security*, *26*(1), 63–72. DOI: 10.1016/j.cose.2006.10.005

Conklin, A. (2006, January). Cyber defense competitions and information security education: An active learning solution for a capstone course. In *Proceedings of the 39th Annual Hawaii International Conference on System Sciences (HICSS'06)* (Vol. 9, pp. 220b-220b). IEEE. https://doi.org/DOI: 10.1109/HICSS.2006.110

Conti, M., Dehghantanha, A., Franke, K., & Watson, S. (2018). Internet of Things security and forensics: Challenges and opportunities. *Future Generation Computer Systems*, *78*, 544–546. DOI: 10.1016/j.future.2017.07.060

Davenport, T. H., & Kirby, J. (2016). *Only humans need apply: Winners and losers in the age of smart machines* (Vol. 1). Harper Business.

Doshi-Velez, F., & Kim, B. (2017). Towards a rigorous science of interpretable machine learning. *arXiv preprint arXiv:1702.08608*. https://doi.org//arXiv.1702.08608DOI: 10.48550

Dwivedi, Y. K., Hughes, D. L., Ismagilova, E., Aarts, G., Coombs, C., Crick, T., Duan, Y., Dwivedi, R., Edwards, J., Eirug, A., Galanos, V., Ilavarasan, P. V., Janssen, M., Jones, P., Kar, A. K., Kizgin, H., Kronemann, B., Lal, B., Lucini, B., & Williams, M. D. (2021). Artificial intelligence (AI): Multidisciplinary perspectives on emerging challenges, opportunities, and agenda for research. *International Journal of Information Management*, *57*, 101994. DOI: 10.1016/j.ijinfomgt.2019.08.002

Endsley, M. R. (2017). From here to autonomy: Lessons learned from human–automation research. *Human Factors*, *59*(1), 5–27. DOI: 10.1177/0018720816681350 PMID: 28146676

Ericsson, K. A., Krampe, R. T., & Tesch-Römer, C. (1993). The role of deliberate practice in the acquisition of expert performance. *Psychological Review*, *100*(3), 363–406. DOI: 10.1037/0033-295X.100.3.363

Floridi, L., Cowls, J., Beltrametti, M., Chatila, R., Chazerand, P., Dignum, V., Luetge, C., Madelin, R., Pagallo, U., Rossi, F., Schafer, B., Valcke, P., & Vayena, E. (2018). AI4People—An ethical framework for a good AI society: Opportunities, risks, principles, and recommendations. *Minds and Machines*, *28*(4), 689–707. DOI: 10.1007/s11023-018-9482-5 PMID: 30930541

Gikandi, J. W., Morrow, D., & Davis, N. E. (2011). Online formative assessment in higher education: A review of the literature. *Computers & Education*, *57*(4), 2333–2351. DOI: 10.1016/j.compedu.2011.06.004

Goodfellow, I., Bengio, Y., & Courville, A. (2016). *Deep learning*. MIT Press.

Guidotti, R., Monreale, A., Ruggieri, S., Turini, F., Giannotti, F., & Pedreschi, D. (2018). A survey of methods for explaining black box models. *ACM Computing Surveys*, *51*(5), 1–42. DOI: 10.1145/3236009

Hadnagy, C. (2018). *Social engineering: The science of human hacking*. Wiley Publication. DOI: 10.1002/9781119433729

Hmelo-Silver, C. E. (2004). Problem-based learning: What and how do students learn? *Educational Psychology Review*, *16*(3), 235–266. DOI: 10.1023/B:EDPR.0000034022.16470.f3

Holland, J. H. (2014). *Complexity: A very short introduction*. OUP Oxford. DOI: 10.1093/actrade/9780199662548.001.0001

Holmes, W. (2019). *Artificial intelligence in education: Promises and implications for teaching and learning*. Center for Curriculum Redesign.

Jennings, N., & Wooldridge, M. J. (Eds.). (1998). *Agent technology: foundations, applications, and markets*. Springer Science & Business Media. DOI: 10.1007/978-3-662-03678-5

Jobin, A., Ienca, M., & Vayena, E. (2019). The global landscape of AI ethics guidelines. *Nature Machine Intelligence*, *1*(9), 389–399. DOI: 10.1038/s42256-019-0088-2

Jordan, M. I., & Mitchell, T. M. (2015). Machine learning: Trends, perspectives, and prospects. *Science*, *349*(6245), 255–260. DOI: 10.1126/science.aaa8415 PMID: 26185243

Kolb, D. A. (1984). *Experiential learning : experience as the source of learning and development*. Prentice-Hall.

Kshetri, N. (2021). *Cybersecurity management: An organizational and strategic approach*. University of Toronto Press. DOI: 10.3138/9781487531249

Lee, J. D., & See, K. A. (2004). Trust in automation: Designing for appropriate reliance. *Human Factors*, *46*(1), 50–80. DOI: 10.1518/hfes.46.1.50.30392 PMID: 15151155

Luckin, R. (2018). *Machine Learning and Human Intelligence. The future of education for the 21st century*. UCL Institute of Education Press.

McAfee, A., & Brynjolfsson, E. (2017). *Machine, platform, crowd: Harnessing our digital future*. WW Norton & Company.

Mirkovic, J., Benzel, T. V., Faber, T., Braden, R., Wroclawski, J. T., & Schwab, S. "The DETER project: Advancing the science of cyber security experimentation and test." In *2010 IEEE International Conference on Technologies for Homeland Security (HST)*, pp. 1-7. IEEE, 2010. https://doi.org/DOI: 10.1109/THS.2010.5655108

Mitchell, M. (2009). *Complexity: A guided tour*. Oxford University Press. DOI: 10.1093/oso/9780195124415.001.0001

MITRE. (2023). *MITRE ATT&CK framework*. MITRE Corporation.

Mittelstadt, B. D., Allo, P., Taddeo, M., Wachter, S., & Floridi, L. (2016). The ethics of algorithms: Mapping the debate. *Big Data & Society*, *3*(2), 2053951716679679. DOI: 10.1177/2053951716679679

NIST. (2023). *Artificial intelligence risk management framework (AI RMF 1.0)*. National Institute of Standards and Technology., DOI: 10.6028/NIST.AI.100-1

OECD. (2021). *OECD framework for the classification of artificial intelligence systems*. OECD Publishing., DOI: 10.1787/cb6d9eca-

Parasuraman, R., Sheridan, T. B., & Wickens, C. D. (2000). A model for types and levels of human interaction with automation. *IEEE Transactions on Systems, Man, and Cybernetics. Part A, Systems and Humans*, *30*(3), 286–297. DOI: 10.1109/3468.844354 PMID: 11760769

Poole, D. L., & Mackworth, A. K. (2010). *Artificial Intelligence: foundations of computational agents*. Cambridge University Press. DOI: 10.1017/CBO9780511794797

Radianti, J., Majchrzak, T. A., Fromm, J., & Wohlgenannt, I. (2020). A systematic review of immersive virtual reality applications for higher education: Design elements, lessons learned, and research agenda. *Computers & Education*, *147*, 103778. DOI: 10.1016/j.compedu.2019.103778

Rahwan, I., Cebrian, M., Obradovich, N., Bongard, J., Bonnefon, J. F., Breazeal, C., Crandall, J. W., Christakis, N. A., Couzin, I. D., Jackson, M. O., Jennings, N. R., Kamar, E., Kloumann, I. M., Larochelle, H., Lazer, D., McElreath, R., Mislove, A., Parkes, D. C., Pentland, A. S., & Wellman, M. (2019). Machine behaviour. *Nature*, *568*(7753), 477–486. DOI: 10.1038/s41586-019-1138-y PMID: 31019318

Rani, V., Kumar, M., Mittal, A., & Kumar, K. (2022). Artificial intelligence for cybersecurity: recent advancements, challenges and opportunities. *Robotics and AI for Cybersecurity and Critical Infrastructure in Smart Cities*, 73-88.

Russell, S., & Norvig, P. (2021). *Artificial intelligence: A modern approach* (4th ed.). Pearson.

Sarker, I. H., Furhad, M. H., & Nowrozy, R. (2021). Ai-driven cybersecurity: An overview, security intelligence modeling and research directions. *SN Computer Science*, *2*(3), 173. DOI: 10.1007/s42979-021-00557-0 PMID: 33778771

Schwab, K. (2017). *The fourth industrial revolution*. Crown Currency.

Shneiderman, B. (2020). Bridging the gap between ethics and practice: Guidelines for reliable, safe, and trustworthy human-centered AI systems. [TiiS]. *ACM Transactions on Interactive Intelligent Systems*, *10*(4), 1–31. DOI: 10.1145/3419764

Siemens, G. (2013). Learning analytics. *The American Behavioral Scientist*, *57*(10), 1380–1400. DOI: 10.1177/0002764213498851

Sommer, R., & Paxson, V. (2010, May). Outside the closed world: On using machine learning for network intrusion detection. In *2010 IEEE Symposium on Security and Privacy* (pp. 305-316). IEEE. https://doi.org/DOI: 10.1109/SP.2010.25

Von Solms, R., & Van Niekerk, J. (2013). From information security to cyber security. *Computers & Security*, *38*, 97–102. DOI: 10.1016/j.cose.2013.04.004

Vygotsky, L. S. (1978). *Mind in society: The development of higher psychological processes* (Vol. 86). Harvard University Press.

Williamson, B., & Eynon, R. (2020). Historical threads, missing links, and future directions in AI in education. *Learning, Media and Technology, 45*(3), 223–235. DOI: 10.1080/17439884.2020.1798995

Wooldridge, M. (2009). *An introduction to multiagent systems*. John Wiley & Sons.

World Economic Forum. (2020). The future of jobs report 2020. *World Economic Forum*

Zawacki-Richter, O., Marín, V. I., Bond, M., & Gouverneur, F. (2019). Systematic review of research on artificial intelligence applications in higher education. *International Journal of Educational Technology in Higher Education, 16*(1), 1–27. DOI: 10.1186/s41239-019-0171-0

KEY TERMS AND DEFINITIONS

Agentic Artificial Intelligence: AI systems capable of autonomous decision-making, reasoning, and action toward predefined goals without continuous human intervention.

Cyber Ranges: Simulated environments that replicate real-world cyber infrastructures for training, testing, and cybersecurity research.

Cybersecurity Education: The structured process of developing knowledge, skills, and competencies required to protect digital systems, networks, and data from cyber threats.

Human–Machine Teaming: Collaborative interaction between human operators and AI systems, combining human judgment with machine intelligence to achieve shared objectives.

Multi-Agent Systems: Computational systems in which multiple intelligent agents interact, coordinate, and collaborate within a shared environment.

Reinforcement Learning: A machine learning approach where agents learn optimal actions through trial-and-error interactions with an environment using feedback signals.

Situational Awareness: The ability to perceive, understand, and anticipate system states and threats in dynamic environments.

Zero Trust Security Model: A cybersecurity framework that assumes no implicit trust and requires continuous verification of users, devices, and systems.

Compilation of References

Abbasi, A. R., & Mohammadi, M. (2026). Engineering a resilient smart grid: Practical defense mechanisms and deployable framework against evolving cyber-threats. *Results in Engineering, 30*, 109893. DOI: 10.1016/j.rineng.2026.109893

Abdelkader, S., Amissah, J., Kinga, S., Mugerwa, G., Emmanuel, E., Mansour, D. E. A., Bajaj, M., Blazek, V., & Prokop, L. (2024). Securing modern power systems: Implementing comprehensive strategies to enhance resilience and reliability against cyber-attacks. In *Results in Engineering* (Vol. 23). Elsevier B.V., DOI: 10.1016/j.rineng.2024.102647

Abouelnaga, Y., Ali, O. S., Rady, H., & Moustafa, M. (2016). CIFAR-10: KNN-based ensemble of classifiers. In *2016 International Conference on Computational Science and Computational Intelligence (CSCI)* (pp. 1192–1195). DOI: 10.1109/CSCI.2016.0225

Acharya, D. B., Kuppan, K., & Divya, B. (2025). Agentic AI: Autonomous intelligence for complex goals—a comprehensive survey. *IEEE Access : Practical Innovations, Open Solutions, 13*, 18912–18936. DOI: 10.1109/ACCESS.2025.3532853

Adabara, I., Sadiq, B. O., Shuaibu, A. N., Danjuma, Y. I., & Maninti, V. (2025a). Trustworthy agentic AI systems: A cross-layer review of architectures, threat models, and governance strategies for real-world deployment. *F1000 Research, 14*(905), 905. DOI: 10.12688/f1000research.169927.1

Adabara, I., Sadiq, B. O., Shuaibu, A. N., Danjuma, Y. I., & Venkateswarlu, M. (2025). A review of agentic AI in cybersecurity: Cognitive autonomy, ethical governance, and quantum-resilient defense. *F1000 Research, 14*, 843. DOI: 10.12688/f1000research.169337.1 PMID: 41169871

Adamski, L., Smith, J., Brown, R., & Wilson, P. (2025, November, 3). *International humanitarian law in focus: Russia's violations and Ukraine's legitimate use of force against energy targets*, PILPG, https://www.publicinternationallawandpolicygroup.org/lawyering-justice-blog/2025/11/3/ international-humanitarian-law-in-focus-russias-violations-andukraineslegitimate-use-of-force-against-energy-targets.

Adebayo, Y., Okunola, C., & Amola, M. (2025). Ethical Implications of Autonomous Decision-Making in Artificial Intelligence: Balancing Innovation and Accountability. *Artificial Intelligence.*

Adesina, P. A. (2021). Why international law and norms do little in preventing non-state cyber attacks. *Journal of Cybersecurity*, *7*(1), tyab009. Advance online publication. DOI: 10.1093/cybsec/tyab009

Adnan, M., Rizwan, K., Ajmal, R. H., Ali, M. W., & Noreen, S. (2025). Strengthening Cybersecurity Trust : Reducing Hallucinations For Reliable Threat Intelligence And Risk Management Across Critical Sectors. *2025 20th International Conference on Emerging Technologies (ICET)*, 1-9. DOI: 10.1109/ICET66147.2025.11321434

Afraji, D. M. A. A., Lloret, J., & Peñalver, L. (2025). Deep learning-driven defense strategies for mitigating DDoS attacks in cloud computing environments. In *Cyber Security and Applications* (Vol. 3). KeAi Communications Co., DOI: 10.1016/j.csa.2025.100085

Agnarsson, G., Greenlaw, R., & Kantabutra, S. (2016). On cyber attacks and the maximum-weight rooted-subtree problem. *Acta Cybernetica (Szeged)*, *22*(3), 591–612. DOI: 10.14232/actacyb.22.3.2016.3

Ahi, K., & Valizadeh, S. (2025). Large Language Models (LLMs) and Generative AI in Cybersecurity and Privacy : A Survey of Dual-Use Risks, AI-Generated Malware, Explainability, and Defensive Strategies. *2025 Silicon Valley Cybersecurity Conference (SVCC)*, 1-8. DOI: 10.1109/SVCC65277.2025.11133642

Ahmad Rana, S. (2026). Adversarial artificial intelligence in industrial control systems: A consequence-oriented gap analysis of MITRE ATLAS. https://doi.org/ DOI: 10.2139/ssrn.6055035

Ahmad, A., Maynard, S. B., & Park, S. (2014). Information security strategies: Towards an organizational multi-strategy perspective. *Journal of Intelligent Manufacturing*, *25*(2), 357–370. DOI: 10.1007/s10845-012-0683-0

Ahmed, F., Rahman, M. D., Alif, M. A., Mumtahina, N., & Mormo, M. I. (2026). *Deep learning–based behavioral biometric authentication using keystroke and touch patterns* (Doctoral dissertation, BRAC University).

Ahronheim, A. (2021, May 27). Israel's operation against Hamas was the world's first ai war. *The Jerusalem Post,* https://www.jpost.com/arab-israeli-conflict/gaza-news/guardian-of-the-walls-thefirst-ai-war-669371

Ajayi, O. O., Adebayo, A. S., & Chukwurah, N. (2024). Ethical AI and autonomous systems: A review of current practices and a framework for responsible integration. *International Journal of Multidisciplinary Research and Growth Evaluation, 1*(1).

Akinrinola, O., Okoye, C. C., Ofodile, O. C., & Ugochukwu, C. E. (2024). Navigating and reviewing ethical dilemmas in AI development: Strategies for transparency, fairness, and accountability. *GSC Advanced Research and Reviews, 18*(3), 050-058.

Akkaya, B. (2025). Current trends in recommender systems: A survey of approaches and future directions. *Computer Science, 10*(1), 53–91.

Akowuah, F., & Kong, F. (2021). Real-time adaptive sensor attack detection in autonomous cyber-physical systems. In 2021 IEEE 27th Real-Time and Embedded Technology and Applications Symposium (RTAS) (pp. 237–250). IEEE. DOI: 10.1109/RTAS52030.2021.00027

Al Farsi, A., Khan, A., Mughal, M. R., & Bait-Suwailam, M. M. (2025). Privacy and security challenges in federated learning for uav systems: A systematic review. *IEEE Access : Practical Innovations, Open Solutions, 13*, 86599–86615. DOI: 10.1109/ACCESS.2025.3570538

Alabi, R. O., Elmusrati, M., Leivo, I., Almangush, A., & Mäkitie, A. A. (2023). Machine learning explainability in nasopharyngeal cancer survival using LIME and SHAP. *Scientific Reports, 13*(1), 8984. DOI: 10.1038/s41598-023-35795-0 PMID: 37268685

Ali, A. H., Charfeddine, M., Ammar, B., Hamed, B. B., Albalwy, F., Alqarafi, A., & Hussain, A. (2024). Unveiling machine learning strategies and considerations in intrusion detection systems: A comprehensive survey. *Frontiers of Computer Science, 6*, 1387354. DOI: 10.3389/fcomp.2024.1387354

Aljoubory, S. H., & Mahdi, M. S. (2025). User Authentication Based on Mouse Dynamics Using an Efficient-Net Model. *Iraqi Journal for Computers and Informatics, 51*(2), 224–242. DOI: 10.25195/ijci.v51i2.612

Alkahtani, H. K., Galiya, Y., Akbayan, B., & Qahmash, A. (2026). Explainable multi agent reinforcement learning framework for secure and adaptive communication in UAV swarm based fanets. *Scientific Reports, 16*(1), 11830. Advance online publication. DOI: 10.1038/s41598-026-39366-x PMID: 41771935

Al-Kamali, F., Chan, F., Bayes, J. H., & D'Amours, C. (2026). Optimizing UAV placement with spatial threat exclusion for secure and Energy-Efficient wireless communications. *IEEE Open Journal of the Communications Society*, *7*, 539–558. DOI: 10.1109/OJCOMS.2026.3650906

Allegra, G. (2025). Best supply chain, manufacturing and aircraft systems identification leveraging a model-based product line engineering approach (Doctoral dissertation, Politecnico di Torino).

Alotaibi, A., & Rassam, M. A. (2023). Adversarial machine learning attacks against intrusion detection systems: A survey on strategies and defenses. *Future Internet*, *15*(2), 62. DOI: 10.3390/fi15020062

Alqahtani, H., & Ahuja, P. (2026). Secure autonomous cyber defense with LLM agents : A systematic review of autonomy, tool-augmented reasoning, and governance constraints. *Computers & Electrical Engineering*, *135*, 111184. DOI: 10.1016/j.compeleceng.2026.111184

Alshamrani, A., & Alghamdi, A. M. (2026). Zero-shot attack detection in UAV networks using foundation models. *Alexandria Engineering Journal*, *136*, 105–124. DOI: 10.1016/j.aej.2025.12.065

Alshehri, M. (2026). Dynamic cyber deception using AI-driven adaptive honeypot networks and context-aware behavioural analysis for proactive threat neutralization. *Ain Shams Engineering Journal*, *17*(4), 104061. Advance online publication. DOI: 10.1016/j.asej.2026.104061

Alshudukhi, K. S., Ali, S., Humayun, M., & Alruwaili, O. (2025). Next-Generation Lightweight Explainable AI for Cybersecurity: A Review on Transparency and Real-Time Threat Mitigation. *Computer Modeling in Engineering & Sciences*, *145*(3), 3029–3085. DOI: 10.32604/cmes.2025.073705

Alsuwaiket, M. A. (2025). ZeroDay-LLM: A large language model framework for zero-day threat detection in cybersecurity. *Information (Basel)*, *16*(11), 939. Advance online publication. DOI: 10.3390/info16110939

Altwaijry, N. (2023). Authentication by keystroke dynamics: The influence of typing language. *Applied Sciences (Basel, Switzerland)*, *13*(20), 11478. DOI: 10.3390/app132011478

Alvarez, J. (2015, February 3). *Stuxnet: The world's first cyber weapon*. Standford Center for International Security and Cooperation, https://cisac.fsi.stanford. edu/news/stuxnet

Alzahrani, A. (2024). Novel Approach for Intrusion Detection Attacks on small Drones using CONVLSTM model. *IEEE Access : Practical Innovations, Open Solutions, 12*, 149238–149253. DOI: 10.1109/ACCESS.2024.3471806

Alzubaidi, A. A. (2025). Systematic Literature Review for detecting intrusions in unmanned aerial vehicles using machine and Deep Learning. *IEEE Access : Practical Innovations, Open Solutions, 13*, 58576–58599. DOI: 10.1109/ACCESS.2025.3552329

Ameedeen, M. A., Hamid, R. A., Aldhyani, T. H., Al-Nassr, L. A. K. M., Olatunji, S. O., & Subramanian, P. (2024). A framework for automated big data analytics in cybersecurity threat detection. *Mesopotamian Journal of Big Data, 2024*, 175–184. DOI: 10.58496/MJBD/2024/012

Amershi, S., Weld, D., Vorvoreanu, M., Fourney, A., Nushi, B., Collisson, P., Suh, J., Iqbal, S. T., Bennett, P. N., Inkpen, K., Teevan, J., Kikin-Gil, R., & Horvitz, E. (2019). Guidelines for human–AI interaction. In *Proceedings of the 2019 CHI Conference on Human Factors in Computing Systems* (pp. 1–13). https://doi.org/ DOI: 10.1145/3290605.3300233

Ananthi, J. V. (2025). Implementation of an energy-efficient secure clustering algorithm with trusted path for flying ad hoc networks. *Wireless Networks, 31*(8), 4929–4943. DOI: 10.1007/s11276-025-04032-z

Andoko, D., Nurisnaeny, P. S., Wicaksono, P., & Widiaty, I. (2024). Women in intelligence: A dynamic and integrative literature review. *Gender Issues, 41*(3), 13. DOI: 10.1007/s12147-024-09331-x

Ang, T. Z., Salem, M., Kamarol, M., Abdolrasol, M. G. M., Ustun, T. S., & Cali, U. (2026). Cyber-resilient control based on soft reinforcement learning for inverter-based PV/FC systems: Real-time implementation and validation. *Energy Reports, 15*, 109241. Advance online publication. DOI: 10.1016/j.egyr.2026.109241

Anisa, G., & Widianingsih, F. (2024). Solarwinds attack: Stages, implications, and mitigation strategies in the cyber age. *Electronic Integrated Computer Algorithm Journal., 2*(1), 47–52. DOI: 10.62123/enigma.v2i1.31

Anthi, E., Williams, L., Burnap, P., & Theodorakopoulos, G. (2021). Adversarial attacks on machine learning cybersecurity systems. *Journal of Information Security and Applications, 58*, 102804. DOI: 10.1016/j.jisa.2020.102717

Appiahene, P., Berchie, O. S., Botchway, E., Ayitey, J. M., Dawson, K. J., Mettle, H. N. A., & Afrifa, S. (2026). Network intrusion detection using hybrid graph-based convolutional network and transformer architecture. *PLoS One*, *21*(1), e0340997. Advance online publication. DOI: 10.1371/journal.pone.0340997 PMID: 41564087

Apruzzese, G., Colajanni, M., Ferretti, L., Guido, A., & Marchetti, M. (2018). On the effectiveness of machine and deep learning for cyber security. 2018 10th International Conference on Cyber Conflict (CyCon), 371-390. DOI: 10.23919/CYCON.2018.8405026

Aristeidis, K., Anastasios, G., Natalia, A., & Christos, K. (2026). Next-Gen Explainable AI (XAI) for Federated and Distributed Internet of Things Systems: A State-of-the-Art Survey. *Future Internet*, *18*(2), 83. DOI: 10.3390/fi18020083

Arslan, S., & Scouza, M. (2023). Regulating Digital Weapons: Autonomous Cyber-attacks, AI Warfare, and International Humanitarian Law. *Legal Studies in Digital Age*, *2*(2), 49–60.

Assante, M. (2016, January 6). Confirmation of a coordinated attack on the Ukrainian power grid. *SANS Industrial Control Systems Security Blog*, https://www.sans.org/blog/confirmation-of-a-coordinated-attack-on-the-ukrainian-powergrid/

Athukorala, T. A. J. S., & Gande, S. (2025). Explainable Personalized Federated Learning for Fitness Recommendation System: Balancing Privacy and Transparency in AI-Driven Personaized Fitness Solutions.

Atmakuru, A. (2025). *Enhancing the performance and transparency of Machine Learning (ML) using MRI-derived data: alternative approaches to ML interpretability-explainability* (Doctoral dissertation, University of Reading).

Atoum, I. (2025). Revolutionizing AI governance: Addressing bias and ensuring accountability through the holistic AI governance framework. *International Journal of Advanced Computer Science and Applications*, *16*(2). Advance online publication. DOI: 10.14569/IJACSA.2025.0160283

Attaullah, H. M., Khan, I. U., Alam, M. M., Ud, M. M. S., & Kaushik, K. (2026). RoboLSTM-IDS: Multi-dataset evaluation of deep learning framework for UAV network. *PeerJ. Computer Science*, *12*, e3500. DOI: 10.7717/peerj-cs.3500

Aydın, E. E., & Bahtiyar, Ş. (2025). AI-Enhanced Phishing Attacks : Understanding the Threat Landscape and Defense Strategies. *2025 IEEE Global Conference on Artificial Intelligence and Internet of Things (GCAIoT)*, 1-6. DOI: 10.1109/GCAIoT68269.2025.11275533

Ayeswarya, S., & Singh, K. J. (2025). Enhancing security and usability with context aware multi-biometric fusion for continuous user authentication. *Scientific Reports*, *15*(1), 30627. DOI: 10.1038/s41598-025-14833-z PMID: 40836057

Azeroual, M., Moughraoui, F. Z., El Iysaouy, L., Mimouni, A., El Amrani, A., & El Markhi, H. (2026). *Cybersecurity challenges and defense strategies for next-generation power systems*. Cyber-Physical Energy Systems., DOI: 10.1016/j.cpes.2025.10.002

Bae, C., Choi, E., Kang, S., Ahn, S., & Lee, S. (2025). Digital twin platform for real-time data communication in UAV environment. *Future Generation Computer Systems*, *175*, 108078. DOI: 10.1016/j.future.2025.108078

Baele, S. J., Bukhari, I., Whyte, C., Cuomo, S., Jensen, B., Payne, K., & Garcia, E. V. (2024). AI IR: Charting international relations in the age of artificial intelligence. *International Studies Review*, *26*(2), viae013. DOI: 10.1093/isr/viae013

Bai, Y., Zhao, H., Zhang, X., Chang, Z., Jäntti, R., & Yang, K. (2023). Toward Autonomous Multi-UAV Wireless Network: A Survey of Reinforcement Learning-Based Approaches. *IEEE Communications Surveys and Tutorials*, *25*(4), 3038–3067. DOI: 10.1109/COMST.2023.3323344

Balasubramanian, P., Liyana, S., Sankaran, H., Sivaramakrishnan, S., Pusuluri, S., Pirttikangas, S., & Peltonen, E. (2025). Generative AI for cyber threat intelligence: Applications, challenges, and analysis of real-world case studies. *Artificial Intelligence Review*, *58*(11), 336. DOI: 10.1007/s10462-025-11338-z

Balleste, R. (2025). Cyberspace domain and legal norms. In *A research agenda for cybersecurity law and policy* (pp. 5–32). Edward Elgar Publishing. DOI: 10.4337/9781803929194.00007

Balunovic, M., & Vechev, M. (2020). Adversarial training and provable defenses: Bridging the gap. In *International Conference on Learning Representations*.

Bandi, A., Kongari, B., Naguru, R., Pasnoor, S., & Vilipala, S. V. (2025). The rise of agentic AI: A review of definitions, frameworks, architectures, applications, evaluation metrics, and challenges. *Future Internet*, *17*(9), 404. DOI: 10.3390/fi17090404

Banerjee, J. (2025). *Feature Selection and Transfer Learning in Network Data: Enhancing Anomaly Detection with Zero-Shot and Few-Shot Learning* (Doctoral dissertation, Staffordshire University).

Bansal, P., & Ouda, A. (2024). Continuous authentication in the digital age: An analysis of reinforcement learning and behavioral biometrics. *Computers*, *13*(4), 103. DOI: 10.3390/computers13040103

Basan, E., Makarevich, O., Lapina, M., & Mecella, M. (2022, November). Analysis of the Impact of a GPS Spoofing Attack on a UAV. *CEUR Workshop Proceedings, 3094*, 6–16.

Bashir, A., Shamszaman, Z. U., Song, Z., & Han, T. A. (2026). Co-evolutionary dynamics of attack and defence in cybersecurity. *Knowledge-Based Systems, 340*, 115750. DOI: 10.1016/j.knosys.2026.115750

Behl, A., & Behl, K. (2012). An analysis of cloud computing security issues. In *2012 World Congress on Information and Communication Technologies* (pp. 109-114). IEEE. https://doi.org/DOI: 10.1109/WICT.2012.6409059

Belenguer, A., Pascual, J. A., & Navaridas, J. (2025). A review of federated learning applications in intrusion detection systems. *Computer Networks, 111023*, 111023. Advance online publication. DOI: 10.1016/j.comnet.2024.111023

Belghachi, M. (2023). A review on explainable artificial intelligence methods, applications, and challenges. [IJEEI]. *Indonesian Journal of Electrical Engineering and Informatics, 11*(4), 1007–1024. DOI: 10.52549/ijeei.v11i4.5151

Bellogín, A., Giudici, P., Larsson, S., Pang, J., Schimpf, G., Sengupta, B., & Solmaz, G. (2025). *Systemic risks associated with agentic ai: A policy brief.* (ACM Europe TPC - Autonomous Systems Subcommittee). Association for Computing Machinery (ACM). https://www.acm.org/binaries/content/assets/public-policy/europe-tpc/system ic_risks_agentic_ai_policy-brief_final.pdf

Berrios Vasquez, S. I., Hermosilla Monckton, P. A., Leiva Muñoz, D. I., & Allende, H. (2025). Zero-day threat mitigation via deep learning in cloud environments. *Applied Sciences (Basel, Switzerland), 15*(14), 7885. Advance online publication. DOI: 10.3390/app15147885

Bhardwaj, V., & Kaur, N. (2021). SEEDRP: A secure energy efficient dynamic routing protocol in fanets. *Wireless Personal Communications, 120*(2), 1251–1277. DOI: 10.1007/s11277-021-08513-0

Bhardwaj, V., Prashar, D., & Rashid, M. (2024). SIRFRM-Secure and Intelligent Routing Fairness Rate Model for Flying Adhoc Networks. *Mobile Networks and Applications, 29*(6), 1828–1838. DOI: 10.1007/s11036-023-02270-z

Bhasin, N., Sharma, S. K., & Mishra, R. (2025). Authentication Using Keystrokes Dynamic For Static Text With Hybrid Deep Learning Technique. *INTERNATIONAL JOURNAL OF ADVANCES IN SIGNAL AND IMAGE SCIENCES*, 573-595.

Biggio, B., & Roli, F. (2018). Wild patterns: Ten years after the rise of adversarial machine learning. In *Proceedings of the 2018 ACM SIGSAC Conference on Computer and Communications Security* (pp. 2154-2156). https://doi.org/DOI: 10.1145/3243734.3264418

Biggio, G. (2025). Regulating non-kinetic effects of cyber operations: The 'loss of functionality' approach and the military necessity-humanity balance under international humanitarian law. *Journal of Conflict and Security Law, 30*(2), 241–263. DOI: 10.1093/jcsl/kraf008

Bilge, L., & Dumitras, T. (2012). Before we knew it: An empirical study of zero-day attacks in the real world. *Proceedings of the 2012 ACM Conference on Computer and Communications Security*, 833-844. DOI: 10.1145/2382196.2382284

Bishop, M., & Frincke, D. A. (2008). Information assurance education: A work in progress. *IEEE Security and Privacy, 6*(5), 54–57. DOI: 10.1109/MSP.2008.123

Biswas, B., & Sarkar, S. (2026). Responsible agentic artificial intelligence governance: Risk, safety, and ethical challenges in autonomous systems. *International Journal of Applied Resilience and Sustainability, 2*(2), 142–167. DOI: 10.70593/deepsci.0202005

Blanchard, A., & Taddeo, M. (2023). The ethics of artificial intelligence for intelligence analysis: A review of the key challenges with recommendations. Digital Society, 2(1), 12.

Bokil, R. (2023). Cyber warfare: Taking war to cyberspace and its implications for international humanitarian law. *International Journal for Multidisciplinary Research, 5*(1), 1–12. DOI: 10.36948/ijfmr.2023.v05i01.1494

Brown, T., Mann, B., Ryder, N., Subbiah, M., Kaplan, J. D., Dhariwal, P., & Amodei, D. (2020). Language models are few-shot learners. *Advances in Neural Information Processing Systems, 33*, 1877–1901. DOI: 10.48550/arXiv.2005.14165

Buczak, A. L., & Guven, E. (2016). A survey of data mining and machine learning methods for cyber security intrusion detection. *IEEE Communications Surveys and Tutorials, 18*(2), 1153–1176. DOI: 10.1109/COMST.2015.2494502

Buksh, W., Guo, Y., Iqbal, S., Qureshi, K. N., & Lloret, J. (2022). Trust-oriented peered customized mechanism for malicious nodes isolation for flying ad hoc networks. *Transactions on Emerging Telecommunications Technologies, 35*(4), e4489. Advance online publication. DOI: 10.1002/ett.4489

Cabaj, K., Domingos, D., Kotulski, Z., & Respício, A. (2018). Cybersecurity education: Evolution of the discipline and analysis of master programs. *Computers & Security*, *75*, 24–35. DOI: 10.1016/j.cose.2018.01.015

Camacho, N. G. (2024). The role of AI in Cybersecurity: Addressing Threats in the Digital Age. *Journal of Artificial Intelligence General Science (JAIGS) ISSN 3006-4023, 3*(1), 143–154. DOI: 10.60087/jaigs.v3i1.75

Cao, L., Jiang, X., Zhao, Y., Wang, S., You, D., & Xu, X. (2020). A survey of network attacks on Cyber-Physical Systems. *IEEE Access : Practical Innovations, Open Solutions*, *8*, 44219–44227. DOI: 10.1109/ACCESS.2020.2977423

Cariello, N., Nguyen, L., Gallagher, R., Kurtzer, I., Balagani, K. S., & Gasti, P. (2026). Keystroke-Aligned Body Motion Patterns for Short-Burst Continuous Smartphone Authentication: A Proof-of-Concept Study Using Motion Capture. *IEEE Transactions on Biometrics, Behavior, and Identity Science*, 1. DOI: 10.1109/TBIOM.2026.3674400

Carter, E., Thompson, M., Rodriguez, A., Brooks, D., & James, A. (2025). Explainable AI Techniques for Enhancing Cybersecurity Transparency.

Casey, B., Santos, J., & Mirakhorli, M. (2024). A large-scale exploit instrumentation study of AI/ML supply chain attacks in Hugging Face models. arXiv preprint arXiv:2410.04490.

Cath, C. (2018). Governing artificial intelligence: Ethical, legal and technical opportunities and challenges. *Philosophical Transactions. Series A, Mathematical, Physical, and Engineering Sciences*, *376*(2133), 20180080. Advance online publication. DOI: 10.1098/rsta.2018.0080 PMID: 30322996

Cavaliere, D., Gallo, M., & Stanzione, C. (2023). Propaganda detection robustness through adversarial attacks driven by explainable AI. In *World Conference on Explainable Artificial Intelligence* (pp. 405–419). Springer. DOI: 10.1007/978-3-031-44067-0_21

Centre for International Governance Innovation. (2023, January, 31). *Cyberwarfare blurs line between civilian and military targets.* https://www.cigionline.org/multimedia/cyberwarfare-blurs-line-between-civilian-and-military- targets/

Ceviz, O., Sen, S., & Sadioglu, P. (2024). A survey of security in UAVs and FANETs: Issues, threats, analysis of attacks, and solutions. *IEEE Communications Surveys and Tutorials*, *27*(5), 3227–3265. DOI: 10.1109/COMST.2024.3515051

Chandaeng, T., Kosolsombat, S., & Ratanavilisagul, C. (2025). Phishing Email Detection Using Large Language Models : A Comparative Analysis of Standalone and Retrieval Augmented Generation Models. *2025 10th International Conference on Computational Intelligence and Applications (ICCIA)*, 133-137. DOI: 10.1109/ICCIA67866.2025.00032

Chander, B., John, C., Warrier, L., & Gopalakrishnan, K. (2025). Toward trustworthy artificial intelligence (TAI) in the context of explainability and robustness. *ACM Computing Surveys*, *57*(6), 1–49. DOI: 10.1145/3675392

Chandola, V., Banerjee, A., & Kumar, V. (2009). Anomaly detection: A survey. *ACM Computing Surveys*, *41*(3), 1–58. DOI: 10.1145/1541880.1541882

Chandrasekar, V., Shanmugavalli, V., Mahesh, T. R., Shashikumar, R., Borah, N., Kumar, V. V., & Guluwadi, S. (2024). Secure malicious node detection in flying ad-hoc networks using enhanced AODV algorithm. *Scientific Reports*, *14*(1), 7818. DOI: 10.1038/s41598-024-57480-6 PMID: 38570527

Chen, Y., Liu, G., Yu, L., Kang, H., Meng, L., & Wang, T. (2024). TBAuth: A continuous authentication framework based on tap behavior for smartphones [SSRN preprint]. DOI: 10.2139/ssrn.4854193

Chen, T. M., & Abu-Nimeh, S. (2011). Lessons from Stuxnet. *Computer*, *44*(4), 91–93. DOI: 10.1109/MC.2011.115

Chen, X., Peng, J., Jiang, L., Cheng, J., & Wu, S. (2026). Defense against multi-path attacks on EV charging networks: A dependency chain analysis and DQN-BASED SOLUTION. *Multimodal Transportation*, *5*(1), 100254. Advance online publication. DOI: 10.1016/j.multra.2025.100254

Cherepanov, A., & Lipovsky, R. (2016, October). BlackEnergy - What we really know about the notorious cyber attacks [Paper Presentation]. VB Conference 2016. Denver, CO, USA. https://www.virusbulletin.com/conference/vb2016/

Chhabra, A., Datta, S., Nahin, S. K., & Mohapatra, P. (2025). Agentic AI security: Threats, defenses, evaluation, and open challenges. arXiv preprint arXiv:2510.23883.

Chinnasamy, P., Yarramsetti, S., Ayyasamy, R. K., Rajesh, E. V. V., Pandey, D., & Lelish, M. E. (2025). AI-driven intrusion detection and prevention systems to safeguard 6G networks from cyber threats. *Scientific Reports*, *15*(1), 37901. DOI: 10.1038/s41598-025-21648-5 PMID: 41162457

Choiniere, M. (2026). *An AI-Driven Risk Quantification Model for Industrial Internet of Things Devices* (Doctoral dissertation, The George Washington University).

Chopra, S., Ahmad, H., Goel, D., & Szabo, C. (2026). ChatNVD : Advancing Cybersecurity Vulnerability Assessment With Large Language Models. *IEEE Access : Practical Innovations, Open Solutions*, *14*, 18595–18610. DOI: 10.1109/ACCESS.2026.3659205

Chriki, A., Touati, H., Snoussi, H., & Kamoun, F. (2019). FANET: Communication, mobility models and security issues. *Computer Networks*, *163*, 106877. DOI: 10.1016/j.comnet.2019.106877

Chulerttiyawong, D., & Jamalipour, A. (2023). SyBil Attack Detection in Internet of Flying Things-IOFT: A Machine Learning approach. *IEEE Internet of Things Journal*, *10*(14), 12854–12866. DOI: 10.1109/JIOT.2023.3257848

CMS. (2025, April 11). *Agentic AI and the EU AI Act*. CMS Legal Services EEIG. https://cms.law/en/aut/legal-updates/agentic-ai-and-the-eu-ai-act2

Coco, A., Dias, T., & Benthem, T. V. (2022). Illegal: The SolarWinds hack under international law. *European Journal of International Law*, *33*(4), 1275–1286. DOI: 10.1093/ejil/chac063

Cola, G., Vecchio, A., & Avvenuti, M. (2021). Continuous authentication through gait analysis on a wrist-worn device. *Pervasive and Mobile Computing*, *78*, 101483. DOI: 10.1016/j.pmcj.2021.101483

Comunale, M., & Manera, A. (2024). *The economic impacts and the regulation of AI: A review of the academic literature and policy actions.*

Cone, B. D., Irvine, C. E., Thompson, M. F., & Nguyen, T. D. (2007). A video game for cyber security training and awareness. *Computers & Security*, *26*(1), 63–72. DOI: 10.1016/j.cose.2006.10.005

Conklin, A. (2006, January). Cyber defense competitions and information security education: An active learning solution for a capstone course. In *Proceedings of the 39th Annual Hawaii International Conference on System Sciences (HICSS'06)* (Vol. 9, pp. 220b-220b). IEEE. https://doi.org/DOI: 10.1109/HICSS.2006.110

Conti, M., Dehghantanha, A., Franke, K., & Watson, S. (2018). Internet of Things security and forensics: Challenges and opportunities. *Future Generation Computer Systems*, *78*, 544–546. DOI: 10.1016/j.future.2017.07.060

Coppi, G., Jimenez, R. M., & Kyriazi, S. (2021). Explicability of humanitarian AI: A matter of principles. *Journal of International Humanitarian Action*, *6*(1), 19. DOI: 10.1186/s41018-021-00096-6

Cupps, N., & Elgazzar, H. (2026, January). Machine Learning Techniques for Continuous User Authentication Based on Mouse and Keystroke Dynamics. In *2026 IEEE 16th Annual Computing and Communication Workshop and Conference (CCWC)* (pp. 0503-0510). IEEE. DOI: 10.1109/CCWC67433.2026.11393691

Cybersecurity and Infrastructure Security Agency. (2026, May 1). *Careful adoption of agentic AI services.* U.S. Department of Homeland Security. https://www.cisa.gov/resources-tools/resources/careful-adoption-agentic-ai-services

da Silva, C. M. R., Feitosa, E. L., & Garcia, V. C. (2020). Heuristic-based strategy for Phishing prediction : A survey of URL-based approach. *Computers & Security, 88*, 101613. DOI: 10.1016/j.cose.2019.101613

Dal Cin, P., Kendzior, D., Seedat, Y., & Marinho, R. (2025). Three essentials for agentic AI security. MIT Sloan Management Review (Online), 1–4.

Daudu, B. O., Osimen, G. U., & Shuaibu, K. (2023). Cyberbullying and social media: Implications for African digital space. In Lahby, M., Pathan, A.-S. K., & Maleh, Y. (Eds.), *Combatting cyberbullying in digital age with artificial intelligence* (pp. 243–253). Chapman and Hall/CRC Press.

Davenport, T. H., & Kirby, J. (2016). *Only humans need apply: Winners and losers in the age of smart machines* (Vol. 1). Harper Business.

Delerue, F. (2020). *Cyber operations and international law.* Cambridge University Press., DOI: 10.1017/9781108780605

Denning, D. E. (2008). The ethics of cyber conflict. In Himma, K. E., & Tavani, H. T. (Eds.), *The handbook of information and computer ethics* (pp. 407–429)., DOI: 10.1002/9780470281819.ch17

Desai, B., Patil, K., Mehta, I., & Patil, A. (2024). Explainable AI in Cybersecurity : A Comprehensive Framework for enhancing transparency, trust, and Human-AI Collaboration. *2024 International Seminar on Application for Technology of Information and Communication (iSemantic)*, 135-150. DOI: 10.1109/iSemantic63362.2024.10762690

DeSimone, A., & Horton, N. (2017). *Sony's nightmare before Christmas: The 2014 North Korean cyber attack on Sony and lessons for US government actions in cyberspace.* Johns Hopkins Applied Physics Laboratory. https://www.jhuapl. edu/sites/default/files/2022-12/SonyNightmareBeforeChristmas.pdf

Devagiri, B. R.Bharatveeranjaneya Reddy Devagiri. (2026). Agentic AI for autonomous cyber defence. *Journal of Information Systems Engineering & Management, 11*(1s, 1S), 1579–1587. DOI: 10.52783/jisem.v11i1s.14327

Diamond, E. (2014). Applying international humanitarian law to cyber warfare. In P. S. Baruch & A. Kurz (Eds.), *Law and national security: Selected issues* (INSS Memorandum No. 138, pp. 67–74). Institute for National Security Studies.

Divakaran, D. M., & Peddinti, S. T. (2025). Large Language Models for Cybersecurity : New Opportunities. *IEEE Security and Privacy, 23*(5), 38–45. DOI: 10.1109/MSEC.2024.3504512

Do, N. Q., Selamat, A., Krejcar, O., Herrera-Viedma, E., & Fujita, H. (2022). Deep Learning for Phishing Detection : Taxonomy, Current Challenges and Future Directions. *IEEE Access : Practical Innovations, Open Solutions, 10*, 36429–36463. DOI: 10.1109/ACCESS.2022.3151903

Duc, D. M., Khang, D. T., Hien, D. T. T., Son, N. D. H., & Duy, P. T. (2025). Phishing Website Detection via Multimodal Learning and Retrieval-Augmented Reasoning. *2025 RIVF International Conference on Computing and Communication Technologies (RIVF)*, 292-297. DOI: 10.1109/RIVF68649.2025.11365186

Dumitraş, T. (2015). Understanding the vulnerability lifecycle for risk assessment and defense against sophisticated cyber attacks. In *Cyber warfare: Building the scientific foundation* (pp. 265–285). Springer. DOI: 10.1007/978-3-319-14039-1_13

Dwivedi, Y. K., Hughes, D. L., Ismagilova, E., Aarts, G., Coombs, C., Crick, T., Duan, Y., Dwivedi, R., Edwards, J., Eirug, A., Galanos, V., Ilavarasan, P. V., Janssen, M., Jones, P., Kar, A. K., Kizgin, H., Kronemann, B., Lal, B., Lucini, B., & Williams, M. D. (2021). Artificial intelligence (AI): Multidisciplinary perspectives on emerging challenges, opportunities, and agenda for research. *International Journal of Information Management, 57*, 101994. DOI: 10.1016/j.ijinfomgt.2019.08.002

Ebert, C., & Beck, M. (2023). Artificial intelligence for cybersecurity. *IEEE Software, 40*(6), 30–31. DOI: 10.1109/MS.2023.3265877

Edelson, D. (2023, July, 17). IDF uses AI in airstrikes. *Ynet Global.,* https://www.ynetnews.com/business/article/r1kngwm53

Ejaz, U., Iqbal, F., Islam, S. M., & Imashev, A. (2025). Behaviour Biometrics Using AI for Continuous Authentication Systems. *Journal of Artificial Intelligence General science (JAIGS), 8*(02), 53-64.

Eleweke, I., Umakor, M. F., Ndubuisi, C. W., Amomo, C. G., & Adeniji, S. (2025). *AI-driven threat detection and prevention in cloud computing environments*. American Journal of Innovation in Science and Engineering., DOI: 10.54536/ajise.v4i3.5041

Elshewey, A. M., Abbas, S., Osman, A. M., Aldakheel, E. A., & Fouad, Y. (2025). DDoS classification of network traffic in software-defined networking SDN using a hybrid CNN-GRU model. *Scientific Reports*. Advance online publication. DOI: 10.1038/s41598-025-13754-1 PMID: 40781265

Endsley, M. R. (2017). From here to autonomy: Lessons learned from human–automation research. *Human Factors*, *59*(1), 5–27. DOI: 10.1177/0018720816681350 PMID: 28146676

Erendor, M. E. (Ed.). (2024). *Cyber security in the age of artificial intelligence and autonomous weapons*. CRC Press. DOI: 10.1201/9781003441700

Ericsson, K. A., Krampe, R. T., & Tesch-Römer, C. (1993). The role of deliberate practice in the acquisition of expert performance. *Psychological Review*, *100*(3), 363–406. DOI: 10.1037/0033-295X.100.3.363

Eshra, S. A., Zohora, F. T., Akter, S., Rasul, I., & Hossain, A. (2025). The role of threat intelligence in preventing financially motivated cyberattacks. *Journal of Engineering and Computational Intelligence Review*, *3*(2), 20–37.

ET. (n.d.). Hong Kong MNC suffers $25.6 million loss in deepfake scam. The Economic Times. Retrieved October 27, 2025, from https://economictimes.indiatimes.com/industry/tech/hongkongmncsuffers256millionlossindeepfakescam/articleshow/107465111.cms?from=mdr

Farzaan, M. A. M., Ghanem, M. C., El-Hajjar, A., & Ratnayake, D. N. (2025). An AI-enabled system for efficient and effective cyber incident detection and response in cloud environments. arXiv: 2404.05602

Feng, X., Han, J., Zhang, R., Xu, S., & Xia, H. (2024). Security defense strategy algorithm for Internet of Things based on deep reinforcement learning. *High-Confidence Computing*, *4*(1), 100167. Advance online publication. DOI: 10.1016/j.hcc.2023.100167

Ferrag, M. A., Maglaras, L., Moschoyiannis, S., & Janicke, H. (2020). Deep learning for cyber security intrusion detection: Approaches, datasets, and comparative study. *Journal of Information Security and Applications*, *50*, 102419. DOI: 10.1016/j.jisa.2019.102419

Feyissa, R., Kassahun, M., Asnake, D., Daniel, N., Gebrie, A., Terefe, S., & Endale, E. (2025). Examining Cyber Warfare in Light of International Humanitarian Law Principles. *Available at SSRN* 5807162.

Finistrella, S., Mariani, S., & Zambonelli, F. (2025). Multi-Agent Reinforcement Learning for Cybersecurity: Classification and survey. In *Intelligent Systems with Applications* (Vol. 26). Elsevier B.V. DOI: 10.1016/j.iswa.2025.200495

Fischer, M. T., Metz, Y., Joos, L., Miller, M., & Keim, D. A. (2024). Multi-case: A transformer-based ethics-aware multimodal investigative intelligence framework. *arXiv preprint arXiv:2401.01955.*

Floridi, L., Cowls, J., Beltrametti, M., Chatila, R., Chazerand, P., Dignum, V., Luetge, C., Madelin, R., Pagallo, U., Rossi, F., Schafer, B., Valcke, P., & Vayena, E. (2018). AI4People—An ethical framework for a good AI society: Opportunities, risks, principles, and recommendations. *Minds and Machines*, *28*(4), 689–707. DOI: 10.1007/s11023-018-9482-5 PMID: 30930541

Fukarel, S. G., Primo Edriatama, O., Aqila, M. R., Ananda Putri Masaling, N., & Chowanda, A. (2025). Phishing Detection with BERT : A Transformer-Based Approach for Cybersecurity. *2025 IEEE International Symposium on Consumer Technology (ISCT)*, 265-271. DOI: 10.1109/ISCT66099.2025.11297271

Gartner, G. (2025). A decade in scientific cartography: Insights and future directions. *International Journal of Cartography*, *11*(2), 166–172. DOI: 10.1080/23729333.2025.2483160

Gattulli, V., Impedovo, D., Pirlo, G., & Volpe, F. (2023). Touch events and human activities for continuous authentication via smartphone. *Scientific Reports*, *13*(1), 10515. DOI: 10.1038/s41598-023-36780-3 PMID: 37386093

Gazit, O., Itzhakev, Y., Elovici, Y., & Shabtai, A. (2025). Real-World adversarial attacks on RF-Based drone detectors. *ArXiv.org*. https://arxiv.org/abs/2512.20712

George, W., & Mark, P. (2025). Explainable Artificial Intelligence (XAI) for Trustworthy Cybersecurity Systems: Investigating Transparency and Interpretability of AI Models in Cyber Defense Decision-Making.

Ghelani, J., Gharia, P., & El-Ocla, H. (2024). Gradient Monitored Reinforcement learning for jamming attack detection in FANETs. *IEEE Access : Practical Innovations, Open Solutions*, *12*, 23081–23095. DOI: 10.1109/ACCESS.2024.3361945

Gikandi, J. W., Morrow, D., & Davis, N. E. (2011). Online formative assessment in higher education: A review of the literature. *Computers & Education*, *57*(4), 2333–2351. DOI: 10.1016/j.compedu.2011.06.004

Gisel, L. (2016). *The principle of proportionality in the rules governing the conduct of hostilities under inter-national humanitarian law – international expert meeting report*. 22–23 June 2016. https://www.icrc.org/sites/default /files/document/ file_list/ 4358_002_ expert _meeting_report_web_1_0.pdf

Gisel, L., Rodenhäuser, T., & Dörmann, K. (2020). Twenty Years On: International Humanitarian Law and the Protection of Civilians Against the Effects of Cyber Operations During Armed Conflicts. *International Review of the Red Cross, 102*(913), 287–334. DOI: 10.1017/S1816383120000387

Goodfellow, I., Bengio, Y., & Courville, A. (2016). *Deep learning*. MIT Press.

Goumiri, S., Riahla, M. A., & Hamadouche, M. (2022). Security issues in self-organized Ad-Hoc networks (MANET, VANET, and FANET): a survey. In *Lecture notes in networks and systems* (pp. 312–324). DOI: 10.1007/978-3-030-96311-8_29

Govindarajan, V., Ahmed, F., Kamaluddin, K., Mushtaq, Z., Alshammari, K., & Khan, F. (2026). *SecureRiskNet: An advanced AI-driven framework for intelligent security risk detection in heterogeneous cloud-fog computing networks*. International Journal of Computational Intelligence Systems., DOI: 10.1007/s44196-025-01117-7

Green, R. (2026). *The cost curve as deterrent: Compound warfare economics, saturation dynamics, and the structural unaffordability of great-power conflict.*

Greiman, V. (2023). Known unknowns: The inevitability of cyber attacks. In *Proceedings of the 22nd European Conference on Cyber Warfare and Security* (Vol. 22). DOI: 10.34190/eccws.22.1.1316

Guembe, B., Azeta, A., Misra, S., Osamor, V. C., Fernandez-Sanz, L., & Pospelova, V. (2022). The emerging threat of AI-driven cyber-attacks: A review. *Applied Artificial Intelligence, 36*(1), 2037254. DOI: 10.1080/08839514.2022.2037254

Guidotti, R., Monreale, A., Ruggieri, S., Turini, F., Giannotti, F., & Pedreschi, D. (2018). A survey of methods for explaining black box models. *ACM Computing Surveys, 51*(5), 1–42. DOI: 10.1145/3236009

Guo, W., Tondi, B., & Barni, M. (2022). An overview of backdoor attacks against deep neural networks and possible defences. *IEEE Open Journal of Signal Processing, 3*, 261–287. DOI: 10.1109/OJSP.2022.3190213

Guo, W., Xiao, Y., Li, D., Cheng, S., Li, Y., Liu, J., Li, W., Wang, L., & Wu, Q. (2026). Byzantine-Resilient Federated Learning with Trust-Aware Task Scheduling for Heterogeneous UAV Swarms. *IEEE Transactions on Consumer Electronics, 1*, 1. Advance online publication. DOI: 10.1109/TCE.2026.3670496

Gupta, A., Barthwal, A., Vardhan, H., Kakria, S., Kumar, S., & Parihar, A. S. (2023). Evolutionary study of distributed authentication protocols and its integration to UAV-assisted FANET. *Multimedia Tools and Applications*, *82*(27), 42311–42330. DOI: 10.1007/s11042-023-15197-0

Guyonneau, R., & Le Dez, A. (2019). Artificial intelligence in digital warfare: Introducing the concept of the cyberteammate. *The Cyber Defense Review*, *4*(2), 103–116.

Hadi, H. J., Cao, Y., Khan, M. K., Ahmad, N., Hu, Y., & Fu, C. (2025). UAV-NIDD: A dynamic dataset for cybersecurity and intrusion detection in UAV networks. *IEEE Transactions on Network Science and Engineering*, *12*(4), 2739–2757. DOI: 10.1109/TNSE.2025.3553442

Hadnagy, C. (2018). *Social engineering: The science of human hacking*. Wiley Publication. DOI: 10.1002/9781119433729

Hafeez, S., Cheng, R., Mohjazi, L., Sun, Y., & Imran, M. A. (2026). Blockchain-enhanced UAV networks for post-disaster communication: A decentralized flocking approach. *Digital Communications and Networks*. Advance online publication. DOI: 10.1016/j.dcan.2026.03.006

Hans, S., Marsella, S., Hirschmann, S., & Gurney, N. (2025). Security logs to AT-T&CK insights: Leveraging LLMs for high-level threat understanding and cognitive trait inference.arXiv: 2510.20930 DOI: 10.54941/ahfe1007047

Hartz, S., & John, J. (2008). Contribution of economic evaluation to decision making in early phases of product development: A methodological and empirical review. *International Journal of Technology Assessment in Health Care*, *24*(4), 465–472. DOI: 10.1017/S0266462308080616 PMID: 18828942

Hasan, M., Hassan, M. M., Akter, S., Hajek, P., & Abedin, M. Z. (2026). Advances in Explainable Big Data Analytics for Enhanced Cybersecurity. *Information Systems Frontiers*, •••, 1–31. DOI: 10.1007/s10796-026-10701-x

Hasan, T., & Jahan, N. (2024). Artificial Intelligence and Ethical Challenges in Financial Services: A Framework for Responsible Data Governance and Algorithmic Transparency. *International Journal of Data Science, Big Data Analytics, and Predictive Modeling*, *14*(8), 16–36.

Hassija, V., Chamola, V., Agrawal, A., Goyal, A., Luong, N. C., Niyato, D., Yu, F. R., & Guizani, M. (2021). Fast, Reliable, and secure drone Communication: A comprehensive survey. *IEEE Communications Surveys and Tutorials*, *23*(4), 2802–2832. DOI: 10.1109/COMST.2021.3097916

He, K., Meng, W., & Xing, X. (2023). Adversarial machine learning for network intrusion detection systems. *IEEE Communications Surveys and Tutorials*, *25*(2), 1413–1451. DOI: 10.1109/COMST.2022.3233793

Hernández-Rivas, A., Morales-Rocha, V., & Sánchez-Solís, J. P. (2024). Towards autonomous cybersecurity: A comparative analysis of agnostic and hybrid AI approaches for advanced persistent threat detection. In *Innovative applications of artificial neural networks to data analytics and signal processing* (pp. 181–219). Springer Nature Switzerland. DOI: 10.1007/978-3-031-69769-2_8

Hersyah, M. H. (2025). *Towards a Risk-Secured Container Ecosystems in Cloud Environment: A Study on System.* Human Insider and Human Capital Perspectives.

Hickling, T., Aouf, N., & Spencer, P. (2023). Robust adversarial attacks detection based on explainable deep reinforcement learning for UAV guidance and planning. *IEEE Transactions on Intelligent Vehicles*, *8*(10), 4381–4394. DOI: 10.1109/TIV.2023.3296227

Hickling, T., Zenati, A., Aouf, N., & Spencer, P. (2023). Explainability in deep reinforcement learning: A review into current methods and applications. *ACM Computing Surveys*, *56*(5), 1–35. DOI: 10.1145/3623377

Hilliard, A., Gulley, A., Kazim, E., & Koshiyama, A. S. (2026). Artificial intelligence policy worldwide: A comparative analysis. *Royal Society Open Science*, *13*(2), 242234. DOI: 10.1098/rsos.242234

Hmelo-Silver, C. E. (2004). Problem-based learning: What and how do students learn? *Educational Psychology Review*, *16*(3), 235–266. DOI: 10.1023/B:EDPR.0000034022.16470.f3

Holland, J. H. (2014). *Complexity: A very short introduction.* OUP Oxford. DOI: 10.1093/actrade/9780199662548.001.0001

Holmes, W. (2019). *Artificial intelligence in education: Promises and implications for teaching and learning.* Center for Curriculum Redesign.

Hossain, M. A. (2025). Deep Q-learning intrusion detection system (DQ-IDS): A novel reinforcement learning approach for adaptive and self-learning cybersecurity. *ICT Express*, *11*(5), 875–880. DOI: 10.1016/j.icte.2025.05.007

Hossain, M. A., Ishtiaq, W., & Islam, M. S. (2025). A comparative analysis of Ensemble-Based machine learning approaches with explainable AI for Multi-Class intrusion detection in drone networks. *Security and Privacy*, *9*(1), e70164. Advance online publication. DOI: 10.1002/spy2.70164

Hosseinzadeh, M., Mohammed, A. H., Alenizi, F. A., Malik, M. H., Yousefpoor, E., Yousefpoor, M. S., Ahmed, O. H., Rahmani, A. M., & Tightiz, L. (2023). A novel fuzzy trust-based secure routing scheme in flying ad hoc networks. *Vehicular Communications, 44*, 100665. DOI: 10.1016/j.vehcom.2023.100665

Hozouri, A., Mirzaei, A., & Effatparvar, M. (2025). A comprehensive survey on intrusion detection systems with advances in machine learning, deep learning and emerging cybersecurity challenges. *Discover Artificial Intelligence, 5*(1), 314. DOI: 10.1007/s44163-025-00578-1

Hruza, P., & Cerny, J. (2017). Cyberwarfare. International conference KNOWLEDGE-BASED ORGANIZATION, 23(1), 155-160. DOI: 10.1515/kbo-2017-0024

Hua, S. (2019). Machine learning weapons and international humanitarian law: Rethinking meaningful human control. *Georgetown Journal of International Law, 51*, 117–146.

Hubinger, E., Denison, C., Mu, J., Lambert, M., Tong, M., MacDiarmid, M., Lanham, T., Ziegler, D. M., Maxwell, T., Cheng, N., Jermyn, A., Askell, A., Radhakrishnan, A., Anil, C., Duvenaud, D., Ganguli, D., Barez, F., Clark, J., Ndousse, K., & Sachan, K. (2024, January 17). Sleeper Agents: Training Deceptive LLMs that Persist Through Safety Training. ArXiv.org. https://doi.org//arXiv.2401.05566DOI: 10.48550

Hughes, L., Dwivedi, Y. K., Malik, T., Shawosh, M., Albashrawi, M. A., Jeon, I., Dutot, V., Appanderanda, M., Crick, T., De', R., Fenwick, M., Gunaratnege, S. M., Jurcys, P., Kar, A. K., Kshetri, N., Li, K., Mutasa, S., Samothrakis, S., Wade, M., & Walton, P. (2025). AI agents and agentic systems: A multi-expert analysis. *Journal of Computer Information Systems, 65*(4), 489–517. DOI: 10.1080/08874417.2025.2483832

Hu, M., Zhang, K., You, R., & Tu, B. (2023). AuthConFormer: Sensor-based continuous authentication of smartphone users using a convolutional transformer. *Computers & Security, 127*, 103122. DOI: 10.1016/j.cose.2023.103122

Humayun, E., Lim, K. C., Krejcar, O., Selamat, A., Do, N. Q., & Zabil, M. H. M. (2025, October). Smart Forensics: A Voting Classifier Approach for Real-Time and Explainable Digital Investigations. In *2025 IEEE International Conference on Computing (ICOCO)* (pp. 430-435). IEEE. DOI: 10.1109/ICOCO67189.2025.11334115

Husom, E. J., Goknil, A., Astekin, M., Shar, L. K., KÃ¥sen, A., Sen, S., Mithassel, B. A., & Soylu, A. (2025). Sustainable LLM Inference for Edge AI : Evaluating Quantized LLMs for Energy Efficiency, Output Accuracy, and Inference Latency. *ACM Trans. Internet Things, 6*(4), 28:1-28:35. DOI: 10.1145/3767742

Hussain, A., Li, S., Hussain, T., Lin, X., Ali, F., & AlZubi, A. A. (2024). Computing Challenges of UAV Networks: A Comprehensive survey. *Computers, Materials & Continua/Computers. Computers, Materials & Continua, 81*(2), 1999–2051. DOI: 10.32604/cmc.2024.056183

Hu, Y., Atta, Z., Rahman, T. U., Qiu, S., Wang, J., Wei, W., Liang, Z., & Zaheer, Q. (2026). Shedding Light on Explainable AI: Insights, Challenges, and the Future of Infrastructure Management. *ISPRS International Journal of Geo-Information, 15*(3), 100. DOI: 10.3390/ijgi15030100

Huynh, T. T., Nguyen, H. T., & Tran, N. H. (2025). A Semantic-Aware Approach to Phishing URL Detection. *Engineering, Technology &. Applied Scientific Research, 15*(6), 29866–29871. DOI: 10.48084/etasr.13187

Ibarra, I., Melentis, J., Summers, D., Stipidis, E., Charchalakis, P., & Ali, F. H. (2008). Through-life capability risk management for evolutionary complex military vetronics. In 2008 3rd IET International Conference on System Safety (pp. 1–6). DOI: 10.1049/cp:20080726

Ibrahim, R. K., & Hoobi, M. M. (2026). Keystroke Dynamics System for User Authentication Using SVM Classifier. *Journal of Intelligent Systems & Internet of Things, 18*(1).

International Committee of Red Cross. (n.d.). *Cyber operations and harmful information* https://www.icrc.org/en/law-and-policy/cyber-and-information- operations.

International Committee of the Red Cross. (2023). *Principle of proportionality: Cyber operations during armed conflict.* https://www.icrc.org/sites/default/files/wysi wyg/war-and-law/04_proportionality-0.pdf

International Court of Justice. (1996). *Legality of the threat or use of nuclear weapons, advisory opinion.* https://www.icj-cij.org/case/95

International Criminal Tribunal for the Former Yugoslavia. (1995). *Prosecutor v. Tadić, Decision on the defence motion for interlocutory appeal on jurisdiction (IT-94-1-A).* https://www.icty.org/x/cases/tadic/acdec/en/51002.htm

Irfan, A. N., Chuprat, S., Mahrin, M. N., & Ariffin, A. (2022). Taxonomy of Cyber Threat Intelligence Framework. *2022 13th International Conference on Information and Communication Technology Convergence (ICTC)*, 1295–1300. DOI: 10.1109/ICTC55196.2022.9952616

Islamov, I., Hashimov, E., Akhundov, R., & Talibov, A. (2025). Hybrid communication models for UAV swarms: Towards scalable and energy-aware network optimization. *Матеріали конференцій МЦНД*, (03.10. 2025; Київ, Україна), 185-195.

Islam, S., Badsha, S., Khalil, I., Atiquzzaman, M., & Konstantinou, C. (2022). A triggerless backdoor attack and defense mechanism for intelligent task offloading in Multi-UAV systems. *IEEE Internet of Things Journal, 10*(7), 5719–5732. DOI: 10.1109/JIOT.2022.3172936

Iturbe, E., Rego, A., Llorente-Vazquez, O., Rios, E., Dalamagkas, C., Merkouris, D., & Toledo, N. (2026). Reinforcement Learning in action: Powering intelligent intrusion responses to advanced cyber threats in realistic scenarios. *Expert Systems with Applications*, *296*, 129168. Advance online publication. DOI: 10.1016/j.eswa.2025.129168

Jabir, R., Le, J., & Nguyen, C. (2025). Phishing Attacks in the Age of Generative Artificial Intelligence : A Systematic Review of Human Factors. *AI*, *6*(8), 174. DOI: 10.3390/ai6080174

Jacobsen, J. T., & Liebetrau, T. (2023). Artificial intelligence and military superiority: How the "cyber-AI offensive-defensive arms race" affects the U.S. vision of the fully integrated battlefield. In Artificial intelligence and international conflict in cyberspace (pp. 135–156). Routledge.

Jacobsen, J. T., & Liebetrau, T. (2023). Artificial intelligence and military superiority: How the cyber-AI offensive-defensive arms race affects the US vision of the fully integrated battlefield. In *Artificial Intelligence and International Conflict in Cyberspace* (pp. 135–156). Routledge. DOI: 10.4324/9781003284093-8

Jaiswal, K., Kumar, S., & Rathore, N. K. (2024, December). Comparative analysis of machine learning application on routing protocols in fanet. In *2024 13th International Conference on System Modeling & Advancement in Research Trends (SMART)* (pp. 706-711). IEEE. DOI: 10.1109/SMART63812.2024.10882526

Jaiswal, K., Kumar, S., & Rathore, N. K. (2025, March). Machine Learning Techniques to Detect a DDoS Attack in Flying AD-HOC Network. In *2025 3rd International Conference on Device Intelligence, Computing and Communication Technologies (DICCT)* (pp. 180-184). IEEE. DOI: 10.1109/DICCT64131.2025.10986407

Jaiswal, K., Kumar, S., & Rathore, N. K. (2026). Machine learning based routing approaches for Flying Ad-hoc Networks (FANETs): A systematic review. *Proceedings of the National Academy of Sciences, India Section A: Physical Sciences*. https://doi.org/DOI: 10.1007/s40010-026-01038-w

Javadpour, A., Ja'fari, F., Benzaïd, C., & Taleb, T. (2025). An optimized reinforcement learning based MTD mutation strategy for securing edge IoT against DDoS attack. *Journal of Information Security and Applications*, *93*, 104138. Advance online publication. DOI: 10.1016/j.jisa.2025.104138

Javaheri, D., Chizari, H., Fahmideh, M., Nadimi-Shahraki, M. H., & Hur, J. (2025). DeepRadar: A cyber-defence interceptor for early warning and defusing malware injection attacks. *Knowledge-Based Systems*, *331*, 114830. Advance online publication. DOI: 10.1016/j.knosys.2025.114830

Jayakrishna, N., & Prasanth, N. N. (2025). Detection and mitigation of distributed denial of service attacks in vehicular ad hoc network using a spatiotemporal deep learning and reinforcement learning approach. *Results in Engineering*, *26*, 104839. Advance online publication. DOI: 10.1016/j.rineng.2025.104839

Jennings, N., & Wooldridge, M. J. (Eds.). (1998). *Agent technology: foundations, applications, and markets*. Springer Science & Business Media. DOI: 10.1007/978-3-662-03678-5

Jeong, J. J., Zolotavkin, Y., & Doss, R. (2022). Examining the current status and emerging trends in continuous authentication technologies through citation network analysis. *ACM Computing Surveys*, *56*(4), 111. Advance online publication. DOI: 10.1145/3533705

Ji, Z., Lee, N., Frieske, R., Yu, T., Su, D., Xu, Y., Ishii, E., Bang, Y. J., Madotto, A., & Fung, P. (2023). Survey of Hallucination in Natural Language Generation. *ACM Comput. Surv.*, *55*(12), 248:1-248:38. DOI: 10.1145/3571730

Jiang, J., Shu, Y., Wang, J., & Long, M. (2022). Transferability in deep learning: A survey. arXiv preprint arXiv:2201.05867.

Jing, R., Niu, Q., Zhao, Q., Shao, J., Li, Z., Qi, B., Chao, G., Ma, Y., Li, D., & Zhou, X. (2026). From UAV imagery to mapping: Detecting sunflower heads in fields using a novel lightweight deep learning network. *European Journal of Agronomy*, *176*, 128018. DOI: 10.1016/j.eja.2026.128018

Jobin, A., Ienca, M., & Vayena, E. (2019). The global landscape of AI ethics guidelines. *Nature Machine Intelligence*, *1*(9), 389–399. DOI: 10.1038/s42256-019-0088-2

Johnson, J. S. (2020). Artificial intelligence: A threat to strategic stability. *Strategic Studies Quarterly*, *14*(1), 16–39.

Jordan, M. I., & Mitchell, T. M. (2015). Machine learning: Trends, perspectives, and prospects. *Science*, *349*(6245), 255–260. DOI: 10.1126/science.aaa8415 PMID: 26185243

Joy, J. (2025). DNS data exfiltration detection using CNN-LSTM with attention mechanism (CLAM) (Doctoral dissertation, National College of Ireland, Dublin).

Kabir, M. H., Siddike, M. A. M., Razib, M., & Uddin, M. R. (2026). A national-scale AI-driven cyber defense framework for protecting US critical infrastructure against nation-state attacks. *Journal of Computer Science and Technology Studies*, *8*(6), 94–107.

Kabir, S., Hannan, N., Shufian, A., & Rahman Zishan, M. S. (2025). Proactive detection of cyber-physical grid attacks: A pre-attack phase identification and analysis using anomaly-based machine learning models. *Array (New York, N.Y.)*, *27*, 100441. Advance online publication. DOI: 10.1016/j.array.2025.100441

Kalakoti, M. K. R.Manoj Kumar Reddy Kalakoti. (2025). AI-augmented self-healing infrastructure: Combining health probes with remediation playbooks. *Journal of Information Systems Engineering & Management*, *10*(58s), 1147–1157. Advance online publication. DOI: 10.52783/jisem.v10i58s.12800

Kalejaiye, A. N. (2022). Reinforcement learning-driven cyber defense frameworks: Autonomous decision-making for dynamic risk prediction and adaptive threat response strategies. [IJETRM]. *International Journal of Engineering Technology Research & Management*, *6*(12), 92–111.

Kalimuthu, N. (2025). Explainable AI (XAI) for Enhanced Cyber Threat Intelligence: Building Interpretable Intrusion Detection Systems. *IJSAT-International Journal on Science and Technology, 16*(4).

Kapoor, S., Kumar, S., & Vardhan, H. (2025). Cyber security of OT networks: A tutorial and overview. *arXiv preprint arXiv:2502.14017*.

Karri, N., & Jangam, S. K. (2025). Security and Compliance Automation. *American International Journal of Computer Science and Technology*, *7*(5), 55–68.

Kasapoğlu, C., & Kırdemir, B. (2019). *Wars of none: Artificial intelligence and the future of conflict*. Centre for Economics and Foreign Policy Studies. https://www.jstor.org/stable/resrep21050

Kass, L., & Jack, J. P. (2014). Combating asymmetric threats: The interplay of offense and defense. *Orbis*, *58*(2), 248–265. DOI: 10.1016/j.orbis.2014.02.004

Katagiri, N. (2022). Two explanations for the paucity of cyber-military, cross-domain operations. *Journal of Cybersecurity*, *8*(1), tyac002. Advance online publication. DOI: 10.1093/cybsec/tyac002

Kavya, S., & Sumathi, D. (2024). Staying ahead of phishers : A review of recent advances and emerging methodologies in phishing detection. *Artificial Intelligence Review*, *58*(2), 50. DOI: 10.1007/s10462-024-11055-z

Kaya, O., Shah, A. S., Karabulut, M. A., Karahan, S. N., Osmanca, M. S., & Acır, N. (2026). Explainable Artificial Intelligence (XAI): Concepts, Applications, Challenges, and Future Perspectives. *IEEE Access : Practical Innovations, Open Solutions, 14*, 27394–27417. DOI: 10.1109/ACCESS.2026.3663161

Kehinde, S. K. (2025). AI in everything, and everything in AI: A review of the ubiquitous role of artificial intelligence in shaping the next technological epoch. *Journal of Computer Allied Intelligence, 3*(5), 17–53. DOI: 10.69996/jcai.2025024

Kempen, A. (2024). WormGPT/FraudGPT: The ugly, dangerous "cousin" of ChatGPT. *Servamus Community-Based Safety and Security Magazine, 117*(11), 19–21.

Kezron, N.Isabirye Edward Kezron. (2024). Securing the AI supply chain: Mitigating vulnerabilities in AI model development and deployment. *World Journal of Advanced Research and Reviews, 22*(2), 2336–2346. DOI: 10.30574/wjarr.2024.22.2.1394

Khalaf, N. Z., Barazanchi, A., Ibraheem, I., Radhi, A. D., Shah, P., & Sekhar, R. (2025). Development of real-time threat detection systems with AI-driven cybersecurity in critical infrastructure. *Mesopotamian Journal of CyberSecurity, 5*(2), 501–513.

Khan, H. U., Khan, R. A., Alwageed, H. S., Almagrabi, A. O., Ayouni, S., & Maddeh, M. (2025). AI-driven cybersecurity framework for software development based on the ANN-ISM paradigm. *Scientific Reports, 15*(1), 13423. DOI: 10.1038/s41598-025-97204-y PMID: 40251237

Khan, M., Karim, D., Kumar, A., & Kabir, J. (2024). Applying Machine Learning to Secure Autonomous Systems from Real-Time Cyber Threats. *European Journal of Applied Science. Engineering and Technology, 2*(6), 270–279.

Khan, S., Devlen, C., Manno, M., & Hou, D. (2024). Mouse dynamics behavioral biometrics: A survey. *ACM Computing Surveys, 56*(6), 1–33. DOI: 10.1145/3640311

Khonji, M., Iraqi, Y., & Jones, A. (2013). Phishing Detection : A Literature Survey. *IEEE Communications Surveys and Tutorials, 15*(4), 2091–2121. DOI: 10.1109/SURV.2013.032213.00009

Killourhy, K. S., & Maxion, R. A. (2009). *Comparing anomaly-detection algorithms for keystroke dynamics. In 2009 IEEE/IFIP international conference on dependable systems & networks*. IEEE.

Kitterman, S. (2014). *Sender Policy Framework (SPF) for Authorizing Use of Domains in Email, Version 1* (Request for Comments RFC 7208). Internet Engineering Task Force. DOI: 10.17487/rfc7208

Klaar, H. T. (2021). *The evolution of the UN group of governmental experts on cyber issues. Cyberstability Paper Series: New Conditions and Constellations in Cyber.* The Hague Centre for Strategic Studies and the Global Commission on Stability of Cyberspace.

Kojukhov, A., & Bovshover, A. (2026). Agentic AI for Cybersecurity: A Meta-Cognitive Architecture for Governable Autonomy. *arXiv preprint arXiv:2602.11897.*

Kolb, D. A. (1984). *Experiential learning : experience as the source of learning and development.* Prentice-Hall.

Kondylakis, H., Osuala, R., Puig-Bosch, X., Lazrak, N., Diaz, O., Kushibar, K., & Lekadir, K. (2025). A review of methods for trustworthy AI in medical imaging: The FUTURE-AI Guidelines. *IEEE Journal of Biomedical and Health Informatics.* PMID: 41021959

Konsta, A.-M., Lluch-Lafuente, A., Spiga, B., & Dragoni, N. (2024). Survey: Automatic generation of attack trees and attack graphs. *Computers & Security, 137,* 103602. DOI: 10.1016/j.cose.2023.103602

Korede, E., & James, M. (2025). Human-AI Collaboration Models in Cybersecurity Operations—Exploring How Human Expertise and AI Systems Can Work Together for Effective Incident Response.

Kosenkov, A. (2016). Cyber conflicts as a new global threat. *Future Internet, 8*(3), 45. DOI: 10.3390/fi8030045

Kostiuk, Y. (2025). Multi-agent system for detecting and counteracting attacks on the enterprise information system. DOI: 10.36690/ITSC

Kostopoulos, G., Davrazos, G., & Kotsiantis, S. (2024). Explainable artificial intelligence-based decision support systems: A recent review. *Electronics (Basel), 13*(14), 2842. DOI: 10.3390/electronics13142842

Kou, T., Zhang, Q., Zhang, C., He, T., & Shen, J. (2023). Integrated MPCAM: Multi-PSF learning for large depth-of-field computational imaging. *Information Fusion, 89,* 452–472. DOI: 10.1016/j.inffus.2022.09.005

Kruti, A., Butt, U., & Sulaiman, R. B. (2023). A review of SolarWinds attack on Orion platform using persistent threat agents and techniques for gaining unauthorized access. arxiv. https://arxiv.org/abs/2308.10294

Kshetri, N. (2021). *Cybersecurity management: An organizational and strategic approach.* University of Toronto Press. DOI: 10.3138/9781487531249

Kshetri, N. (2025). Transforming cybersecurity with agentic AI to combat emerging cyber threats. *Telecommunications Policy, 49*(6), 102976. DOI: 10.1016/j.telpol.2025.102976

Kucherawy, M., & Zwicky, E. (2015). *Domain-based Message Authentication, Reporting, and Conformance (DMARC)* (Request for Comments RFC 7489). Internet Engineering Task Force. DOI: 10.17487/rfc7489

Kucherawy, M., Crocker, D., & Hansen, T. (2011). *DomainKeys Identified Mail (DKIM) Signatures* (Request for Comments RFC 6376). Internet Engineering Task Force. DOI: 10.17487/rfc6376

Kulkarni, A., Balachandran, V., Divakaran, D. M., & Das, T. (2025). From ML to LLM : Evaluating the Robustness of Phishing Web Page Detection Models against Adversarial Attacks. *Digital Threats, 6*(2), 10:1-10:25. DOI: 10.1145/3737295

Kumar Kakarala, M. R., & Rongali, S. K. (2025). Existing challenges in ethical AI: Addressing algorithmic bias, transparency, accountability and regulatory compliance.

Kumar, P., & Kumar, S. (2026). Designing Trustworthy Artificial Intelligence: Ethical Frameworks, Transparency, and Accountability in AI Systems. In *AI-Driven Hardware Security: Architectures, Chips, and Trust* (pp. 1-30). IGI Global Scientific Publishing.

Kumar, S., Singh, P., & Shrivastva, A. (2026) Energy-Efficient Routing Approaches in FANETs: An Extensive Survey. *Proceedings of the National Academy of Sciences, India Section A: Physical Sciences*. DOI: 10.1007/s40010-026-01120-3

Kumar, A., & Dadhich, H. (2024). Regulatory frameworks for artificial intelligence in law: Ensuring accountability and fairness. *NUJS J. Regul. Stud., 9*(2), 13. DOI: 10.69953/njrs.v9i2.7

Kumar, R., Sharma, B., & Athithan, S. (2023). TBMR: Trust based multi-hop routing for secure communication in flying ad-hoc networks. *Wireless Networks*. Advance online publication. DOI: 10.1007/s11276-023-03480-9

Kumar, S., Tiwari, A., Ahirwar, Y., Kumar, G., & Arafat, M. Y. (2025a). The Rise of UAV-Based Smart Surveillance: A Systematic Review of Trends and Technologies. *IEEE Access : Practical Innovations, Open Solutions, 13*, 181553–181575. DOI: 10.1109/ACCESS.2025.3621736

Kumar, V., Asthana, A., & Tripathi, G. (2025b). Enhancing Data Security in IOT-based UAV Networks through Blockchain Integration. *Engineering Technology & Applied Science Research, 15*(2), 21800–21804. DOI: 10.48084/etasr.9922

Kundu, J., Alam, S., Das, J. C., Dey, A., & De, D. (2024). Trust-Based Flying Ad Hoc Network: A survey. *IEEE Access : Practical Innovations, Open Solutions, 12*, 99258–99281. DOI: 10.1109/ACCESS.2024.3419904

Kurra, P. (2025). Securing the cloud with AI: The future of autonomous threat detection. *World Journal of Advanced Research and Reviews, 26*(01), 756–762. https://journalwjarr.com/sites/default/files/fulltext_pdf/WJARR-2025-1081.pdf

Kwubeghari, A., & Ezeji, N. G. (2025). Designing an Explainable Intrusion Detection System (X-Ids) Using Machine Learning: A Framework for Transparency and Trust. [AJERD]. *ABUAD Journal of Engineering Research and Development, 8*(2), 319–328. DOI: 10.53982/ajerd.2025.0802.32-j

Lahmann, H. (2022). *The future digital battlefield and challenges for humanitarian protection: A primer* (Working Paper), Geneva Academy of International Humanitarian Law and Human Rights. https://archives.geneva-academy.ch/ joomlatools-files/ docman-files/workingpapers/The%20Future% 20Digital %20Battle field%20.pdf

Lakshmi, R. P., & Jayanthi, V. E. (2025). Cybersecurity Analytics: A Review of Challenges and the Role of Machine Learning and Deep Learning in Threat Detection. *Cybersecurity Unlocked: Cryptography, Network Security, Data Protection*, 103.

Landolt, C. R., Würsch, C., Meier, R., Mermoud, A., & Jang-Jaccard, J. (2025). Multi-agent reinforcement learning in cybersecurity: From fundamentals to applications. arXiv: 2505.19837

Lanzoni, N. (2025). The role of expert groups in shaping international cyberlaw: A case study of the Tallin Manuals and international law-making. *Journal of Conflict and Security Law, 30*(3), 341–358. DOI: 10.1093/jcsl/kraf013

Lazer, J. S., Aryal, K., Gupta, M., & Bertino, E. (2026). A survey of agentic AI and cybersecurity: Challenges, opportunities and use-case prototypes. https://arxiv.org/abs/2601.05293

Lee, C. H., Thiessen, C., Van Bossuyt, D. L., & Hale, B. (2022). A systems analysis of energy usage and effectiveness of a Counter-Unmanned aerial system using a Cyber-Attack approach. *Drones (Basel), 6*(8), 198. DOI: 10.3390/drones6080198

Lee, J. D., & See, K. A. (2004). Trust in automation: Designing for appropriate reliance. *Human Factors, 46*(1), 50–80. DOI: 10.1518/hfes.46.1.50.30392 PMID: 15151155

Lewis, P., Perez, E., Piktus, A., Petroni, F., Karpukhin, V., Goyal, N., Küttler, H., Lewis, M., Yih, W., Rocktäschel, T., Riedel, S., & Kiela, D. (2020). Retrieval-augmented generation for knowledge-intensive NLP tasks. *Proceedings of the 34th International Conference on Neural Information Processing Systems, NIPS '20*, 9459-9474. https://dl.acm.org/doi/10.5555/3495724.3496517

Li, R., Ben Allal, L., Zi, Y., Muennighoff, N., Kocetkov, D., Mou, C., Marone, M., Akiki, C., Li, J., Chim, J., ... (2023). StarCoder: May the source be with you. arXiv preprint arXiv:2305.06161.

Li, B., Jin, X., Ba, T., Pan, T., Wang, E., & Gu, Z. (2025). Deceptive cyber-resilience in PV grids: Digital twin-assisted optimization against cyber-physical attacks. *Energies, 18*(12), 3145. DOI: 10.3390/en18123145

Li, B., Li, J., & Jia, M. (2025). ADFCNN-BiLSTM: A deep neural network based on attention and deformable convolution for network intrusion detection. *Sensors (Basel), 25*(5), 1382. DOI: 10.3390/s25051382 PMID: 40096198

Li, D., & Li, Q. (2020). Adversarial deep ensemble: Evasion attacks and defenses for malware detection. *IEEE Transactions on Information Forensics and Security, 15*, 3886–3900. DOI: 10.1109/TIFS.2020.3003571

Lin, H. (2012). Cyber conflict and international humanitarian law. *International Review of the Red Cross, 94*(886), 515–531. DOI: 10.1017/S1816383112000811

Lin, L. S. F. (2025). Examining the role of deepfake technology in organized fraud: Legal, security, and governance challenges. *Frontiers in Law, 4*, 6–17. DOI: 10.6000/2817-2302.2025.04.02

Li, T., & Zhang, Y. (2025). Adaptive trust evaluation model based on container security analysis in the Docker platform. *International Journal of Information Security, 24*(5), 190. DOI: 10.1007/s10207-025-01108-x

Li, T., & Zhu, Q. (2025). Agentic AI for cyber resilience: A new security paradigm and its system-theoretic foundations. arXiv: 2512.22883

Liu, Y., Deng, G., Li, Y., Wang, K., Wang, Z., Wang, X., Zhang, T., Liu, Y., Wang, H., Zheng, Y., ... (2023). Prompt injection attack against LLM-integrated applications. arXiv preprint arXiv:2306.05499.

Liu, Y., Jia, Y., Geng, R., Jia, J., & Gong, N. Z. (2024). Formalizing and benchmarking prompt injection attacks and defenses. *Proceedings of the 33rd USENIX Conference on Security Symposium, SEC '24*, 1831-1847.

Lohn, A. J. (2025). *The impact of AI on the cyber offense-defense balance and the character of cyber conflict. arXiv preprint arXiv:2504.13371.*

Lu, Z., Li, Z., Chiang, C.-W., & Yin, M. (2023). Strategic adversarial attacks in AI-assisted decision making to reduce human trust and reliance. In IJCAI (pp. 3020–3028).

Lucas, G. R. (2017). Ethics and cyber warfare. In Allhoff, F., Henschke, A., & Strawser, B. (Eds.), *Routledge handbook of ethics and war.*, DOI: 10.4324/9781315509730-28

Lucas, G. R. (2017). *Ethics and cyber warfare: The quest for responsible security in the age of digital warfare.* Oxford University Press. DOI: 10.1093/acprof:oso/9780190276522.001.0001

Luckin, R. (2018). *Machine Learning and Human Intelligence. The future of education for the 21st century.* UCL Institute of Education Press.

Luo, F., Xu, T., Li, J., & Xu, F. (2025). MDP-AD: A Markov decision process-based adaptive framework for real-time detection of evolving and unknown network attacks. *Alexandria Engineering Journal, 126*, 480–490. DOI: 10.1016/j.aej.2025.04.091

Madireddy, V. T. (2025). Graph neural network-based adaptive threat detection for cloud identity and access management logs. https://arxiv.org/abs/2512.10280

Malatji, M., & Tolah, A. (2025). Artificial intelligence (AI) cybersecurity dimensions: A comprehensive framework for understanding adversarial and offensive AI. *AI and Ethics, 5*(2), 883–910. DOI: 10.1007/s43681-024-00427-4

Maréchal, L., Mermoud, A., David, D. P., & Humbert, M. (2024). Measuring the performance of investments in information security startups: An empirical analysis by cybersecurity sectors using Crunchbase data. arXiv preprint arXiv:2402.04765.

Mareedu, A. (2025). Autonomous Security Operations Centers (SOC): AI Agents for Threat Triage, Response, and Orchestration. *International Journal of Emerging Research in Engineering and Technology, 6*(2), 63–70.

Margulies, P. (2006). Sovereignty and cyber attacks: Technology's challenge to the law of state responsibility. *Michigan Telecommunications and Technology Law Review, 14*(1), 17–56. https://law.unimelb.edu.au/__data/assets/pdf_file/0006/1687488/05Margulies-Depagina ted .pdf

Marimuktu, P., & Subramanian, R. R. (2025, May). Federated learning-based human-robot collaboration with explainable AI: A framework for secure and transparent interaction. In *2025 International Conference on Computational Robotics, Testing and Engineering Evaluation (ICCRTEE)* (pp. 1-5). IEEE. DOI: 10.1109/ICCRTEE64519.2025.11052945

Markevych, M., & Dawson, M. (2023, June). A review of enhancing intrusion detection systems for cybersecurity using artificial intelligence (AI). In *International Conference Knowledge-Based Organization* (Vol. 29, No. 3, pp. 30–37). DOI: 10.2478/kbo-2023-0072

Marks, T., & Fuger, K. (2025). Using generic cities to assess flying ad-hoc network (FANET) performance. *CEAS Aeronautical Journal, 16*(1), 377–398. DOI: 10.1007/s13272-024-00801-2

Martins, A., Dias, T., Dias, A., Vitorino, J., Maia, E., & Praça, I. (2025). Keystroke dynamics for intelligent biometric authentication with machine learning. *Discover Applied Sciences, 7*(9), 992. DOI: 10.1007/s42452-025-07449-5

Mathew, D. E., Ebem, D. U., Ikegwu, A. C., Ukeoma, P. E., & Dibiaezue, N. F. (2025). Recent emerging techniques in explainable artificial intelligence to enhance the interpretable and understanding of AI models for human. *Neural Processing Letters, 57*(1), 16. DOI: 10.1007/s11063-025-11732-2

Matisoft Cyber Security Labs. (n.d.) *Stuxnet.* https://www.matisoftlabs.com/case-studies/stuxnet

McAfee, A., & Brynjolfsson, E. (2017). *Machine, platform, crowd: Harnessing our digital future.* WW Norton & Company.

Medvedev, V., Budžys, A., & Kurasova, O. (2025). A decision-making framework for user authentication using keystroke dynamics. *Computers & Security, 155*, 104494. DOI: 10.1016/j.cose.2025.104494

Mekruksavanich, S., & Jitpattanakul, A. (2021). Deep learning approaches for continuous authentication based on activity patterns using mobile sensing. *Sensors (Basel), 21*(22), 7519. DOI: 10.3390/s21227519 PMID: 34833591

Menon, U. V., Kumaravelu, V. B., Kumar, C. V., Rammohan, A., Chinnadurai, S., Venkatesan, R., Hai, H., & Selvaprabhu, P. (2025). AI-powered IoT: A survey on integrating artificial intelligence with IoT for enhanced security, efficiency, and smart applications. *IEEE Access : Practical Innovations, Open Solutions.*

Military Drones Industry Outlook to 2030: U.S. and China Lead Market Growth with Double.Digit CAGRs, GlobeNewswire, Jul. [Online]. Available: 2025. Accessed: Oct. 17, 2025.

Miller, C. (2007). The legitimate vulnerability market: The secretive world of 0-day exploit sales. *Proceedings of the 6th Workshop on the Economics of Information Security*. DOI: 10.2139/ssrn.1009125

Mirkovic, J., Benzel, T. V., Faber, T., Braden, R., Wroclawski, J. T., & Schwab, S. "The DETER project: Advancing the science of cyber security experimentation and test." In *2010 IEEE International Conference on Technologies for Homeland Security (HST)*, pp. 1-7. IEEE, 2010. https://doi.org/DOI: 10.1109/THS.2010.5655108

Mishra, R., Varshney, G., & Singh, S. (2025). Jailbreaking Generative AI : Empowering Novices to Conduct Phishing Attacks. *2025 55th Annual IEEE/IFIP International Conference on Dependable Systems and Networks - Supplemental Volume (DSN-S)*, 251-252. 2025 55th Annual IEEE/IFIP International Conference on Dependable Systems and Networks - Supplemental Volume (DSN-S). DOI: 10.1109/DSN-S65789.2025.00022

Mishra, O. P. (2025). *An Ai-Powered Automation Framework For Real Time Cybersecurity Risk Governance And Resilience*. Digital Repository of Theses.

Mitchell, M. (2009). *Complexity: A guided tour*. Oxford University Press. DOI: 10.1093/oso/9780195124415.001.0001

MITRE. (2023). *MITRE ATT&CK framework*. MITRE Corporation.

Mittelstadt, B. D., Allo, P., Taddeo, M., Wachter, S., & Floridi, L. (2016). The ethics of algorithms: Mapping the debate. *Big Data & Society*, *3*(2), 2053951716679679. DOI: 10.1177/2053951716679679

Modalavalasa, G., & Yadav, P. (2025, June). A hybrid approach to cloud database security: Integrating DL and machine learning for threat detection and prevention. In *2025 3rd International Conference on Inventive Computing and Informatics (ICICI)* (pp. 1147–1154). IEEE.

Mohamed, N. (2023). Current trends in AI and ML for cybersecurity: A state-of-the-art survey. *Cogent Engineering*, *10*(2), 2272358. DOI: 10.1080/23311916.2023.2272358

Mohammad, A. A. S., Mohammad, S. I. S., Al Oraini, B., Vasudevan, A., Hindieh, A., Altarawneh, A., Alshurideh, M. T., & Ali, I. (2025). Strategies for applying interpretable and explainable AI in real world IoT applications. *Discover Internet of Things*, *5*(1), 71. DOI: 10.1007/s43926-025-00155-z

Mohammed, A. M., & Hoomod, H. K. (2026). A two-stage hybrid intrusion detection framework based on hierarchical attack mapping and pruned CNN-GRU models. *Engineering, Technology &. Applied Scientific Research, 16*(1), 32342–32347. Advance online publication. DOI: 10.48084/etasr.16210

Mollick, E. (2024). *Co-Intelligence: Living and working with AI.* Portfolio.

Monastyrska, E. (2025). *Machine learning techniques for biometric authentication based on keystroke dynamics* (Doctoral dissertation, Vilniaus universitetas.).

Monrose, F., & Rubin, A. D. (2000). Keystroke dynamics as a biometric for authentication. *Future Generation Computer Systems, 16*(4), 351–359. DOI: 10.1016/S0167-739X(99)00059-X

Montufar, A. H. A., Romero, C. T., Ortiz, J. H., Timaná, L. C. R., Varela, F. V., & Gamboa-Cruzado, J. (2025). FANET and MANET, a support and composition relationship. *Computers, Materials & Continua/Computers. Computers, Materials & Continua, 82*(2), 1699–1732. DOI: 10.32604/cmc.2025.056400

Morris, A., Procter, R., & Wallbank, C. (2025). Evaluating reinforcement learning agents for autonomous cyber defence. *Applied AI Letters, 6*(3), e125. Advance online publication. DOI: 10.1002/ail2.125

Morshedi, R., & Matinkhah, S. M. (2025). Cybersecurity Challenges and solutions in Unmanned Aerial Vehicles (UAVs). *Journal of Field Robotics, 43*(1), 314–329. DOI: 10.1002/rob.70040

Mosca, E., Szigeti, F., Tragianni, S., Gallagher, D., & Groh, G. (2022, October). SHAP-based explanation methods: a review for NLP interpretability. In *Proceedings of the 29th international conference on computational linguistics* (pp. 4593-4603).

Moss, J., Gordon, J., Duclos, W., Liu, Y., Wang, Q., & Wang, J. (2025). Explainable AI in IoT: A Survey of Challenges, Advancements, and Pathways to Trustworthy Automation. *Electronics (Basel), 14*(23), 4622. DOI: 10.3390/electronics14234622

Mouratidis, H., & Kang, M. (2012). Secure by design. In Developing and evaluating security-aware software systems (p. 1). DOI: 10.4018/978-1-61350-456-7.ch108

Mowla, M. N., Asadi, D., & Sohel, F. (2025). Real-time fault detection in multirotor UAVs using lightweight deep learning and high-fidelity simulation data with single and double fault magnitudes. *Complex & Intelligent Systems, 12*(2), 62. Advance online publication. DOI: 10.1007/s40747-025-02195-y

Mowla, N. I., Tran, N. H., Doh, I., & Chae, K. (2020). AFRL: Adaptive federated reinforcement learning for intelligent jamming defense in FANET. *Journal of Communications and Networks (Seoul)*, *22*(3), 244–258. DOI: 10.1109/JCN.2020.000015

Muralidharan, A., Eaman, A., & Hassan, E. (2025). A Comparative Analysis of Machine Learning Models for Behavioral Biometric Authentication using Keystroke Dynamics. *Procedia Computer Science*, *265*, 116–123. DOI: 10.1016/j.procs.2025.07.163

Muravev, M., Brazhenko, D., Somenkova, A., Golovkov, A., & Sergunin, I. (2025). MLOps architecture as a future of machine learning. *Journal of Computer Information Systems*, •••, 1–13. DOI: 10.1080/08874417.2025.2483826

Murugesan, S. (2025). The rise of agentic AI: Implications, concerns, and the path forward. *IEEE Intelligent Systems*, *40*(2), 8–14. DOI: 10.1109/MIS.2025.3544940

Nadhir, A. M., Mounir, B., Abdelkader, L., & Hammoudeh, M. (2025). Enhancing Cybersecurity in Healthcare IoT Systems Using Reinforcement Learning. *Transportation Research Procedia*, *84*, 113–120. DOI: 10.1016/j.trpro.2025.03.053

Nagalakshmi, T., Gnanasekar, A., Ramkumar, G., & Sabarivani, A. (2021). Machine learning models to detect the blackhole attack in wireless adhoc network. *Materials Today: Proceedings*, *47*, 235–239. DOI: 10.1016/j.matpr.2021.04.129

Nagila, A., Appalakonda, M. V., Kurumeti, N. K., Poornavalli, R., Dube, A. P., Anandh, A., Parimala, R. S., & Jain, A. K. (2025). Optimizing cybersecurity decision making: A framework for balancing short-term costs and long-term benefits. *International Journal of Environmental Sciences*, *11*(10s), 408–422. DOI: 10.64252/jep5hy65

Naif Alatawi, M. (2025). Enhancing intrusion detection systems with advanced machine learning techniques: An ensemble and explainable artificial intelligence (AI) approach. *Security and Privacy*, *8*(1), e496. DOI: 10.1002/spy2.496

Najafinia, S., Wang, S., & Lai, C. C. (2026). More Than a Mobile Client: A systematic literature review of architectures, applications, and challenges of UAV-Enabled Federated Learning. *IEEE Access : Practical Innovations, Open Solutions*, *14*, 12930–12959. DOI: 10.1109/ACCESS.2026.3656665

Narula, S., Ghasemigol, M., Carnerero-Cano, J., Minnich, A., Lupu, E., & Takabi, D. (2025). Exploring AI security: A systematic mapping study. *IEEE Access : Practical Innovations, Open Solutions*, *13*, 84057–84080. DOI: 10.1109/ACCESS.2025.3567195

Nastoska, A., Jancheska, B., Rizinski, M., & Trajanov, D. (2025). Evaluating trustworthiness in AI: Risks, metrics, and applications across industries. *Electronics (Basel), 14*(13), 2717. DOI: 10.3390/electronics14132717

Nawaz, S. (2024). *Agentic AI vs AI agents: A detailed comparison*. Ampcome. Retrieved April 24, 2025, from https://www.ampcome.com/post/agentic-ai-vs-ai - agents-a-detailed-comparison.

News, M. I. T. (2016). System predicts 85 percent of cyberattacks using input from human experts. Retrieved October 27, 2025, from https://news.mit.edu/2016/ai -system-predicts-85-percent-cyberattacks-using-input-human-experts-0418

Nguyen, D. C., Ding, M., Pathirana, P. N., Seneviratne, A., Li, J., & Poor, H. V. (2021). Federated Learning for Internet of Things: A Comprehensive survey. *IEEE Communications Surveys and Tutorials, 23*(3), 1622–1658. DOI: 10.1109/COMST.2021.3075439

NIST AI. (2024). *A plan for global engagement on AI standards*. National Institute of Standards and Technology.

NIST. (2023). *Artificial intelligence risk management framework (AI RMF 1.0)*. National Institute of Standards and Technology., DOI: 10.6028/NIST.AI.100-1

Nobles, C. (2024). The weaponization of artificial intelligence in cybersecurity: A systematic review. *Procedia Computer Science, 239*, 547–555. DOI: 10.1016/j.procs.2024.06.206

Ntizikira, E., Lei, W., Alblehai, F., Saleem, K., & Lodhi, M. A. (2023). Secure and Privacy-Preserving intrusion detection and prevention in the internet of unmanned aerial vehicles. *Sensors (Basel), 23*(19), 8077. DOI: 10.3390/s23198077 PMID: 37836907

Nyangaresi, V. O. (2023). Provably secure authentication protocol for traffic exchanges in unmanned aerial vehicles. *High-Confidence Computing, 3*(4), 100154. DOI: 10.1016/j.hcc.2023.100154

O'Neill, J., Subramanian, S., Lin, E., Satish, A., & Mugunthan, V. (2024). GuardFormer: Guardrail instruction pretraining for efficient safeguarding. In NeurIPS Safe Generative AI Workshop 2024.

Odukoya, O., Sanusi, M. A., & Adenekan, S. (2025). A comparative study of machine learning algorithms for real-time DDoS detection in cloud environments. *International Journal of Advance Research, Ideas and Innovations in Technology*. https://www.ijariit.com/manuscript/a-comparative-study-of-machine-learning-algorithms-for-real-time-ddos-detection-in-cloud-environments/

OECD. (2021). *OECD framework for the classification of artificial intelligence systems*. OECD Publishing., DOI: 10.1787/cb6d9eca-

Ogab, M., Zaidi, S., Bourouis, A., & Calafate, C. T. (2025). Machine learning-based intrusion detection systems for the Internet of Drones: A systematic literature review. *IEEE Access : Practical Innovations, Open Solutions, 13*, 96681–96714. DOI: 10.1109/ACCESS.2025.3575236

Oh, C., & Kang, S. (2026). LSTM-Based Early Jamming Threat Detection Scheme for Drone Ad-Hoc Networks. *Applied Sciences (Basel, Switzerland), 16*(6), 3046. DOI: 10.3390/app16063046

Ojha, Y. (2025). Artificial intelligence in armed conflict: Perspectives from international humanitarian law. *Unity Journal., 6*(1), 34–47. DOI: 10.3126/unityj.v6i1.75547

Oli, A., & Mahalal, E. (2025). *UAV security: Attacks, defenses, and open challenges*. IEEE., DOI: 10.1109/ACCESS.2025.3647023

Onyilo, J., & Uzuegbu, V. C. (2025). Explainable AI Intrusion Detection System: Improving Transparency and Trust in Cybersecurity. *Nature Journal of Emerging Sciences Technologies and Innovations, 1*(1).

Oprea, A., & Vassilev, A. (2023). *Adversarial machine learning: A taxonomy and terminology of attacks and mitigations (Technical report)*. National Institute of Standards and Technology. DOI: 10.6028/NIST.AI.100-2e2023.ipd

Orend, B. (2014). Fog in the fifth dimension: The ethics of cyber-war. In Floridi, L., & Taddeo, M. (Eds.), *The ethics of information warfare* (pp. 3–24)., DOI: 10.1007/978-3-319-04135-3_1

Osimen, G. U., Newo, O., & Fulani, O. M. (2024). Artificial intelligence and arms control in modern warfare. *Cogent Social Sciences, 10*(1), 2407514. DOI: 10.1080/23311886.2024.2407514

Oubbati, O. S., Atiquzzaman, M., Ahanger, T. A., & Ibrahim, A. (2020). Softwarization of UAV Networks: A survey of applications and Future Trends. *IEEE Access : Practical Innovations, Open Solutions, 8*, 98073–98125. DOI: 10.1109/ACCESS.2020.2994494

Ouiazzane, S., Addou, M., & Barramou, F. (2023, January). Dos and ddos cyberthreats detection in drone networks. In *The International Conference on Intelligent System and Smart Technologies* (pp. 109-119). Cham: Springer International Publishing.

Owen, O. (2025). Model Interpretability and Explainability: Foundations, Approaches, Challenges, and Future Directions in Responsible AI. *Approaches, Challenges, and Future Directions in Responsible AI (September 30, 2025).*

Palma, Á., Antunes, M., Bernardino, J., & Alves, A. (2025). Multi-class intrusion detection in Internet of Vehicles: Optimizing machine learning models on imbalanced data. *Future Internet, 17*(4), 162. DOI: 10.3390/fi17040162

Pang, T., Du, C., Dong, Y., & Zhu, J. (2018). Towards robust detection of adversarial examples. *Advances in Neural Information Processing Systems,* •••, 31.

Papavasileiou, I., Qiao, Z., Zhang, C., Zhang, W., Bi, J., & Han, S. (2021). GaitCode: Gait-based continuous authentication using multimodal learning and wearable sensors. *Smart Health (Amsterdam, Netherlands), 19,* 100162. DOI: 10.1016/j.smhl.2020.100162

Parasuraman, R., Sheridan, T. B., & Wickens, C. D. (2000). A model for types and levels of human interaction with automation. *IEEE Transactions on Systems, Man, and Cybernetics. Part A, Systems and Humans, 30*(3), 286–297. DOI: 10.1109/3468.844354 PMID: 11760769

Patil, K., Gupta, P., Nagre, H., & Hadule, H. (2025). Layer Zero : The Safeguard against Malicious Prompts. *2025 1st International Conference on Advancement in Futuristic Technologies (ICAFT),* 1-6. DOI: 10.1109/ICAFT66710.2025.11452809

Patil, S., & Wadhwa, K. (2026, April 2). *Agentic AI and India's nuclear security: Threat, opportunity, and doctrine.* Observer Research Foundation. https://www.orfonline.org/expert-speak/agentic-ai-and-india-s-nuclear-security-threat-opportunity-and-doctrine

Patil, S., Varadarajan, V., Mazhar, S. M., Sahibzada, A., Ahmed, N., Sinha, O., Kumar, S., Shaw, K., & Kotecha, K. (2022). Explainable artificial intelligence for intrusion detection system. *Electronics (Basel), 11*(19), 3079. DOI: 10.3390/electronics11193079

Patil, V., Naik, A., Oswal, A., Ghonge, V. D., Nayakwadi, V., & Pawar, Y. (2026, March). User Authentication through Mouse Dynamics Using Gameplay Data. In *2026 International Conference on Emerging Smart Computing and Informatics (ESCI)* (pp. 1-7). IEEE. DOI: 10.1109/ESCI68015.2026.11493277

Paulraj, J., Raghuraman, B., Gopalakrishnan, N., & Otoum, Y. (2025, June). Autonomous AI-based cybersecurity framework for critical infrastructure: Real-time threat mitigation. In *2025 IEEE/ACIS 29th International Conference on Software Engineering, Artificial Intelligence, Networking and Parallel/Distributed Computing (SNPD)* (pp. 925-931). IEEE.

Pawlicki, M., Pawlicka, A., Kozik, R., & Choraś, M. (2024). Advanced insights through systematic analysis: Mapping future research directions and opportunities for XAI in deep learning and artificial intelligence used in cybersecurity. *Neurocomputing*, *590*, 127759. DOI: 10.1016/j.neucom.2024.127759

Payne, K. (2018). Artificial intelligence: A revolution in strategic affairs. *Survival*, *60*(5), 7–32. DOI: 10.1080/00396338.2018.1518374

Pinto, A., Gonçalves, G., Ferreira, J. C., & Tovar, E. (2023). Survey on intrusion detection systems based on machine learning techniques for critical infrastructure protection. *Sensors (Basel)*, *23*(5), 2415. DOI: 10.3390/s23052415 PMID: 36904618

Pipyros, K. (2026). Artificial Intelligence in Cybersecurity: Legal Accountability, Explainability, and Governance Challenges in the Digital Age. In *Legal and Regulatory Impacts on AI Development* (pp. 225-258). IGI Global Scientific Publishing.

Pirayesh, H., & Zeng, H. (2022). Jamming Attacks and Anti-Jamming Strategies in Wireless Networks: A Comprehensive survey. *IEEE Communications Surveys and Tutorials*, *24*(2), 767–809. DOI: 10.1109/COMST.2022.3159185

Pollard, M. (2024). A case study of Russian cyber-attacks on the Ukrainian power grid: Implications and best practices for the United States, *Pepperdine. Policy Review*, *16*, 1–25.

Poole, D. L., & Mackworth, A. K. (2010). *Artificial Intelligence: foundations of computational agents*. Cambridge University Press. DOI: 10.1017/CBO9780511794797

Poorvi, J., Kalita, A., & Gurusamy, M. (2025). Reliable and efficient data collection in UAV-Based IoT networks. *IEEE Communications Surveys and Tutorials*, *28*, 2531–2571. DOI: 10.1109/COMST.2025.3550274

Premkumar, M., Ashokkumar, S. R., Anupallavi, S., Srinivasan, D., Prema, K., & Kiran, A. (2025). AI-based strategic decision framework for precise e-commerce applications and ensuring consumer trust through tactical precision and decision-driven strategies. *Results in Engineering*, *28*, 108191. DOI: 10.1016/j.rineng.2025.108191

Priyadharshini, S., & Balamurugan, P. (2024). An efficient DDoS attack detection and prevention model using fusion heuristic enhancement of deep learning approach in FANET sector. *Applied Soft Computing*, *167*, 112438. DOI: 10.1016/j.asoc.2024.112438

Pum, M. (2024). Autonomous weapons systems: ethical concerns and international regulation in the use of AI in military applications. University of Chicago. https://www.researchgate.net/publication/387383028_Autonomous_Weapons_Systems_Ethical_Concerns_and_International_Regulation_in_the_Use_of_AI_in_Military_Applications

Purves, T., Kyriakopoulos, K. G., Jenkins, S., Phillips, I., & Dudman, T. (2024). Causally aware reinforcement learning agents for autonomous cyber defence. *Knowledge-Based Systems*, *304*, 112521. Advance online publication. DOI: 10.1016/j.knosys.2024.112521

Radanliev, P. (2026). Transparent by Design: Ensuring Safety in Agentic AI Through Decision Traceability. In *Ethical AI and Data Science* (pp. 1-20). Auerbach Publications.

Radanliev, P., Santos, O., & Ani, U. D. (2025). Generative AI cybersecurity and resilience. *Frontiers in Artificial Intelligence*, *8*, 1568360. DOI: 10.3389/frai.2025.1568360 PMID: 40529644

Radianti, J., Majchrzak, T. A., Fromm, J., & Wohlgenannt, I. (2020). A systematic review of immersive virtual reality applications for higher education: Design elements, lessons learned, and research agenda. *Computers & Education*, *147*, 103778. DOI: 10.1016/j.compedu.2019.103778

Rahmani, S. (2025). AI's dual-use paradox in financial fraud: Navigating offense and defense in the digital era. *Sociedad & Tecnología*, *8*(4), 673–692. DOI: 10.51247/st.v8i4.666

Rahman, M. H., Sejan, M. S., Aziz, M. A., Tabassum, R., Baik, J., & Song, H. (2024). A Comprehensive survey of unmanned aerial vehicles detection and classification using Machine learning approach: Challenges, solutions, and future directions. *Remote Sensing (Basel)*, *16*(5), 879. DOI: 10.3390/rs16050879

Rahwan, I., Cebrian, M., Obradovich, N., Bongard, J., Bonnefon, J. F., Breazeal, C., Crandall, J. W., Christakis, N. A., Couzin, I. D., Jackson, M. O., Jennings, N. R., Kamar, E., Kloumann, I. M., Larochelle, H., Lazer, D., McElreath, R., Mislove, A., Parkes, D. C., Pentland, A. S., & Wellman, M. (2019). Machine behaviour. *Nature*, *568*(7753), 477–486. DOI: 10.1038/s41586-019-1138-y PMID: 31019318

Rajpoot, A., Sharma, N., Sahu, S., Anand, V., Bhalerao, S., & Yadav, S. (2025). Real-Time Multi-User Authentication Using Mouse Dynamics Behavioural Biometrics. In *2025 International Conference on Emerging Technologies and Innovation for Sustainability (EmergIN)* (pp. 466-471). IEEE. DOI: 10.1109/EmergIN67762.2025.11450662

Rangappa, A. S. (2025). Agentic AI and cyber security: Autonomous threat hunting, intrusion detection, and adaptive defense mechanisms in a world of increasingly sophisticated cyber attacks. *Journal of Digital Security and Forensics*, *2*(1), 128–138.

Rani, V., Kumar, M., Mittal, A., & Kumar, K. (2022). Artificial intelligence for cybersecurity: recent advancements, challenges and opportunities. *Robotics and AI for Cybersecurity and Critical Infrastructure in Smart Cities*, 73-88.

Reddy, K. Y., & Lingam, G. S. (2025). Scalable and adaptive framework for AI-based intrusion detection systems. *Measurement : Journal of the International Measurement Confederation*, *254*, 117955. DOI: 10.1016/j.measurement.2025.117955

Risto, H. N., & Graven, O. H. (2024). Fixed-text keystroke dynamics authentication data set—Collection and analysis. *Annales des Télécommunications*, *79*(11), 731–743. DOI: 10.1007/s12243-024-01039-z

Robinson, M., Jones, K., & Janicke, H. (2015). Cyber warfare: Issues and challenges. *Computers & Security*, *49*, 70–94. DOI: 10.1016/j.cose.2014.11.007

Rongali, S. K., & Kumar Kakarala, M. R. (2024). Existing challenges in ethical AI: Addressing algorithmic bias, transparency, accountability and regulatory compliance.

Roy, I. (2026). *Securing Graphical Authentication Using Keystroke Dynamics* (Doctoral dissertation, © University of Dhaka).

Russell, S., & Norvig, P. (2020). Artificial intelligence: a modern approach, 4/E.

Russell, S., & Norvig, P. (2010). *Artificial intelligence: A modern approach* (3rd ed.). Pearson.

Saltini, A. (2024). Navigating cyber vulnerabilities in ai enabled military systems. European Leadership Network. https://europeanleadershipnetwork.org/commentary/navigating-cyber-vulnerabilities-in-ai-enabled-military-systems/

Saripalli, S., & Yeshwanth, P. (2025, August 5). *Agentic AI and cybersecurity: Challenges and key consideration*. PwC India. https://www.pwc.in/blogs/agentic-ai-and-cybersecurity-challenges-and-key-considerations.html

Sarker, I. H., Furhad, M. H., & Nowrozy, R. (2021). Ai-driven cybersecurity: An overview, security intelligence modeling and research directions. *SN Computer Science, 2*(3), 173. DOI: 10.1007/s42979-021-00557-0 PMID: 33778771

Sarker, I. H., Janicke, H., Mohsin, A., Gill, A., & Maglaras, L. (2024). Explainable AI for cybersecurity automation, intelligence and trustworthiness in digital twin: Methods, taxonomy, challenges and prospects. *ICT Express, 10*(4), 935–958. DOI: 10.1016/j.icte.2024.05.007

Sarraf, G., & Pal, V. (2025). Autonomous threat detection and response in cloud security: A comprehensive survey of AI-driven strategies. *International Journal of Emerging Research in Engineering and Technology*.arXiv: 2601.03303

Sathaporn, P., Krungseanmuang, W., Chaowalittawin, V., Benjangkaprasert, C., & Purahong, B. (2025). DDoS detection using a hybrid CNN-RNN model enhanced with multi-head attention for cloud infrastructure. *Applied Sciences (Basel, Switzerland), 15*(21), 11567. Advance online publication. DOI: 10.3390/app152111567

Schmitt, M. N. (Ed.) (2017). Tallinn manual 2.0 on the international law applicable to cyber operations. Cambridge University Press.

Schmitt, M. N. (2012). Classification of cyber conflict. *Journal of Conflict and Security Law, 17*(2), 245–260. DOI: 10.1093/jcsl/krs018

Schmitt, M. N. (2012). International law in cyberspace: The Koh Speech and Tallinn Manual juxtaposed. *Harvard International Law Journal, 54*, 13–37.

Schröer, S. L., Apruzzese, G., Human, S., Laskov, P., Anderson, H. S., Bernroider, E. W. N., Fass, A., Nassi, B., Rimmer, V., & Roli, F.. (2025). SoK: On the offensive potential of AI. In *2025 IEEE Conference on Secure and Trustworthy Machine Learning (SaTML)* (pp. 247–280). IEEE. DOI: 10.1109/SaTML64287.2025.00021

Schwab, K. (2017). *The fourth industrial revolution*. Crown Currency.

Schweitzer, N., Dvir, A., & Stulman, A. (2023). Network wormhole attacks without a traditional wormhole. *Ad Hoc Networks, 151*, 103286. DOI: 10.1016/j.adhoc.2023.103286

Selçuk, A. A. (2019). A guide for systematic reviews: PRISMA. *Turkish Archives of Otorhinolaryngology, 57*(1), 57–58. DOI: 10.5152/tao.2019.4058 PMID: 31049257

Sepehrzad, R., Hosseinalibeiki, H., Taghinezhad, N., Khosravi, N., al Durra, A., & Sadabadi, M. S. (2026). Enhanced cyber-resilience in flexible energy markets for microgrids: A trust-aware federated deep reinforcement learning framework. *Applied Energy*, *406*, 127282. Advance online publication. DOI: 10.1016/j.apenergy.2025.127282

Shafi, M. M., Lashkari, A. H., Rodriguez, V., & Nevo, R. (2024). Toward generating a new cloud-based DDoS dataset and cloud intrusion traffic characterisation. *Information (Basel)*, *15*(195). Advance online publication. DOI: 10.3390/info15040195

Shafique, A., Mehmood, A., & Elhadef, M. (2021). Detecting signal spoofing attack in UAVs using machine learning models. *IEEE Access : Practical Innovations, Open Solutions*, *9*, 93803–93815. DOI: 10.1109/ACCESS.2021.3089847

Shahriar, A., Rahman, M. N., Ahmed, S., Sadeque, F., & Parvez, M. R. (2025). A survey on agentic security: Applications, threats and defenses. *arXiv preprint arXiv:2510.06445.*

Shakhatreh, H., Sawalmeh, A. H., Al-Fuqaha, A., Dou, Z., Almaita, E., Khalil, I., Othman, N. S., Khreishah, A., & Guizani, M. (2019). Unmanned Aerial Vehicles (UAVs): A survey on civil applications and key research challenges. *IEEE Access : Practical Innovations, Open Solutions*, *7*, 48572–48634. DOI: 10.1109/ACCESS.2019.2909530

Shapovalov, V., Tran, Q. K., Groussis, M., Jasani, G., Tilley, L., & Pourmand, A. (2024). Analyzing unmanned aerial vehicle (drone) attacks; a disaster medicine perspective. *The American Journal of Emergency Medicine*, *84*, 135–140. DOI: 10.1016/j.ajem.2024.08.001 PMID: 39116674

Sharma, M., Singh, M., Walia, K., & Kaur, K. (2019, October). A comprehensive study of performance parameters for MANET, VANET and FANET. In *2019 IEEE 10th Annual Information Technology, Electronics and Mobile Communication Conference (IEMCON)* (pp. 0643-0646). IEEE.

Sharma, V., Shah, D., Sharma, S., & Gautam, S. (2024). Artificial intelligence-based intrusion detection system: A detailed survey. *ITM Web of Conferences, 65*, 04002. DOI: 10.1051/itmconf/20246504002

Sharma, A., Jureček, M., & Stamp, M. (2025). Keystroke dynamics for user identification. In *Machine Learning, Deep Learning and AI for Cybersecurity* (pp. 601–622). Springer Nature Switzerland. DOI: 10.1007/978-3-031-83157-7_21

Sharma, D., & Jameel, A. (2019). Enhancement of security in flying AD-HOC network using a trust based routing mechanism. *International Journal of Innovative Technology and Exploring Engineering*, *9*(1), 253–257. DOI: 10.35940/ijitee.A4010.119119

Sharmin, Z., Uddin, M. P., Xiang, Y., & Chen, F. (2026). A systematic literature review on federated cyber-attack detection for edge intelligence: Challenges, approaches, and future directions. *Computer Science Review*, *61*, 100965. DOI: 10.1016/j.cosrev.2026.100965

Shen, S., Jin, G., Gao, K., & Zhang, Y. (2017). APE-GAN: Adversarial perturbation elimination with GAN. arXiv preprint arXiv:1707.05474.

Shevchenko, A. I., Kondratenko, Y. P., Slyusar, V. I., Atamanyuk, I. P., Kondratenko, G. V., & Yeroshenko, T. V. (2024). Analysis of the prospect domains in AI implementation: Nationals, NATO and Ukraine AI strategies. In *Research Tendencies and Prospect Domains for AI Development and Implementation* (pp. 1–27). River Publishers. DOI: 10.1201/9788770046947-1

Shneiderman, B. (2020). Bridging the gap between ethics and practice: Guidelines for reliable, safe, and trustworthy human-centered AI systems. [TiiS]. *ACM Transactions on Interactive Intelligent Systems*, *10*(4), 1–31. DOI: 10.1145/3419764

Shokri, R., Stronati, M., Song, C., & Shmatikov, V. (2017). Membership inference attacks against machine learning models. In *2017 IEEE Symposium on Security and Privacy (SP)* (pp. 3–18). IEEE. DOI: 10.1109/SP.2017.41

Shorten, C., Khoshgoftaar, T. M., & Furht, B. (2021). Text data augmentation for deep learning. *Journal of Big Data*, *8*(1), 101. DOI: 10.1186/s40537-021-00492-0 PMID: 34306963

Shrivastava, G., Veeraiah, V., Praveenkumar, S., Pathak, P., Sharma, T., & Gupta, A. (2024, June). Explainable AI in NLP: Interpretable models for transparent decision making. In *2024 15th International Conference on Computing Communication and Networking Technologies (ICCCNT)* (pp. 1-6). IEEE.

Shu, H., Zhao, H., Yang, Y., & Tang, Y. (2026). Defense strategy against cyber-physical coordinated false data injection attacks in cyber-physical power systems. *Results in Engineering*, *29*, 109424. Advance online publication. DOI: 10.1016/j.rineng.2026.109424

Shukla, P. K., Raghuvanshi, C. S., & Sharan, H. O. (2024). AI-enhanced cybersecurity: Leveraging artificial intelligence for threat detection and mitigation. *Journal of Computational Analysis and Applications*, *33*(8).

Siddiqui, E. F., Haleem, M., Ahmad, S. F., Salhi, A., Zamani, A. T., & Varish, N. (2025). A multi-layered AI-driven cybersecurity architecture: Integrating entropy analytics, Fuzzy reasoning, game theory and multi-agent reinforcement learning for adaptive threat defense. *IEEE Access : Practical Innovations, Open Solutions, 13*, 170235–170257. DOI: 10.1109/ACCESS.2025.3610526

Siemens, G. (2013). Learning analytics. *The American Behavioral Scientist, 57*(10), 1380–1400. DOI: 10.1177/0002764213498851

Silvola, H. (2008). Do organizational lifecycle and venture capital investors affect the management control systems used by the firm? *Advances in Accounting, 24*(1), 128–138. DOI: 10.1016/j.adiac.2008.05.013

Singer, P. W. (2015). Stuxnet and its hidden lessons on the ethics of cyberweapons. *Case Western Reserve Journal of International Law, 47*(1), 79–86.

Singh, R., Nishad, D. K., Khalid, S., & Chaudhary, A. (2025). A review of the application of fuzzy mathematical algorithm-based approach in autonomous vehicles and drones. *International Journal of Intelligent Robotics and Applications, 9*(1), 344–364. DOI: 10.1007/s41315-024-00385-4

Slack, D., Krishna, S., Lakkaraju, H., & Singh, S. (2023). Explaining machine learning models with interactive natural language conversations using TalkToModel. *Nature Machine Intelligence, 5*(8), 873–883. DOI: 10.1038/s42256-023-00692-8

Smail, B. (2024). Cyberattacks between the strategic and humanitarian implications and legal and ethical challenges. *Aabhath Review*, 9 (2) 277, 275-83.

Sommer, R., & Paxson, V. (2010, May). Outside the closed world: On using machine learning for network intrusion detection. In *2010 IEEE Symposium on Security and Privacy* (pp. 305-316). IEEE. https://doi.org/DOI: 10.1109/SP.2010.25

Song, L., Shokri, R., & Mittal, P. (2019). *Membership inference attacks against adversarially robust deep learning models. In 2019 IEEE Security and Privacy Workshops*. SPW.

Sowmya, T., & Anita, M. E. A. (2023). A comprehensive review of AI-based intrusion detection systems. *Measurement. Sensors, 28*, 100827. DOI: 10.1016/j.measen.2023.100827

Spring, J. M., & Illari, P. (2018). Building general knowledge of mechanisms in information security. *Philosophy & Technology, 31*(4), 555–579. DOI: 10.1007/s13347-017-0279-z

Spring, J. M., Illari, P., Luta, A., & Parkin, S. (2021). Why the attackers have the advantage: A cybersecurity thought experiment. *Science and Engineering Ethics, 27*, 24. DOI: 10.1007/s11948-021-00288-z

Srinivas, S., Kirk, B., Zendejas, J., Espino, M., Boskovich, M., Bari, A., Dajani, K., & Alzahrani, N. (2025). AI-Augmented SOC : A Survey of LLMs and Agents for Security Automation. *Journal of Cybersecurity and Privacy, 5*(4), 95. DOI: 10.3390/jcp5040095

Srivastava, A., & Prakash, J. (2020). Future FANET with application and enabling techniques: Anatomization and sustainability issues. *Computer Science Review, 39*, 100359. DOI: 10.1016/j.cosrev.2020.100359

Steinberg, S., Stepan, A., & Neary, K. (2021). *The hacking of Sony Pictures: A Columbia University case study.* School of International and Public Affairs, Columbia University, https://www.sipa.columbia.edu/sites/default/files/2022-11/Sony%20-%20Written% 20 Case.pdf.

Stragapede, G., Delgado-Santos, P., Tolosana, R., Vera-Rodriguez, R., Guest, R., & Morales, A. (2024). TypeFormer: Transformers for mobile keystroke biometrics. *Neural Computing & Applications, 36*(29), 18531–18545. DOI: 10.1007/s00521-024-10140-2

Stylios, I., Chatzis, S., Thanou, O., & Kokolakis, S. (2023). Continuous authentication with feature-level fusion of touch gestures and keystroke dynamics to solve security and usability issues. *Computers & Security, 132*, 103363. DOI: 10.1016/j.cose.2023.103363

Stylios, I., Skalkos, A., Kokolakis, S., & Karyda, M. (2022). BioPrivacy: A behavioral biometrics continuous authentication system based on keystroke dynamics and touch gestures. *Information and Computer Security, 30*(5), 687–704. DOI: 10.1108/ICS-12-2021-0212

Subash, A., Song, I., Lee, I., & Lee, K. (2025). AgeGen Bio Track: Continuous Mouse Behavioral Biometrics-Based Age and Gender Profiling in Online Education Platforms. In *ICAART (3)* (pp. 383-393).

Sudha, R., & Premkumar, M. (2025). Securing wireless sensor networks: A survey of challenges and innovations. *Franklin Open*, •••, 100470.

Su, G., Dai, M., Chen, B., & Lin, X. (2024). Deep reinforcement learning aided secure UAV communications in the presence of moving eavesdroppers. *Journal of King Saud University. Computer and Information Sciences, 36*(4), 102047. DOI: 10.1016/j.jksuci.2024.102047

Suleyman, M., & Bhaskar, M. (2023). *The coming wave: Technology, power and the twenty-first century's greatest dilemma*. Crown.

Sullivan, C. (2016). The 2014 Sony hack and the role of international law. *Journal of National Security Law and Policy*, *8*, 437–468.

Sullivan, J. E., & Kamensky, D. (2024). Putin's power play: Russia's attacks on Ukraine's electric power infrastructure violate international law. *The Electricity Journal*, *37*(2), 107371. DOI: 10.1016/j.tej.2024.107371

Sweet, C. (2014). Tallinn Manual on the International Law Applicable to Cyber Warfare. Europe-Asia Studies, 66(4), 669–670. https://doi.org/. 2014 .897423.DOI: 10.1080/ 09668136

Swetha, T., Kumaran, U., Meena, V. P., & Hameed, A. I. (2025). Leveraging AI for enhanced cybersecurity: A comprehensive review. *Discover Applied Sciences*, *7*(6), 584. Advance online publication. DOI: 10.1007/s42452-025-06773-0

Taddeo, M. (2019). Three ethical challenges of applications of artificial intelligence in cybersecurity. *Minds and Machines*, *29*(2), 187–191. DOI: 10.1007/s11023-019-09504-8

Taddeo, M., & Floridi, L. (2018). How AI can be a force for good. *Science*, *361*(6404), 751–752. DOI: 10.1126/science.aat5991 PMID: 30139858

Tao, X., Huang, Y., Liu, J., Wang, T., Zhao, W., Wang, C., & Fu, J. (2026). User Identity Authentication via Spatiotemporal Mouse Dynamics Modeling. *Available at SSRN* 6193851. DOI: 10.1016/j.comnet.2026.112502

Tayseer Jafar, M., Yang, L. X., Li, G., Doss, R., Mouzakis, K., Vasa, R., Janicke, H., Ibrahim, A., Mohsin, A., Sarker, I. H., Moore, K., Camtepe, S., & Goel, D. (2026). Mitigating malware prevalence in networks with arbitrary topologies: A Flip-It cyber game approach integrated with epidemic modeling. *Information Sciences*, *726*, 122753. Advance online publication. DOI: 10.1016/j.ins.2025.122753

Teo, C. S. M., Claire, C. A., Lopez, V., & Shorey, S. (2019). Pressure injury prevention and management practices among nurses: A realist case study. *International Wound Journal*, *16*(1), 153–163. DOI: 10.1111/iwj.13006 PMID: 30273984

The Stuxnet Virus. Case study. https://www.afahc.ro/ro/erasmus/DDHE/Courses/Information%20Warfare/case_study_5__the_stuxnet_virus.html

Torkjazi, M., & Raz, A. K. (2024). A review on integrating autonomy into system of systems: Challenges and research directions. *IEEE Open Journal of Systems Engineering*, *2*, 157–178. DOI: 10.1109/OJSE.2024.3456037

Torr, P. (2005). Demystifying the threat modeling process. *IEEE Security and Privacy, 3*(5), 66–70. DOI: 10.1109/MSP.2005.119

Tripathy, S. S., & Behera, B. (2023). Performance evaluation of machine learning algorithms for intrusion detection system. *arXiv preprint arXiv:2310.00594.*

Truong, T. C., Diep, Q. B., & Zelinka, I. (2020). Artificial intelligence in the cyber domain: Offense and defense. *Symmetry, 12*(3), 410. DOI: 10.3390/sym12030410

Tsao, K., Girdler, T., & Vassilakis, V. G. (2022). A survey of cyber security threats and solutions for UAV communications and flying ad-hoc networks. *Ad Hoc Networks, 133*, 102894. DOI: 10.1016/j.adhoc.2022.102894

Tulembayev, A., Dolya, A., Kuttybayeva, A., Jussupbekov, T., & Tazhen, K. (2026). Energy-Aware Adaptive Communication Topology with Edge-AI Navigation for UAV Swarms in GNSS-Denied Environments. *Drones (Basel), 10*(4), 273. DOI: 10.3390/drones10040273

Tursunalieva, A., Alexander, D. L., Dunne, R., Li, J., Riera, L., & Zhao, Y. (2024). Making sense of machine learning: A review of interpretation techniques and their applications. *Applied Sciences (Basel, Switzerland), 14*(2), 496. DOI: 10.3390/app14020496

Tyugu, E. (2011). Artificial intelligence in cyber defense. 2011 3rd International Conference on Cyber Conflict, 95-105. https://doi.org/DOI: 10.1109/CYCON.2011.18

Uddin, M. A., Mahiuddin, M., & Sarker, I. H. (2024). *An Explainable Transformer-based Model for Phishing Email Detection : A Large Language Model Approach.* DOI: 10.2139/ssrn.4785953

Ullah, A., & Xinlei, L. (2025). Great power divergence: Military primacy versus economic engagement in the Israeli–Palestinian conflict: A theoretical reexamination of realist paradigms. *Chinese Political Science Review*, •••, 1–28. DOI: 10.1007/s41111-025-00287-1

United Nations Office for Disarmament Affairs. (2024). *ICT security.* United Nations. https://disarmament.unoda.org/ict-security

Valikhanli, O. (2024). UAV networks DoS attacks detection using artificial intelligence based on weighted machine learning. *Results in Control and Optimization, 16*, 100457. DOI: 10.1016/j.rico.2024.100457

Vielberth, M., Böhm, F., Fichtinger, I., & Pernul, G. (2020). Security Operations Center : A Systematic Study and Open Challenges. *IEEE Access : Practical Innovations, Open Solutions, 8*, 227756–227779. DOI: 10.1109/ACCESS.2020.3045514

Von Solms, R., & Van Niekerk, J. (2013). From information security to cyber security. *Computers & Security, 38*, 97–102. DOI: 10.1016/j.cose.2013.04.004

Vouros, G. A. (2022). Explainable deep reinforcement learning: State of the art and challenges. *ACM Computing Surveys, 55*(5), 1–39. DOI: 10.1145/3527448

Vyas, S. D., & Dey, S. (2024). Reinforcement Learning-based Adversarial Attack Generation Examples in Connected and Autonomous Vehicles: A Case Study on Vehicular Platoons. *IFAC-PapersOnLine, 58*(28), 78–83. DOI: 10.1016/j.ifacol.2024.12.014

Vygotsky, L. S. (1978). *Mind in society: The development of higher psychological processes* (Vol. 86). Harvard University Press.

Wang, C., You, X., Gao, X., Zhu, X., Li, Z., Zhang, C., Wang, H., Huang, Y., Chen, Y., Haas, H., Thompson, J. S., Larsson, E. G., Di Renzo, M., Tong, W., Zhu, P., Shen, X., Poor, H. V., & Hanzo, L. (2023). On the Road to 6G: Visions, Requirements, Key Technologies, and Testbeds. *IEEE Communications Surveys and Tutorials, 25*(2), 905–974. DOI: 10.1109/COMST.2023.3249835

Wang, H., Guo, S., He, J., Liu, H., Zhang, T., & Xiang, T. (2025). Model supply chain poisoning: Backdooring pretrained models via embedding indistinguishability. In *Proceedings of the ACM Web Conference 2025* (pp. 840–851). DOI: 10.1145/3696410.3714624

Wang, J., & Zhang, H. (2019). Bilateral adversarial training: Towards fast training of more robust models against adversarial attacks. In *Proceedings of the IEEE/CVF International Conference on Computer Vision (ICCV)*. DOI: 10.1109/ICCV.2019.00673

Wang, X., Shi, Y., Zheng, K., Zhang, Y., Hong, W., & Cao, S. (2022). User authentication method based on keystroke dynamics and mouse dynamics with scene-irrelated features in hybrid scenes. *Sensors (Basel), 22*(17), 6627. DOI: 10.3390/s22176627 PMID: 36081085

Wang, X., Wang, X., Zhang, M., & Wang, S. (2023). Detection-based active defense of biased injection attack based on robust adaptive controller. *Internet of Things and Cyber-Physical Systems, 3*, 14–23. DOI: 10.1016/j.iotcps.2023.01.004

Wang, X., Zhao, Z., Yi, L., Ning, Z., Guo, L., Yu, F. R., & Guo, S. (2024). A survey on security of UAV swarm networks: Attacks and countermeasures. *ACM Computing Surveys, 57*(3), 1–37.

Warwick, K. (2012). *Artificial Intelligence: The basics*. Routledge.

Wei, J., Li, F., Sun, J., Zhu, Z., Shi, R., Shi, J., & Sun, K. (2024). Modified tracheal traction exercise reduces the incidence of dysphagia in patients with multilevel anterior cervical discectomy and fusion. *Orthopaedic Surgery*, *16*(10), 2391–2400. DOI: 10.1111/os.14166 PMID: 39030809

Wei, J., Wang, X., Schuurmans, D., Bosma, M., Ichter, B., Xia, F., Chi, E. H., Le, Q. V., & Zhou, D. (2022). Chain-of-thought prompting elicits reasoning in large language models. *Proceedings of the 36th International Conference on Neural Information Processing Systems, NIPS '22*, 24824-24837. DOI: 10.52202/068431-1800

Whyte, C. (2020). Problems of poison: New paradigms and 'agreed' competition in the era of AI-enabled cyber operations. 2020 12th International Conference on Cyber Conflict (CyCon), 215-232. DOI: 10.23919/CyCon49761.2020.9131717

Willett, M. (2021). Lessons of the SolarWinds hack. *Survival*, *63*(2), 7–26. DOI: 10.1080/00396338.2021.1906001

Williamson, B., & Eynon, R. (2020). Historical threads, missing links, and future directions in AI in education. *Learning, Media and Technology*, *45*(3), 223–235. DOI: 10.1080/17439884.2020.1798995

Woltag, J. C. (2015). Cyber Warfare. In *Max Planck encyclopedia of public international law* (pp. 231690–e280). Oxford University Press., https://opil.ouplaw.com/display/ 10.1093/law:epil/9780199231690/law-9780199

Wooldridge, M. (2009). *An introduction to multiagent systems*. John Wiley & Sons.

World Economic Forum. (2020). The future of jobs report 2020. *World Economic Forum*

Wullman, I. (2026, April 3). *The first AI war? How algorithms and data are reshaping the war with Iran*. Ynet. https://www.ynetnews.com/tech-and-digital/article/sjksd11 ikbg.

Xie, M., & Zeng, M. (2026). A multimodal reinforcement learning-based access control model for power systems under zero-trust architecture. *Alexandria Engineering Journal*, *141*, 269–283. DOI: 10.1016/j.aej.2026.03.017

Xiong, R., Xiong, L., Shan, F., & Luo, J. (2021). SBHA: An undetectable black hole attack on UANET in the sky. *Concurrency and Computation*, *35*(13), e6700. Advance online publication. DOI: 10.1002/cpe.6700

Xu, J., Cai, Z., & Shen, W. (2019). Using FGSM targeted attack to improve the transferability of adversarial example. In 2019 IEEE 2nd International Conference on Electronics and Communication Engineering (ICECE) (pp. 20–25). DOI: 10.1109/ICECE48499.2019.9058535

Xu, C., Shen, J., Du, X., & Zhang, F. (2018). An intrusion detection system using a deep neural network with gated recurrent units. *IEEE Access : Practical Innovations, Open Solutions*, *6*, 48697–48707. DOI: 10.1109/ACCESS.2018.2867564

Xu, H., Ma, Y., Liu, H.-C., Deb, D., Liu, H., Tang, J., & Jain, A. K. (2020). Adversarial attacks and defenses in images, graphs and text: A review. *International Journal of Automation and Computing*, *17*(2), 151–178. DOI: 10.1007/s11633-019-1211-x

Xu, Y., Zha, J., Hong, W., Yi, X., Chen, G., Zheng, J., Hsia, C., & Chen, X. (2026). Scalable UAV Multi-Hop Networking via Multi-Agent Reinforcement Learning with Large Language Models. *IEEE Transactions on Mobile Computing*, *25*(7), 1–17. DOI: 10.1109/TMC.2026.3669346

Yadav, T., & Masum, M. (2026). HRIT : A Human-Readable Framework for Phishing URL Detection using Large Language Models. *2026 IEEE 5th International Conference on AI in Cybersecurity (ICAIC)*, 1-6. DOI: 10.1109/ICAIC67076.2026.11395727

Yan, B., Yang, C., Shi, C., Fang, Y., Li, Q., Ye, Y., & Du, J. (2023). Graph mining for cybersecurity: A survey. *ACM Transactions on Knowledge Discovery from Data*, *18*(2), 1–52. DOI: 10.1145/3610228

Yang, L., & Shami, A. (2023, November). Towards autonomous cybersecurity: An intelligent AutoML framework for autonomous intrusion detection. In *Proceedings of the Workshop on Autonomous Cybersecurity* (pp. 68–78). DOI: 10.1145/3689933.3690833

Yang, L., & Shami, A. (2025). Toward autonomous and efficient cybersecurity: A multi-objective AutoML-based intrusion detection system. *IEEE Transactions on Machine Learning in Communications and Networking*, *3*, 1244–1264. DOI: 10.1109/TMLCN.2025.3631379

Yang, X., Howley, E., & Schukat, M. (2024). ADT: Time series anomaly detection for cyber-physical systems via deep reinforcement learning. *Computers & Security*, *141*, 103825. Advance online publication. DOI: 10.1016/j.cose.2024.103825

Yan, Y., Huang, K., & Siegel, M. (2025). ISSF: An intelligent security service framework for cloud-native operations. *Journal of Web Engineering*. Advance online publication. DOI: 10.13052/jwe1540-9589.2447

Yao, J., & Wang, D. (2026). StrokePIN: Enhancing PIN Authentication with Keystroke Dynamics for Mobile Devices. *IEEE Transactions on Dependable and Secure Computing, 23*(3), 6797–6814. DOI: 10.1109/TDSC.2026.3667918

Ynet. (2024, April 4). *IDF's AI-based system identifies 37,000 targets, report.* https://www.ynetnews.com/business/article/b14nkao1r

Yuvaraja, T., Sumithra, S., Jeyalakshmi, M., & Premkumar, M. (2024). A combined scheme based on artificial immune system for selective forwarding attack detection in event-driven wireless sensor networks. *Tehnički Vjesnik (Strojarski Fakultet), 31*(1), 156–161.

Zawacki-Richter, O., Marín, V. I., Bond, M., & Gouverneur, F. (2019). Systematic review of research on artificial intelligence applications in higher education. *International Journal of Educational Technology in Higher Education, 16*(1), 1–27. DOI: 10.1186/s41239-019-0171-0

Zeng, J., Wu, S., Chen, H., Han, C., & Shi, Y. (2019). Survey of attack graph analysis methods from the perspective of data and knowledge processing. *Security and Communication Networks, 2031063*, 1–16. Advance online publication. DOI: 10.1155/2019/2031063

Zetter, K. (2016a, January 20). *Everything we know about Ukraine's power plant hack.* Wired. January 20, 2016. https://www.wired.com/2016/01/everything-we-know-about-ukraines-powerplant-hack/

Zetter, K. (2016b, March 3). *Inside the cunning, unprecedented hack of Ukraine's power grid.* Wired. https://www.wired.com/2016/03/inside-cunning-unprecedented-hackuk raines-power-grid/

Zhai, W., Liu, L., Ding, Y., Sun, S., & Gu, Y. (2023). ETD: An efficient Time delay Attack Detection framework for UAV networks. *IEEE Transactions on Information Forensics and Security, 18*, 2913–2928. DOI: 10.1109/TIFS.2023.3272862

Zhang, C., & Liu, L. (2025). Machine learning prediction model for medical environment comfort based on SHAP and LIME interpretability analysis. *Scientific Reports, 15*(1), 39269. DOI: 10.1038/s41598-025-22972-6 PMID: 41214038

Zhang, J., Wu, P., London, J., & Tenney, D. (2025). Benchmarking and Evaluating Large Language Models in Phishing Detection for Small and Midsize Enterprises : A Comprehensive Analysis. *IEEE Access : Practical Innovations, Open Solutions, 13*, 28335–28352. DOI: 10.1109/ACCESS.2025.3540075

Zhang, Y., Dong, Y., Zhang, S., Min, T., Su, H., & Zhu, J. (2024). Exploring the transferability of visual prompting for multimodal large language models. In *Proceedings of the IEEE/CVF Conference on Computer Vision and Pattern Recognition* (pp. 26562–26572). DOI: 10.1109/CVPR52733.2024.02508

Zhou, S., Liu, C., Ye, D., Zhu, T., Zhou, W., & Yu, P. S. (2022). Adversarial attacks and defenses in deep learning: From a perspective of cybersecurity. *ACM Computing Surveys*, *55*(8), 1–39. DOI: 10.1145/3547330

Zhou, Y., Cheng, G., Jiang, S., & Dai, M. (2020). Building an efficient intrusion detection system based on feature selection and ensemble classifier. *Computer Networks*, *174*, 107247. DOI: 10.1016/j.comnet.2020.107247

About the Contributors

Bahaa Eddine Elbaghazaoui is a professor at ENSA Beni Mellal and a PhD holder in Computer Science and Artificial Intelligence. With extensive experience in software engineering, he specializes in full-stack development, microservices, AI integration, and cloud computing. As a project manager and trainer, he has led and contributed to innovative solutions in telecommunications, insurance, and government sectors. His research focuses on data profiling and predictive analytics, with numerous publications in high-impact journals. Passionate about technology and education, he actively mentors, reviews scientific work, and advances cutting-edge software solutions.

***

Sourabh Aggarwal is a cybersecurity educator, Faculty Fellow at Westcliff University, and a PhD candidate in Management (Technology, Innovation, and Entrepreneurship) at IAE Business School. He teaches cybersecurity, artificial intelligence, and information systems across graduate and undergraduate programs. His research focuses on agentic artificial intelligence, cybersecurity education, and entrepreneurial ecosystems, with an emphasis on preparing the workforce for autonomous and AI-driven digital environments. His work integrates technical expertise with innovation and pedagogy to advance modern cybersecurity learning.

Mohammad Al-Khaldy is an Assistant professor of Business Intelligence and Data Analytics at University of Petra, Jordan. He completed his PhD in Atrificial Intelligence and Data Science for the University of Hull -United Kingdom - 20017. Alkhaldy's research interests include data analytics, machine learning, predictive analytics, NLP, and decision support systems. His research has been published extensively in academic journals and conferences. Alkhaldy taught a variety of courses in Artificial intelligence and business intelligence, including Data Mining,

Business Analytics, Computer Programming, Intelligent business systems, Data Visualization, and machine learning. Alkhaldy is a member of Jordan Computers Society, and Arab Robotics & AI Association. He also a reviewer for several other academic conferences and journals.

Lakshmi D is presently designated as a Senior Associate Professor in the School of Computing Science and Engineering (SCSE) & Assistant Director, at the Centre for Innovation in Teaching & Learning (CITL) at VIT Bhopal. She has 17 international conference presentations, and 21 international journal papers inclusive of SCOPUS & SCI (cumulative impact factor 31). 3 SCOPUS inee book chapters. A total of 24 patents are in various states and 18 patents have been granted at both national and international levels. One Edited book with Taylor & Francis (SCOPUS Indexed). She has won two Best Paper awards at international conferences, one at the IEEE conference and another one at EAMMIS 2021. She received two awards in the year 2022. She received two awards in the year 2022. She has addressed innumerable guest lectures, acted as a session chair, and was invited as a keynote speaker at several international conferences. She has conducted FDPs that cover approximately ~80,000 plus faculty members including JNTU, TEQIP, SERB, SWAYAM, DST, AICTE, MHRD, ATAL, ISTE, Madhya Pradesh Government-sponsored, and self-financed workshops across India on various titles.

Ismail El Bazi holds a Doctorate in Computer Science from Hassan 1er University and an Engineering degree in Computer Engineering from Cadi Ayyad University. After 12 years of professional experience in the field of Software Engineering with International IT companies, he joined the Sultan Moulay Slimane University in 2019 as Associate Professor. His research focuses are Arabic Natural Language Processing, Data Science, and Agentic Intelligence.

Jamal Ezzine is a professional translator, interpreter, and founder of ItalArabo Consult Group S.a.r.L. With over fifteen years of experience, he specializes in certified legal and technical translation across Arabic, Italian, English, and French. He is a member of several international professional translation associations and holds a PhD from the University of Calabria. His current research interests include Natural Language Processing (NLP), Large Language Models (LLMs), and Agentic Intelligence.

Silambarasan G possesses a comprehensive academic foundation, holding a Bachelor of Computer Applications (BCA) and a Master of Computer Applications (MCA), and is currently pursuing a Ph.D. (Full-Time) in the Department of Computer Science at Periyar University, Salem, Tamil Nadu, India. With over 08 years of teaching experience and 02 years of industry exposure, he has consistently demonstrated excellence in both academic and technical domains. His professional journey reflects a strong commitment to research, innovation, and pedagogical advancement in the rapidly evolving field of computer science. Renowned for his expertise in network administration, system architecture, virtualization, and emerging computing technologies, Silambarasan G continues to contribute significantly to the integration of theory and practical application. His academic and research pursuits exemplify a passion for technological innovation and a steadfast dedication to advancing the frontiers of computer science education.

Brahim Ghazoui is a Computer Science Engineer, graduated from the National Institute of Posts and Telecommunications (INPT), Morocco. Since 2022, he has pursued his Ph.D. at the LGS Laboratory, Department of Computer Science, Faculty of Sciences and Techniques, Sultan Moulay Slimane University, Morocco. His research interests include machine learning and deep learning for natural language processing and its applications

Khushbu Jaiswal received the BCA and Master of Computer Applications (MCA) degrees from Indira Gandhi National Tribal University (A Central University), Madhya Pradesh, India, in 2018 and 2021, respectively. Currently, she is pursuing a Ph.D. in the emerging area of designing secure frameworks for FANETs from the Department of Computer Science at Indira Gandhi National Tribal University, Madhya Pradesh, India. Her research interests include the emerging technologies of FANETs, UAV networks, next-generation network security issues, and AI/ML Applications in wireless communication networks.

Jasdeep Kaur is doctorate in Law, a vehement educator with a teaching experience of more than 17 years and presently working as Professor in Law, Chitkara Law School, Chitkara University, Punjab. Her research aptitude has given her the recommendation through citations in Springer journal, Heinonline publications. Her fervour for academics is demonstrated through her commendable endeavours in organizing and Convening Moot Courts and National Conferences apart from presenting and publishing in National and International Journals. She has been awarded with Award of Innovative Teaching by ZIIEI and Best Global Teaching Excellence Award, Kiteskraft Production and Research Excellence award by Institute of Scholars, An ISO 9001:2015 certified institute by International Accurate Certification. She is applauded for her upskill and exploration in scholarly world.

Sangeeta Taak is a Assistant Professor of Law at Rajiv Gandhi National University of Law, Punjab, India. She has a teaching experience of more than 19 years at the Rajiv Gandhi National Law University, Punjab. She was a Research

Fellow at Central Asian Legal Research (CALR), Tashkent State University of Law (TSUL), at Tashkent, Uzbekistan, from December 2023- September 2024. She is a visiting Lecturer at School of International ad Advanced Problems of Private Law Faculty of Law and Administration University of GDANSK, 2024. She has various publications in Scopus indexed journal and UGC care listed Journals.

Sudesh Kumar received Ph.D. degree in Computer Science in 2021. He is currently an Assistant Professor in the Department of Computer Science at Indira Gandhi National Tribal University, A Central University in Amarkantak, Madhya Pradesh, India. He completed M.E. (Computer Science & Engineering) and M.Sc. (Mathematics) in 2009 and 2005, respectively. He has worked as an Assistant Professor in the Department of Computer Science and Engineering at the Central University of Rajasthan, India. He has more than 15 years of teaching, administrative and research experience. He has organised many conferences, seminars, and Workshops at the national and International levels. He has delivered many expert and Invited Lectures at National and International levels. Dr Kumar has published more than 30 research papers with high impact factors in reputable international journals and Conferences, including IEEE, Elsevier, Springer, Wiley & Sons, Taylor & Francis, and Inderscience. His current research interests include Flying Ad-hoc Networks, UAV Applications, Vehicular Ad-hoc Networks, Healthcare Industry 5.0, and IoTs.

Premkumar M is presently working as an Professor in the Department of Artificial intelligence and data science. He completed his Ph.D. in Wireless Sensor Networking at Anna University year of 2022. He has more than fifteen years of teaching experience and has published research papers and book chapters in reputed national and international journals. Her areas of interest include Wireless Communication, Networking, and Digital Systems.

Aquil Mohammed is a researcher and educator specializing in AI, AIoT, robotics, sensor networks, and medical imaging. Since 2025, he has been Dean and Professor at Liaoning Technical University, China. He is also a Senior Lecturer at PolyU, teaching courses like Programming Fundamentals and AIoT, with high student feedback. Between 2021 and 2023, he led projects on wall-climbing robots, autonomous drones, and smart monitoring systems. He is an IEEE senior member. He began his career with research and academic roles at IIT Delhi and BITS Pilani. He holds a Ph.D. in Computing from PolyU, with master's degrees from KAUST and IIIT-Hyderabad. His research has been funded by major grants, and his work has earned several awards such as the IEEE Best Student Papers. With a strong academic background and innovative research, he continues to advance the fields of intelligent systems and robotics, inspiring future engineers.

Hitesh Mohapatra received the B.E. degree in Information Technology from Biju Patnaik University of Technology (BPUT), Odisha in 2006, and the MTech. Degree in CSE from Odisha University of Technology and Research (OUTR) University, Odisha in 2009. He received his Ph.D. in Computer Science & Engineering in 2021 from Veer Surendra Sai University of Technology (VSSUT), Burla, India. He has contributed 150+ SCI and Scopus indexed research articles. He has authored two books on Software Engineering and C Programming respectively. He has 15 years of teaching experience both in industry and academia. He has served the research community with various capacities like session chair, technical chair, keynote speaker etc. His research interests include wireless sensor network, smart city, smart grid and smart water. Currently he is working as Associate Professor at School of Computer Engineering, KIIT (Deemed to be) University, Bhubaneswar, Odisha, India.

Sudha R is presently working as an Assistant Professor in the Department of Electronics and Communication Engineering at SSM Institute of Engineering and Technology (Autonomous), Dindigul. She has been pursuing her Ph.D. in Wireless Sensor Networking at Anna University since 2021. She has more than three years of teaching experience and has published research papers and book chapters in reputed national and international journals. Her areas of interest include Wireless Communication, Networking, and Digital Systems.

Neeraj Rathore is a Professor in the Department of Computer Science and Engineering at the National Institute of Technical Teachers Training and Research (NITTTR), Bhopal, Madhya Pradesh. He previously served as Dean (2024–2026) and Head (2022–2025) of the Faculty of Computer Science at Indira Gandhi National Tribal University, Amarkantak, a Central University, during the period 2021–2026. He also held the position of Vice President (2025–2026) of the Teachers' Association at the same university. Prior to this, he served at Shri Govindram Seksaria Institute of Technology and Science (SGSITS), Indore, an autonomous state government institution, from 2018 to 2021, and at Jaypee University of Engineering and Technology, Guna, from 2010 to 2018. He earned his Bachelor of Engineering in 2006 from the University of Rajasthan, Rajasthan, and completed his Master of Engineering (2008) and Ph.D. (2014) in Computer Science and Engineering from Thapar University. He also qualified GATE in 2006, securing an All India Rank of 241. Prof. Rathore has over 18 years of combined experience in teaching and industry across various state and central government universities and institutions.

His academic contributions include more than 90 publications, comprising 23 SCI-indexed papers, 7 patents, and 8 books, along with numerous articles in reputed journals and conference proceedings. His research has received over 1,300 citations, with an h-index of 21 and an i10-index of 42. He has successfully supervised 4 Ph.D. scholars, with 4 more currently pursuing their doctoral research under his guidance. Additionally, around 30 postgraduate and 90 undergraduate students have completed their projects under his supervision. He has delivered more than 50 expert lectures, keynote addresses, and invited talks at national and international platforms. He is actively associated with prominent national agencies such as NTA, MPPSC, CGPSC, MP Vyapam and CG Vyapam for various professional assignments and has received several prestigious awards in recognition of his contributions. Prof. Rathore is affiliated with numerous universities and institutions as an external Ph.D. examiner, paper setter, Board of Studies member, Doctoral Research Committee expert, interview panel member, and council member. He has chaired and coordinated over 50 workshops, conferences, and technical sessions. Beyond academics, he has actively participated in extracurricular activities and has earned accolades in sports including cricket, volleyball, and kabaddi. He has also performed various government duties, serving as an observer and coordinator for different organizations. In addition to his academic and administrative roles, Prof. Rathore is actively associated with several professional bodies and agencies, serving as an Editorial Board Member, Technical Program Committee Member, Program Chair, Advisory Member, Adjunct Faculty, and Reviewer. He has undertaken significant responsibilities at both departmental and university levels and has served as Chair or Member of more than 100 committees at institutional and university levels. These responsibilities include roles such as Coordinator of NBA Coordinator, Examination Superintendent, Cyber Cell Coordinator, Discipline Committee, Academic Council, SWAYAM and MOOC Advisory Committee, WiFi Committee, IQAC and NAAC Committee, Doctoral Research Committee (DRC), Alumni Cell, Scholarship Authority, and Board of Studies (BoS), among others. Prof. Rathore's distinguished career reflects his unwavering commitment to academic excellence, research innovation, leadership, and professional service.

Asha S is an Assistant Professor in the Department of Computer Science and Engineering at SR University. She obtained her Ph.D. in Computer Science from Avinashilingam University and has five years of research experience in the field of Computer Science. Her research interests include cybersecurity, artificial intelligence, and behavioral biometrics. She received the Vijayalakshmi Purushothaman Award for securing university rank in Master of Science in Information Technology. Her research contributions include publications in SCIE Q1 top 10% journals, Scopus-indexed conference proceedings, and book chapters. She has also presented her research work at various research conventions and academic forums. In addition, she has published two patents and two copyrights, and has actively contributed to three funded research projects.

Gautam Shivaraj, with a comprehensive academic background including a Bachelor's in Mechanical Engineering, Master of Engineering Management (Australia), MBA and also pursuing Ph.D., brings an impressive 07 years of teaching experience alongside a brief stint in the industry of 5 years. Currently serving as an Assistant Professor at the Adarsh Institute of Management and Information Technology in Bangalore, Karnataka, India, he has distinguished himself in the academic and research fields. Prof.Gautam Shivaraj professional journey is a testament to his dedication to academia, research, in the evolving world.

Vineeta Singh is presently associated with Department of Computer Science & Engineering, School of Engineering and Technology, Chhatrapati Shahu ji Maharaj University Kanpur, India. She has more than 10 years of teaching experience in different Engineering and Technological Institutions. She has guided more than 220 B.Tech. level projects and more than 2 M.Tech. level Projects. She is Ph.D. in CSE from the Harcourt Butler Technical University Kanpur, India and M.Tech from Dr. APJ Abdul Kalam Technical University Lucknow as well as B.Tech with honours from UPTU Lucknow India. Her area of research includes Deep learning, Image Processing, Cyber Security, Data Mining and Biometrics. She has 47+ Scopus/ SCIE Publications and 20+ are in pipeline. She also worked as reviewer in different international conferences organized by IIT BHU (ANTIC-BHU) Varanasi and NIT Arunachal Pradesh. She is also working as reviewer in SCIE indexed journals such as IET Image Processing, Scientific Reports, Signal Image and Video Processing, Journal of Scientific and Industrial Research and many more. She is also associated as an editor with five ongoing projects as edited Books pertaining to renowned publishers such as Bentham Science, Wiley Scrivener. She has two edited Books published with IGI Global Scientific Publishing. She has two Indian Granted Patents "Artificial Tree for oxygen production and atmospheric purification" and SMART BOOK FOR TRACKING STUDENTS' LEARNING PROGRESS and third one is in process. She has seven design based grants accepted and 2 in process. She has one UK design grant. She is currently guiding one PhD Student in the area of Natural Language Processing.

Index

A

B

C

S

T

U

V

W

Z

www.ingramcontent.com/pod-product-compliance
Lightning Source LLC
LaVergne TN
LVHW062333300926
849161LV00007B/1672